To
James,
with gratitude
forever friendship and our
years of shared mess!

Don Loose

February, 2011

AN ACT OF PROVIDENCE

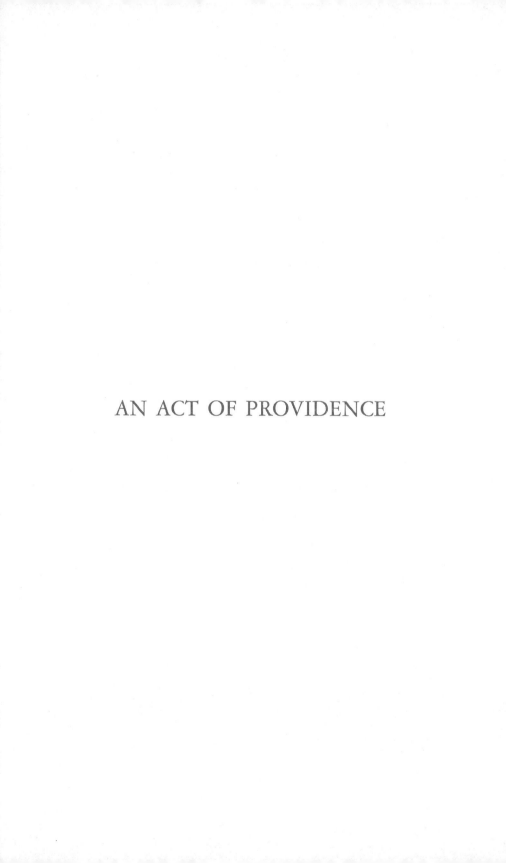

AN ACT OF PROVIDENCE

A History of Houston Baptist University,
1960-2010

Don Looser, PhD
Vice President Emeritus
Houston Baptist University

First Edition
Printed in The United States of America

ISBN 978-1-931823-55-5

Halcyon Press Ltd.
P.O. Box 260
Pearland Texas 77588

www.halcyonpress.com

Library of Congress Cataloging-in-Publication Data
available upon request

CONTENTS

PHOTOGRAPHS

Preface

Robert B. Sloan, Jr.

It is my privilege to serve as the president of Houston Baptist University during the institution's 50th anniversary. HBU represents the dreams of a group of men and women who first conceived the possibility of a great Christian college in the thriving and growing metropolis of Houston. They knew that Christian schools typically are located far away from the temptations of city life, but had the idea that the college they would found would be integrated with the everyday affairs of Houston. In their minds, HBU could provide a witness for the gospel of Jesus Christ in higher education to the people of the city.

When I came to HBU in 2006, Don Looser and I discussed his desire to write a history of the University. He was a perfect choice, having served 44 years in a variety of positions as both a faculty member and an administrator. Don capped his long and successful career with many years as HBU's vice president for academic affairs. I knew that no one else could bring the same degree of insider knowledge and expertise to the task of writing our history.

You will find that Don has made all the right decisions in putting together this history. He has opted for facts and detail over sweeping themes, and that is for the good. An institutional history creates an opportunity to remember the people and events who helped build a university literally out of nothing. I know I learned a great deal about the people who labored tirelessly to fund the University, the professors who made a lasting impression on their students, the leaders of campus life who formed the substance of programs and traditions, and our outstanding alumni. I also learned about the trials and triumphs of a Christian school in southwest Houston.

I hope people will read the book and be inspired by the example of men and women who made special contributions. In these pages we encounter an indomitable Stewart Morris, a hard-driving Gilbert Turner, an exacting H. B. Smith, the entrepreneurial W. H. Hinton, and the stabilizing and renewing strength of Doug Hodo. I was also deeply inspired by the sacrificial commitments of Ross Dillon, Rex Baker, and Jake Kamin. And no former colleague or student of Opal Goolsby's or Joyce Fan's will ever forget their enthusiasm for their work or their passion for teaching students. These are people who devoted much of their lives to building the HBU we know today. All of us who are involved with the University can learn from their example. Those who have not invested themselves here or with some other great errand of Christian service should find much to stimulate their imagination and their efforts as they read this history.

Perhaps the greatest contribution of this book is that it demonstrates the virtue of the perseverance shown by many of HBU's stalwart supporters and dedicated faculty and staff over the years. Despite the challenges facing a university founded in the sixties, HBU has continued to grow as a Christian institution. Its record of accomplishment depends heavily on the people whose stories are chronicled here by Don Looser.

Finally, I am thankful for the work of W. H. Hinton and Doug Hodo as my predecessors. Don Looser's history of HBU has given me a greater sense still of the privilege I have to serve at this university in the city of Houston. Through the Ten Pillars vision, I am committed to moving HBU to the next level—as a comprehensive, national university where Athens and Jerusalem truly come together. I also know that because of the persevering efforts of the current stars on our faculty, staff, and administration—individuals like Paul Bonicelli, Sharon Saunders, Sandy Mooney, Charles Bacarisse, James Steen, Steve Moniaci, Doris Warren, David Capes, Bob Stacey, Lou Markos, and so many others—the next half century at HBU will prove worthy of the years that went before it.

ONE

September, 1963

*This is a story written as much by the lives of people
as by the events they shared. It is a story of faith;
it is a story of confidence; it is a story of inspiration;
it is a story of courage. More than anything else,
it is a story of Providence.*

September 17, 1963, dawned still hot from summer. In the space capital of the nation, a new Christian college was beginning its miraculous life. Some sixty-five freshmen students had moved into new dormitories the previous week. Others of the 190 freshmen found their way to the campus in remote southwest Houston out Bellaire Boulevard or the feeder road of the uncompleted Southwest Freeway.[1] The campus was an island of development in a sea of raw land. Beechnut Street terminated at the new freeway site. A short stretch of Fondren Road reached only as far north as Clarewood Drive and only slightly beyond the campus on the south. Aerial photographs of the era documented undeveloped land south, west, and north from the campus. R. E. "Bob" Smith's ranch stretched south from Westheimer Road across Bellaire Boulevard and Bissonnet Street to the city of Sugar Land, creating a virtual no-man's land on the city's southwest side. The new Sharpstown Mall and the area's first few homes marked the southwestern edge of Houston's residential development.

Despite the determined efforts of trustees and construction forces, the Houston Baptist College campus was not an attractive sight for the first campus residents. The land was flat and barren—dusty when dry, and marshy when wet.[2] However, an academic quadrangle rose from the prairie marking the center of the new campus. This modern, compact facility contained the M. D. Anderson Student Center with its bookstore and cafeteria; two academic wings containing classrooms, the College library, faculty and administrative offices, science labs, and music and art studios; and Denham Hall—a small theater that served variously for chapel, drama, and trustee meetings. Under construction but not yet

---

1. Fred King, "Backers to celebrate the anniversary of HBU," *Houston Post,* 24 Apr. 1983, sec. C, p. 1.
2. "Landscaping in Progress at Houston Baptist College," *Houston Baptist College News,* Aug. 1963, 4. Photo.

completed were the Atwood Theology Building and the Sharp Gymnasium.

The new campus boasted state-of-the-art facilities. Closed-circuit television connected all instructional facilities. New Steinway pianos afforded students the finest keyboard instruments for practice and performance. The buildings all incorporated the concept of a quadrangle or atrium that could be more quickly landscaped than the campus-at-large. Dorms were arranged in suites opening onto a central courtyard that provided natural light and green space for the residents. The residential area anchored the east side of the campus with entry from Beechnut. The location provided easy street access and restricted campus vehicular traffic to the perimeter. Students quickly discovered, however, that the long walk from the dorms to the M. D. Anderson cafeteria was miserable in cold or rainy weather and inconvenient year-round.[3]

Trustees had actually been working since the 1950s on campus land acquisition, raising funds, seeking authorization from the Baptist General Convention of Texas, and drafting documents stipulating the nature of the College. The first administrators, appointed in 1962, had been working with the Board of Trustees to attract the original faculty, recruit the first students, establish broad curriculum outlines, and supervise construction of the first campus facilities. Most members of the first faculty had been on the payroll since the early summer of 1963; they moved, became acquainted, developed the first curriculum, created policy, acquired library resources, and established relationships with administrative personnel.

The 190 freshmen represented fifty-six different high schools and fifteen colleges. Bellaire High School in Houston contributed a significant number of students to the freshman class, as did Lamar, Reagan, Sam Houston, Milby, Waltrip, and San Jacinto high schools. Freshmen also came from Detroit, El Paso, Louisville, Memphis, New Orleans, Texarkana, California, Mississippi, New York, and Japan. College transfer students moved from Baylor University, Carson Newman College, Texas A&M University, Texas Christian University, the University of Corpus Christi, and the University of Houston. Of these 190 freshmen and transfers, a committed eighty students would one day graduate from Houston Baptist College leaving their mark as those who had pioneered every course required for the degree.

---

3. *The Collegian*, 14 Feb. 1968, p. 4. Photo.

§

The freshmen class of 1963 was a remarkable group of students. They had wide-ranging choices of other colleges to attend. Their decision to enroll at HBC was an act of faith. As each considered a college choice, there was no visible campus. There were no upperclassmen. There was neither faculty nor curriculum. There was no accreditation and only the prediction of specific programs of study. Yet from these dedicated students came the establishment of every "first" organization, event, and tradition in emerging institutional history. Nearly fifty years after their freshman year, these first students remain among the University's most active alumni. Some members of the first class were viewed by faculty in later years as among the most gifted in institutional history.

Most students chose HBC because of their desire to attend a Christian college and the excitement of being a part of a new venture. Many of these freshmen were profiled in a series of articles in the official College publication, the *Houston Baptist College News*.[4] A "Christian Rice" was the way Judy Bennatte (Ferguson) remembers hearing the vision described. Other students, particularly in music and later athletics, were recruited especially for their talent and giftedness. A 2008 survey of these pioneering students revealed that many first heard about HBC through church sources. Others learned of the new college from high school principals, from the HBC faculty during the summer of 1963, by announcement of scholarships, newspaper ads, and the influence of trustees, coaches, family, and friends.[5]

The first College faculty members were even greater risk-takers. They confronted all the same issues as freshmen—no visible campus or observable history. Additionally, in the case of faculty, major career and financial choices were at stake. Virtually all of these faculty members had served well-established colleges and universities. Most were in the prime of their professional careers. Many had families with children and were coming to an assignment with multiple unknowns.

Faculty members were drawn by the persuasive vision of the College administration and trustees. They were also drawn by the prospects of

---

4. "Sampling of Accepted Students Listed," *Houston Baptist College News*, April 1963, 4; "Student Enrollment Increases Daily," *Houston Baptist College News*, May 1963, 4; "HBC Announces Scholarship Recipients," *Houston Baptist College News*, July 1963, 4.

5. (Survey of freshmen of 1963, Dr. Don Looser, Nov. 2008).

high standards of academic achievement, unswerving Christian commitment, entrepreneurial opportunity in a city enjoying explosive growth, and the opportunity—perhaps once in a lifetime—to be a part of a new academic venture. In a 1991 Founders' Day address, faculty member Dr. A. O. Collins recalled,

> From the beginning, I was impressed by the caliber and commitment of the faculty and administration. We had come from all over, and we believed in the school. It was not easy. At times, we wondered if the payroll would be met. There were some turbulent times, as in any worthwhile endeavor, but we were sold on what we were doing. We were not like any other school in Texas and didn't want to be. We wanted to be the best of what others had, yet be ourselves.

The enthusiastic faculty held degrees from Duke University, Florida State University, Fordham University, Indiana University, Louisiana State University, Peabody College, Rice University, Syracuse University, Tulane University, University of Iowa, University of Oklahoma, University of South Carolina, the University of Texas, as well as Southern and Southwestern Baptist Theological Seminaries. They moved from academic appointment at Auburn University, Carson Newman College, Erskine College, Howard Payne College, Mississippi College, Peabody College, Purdue University, University of Houston, Vanderbilt University, William Carey College, Yankton College, New Orleans and Southwestern Baptist Theological Seminaries, as well as the pastorate. These faculty members came from competitive positions and had to be wooed to the new College by the promise of security as well as vision. Nine were deans or chairs of departments at their previous institutions. Their mean age was forty-one years with a span from the mid-thirties to the mid-fifties.

The Board of Trustees had secured the consultancy service of Dr. Howard Bruce, President of East Texas Baptist College, to serve as an interim executive officer and assist in planning matters of institutional operation.[6] One of the first responsibilities of the new Board was to find leadership for the new College. A committee "to search for a new president" was appointed consisting of Chairman Dr. James Riley, L. D.

---

6. (Dr. Howard Bruce, Consultant to Houston Baptist College Board of Trustees, 30 Nov. 1962). "I think you are in the best position financially and otherwise for starting a college than any of the institutions with which I have been associated."

Morgan, Cecil Cook, George Duncan, and Dr. James E. Williamson.[7] In 1961, after several months of search and deliberation, Dr. Ralph Phelps, President of Ouachita Baptist, was invited to come for an interview for the position of President. Phelps had spoken for a convocation that marked the initiation of fund raising in March 1960 and was known to the members of the Board of Trustees. Discussion was held with Dr. Phelps regarding commitment to the new Preamble to the Bylaws, fund raising, and "Bible teaching in Baptist colleges." It was reported that Phelps "would be interested in considering the Presidency of HBC."[8] Ultimately, an offer was made to him in the spring of 1961 stating that the trustees held him in high esteem and felt that he was "needed at Houston Baptist College."[9] Chairman Denham wrote the trustees in late July, "We are encouraged over the possibility that Dr. Phelps may give an affirmative answer."[10] However, Phelps ultimately declined the offer—by telegram. The Search Committee reported, "Dr. Phelps did not at this time have a feeling of definite conviction that he should accept the responsibilities of the presidency of the Houston Baptist College."[11] Phelps expressed concerns to the Arkansas news media about the debt-elimination timetable on the HBC campus land, the lagging payment of pledges by churches, uncertainty about payments from the Baptist General Convention of Texas for college operations, and concern that the College would not be open by fall 1963.[12]

The trustees were both shocked and disappointed. Pastor Denham encouraged his colleagues.

> Let me underscore the abiding conviction that God has guided us thus far in the splendid developments which have taken place. We believe that these next months will bring additional desirable answers to our problems. Your continuing loyalty and devotion is a matter of tremendous gratification. We can rest assured that God's guidance will continue to be upon the projects in which He is concerned.[13]

---

7. Houston Baptist College, Minutes of Meetings of the Board of Trustees, Meeting on 17 Jan. 1961.

8. Houston Baptist College, Minutes of Meetings of the Board of Trustees, Meeting on 1 June 1961.

9. Ibid.

10. (Dr. William Denham, Chairman, to members of the Houston Baptist College Board of Trustees, July 28, 1961).

11. Houston Baptist College, Minutes of Meetings of the Board of Trustees, Meeting on 7 Sept. 1961.

12. Houston Baptist College, Minutes of Meetings of the Board of Trustees, Meeting on 2 Nov. 1961.

13. (Dr. William Denham, Chairman, to members of the Houston Baptist College Board of Trustees, Sept. 8, 1961).

Subsequently, the Board voted "to rescind the action taken by the trustees in the meeting of September 23, 1961, in which Dr. Ralph Phelps was elected President of the Houston Baptist College."[14]   Apparently, the Board wished to be on record only as having elected a first President who accepted its invitation. The Phelps offer in essence was annulled.

The Presidential search continued over the next year and ultimately focused on Dr. William H. Hinton, President of Texarkana Junior College. In May 1962, Hinton agreed to meet at Love Field in Dallas with Dr. Riley and members of the search committee. "They painted pictures of faith and excitement," Dr. Hinton recalled. Later at a Ramada Club reception in downtown Houston, Dr. and Mrs. Hinton met with members of the Board of Trustees and their wives. A "full exchange of concepts, expressions, and beliefs" ensued.[15]   Both the Board and the Hintons felt God's leadership to enter into an agreement to serve. Therefore, at the May 19, 1962, trustee meeting at the First City National Bank, John Baugh moved that Dr. William Harwood Hinton be invited to become the President of Houston Baptist College. Pastor L. D. Morgan seconded the motion that was unanimously approved.[16] Dr. Hinton responded to his election in several local news reports. "I was influenced to accept the position by two things: first, the Christian commitment of the Board of Trustees to be an institution of excellence; and second, the enthusiasm and the ability to get things done on the part of the College Property Committee."[17] Dr. Hinton was later presented to the 1962 Annual Session of the Union Baptist Association by Dr. Ross Dillon.[18] Founder John Baugh later recalled in a Founders' Day speech in 1991,

> I never doubted Dr. Hinton's capabilities to wrest these facilities from the barren ground, but I inwardly questioned the mental state of a man who would accept such an awesome undertaking. Our founding president was the man for this work. God had granted him the abilities and characteristics to accomplish every task—as educator, athlete, administrator, remarkable promoter in the finest sense of the word, and generous encourager of all persons.[19]

14. Houston Baptist College, Minutes of Meetings of the Board of Trustees, Meeting on 2 Nov. 1961.
15. Houston Baptist College, Minutes of Meetings of the Board of Trustees, Meeting on 19 May 1962.
16. Ibid.
17. Rabun L. Brantley, "Hinton Begins Presidency of Houston College," *Southern Baptist Educator*, June 1962, 10.
18. Union Baptist Association of Texas, Minutes of the 122nd Annual Session, 1962, pp. 56-58.
19. John Baugh, "Founders' Day Address," *HBU News*, Feb. 1992, 8-11.

Dr. Hinton had served as President at both Texarkana and Northeast Mississippi Junior College after serving as Executive Vice-President at Howard Payne College in Texas.[20] He held the BA from Howard Payne College, the MA from Hardin-Simmons University, and EdD from the University of Texas in Austin. He and Mrs. Hinton had two teen-age daughters, Julie and Linda;[21] the Hinton family moved initially into temporary housing at 7711 Hiawatha Street near the College while a campus home was under construction.[22] Dr. Hinton was 41 years old at the time of his appointment.[23]

Hinton lost no time in appointing Dr. Herbert B. Smith, Dean of Faculties at Hardin-Simmons University, as the first Vice President for Academic Affairs in August of 1962. Dr. Smith, 54, held the BA in biology from Georgetown College in Kentucky and an MA and EdD from the University of Cincinnati.[24] H. B. Smith became the chief architect of the HBC curriculum—a unique combination of models from across the nation. He was a keen academician with a personal, folksy demeanor more akin to his native Kentucky or to West Texas than to urban Houston. Yet, he was a man of expertise, acumen in higher education, and dogged determination.

Troy Womack was appointed the first Business Manager and Controller and later Vice President for Financial Affairs. Womack, a graduate of Baylor University and the University of Kentucky, was a Certified Public Accountant and had served with Hinton in Texarkana. At the same time, Dr. Thomas V. Jenkins, also from Texarkana, was named Assistant to the President.[25]

Dr. Ross E. Dillon, Executive Director of the Union Baptist Association (UBA), was named Director of Development at HBC in 1963

---

20. "Hinton Houston School President," *Abilene Reporter-News*, 1 June 1962, sec. A, p. 2.

21. Ruth Rosenfeld, "Hinton House: Gracious New Home for A College President," *Bellaire Texan*, 28 Aug. 1963, p. 4. Furnishings for the home were purchased from Kamin Furniture under the design guidance of Mrs. Henry (Mary) Buchanan, thereafter a lifelong friend of the College.

22. Houston Baptist College, Minutes of Meetings of the Board of Trustees, Meeting on 13 July 1962. The purchase price of the house was $31,650.

23. "Introducing Houston Baptist College Executive Officers," *Houston Baptist College News*, Vol. 1, No. 1, 1. No date. Biography with photo.

24. Ibid.

25. "Only Dedicated Christians Sought for Faculty," *Houston Baptist College News*, Dec. 1962, 1. Biography with photo.

upon his retirement from the Association.[26] Dr. Dillon had been part of the developing College vision since the early 1950s. He was instrumental in many of the early fund-raising and land-development activities that addressed the requirements for establishing the new college. Known as a "tenacious bulldog" for his work for the UBA, Dr. Dillon ultimately proved to be a "political genius with governments, churches, civic organizations, and faith constituencies."[27] Joining Dr. Dillon in the area of corporate support was William C. Bolton, a Houston resident with news media and fund-raising experience.[28]

This group of experienced, dedicated professionals formed the first administrative cabinet that was to lead the College through some of its most difficult years. Offices were set up initially in the T. J. Bettis Building at 3910 Travis Street in downtown Houston. Trustee Stewart Morris called upon young home-builder Bruce Belin, Jr. to propose temporary housing for college operations. Belin constructed a two-story frame residence on the campus at 7502 Fondren Road that served to house the administrative offices for the College until September 1963.[29] Many of the original faculty and staff interviewed for positions in that house which later became the home of the Superintendent of Buildings and Grounds.[30]

Long before the opening of the new College in 1963, however, was a significant and complex history of institutional development.

---

26. "Dr. Dillon Retires; Accepts Position on HBC Staff," *Houston Baptist College News,* Feb. 1963, 1. Biography with photo.

27. Marilyn Sibley, *To Benefit a University: the Union Baptist Association Property Committee, 1958-1975* (Houston: Houston Baptist University, 1978), 20-21.

28. "Bolton Named Houston College Vice President," *Texas Baptist Press,* 30 July 1963; "College Advancement Program Gains Momentum," *Houston Baptist College News,* July 1963, 1. Biography with photo.

29. *Houston Baptist College Collegian,* 4 Sept. 1986, p. 5. Photo.

30. (Dr. Bruce J. Belin to Dr. Don Looser, Sept. 8, 2010). The house stood where the Bank of America stands in 2010. Mr. J. W. Youngblood, the first Superintendent of Buildings and Grounds, and his family lived in the house for his entire career with the College.

TWO

1908-1963

The 112th annual session of the Union Baptist Association, meeting on October 14, 1952, appointed a Special College Committee chaired by Dr. William E. Denham, pastor of River Oaks Baptist Church, to consider the efficacy of establishing a Baptist college in Houston. Members of the Committee were Dr. Denham, Milton Bailey, Tom Burr, R. G. Commander,[1] J. T. Draper, W. R. Estep, Gabriel Fransee, Earl Hankamer, W. M. Harrell, R. V. Mayfield, L. D. Morgan, Al Novak, J. H. Russell, Joseph Stiles, and O. A. Taylor.[2]

The establishment of a new college was not a new idea; as early as 1908, the *Galveston Daily News* reported, "Especially will the needs of the Baptist Sanitarium at Houston, Palacios Baptist College at Palacios, and the need of a Baptist paper for the section of the state above mentioned be considered."[3]   In 1921, Pastor J. W. Anderson from Goose Creek pledged $1,000 toward the "establishment of a Baptist school in South Texas."[4] On the motion of Pastor L. D. White of Magnolia Park Church, Houston, the Association appointed a committee chaired by A. D. Foreman "to look into the matter with a view to establishing a Baptist school in Union Association."[5] Minutes of the 82nd Annual Session of the Union Baptist Association October 11-12, 1922, recorded, "M. M. Wolf read the report of the committee appointed in 1921 to take steps looking to the establishment of a Union Association Baptist school. The committee for the Union Baptist School, composed of Chairman A. D. Foreman, M. M. Wolf, J. B. Leavell, E. P. West, and E. F. Adams, was

---

1. "Obituaries," *Rocky Mountain News*, 22 Feb. 1998, sec. B, p. 10. Commander was the pastor of the First Baptist Church Rosenberg, Eastwood, and Oak Forest Baptist churches. For a period of time in the 1960s, he worked in the Houston Baptist College Development Office.
2. Elaine Lowry, "The History of Houston Baptist College," (Senior Seminar Paper, Houston Baptist College, 1967), p. 7. On file in the Moody Library.
3. "Crowds Attend Services in Palacios Auditorium," *Galveston Daily News*, 11 July 1908, p. 7. Rev. M. M. Wolf of Palacios was appointed to a committee to review the needs of the Palacios College. Wolf was later appointed to a committee in 1921 to look into the "establishment of a Union Baptist School."
4. Union Baptist Association of Texas, Minutes of the 81st annual session, 1921, agenda item No. 36.
5. Ibid.

appointed for another year."[6] In 1923, the same committee was re-appointed. Thereafter, the topic of a new "school" is absent from the UBA minutes. R. G. Commander recorded, "the college item was postponed (in 1923) in favor of the 'Seventy-five Million Campaign.'"[7] The Great Depression and the advent of World War II may have diverted the resources and attention of the Association to more pressing matters. Commander reflected, "It was also sobering to read the list of casualties among schools that had failed because of a lack of support, but the idea never died."[8]

Dr. Harry Leon McBeth, in his sesquicentennial history of Texas Baptists, described the state of Texas Baptist higher education in the 1950s:

> Texas Baptist colleges grew up much like Topsy, largely regional enterprises with no statewide planning as to location. . . . By the 1950s, it became obvious that Baptists had no colleges in the major metropolitan centers where over 50 percent of Texas Baptists lived. . . . Major cities without a Baptist college included Dallas, Houston, and San Antonio. . . . James H. Landes . . . reported in 1956 that in ten years the number of Baptist collegians in Texas would double, and he moved "to continue studying the possibilities of expansion into metropolitan areas not adequately served by existing institutions."[9]

Prior to the 1952 appointment of the UBA Special College Committee, the relocation of a Southern Baptist college from Beeville, Texas to Houston had been discussed. A committee was appointed by the Union Baptist Association to investigate such a possibility with representatives of the Baptist General Convention of Texas. However, the committee discovered that previous discussion had been held between the Beeville College and a committee from Corpus Christi. The Houston delegation demurred. The University of Corpus Christi eventually emerged and was chartered on April 1, 1947.[10]

From 1952 until the election of the first official college trustees in 1960, the work of this UBA Special College Committee and its associat-

---

6. Union Baptist Association of Texas, Minutes of the 82nd annual session, 1922, agenda item No. 39.

7. R. G. Commander, *The Story of Union Baptist Association* (Houston: D. Armstrong Publishers, 1977), 76-77.

8. Commander, 76.

9. Harry Leon McBeth, *Texas Baptists: A Sesquicentennial History* (Dallas: Baptistway Press, 1998), 264-265.

10. E. C. Routh, "Romance of a College," *Baptist Standard*, October 1956, 12.

ed sub-committees was the driving force toward the realization of a new college. The appointment of Ross E. Dillon as Executive Director of the UBA in 1948 provided the impetus for the realization of a dream held by many Houstonians for a number of years.

During the 1950s, new patterns of urban expansion began to develop in Houston. Annexation of land by the city attempted to maintain pace with dispersion of housing developments. Both Houston and Harris County increased their populations by fifty percent from 1950 to 1960. The era became described as the "Fabulous Fifties" and the "Dynamic Decade." In 1954, Dr. Denham reported to the UBA that consultant Dr. Freeman Beets from the Southern Baptist Convention Educational Commission had advised that a new college would complement rather than compete with other Baptist colleges in the state. Such a college could ride the crest of the explosive growth occurring in Harris County, might attract as many as 500 freshmen the first year, and would offer a distinctly Christian college for the residents of southeast Texas. It was Beets' opinion that Houston "offered the best opportunity of any metropolitan area in the Southern Baptist Convention."[11]

He further applauded the merits of early planning and stated that this investigative look at the prospects for a new college in Houston was to his knowledge "the first attempt ever to determine the needs of a community for a Baptist college prior to making a decision to establish that college."[12] This observation was particularly gratifying to the Houston planners in view of other urban Baptist colleges that were established about the same time—Atlanta Baptist College (1964-1972), Baptist College at Charleston (1960-), Dallas Baptist College (1965-), Kentucky Southern College in Louisville (1961-1969), Missouri Baptist College in St. Louis(1963-), and Mobile College (1961-).[13]

The study report of the Special College Committee was sent to the Education Commission of the Baptist General Convention of Texas in November 1956.[14] Dr. Harold Haswell, Chair of the Education

---

11. Houston Baptist College, Minutes of the Board of Trustees, Meeting on 26 Nov. 1963.

12. Sibley, 3-4.

13. Higher Education Directory Research Service, "Custom Report for HBU: Comparative study of 1984 and 2008 College Databases," 2008. Other Christian colleges founded between 1955 and 1968 still extant in 2010 include University of Dallas (1955), Lubbock Christian College (1957), Eckerd College (1959), Oral Roberts University (1965), and Palm Beach Atlantic College (1968).

14. "Anniversary of a Dream," *Houston Baptist College News*, Sept. 1964, 2.

Commission, was a supporter of metropolitan locations for new colleges.[15] In December, Dr. Denham and members of the College Committee were invited to meet with the Education Commission of the BGCT to discuss another possibility—the creation of Baptist junior colleges in Houston, Dallas, Ft. Worth, and San Antonio.[16] Denham later reported, "The (College) Committee feels that the Houston school should not be (a two-year institution or) affiliated with any existing Baptist school, because action taken by the Union Baptist Association presupposes a separate institution." McBeth reports that as a result, "All thought of starting with a junior college or of making the Houston school a branch of Baylor University had . . . been dropped."[17] A name, *Texas Baptist College*, was selected by the UBA in 1956.[18] Dr. Dillon later recalled that Baylor's President W. R. White and many Houston Baylor alumni "did not want a college to be established in Houston."[19] Nonetheless, the Education Commission responded favorably to the UBA proposal, but required that the new college-backers raise $3,000,000—half for facilities and equipment and half for endowment. Additionally, the UBA was to acquire a campus site of no less than 100 acres.[20] McBeth records, "The (BGCT Executive) Board established stringent minimum requirements for the site and local funding; after the University of Corpus Christi, they wanted no more 'shoe string' colleges."[21] A fifty-acre site near Kemah had earlier been offered to the Association as a possible location for the new college there, but was judged too small and too remote.[22] R. G. Commander, in his history of the UBA, reported that "the old Sam Houston High School was considered as a place to start, also the Kincade (sic) School, but neither site would answer the real need of the college."[23]

Dr. Dillon and Dr. Haswell sought the counsel of the Secretary of the City of Houston Planning Commission in considering a campus site. Citizens of the City of Pasadena made the location something of a civic effort and petitioned that the college be located there. The Planning Commission Secretary surveyed the greater Houston area noting the

15. Sibley, 5.
16. "Baptist Group to Hold Parley on New Schools," *Houston Chronicle*, 14 Dec. 1956, sec. B, p. 1.
17. McBeth, 265.
18. Ibid.
19. Lowry, p. 20.
20. "Anniversary of a Dream," *Houston Baptist College News*, Sept. 1964, 2; Sibley, 5-6.
21. McBeth, 265.
22. Union Baptist Association of Texas, Minutes of the 113th Annual Session, 1953, p. 35.
23. Commander, 79.

location of high schools, the percentage of college-bound students within geographical areas, the economic vitality of various sections of the city, and the availability of large tracts of land.[24] The consensus was that a site should be sought in the western or southwestern area of the city.[25]

By the end of the 1950s, the population growth of Houston moved the city from 14th to 6th largest in the nation.[26] As the city expanded, it quickly became apparent that the automobile would be essential to Houston's growth. Houston's first freeway, the Gulf Freeway, had opened in 1948. With the passage of funding for the Interstate Highway System under President Eisenhower in 1956, a freeway lifestyle was assured for cities like Houston. The Gulfgate Mall opened in 1956 as the city's first urban shopping center.[27] At that same time, Houston land developer Frank Sharp was planning a 4,000-acre community in southwest Houston that was favorably located in the path of city expansion.[28] Sharp donated right-of-way for the new U.S. Highway 59 Southwest Freeway to assure access to his new Sharpstown Center, the first air-conditioned mall in Houston.[29] In 1957, Sharp offered the Union Baptist Association a 250-acre campus site in Sharpstown with a financing proposal that ultimately proved unacceptable.[30] However, when serious cash flow problems later developed for Sharp, he offered 390 acres of land on the Freeway for $760,000, but required cash.[31] The land was a rare bargain; at $2,000 an acre, the price represented only forty percent of what the UBA had paid Sharp for the site of the Sharpstown Mission.[32] Moreover, the campus would profit from the route of the new Southwest Freeway providing easy access from both north and south. Nonetheless, the UBA did not have the money in ready cash. At its December 1957 meeting at Youngblood's Chicken Shack on South Main, Rex Baker, Sr. recommended that the UBA College Committee appoint a development committee "to work out a contract with the Sharpstown landowners whereby the UBA will acquire the 390 acres of land in Sharpstown . . . for the

24. Lowery, p. 24.
25. Ibid.
26. Ray Miller, *Ray Miller's Houston* (Austin: Capital Printing, 1982), 187.
27. Miller, 183.
28. Sibley, 7.
29. Miller, 184.
30. Union Baptist Association of Texas, Minutes of Meetings of the Association, Meeting on 14 May 1957.
31. Sibley, 7-8.
32. Commander, 79.

View of the undeveloped campus tract looking east in 1960. Bellaire Boulevard is to the left of center; Beechnut is to the right. Downtown Houston is in the upper left-hand corner.

purpose of establishing a Baptist college."[33] Dr. O. D. Martin later mused, "The committee went to that meeting not owning a postage stamp and came out owing $760,000."[34]

In her history of the UBA Property Committee, Dr. Marilyn Sibley reported that Ross Dillon and Baker made the request for a bank loan to purchase the land, but were denied because there was no payback plan.[35] The two men sought the advice of Houston businessman Jake Kamin who recommended that Don McGregor, Executive Vice President of the T. J. Bettis Company, serve as a team member. McGregor suggested that half the property might be developed residentially to pay off the other half that could serve as a campus site. McGregor further recommended Stewart Morris, the President of Stewart Title Company, as one who could accomplish the enormous task of project leadership. The Special College Committee asked Kamin to talk to Morris. Ultimately, Morris

---

33. Union Baptist Association of Texas, Minutes of Meetings of the College Committee, Meeting on 17 Dec. 1957; Commander, 79-80.
34. Commander, 80. Commander's UBA history uses the incorrect figure of $780,000.
35. Sibley, 8.

agreed to assume the project provided Kamin and McGregor would work with him on a small committee given a high level of autonomy.[36]

Stewart Morris had been born in Houston and educated as an attorney. His business career had centered in the development of Stewart Title Company. His knowledge of the dynamics of the city and of the real estate business along with his commitment to the realization of a Christian college made him the gifted leader and advocate the project required.[37] Jake Kamin was a business partner with Morris in several ventures. Kamin was founder, Chairman of the Board, and Chief Executive Officer of American Mortgage Company and had achieved success as a financier and real estate developer. Kamin would subsequently create the residential and commercial venture of Nassau Bay adjacent to NASA and develop Sugar Creek in Fort Bend County.

Other influential laymen also became associated with the Special College Committee including attorneys Cecil Cook and Howard C. Lee, Sr.[38] Cook was a partner in the law firm of Butler, Binion, Rice, Cook and Knapp. He had been President of the Houston Bar Association and was a well-known and published expert in the field of petroleum law.[39] Lee was a partner in the law firm Carl & Lee and was founder of the Commercial Title Company. Lee had long been involved in assisting the Union Baptist Association to secure new church sites in the growing city. Denham named Morris as chair both of a development committee along with Kamin and McGregor and of a legal committee along with Cook and Lee. In time these two committees fused into a working unit called the College Property Committee that was officially approved by the Union Baptist Association in the 1962 annual session.[40]

Newton Rayzor, a member of the Rice Institute Board of Governors, knew of the proposal from Frank Sharp and volunteered that Rice had funds available and might be able to finance the land purchase for the Baptists. Not only was this good news, but the association with Rice was viewed as helpful in establishing the visibility and credibility of the project. Contractor Walter Mischer, Newton Rayzor, Ross Dillon, and

36. Sibley, 2.
37. Zarko Franks, "Helping Mankind More Important Than Riches to Stewart Morris," *Houston Chronicle*, 6 Aug. 1967, sec. 2, p. 1.
38. Sibley, 6.
39. *Who, Houston '80* (Houston: Who Houston, Inc., 1980), 92.
40. Union Baptist Association of Texas, Minutes of Meeting of the 121st Annual Session, Meeting in Nov. 1962, pp. 48-50.

Stewart Morris presented the loan opportunity to C. A. Dwyer, Business Manager at Rice.[41] The Institute agreed to lend $500,000 at six percent interest for five years using the land as collateral. However, there was still a shortfall of $260,000. Stewart Morris suggested a solution whereby the Bank of the Southwest that held the mortgage on the Sharp land might be approached to lend $260,000 based on the personal guaranty of a number of local businessmen. A. G. McNeese, President of the Bank, responded affirmatively to the proposal. Armed with the confidence of a certain funding mechanism, Morris pressed for the superior solution in his mind by requesting the total $760,000 from the Rice Institute, guaranteeing the top $260,000 with personal notes, and giving the 390 acres as collateral for the remaining $500,000. Rice agreed.

Ultimately, some twenty-five men would sign personal notes for $10,000. Rex Baker, Sr. committed to be responsible for $20,000. These founders were Rex G. Baker, Sr., the members of the Property Committee—Cecil Cook, Jake Kamin, Howard C. Lee, Sr., Don McGregor, and Stewart Morris—as well as Keith Beeman, Lloyd Bentsen (later U. S. Senator from the State of Texas,) W. D. Black, Jr., Stewart Boyle, Frank Breaker, Lester Cain, Ed Crocker, Tom S. Gandy, R. Graham Jackson, Ralph Lee, Milton McGinty, Don McMillian, Freeland Murphy, Robert Ray, Newton Rayzor, Joseph Russell, O. R. Smith, John Wooters, and W. M. Wright.[42] In time, these men would become known and remembered as the Founders of the College whose bold action, born of conviction, is commemorated each fall on or near the anniversary of the official chartering of the College.[43] The first Founders' Day ceremony was held November 16, 1964, and featured Stewart Morris as speaker.[44] The Founders were acknowledged in 1968 by a formal resolution of appreciation from the HBC President's Council and by a bronze plaque that marks the entrance to the Brown Academic Quadrangle.[45] Sibley reported that by 1961, "the property the founders had bought by the acre was selling by the square foot with prices still rising."[46]

41. (Dr. Stewart Morris, "Introduction of Martha Turner," Houston Baptist University Convocation, March 3, 2010).
42. Sibley, 10-11.
43. A copy of the Guaranty document was prepared for each founder. A copy of the Howard C. Lee, Sr. document is on file in the University archives.
44. "Founders' Day," *Houston Baptist College News,* Dec. 1964, pp. 1-2.
45. "Houston Baptist College President's Council Acknowledgement of Appreciation to the Founding Fathers of Houston Baptist College." Copy of document on file in University archives.
46. Sibley, 33.

The minutes of the Union Baptist Association in October 1958 acknowledged, "The most significant forward step in the establishment of a Baptist college in Houston achieved in the past year was the purchase of the 390-acre tract in Sharpstown."[47] The original tract of land was 419.63 acres less six parcels of property contained within. Of these six tracts, an eight-acre tract was owned by the Houston Independent School District; other parcels of land varied in size from 1.7 to 5.28 acres. These tracts had "either never been owned by the Grantor or had been theretofore conveyed by the Grantor by deeds of record."[48] In June, Cecil Cook reported a favorable Internal Revenue Service ruling that extended the tax-exempt status of the Union Baptist Association to the work of the Property Committee. "Any profit derived by the UBA from the sale of any or all of the tract of land of 390.6875 acres out of the J. R. Black, James Wells, and HT&BRR Company Section 2 survey Harris County, Texas would be exempt from the imposition of tax on unrelated business income."[49] The campus site of approximately 200 acres would be a triangular tract of land bordering the proposed route for the Southwest Freeway. The Union Baptist Association authorized the sale of as much of the land south of Beechnut as necessary to eliminate all financial obligations on the whole tract.[50]

The development of the remaining 190 acres as residential property, however, was to be fraught with difficulty. A twelve-acre tract within the college property was privately held and ultimately had to be purchased for $170,000—seven times the incremental value of the original tract.[51] A north-south easement at Bonhomme Road owned by Crown Central Petroleum had to be renegotiated.[52] Previously-approved city street layouts had to be legally abandoned in order to locate new streets for residential development.[53]

The City of Houston refused to install water and sewer service that had already been approved in a bond issue in 1956. Efforts to leverage response on these issues were greeted in the local press by charges of City

47. Sibley, 6.

48. General Warranty Deed #1880801, Harris County, State of Texas.

49. Union Baptist Association of Texas, Minutes of the Meetings of the College Committee, Meeting on 14 Apr. 1959.

50. Walker L. Knight, "Minding BGCT Business," *Baptist Standard*, June 1959, Vol. LXXI, No. 24, 6.

51. Commander, 80.

52. Union Baptist Association of Texas, Minutes of the Meetings of the College Committee, Meetings on 9 May 1958 and 16 Mar. 1959.

53. *Houston Post*, 24 Apr. 1983, sec. C, p. 1. Photo.

Hall favoritism and church-state compromise. When it was discovered that the city's inaction was due to a political feud that had nothing to do with the College, Ross Dillon established a virtual "sit-in" vigil at City Hall to get action on pending city services. Ultimately, sewer and water lines were laid—only to be followed by similar delays in getting street lighting installed. Dillon's tenacity and his reputation for securing positive response soon earned him the admiration and gratitude of the Committee and the affectionate nickname of "Bulldog Dillon."[54] In later meetings, the new Board of Trustees would express particular gratitude to Don McGregor for "hours spent in handling financial concerns and for securing the support of Mayor Lewis Cutrer to support water and sewer efforts."[55] Additional gratitude was expressed to contractor Walter Mischer for "his gracious cooperation and generosity evidenced through his work with and interest in the Houston Baptist College."[56] Mischer became a lifetime friend of Dr. Hinton and the College.

Adding to the difficulties in developing the residential acreage was the state of the Houston economy in 1958. Sibley observed that growth had slowed, construction was at a virtual standstill, and housing developers had begun abandoning projects.[57] The City of Houston was facing the same economic factors that had forced Sharp to sell the land in the first place. However, about the time the College lots were ready to be sold, the economy suddenly improved. Builders began looking for lots that were ready for construction. Howard Lee recalled that the College lots in Sharpstown were among the few in the city ready for immediate sale. The report of the Committee to the Union Baptist Association in 1959 projected that the 200-acre campus site would be debt-free within the next two years.[58]

A sub-committee from the Special College Committee met in June 1958 to address ten significant issues that would guide the development of the new College from planning to implementation. These decisions included the formulation of the exact plat for the campus site, the nature of the curriculum, the desire for a four-year institution with residential facilities, the role of intercollegiate athletics, the projected size of the student body, provision for parking, and the geographical orientation of the

54. "Reflections: HBC Beginning and HBC Today," *Houston Baptist College News,* Fall 1986, 13.
55. Houston Baptist College, Minutes of Meetings of the Board of Trustees, Meeting on 6 May 1961.
56. Houston Baptist College, Minutes of Meetings of the Board of Trustees, Meeting on 7 Sept. 1961.
57. Sibley, 20.
58. Sibley, 21.

campus on the land.[59] In time, the new Board of Trustees appointed two architectural firms to work together on the design the first campus buildings—Milton McGinty and Associates[60] and Lloyd and Morgan.[61]

§

In June 1958, the finance sub-committee determined to mount a fund-raising campaign in the spring of 1960 following the completion of several other major not-for-profit campaigns in the city.[62] Rex Baker, Sr. was finishing a period of elected alumni leadership at the University of Texas and agreed to serve as chair of the UBA campaign along with Denham and Don McGregor.[63] Although the BGCT requirement was for $3,000,000 to fund construction and endowment, the committee set a goal of $3,500,000:

> The campaign was officially launched . . . on March 30. . . . More than 2,000 Houston-area Baptists attended a special convocation marking "the birth of a college that could become one of Southern Baptists' foremost institutions.". . . Principal speaker, Ralph Phelps, President of Ouachita College . . . told the delegates that Houston Baptists have the need, opportunity, and resources to build a great Baptist college.[64]

Dr. Forrest Feezor, Executive Secretary of the BGCT, told campaign workers that "the college not only will fill the needs of Baptists, but of the entire Houston community."[65]

The firm Associated Consultants for Education was employed to help plan for curriculum, faculty, and administrative needs.[66] Former Florida State University President Dr. Doak Campbell served as consultant to the Special Committee.[67] The *Birth of a College* campaign published an attrac-

---

59. Union Baptist Association of Texas, Minutes of the Meetings of the College Committee, Meeting on 25 June 1958.

60. *Who Houston*, 287.

61. Houston Baptist College, Minutes of Meetings of the Building Committee of the Board of Trustees, Meeting on 19 May 1962.

62. Union Baptist Association of Texas, Minutes of the Meetings of the College Finance Committee, Meeting on 16 June 1958.

63. "College Chairman Named," *Baptist Standard*, Feb. 1960, Vol. LXXII, No. 6, 10.

64. "Baptists Start Drive for Houston College," *Paris (Texas) News*, 24 Mar. 1960, p. 17; Lowry, pp. 39-40.

65. "Houston Baptist College Proposed," *Odessa American*, 23 Mar. 1960, p. 7.

66. "Blueprint for Houston," *Baptist Standard*, Apr. 1959, Vol. LXXXXI, No. 15, 10.

67. Union Baptist Association of Texas, Minutes of the Meetings of the College Committee, Meeting on 20 Feb. 1959.

tive, fact-filled prospectus stating the rationale for the new college and describing its basic objectives.[68] The Education Commission of the BGCT had made prior commitments of its resources from 1955 to 1960 to support the efforts of East Texas Baptist College, Howard Payne College, and the University of Corpus Christi to become accredited.[69] However, those funds were to become available to the Houston committee in 1960.

Rex G. Baker, Sr., Vice-President and General Counsel for Humble Oil, was a staunch advocate for an institution of academic excellence.[70] Baker was active in University of Texas affairs and was experienced in matters of academic management and institutional governance. Baker had been appointed Chair of the University of Texas "Committee of 75" whose 1958 report helped catapult that University beyond its regional reputation into the top tier of American research universities.[71] Baker was named the Outstanding University of Texas Alumnus in 1963.[72] He had a stellar reputation in the Houston business community, and his engagement with the project opened many doors of support. The other important early team member with Dr. Dillon and Mr. Baker was O. D. Martin, the UBA District Superintendent of Missions, who had strong influence with the Baptist churches in the area.[73]

The geographical boundaries of the Union Baptist Association extended far beyond the limits of the city of Houston. Therefore, the campaign focused on Baptist churches in southeast Texas—primarily those in Districts 3, 4, and 15 that encompassed some 400,000 church members. "One-fourth of the population of Texas lived in a radius of 100 miles of Houston."[74] Churches initially were asked to raise the money needed for the first year's interest on the Rice loan. The UBA contracted with the New York firm of Ward, Freshmen & Reinhardt to organize and conduct the campaign. The consultant's fee was to be privately underwritten and not charged against the campaign. Under Baker's leadership, the campaign was successfully completed by gifts and pledges

---

68. *Birth of a College* (Houston: Union Baptist Association, 1960).
69. Walker L. Knight, *Baptist Standard*, Dec. 1956, Vol. LXVIII, No. 50, 9.
70. "Meet the Trustees: Rex. G. Baker," *Houston Baptist College News*, May 1963, 3.
71. Marc Schwartz, "Change in Course: the Committee of 75," *McCombs School of Business, University of Texas at Austin, Fall/Winter 2002 Magazine*, Dec. 2002.
72. The University of Texas Alumni Association, "Distinguished Alumnus Award Recipients: Rex. G. Baker, Sr., 1963," University of Texas Alumni Association, www.texasexes.org (accessed January 16, 2009).
73. Sibley, 3-4.
74. Commander, 81.

prior to the annual meeting of the Union Baptist Association in October 1960. The Special Committee reported to the Association that approval for the new college was expected at the annual BGCT meeting in November. In anticipation of the appointment of the first college trustees by the BGCT, the final report from the Special College Committee, first appointed in 1952, expressed particular appreciation to Rex Baker, Sr., Cecil Cook, Don McGregor, Stewart Morris, Robert Ray, James S. Riley, and Hermond Westmoreland—all of whom would later serve on the College Board of Trustees.[75] In 1955, the personnel of the committee was increased to include Rex Baker, Jr., R. G. Commander, O. D. Martin, Donald McGregor, Carloss Morris, James W. Parker, Newton Rayzor, W. E. Sampson, E. H. Westmoreland, K. Owen White, Stanley Wilkes, Kyle M. Yates, and R. P. York.[76] By 1957, the members of the Special College Committee included Chair William E. Denham, Joe Allbritton, Milton Bailey, Rex G. Baker, Sr., Rex G. Baker, Jr., John Baugh, W. S. Boyle, Tom Burr, L. D. Cain, R. G. Commander, Cecil Cook, Paul Denny, Gabriel Fransee, Earl Hankamer, William M. Harrell, Sterling Hogan, Paul Jeffrey, Jake Kamin, Roy E. Ladd, Donald McGregor, Ray Mayfield, Jr., O. D. Martin, L. D. Morgan, Stewart Morris, Freeland Murphy, J. W. Parker, A. B. Penny, Robert H. Ray, J. Newton Rayzor, James S. Riley, O. A. Taylor, E. H. Westmoreland, K. Owen White, and J. E. Williamson.[77]

The Special College Committee recommended that the institution be a co-educational liberal arts college with "special emphasis on religion and the natural sciences."[78] Among those tenets set forth by the Committee were a belief in the Bible as the inspired Word of God and the desire for a faculty "of highest academic competency" committed to a Christian life "which is deliberate, unapologetic and Baptist where possible."[79] There were additional commitments that the College teach the dignity and freedom of the individual under God, that students be chosen on the basis of Christian character and scholarship, that the moral and spiritual development of the student be of paramount importance, and that teaching

75. Lowry, pp. 33-36, 42.
76. Commander, 77-78,
77. Union Baptist Association of Texas, Minutes of the Meetings of the College Committee, Meeting on 17 Dec. 1957.
78. Sibley, 2, 6.
79. Baptist Press, "Houston Launches Fund Drive," *Baptist Standard*, Vol. LXXII, No. 13, 11.
80. Ibid.

include the responsibility of every individual to God and country.[80] "Believing that no incongruity need exist between profound spirituality and the highest scholastic standards, we propose that the aim of the College shall be to excel both in scholarship and in Christian training."[81] This early period of College planning history is the subject of the book, *To Benefit a University: the UBA College Property Committee 1958-1975*, by Dr. Marilyn Sibley, later Chair of the HBU Department of History at the time of its writing in 1978.[82]

Dr. E. N. Jones, Secretary of the Christian Education Commission of the BGCT, visited with the College Committee in October 1960. Dr. Jones, the former President of Texas Tech University, expressed particular concern about operating funds for the first five years. The general, acknowledged anxiety about the actual payment of pledges by churches led to extended discussion with Dr. Jones about how church pledges had been acquired, how they had been approved by local congregations, and how they had been legally documented. Baker explained that a major gift of $350,000 from the M. D. Anderson Foundation that was included in the $3,000,000 total was a certainty but would not be forthcoming until the Foundation's new fiscal year.[83] Cash, pledges, and assets totaled $3,151, 264, but cash on hand represented only $208,646.[84] In preparation for the BGCT meeting in November, the Christian Education Commission drafted the motion, "While the criteria have not been met in the letter of the law, yet it (sic) has been met in spirit, therefore: This Commission recommends to the Executive Board that the Union Baptist Association will be considered as having met the criteria and that the charter be granted."[85] There was great elation in Houston over the Commission's recommendation.

The previous August, a trustee nominating committee had been announced composed of W. M. Harrell, Houston; Milton W. Bailey, Houston; Arthur L. Jordan, Baytown; Roy E. Ladd, Houston; and Ralph M. Smith, Rosenberg.[86] In November 1960, meeting in convention in

81. Lowry, pp. 40-41.
82. Marilyn Sibley, *To Benefit a University: the Union Baptist Association Property Committee, 1958-1975* (Houston: Houston Baptist University, 1978).
83. Union Baptist Association of Texas, Minutes of the Meetings of the College Committee, Meeting on 28 Jul. 1960.
84. Houston Baptist College, Minutes of Meetings of the Board of Trustees, Meeting on 17 Jan. 1961.
85. Union Baptist Association of Texas, Minutes of the Meetings of the College Committee, Meeting on 21 Oct. 1960.
86. "Nominating Committee Announced," *Baptist Standard*, Aug. 1960, Vol. LXXII, No. 33, 11.

Lubbock, the Baptist General Convention approved the plans for the new college and appointed its first Board of Trustees[87] that included Rex G. Baker, Sr.,[88] John Baugh,[89] Cecil Cook,[90] Dr. William Denham,[91] Roy Dolen, George Duncan,[92] A. L. Jordan,[93] Jake Kamin,[94] Clyde Kennelly,[95] Ray V. Mayfield, Jr.,[96] Donald McGregor,[97] L. D. Morgan,[98] Stewart Morris,[99] Freeland M. Murphy,[100] John Newton,[101] James W. Parker,[102] Robert Ray,[103] James S. Riley,[104] J. J. Slone,[105] Florence Oldham Weaver,[106] and James E. Williamson.[107] Following the approval of the CECB motion by the Baptist General Convention of Texas, the *Articles of Incorporation of Houston Baptist College* was signed in the first meeting of the new trustees on November 15, 1960, and was carried to Austin the next day by Rex Baker, Sr. to be recorded with the Secretary of State Zollie Steakely as Charter #169920.[108] These signatures were duly notarized by the well-known, long-time UBA secretary Jane Elder. According to meeting minutes, others present for the signing for whom the new college was a long-held dream included Dub Black, Edwin Crawford,[109] Ross Dillon, W. M. Harrell, and O. D. Martin. The College Property Committee continued "to act as trustee for the UBA in the holding, management, and development of real estate with the profits and proceeds to

---

87. "Found Faithful is Convention Theme," *Lubbock Avalanche Journal*, 31 Oct. 1960, sec. D, p. 1.

88. "Meet the Trustees," *Houston Baptist College News*, May 1963, 3. Biography with photo.

89. "Council Anniversary," *Houston Baptist College News*, Nov. 1964, 4. Photo.

90. "Meet the Trustees," *Houston Baptist College News*, Feb. 1963, 3. Biography with photo.

91. "Meet the Trustees," *Houston Baptist College News*, Vol. 1, No. 1, 3. Biography with photo.

92. "Meet the Trustees," *Houston Baptist College News*, Aug. 1963, 3. Biography with photo.

93. "Meet the Trustees," *Houston Baptist College News*, May 1963, 3. Biography with photo.

94. Sibley, 80.

95. "Meet the Trustees," *Houston Baptist College News*, Aug. 1963, 3. Biography with photo.

96. "Meet the Trustees," *Houston Baptist College News*, Feb. 1963, 3. Biography with photo.

97. "Meet the Trustees," *Houston Baptist College News*, June 1963, 3. Biography with photo.

98. "Meet the Trustees," *Houston Baptist College News*, Apr. 1963, 3. Biography with photo.

99. "Meet the Trustees," *Houston Baptist College News*, July 1963, 3. Biography with photo.

100. Freland Murphy was a member of Baptist Temple Church. He was an inventor and held patents in both the United States and Canada. "Obituary: Laura Belle Murphy," *Houston Chronicle*, 16 July 2002, sec. A, p. 3, three-star ed.

101. "Meet the Trustees," *Houston Baptist College News*, Apr. 1963, 3. Biography with photo.

102. "Meet the Trustees," *Houston Baptist College News*, July 1963, 3. Biography with photo.

103. "Meet the Trustees," *Houston Baptist College News*, Dec. 1962, 3. Biography with photo.

104. "Meet the Trustees," *Houston Baptist College News*, June 1963, 3. Biography with photo.

105. Sibley, 12, 24, 86. Photo.

106. Sibley, 83-84.

107. "Dr. Williamson Heads Mathematics Department," *Houston Baptist College News*, June 1963, 1-2. Photo.

108. Union Baptist Association of Texas, Minutes of the Meetings of the College Committee, Meeting on 15 Nov. 1960; Sibley, 24.

109. "Around the State: Deaths," *Baptist Standard*, 6 Jan. 2003. In 1960, Crawford was a founding trustee and was pastor of West End Baptist Church.

benefit the college." Within the annals of the Education Commission of the Southern Baptist Convention of Texas, Houston Baptist College became institution 72; Mobile College followed in 1961 as institution 73.[110]

§

As early as June 1959, minutes of the UBA College Committee record the first draft of an institutional purpose statement including commitments to a Christian faculty, students of good character, focus on liberal arts education, assurance of quality, a campus of the "highest order," and emphasis on high moral and spiritual values "that exemplify the Christian principles of Baptists."[111] At this time, the new college planned to open in 1962.[112] The committee described a business plan that would provide for a freshman class of 250 to 300 students in the first year with advanced study to be added one year at a time until a four-year program was realized. The committee further projected an ultimate student body of 1200 students.[113]

Shortly after the 1960 chartering, Dr. Denham, the Chairman of the new HBC Board, asked a task force to draft a formal statement describing the nature of the new institution. Those appointed were Chairman Cecil Cook, Rex Baker, Sr., Edwin Crawford, Stewart Morris, and James Parker.[114] Stewart Morris recalled that some early efforts at wording were so amorphous as to lack specificity about matters of doctrine. Similar statements from other colleges were reviewed. Ultimately, drafts were submitted to Chairman Cook by Morris and by Baker. This statement came to be called the Preamble to the By-Laws of the new College. The Preamble was unanimously approved by the Board of Trustees in February 1961 and has since consistently appeared in the College and University documents as a constant reminder of its tenets.

---

110. *Southern Baptist Educator*, July/August 1962, 10.
111. Union Baptist Association of Texas, Minutes of the Meetings of the College Committee, Meeting on 27 June 1959.
112. "Charter Application Made for New College," *Waco Tribune*, 17 Nov. 1960, p. 7.
113. Union Baptist Association of Texas, Minutes of the Meetings of the College Committee, Meeting on 10 Feb. 1959.
114. Houston Baptist College, Minutes of Meetings of the Board of Trustees, Meeting on 15 Feb. 1961; Sibley, 26.

PREAMBLE TO THE BY-LAWS

The Houston Baptist College is a Christian liberal arts college. Its purpose is to offer a curriculum of studies and a program of student activities dedicated to the development of moral character, the enrichment of spiritual lives, and the perpetuation of growth in Christian ideals. Founded under the providence of God and with the conviction that there is a need for a college in this community that will train the mind, develop the moral character, and enrich the spiritual lives of all people who may come within the ambit of its influence, HOUSTON BAPTIST COLLEGE shall stand as a witness for Jesus Christ, expressed directly through its administration, faculty, and students. To assure the perpetuation of these basic concepts of its founders, it is resolved that all those who become associated with Houston Baptist College as a trustee, officer, member of the faculty or of the staff, must believe in the divine inspiration of the Bible, both the Old Testament and New Testament, that man was directly created by God, the virgin birth of Jesus Christ, our Lord and Saviour, as the Son of God, that He died for the sins of all men and thereafter arose from the grave, that by repentance and the acceptance of and belief in Him, by the grace of God, the individual is saved from eternal damnation and receives eternal life in the presence of God; and it is further resolved that the ultimate teachings in this college shall always be consistent with the above principles.[115]

In view of the divisive theological debates among Baptists over the course of the next twenty years, it is significant to note that this Preamble statement was written in 1961, two years before the College opened. Written by the first trustees, the Preamble was a spontaneous expression of doctrine that was reflective of evangelical orthodoxy in an increasingly secular age. The Preamble was not reactive to any threatening challenge but rather was penned without pressure from any external source. Trustee Howard Lee, Sr. described the Preamble as "pro-Christian, not anti-any-thing."[116] Stewart Morris called the Preamble "the steel" that held together the very foundation of the new College. Morris contended, "Millions of dollars and the tens of thousands of man hours have been given in support of the precepts and the concepts encompassed by our Preamble."[117]

---

115. Houston Baptist College, *Bulletin of Information* 1963 (Houston: Houston Baptist College, 1962), 6.
116. Sibley, 30.
117. Sibley, 31.

25

§

The primary task of the College Board of Trustees was to fulfill the requirements of the Baptist General Convention of Texas for approval and funding. As negotiations began for design and construction of campus buildings, Baker reported that payments on church pledges were approximately $1,000,000 less than anticipated. However, Stewart Morris reported for the Property Committee that an audit showed the "College property to be quite out of the woods. We have $500,000 of assets in excess of paying the indebtedness to Rice."[118] In the face of the church payment shortfall, at the February 1962 meeting of the trustees, Dr. Dillon proposed a campaign designed to raise $2,000,000 outside the churches as a *Crusade for Christian Education* spearheaded by consultant Joe L. Mayes.[119] In further action Dr. Dillon and Florence Weaver presented a resolution conveying a major gift from Miss Enla V. Atwood to establish a School of Theology on the campus.[120] Miss Atwood was President of the Houston Developers and Builders, Inc. and a member of Second Baptist Church.[121]

In an act that portended many discussions in the future, Cecil Cook moved that a committee be appointed to study the feasibility of changing the name of the College; John Baugh was named chair of a committee that included Rex G. Baker, Sr. and L. D. Morgan.[122] Discussion centered both upon the possibility of renaming the institution in response to a major gift and upon the efficacy of the name "college" to communicate to the public the academic aspirations the trustees held. Rice Institute had experienced similar confusion in the public eye in the 1950s resulting in its decision to change its name to Rice University in 1960. The name-change topic was introduced into board meetings many times over the next several years and resulted ultimately in changing the institutional name to Houston Baptist University in 1973.

Meanwhile, final decisions regarding campus construction were determined. A proposed site plan for campus development was presented by architect Milton McGinty; George Duncan projected construction

---

118   Sibley, 33.
119   Houston Baptist College, Minutes of Meetings of the Board of Trustees, Meeting on 13 Feb. 1962.
120   Ibid.
121   "$1 million given HBC for '62 startup," *Houston Post,* 21 May, 1962. Photo of Governor Price Daniel turning first spade of earth.
122   Ibid.

Groundbreaking ceremonies included Dr. Dillon, Dr. Denham, D. K. Harrell, Dr. Williamson, Gov. and Mrs. Price Daniel, Miss Enla Atwood, and Mrs. Florence Woltman.

costs to be approximately $16 per square foot. An estimate of $1,050,000 was proposed by the Building Committee to construct the academic quadrangle excluding equipment, roads, underground utilities, and architectural fees.[123] The Board approved the construction and moved forward with development of construction documents. At a meeting in May 1962, architect Herman Lloyd presented final architectural drawings, and the Board approved a construction budget of $1,100,000, or $14.14 per square foot.[124]

The formal groundbreaking ceremony for the academic quadrangle was planned by consultant Dr. Howard Bruce. Governor Price Daniel, a Baptist layman, brought the address for the groundbreaking held on May

123. Ibid.
124. Houston Baptist College, Minutes of Meetings of the Board of Trustees, Meeting on 15 May 1961.
125. *Houston Post*, 17 May 1972; *Houston Press*, 18 May 1962. Houston Baptist College archives newspaper clipping file.

20, 1962. "If Houston and Southwest Texas continue to grow and to develop as they are expected to do, there will be a very large role for the new college to fill."[125] The event was reported in the *Houston Post* and by KPRC-TV and KHOU-TV marking an auspicious beginning for awareness of the new college by the local media.[126]

In July 1962, H. A. Lott, Inc. was approved as contractor for the first buildings that were to cost $1,116,171.[127] About this same time, the first of the new administrative officers were joining the college team. President Dr. W. H. Hinton was quickly assimilated into the rapid pace of activity. One of Hinton's first acts was to recommend that the College Property Committee be given responsibility for all property development, not just the Sharpstown campus project.[128] These holdings ultimately included Atwood properties on Kirby Drive and on Memorial Drive at Brittmoore, land in the Sharpstown Industrial Park that secured the Sharp Gym gift, and a twelve-acre tract on the Southwest Freeway between Gessner Road and Beechnut Street where KPRC-TV would later be built. Future action by the College Property Committee would ultimately develop Inwood Forest, Inwood Pines, Bellaire-West, land along the Southwest Freeway, and consummate the sale of campus property to Memorial Hospital for relocation of the downtown hospital facility.

In 1961, Texas Baptists mounted a ten-year financial campaign in support of higher education that was called the *Decade of Decision: Texas Baptist Crusade for Christian Education*.[129] Dr. E. N. Jones, Secretary of the Christian Education Commission, called for restoration of Texas Baptist colleges "to the place of respect and leadership in education they once held."[130] A book and promotional film described the $28,000,000 campaign that included a potential $2,000,000 allocation for Houston Baptist College.[131] Among Texas Baptist colleges at that time, the University of Corpus Christi was still operational, and Dallas Baptist College had not yet become a reality.

In November 1962, the firm Lloyd, Morgan and Jones was approved to serve as coordinating architects for the Sharp Gymnasium as well as the

---

126. (Letter from consultant Joe L. Mayes to Rex Baker, June 23, 1962).
127. Houston Baptist College, Minutes of Meetings of the Board of Trustees, Meeting on 20 July 1962.
128. Sibley, 43.
129. Dr. E. N. Jones, "Decade of Decision: 1961-1970," *Decade of Decision* (Dallas: Baptist General Convention of Texas, 1960), 11.
130. Ibid.
131. "Baptist Secretary Places Emphasis on Inner Space," *Amarillo Globe-Times*, 9 Nov. 1961, p. 6.

The 1962 view north from Beechnut at the freeway frontage road. Dr. Hinton and Dr. Dillon stand beneath the announcement of the new college.

Atwood Theology Building. The Board authorized funds not to exceed $400,000 for the gym and $70,000 for a President's home on campus.[132] Interim funding was needed for both projects. Eventually, permanent financing was secured with Southwestern Savings.[133] Rex Baker, Sr. recommended that the student center be named for the M. D. Anderson Foundation in gratitude for their gift of $350,000. Additionally, in a move that would direct the path of campus development over at least the next fifty years, Stewart Morris urged "that only *permanent* structures be put on the campus, else we might fall in the trap of never getting rid of temporary structures."[134] By December 1962, construction was underway on the academic quadrangle. By February, work began on the dormitories;[135] in the spring, construction started on the President's

---

132. Houston Baptist College, Minutes of Meetings of the Board of Trustees, Meeting on 13 Sept. 1962.

133. Houston Baptist College, Minutes of Meetings of the Board of Trustees, Meeting on 13 Nov. 1962.

134. Ibid.

135. "Construction Begins on New Dorms," *Houston Baptist College News,* Feb. 1963, 1, 4. Photos.

The first campus building served as administrative offices.

Home.[136] A February article in the *Houston Post* reported on campus construction and plans for the fall 1963 opening.[137]

Work had also begun to assemble the opening day collection of the new College library. Dr. Jefferson Caskey was appointed in 1962 to begin selection, purchase, solicitation, and processing of new books. Library operations were set up in temporary headquarters in the Sharpstown State Bank Building awaiting completion of the academic quadrangle.[138] In trustee meetings, J. J. Slone presented a curriculum plan that was the product of the new Vice President H. B. Smith, consultant Doak Campbell, and President Hinton. A. L. Jordan proposed an academic calendar of two semesters for the first year. Rex Baker, Sr. proposed the first year's tuition and fees. Stewart Morris proposed basic admissions

136. "From this to this," *Houston Baptist College News,* Feb. 1963, 2. Photos.
137. "Houston Baptist College Plans To Open Sept 16," *Houston Post*, 8 Feb. 1963, sec. 1, p. 2.
138. "Librarian Hard at Work Preparing for September Opening," *Houston Baptist College News*, Mar. 1963, 3.

policies.[139]   Dr. James E. Williamson presented text for the first college catalog as a report from the trustee Academic Committee.[140]

In January 1963, Dr. Hinton reported that twenty-six faculty members had been employed, twenty-two of whom held the doctorate. Dr. James E. Williamson, UBA College Committee member and founding trustee, submitted his resignation from the Board of Trustees in order to accept faculty appointment beginning on June 1.[141] In University history, only three other trustees later served as full-time members of the faculty: Dr. James Riley, Dr. Bill West, and Dr. Robert Creech.

Construction of two dormitories was approved with a budget of $800,000 to include landscaping and a walk with gas lights from the dorms to the main academic quadrangle.[142] Construction of the Atwood Theology Building was also approved pending negotiations with the Baptist Foundation of Texas for management of the Atwood property located on Kirby Drive, as well as the Memorial Oaks subdivision.

The first draft of a proposed *Manual of Organization* was prepared by Dr. H. B. Smith and presented to Dr. Hinton for approval on January 24, 1963. The document contained job descriptions, delineated responsibilities for standing committees, and provided "General Information" detailing operation policies, i.e., "The College will not at this time operate a campus post office, but mail will be distributed at the Information Window in the Administration Building."[143] The *Manual* also included policy on such professional issues as absences, academic freedom, appointments and contracts, chaperones, consulting, faculty evaluation, insurance, payroll, professional growth, rank, teaching load, tenure, and "full tuition discounts for children of full-time employees."[144]

The trustees discussed the efficacy of a college advisory board to attract and hold the interest of members of the community. Many of the suggested members later became trustees or played important roles in the life of the young college. These included Bruce Belin, Jr., Warren Bellows, Charles Bybee, Harry Chavanne, Frank Cornelius, W. T.

---

139. Houston Baptist College, Minutes of Meetings of the Board of Trustees, Meeting on 13 Nov. 1962.

140. Houston Baptist College, Minutes of Meetings of the Board of Trustees, Meeting on 3 Jan. 1963.

141. (Dr. James Williamson to Dr. William Denham filed with Minutes of the Houston Baptist College Board of Trustees, Meeting on 5 Feb. 1963).

142. Houston Baptist College, Minutes of Meetings of the Board of Trustees, Meeting on 3 Jan. 1963.

143. Dr. H. B. Smith, *Manual of Organization* (Houston: Houston Baptist College, 24 Jan. 1963). An attached and undated memo reads, "Attached is a first of draft of a work copy of a Manual of Organization for our campus."

144. Houston Baptist College, *Manual of Organization*, 11-23.

Doherty, James A. Elkins Jr., Tom Gandy, Earl Hankamer, Leon Jaworski, John T. Jones, Jr., James E. Lyon, Mrs. R. Thomas McDermott, Kline McGee, Al Parker, Newton Rayzor, Frank Sharp, Gilbert Turner, Clyde Verheyden, and Joe Wessendorf.[145]

On February 14, 1963, the final payment was made to Rice Institute. The land had greatly increased in value since its purchase in 1958. What had been raw land was now residential and campus property. The city was rapidly moving in the direction of the college. The 2010 dollar equivalent of the undeveloped campus tract on the uncompleted Southwest Freeway, purchased for $760,000 in 1958, is estimated to be over $6,000,000.[146] However, the 2010 appraised value of the 390 acres is approximately $125,000,000.[147]

Ross Dillon wrote a letter of appreciation to Stewart Morris on the occasion of this final payment:

> I thank God for what you mean to the development of Houston Baptist College and to me personally. My high regard for you as a Christian, as a business man, and as a layman in the Lord's work has deepened more and more as the months have passed. The coming into being of Houston Baptist College is due in large measure to your devotion and business acumen. May God continue to bless you daily.[148]

The Board of Trustees sought to be financially competitive in the academic marketplace in order to secure the best faculty possible. Incentives for faculty—including fringe benefits, housing reimbursement, and moving expenses—were important in faculty recruitment, as were provisions for sabbatical leave, tenure, and professional growth. In April, the Board approved a faculty retirement policy that provided ten percent matching funds to supplement a five percent personal contribution with an escalation to a fifteen percent college contribution upon the attainment of tenure.[149] This benefit, however, did not extend to staff until many years later. This generous plan recognized the senior stature of this first faculty, affirmed the Board's plan to develop an institution of academic excellence, and enhanced the success of faculty recruiting.

---

145   Houston Baptist College, Minutes of Meetings of the Board of Trustees, Meeting on 19 Feb. 1963.
146. Consumer price index used for comparison. (accessed Feb. 7, 2010).
147. (Assistant Vice President of Treasury Operations Hugh McClung to Dr. Don Looser, Oct. 5, 2009).
148. Sibley, 44.
149. Houston Baptist College, Minutes of Meetings of the Board of Trustees, Meeting on 9 Apr. 1963.

§

The Board continued to try to exploit the financial capabilities of property along the Freeway while developing a campus plan that would be the model for years to come. Professor Robert Rucker was approved as the land-planning consultant and landscape architect for the new campus.[150] Rucker was a member of the faculty in landscape design at both Oklahoma State University and, later, Texas A&M University. Rucker's plan, adopted by the Building Committee on July 19, 1963, still remains the foundational model for campus development.[151]

In these early days of property development, discussion about a "senior citizen project" ensued among the board members.[152] A model of such a proposed project for the triangle at Fondren, Guildford Road, and the Southwest Freeway was constructed and went on display in the Sharpstown State Bank lobby. At the May 1963 meeting of the Board, the members of the College Property Committee were appointed to serve as directors of a wholly-owned subsidiary to "lease, own, and/or operate" such a senior citizens' development.[153] At the same meeting, the Board created an HBC Foundation that could receive gifts on behalf of the College. Serving as members of the Foundation were Rex Baker, Sr., Don McGregor, Stewart Morris, Robert Ray, plus several "non-Baptist" members—Charles Bybee (Houston Bank and Trust), Joe Woodward (South Coast Life Insurance), and Clyde Verheyden (The Good Samaritan Foundation).[154]

By the summer of 1963, the Board began to see the tangible fruits of its labor. James Riley announced the June 1 arrival of the first new faculty. Over 120 students had been admitted. Registrar Bobbie Hinton documented the admission of the first of the new freshmen including Judy Bennatte, Timothy Brown, William Crump, Martha Failing, Diane

150. "Through These Portals: Proposed Entrance to Campus," *Houston Baptist College News,* Mar. 1965, 3. Photo.

151. Houston Baptist College, Minutes of the Meetings of the Building Committee of the Board of Trustees, Meeting on 19 July 1963.

152. Houston Baptist College, Minutes of Meetings of the Board of Trustees, Meeting on 13 July 1962 and on 3 Jan. 1963.

153. Houston Baptist College, Minutes of Meetings of the Board of Trustees, Meeting on 29 May 1963.

154. Houston Baptist College, Minutes of Meetings of the Board of Trustees, Meeting on 3 Jan. 1963.

155. Lowry, p. 84. (Interview with Registrar Bobbie Ruth Hinton, 9 Dec. 1966).

156. "College Store Preparing for September Opening," *Houston Baptist College News*, Aug. 1963, 1. Photo.

157. Ruth Rosenfeld, "Hinton House: Gracious New Home for A College President," *Bellaire Texan,* 28 Aug. 1963, p. 4.

Halbert, John Robert Hubbard, Elaine Lowry, and Bill Myers.[155]   The College Bookstore found a manager, Dorothy Jackson, who began setting up that vital operation over the summer.[156]   The President's Home was nearing early-summer completion;[157] the academic quadrangle facilities were projected to be completed by July 15; the dormitories were to be ready for fall occupancy; and the gymnasium was anticipated by late September.   Marshall Construction was at work on the Atwood Theology Building.[158]   In May, the Board reviewed the accomplishments of the first five years and gave thanks for extraordinary leadership, personal sacrifice, and providential guidance.   In relief and gratitude, the Board gave a standing ovation to Chairman Denham for "securing the cooperation of Texas Baptists in the establishment of the College and his efforts in leading the trustees."[159]

§

The chronicle of personal commitment of time, resource, and energy by these first business leaders and pastors is a remarkable record of achievement.   Many of these founders laid aside their personal career and business activities for months at a time to respond to the extraordinary needs of the new college.   On many occasions—some recorded and many doubtless unrecorded—trustees personally paid College expenses.   When construction funds ran short on the Sharp Gymnasium project, contractor H. A. Lott absorbed the additional construction costs to build the facility as the architect had originally designed it.[160]   Committee minutes document an early loan interest payment made quietly by Don McGregor because College funds had been depleted.   Tennis court repairs at one point were funded by architects Herman Lloyd, Milton McGinty, and trustee Robert Ray.[161]   Stewart Morris recalls one memorable meeting of trustee leadership at his home where it was suggested that the College declare bankruptcy and cut its losses.   Founding trustee Robert Ray responded, "We will mortgage our own homes before taking such a course.   No more of such talk!"[162]   It may never be known how much per-

---

158. Houston Baptist College, Minutes of Meetings of the Board of Trustees, Meeting on 29 May 1963.
159. Ibid.
160. (H. A. Lott to Dr. W. H. Hinton, Nov. 22, 1963).
161. Houston Baptist College, Minutes of Meetings of the Building Committee, Board of Trustees, Meeting on 9 June 1964.
162. (Dr. Stewart Morris to Dr Don Looser, Jan. 15, 2010).

sonal financial contribution was made by these first trustees with little acknowledgement or fanfare. Equally significant was the provision of professional expertise provided by these trustees to the waves of unanticipated problems that beset the founding of the College.

There were those leaders whose names continually appear in written records; it also seems apparent that there were countless contributions by other trustees that were never formally reported. It is noteworthy, however, that all of these entrepreneurial founders, most of whom were accustomed to high levels of personal autonomy in their own professional domains, fell easily into harness with each other to pull together toward a common goal with little regard for rank, title, or position.

It is a beautiful story.

THREE

1963-1965

In 1963, with the opening of the new College, the Board of Trustees moved to redefine its role from one of developing an idea whose realization was still in the future to one of responding to a functional institution with its own set of immediate requirements. Students had to be fed and housed. Faculty had to be paid. Funding for the immediate operational demands now became pressing; cash flow became an operational concern. In August 1963, the trustees authorized borrowing $37,000 to meet the monthly payroll for faculty and staff who had been working since June 1. Payment of church pledges by local Baptist congregations toward the $3,500,000 goal was slow. These pledges had been made in 1960 as a result of the campaign to meet the requirements of the Baptist General Convention of Texas. In late summer 1963, William Bolton reported that only $50,000 of a currently-needed $200,000 had been paid to date. BGCT funding contributed $62,000 in 1962 and $120,000 in 1963.[1]

From the outset, the College had been blessed by the participation of trustees who had not only exceptional business acumen, but who also volunteered massive amounts of time and energy to birth the new enterprise. Part of the maturation process for the Board was passing the operation of the College to the administration, faculty, and staff. Expectation was high. Idealism confronted practical reality. Stress permeated the difficulty of day-to-day discovery of new need. Control gave way to shared responsibility and authority.

Varying views of institutional reality were held by students, faculty, administrators, and trustees as revealed in the minutes of faculty meetings, those of the Board of Trustees, and the *Collegian*. Students had their own sense of what was happening, what was important, and what was needed for the collegiate experience. Faculty members shared curriculum and learning environment with students, but had their own perspective rooted in professional issues—tenure, sabbatical leave, housing, fringe benefits, academic support, professional growth, and academic freedom.

---

1. Houston Baptist College, Minutes of Meetings of the Board of Trustees, Meeting on 13 Sept. 1962.

The College administration shared the concerns of students and faculty but had additional responsibility for the development of policy, operational objectives, morale, team-building, and inculcation of the dream. More immediate was the responsibility of the administration to make the available resources stretch to address the unpredictable demands of the unfolding campus operation.

The Board of Trustees struggled financially to sustain the College and understand the faculty's need for academic autonomy and a secure work environment. Other than Baker and Denham, few of the trustees had previous collegiate governance experience. With the opening of the College in 1963, trustees were confronted with many new realizations about academic operation—academic hierarchy, shared decision-making, academic freedom, and the authority of the faculty in curricular matters. Some of the accreditation requirements by the Southern Association of Colleges and Schools challenged the autonomy with which the Board had operated in its years of planning and development. The concept of "shared governance" was new to many trustees.

The College opening was exhilarating and exhausting. Faculty contracts had begun on June 1—a particularly critical date—because the faculty had only three months to develop curriculum for the freshman courses before classes actually began. The new faculty had been offered residential lots on Beechnut Street across from the campus. Drs. Duncan Tidwell,[2] Arthur Travis,[3] Claude Rhea,[4] Wayne Barton, and Chris Jordan purchased lots and built custom homes, establishing a handsome 'faculty row.'[5] Most other faculty members took advantage of special arrangements made by the College with selected home builders and settled in the Sharpstown area, many west of the proposed Southwest Freeway. A series of illuminating personal interviews with the new faculty was printed in successive issues of the *Bellaire Texan* during the summer of 1963.[6]

---

2. Ruth Rosenfeld, "Dr. Tidwell Dept. Of Christianity Head at New Houston Baptist College," *Bellaire Texan,* 31 July 1963, p. 4.

3. Ruth Rosenfeld, "Houston Baptist College Prof. Has Served Local Pastorates," *Bellaire Texan,* 17 July 1963, p. 4.

4. Ruth Rosenfeld, "Meet the Musical Rheas," *Bellaire Texan,* 9 Oct. 1963, p. 4.

5. Houston Baptist College, Minutes of Meetings of the Executive Committee of the Board of Trustees, Meeting on 17 Mar. 1964.

6. Ruth Rosenfeld, "Language Instructor's Home Filled With Travel Mementos," *Bellaire Texan,* 14 Aug. 1963, p. 4; "Milton Enthusiast Heads Language Arts Division at Houston Baptist," *Bellaire Texan,* 4 Dec. 1963, p. 4; "Students, Approach To Education Is Vital, Says Dr. Josserand," *Bellaire Texan,* 7 Aug 1963, p. 4.

The first faculty meeting was held July 9, 1963, in the Sharpstown State Bank Conference Room.[7] No buildings on campus were yet completed. Extensive information was conveyed to the faculty; operational questions were addressed. The liberal arts core was to be at the heart of all curricula; no night classes would be scheduled; no graduate programs were planned; continuing study opportunities for faculty would be encouraged. Faculty office space would be in short supply until completion of the Atwood Theology Building and the Sharp Gymnasium. The first interdisciplinary-course teaching team was appointed with the responsibility to create *The Developing Social Order* syllabus by fall. Additionally, Dr. Hinton announced, "We need a symbol, a mascot, a nickname, and an Alma Mater."[8]

The founding faculty included Dr. Wayne Barton in Christianity (1963-65),[9] Dr. Glen Cain in Christianity (1963-84), Librarian Jefferson Caskey (1963-70),[10] Dr. A. O. Collins in Christianity (1963-91),[11] Dr. William Dacres in biology (1963-91),[12] Dr. Joyce Fan in chemistry (1963-82),[13] Dr. Wayne Ford in mathematics (1963-65), Mrs. Opal Goolsby in English and French (1963-76),[14] R. Paul Green in choral music (1963-78),[15] Don Hardisty in music (1963-64),[16] Dr. Clif Harris in mathematics (1963-68),[17] Dr. James Herring in German (1963-67), Dr. John Hoskins in sociology (1963-65),[18] Dr. Calvin Huckabay in English (1963-94),[19] Anna Ley Ingraham in physical education (1963-68),[20] Kenneth

7. Houston Baptist College, Minutes of Meetings of the Faculty, Meeting on 9 July 1963.
8. Ibid.
9. "Dr. Tidwell Chairmans (sic) Christianity Department," *Houston Baptist College News*, May 1963, 1-2. Biography with photo.
10. "Quality Library is Houston Baptist College Aim," *Houston Baptist College News*, July 1963, 3. Biography with photo.
11. "Dr. A. O. Collins," *Houston Baptist College News*, May 1963, 2. Biography with photo.
12. "'Dr. Albert Myers Heads Division of Science," *Houston Baptist College News*, May 1963, 1-2. Biography with photo.
13. Ibid.
14. "Huckaby (sic) is Chairman of Language Arts Division," *Houston Baptist College News*, June 1963, 2. Biography with photo.
15. "Four Appointed to Music Department," *Houston Baptist College News*, Apr. 1963, 2. Biography with photo.
16. Ibid.
17. "Dr. Williamson Heads Mathematics Department," *Houston Baptist College News*, June 1963, 1-2. Biography with photo.
18. "Hoskins to Head Social Sciences," *Houston Baptist College News*, Apr. 1963, 1. Biography with photo.
19. "Huckaby (sic)," *Houston Baptist College News*, June 1963, 1. Biography with photo.
20. "Meet the Faculty: Miss Ingraham," *Houston Baptist College News*, Oct. 1963, 3. Biography with photo.

Jones in economics (1963-64),[21] Dr. Chris Jordan in biology (1963-67),[22] Dr. Frank Josserand in history (1963-65),[23] Jack Mullins in political science (1963-64),[24] Dr. Albert Myers in chemistry (1963-67),[25] Dr. Robert Parker in music (1963-73),[26] Dr. Claude Rhea in music (1963-67),[27] Dr. Milton Smith in English (1963-67),[28] Jim Stoker in art (1963-66),[29] Mac Sutton in physical education (1963-67),[30] Dr. Duncan Tidwell in Christianity (1963-71),[31] Dr. Arthur Travis in Christianity (1963-74),[32] John Welch in drama (1963-64), Dr. James E. Williamson in mathematics and Dean of Student Life (1963-71),[33] and Marion Young in English (1963-69).

At that first faculty meeting in 1963, a question arose about the admission of "colored groups." As recorded in the faculty meeting minutes, Dr. Hinton's response was, "When a qualified person applies, he will be presented to the Board for approval. The feeling is that he will be admitted. Our hope is that it will be a smooth process and just routine."[34] Not surprisingly for the era, the Board had talked with presidential candidate Ralph Phelps in 1961 about "integration of the races."[35] Minutes of the Board of Trustees in August 1963 record that a study committee was appointed "to investigate all implications of the questions involved regarding the matter of admitting students to the College . . . in light of her charter and the purposes involved therein."[36] The trustees sought the counsel of Cecil Cook who advised the Board, "If we are to serve our community as we wish, we should be open to all who want to come here."[37] By the opening of the College in September, it was freely communicated

21. "Williamson," *Houston Baptist College News,* June 1963, 2. Biography with photo.

22. "Myers," *Houston Baptist College News,* May 1963, 2. Biography with photo.

23. "Hoskins," *Houston Baptist College News,* Apr. 1963, 2. Biography with photo.

24. Ibid.

25. "Myers," *Houston Baptist College News,* May 1963, 1. Biography with photo.

26. "Four Appointed to Music Department," *Houston Baptist College News,* Apr. 1963, 2. Biography with photo.

27. Ibid.

28. "Huckaby (sic)," *Houston Baptist College News,* June 1963, 2. Biography with photo.

29. Honey Harrison, "Art Exhibit on View," *The Collegian,* 28 Jan. 1966, p. 2.

30. "Meet the Faculty: Mr. Sutton," *Houston Baptist College News,* Oct. 1963, 3. Biography with photo.

31. "Dr. Tidwell Chairmans (sic) Christianity Department," *Houston Baptist College News,* May 1963, 1. Biography with photo.

32. Ruth Rosenfeld, "Houston Baptist College Prof. Has Served Local Pastorates," *Bellaire Texan,* 31 July 1963, p. 4; "Dr. Arthur E. Travis" *Houston Baptist College News,* May 1963, 2. Biography with photo.

33. "Williamson," *Houston Baptist College News,* June 1963, 1. Biography with photo.

34. Houston Baptist College, Minutes of the Meetings of the Faculty, Meeting on 9 July 1963.

35. Houston Baptist College, Minutes of Meetings of the Board of Trustees, Meeting on 1 June 1961.

36. Houston Baptist College, Minutes of Meetings of the Board of Trustees, Meeting on 13 Aug. 1963.

37. (Dr. Stewart Morris, Sr. to Dr. Don Looser, June 27, 2008).

on campus that the College did not discriminate on the basis of race in student admission or employment.

The HBC position was a significant stand in 1963 and well ahead of its time. As early as 1952, Billy Graham had startled delegates to the Southern Baptist Convention by "asserting that it was the Christian duty of every Baptist college to welcome academically qualified Negro students. The moral stature of the Baptist people can rise no higher than the policies of the Baptist educators.'"[38] In July 1963, the First Baptist Church of Houston was the scene of a picket line by the Congress of Racial Equality because of its membership policy. Although Hattie Mae White was the first African-American to be elected to the Houston Independent School District School Board in 1959, the Houston Independent School District was still predominantly racially segregated until 1970. Only in 1962 had Rice University determined to admit students of all races.

HBC's decision was quietly implemented but resolute from the first day of student matriculation. Despite its non-discrimination policy, however, it was 1966 before the first African-American students enrolled. Professor A. O. Collins recalled, "I remember the first black student who enrolled—how pleased I was that there was no problem as he was immediately accepted as a member of the Coreons fraternity and occupied a position on the BSU Council."[39] In later years, a 1998 *Collegian* article on racial harmony recorded the recollections of a number of the first African-American students in the campus community including artist Robert Gholston, 1969 "Campus Favorite" Rufus Burns, and fellow basketball stars Eddie Brown and E. C. Coleman.[40]

The new freshman class first met together at the Shamrock Hotel Castilian Room on August 23; students received copies of the first *Bulletin of Information*.[41] The new college intentionally created a unique lexicon reflective of its innovative spirit. There was a "Bulletin," not a "Catalog." There were "quality points," not "grade points." A double major with integrated *Senior Seminars* in each of the two fields of study was required. All governing committees included student members with full voting privileges. The lower-division curriculum was highly specific, requiring

---

38. Martin, William. *A Prophet with Honor: The Billy Graham Story.* New York: William and Co., 1991, p. 169; "Negroes Picket Houston First Baptist Church," *Baptist Press,* http://media.sbhla.org.s3.amazonaws.com/1766.30-Jul-1963.pdf (accessed Feb. 9, 2010).
39. Dr. A. O. Collins, "Founders' Day," *HBU News,* Feb. 1991, 10.
40. Nicole Broussard, "Remembering integration," *The Collegian,* 19 March 1998, p. 4.
41. Houston Baptist College, Minutes of Meetings of the Faculty, Meeting on 23 Aug. 1963.

Trustees George Duncan and Jake Kamin set the cornerstone.

most students to take exactly the same courses for the better part of the first sixty hours of work. Team-teaching, interdisciplinary organization, and diverse pedagogical techniques were integral parts of the learning model. To foster the interdisciplinary commitment, the College was organized into "Divisions," not "Departments," headed by Chairmen—a term not yet thought to be sexist. Divisions of Christianity, Fine Arts, Languages, Science and Mathematics, and Social Sciences were established. Review of early printed documents reveals that the absence of upperclassmen initially caused the freshmen to retain much of their high school vocabulary. There were "boys'" and "girls'" dorms. The student newspaper occasionally referred to students as "pupils."

Following a retreat for the faculty from all Baptist colleges across the state at Howard Butt's Laity Lodge, the HBC faculty returned to campus for the first of the ceremonial events marking the establishment of the new institution—the laying of the cornerstone on September 8, 1963.[42] The events of the next several weeks would prove a unifying experience for the new college family. The cornerstone-laying ceremony was led by

42. "New Houston Baptist College To Be Dedicated in Sunday Rite," *Galveston News,* 7 Sept. 1963, p. 3; "Dr. Denham To Dedicate Baptist College Sunday," *Houston Post,* 6 Sept. 1963, sec. 4, p. 14.

trustees Rex G. Baker, Sr., John Baugh, George Duncan, Jake Kamin, L. D. Morgan, and James Parker. Stewart Morris thanked the business and corporate community of Houston for its support of the new enterprise. President Hinton expressed his gratitude for the thousands of Baptists and friends who had made the day a reality.[43] Some 3500 "hat-and-glove" guests including Mayor Lewis Cutrer, Rice President Kenneth Pitzer, and University of Houston President Philip Hoffman heard an address by Dr. William E. Denham, Chairman of the Board of Trustees. Denham noted, "A liberal arts college must do more than expose students to the facts of the new frontiers of space, genetics, biochemistry, and psychology. Perspective must be provided from the past—all that mankind has thought, believed, and produced. There is history, art, literature, and religion."[44] Trustees Duncan, Kamin, Baugh, Morgan, and Parker assisted with the setting of the cornerstone that was inscribed with the College scripture from John 14:6, "I am the way, the truth, and the life; no man cometh unto the Father, but by me."[45] Among the establishment of early traditions for the new College was the singing of the hymn *Lead On, O King Eternal* that became the official hymn of the new enterprise and was sung thereafter as a regular part of major College ceremonial events.

The dormitories opened on September 14. Lynda Uphouse from Sherman was the first student to move into the new facilities.[46] The first student registration was held September 16; Ted Bosworth of Seguin enjoyed news coverage in the *Houston Press* as the first student to register.[47] The first year's institutional budget was $530,000. The Board minutes of September 19, 1963, reported a tuition shortfall of $140,000 because 400 freshmen had been anticipated.[48] Tuition in 1963 was $19 per credit hour plus fees or a total of approximately $300 per semester for enrollment in fifteen semester hours of work. Many students were receiving significant institutional financial aid. Trustees had long dealt with the difficult and exhausting financial requirements of the new College; the

43. "Opportunity, Tension, Commitment Ingredients of Christian Education, Says Dr. Denham," *Bellaire Texan,* 1 Sept. 1963, p. 9.

44. "Thousands Attend Dedication Ceremony at HBC," *Houston Baptist College News,* Sept. 1963, 1-2; *Houston Post,* 9 September 1963, sec. 3, p. 16.

45. "Cornerstone Ceremony Sunday at Baptist College," *Bellaire Texan,* 6 Sept. 1963; *Ornogah 1964,* 66-67; Sibley, 46-47. Photos. The cornerstone greets campus visitors at the main entrance to the Brown Academic Quadrangle.

46. "First Student in Women's Hall, Houston College," *Baptist Standard,* 2 Oct. 1963. Photo.

47. Jim Cox, "Student No. 1 At Baptist College Takes Look Around," *Houston Press,* Sept. 1963. Clipping from the Houston Baptist College archive. Photos.

48. Houston Baptist College, Minutes of Meetings of the Board of Trustees, Meeting on 19 Sept. 1963.

The first students moved into the new dormitories, 1963.

Board was determined not to borrow additional funds to address the shortfall but to consider refinancing the total accumulated indebtedness. The value of the campus plant in 1963 was estimated to be $9,000,000.[49]

With the advent of the first year of operation, a tradition of opening each fall term with a convocation featuring formal academic attire was established. Setting a lofty academic tone for the year—especially in the eyes of new freshmen—seemed particularly appropriate since no formal commencement ceremony would be held for four years. On September 19, 1963, the first Fall Convocation was held in the M. D. Anderson Student Center and featured an address by Dr. Ross Dillon.[50]

The most exciting event of the fall was the appearance by Dr. Billy Graham on October 30 as a part of Religious Emphasis Week.[51] The new President's Home had been rushed to completion in July by builder Glenn McMillan[52] and was the scene of an evening campus reception for

49. Ibid.

50. "Dillon Addresses First Convocation," *Houston Baptist College News,* Sept. 1963, 3; *Ornogah 1964,* 68-69.

51. "Billy Graham Is Religious Emphasis Speaker," *Houston Baptist College News,* Oct. 1963, 1-2. Photos.

52. Ruth Rosenfeld, "Pace Quickens for Houston Baptist College President W. H. Hinton," *Bellaire Texan,* 21 Aug. 1963, p. 4.

trustees and friends of the College honoring Dr. Graham.[53]   Among the guests were HBC faculty member Dr. Joyce Fan and her husband Paul who held the distinction of being the first couple ever married by Dr. Graham.[54]   An address by Dr. Graham the next morning before 5,000 guests in the academic quadrangle[55] was followed by a noon speech to the Houston Kiwanis Club attended by Texas Governor John Connally.[56]

Billy Graham Day ceremonies at HBC were attended by 3,000 high school seniors invited for a first look at the new campus.[57]   Stewart Morris persuaded Houston ISD Superintendent G. C. Scarborough to dismiss seniors at 1:00 p.m.[58]   Malcolm Morris served as a high school chauffeur for Graham.   Upon arrival on campus for the ceremonies, Graham detoured to speak to workers who were completing campus landscaping. Morris recalled, "Graham knelt and thanked them.   He told them what they were doing would be attracting the students that would one day be leading America."[59]

Music by Dr. Claude Rhea and the new College Choir under the direction of R. Paul Green featured the resources of the new faculty.[60] Graham's passion and commitment to ministry in major urban settings around the globe resonated with the mission of the new college.   His encouragement has served as inspiration and challenge to the University's leadership throughout all the years since his historic visit.

It is a great privilege for me to be here today and participate in this historic occasion at the beginning of a great new Christian institution in the city of Houston. . . . To the choir, it is tremendous for the first year to get these students to sing that way. . . . I appreciate Dr. Rhea for this beautiful song he has sung for us that I know comes from his heart. . . . I want to say a word about how delighted I am at this tremendous enterprise here in Houston. . . . Thank God for institutions that have purpose and meaning, where there is a belief in God—where whatever course

---

53   Houston Baptist College, Minutes of Meetings of the Board of Trustees, Meeting on 29 Oct. 1963.
54   *Ornogah 1964*, 77.
55   "Billy Graham Challenges Students to Commitments," *Houston Baptist College News,* Nov. 1963, 1.   Text of address reprinted from *Houston Chronicle.*
56   "Billy Graham," *San Antonio Express/News,* 27 Oct. 1963, sec. A, p. 6.
57   Ruth Rosenfeld, "Over 3000 Hear Billy Graham at Houston Baptist College," *Bellaire Texan,* 6 Nov 1963, p. 7.
58   (Dr. Stewart Morris to Dr. Don Looser, June 7, 2010).
59   Brian Horn, "Opening Doors," *Smart Business,* Dec 2009, 1.   Recollection of Malcolm Morris, Graham's driver on Oct. 30, 1963.
60   "Musical Choir and Ensemble," *Houston Baptist College News,* May 1964, 8.   Photo.

you are taking is taught within the Christian framework, where they recognize that the Creator of the universe is a supreme being that we call God. This is an institution that stands without any apology for the Christ, who is the redeemer and reconciler of the world. . . . This institution is dedicated not only to training the mind but to converting the character and building splendid men and women who will go out with purpose and meaning in their lives. So it is a great delight for me to participate in this great event here today.[61]

Dr. Billy Graham, speaking for HBC Religious Emphasis Week, 1963.

Graham received a hard-hat tour of the Astrodome under construction from Judge Roy Hofheinz, the guiding genius behind the realization of the project. Graham's visit was a prelude to his 1965 Houston Crusade in the Astrodome. A 1963 photograph also documents a golf game for Dr. Graham, Dr. Hinton, and golf professionals Jimmy Demerit and Jackie Burke that was somehow worked into his busy schedule.[62]

---

61   "Billy Graham Challenges Students To Commitments," *Houston Baptist College News,* Nov. 1963, 1-3.
62   *Ornogah 1986,* 9.

Student life on campus began to take root as the freshmen sensed elements of college culture that needed to be established. The first issue of the student newspaper was published on October 30. Suggestions for an appropriate name for the publication were solicited. The *Houston Baptist Collegian* was the popular choice, and the flag has carried the name *Collegian* since October 1963.[63] The first issues reported thirty "girls" and thirty-five "boys" in the dorms and observed that a proposed school song was "hard to learn."[64] The publication was intended to be bi-monthly. A staff of sixteen students—including Editor Mary K. Heye, Suzanne Clark, John Gillespie, John Goodwin, Judy Bennatte, and Henry Maxwell—was sponsored by C. C. Risenhoover[65] who also served as the College public relations press officer, managing editor of the *Houston Baptist College News*, and later volunteer baseball coach.[66]

To aid social interaction, a Campus Club was organized on October 11, 1963, composed of female faculty, faculty spouses, and wives of administrators.[67] At an early meeting, Helen Cain sang "Moonlight and Roses;" Margaret Collins sang "Silver Threads among the Gold;" and the women told anecdotes about their husbands with "much laughter." Among the early voluntary leaders were Thelma Tidwell, Twinkle Hoskins, Katherine Myers, Jewel Travis, Gertrude Dacres, Virginia Smith, Bobbie Ruth Hinton, and Rose Dillon. The Club hosted the first of its covered-dish dinners in November 1965 that drew sixty-five attendees, was labeled "a huge success," and continued to be held quarterly thereafter.[68] Single men were asked only to bring bread!

The fall semester was highlighted by the first Halloween Hoot'nanny,[69] the first drama production—*The Corn is Green*,[70] the first

---

63. Flag (Masthead), *Houston Baptist Collegian*, 30 Oct. 1963, p. 1.

64. "Dorm Councils," *Houston Baptist Collegian*, 30 Oct. 1963, p. 2. "Nearly every night after curfew, all the girls stand outside their rooms and sing one or two hymns and have a moment of silent prayer before studying."

65. *Baptist Standard* archives, 25 May 2007. http://www.baptiststandard.com/index.php?option=com_content&task=view&id=6521&Itemid=135 (accessed Feb. 3, 2010). Risenhoover later played semi-professional baseball and went on to become the author of more than 20 books including six best sellers. He also served on the journalism faculty at Southern Methodist University and on the staff of both the Baptist General Convention of Texas and the Radio Television Commission of the Southern Baptist Convention. In 2010, he was pastor of Gateway Community Church in Granbury, Texas.

66. "Risenhoover Now at Baylor," *Houston Baptist Collegian*, 25 Oct. 1966, p. 4; *Ornogah 1964*, 113, 136.

67. Houston Baptist College, Minutes of the Meetings of the Campus Club, Meeting on 11 Oct. 1963. Scrapbook in Houston Baptist University Archives.

68. "Calendar of Events," *HBC News*, Mar. 1966, 5.

69. *Ornogah 1964*, 78-79.

70. "First College Play," *Houston Baptist College News*, Oct. 1963, 2.

official Thanksgiving turkey dinner,[71] and the first faculty and staff Christmas dinner. The Christmas event provided opportunity to enjoy music, food, and fellowship, to present awards to faculty for academic excellence, and to hear a dramatic reading by students from the Gallery Theatre Players.[72]

The Board of Trustees approved initiating the first intercollegiate athletic programs in baseball and basketball in 1964. Over twenty men "walked on" as prospective team members.[73] In basketball, the first four games were cancelled because the gymnasium was not yet completed. It was also difficult to find collegiate competitors because game schedules were already set for the 1963-64 year. Nonetheless, the basketball program, coached by Mac Sutton, compiled a 1-7 record for the first year. The baseball team canceled four games, had no field, and finished with a 0-5 season. The first cheerleaders were elected—Sharon Crutcher, Jimmie Lee, Vicki Pomorski, Doug Tipps, and Joyce Watts. In all these student activities, freshmen responded to need, set aside physical constraints, and exhibited the kind of determination and strong sense of

1964-65 Houston Baptist College Spartans

71. "Turkey Dinner," *Houston Baptist Collegian*, 22 Nov. 1963, p. 1.
72. *Ornogah 1964*, 80-81.
73. *Ornogah 1964*, 134.

responsibility that characterized the first years of the new institution. These bold student pioneers carved a niche in the history of the College that remains a living tribute to their commitment and maturity.

§

Houston in the 1960s was experiencing unprecedented growth in population, commercial development, and proliferation of cultural activity. In the downtown area, work was underway on the 44-story Humble Building, the First City National Bank Tower, a World Trade Center, the 33-story Tennessee Gas headquarters, the 47-story One Shell Plaza, a new Federal Office Building, and a new central Post Office. Kenneth Schnitzer was developing Greenway Plaza; the seven-acre $100,000,000 Cullen Center was under construction.[74] The Houston Grand Opera was newly formed; Sir John Barbirolli was named conductor of the Houston Symphony; and Bud Adams negotiated an American Football League franchise for the city. In 1961, voters approved construction of a new domed stadium to house a new National League baseball franchise.[75] The $50,000,000 *Astrodome,* opened in 1965, came to symbolize the economic boom of the Gulf Coast area and the willingness of its residents to pioneer new enterprise.[76]

On September 19, 1961, the most significant event in Houston's postwar development took place when the National Aeronautics and Space Administration (NASA) announced that the city had been designated as the site of a new center for the nation's space exploration program. The Space Center would be built at Clear Lake southeast of the city on land provided by Humble Oil conveyed as a gift through Rice Institute to NASA. Houston had been selected over twenty other cities due in large measure to its industrial complex, ship channel and port facilities, its intellectual capital, and the advocacy of then-Senator Lyndon Johnson, Chairman of the National Space Committee.[77]

§

74. Miller, 187.
75. Miller, 190.
76. Marvin Hurley, *Decisive Years for Houston* (Houston: Houston Chamber of Commerce, 1966), 234.
77. Miller, 188.

In the 1960s, Houston boasted more private colleges than at any time in the city's history. Rice Institute, the city's best-known academic center, had been founded in 1912 and later became Rice University in 1970. The University of Houston (UH) initially was a private university, founded in 1927, that was the object of frequent, lavish gifts from oilman Hugh Roy Cullen in the years following World War II. Later in 1963, UH was assimilated into the Texas system of public universities.[78] Sacred Heart Dominican College, founded in 1945 by the Sisters of St. Dominic of the Congregation of the Sacred Heart, was an outgrowth of the congregation's teacher training program that offered strong programs in art, music, education, and nursing until the college ceased operations in 1975.[79] Thereafter, the University of St. Thomas, founded in 1947 by Basilian priests, served as the only Catholic higher education institution in the Galveston-Houston Catholic Diocese. The chartering of Houston Baptist College in 1960 marked the newest establishment of a private institution of higher education in Houston. Shortly thereafter in 1967, the South Texas Junior College was established as the only private junior college in the state. The University of Houston ultimately purchased South Texas Junior College that became the University of Houston–Downtown in 1974. By 1976, only Rice, St. Thomas, and HBU remained as private colleges in the city.

§

In the midst of a booming regional economy, the HBC Board of Trustees continued to grapple with ongoing financial struggles during the first year of College operation. A comprehensive refinancing plan was completed in the fall of 1963 with a loan from Houston First Federal Savings and Loan that paid off existing loans and provided $260,000 for current operations. The trustees were unwavering in their commitment to an institution of the highest academic order despite the financial concerns.

Dr. William Denham accepted a new pastorate at the First Baptist Church of Austin in the fall of 1963 and resigned as Chair of the Board of Trustees. Denham's departure marked the conclusion of his unparalleled leadership to establish a new college that began in the 1950s. His depar-

---

78. Miller, 192-193.
79. *The Handbook of Texas: Dominican College.*
http://www.tshaonline.org/handbook/online/articles/DD/kbd10.html (accessed Feb. 9, 2010).

ture represented the first major change of leadership in College history. It was Dr. Denham, for whom Denham Hall is named, who had marshaled forces to begin consideration of a new Christian college in Houston. To Denham had been given a particular set of strengths that served him well in his leadership role—his scholarly character, imposing physical bearing, and personal warmth. Denham was the son of a Southern Baptist Theological Seminary professor and a graduate of Washington University in St. Louis, a scholar in his own right.[80] He pastored an affluent congregation of influential Houston leaders and was well-respected both in denominational and community circles. It was Dr. Denham and Rex G. Baker, Sr. who provided the principal academic leadership for the new college.

A resolution of appreciation to Dr. Denham, reflected in the November 26, 1963, minutes of the Board, reads in part,

> To him [Dr. Denham] more than to any single individual among Baptists we owe our tribute of thanks and honor. . . . His standing as a scholar, his influence as a pastor, and his ability in interpreting the need for a college . . . accounted for bringing together the resources to birth the new college.[81]

The torch passed to Robert H. Ray, the succeeding chair of the College Board of Trustees.

§

During the first fifty years of its history, the Board of Trustees has gathered on several occasions at times that coincided with moments of national tragedy. On the first such occasion in November 1963, trustees arrived for a scheduled meeting on November 22 to be greeted with the shocking news of the assassination of President John F. Kennedy. More than 4,000 Houstonians had heard President Kennedy speak in Houston only the night before at a Coliseum dinner honoring Congressman Albert Thomas.[82] Appropriately, the trustees held a time of prayer for the Kennedy family and the nation and quietly adjourned to reassemble at a later date.[83]

§

---

80. Commander, 82.
81. Houston Baptist College, Minutes of Meetings of the Board of Trustees, Meeting on 26 Nov. 1963.
82. Hurley, 218.
83. Houston Baptist College, Minutes of Meetings of the Board of Trustees, Meeting on 22 Nov. 1963.

In September 1963, some ninety women drawn chiefly from the ranks of Baptist Women's Missionary Unions throughout the city attended the opening meeting of the Ladies Auxiliary, an organization first begun by Mrs. Hinton on April 29, 1963.[84] Dona Williamson, wife of Dean of Students James E. Williamson, served as the first President of the organization. The 1963-64 members' directory listed some 150 current members and their church home.[85] Over the course of the organization's lifetime, the Auxiliary was to play a significant role in the financial support of the institution including the funding of such projects as campus lighting, landscaping, furnishings, library acquisitions, dorm beautification, and academic support.

During the fall semester of 1963, faculty members were heavily engaged in the planning and writing of curricula for all the new courses. Because of the interdisciplinary emphasis of so much of the curriculum, the decision had been made to begin with a freshman class and add a new freshman class each year until the four years were accomplished. This schedule allowed the faculty time to stay ahead of the students in developing the new curriculum.

Dr. H. B. Smith was the architect for the development of the new degree requirements. Curricular models across the nation at Florida Presbyterian College (now Eckerd), at Colorado College, Denison, and Austin College provided fresh perspectives. A Bachelor of Arts degree of 130 semester hours was to be offered that featured a double major required of all students. Emphasis was to be placed on broad multi-disciplinary understandings of self, faith, the world, and breadth of knowledge. A foundation in the liberal arts was to be required of all students. The prescriptive curriculum provided the same basic sequence of courses for all students for the first two years. Faculty members were organized into broad divisions, some without departments, in order to promote interdisciplinary thought.

Four years of team-taught, interdisciplinary courses were envisioned as foundational. These were originally called *Basic Courses*, but soon came to be known as CORE in the student lexicon. CORE later gave way to INDC (interdisciplinary course) when the acronym CORE became

---

84. "Ladies Auxiliary Now Being Organized," *Houston Baptist College News,* Feb. 1963, 3.
85. Houston Baptist College, *Ladies Auxiliary Directory, 1963-64.* The official name eventually became the Houston Baptist College Auxiliary.

associated in the public mind with the Congress of Racial Equality.[86] The first year of the *Basic Courses* was designed to provide self-examination based in the social sciences. *The Developing Social Order* was a two-semester course covering six areas of study. Classes were organized into both large lecture sections and small discussion groups and were team-taught by as many as five professors.[87] Two semesters of freshman English titled *The Nature and Function of Language* and *Composition and Rhetoric* focused heavily on the development of written communication skills. *Old Testament* and *New Testament*, two semesters of a laboratory science, and physical education completed the freshman year component. Limited space was available for electives or for initiating majors such as music that had four-year linear curriculum models.

The fall of 1963 seemed a blur to everyone. For faculty and students, so much was new; so much demanded creative thought; so much needed to be accomplished. Moreover, the players were new to each other. Faculty scrambled to write the new curricula. Students struggled with the demand for abstract thinking and higher-level learning skills. Some stresses resolved themselves as time passed. In the faculty ranks, however, misunderstandings involving finance and recruiting promises became an issue. Moving expenses, housing subsidies, institutional communication, and faculty autonomy were of particular concern. At a December 1963 faculty meeting, Dr. Hinton addressed morale, fatigue, and enthusiasm. He announced a $100,000 scholarship endowment and urged faculty "not to be discouraged in their initial but very important efforts to carry out their responsibilities."[88] Later at an April 1964 faculty meeting, heated discussion of alleged promises regarding faculty housing reimbursement ensued.[89]

In the 1960s, academic leadership styles were changing to become more participative. This was an era that marked the final chapter of "administration" as a leadership style in higher education; however, the word "management" remained an alienating term to many faculty mem-

86. Houston Baptist College, Minutes of the Meetings of the Faculty, Meeting on 14 Oct. 1965.

87. "Heart of the Core: Chairman Reviews Progress," *Houston Baptist College News,* Sept. 1964, 3-4. A year-end assessment revealed "some lack of student familiarity with levels of abstract thought, immature study habits, and faculty growth of knowledge through team teaching. The most serious-minded students benefitted more than others."

88. Houston Baptist College, Minutes of the Meetings of the Faculty, Meeting, on 12 Dec. 1963.

89. Houston Baptist College, Minutes of the Meetings of the Faculty, Meeting on 23 Apr. 1964. This divisive issue in time became the root of such contention with a few faculty members that it resulted in the termination of several whose conduct was viewed to have become insubordinate.

bers, particularly those outside the field of business. To some of the faculty, administrative practice at HBC was more directive, less flexible, and more authoritarian than had been their previous experience. Formal lines of communication between constituent groups were still forming, and the administrative triumvirate of Hinton, Smith, and Womack appeared to some faculty to be needlessly dismissive and autocratic. Although this style might be understandable within the pressure of a new College setting, the situation was no less onerous or unacceptable to many faculty members.

In time, management style became a festering issue. Matters of appropriate governance were not clear to some faculty and trustees who wanted direct access to each other and viewed the administration as a barrier. Some trustees continued to view their role as managerial rather than policy-making. Professional issues for certain faculty members continued to ferment. A current of complaint about administrative practice from some faculty members was expressed directly to members of the Board of Trustees. Though individual incidents may have been relatively insignificant, the cumulative effect of perceived administrative demeanor toward faculty opinion and professional respect began to emerge as a serious challenge to effective working relationships.

The second semester of the first year was highlighted by a continual stream of "firsts." In January, Tracy and Lee Lawrence announced the gift of a new Rogers organ to the College in memory of their daughter, Sandra Lee Lawrence. The organ was installed in the gymnasium for use in chapel and for teaching, recitals, and ceremonial events.[90] The first "Sweetheart of HBC," Bonnie Bates, was chosen to reign over a Valentine Banquet with her court of Lynda DeLoach, Bonnie Miller, Mary Lynn Naye, Viki Pomorski, Joyce Watts, and Mary Edith Whitelock.[91] Discussions were held regarding a missionary-in-residence program and proposal of both a retirement facility and a shopping center on the Southwest Freeway.[92] Dr. Hinton presented sketches of a proposed College chapel and fine arts building projected to cost $250,000 and $5,500,000 dollars respectively.[93]

The first official visit from the Southern Association of Colleges and Schools occurred on February 3, 1964, with the visit of Dr. Gordon Sweet,

---

90. *Ornogah 1964*, 89.
91. *Ornogah 1964*, 98.
92. Houston Baptist College, Minutes of Meetings of the Board of Trustees, Meeting on 26 Nov. 1963.
93. "Fine Arts Complex Next Major Effort," *HBU News,* June 1976, 1; Houston Baptist College, Minutes of Meetings of the Board of Trustees, Meeting on 27 Feb. 1964.

Executive Secretary of the Commission on Colleges. The February minutes of the Executive Committee of the trustees contain a report of the visit:

> Dr. Sweet gave a very detailed report to the committee. . . . He stressed the new approach to accreditation which is officially called *Admission to Candidacy* for new colleges, indicating that Houston Baptist College would be permitted to apply for this program in the fall of the third year (1965). . . . Dr. Sweet seemed impressed with the College.[94]

The spring 1964 enrollment was up to 210 students with seventy-seven students living on campus.[95] Houston businessman Gilbert Turner, not yet a trustee, gave a greatly-needed metallic building to the College that was erected behind the gymnasium for housing campus maintenance operations.[96] The Gallery Theatre celebrated the 400th anniversary of Shakespeare's birth,[97] and the College Choir gave its first spring campus concert. The first College yearbook, *Ornogah*—"shining light" in Hebrew—edited by Jo-Jo Stephens, was published under the sponsorship of biology faculty member Dr. Bill Dacres.[98] Dr. Cary Croneis of Rice Institute delivered the address for the first Awards Day in May.[99]

Three events in the first spring shaped the direction of the College for many years to come: the dedication of the Frank and Lucille Sharp Gymnasium, the dedication of the Atwood Theology Building, and the inauguration of the College's first president, Dr. W. H. Hinton. On March 20, 1964, the Frank and Lucille Sharp Gymnasium was dedicated.[100] The Honorable Albert Thomas, Congressman from the State of Texas, delivered the principal address.[101] It was from Sharp on April 10, 1958, that the Union Baptist Association had bought 390 acres of land in the new Sharpstown development for the college campus. President Hinton presented the three Sharp grandchildren with ceremonial lifetime

---

94. Houston Baptist College, Minutes of Meetings of the Executive Committee of the Board of Trustees, Meeting on 4 Feb. 1964.

95. Houston Baptist College, Minutes of Meetings of the Executive Committee of the Board of Trustees, Meeting on 18 Feb. 1964.

96. Houston Baptist College, Minutes of the Meetings of the Executive Committee of the Board of Trustees, Meeting on 17 Mar. 1964.

97. "The Gallery Theatre," *Houston Baptist College News,* June 1964, 7; *Ornogah 1964,* 110-112.

98. *Ornogah 1964,* 126-7.

99. "Awards: Quality Recognized," *Houston Baptist College News,* May 1964, 7; *Ornogah 1964,* 94-95.

100. "Dedicate Baptist College Building," *Houston Chronicle,* 21 Mar. 1964, sec. A, p. 2. Photo of Mr. and Mrs. Sharp and Rep. and Mrs. Albert Thomas.

101. "First President of College," *Houston Baptist College News,* May 1964, 3-4; *Ornogah 1964,* 84-85. Photos.

passes for all events scheduled in the future for the Sharp Gym. This building was critical to the completion of the original campus complement of facilities. Both intercollegiate athletics and the physical education program of the College now had a home. Moreover, as campus growth continued, the gym served as a surrogate auditorium for the next forty-three years, housing weekly chapel and convocation programs, commencements and concerts, as well as athletic events.

The principal campus academic facility, the Atwood Theology Building, was dedicated on May 3, 1964.[102] Miss Enla V. Atwood conveyed a large gift to fund this facility and to provide for future buildings as well. Miss Atwood had begun development of Houston residential subdivisions late in the 1930s. Her personal home-site occupied the southwest corner of Kirby Drive and Richmond Avenue. In the throes of the depression, Miss Atwood had prayed that if allowed to maintain her land holdings, she would return the gain "for the glory of the Father." She had planned to establish a seminary in Houston. However, through a friendship with trustee Florence Weaver and Dr. Ross Dillon, she was encouraged to fund facilities on the campus for study of the Bible. The building dedication plaque reads, "Dedicated to and to be used for the teaching of the gospel of Jesus Christ our Lord and Savior through the study of the Bible—the Word of God." The Atwood Theology building was given in memory of her mother and father, Ida L. and T. J. Atwood.[103]

The new Atwood Theology Building was designed to accommodate the distinctive instructional program of the new college. Two large classrooms with theater-seating for 168 persons came to be known as the Red Room and the Blue Room. Students in the *Basic Courses* gathered in these rooms for large group instruction by the teaching teams and then dispersed into small discussion groups of ten to twelve students with a faculty mentor. Closed-circuit television allowed presentations in one room to be viewed in real time anywhere on the campus. A distinctive element of the design of the Atwood Building was an interior court featuring natural sunlight, a bubbling fountain, and a Biblical garden featuring plants mentioned in the Old Testament—sycamore, aloe, bulrush, and palm.[104] A small prayer room, faculty offices, and additional classrooms complet-

---

102. "Dedication: A Biblical Emphasis," *Houston Baptist College News,* May 1964, 5-6. Photos.

103. "Atwood Dedication: Gift of Love," *Houston Baptist College News,* June 1964, 6. Photo.

104. "Courtyard: The Plants of the Bible," *Houston Baptist College News,* May 1964, 5-6; *Ornogah 1964,* 86-88. Photo.

ed the facility. Miss Atwood died August 30, 1965, only a year after the realization of her dream.[105] Her estate later funded a second Atwood building on the campus.

The third major event of the spring semester was the inauguration of the first president of the College, Dr. William Harwood Hinton. Following the first spring choral concert dedicated to Dr. Hinton,[106] the inaugural ceremony was held the next day on May 8, 1964, in the Sharp Gymnasium. Former governor The Honorable Allan Shivers brought the principal address.[107] Dr. H. B. Smith and Board Chair Robert Ray performed the official investiture.[108] Lunch followed at the Sharpstown Country Club.[109]

The first year drew to a close with an Awards Day Convocation on May 21, 1964. The award nomenclature from this event convey the social conventions of the era—"Outstanding Boy," "Outstanding Girl," "Christian Witness," "Freshman Composition," "Outstanding Organization," and "Scholastic Achievement" awards.[110] The College Singers, voted "Most Outstanding Campus Organization,"[111] also became the talk of the city with the organization's pursuit of its public relations mission for the College. *The Collegian* reported, "The Choir, small in number but large in quality, has astonished crowds in the city with its professional excellence ever since its auspicious debut on Billy Graham Day."[112] So frequently honored was the College Singers organization over the next several years that student Merrill Blackburn wrote in the *Collegian*, "The College Singers are so outstanding, they will be in next year's Cotton Bowl."[113]

It had been a momentous first year. Campus guests had included George H. W. Bush, Billy Graham, Ann Landers, and Andre Previn.[114] Significant academic foundations had been established. H. B. Smith urged faculty to "encourage students in independent study and self-

---

105. "In Memoriam," *Houston Baptist College News,* Sept. 1965, 1. Photo.
106. "Musical Choir and Ensemble," *Houston Baptist College News,* May 1964, 8. Photo.
107. "Walton Due at Events for Houston Baptist College," *Abilene Reporter-News,* 2 May 1964, sec. A, p. 2.
108. "Challenge of Change," *Houston Baptist College News,* June 1964, 4. Photo.
109. "Luncheon: The Closing Event," *Houston Baptist College News,* May 1964, 4; "Luncheon: Responsibility for Truth," *Houston Baptist College News,* June 1964, 5; *Ornogah 1964,* 90-93; *Ornogah 1965,* 5.
110. "Awards Day: Outstanding Students," *Houston Baptist College News,* June 1964, 8; *Ornogah 1964,* 94-97.
111. *Ornogah 1964,* 123-25.
112. Suzanne Clark, "Looking Back," *Houston Baptist Collegian,* 22 May 1964, p. 1.
113. Merrill Blackburn, "Moments with Merrill," *Houston Baptist Collegian,* 18 Jan. 1967, p. 3.
114. *Ornogah 1964,* 140.

learning."[115] Students had responded to classroom rigor with outstanding performance. The first academic honor society, Alpha Sigma Epsilon, was formed by Judy Bennatte, Linda Cecil, Suzanne Clark, Lynda DeLoach, John Gillespie, Mary K. Heye, John Kadz, Bill Myers, and Mary Lynn Naye. The Student Association drafted its first constitution with the leadership of Lynda DeLoach, John Gillespie, Jon Green, and Diane Halbert Smith. Dorm councils were organized for Jordan Hall honoring Director Alma Jordan[116] and Herring Hall honoring faculty Director Dr. James Herring. Intramurals, drama, art, and music activity became rooted.[117] The first faculty and administration served well and boldly. The trustees had kept the financial ship afloat for the first year of operation.

§

Some early decisions ultimately were reversed. The first school song, *Onward HBC,* met with general student disaffection[118] and was replaced in 1968 with an alma mater, *Hail the Orange and Blue.*[119] The original mascot name "Spartans," chosen over "Bobcats," proved problematic.[120] By referendum on May 11, 1965, students voted to adopt "Huskies" as the name for a new mascot.[121] However, a remarkable number of early decisions remained in place throughout the history of the College. Dr. Hinton told the story of meeting with a group of students late in the spring of 1964. He was asked who had selected the official colors of orange and blue. Hinton replied that the colors were of his selection. The follow-up question was, "Can anything be done about it?"[122]

No summer classes were offered for several years. Initially, during the summer faculty members caught their breath from the year just concluded. Twelve-month contracts provided summer time for curriculum writing and class preparation for the coming year. Over the course of the 1964 summer, a Basic Course team worked on the sophomore INDC

115. Houston Baptist College, Minutes of the Meetings of the Faculty, Meeting on 14 May 1964.

116. "Meet Mrs. Jordan," *Houston Baptist College News,* Nov. 1964, 3; *Ornogah 1964,* 106-107.

117. *Ornogah 1964,* 108-9.

118. *Ornogah 1964,* 36. Words by Dr. Milton S. Smith; music by Dr. Claude Rhea. Full text.

119. "Alma Mater Competition," *Houston Baptist Collegian,* 15 Dec. 1968, p. 2.

120. Wayne Webb, "Letter to the Editor," *Houston Baptist Collegian,* 17 May 1965, p. 7.

121. William C. Bolton, "Letters to the Editor," *Fairbanks (Alaska) Daily News-Miner,* 13 Nov. 1965, p. 4.

122. Louis Detwiler, "Spartans, Alligators, Huskies, Mystery Colors Disclosed," *Houston Baptist Collegian,* 10 Sept. 1970, p. 2.

course *Cultural and Human Experience* that addressed art, music, drama, literature, and Christianity.[123] This course was "designed to acquaint each student with man's cultural and artistic accomplishment and to encourage an appreciation of them."[124] The sophomore year also required two semesters of *World Literature* that paralleled the global orientation of *Culture and Human Experience.* Two years of foreign language beginning in the sophomore year were required of all students. Some opportunity for elective study and exploration of potential majors was incorporated into the sophomore curriculum.

Trustees met through the summer of 1964 to deal with continuing financial shortfalls. In July, they borrowed $105,000 to bridge the cash flow shortage for the next several months. A summer report indicated that $2,000,000 was owed on academic buildings and some $850,000 on dormitories. The financial obligation for housing was designed to be self-amortizing, but needed full occupancy to be viable.

Four of the original faculty did not return in the fall of 1964. Eight new faculty members joined the ranks; some represented new areas of curriculum that were to begin in the coming junior year. New faculty members included Dr. Henry Eason, Drama (1964-1967);[125] Ruth Jackson, Music (1964-1968); Ralph Liese, Music (1964-1969); Don Looser, Music (1964-2010); Roy Turner, Biology (1964-1967); Peck Vass, Physical Education (1964-1967); Frank Wright, English (1964-1965); Carolyn Yarbrough, Speech (1964-1968); and Dr. Robert Young, Physics (1964-1969).[126]

Enrollment increased as 478 students were registered in the fall—259 new freshmen, 148 returning students, and seventy-one transfer students. Of these, seventy-nine were reported to be ministerial students; seventy-one percent were Baptist. The women's dorm was full at 128; the men's dorm housed eighty-two residents.[127] The Board employed architect Wiley Vale of Rustay, Martin and Vale to design a second women's dorm

---

123. "News Notes," *Houston Baptist College News,* June 1964, 7. Faculty members included Chair Dr. Claude Rhea in music, Jim Stoker in art, John Welsh in theatre, Dr. A. O. Collins in theology, and Dr. Calvin Huckabay in literature.
124. "Sophomore Core," *Houston Baptist Collegian,* 21 May 1964, p. 2.
125. "Gallery Theatre Presents," *Houston Baptist College News,* Nov. 1964, 2.
126. "New Staff and Faculty Join Houston Baptist," *Houston Baptist College News,* Sept. 1964, 8. Biographies and photographs of new employees.
127. "Enrollment More Than Doubled," *Houston Baptist College News,* Oct. 1964, 1. The issue was mislabeled as October 1965; however, the article states the "second school year for the College."

and the firm of Lloyd, Morgan, Jones to design a new library building.[128] In December, architects presented a concept for a proposed dormitory that included 256 beds, a cafeteria, Board of Trustees room, banquet space, and a student lounge for an estimated cost of $1,100,000.[129] In 1966, the plan was modified to include housing for 308 students, but no provision was made for a cafeteria.[130]

Another of the "firsts" in 1964 was the President's Council Dinner that was held at the Warwick Hotel. The President's Council consisted of businessmen pledged to support the cause of Christian higher education in the city. These semi-annual, black-tie events came to garner extensive publicity and featured a tradition of outstanding celebrity speakers. Through such events in institutional history, HBC increased credibility and visibility in the Houston community. Lacking alumni or a significant athletic or fine arts legacy in these early years, these highly-visible public events well-served the development purposes of the College. An enthusiastic 350 guests attended this first President's Council Dinner in 1964 and heard an address by Dr. Kenneth McFarland.[131]

§

Since 1962, the development of a retirement village at the corner of Fondren Road and the Southwest Freeway had been the object of extended discussion and planning in the Board of Trustees. Dr. Dillon also reported interest for a shopping center on this same site as early as January 1964.[132] A report by Stewart Morris to the UBA confirmed a favorable IRS ruling for the "senior citizen project." However, in December 1964 the College Property Committee of the UBA reached a decision to postpone the College Gardens project. "It was felt by this committee that its abilities could better serve the College by working on a major project that would enhance the financial structure of the College much sooner."[133] Helping to explain the committee's decision, Jake

---

128. Houston Baptist College, Minutes of Meetings of the Board of Trustees, Meeting on 20 Nov. 1964.

129. Houston Baptist College, Minutes of Meetings of the Board of Trustees, Meeting on 23 Dec. 1964; "Proposed New Girl's Dormitory," *Houston Baptist College News,* Mar. 1965, 4. Photo.

130. Houston Baptist College, Minutes of Meetings of the Building Committee of the Board of Trustees, Meeting on 12 Jan. 1966.

131. "Council Anniversary," *Houston Baptist College News,* Nov. 1964, 1.

132. Houston Baptist College, Minutes of Meetings of the Executive Committee of the Board of Trustees, Meeting on 21 Jan. 1964.

133. Sibley, 52-53; Houston Baptist College, Minutes of Meetings of the Executive Committee of the Board of Trustees, Meeting on 8 Dec. 1964.

Kamin reported on completion of a $4,600,000 loan for twenty years to refinance existing College loans and ease cash-flow problems; 122 acres of campus land were pledged as collateral. In 1965, Florence Weaver was added to the UBA Committee membership replacing Donald McGregor who resigned for reasons of health. Weaver had first been elected a trustee in 1961 and was the first woman ever to serve on the College Board of Trustees.

Highlights from the spring of 1965 included a production of Euripides's *Medea* starring Houston actress Jeannette Clift. The production received a glowing review in the *Houston Chronicle* featuring the headline, "Baptist College Cast's 'Medea' Rates Applause."[134] In February, the Captain Theodore C. Freeman Library of Astronautics was dedicated in memorial services on campus honoring astronaut Ted Freeman who had been killed while a NASA pilot.[135] Stewart Morris made the presentation of the library to the College; Captain David Scott gave the address that concluded with the reading of a telegram from President Lyndon B. Johnson.[136]

A Spring Gala at the Music Hall in downtown Houston gave opportunity for the city-at-large to hear College music faculty, students, and music ensembles in concert. Featured performers included the College Singers, faculty members David Appleby, Don Looser, Claude Rhea, and Ray Fliegel's string quartet from the Houston Symphony.[137] Fliegel was concertmaster of the Houston Symphony Orchestra, taught violin at HBC, and was instrumental in securing members of the Houston Symphony to teach private lessons for the College as affiliate artists. The Symphony musicians excelled as student recruiters. In 1965, three HBC students—John Kadz, Milford Kuhn, and Larry Long— played with Sir John Barbirolli and the Houston Symphony in a performance of Bruckner's Ninth Symphony.[138]

The spring 1965 President's Council Dinner featured Meredith Willson, composer of the Broadway hit *The Music Man*.[139] Mayor Louie

---

134. Donna Jean Hobby, "Baptist College Cast's 'Medea' Rates Applause," *HBC News*, Feb. 1966, 6; *Ornogah 1966*, 158; Houston Baptist College, Minutes of the Meetings of the Faculty, Meeting on 7 Jan. 1966.

135. "Library of Astronautics Dedicated January 21," *Houston Baptist College News*, Feb. 1965, 1, 2; "Dead Astronaut Honored," *San Antonio Express*, 22 Jan. 1965, sec. A, p. 13. Photo.

136. "Library of Astronautics Dedicated Jan. 21," *HBU News*, Feb. 1965, 1. Photo.

137. "High Praise for Fine Arts Benefit," *Houston Baptist College News*, June 1965, 1-2; *Ornogah 1965*, 111-113.

138. "Houston Symphony: College is Well Represented," *Houston Baptist Collegian*, 16 Nov. 1965, p. 3. Photo with conductor Sir John Barbirolli.

139. "'Music Man' To Visit Campus in April," *Houston Baptist College News*, Apr. 1965, 2; "Willson and Wife Make A Hit with High School Bands," *Houston Baptist College News*, May 1965, 3.

Welch proclaimed the day "Meredith Willson Day" in Houston and joined Willson and massed high school musicians on campus in conducting a rousing performance that climaxed with 76 trombones playing the song of the same name. That evening at a dinner at the Houston Club, Willson joined with the College Singers in a premiere performance of a medley of songs from *The Music Man* arranged especially for the Singers.[140] The College Singers was also honored to be selected to present the world premiere of a new choral work by composer Ron Brown, *What is Man?*, for the 1965 meeting of the Baptist World Alliance in Miami.[141] The year 1964-65 had been a marathon year for the Singers consisting of a 105 performance appearances during the nine months.[142]

The *Houston Baptist Collegian* struggled to survive during 1964-65, publishing intermittently, sometimes even in mimeographed form, but featured stimulating editorial writing by John Gillespie who observed and critiqued the changing campus environment. Chapel and Assembly

The 1964-65 College Singers en route to the Baptist World Alliance in Miami

---

140. Judy Bennatte, "'Mr. Music Man' at HBC," *Houston Baptist Collegian*, 29 Apr. 1965, p. 1. *Ornogah 1965*, 86-87.

141. "Modern Man's Uncertainty Oratorio Theme," *Miami Herald*, 25 June 1965, sec. E, p. 2; "College Singers to Perform for SBC," *Houston Baptist College News*, May 1965, 2; "HBC goes to SBC and BWC," *Houston Baptist Collegian*, 15 Sept. 1965, p. 4. Photo.

142. Houston Baptist College, Minutes of the Meetings of the Faculty, Meeting on 11 Feb. 1965 and 11 Mar. 1965. Faculty meetings in February and in March focused on the frequent absence of the College Singers from classes.

programs continued to feature a roster of speakers and performers who stimulated the mind, strengthened the spirit, and helped unify the new College family. In March, Miss America of 1965, Vonda Kay Van Dyke, delighted students and 300 invited high school National Honor Society students with her ventriloquism and her Christian testimony.[143]

Sophomores now joined freshmen who appeared in traditional beanies and endured innocent, non-threatening harassment. Freshman courses benefited from the sophomores who had gone before. The faculty began to be more confident of the grand academic design and place a personal imprint on its manifestation. In the *Collegian*, the ChucWagun #14 at the corner of Beechnut and Bissonnet advertised a "Sunday Night Hunger" campaign to dorm students for whom there was no Sunday night campus meal service. The ChucWagun advertised one free drink with the purchase of one "Wheelburger" for HBC students.[144] Students in groups made the mile-long walk for weekend food. More mobile students could drive down Bissonnet to Youngblood's Fried Chicken where a student special would yield three pieces of chicken, mashed potatoes, and hot bread for seventy-five cents. As the city continued to develop in the southwest quadrant, the Southwest Freeway construction pressed ever closer toward Fort Bend County. The Hillcroft overpass on the Southwest Freeway opened in April 1969, provided much greater ease in reaching the campus, and significantly reduced the drive time for students and faculty.[145]

§

The year 1964 had begun with overt signs of faculty-administration antipathy. An early-year faculty meeting had resulted in shouts, finger pointing, and heated accusations. It should have come as no surprise, therefore, when Dr. Hinton announced in March 1965 that he would be holding individual conferences with all faculty members addressing the concerns of "supporting the Preamble, professional growth, innovation, breaking ties with former institutions, and loyalty to the College."[146] He further stated that commitment to the College should be in "action, word, and deed."[147] In the April faculty meeting, he issued a strong challenge to

---

143. "Miss America Thrills Students with Testimony," *Houston Baptist College News,* Apr. 1965, 1, 4. Photo.
144. "Chuc Wagun #14," *Houston Baptist Collegian,* 13 Nov. 1964, p. 5.
145. "Freeway to Open," *Houston Baptist College News,* Apr. 1965, 4.
146. Houston Baptist College, Minutes of the Meetings of the Faculty, Meeting on 22 Mar. 1965.

faculty members to examine their individual commitment to the College. Dr. Hinton later announced the resignation of two faculty members to accept positions at other colleges and revealed his decision not to renew the contracts of two Division Chairmen.[148] Presidential correspondence and faculty minutes from the period confirm the shock of this action on the faculty.[149] Nonetheless, most faculty members agreed that open challenges of the President in faculty meetings and of his authority directed to individual trustees were unprofessional and unacceptable. Nonetheless, these non-renewals coupled with ongoing reports of limited administrative communication with faculty caused the Board to request reassurance from Dr. Hinton that means of more effective dialogue would be developed. Effective communication also became one of the objects of concern for the Southern Association of Colleges and Schools on the agency's first accreditation visit. As a result of anxiety emanating from these personnel decisions, the faculty Professional Growth Committee recommended that the American Association of University Professors (AAUP) *1940 Statement on Academic Freedom* that dealt with notice for non-reappointment be added to the College *Manual of Board Policy*.[150]

The summer of 1965 was defined by work toward courses in the junior year, the creation of two new divisions in education[151] and business, a successful first Texas Baptist Youth Music Camp in June, and the death of Miss Atwood in August. Faculty members remained on twelve-month contracts. With the prospects of no summer tuition income, the Executive Committee in March authorized the President "to make arrangements" to meet the summer payroll.[152]

§

Rex Baker, Sr. frequently used the expression, "where the water hits the wheel." On campus, it was with the person of Dr. H. B. Smith that the water most often hit the wheel. Smith ran a tight ship. Dr. Smith

---

147. Ibid.
148. Houston Baptist College, Minutes of Meetings of the Board of Trustees, Meeting on 1 Apr. 1965.
149. Houston Baptist College, Minutes of the Meetings of the Faculty, Meeting on 2 Apr. 1965; (Confidential correspondence to Dr. W. H. Hinton from several non-renewed faculty members).
150. Houston Baptist College, Minutes of the Meeting of the Faculty, Meeting on 8 Oct. 1964.
151. "Division of Education to open this fall with Harris as Chairman," *Houston Baptist College News*, May 1965, 1.
152. Houston Baptist College, Minutes of Meetings of the Executive Committee of the Board of Trustees, Meeting on 17 Mar. 1965.

commonly took faculty attendance at chapel, published the list of those absent from faculty meetings, challenged any skewed grading distributions, and seasonally removed from faculty offices any library books that were overdue or furniture acquired by what he called "midnight requisition." He deferred from reading a memo that was not signed and dated. He was a man of the "old school." Many faculty members took issue with his administrative style but did not fault his sincerity and commitment.

The 1960s were an era of challenge of authority and redefinition of academic leadership style into a more corporate model. Nonetheless, the breadth of Smith's academic vision, the tenacity of his curricular research, and the power of his ability to motivate scholarship among faculty and students made him an effective first chief academic officer. During his career, H. B. Smith left a legacy in the person of a number of academicians he had mentored.[153] For those whom he mentored, he was a model of consistency, sound practice, practical wisdom, and institutional dedication.

---

153. These included Dr. Calvin Huckabay and Dr. Alma Leavell with whom he had worked at Hardin Simmons University and a generation of young academics whom he mentored in Houston.

FOUR

1965-1969

"Chance favors the prepared mind."
—Louis Pasteur

In 1965, the third class of freshman began its academic studies. Student enrollment totaled 674 of which the majority was male. In years thereafter, females would represent sixty percent or more of the student population. Dr. Stanley Olsen, Dean of Baylor College of Medicine, delivered the address for the fall 1965 opening convocation. A complement of fourteen new faculty members joined the College. Dr. Smith gave specific instructions in the opening faculty meeting that mandated faculty office hours from 8 a.m. to 4 p.m. daily, faculty attendance for Chapel and Assembly, and continued attention to institutional commitment.[1] Faculty members from various disciplines were assigned to intermixed office locations to enhance interdisciplinary dialog.

By this third year, the campus community was becoming functionally cohesive. Coffee was served each morning until 10:30 in the cafeteria dining room that was regularly populated by most of the faculty and staff who were not actually in class. A Faculty Coffee Club was formed by Dr. Joyce Fan who also served as chair and collected monies for the coffee service. Dr. H. B. Smith was a regular participant and had only the rule that no business could be discussed at Coffee Club. Most classes were completed by noon, enabling faculty and staff to eat lunch together as well.

The new faculty was charged with expansion of the curriculum into upper-division courses and the development of majors in professional fields. In 1965, those new faculty included Elsa Jean Albritton, English (1965-1969); Dr. David Appleby, Music (1965-1969); Virginia Babikian, Music (1965-1982); Jeannette Clift, Drama (1965-1968); Dr. Daniel Craver, Education (1965-1966); Dr. Sam Davis, Economics (1965-1993); Dr. Thomas Foster, Chair, Business (1965-1966); Dr. Jack Gunn, Chair,

---

1. Houston Baptist College, Minutes of the Meetings of the Faculty, Meeting on 19 Sept. 1965.

History (1965-1967); Marilyn Henson, Physical Education (1965-1968); Dr. A. E. Kannwischer, Chair, Social Studies (1965-1974); Dr. James Leavell, Christianity (1965-1973); Dr. Alma Malone, Chair, Education (1965-1983); Dr. Ronald E. Roberts, Political Science (1965-1968); David Thomas, Speech (1965-1966); Richard Webb, German (1965-1968); Dr. Lew Zailer, Music (1965-1976); Adella Chris Mitchell, Art (1965-1968); Dr. Wallace Hooker, English (1965-1990); Steve Ligh, Mathematics (1965-1966); Fran Rogers, Music (1965-1968); and Jean Tilton, Art (1965-1968).

Dr. Irwin Abrams, an academic consultant from Antioch College, spent several days with the faculty during the fall planning for the fourth-year's *Senior Seminar* capstone courses that focused on research methods and modes of formal presentation.[2] The new Division of Education chaired by Dr. Clif Harris offered its first education classes to junior students.[3] A new fight song, "Get Up and Go, You Mighty Huskies," was composed by HBC musicologist Dr. Robert Parker.

> *Get up and go, you mighty Huskies*
> *Give it a fight for HBC.*
> *Whenever the goin' is rough and things are tough,*
> *Don't give up the fight.*
> *Shoulder the load, hold to the road,*
> *Pull with all your might.*
>
> *Get up and go, you mighty Huskies*
> *Give it a haul for orange and blue.*
> *Get ready to meet the test, show your best,*
> *Drive until you've made*
> *History with victory.*
> *You'll win for HBC.*
>
> *Robert L. Parker*

§

---

2. "Senior Seminar Session Held," *Houston Baptist Collegian*, 16 Nov. 1965, p. 1.
3. "Division of Education to Open This Fall with Harris as Chairman," *HBC News*, May 1965, 1.

In the city's cultural community, Mrs. Charles Bybee became enamored with the idea of establishing a decorative arts museum on the campus. On September 23, 1965, Mrs. Bybee chaired a "flea market" at her River Oaks home as a fund-raiser to aid such an undertaking. Helen Tinch, author of *Days in Colonial Texas*,[4] had been employed by the College in 1964 to begin assembling a museum collection that would "encompass all phases of American architecture, restoration, decorative arts and crafts, and domestic life in America, especially Texas."[5] Christine Imber was elected the first president (executive committee chair) of the new Museum Society.[6] An advisory committee was composed of Mrs. J. R. Imber, Mrs. Charles Bybee, Mrs. James E. Lyon, Mrs. R. T. McDermott, Mrs. John W. Mecom, Jr., Mrs. Robert Ray, Mrs. Earl Sheffield, Mrs. R. E. "Bob" Smith, and Mrs. Knox Tyson. No location was yet available for a museum on campus although artifacts including the Theo Redwood Blank Doll Collection were being acquired and stored awaiting future display.[7] In December, Mrs. Bybee appeared before the College Board of Trustees to propose the formal establishment of a Museum of Fine Arts.[8] She returned in January to suggest a Yale University model that united its School of Theology, School of Art, and University Museum into one interdisciplinary organization. In the January meeting, the Board approved a resolution that created such a museum at HBC:

> Be it resolved that we, the Board of Trustees of Houston Baptist College, establish a museum to be known as the Museum of American Architecture and Decorative Arts as a department of the Division of Fine Arts of the College. Be it further resolved

4. Helen Tinch, *Days in Colonial Texas* (Houston: Houston Baptist College American Museum Society, c. 1963).

5. "Museum Effort Gains Ground," *HBC News*, Feb. 1968, 2-3. Museum Society Scrapbook in University Archives: "Clubs," *Houston Chronicle*, 26 Sept. 1965; "Society Eyes Flea Market," *The Houston Post*, 24 Sept. 1965, sec. 2, p. 3; "New Museum Society," *Houston Tribune*, 23 Sept. 1965, p. 9; "Museum Plans 'Flea Market,'" *The Mirror*, 29 Sept. 1965, p. 12.

6. "New-Houston fascination in Houston heritage," *Houston Tribune*, 25 Aug. 1966, p. 2; *American Museum Society Year Book 1972* (Houston: Houston Baptist College American Museum Society, 1972-73), 6.

7. "Simpson College," *Des Moines Sunday Register*, 24 Dec. 1967, p. 5. Photo of Mrs. Blank. "Several years ago, she gave a valuable collection, known as the Theo Redwood Blank collection of about 1500 dolls, some dating from 1500 B. C., to Houston (Texas) Baptist College Museum. (She stated) there is no place in Des Moines for them."

8. Houston Baptist College, Minutes of Meetings of the Board of Trustees, Meeting on 30 Dec. 1965.

that the said museum shall be located on the campus and shall be controlled and operated under the authority vested in the Board of Trustees.[9]

Dr. Claude Rhea shepherded the museum project as a part of his responsibilities as Chair of the Division of Fine Arts. In February 1966, the newly-formed American Museum Society hosted a Silver Tea chaired by Mrs. Carloss Morris, Mrs. Charles Bybee, and Mrs. R. Thomas McDermott.[10] In the spring, the Museum Society sponsored a tour of the Texas "Painted Churches" near Schulenburg that concluded at Mrs. Bybee's log house at Round Top.[11] The Society continued to build interest, to assist in establishing a permanent museum collection, and to press for a campus site.

§

The payment of financial pledges by churches continued to lag. In a speech before the UBA in 1965, Dr. Hinton pleaded for churches to make good on their pledges to pay for the original campus buildings. "Only 92 churches are now giving any financial assistance to the College. The need of $15,000 monthly is imperative."[12] UBA real estate development, however, continued to flourish. The UBA Executive Committee authorized the acquisition of 200 acres of land on Bellaire Boulevard, later known as Alief, from the Jackson-Bellaire West Corporation.[13] By December, the UBA Property Committee was reporting extensive real estate development activity in Bellaire West, Imperial Point, Memorial Grove, and on the Atwood homestead on Kirby.[14]

The most light-hearted news of the fall centered on a report that indicated "a solid brass Mexican cannon filled with gold, diamonds, and

9. Houston Baptist College, Minutes of Meetings of the Executive Committee of the Board of Trustees, Meeting on 10 Jan. 1966; Houston Baptist College, Minutes of Meetings of the Board of Trustees, Meeting on 14 Jan. 1966.

10. Betty Ewing, "Girls Will Always Have Their Heroes," *Houston Chronicle,* 3 Feb. 1966, sec. 3, p. 1; "Furthering the Fine Arts," *Houston Post,* 6 Feb. 1966, sec. 7, p. 7; Maurine Eastus, "Houston Diary," *Houston Tribune,* 10 Mar. 1966, sec. 3, p. 2.

11. *Houston Post,* 23 May 1966, sec. 2, p. 6; "On Our Cover," *River Oaks Times,* Vol. 21, #42, cover photo of Doris Morris, Faith Bybee, and Ethel McDermott.

12. Union Baptist Association of Texas, Minutes of the Annual Conference, *HBC Reports,* 1965, 13-14.

13. Ibid; Houston Baptist College, Minutes of Meetings of the Board of Trustees, Meeting on 24 Sept. 1965.

14. Houston Baptist College, Minutes of Meetings of the Executive Committee of the Board of Trustees, Meeting on 6 Dec. 1965.

pearls" was buried on the campus near Beechnut and the men's dorm.[15] Digging for the buried treasure began immediately. KHOU-TV interviewed Fine Arts Division Chairman Dr. Claude Rhea who pledged any monies recovered would be used to help fund a proposed new fine arts center.[16] However, to the frustration and disappointment of all, the excavation repeatedly filled with quicksand and ultimately had to be abandoned.[17] No cannon or buried treasure has ever been found.

Student life on campus continued to mature and flourish. Late in the fall, Houston Symphony conductor Andre Previn and *Tonight Show* band leader Doc Severinsen were campus guests for a Stage Band Clinic arranged by faculty member Ralph Liese. Previn also offered a master class for pianists while Severinsen appeared in concert with the HBC Stage Band. At his request, in lieu of an honorarium, Severinsen was presented a Palomino colt quarter-horse sired by "Sure Cash" at the J. B. Clifton Ranch in Wharton.[18] Both Previn and Severinsen generously

Mr. "Music Man," Meredith Willson, conducting "Seventy-Six Trombones."

Dr. Hinton and B. J. Clifton present Palomino colt to Doc Severinsen.

15. "Digging for treasure," *HBU News,* Feb. 1991, 10. Alice Murphy, "Drillers Hunt Treasure Under College Campus, *Houston Post*; "Quicksand Spoils Hunt for Buried Treasure," *Houston Chronicle.*
16. "Proposed Fine Arts Complex: Houston Baptist College," *Houston Baptist College News,* Feb. 1965, 4. Photo.
17. "Quicksand Halts Search for Phantom Cannon," *Houston Baptist Collegian,* 2 Nov. 1965, p. 1; "Notoriety," *HBC News,* Nov. 1965, 4; *Ornogah 1966,* 153. Photos.
18. "HBC to Host Stage Band Clinic," *HBC News,* Nov. 1965, 3; "Band Clinic Very Successful," *HBC News,* Dec. 1965, 3; *Ornogah 1966,* 169; "Band Festival Awards Prizes," *Houston Baptist Collegian,* 18 Jan. 1966, p. 3.

returned to the campus for workshops a number of times over the next several years.[19]

Representatives from the Student Government were invited to attend a meeting of the Board of Trustees for the first time in December 1965.[20] The Triceans was chartered as the first "girls" service club on campus.[21] Sophomore Julia Keith was named "Miss Houston 1965,"[22] and Brenda Hodges was crowned "Queen of the Bluebonnet Bowl."[23]

Traditions took root and were passed from one class to the next. Film of Billy Graham Day in 1963 documents the establishment of the tradition of standing to honor a guest speaker on campus.[24] The Coreons fraternity established the tradition of a tug-of-war between freshmen and sophomores to determine how long freshman beanies must be worn. The tradition of a bonfire before the first basketball game of the year was also established. One spontaneous tradition that developed consisted of dunking a newly-engaged man into one of the pools of the academic quadrangle.[25] Early in 1966, the precedent was set that faculty also be included in this new tradition. In 34-degree January weather, music faculty member Don Looser was the first of the faculty so honored. This immersion resulted from his engagement to fellow faculty member Elsa Jean Albritton and was duly recorded in that year's edition of the *Ornogah*.[26] This tradition continued well into the 1980s and became a matter of great pride for many male alumni. Ultimately, concern for the safety of the man and increasing awareness of institutional liability terminated the practice.

§

The presence of the arts in these early years profoundly shaped the campus community. An active music program consisting of faculty recitals, guest artists, and ensemble performances belied the youth of the

19. "Severinsen, Smith Hold Spring Band Festival at HBC," *Houston Baptist Collegian*, 22 Feb. 1967, p. 1.

20. Houston Baptist College, Minutes of Meetings of the Board of Trustees, Meeting on 10 Dec. 1965.

21. "Tricean Charter Accepted At Service Tea," *Houston Baptist Collegian*, 15 Feb. 1966, p. 1.

22. "HBC Beauty Named Miss Houston," *Houston Baptist Collegian*, 15 Sept. 1965, p. 4.

23. Joe Tulloch, "Brenda Hodges Earns Miss Bluebonnet Title," *Houston Baptist Collegian*, 14 Dec. 1965, p. 1; "Brenda Hodges," *HBC News*, June 1966, 2. Photo.

24. Houston Baptist College, "A New Dimension in Christian Culture," 1963. Promotional film housed in University archives.

25. "Cold Water Treatment for the Engaged Man," *The Collegian*, 22 Nov. 1967, p. 1.

26. "Miss Albritton-Looser Announce Engagement," *The Collegian*, 18 Jan. 1966, p. 4; *Ornogah 1966*, 33. Photo.

new college in quality and diversity. Gallery Theatre drama productions of *Agamemnon*,[27] *Waiting for Godot*,[28] and *Twelfth Night*[29] enriched the campus academic environment. The drama program not only supplemented formal academic courses with cultural enrichment but, with its campus performances, also added a cohesive dimension for resident students. The College Singers recorded Mary Caldwell's *Of Time and Eternity* for the Broadman Press in January 1966[30] and presented both the television premier on KPRC-TV[31] and the world premier performance in April.[32] This marked the Singers' first commercial recording.[33]

The remarkable fine arts program of the College can largely be credited to the leadership of Dr. Claude Rhea, Chair of the Division of Fine Arts. Rhea had been recruited by Dr. Hinton from his position as Dean of the School of Music at New Orleans Baptist Theological Seminary. He was an internationally-recognized oratorio tenor who had a number of recordings among his professional credits.[34] Rhea was responsible for recruiting the outstanding faculty in fine arts that included R. Paul Green, former conductor of the Southwestern Singers and the Baptist Hour Choir; Dr. David Appleby, noted concert pianist and member of the faculty at the Interlochen Center for the Arts; Virginia Babikian, artist-in-residence and acclaimed soprano soloist for the Houston Symphony Orchestra under Leopold Stokowski and John Barbirolli; Raphael Fliegel, Concertmaster of the Houston Symphony Orchestra; Jeannette Clift, Alley Theatre actress and later founder of the A. D. Players; Ralph Liese, Principal Trombonist of the Houston Symphony Orchestra and President of the Houston American Federation of Musicians; and Jim Stoker, a widely-recognized Texas artist. These faculty members were largely responsible for recruitment of an outstanding group of one hundred students that majored in the arts. As an effective cultural ambassador for the College, Rhea ultimately was also responsible

---

27 "Agamemnon," *HBC News*, June 1965, 2.

28 *HBC News*, Oct. 1965, 4; *Ornogah 1966*, 159. Photo.

29 *Houston Baptist Collegian*, 26 Apr. 1966, p. 1, photo; "Calendar of Events," *HBC News*, Sept. 1969, 4.

30 "Singers to Make Record," *HBC News*, Oct. 1965, 2; "HBC Singers Record 'Of Time and Eternity,'" *Houston Baptist Collegian*, 10 Oct. 1965, p. 1; "College Singers Album Is Released To Public," *Houston Baptist Collegian*, 15 Feb. 1966, p. 1. The cantata recording was produced by HBC faculty members R. Paul Green, conductor, and Don Looser, organist.

31 "Recent News Worth Noting," *HBC News*, May 1966, 3.

32 "At First Baptist Church Singers to Present Cantata," *Houston Baptist Collegian*, 5 Apr. 1966, p. 4.

33 "Fine Arts Festival Scheduled," *HBC News*, May 1966, 1.

34 Ruth Rosenfeld, "Meet the Musical Rheas," *Bellaire Texan*, 9 Oct. 1963, p. 4; *HBC News*, Oct. 1965, 4. Photo.

for helping organize several national symposia on architectural preservation, was the founding administrator for the College Museum, and was an
effective fund raiser in the city's cultural community.

An environment of elevated enrichment characterized the campus
through the quality of Chapel and Assembly guests, the success of music
and drama performances, the coming of age of the *Collegian*, the growth of
intercollegiate athletics, and the establishment of social, service, and academic organizations within the student body. This level of intellectual and
cultural richness in only the third year of institutional life bore witness to
the significant contributions of the early faculty, staff, and students.

The 1966 spring semester marked several mileposts. Westward Ho
Day emerged as the traditional spring day of campus festivity. The first
study-abroad trip was announced by faculty sponsor Dr. James Leavell.
The program of twenty-one days in the Holy Land that included air travel and all meals cost participants $1478.[35] The first HBC summer school
was planned following a student interest survey.[36] The first College forensics students, coached by Dr. Jerry Reynolds, won recognition at the
forty-eight-college Baylor University tournament.[37] An apparent one-
time student literary publication called *The Binding Cord* was issued in
1965-66.[38] However, first mention of a literary anthology called *The Raft*
was subsequently made in a March 1966 *Collegian*.[39] The anthology was
edited by student Dan Elkins and sponsored by faculty member Richard
Webb. The following year's edition was edited by Dale Ratheal and
Honey Harrison with the assistance of Dr. Wallace Hooker.[40] With the
1968 publication of *The Raft* edited by Don Hendrix and Honey
Harrison, the anthology established a continuum of publication.[41]

Stewart Morris funded a promotional film by Bob Bailey, *A New
Dimension*,[42] that reflected the institutional slogan *A New Dimension in*

35. "James Leavell To Offer Tour Of Holy Land," *Houston Baptist Collegian*, 1 Mar. 1966, p. 3.
36. Houston Baptist College, Minutes of the Meetings of the Faculty, Meeting on 13 Jan. 1966; "Summer
Classes Announced," *HBC News*, Mar. 1966, 6; "College Holds Summer School for First Time," *Houston Baptist
Collegian*, 15 Mar. 1966, p. 1; "Summer Schedule Is Completed," *Houston Baptist Collegian*, 26 Apr. 1966, p. 1.
37. "Gibson, Tambrella Lead HBC to Tournament Win," *Houston Baptist Collegian*, 15 Feb. 1967, p. 1. Photo.
38. *The Binding Cord* (Houston: Houston Baptist College, 1965-66).
39. Dan Elkins, "Literary Anthology," *Houston Baptist Collegian*, 1 Mar. 1966, p. 2.
40 Dale Ratheal, ed., *The Raft*, (Houston: Houston Baptist College, 1967). Personal collection of Dr. Wallace
Hooker.
41 "Raft Accepts Entries," *The Collegian*, 14 Feb. 1968, p. 1.
42 Houston Baptist College, Minutes of Meetings of the Board of Trustees, Meeting on 7 Feb. 1966.

Christian Culture.[43] Over the next several years, the film enjoyed repeated viewings in churches and civic organizations to encourage student inquiry and financial support. At the March 1966 meeting of the Board of Trustees, Dr. Hinton "discussed the necessity of intensified student recruitment, increased operating funds, strengthening of the faculty, construction of additional dorm space . . . and consideration of a change in the name of the College."[44] The Board postponed action on a long-planned additional dormitory and purchased instead the Heritage Manor Apartments across Beechnut Street at Fondren Road for $450,000.[45] The apartments were to house 220 junior and senior women.[46]

In April, tenure was granted to the first faculty members.[47] All of the upper ranks of the original faculty members plus Opal Goolsby and Marion Young were awarded tenure and received increased retirement benefits.[48] Work toward initial accreditation continued, and the Southern Association reported that a new library facility would be a requirement for approval.[49] Trustees approved budgeting for a new Office of Student Enlistment. The new operation centered on student recruiting, particularly in selected urban centers along the East Coast where the appeal of a small Christian college in the urban Sun Belt setting might find resonance.[50]

In the spring of 1966, a Houston pastor-trustee mounted a campaign to limit the period of interim church service by faculty and staff. In a highly controversial and divisive action, the Board established a policy stating that no faculty member could serve a church appointment of more than six months.[51] The policy ostensibly would result in Christianity and music faculty being available for interim service to more churches in the com-

---

43 Houston Baptist College, Minutes of the Meetings of the Faculty, Meeting on 14 Nov. 1963. The slogan "A New Dimension in Christian Culture" was used on campus billboards along the feeder road of the proposed Southwest Freeway.

44 Houston Baptist College, Minutes of Meetings of the Board of Trustees, Meeting on 11 Mar. 1966.

45 Houston Baptist College, Minutes of Meetings of the Executive Committee of the Board of Trustees, Meeting on 15 Mar. 1966; Houston Baptist College, Minutes of Meetings of the Board of Trustees, Meeting on 12 Apr. 1966; "Apartment units purchased," *HBC News,* Sept. 1966, 6.

46 Houston Baptist College, Minutes of the Meetings of the Faculty, Meeting on 14 Apr. 1966.

47 "19 Members Of Faculty Given Tenure," *Houston Baptist Collegian,* 26 Apr. 1966, p. 1.

48 Houston Baptist College, Minutes of the Meetings of the Academic Committee of the Board of Trustees, Meeting on 24 Feb. 1966. Those receiving tenure were Cain, Caskey, Collins, Dacres, Fan, Goolsby, Green, Harris, Herring, Huckabay, Ingraham, Jordan, Myers, Parker, Rhea, Milton Smith, Sutton, Tidwell, Travis, Williamson, and Young.

49 Houston Baptist College, Minutes of Meetings of the Board of Trustees, Meeting on 12 April 1966.

50 Houston Baptist College, Minutes of Meetings of the Board of Trustees, Meeting on 11 Mar. 1966.

51 Houston Baptist College, Minutes of Meetings of the Academic Committee of the Board of Trustees, Meeting on 24 Feb. 1966; Houston Baptist College, Minutes of Meetings of the Board of Trustees, Meeting on 11 Mar. 1966.

munity. The response from faculty members was strong and negative.[52] Christianity faculty responded that the term of interim appointments could not be predicted. Music faculty members reported that churches would not appoint musicians who had only six months to serve. The action was viewed as discriminatory because it did not define policy governing the extra-curricular activity of faculty members in other disciplines.

The genesis of the policy emanated from the employment of one prominent HBC music faculty member by a large Houston church to the dissatisfaction of another large Houston church whose pastor served on the HBC Board of Trustees. Ultimately, the policy was modified to become a practice of reporting such service to the Office of the President as a part of annual contract renewal and was extended in scope to include consultancy service and appointment to publicly-held boards. At the time, however, the policy created additional stress on faculty/administration relations and ran counter to the historical involvement of faculty members in the professional practice of their academic disciplines.[53]

§

HBC juniors were presented drawings of a newly-designed senior ring in the spring semester of 1966. The ring design featured the Christian symbols of a triangle representing the Holy Trinity,[54] an open Bible and cross from the College seal, and a shield of faith surrounded by a chain signifying unity, security, and strength. Laurel leaves rested upon the founding date of "1960" and symbolized achievement and leadership. The ring was described by the Balfour Company as one of "simple dignity."[55] The student response to the design was strongly positive, and some sixty rings were ordered.[56]

Summer 1966 marked the realization of the first Symposium on Historical Preservation on campus. Featuring twelve speakers from the National Trust for Historical Preservation, the Symposium was organized by Mr. and Mrs. Stewart Morris and Mrs. Charles Bybee. Speakers

---

52. Houston Baptist College, Minutes of the Meetings of the Faculty, Meeting on 14 Apr. 1966 and on 8 Dec. 1966.

53. Houston Baptist College, Minutes of Meetings of the Academic Committee of the Board of Trustees, Meeting on 21 Oct. 1967.

54. Rudolf Koch, The Book of Signs (New York: Dover Publications, Inc., 1965), 8.

55. "Houston Baptist College Ring Design Proposal," L. G. Balfour, Inc., 15 Apr. 1966.

56. "HBC Ring Design Distinctive," HBC News, Oct. 1966, 6; "Senior Rings Arrive," Houston Baptist Collegian, 25 Oct. 1966, p. 3.

included Dr. Edward Alexander, Vice President of Colonial Williamsburg; Jonathan Fairbanks, DuPont Winterthur Museum; Penelope Harshore, National Park Services; Dr. William Murtaugh, National Trust for Historical Preservation; Dr. Charles Peterson, Philadelphia architectural historian;[57] Robert Raley, White House restoration consultant; and David Warren, Curator of Bayou Bend.[58] Peterson had first delivered a lecture for the College on May 4, 1964, on the topic "Restoration of Old Philadelphia" that drew the interest of Ima Hogg and opened a path for future symposia on historic preservation.[59] Miss Hogg hosted the symposium guests on a tour of Bayou Bend and was an active participant in the daily lectures. Extensive press coverage was afforded the Symposium by the *Houston Post*, the *Houston Chronicle*, the *Houston Tribune*, and *Houston Town and Country* magazine. Participants were attracted from across the nation. The Symposium resulted in heightened visibility for HBC in the city, in national recognition for the Symposium itself, and in hastening the establishment of a campus museum.

§

For all the victories and successes, however, these early years continued to be difficult for the new college. Sensitive to this fact and grateful for the College leadership, trustee John Baugh expressed a tribute on behalf of the trustees to Dr. Hinton "who faces all the difficulties of this new school."[60] Mr. Baugh expressed his "admiration, respect, and love" for Dr. Hinton whose nomination for the presidency Baugh had made four years earlier. In a move characteristic of the dedication of the trustees to the new College, Baugh announced he was foregoing membership on the board of the Baptist Foundation of Texas in order to remain active on the HBC Board of Trustees.

---

57. "Restoration in Old Philadelphia," *HBC News*, May 1964, 7.
58. Ibid; Maurine Eastus, "Houston Diary: Texas Restoration Symposium," *Houston Tribune*, 19 May 1966, p. 2; "Unique in Texas: Historic Preservation Will Be Topic of June Symposium," *Houston Chronicle*, 22 May 1966, sec. 7, p. 5; "Houston Society," *Houston Town and Country Magazine*, May 1966; "Architecture and the Arts," *Houston Chronicle*, 3 June 1966, sec. 3, p. 8; Carolie Allgood, "Symposium Urges Restoration in Area," *Houston Chronicle*, 6 June 1966, sec. 3, p. 2; Maurine Eastus, "Symposium: The surge of historic preservation," *Houston Tribune*, 9 June 1966.
59. "Restoration in Old Philadelphia," *HBC News*, May 1964, 7; *HBC News*, June 1964, 7. Photo of Miss Hogg, Mrs. Charles Bybee, Dr. Charles Peterson, and Dr. Claude Rhea.
60. Houston Baptist College, Minutes of Meetings of the Board of Trustees, Meeting on 12 Apr. 1966.

The fourth year began with a student enrollment of 825. Faculty members attended the Texas Baptist Faculty Workshop at Lakeview Assembly near Palestine.[61] Student residential housing was crowded; in the men's dorm, ten men were assigned to suites designed for eight.[62] Reaction to the new apartments was mixed; women felt more removed from the campus; security was a concern; and the walk to class was longer.[63] An additional 200 parking spaces were added to the Fondren West lot over the course of the summer.[64] In this era of process management by paper, class registration consumed several days. Faculty at tables in Sharp Gym distributed computer punch cards and counseled students enrolling for courses.[65]

For the first senior year, new faculty included Eleanor Powers Beebe, French (1966-1970); Dr. Ed Billings, Chair, Physical Education and Athletic Director (1966-1989); Marjorie Dyer, Mathematics (1966-1973); Dr. Dean Kellums, Political Science (1966-1968); Anita Magafas, Physical Education (1966-1969); Dr. Edwin D. Martin, Education (1966-1973); Dr. Jerry Reynolds, Chair, Speech (1966-1972); Dr. Joe Rice, English (1966-1968); Dr. Jerry Robinson, Sociology (1966-1971); Dr. Marilyn Sibley, Chair, History (1966-1984); Dr. Marvin Sipe, Accounting (1966-1970); Cynthia Stadeager, French (1966-1969); Dr. Molly Wieting, English (1966-1974); Ken Williams, Music (1966-1968); and Dr. Stephen G. Williams, Psychology (1966-1990).

A five-year enrollment goal of 2500 students by 1971 was announced in the fall of 1966. To accomplish this goal, notice was directed to the rising number of transfer students coming to the College. Dr. Hinton called for a review of the liberal arts core. "Due to economic factors, the entire academic program must undergo restudy. The curriculum must be made more attractive to junior college transfers."[66] In the spirit of this request, the Academic Affairs Committee reduced the Christianity requirement from four to three courses with the assurance of a Christianity component in the six semesters of the *Basic Courses*.[67] The existing sixty-hour resi-

---

61. Houston Baptist College, Minutes of the Meetings of the Faculty, Meeting on 31 Aug. 1966.
62. Houston Baptist College, Minutes of the Meetings of the Faculty, Meeting on 12 May 1966.
63. "Student Opinion on Apartments," *Houston Baptist Collegian*, 18 Oct. 1966, p. 2.
64. *HBC News*, Sept. 1966, 5. Photo only.
65. *HBC News*, Oct. 1966, 5. Photo only.
66. Houston Baptist College, Minutes of Meetings of the Academic Committee of the Board of Trustees, Meeting on 12 Sept. 1966.
67. Houston Baptist College, Minutes of Meetings of the Academic Affairs Committee of the Board of Trustees, Meeting on 2 Nov. 1966.

dency requirement for graduation was reduced to a more-common thirty-two semester hours[68] with a minimum of ten semester hours at HBC required in each major.[69]

A second women's club, Epsilon Delta Pi, was founded "to encourage academic excellence, promote social life, and render service."[70] The first Circle K club in the city of Houston was chartered sponsored by the Houston Kiwanis Club.[71] These organizations joined the Triceans and the Coreons as the pioneer student social/service clubs on campus. The faculty voted to require the Graduate Record Examination or the National Teachers Examination of all seniors in an effort to assess the quality of the first graduating classes.[72] An honors program for students began to be discussed, and a protocol for formal evaluation of faculty performance was developed by the Professional Growth Committee.

Although a seminal course in the curriculum, the interdisciplinary *Basic Courses* presented problems for transfer students. In order to qualify for transfer credit, the courses required study in several traditional disciplines for content equivalency. The study, however, revealed the INDC courses were regarded as one of the key distinctives of an HBC degree. A survey of student opinion about the *Basic Courses* revealed that the courses were viewed by many to be among the best they had ever taken.[73] Former student Lillian Turner wrote her trustee father, "I have told everyone I've talked to that the HBC years were the best because of the excellence of the courses they offer to freshmen and sophomores, especially those CORE courses."[74] Many alumni from this era view the *Basic Courses* (CORE) as one of their finest collegiate intellectual experiences. Alumni from this era also recall the mantra drilled into their consciousness by the faculty in CORE, "Chance favors the prepared mind."[75]

---

68. Houston Baptist College, Minutes of the Meetings of the Faculty, Meeting on 10 Nov. 1966.

69. Houston Baptist College, Minutes of the Meetings of the Faculty, Meeting on 12 Oct. 1967.

70. Cheryl Hammock, "Spotlight '67," *Houston Baptist Collegian*, 1 Nov. 1966, p. 3.

71. "First Circle K Club Here is Given Charter," *Houston Chronicle*, 26 May 1965, Southwest section, p. 1; "What's Happening in November," *HBC News*, Oct. 1966, 4; *Ornogah 1965*, 105, 126-127.

72. Houston Baptist College, Minutes of the Meetings of the Faculty, Meeting on 13 Oct. 1966. The aggregate scores for all graduates were compared to national norms. Subject matter exams were also administered particularly for students applying to graduate and professional schools. In 1973, the GRE exam was replaced as a graduation requirement by field tests from the Undergraduate Record Program.

73. "Student Views On Basic Course," *Houston Baptist Collegian*, 25 Oct. 1966, p. 2.

74. (Gilbert Turner to Dr. W. H. Hinton, May 6, 1969).

75. "Beyond the New Dimension," *HBColleague*, Sept. 1972, p. 11. Alumni from the first four years remember this quote from Louis Pasteur as one of their most abiding recollections.

Students complained that the courses did not transfer easily. They disliked the occasional use of closed-circuit television for large CORE lecture sections. However, the small discussion groups were reported to be stimulating and effective. Students further suggested that these courses contained too much content material and carried too little credit. Moreover, they proposed that three years of the *Basic Courses* were too much. The sophomore course *Culture and Human Experience* was popular; the junior course *Philosophy of Science* was not. In the spring of 1967, the *Philosophy of Science* was eliminated from the sequence of required courses. Some of the content areas such as the use of symbolic language, the history of scientific thought, and the philosophy of science were incorporated into the other *Basic Courses*. Popular *Collegian* humorist Merrill Blackburn wrote, "It was the semester when the administration finally decided that Junior Core was like LBJ, in that it never accomplished anything. It was just a lot of words."[76]

§

Dr. Hinton leaned heavily on Vice President Womack to implement his presidential priorities. As a result, Womack exerted considerable influence on academic decision-making. His roles as secretary of the Academic Affairs Committee and later as Director of Student Admissions blurred the lines between financial management and academic autonomy. Womack also regularly met with the Academic Committee of the Board. These roles in time became matters of concern. SACS required separation of academic and financial areas of responsibility to ensure appropriate balance of power and to avoid conflict of interest.

Womack also exerted powerful influence by his control of purchasing. He was known on the campus for holding rather than denying those financial requisitions with which he did not personally agree. Requested academic items simply never arrived. The story was told of a standard musicology reference book in German that was ordered for the first offering of *Music History* in the junior year. When the book never arrived, it was discovered it had never been ordered—because, Womack purported, "No one around here speaks German." Womack's "bottom desk drawer" did, in fact, exist and became a legendary euphemism for unapproved requests of

---

76. Merrill Blackburn, "Moments with Merrill," *Houston Baptist Collegian*, 18 Jan. 1967, p. 3.

all kinds. In a column on automobile bumper stickers, Merrill Blackburn suggested that Womack's sticker read, "A penny saved is a penny." Other stickers included those of Joyce Fan, "Made in China by Chinese" and Christianity professor Arthur Travis's, "You only live twice."[77]

The first senior year was enriched with art exhibits by faculty member Arthur Turner, music concerts by Houston Symphony affiliate faculty Ray Fliegel, Don Slocomb, and Richard Pickar, and drama productions of *All My Sons*,[78] *Phaedra*,[79] and *Murder in the Cathedral*.[80] A young member of the House of Representatives, George H. W. Bush, spoke for Assembly.[81] Pat Boone and H. L. Hunt highlighted the Spring President's Council Dinner for six hundred guests at the Warwick Hotel.[82]

A new Alaskan malamute mascot named Toby became a campus resident.[83] Basketball and baseball matured under coaches Mac Sutton and Peck Vass, and in the spring of 1967, Gerald Myers was announced as the first full-time athletic coach ever recruited for the new College.[84] Myers, a former all-Southwest Conference star at Texas Tech, was one of the "winningest coaches in schoolboy history during a seven-year stint at Monterey High School in Lubbock where he compiled a 153-50 record."[85]

In December 1966, the College was admitted to candidacy status with the Southern Association of Colleges and Schools at its annual meeting in Atlanta.[86] During the meeting, the Moody Foundation of Galveston announced a gift of $500,000 to be used for construction of a new library that would help meet one of the requirements for institutional accreditation.[87] John Baugh, Chair of the trustee Academic Committee, expressed appreciation for the gift but reminded the Board

77. Merrill Blackburn, "Moments with Merrill," *The Collegian*, 16 Jan. 1968, p. 3.

78. "'All My Sons' Currently In Gallery," *Houston Baptist Collegian*, 6 Dec. 1966, p. 1; "Gallery Extends Production Run," *Houston Baptist Collegian*, 14 Dec. 1966, p. 1.

79. "What's Happening in February," *HBC News*, Feb. 1967, 4; "Phaedra on Stage in Gallery," *Houston Baptist Collegian*, 18 Jan. 1967, p. 1; "This Was Phaedra," *Houston Baptist Collegian*, 15 Feb. 1967, p. 3; *Ornogah 1967*, 160-61. Photos.

80. "Eliot's 'Murder' Now in Gallery," *Houston Baptist Collegian*, 8 Mar. 1967, p. 1.

81. "Grover, Miller, Bush To Speak Here," *Houston Baptist Collegian*, 1 Nov. 1966, p. 1; *Ornogah 1964*, 140.

82. "Hunt and Boone Challenge Council," *HBC News*, April 1967, 1; "HLH Speaks to Council, Students," *Houston Baptist Collegian*, 12 Apr. 1967, pp. 1, 3. Photos.

83. *HBC News*, June 1966, 3. Photo of Toby.

84. "Myers Named Basketball Coach," *HBC News*, Apr. 1967, 2; "Myers Husky Basketball Mentor," *Houston Baptist Collegian*, 12 Apr. 1967, p. 4.

85. Burle Pettit, "Gerald Myers Named Cage Coach at Houston Baptist," *Lubbock Avalanche Journal*, 18 Mar. 1967, p. 25.

86. "College Moves Toward Accreditation," *HBC News*, Feb. 1967, 1.

87. "Moody's Grant $500,000," *HBC News*, Apr. 1967, 1; Houston Baptist College, Minutes of Meetings of the Board of Trustees, Meeting on 24 May 1968.

of the critical need for a chapel and facilities for science and fine arts.

The student newspaper inexplicably changed its masthead flag to the *Fourth Estate* in September 1967. Then with the October 12, 1967 issue, the publication re-assumed the title *Collegian* that it has maintained all the years since. Merrill Blackburn, in another of his *Collegian* articles entitled, "Happiness Is," recorded the first known printed reference to Bertha Wilson, a revered cook in the cafeteria and, in later years, the acknowledged monarch of the student center snack bar. In parody of Linus and Snoopy, Blackburn's "Happiness is another Bertha Burger" preserved forever the undying student, faculty, and staff appreciation for Bertha's culinary skills.[88] In the summer when the cafeteria was closed, Bertha would cook "comfort" food in the snack bar; the selection typically included turnip or collard greens and corn bread. The Southern gentlemen, Dr. Smith and Dr. Huckabay, were usually the first ones in line for lunch at Bertha's that would often be sold out by 12:30 p.m. Blackburn's homage to Bertha Wilson was directly opposite to his stance on traditional campus cafeteria food about which he reported, "This was the semester when one of the worst crimes in history took place right here on our campus. The cafeteria decided to kill us off—slowly."[89]

§

The Executive Committees of both the College and the Memorial Baptist Hospital met in joint session in December 1966 to discuss the possibility of creating a Bachelor of Science in Nursing degree to be developed from the diploma program at Memorial's Lillie Jolly School of Nursing. There were four principal points of discussion: 1) higher clinical instructional costs rooted in a mandated 10:1 student/faculty ratio; 2) physical housing for the clinical program in the junior and senior years; 3) the need for a tuition subsidy to the Lillie Jolly tuition to equal the College's; and 4) the need for further financial analysis.[90]

In April, twenty-two students under the mentoring of Dr. Calvin Huckabay left for four weeks of study at the Shakespeare Institute in Stratford-upon-Avon, England. The 1967 program was tailored solely for

---

88. Merrill Blackburn, "Moments with Merrill," *Houston Baptist Collegian,* 22 Nov. 1966, p. 3; Merrill Blackburn, "Moments with Merrill," *The Collegian,* 26 Oct. 1967, p. 3.

89. Merrill Blackburn, "Moments with Merrill," *Houston Baptist Collegian,* 18 Jan. 1967, p. 3.

90. Houston Baptist College, Minutes of Meetings of the Executive Committee of the Board of Trustees, Meeting on 5 Dec. 1966.

the HBC students by Dr. T. J. B. Spencer, Director of the Institute, and provided a period of study that included the annual celebration of Shakespeare's birth.[91] Faculty in other courses in which these students were enrolled accommodated assignments to support this unusual opportunity.

Groundbreaking for the new Moody Library

Groundbreaking for the new Moody Library was held on May 28, 1967 in conjunction with baccalaureate and commencement ceremonies. Mrs. Mary Moody Northen, Mr. W. L. Moody IV, Stewart Morris, and Building Committee Chairman Otis Brigman turned the first earth for the new facility.[92] Following the library groundbreaking, the first baccalaureate service was held at 3 p.m. with Dr. James L. Sullivan, Executive Secretary of the Sunday School Board of the Southern Baptist Convention, delivering the sermon. That evening, a buffet dinner honored the first graduating seniors and their guests.

---

91 "British Trip Is Scheduled By HBC English Students," *Houston Baptist Collegian,* 6 Dec. 1966, p. 1; "Study Abroad Plans Set," *Houston Baptist Collegian,* 18 Jan. 1967, p. 1; *Ornogah 1967,* 173.
92 *HBC News,* June 1967, 2; *Ornogah 1967,* 189. Photo.

The first commencement was held the next day on May 29, 1967. A proud fifty-nine graduates received the Bachelor of Arts degree. U. S. Senator John Tower addressed the Class of 1967 and the assembled guests in the Sharp Gymnasium. Some fifty-four faculty members participated in these ceremonies. Of these, nineteen were members of the original faculty.[93] Michael Anderson BA '67 received the first diploma.[94] Never again would there be another first class. An alumni association was immediately formed with Charlie Bonds elected President and Peggy Turman Vice President. The Alumni Association was chartered on November 14, 1968, by the State of Texas as a non-profit organization.[95] In a letter of notification from the Alumni Association to trustees was this strong affirmation, "The alumni have found the liberal arts education provided by Houston Baptist College to be invaluable preparation for meeting challenges in their academic, professional, and personal lives. *We are eager to insure the continuance of this uniquely structured program of studies for future generations of students.*"[96]

The choice of the library project by the Moody Foundation was critical to initial accreditation. Since 1963, the library had been located on the first floor of the south wing of the academic quadrangle. The new 25,000 square-foot building was designed to provide study space for up to 400 students, shelving space for 50,000 volumes, a lecture room, a Board of Trustees Room, library offices, and technical-service space. The location of the library marked for the first time the southern edge of what would become the Holcombe Mall.[97] Trustees approved construction of an extension of the campus steam tunnel system on the south side of the academic quadrangle to contain utility service provision for the new library and future construction.[98] In additional acts of trustee generosity, Otis Brigman offered to construct the tunnel for $20,000 less than the

93. "First Graduation Exercises to be held May 28-29," *HBC News,* May 1967, 1; "The Class of 1967," *HBC News,* June 1967, 1; Sibley, 49.

94. *Ornogah 2003,* 99; "Generation to Generation," *HBU News,* Dec. 2002, 13.

95. "Dear Trustee," *HBColleague,* Spring 1969, p. 3.

96. Ibid.

97. "Mall Plans Revealed," *HBC News,* Oct. 1968, 1. Photo.

98. Houston Baptist College, Minutes of Meetings of the Building Committee of the Board of Trustees, Meeting on 16 Feb. 1968; Houston Baptist College, Minutes of Meetings of the Executive Committee of the Board of Trustees, Meeting on 18 Mar. 1968.

low bid,[99] and Gilbert Turner contributed another $20,000 of supplies for related campus drainage.[100]

This was to be the last year of service for several influential faculty members. Dr. Claude Rhea, later to become President of Palm Beach Atlantic College, resigned in 1967 to join the staff of the Foreign Mission Board;[101] Dr. Albert Myers, Chairman of the Division of Science and Mathematics, resigned to return home to Carson Newman College.[102] Along with Dr. John Hoskins, Chair of the Division of Social Studies, these faculty members had been among the chief architects of the original curriculum, were profound scholars, and brilliant, revered teachers.

Reflection on this first erosion of leadership from the original faculty ranks invites analysis. Many of the first faculty members, like these three, represented the finest examples of scholarship and dedication to teaching. They have rarely been equaled over fifty years and perhaps never surpassed. Their contribution to an institution at any point in its history would have been significant. Coming as they did, however, to a new academic program that they could design and call their own, these faculty members had opportunity for contribution and significance at a unique moment in time. Their influence was profound despite their relatively brief tenure. Their departure was a source of considerable loss.

Not all of the Class of 1963 completed the degree in 1967; a number of students from the first class graduated in 1968. Additionally, four students who transferred to the College after 1963 completed the degree in 1967.[103] Perhaps the most persevering of all the members of the freshman class of 1963, Frances Vargas Velasco completed her degree work in 1998 with her family present to share the proud moment. Of the original class of approximately 190 students, ninety completed their degree at Houston Baptist College as a part of the "first" pioneering graduates.

Among the early classes, student scholarship was strong. Milford Kuhn was reported to be the "first alumnus to receive a Masters degree."[104] John Gillespie was selected to study philosophy at Heidelberg University following his senior year. Gillespie, along with other seniors

---

99. Houston Baptist College, Minutes of Meetings of the Executive Committee of the Board of Trustees, Meeting on 20 May 1968.

100. Houston Baptist College, Minutes of Meetings of the Board of Trustees, Meeting on 29 Sept. 1967.

101. Claude H. Rhea, *With My Song I Will Praise Him* (Nashville: Broadman Press, 1977), 41-43.

102. "Faculty Changes Announced," *HBC News,* May 1967, 1.

103. Based on comparison of *1964 Ornogah* freshman class photos and *Alumni Student Directory 1992-93,* 134.

104. "Class of '67," *HBColleague,* Sept. 1968, p. 7.

Bill Myers and Sam Ferguson, would later be the first HBC graduates to gain the PhD in their fields of study at Indiana University, the University of Florida, and Duke University respectively. Myers and Ferguson were selected for Atomic Energy Commission honors programs during the summer of 1967.[105] From this first class emerged a number of outstanding community leaders who would also take positions of professional leadership. Eight became corporate executives; eighteen became educators; six became pastors; three, professional musicians; two became doctors; and two, psychologists. Others moved into health care administration, professional golf, real estate, and public safety.

An extraordinarily close bond existed among students, faculty, and staff in these first four years. Because all shared in the pioneering task of institutional establishment, the College community was at once appropriately professional and, at the same time, remarkably personal. Dr. Hinton repeatedly voiced his contention, "It is all about people." His successful relationship with various College constituencies set the model for strong personal relationships. Alumni recollections both affirm the awe students had for the faculty and confirm the remarkable personal relationship students enjoyed.

> I was privileged to take a John Milton senior seminar from Dr. Calvin Huckabay under his scholarly eye and even had the nerve to take him a plate of homemade cookies at one of our one-on-one sessions. What was I thinking?[106]

> Botany professor, Dr. Cynthia Rogers, was my age at most, and during the course of my semester with her, I was privileged to host a baby shower for her at my home.[107]

> Dr. Daton Dodson's *World Literature* class opened new worlds to me. I was excited to read everything and more excited to go to class. He was a tough, demanding professor, but I didn't mind a bit. I thrived on doing my best to live up to his standards. Moreover, he gave me some advice I've never forgotten. He encouraged me to do what I loved and never to lose my idealism. He helped me to find the courage to do what I really wanted, and I have never regretted it.

105. *HBC News,* Feb. 1967, 5. Photo.
106. "Favorite HBU Memory," www.hbu.edu/hbu/Alumni_Favorite_HBU_Memory.asp?SnID=2 (accessed April 28, 2010).
107 Ibid.

Dr. Fan's refrain of "Chemistry is easy; chemistry is fun!" got on my nerves at the beginning. I didn't believe it. But her joy both in teaching and in living was infectious. Her skills were magical, and she never gave up on anyone. I got to where I actually enjoyed doing chemical equations. She taught me that attitude is everything, and it is a lesson I never forgot.

I remember sitting in Dr. Arthur Travis' *Christian Doctrine* class and hating it—I even made a "D." But this man was incredible, and it was in his class that I was converted.

§

In June 1967, the second Historical Preservation Symposium, "Architecture and the Arts II," was held.[108] "Four days of lectures, demonstrations, round-table discussion, and trips—all by the most noted men in the field of restoration, including Dr. Harold J. Plenderleith of Rome and his account of the recent flood in Florence— impressed everyone."[109] Chaired by Faith Bybee and again underwritten by the National Trust for Historic Preservation and the Galveston Historical Foundation, the Symposium drew experts from Rome, London, San Juan, and Mexico.[110] Many years later, these early symposia bring vivid memories to the minds of many participants and mark their first association with Houston Baptist College.[111]

In July 1967, a strategic new model emerged for augmenting endowment funds. The College was approached by the Riverside Baptist Church that was located in a declining neighborhood and in the process of disbanding. Funds from the sale of the church property legally had to be conveyed to another tax-exempt entity. A model was developed to fund a Riverside Scholarship at HBC that would perpetuate the name of the church and provide financial support for future generations of students planning to attend seminary.[112] This model emerged to become an opportunity for churches in similar circumstance to perpetuate the name

---

108. "Symposium Slated On Restoration for Early Summer," *Houston Baptist Collegian,* 24 May 1967, p. 2; *HBC News,* Sept. 1966, 4. Photo.

109. Lucille Stewart Krisch, "Twigs, Trees: Symposium Success," *San Antonio Light,* 18 June 1967, sec. F, p.13.

110. Diane Casler, "Historical Symposium Planned," *Galveston News,* 19 Mar. 1967, sec. A, p. 12. Photo.

111. Pat Purdie, "Socially Peeking," *Houston Post,* 9 June 1967, sec. 2, p. 2. Photos.

112. Houston Baptist College, Minutes of Meetings of the Executive Committee of the Board of Trustees, Meeting on 23 June 1967; Houston Baptist College, Minutes of Meetings of the Board of Trustees, Meeting on 14 July 1967.

of the church and also invest in the lives of young people. A Texas Avenue Baptist Church fund was similarly established shortly thereafter.[113]

In 1967, Dr. H. B. Smith reported to the Board that fifty-four faculty would be in place in the fall with twenty-seven holding the doctorate. He cautioned that faculty salaries were falling behind the original benchmarks established by the trustees. Smith further reported that church WMU organizations were being asked, in response to budget cuts, to help buy library books needed for the coming year.[114] A new "Xerox" machine was installed "in the duplicating office under the aegis of the Secretarial Pool freeing up the A. B. Dick duplicator press for longer runs."[115]

§

The 1967 fall semester opened in the context of campus riots across the nation over the Viet Nam War.[116] HBC opened without its first graduates and with only half of its original faculty. It was a time of fresh perspective and new energy. The college mascot Toby had been stolen during the summer, and a new ten-year-old Samoyed named Buttons had been acquired by the Coreons fraternity.[117] An innovative tuition plan for students capped at $500 that allowed students to take more than fifteen hours at no additional cost[118] and encouraged both academic enrichment and timely degree completion.

For the fifth year in 1967, a number of the new faculty and staff were recruited who ultimately contributed many years of service to the institution. These included Daton Dodson, English (1967-2003); Dr. Jules Ladner, Chemistry (1967-2000); Elysee Peavy, English (1967-1997); Ken Rogers, Financial Aid (1967-2008); and Cynthia Rogers, Biology (1967-2005). Smith encouraged the faculty to be more "venturesome" in areas such as pedagogy, study-abroad, internships, honors programs, flexible academic calendars, research, and service.[119] Dr. Hinton expressed his appreciation for Smith to the Board of Trustees and acknowledged Smith

113. "Ill Wind Brings HBC Windfall," *HBC News,* Sept. 1967, 3.

114. Houston Baptist College, Minutes of Meetings of the Board of Trustees, Meeting on 8 Aug. 1967.

115. *Flashes & Dashes,* 1 Sept. 1967, p. 1.

116. Don Hendricks, "Editorial: Viet Nam," *The Collegian,* 12 Oct. 1967, p. 2.

117. "Buttons," *The Collegian,* 16 Jan. 1968, p. 7, photo; "Huskies Open Basketball Season November 18," *HBC News,* Nov. 1967, 2-3.

118. "HBC Students Question New Tuition Boost," *Houston Baptist Collegian,* 22 Feb. 1967, p. 2; "Sutton Explains Tuition Hike," *Houston Baptist Collegian,* 8 Mar. 1967, p. 2.

119. Houston Baptist College, Minutes of the Meeting of the Faculty, Meeting on 6 Sept. 1967.

as "the dynamic force behind leading the faculty and in developing the curriculum. He is a man who is fully dedicated to Christian education and who is held in high esteem by his peers."[120]

In September 1967, a review committee from the Southern Association of Colleges and Schools made its first campus visit. The College was well prepared, and the review went smoothly.[121] A subsequent called faculty meeting in early October communicated three assignments from the visiting committee: 1) the drafting of an academic purpose statement separate from the existing "History and Purpose" statement; 2) attention to matters of policy relating to tenure, dismissal, retention, and academic freedom; and 3) the delineation of criteria for the evaluation of faculty performance as it affected raises and promotions.[122] The original history/purpose statement as printed in the *Bulletin* was no longer accurate, i.e., "Curriculum will be limited in scope since no professional or applied courses are anticipated." In fact, two professional divisions of business and education were flourishing. From a review of presidential correspondence, the visiting committee also manifested concern about the Board of Trustees' understanding of its role as a policy-making entity rather than a management operation.[123] Dr. Hinton conveyed the suggestion of the visiting SACS team that an "independent organization of the faculty" needed to be formed.[124]

These SACS requests resulted in specific recommendations from the faculty to the Board of Trustees. The history of the College in the *Bulletin* was updated. A separate purpose statement was drafted that reflected learning outcomes; many trustees had felt that the Preamble to the By-Laws served as a suitable purpose statement.[125] The Preamble thereafter was carried in the *Bulletin of Information* under the title "The Nature of the College."[126] The faculty proposed a promotion and salary policy that established merit pay, created steps within rank related to years of service, and provided peer review for promotions. The "B" category of average salaries on the annual AAUP survey was suggested as the benchmark for the College.[127] Finally, in a move to curtail unbudgeted employment,

120. Ibid.
121. "Gird your loins," *Flashes & Dashes,* 15 Sept. 1967, p. 1.
122. Houston Baptist College, Minutes of the Meeting of the Faculty, Meeting on 2 Oct. 1967.
123. Houston Baptist College, Minutes of Meetings of the Board of Trustees, Meeting on 29 Sept. 1967.
124. Houston Baptist College, Minutes of the Meeting of the Faculty, Meeting on 2 Oct. 1967.
125. Houston Baptist College, Minutes of Meetings of the Board of Trustees, Meeting on 29 Oct. 1967.
126. Houston Baptist College, *Bulletin 1968-1969,* 6.

the Board also directed the administration to develop policy that would more clearly define standards for faculty employment integrally related to the budget process.[128]

A Friends of the Library organization was formed in September "to stimulate public interest and seek benefactions to fill the shelves of the new library."[129] Trustee Freland Murphy was elected President of the Friends to work with a board consisting of Clay Bailey, Dona Williamson, Willard Russell, Dan Elkins, Mrs. Edwin Martin, Marie Kern, Jessie Millsaps, and Harry Chavanne. HBC Librarian Jefferson Caskey served as an ex-officio member. Significantly, each of these individuals ultimately became personally involved with the college as donors, faculty spouses, parents of students, and founding members of the Auxiliary and the President's Advisors.

The written progress report from the SACS Visiting Committee was received in November. In addition to the matters already anticipated, the SACS committee directed that a faculty admissions committee be appointed to evaluate and approve all students for admission. Since 1963, admission had been largely an administrative process that had been colored, in the eyes of the visiting SACS committee, by the financial exigency of the institution in deference to the institutional claims of academic selectivity. The President's wife was currently serving as Registrar; both she and CFO Womack had served as Directors of Admissions.[130] In response to the SACS mandate, Frank Fisher was appointed Registrar in 1967.[131] The faculty developed a set of admissions policies and procedures under the management of a faculty admissions committee.[132] There remained SACS' concern for the lack of faculty doctoral credentials in several departments.[133]

Buoyed by four years of extraordinary accomplishment, the College administration fully expected the Southern Association to approve accreditation following the graduation of its first class. However, in its annual meeting in December 1967, the Southern Association declined to

127. Houston Baptist College, Minutes of the Meeting of the Faculty, Meeting on 12 Oct. 1967.

128. Houston Baptist College, Minutes of the Meetings of the Academic Committee of the Board of Trustees, Meeting on 15 Sept. 1967.

129. "Drive Scheduled To Fill Moody-Funded Library," Galveston Daily News, 18 Sept. 1967, sec. B, p. 7.

130. Houston Baptist College, Minutes of the Meeting of the Faculty, Meeting on 6 Sept. 1967.

131. "Nine Faculty Members Are Employed By HBC," The Fourth Estate, 11 Sept. 1967, p. 3. This seems to be the only issue in which this title was ever used. Thereafter, the banner read The Collegian. The paper did begin carrying the byline "Student Voice of Houston Baptist College."

132. Houston Baptist College, Minutes of the Meeting of the Faculty, Meeting on 9 May 1968.

133. Southern Association of Colleges and Schools, Report of the Visiting Committee to HBU, Nov. 1967.

approve HBC for institutional accreditation. "Implicit to the decision is the conclusion that HBC has not demonstrated its acceptability under the *Standards of the College Delegate Assembly.*" Although accreditation was to be retroactive to the first graduates in 1967, the SACS decision was a particular though momentary disappointment to the campus community, as well as the first alumni.[134]

The SACS decision forced attention to a number of issues. The SACS visiting committee clarified the appropriate role of the trustees. Faculty and administrators were encouraged to plan together and agree on mutually-satisfying solutions to enumerated concerns. The SACS recommendations suggested remedies leading to better understanding, cooperative planning, and shared ownership of decisions. Moreover, the recommendations helped the University move beyond a chapter of intense struggle for institutional survival characterized both by sound decisions and by occasional errors of judgment by all players. The very survival and growth of Houston Baptist College in the face of a pattern of closure and merger by many other colleges that were founded in the 1960s were matters of significance and prayerful gratitude.

§

The academic program continued to mature. Rex Fleming, a national Debate Coach of the Year, joined the faculty to direct the debate team that in 1967 bested Southern California, Pittsburgh, and Miami in national tournaments.[135] Dr. Jerry Robinson established a College Research Center with an initial grant from the Hogg Foundation.[136] Those funds were followed by a grant of $176,898 from the National Institute of Mental Health.[137] Scholarly books were published by Dr. David Appleby, Dr. Joyce Fan, Dr. Calvin Huckabay, Dr. Robert Parker, Dr. Marilyn Sibley, Dr. Duncan Tidwell, and Richard Webb.[138]

---

134. Dr. W. H. Hinton, "President's Report," *HBC News,* Feb. 1968, 1; Houston Baptist College, Minutes of the Meeting of the Faculty, Meeting on 11 Jan. 1968.

135. "Defending State Collegiate Champs Aim To Repeat," *The Collegian,* 12 Oct. 1967, p. 4.

136. Houston Baptist College, Minutes of Meetings of the Board of Trustees, Meeting on 17 Nov. 1967.

137. "Grant Received," *HBC News,* May 1968, 4.

138. "Authors Abound Among HBC Faculty," *HBC News,* Dec. 1967, 3. Popular faculty member Richard Webb wrote four books while on the faculty before his life was tragically cut short: *Thoughts of a 20th Century Man; Mosaic of Man; The Executioner;* and *What is Truth?, The Crucifixion of Christ as seen through Roman Eyes.*

Artist-in-Residence Jeannette Clift founded her renowned After Dinner Players on the HBC campus in 1967.[139] "I wanted to find a way to relate Biblical scripture which has been so vital in my life to individuals who had never come under its influence."[140] Beginning with some twenty students, Clift developed a new concept of relating her faith though drama that differed significantly from standard "Christian drama" in the church and seminary. She felt that many scripts failed to convey their spiritual message to a contemporary world. Her first attempt as an author for the kind of script she sought was a play called *Ibid* that enjoyed its premier performance at Houston's Chinese Baptist Church.[141] HBC professor Dr. Joyce Fan translated the script into Chinese for the bi-lingual congregation. *Ibid* was a conceptual breakthrough and was taped for television broadcast.[142] The A. D. Players, as they came to be known, celebrated their 40th anniversary in 2007, proudly remembered their HBC roots, and revealed plans for construction of a new performing and instructional complex in Houston.[143]

Paul Harvey, nationally syndicated commentator, addressed the Fall 1967 President's Council Dinner at the Warwick Hotel.[144] Distinguished service medallions were given to Rex Baker, Sr., John Baugh, Bill Denham, Curtis Hankamer, Jake Kamin, and Clyde Kennerly.[145] Other campus guests that fall included Texas Senator Barbara Jordan,[146] Dr. Chester Swor,[147] pianist Jacque Abram,[148] and jazz musician Doc Severinsen.[149] For alumni, the first College Homecoming in history was held in December 1967;[150] twenty-four of the fifty-nine first graduates

---

139. Ron Durham, "Directed by Houston actress, Religious dramatists do their thing," *Houston Post,* 11 Oct. 1969, sec. 2, p. 12.
140. "A. D. Players," *Houston Town and Country Magazine*, Dec. 1975, 35.
141. *Ornogah 1968*, 74-75.
142. Jeannette Clift, *Ibid,* First Baptist Church Dallas, 5, May 1968. Performance program. The program cover reads "After Dinner Players" and "Houston Baptist College."
143. Ralph Bivins, "Purchase by theater group moves tract to center stage," *Houston Chronicle,* 15 Jan. 2003, sec. B, p. 1.
144. "Paul Harvey to Speak at HBC President's Council Fall Dinner," *The Collegian,* 9 Nov. 1967, p. 1. Photo.
145. "Council Dinner Announced," *HBC News,* Nov. 1967, 3; "500 Enjoy Council Dinner," *HBC News,* Dec. 1967, 1. Photo.
146. "Coming Campus Events," *HBC News,* Oct. 1969, 4.
147. "Chester Swor Challenges Students To Use Time," *The Collegian,* 18 Oct. 1968, p. 3.
148. "Abram Is To Present Concert Here In March," *The Collegian,* 15 Mar. 1968, p. 6; "Coming Campus Events," *HBC News,* Mar. 1968, 1.
149. "Severinsen, Smith Hold Spring Band Festival at HBC," *Houston Baptist Collegian,* 22 Feb. 1967, p. 1.
150. "Houston Baptist College Welcomes Home First Graduating Class," *The Collegian,* 8 Dec. 1967, pp. 1, 3, 6, 7. Individual Photos of Class of '67; "Homecoming," *HBC News,* Nov. 1967, 3; *Ornogah 1968,* 62-63.

Jan Stephenson, Homecoming Queen 1967,
with Carol Ann Halliday, J. C. Clarke, Dan Elkins, and Pat Ellis.

returned for the weekend that was highlighted by the crowning of the first Homecoming Queen, Jan Stephenson.[151]

The HBC Board of Trustees remained focused on innovative financial strategies and considered proposals for development of a freeway motel and heliport, apartment projects, commercial retail developments, the development of Bellaire-West, and new properties in Inwood Forest on Antoine Road. Stewart Morris issued a challenge to the members of the Board at the November meeting:

> The development of the land assets of the College are looked to for the retirement of this indebtedness. You are part of a unique institution of higher quality liberal arts. The progress of the College to this date has been the result of the united effort of Christian men to build a Christ-centered institution to perpetuate the highest ideals of our country. You are chosen carefully; you are NOT an honorary board, but a working one.[152]

New members taking seats on the Board at that meeting included Gilbert Turner, Curtis Hankamer, J. Bruce Belin, Jr., Grayson Glass, and Mrs. R. Thomas McDermott. In retrospect, it is clear that these trustees were selected for their strategic value to the Board. They became among the most active in history.

151. "First Alumni Homecoming Held," *HBC News,* Feb. 1968, 4. Photo.
152. Houston Baptist College, Minutes of Meetings of the Board of Trustees, Meeting on 17 Nov. 1967.

The trustees voted to approve the Bachelor of Science degree in nursing on the condition that scholarship monies be raised to fund the program for a minimum trial period of four years.[153] Subsequently, a grant of $668,000 from The Houston Endowment, Inc. was announced to fund nursing scholarships.[154] Additional grants were received from the Rockefeller Foundation and the Cullen Foundation. [155] The former Lillie Jolly School of Nursing diploma program expanded to become a four-year baccalaureate degree program.[156] Faculty from the Lillie Jolly School and its Dean, Dr. Glendola Nash, joined the College faculty in 1968.[157]

In February 1968, the Constitution and By-Laws for a new Faculty Assembly were approved, fulfilling one of the SACS requirements for accreditation.[158] Dr. Robert Parker served as the first Chair of the Assembly.[159] In one of the Assembly's first acts, the faculty delivered a resolution calling for a faculty representative as an ex-officio member of the trustee Academic Committee and boldly asked that a "representative go with Dr. Hinton to the Board to make the request . . . in the interest of continuing the development of effective communication and mutual understanding between the faculty and the governing bodies of the College."[160] In May, the Board "acknowledged" but did not respond to the Assembly resolutions.[161]

The Faculty Assembly issued a charge that HBC's 1967 SACS progress report had "inaccurately conveyed" the written statements approved by the faculty on matters of academic freedom, tenure, and compensation. The recommended goal of a "B" standard for average salaries had been changed to a "C" standard by the Trustees. Moreover, the proposed salary policy had been altered by the deletion of cost-of-

153. Houston Baptist College, Minutes of Meetings of the Board of Trustees, Meeting on 14 July 1967; Houston Baptist College, Minutes of Meetings of the Executive Committee of the Board of Trustees, Meeting on 22 Jan. 1968.

154. Houston Baptist College, Minutes of Meetings of the Academic Committee of the Board of Trustees, Meeting on 24 Jan. 1968; Houston Baptist College, Minutes of Meetings of the Board of Trustees, Meeting on 24 May 1968.

155. Ibid.

156. Ted Francis and Carole McFarland, *The Memorial Hospital Systems: the first Seventy-five years* (Houston: Larkadale Publishing, 1982), 76.

157. The Lillie Jolly School of Nursing dates from 1907 when the Baptist Sanitarium opened with the first chartered school of nursing in Houston. The School was named for the first director of the school, Mrs. J. P. (Lillie) Burnett who later became the wife of Robert Jolly, superintendent of the Baptist Sanitarium from 1921 to 1945. In 1946, the name of the institution was changed to Memorial Baptist Hospital.

158. Houston Baptist College, Minutes of the Meetings of the Faculty, Meeting on 8 Feb. 1968.

159. "Faculty Organizes," *HBC News,* Mar. 1968, 2.

160. Houston Baptist College, Minutes of the Meetings of the Faculty Assembly, Meeting on 12 Mar. 1968.

161. Houston Baptist College, Minutes of Meetings of the Board of Trustees, Meeting on 24 May 1968.

living considerations and the elimination of a graded-step model within each academic rank.[162] The Chair of the trustee Academic Committee, Howard Lee, Sr., responded to the objection of the Faculty Assembly that a revised document had been subsequently submitted to the Southern Association that was clearly labeled, "written by the administration and approved by the Academic Committee of the Board."[163] Another Board-altered policy statement in the SACS response, "Tenure shall be granted at the discretion of the Board upon the recommendation of the President," was later to give rise to action that placed the institution on the censure list of the AAUP.

The submittal of these administrative revisions to the Southern Association without notice to the campus SACS steering committee exacerbated the level of tension that existed between the faculty and the College administration. In the fall, Howard Lee, Sr., Chair of the trustee Academic Committee, met with six representatives from the Faculty Assembly to discuss the several SACS report issues.[164] At that time, the Faculty Assembly further requested the establishment of a sabbatical leave policy and the elimination of the "six-month rule."[165]

The Student Association, meanwhile, requested opportunity to speak at a meeting of the Board of Trustees. In an effort to reduce student angst, the Student Association President Mark Fowler was invited to speak before the Board in November 1968. Fowler outlined five requests of the trustees: 1) that salaries be provided for several major student officers including Association President and editors of the *Ornogah* and the *Collegian*; 2) that responsibility for student publications be placed with the Student Senate rather than a faculty editorial policy committee; 3) that Baccalaureate and Commencement ceremonies be changed to a weekend format; 4) that a spring break be established for students and faculty; and 5) that the academic calendar be changed to complete the fall semester before the Christmas holiday.[166] None of the requests fell within the designated responsibilities of the Board of Trustees. Yet, the Board had acted courteously to the students' request to be heard. Subsequently,

---

162. Houston Baptist College, Minutes of the Meetings of the Faculty Assembly, Meeting on 14 May 1968.
163. Houston Baptist College, Minutes of the Meetings of the Executive Committee of the Board of Trustees, Meeting on 16 Sept. 1968.
164. Houston Baptist College, Minutes of Meetings of the Executive Committee of the Board of Trustees, Meeting on 21 Oct. 1968.
165. Houston Baptist College, Minutes of the Meetings of the Faculty Assembly, Meeting on 14 May 1968.
166. Houston Baptist College, Minutes of Meetings of the Board of Trustees, Meeting on 22 Nov. 1968.

the faculty Academic Affairs committee voted to end the fall semester in December and to create a January short term. Most of these requests ultimately were implemented with the exception of the recommendation for student publication management; that remained under a faculty-staff editorial board.

Gift and grant income continued to be under-realized. The trustee Finance Committee reported,

> Our most crucial problem remains the collection of budgeted gifts and grants. In order to fully realize our budget projection we must receive $138,622 from gifts and grants during the remaining three months. The BGCT allocation is $28,388 less than budgeted due to the change in the allocation formula.[167]

One section of a report commissioned by the BGCT showed HBC's gifts to be only approximately ten percent of institutional income; the average income from gifts at other BGCT institutions was closer to twenty-five percent.[168] Low revenue from gifts and grants remained a historic institutional problem.

§

In 1968, the Board undertook a significant campus landscaping initiative and purchased some 250 large magnolia trees for the campus.[169] Additionally, 200 live oaks donated by area churches were planted.[170] The March 1968 meeting of the Board included library construction reports, the offer of more trees for the campus from Tracy Lawrence,[171] an offer of stock from Frank Sharp to construct a bell tower,[172] plans for a

---

167. Houston Baptist College, Minutes of Meetings of the Finance Committee of the Board of Trustees, Meeting on 29 Feb. 1968.

168. "Carden expresses concern for liberal arts colleges," *The Collegian* 19 Feb. 1969, p. 3.

169. "Trees for Campus," *Houston Baptist College News,* Apr. 1965, 2; "Ah, Spring," *Houston Baptist College News,* May 1968, 2. Temple Hargrove harvested these mature trees from his tree farm near Slidell on the banks of Lake Pontchartrain for planting on the HBC campus. They had been root pruned and moved numerous times to prepare the trees for transplanting.

170. "Dr. Dillon, David Elkins, and Ray Mayfield Participate in Planting," *The Collegian,* 14 Feb. 1968, p. 1. Photo.

171. "Trees for Campus," *Houston Baptist College News,* Apr. 1965, 2. An earlier gift provided 400 trees for the new campus.

172. Houston Baptist College, Minutes of Meetings of the Executive Committee of the Board of Trustees, Meeting on 18 Mar. 1968; (Dr. W. H. Hinton to College Trustees, March 15, 1968). The building was to be funded by a gift of Sharp land. The first floor was to contain museums; the carillon was projected to be one of the largest in the world.

proposed mall between the library and the academic quadrangle,[173] and reports on both a proposed American Historical Center[174] and an Arabic Culture Center. President Hinton explained the Center for Arabic Studies was to be built on a ten-acre campus site and was to teach "language, history, economics, archeology, music, and art of the Arab people." He predicted the Center could have "great influence in reshaping American foreign policy toward the Arab States."[175] Though the Center never came to fruition, the concept garnered the attention of the national media including the *New York Times*.[176]

Rex Fleming's debate team of Robert Hemfelt, Wendell Odom, Tom Pearson, Kenneth Hooper, Brenda Cherry, and Philip Butler finished first and second at the University of Houston Tournament[177] and went on to win against Northwestern University at a Tulane tournament. The National Forensics League named Fleming "The coach who has done the most for college debate, 1971-72."[178] The Gallery Theatre offered Christopher Fry's *A Phoenix Too Frequent* and Peter Shaffer's *The Public Eye* directed by Jeannette Clift.[179] Productions of Shakespeare's *Midsummer Night's Dream*[180] and Shaw's *Arms and the Man* featured future film and Broadway stars Brent Mintz (Spiner) and Trey Wilson.[181]

In the spring of 1968, the Association of Women Students held the first Women's Day to recognize honorees selected for outstanding leadership and contribution. The first Woman of the Year, Elsa Jean Looser, was joined by the first Faculty Woman of the Year, Opal Goolsby, and by the first women of the year from each class—Carol Ann Halliday, Carol Joyce Crumm, Linda Leazar, and Brenda Cherry.[182] In 1969, the literary anthology *The Raft*[183] became the *Shank's Mare* ("to go on one's own two

---

173. Houston Baptist College, Minutes of Meetings of the Executive Committee of the Board of Trustees, Meeting on 18 Mar. 1968.
174. Ibid. (Dr. W. H. Hinton to College Trustees, March 15, 1968). "The proposal is for a communication center which would house historical information about our country which could be transmitted through electronic equipment on call to various colleges in America. This project would work with Rice in the pilot program."
175. "Arabic Studies Unit Planned by College," *New York Times*, 10 Mar. 1968, p. 15.
176. Ibid.
177. "Debate Team Takes Three of Four at UH," *The Collegian*, 22 Nov. 1967, pp. 1, 3; "Hip deep in hardware," *Flashes & Dashes*, 1 Feb. 1968, p. 1.
178. Houston Baptist College, *President's Report of Houston Baptist College 1971-72*, p. 4.
179. Don Hendrix, "Drama," *The Collegian*, 8 Dec. 1967, p. 3.
180. "Editorials: Drama Department," *The Collegian*, 13 Nov. 1968, p. 3.
181. "The Play's the Thing," *HBC News*, Oct. 1968, 1; *Ornogah 1968*, 76-77.
182. *HBC News*, May 1968, 3; *Ornogah 1968*, 120-121, 132. Photos.
183. "Raft Accepts Entries," *The Collegian*, 14 Feb. 1968, p. 1. Co-editors Don Hendrix and Honey Harrison.

feet").[184]   Chapters of the fraternities Alpha Pi Kappa,[185] Phi Kappa Epsilon[186], and Sigma Phi Chi[187] were established. The Men's Honorary Leadership Society was formed by Dean James E. Williamson with the expressed purpose of petitioning Omicron Delta Kappa for affiliation with the national society.[188] The speculative student recruiting program on the east coast was discontinued, and new administrative leadership was sought for the College admissions operation.[189] At the same time, students for the new nursing program were recruited through radio and television commercials on local stations.[190] Board minutes from 1968 also reflect the first recorded trustee conversation about dancing that resulted in approval for an off-campus graduation dance given by the junior class to honor seniors.[191]

§

Students and faculty from the first years of the College history had an unusually close personal working relationship with many members of the College staff. Job titles during these years seemed comparatively unimportant as all members of the College family struggled together to establish the new institution. Among those significant long-term staff members from those early years were Frances Arnold, Development (1962-1971); Judy Babb, President's Office and Financial Aid (1963-1991); Mildred Boone, Switchboard (1967-1993); Virginia Crosno, Development (1964-1977); Frances Curtis, Student Affairs (1968-2008); Wanda Green, President's Office (1963-1969); Sue Hart, Public Relations (1965-1974); Mary Lou Moore, Secretarial Services (1969-1979); Kathleen Strom, Library (1964-1999); Helen Tinch, Museum

---

184. *Ornogah 1970*, 182. Editor Jerry Aldridge wrote in 1969, "Generally speaking, Shank's Mare means to be independent, or on one's own. The students were on their own when they wrote; we were on our own when we published; and now, you are on your own as you read."

185. *Ornogah 1970*, 192-93.

186. *Ornogah 1970*, 194-5.

187. *Ornogah 1970*, 196-7.

188. *Ornogah 1967*, 82; *Ornogah 1968*, 138-9; "ODK Gets Charter and New Members," *The Collegian*, 11 May 1972, p. 2. ODK received its national charter in 1972.

189. Houston Baptist College, Minutes of Meetings of the Executive Committee of the Board of Trustees, Meeting on 15 Apr. 1968; Houston Baptist College, Minutes of Meetings of the Academic Committee of the Board of Trustees, Meeting on 30 Sept. 1968.

190. Houston Baptist College, Minutes of Meetings of the Executive Committee of the Board of Trustees, Meeting on 15 Apr. 1968.

191. Houston Baptist College, Minutes of Meetings of the Executive Committee of the Board of Trustees, Meeting on 18 Mar. 1968.

(1964-1978); Marie Wetzel, Academic Affairs (1962-1974); Nada Wilkins, Development (1964-1976); Jackie Williams, Controller (1962-1995); J. W. Youngblood, Plant Operations (1963-1976);[192] and Ellouise Zapalac, Bookstore (1967-1993).

At the second annual Baccalaureate and Commencement in 1968, Dr. Baker James Cauthen, Secretary of the Foreign Mission Board, and U. S. Representative Walter H. Judd addressed the ninety graduates of the class of 1968.[193] In July, the College Singers, under the direction of R. Paul Green, departed for the Seventh Baptist World Youth Conference in Bern, Switzerland,[194] meeting HBC alumnus John Gillespie who was in post-baccalaureate study in Germany.[195] The Singers continued a concert tour that included Rome, Florence, Venice, and Paris.

The third annual historical preservation symposium, "Architecture and Arts on the Southern Frontier," was held on the campus May 8-10, 1968.[196] Sponsored by the National Trust for Historic Preservation, experts from the du Pont Winterthur Museum, Smithsonian Institution, American Institute of Architects, University of California, SMU, Tulane, University of Texas, Texas A&M, and HBU presented twenty-four lectures in the course of three days. Chair Faith Bybee again served with Joella and Stewart Morris who hosted Houston symposium leaders with a buffet dinner in their Rivercrest home.[197] All three symposia attracted significant national attention. However, the 1968 meeting proved to be the final installment of these symposia of prominence and academic enrichment. The symposia were symbolic of the lofty aspirations of the leaders of the young institution and helped shape the image of the College in both the local and the national cultural community.

In June 1968, Dr. Ross Dillon announced his retirement as Vice President for Development.[198] The *1966 Ornogah* was dedicated to him:

Dr. Dillon was a man with the vision of a College in Houston, established on Christian ideals and dedicated to God . . . a man

---

192. "Pin a Medal on our Unsung Hero," *HBC News,* Oct. 1968, 3.

193. "Graduation Gallery," *HBC News,* June 1968, 2-3. Photo.

194. Houston Baptist College, Minutes of Meetings of the Board of Trustees, Meeting on 17 Nov. 1967; "Singers Enjoy Tour," *HBC News,* Sept. 1968, 1. Photo.

195. "John Gillespie to Study at German School," *Houston Baptist Collegian,* 24 May 1967, p. 4.

196. "Third Houston Symposium Was Held in May, Had Noted Talks," *Antique Quarterly,* Summer 1968, 16; Houston Baptist College, Minutes of Meetings of the Academic Committee of the Board of Trustees, Meeting on 15 Sept. 1967.

197. Nancy Thobae, "Antiquary Lovers," *Houston Tribune,* 18 Apr. 1968, p. 2.

198. "Dillon to Retire," *HBC News,* June 1968, 1.

with the forethought and ingenuity to see his dream realized . . .
a man whose life is centered in furthering the standards of
Houston Baptist College . . . a man respected by all who know
him.

Part of the genius of the early leadership of Houston Baptist College
was the structural integrity of the team that resulted from the unique contributions each player could make to the enterprise. Stewart Morris, Ross
Dillon, William Denham, and O. D. Martin each offered differing qualities, perspectives, and capabilities that ultimately contributed to the success of their joint venture.[199] Ross Dillon was a prototypical southern gen-
tleman with deep roots in Alabama and an accent to match. Yet, he possessed a tenacity born of conviction that served the cause of Christ in every
assignment he addressed. His work with land acquisition and local governments to acquire new church sites for the UBA prepared him for the
unexpected demands of the early years of the College. His affinity with
the College Property Committee provided him an influential, authorita-
tive, and comprehensive platform from which to amplify his effectiveness.

Dillon's retirement enhanced the occasion of his 50th wedding
anniversary to his beloved Rose. Rose Dillon played her own role in history—helping organize the Women's Auxiliary, encouraging its fund-raising activities, and working through women in the church community to
support the new College. In tribute to the leadership of this couple at
Houston Baptist College, a section of the Hinton Center honors their
memory. The wing contains a large meeting room that houses the square
grand Steinway piano from the home of Rose and Ross Dillon, portraits of
both of them, and a commemorative plaque identifying their role in HBC
history. Of her husband, Rose once confided, "I've never said this publicly,
but Houston Baptist College was born on the knees of Ross Dillon."[200]
Following Dr. Dillon's retirement, Dr. O. D. Martin was appointed to
head the development program of the College.[201] Senator Hank Grover
was also added to the development staff to deal with foundation and corporate support.[202]

199. Sibley, 20.
200. "Reflections," *HBC News,* Fall 1986, 13.
201. "Martin Named in Development," *HBC News,* Oct. 1968, 1.
202. *Flashes & Dashes,* 15 Aug. 1967, p. 2.

With the fall of 1968 came the opening of the new Moody Library.[203] Librarian Jefferson Caskey and his staff began moving books to the new facility in late summer. At the same time, the library staff completed conversion of the catalog from the Dewey Decimal to the Library of Congress system.[204] On September 20, the Board of Trustees held its first meeting in the new Moody Library Board Room. Dr. Hinton introduced O. D. Martin and Don Looser as newly-appointed administrative personnel. New faculty in the fall who ultimately served long years of service included Donna LeRoux, Nursing (1968-1984); Georgena Prator, Library (1968-1990); Dr. Glendola Nash, Dean of Nursing (1968-1990); Dr. William B. Crittenden, Education (1968-1980); Dorothy Allen, Library (1968-1995); Dr. Marion Webb, Spanish (1968-1991); Jan Edds, Physical Education (1968-1982); Rex Fleming, Speech and Debate (1968-1994); Dr. Florence Gould, Political Science (1968-1986); Dr. William Guthrie, Music (1968-1980); Dr. James Tsao, Political Science (1968-1998); and Dr. Doris Warren, Chemistry (1968-).

Fall 1968 enrollment totaled 1009 students, 300 of whom were in campus housing. This included 162 nursing students enrolled for the first year of the BSN program. Responding to heightened financial pressures, the Board changed the beginning of the annual faculty contract period from June 1 to September 1 marking the end of the provision of summers to draft new curriculum.[205]

On December 4, 1968, initial accreditation of Houston Baptist College was granted by the Southern Association of Colleges and Schools.[206] After a year's delay in the anticipated action, the news was all the more gratifying. On the historic day, the chief administrators Hinton, Smith, and Womack were absent from the campus attending the SACS annual meeting in Atlanta. In recalling the milestone moment, this author later wrote,

We all had shared the roller coaster ride of the first years. We traversed the highs of student giftedness, of extraordinary faculty depth, of the exhilaration of being a part of the first time everything had been done, and the gratification of pioneering new academic models in a new place. Interwoven were the anxieties of

---

203. Houston Baptist College, Minutes of Meetings of the Board of Trustees, Meeting on 20 Sept. 1968.
204 "Expectations Rise with Moody Library," *HBC News*, Apr. 1968, 3. Photo.
205 Houston Baptist College, Minutes of the Meetings of the Faculty, Meeting on 12 Dec. 1968.
206 "HBC accredited by Southern Association," *The Collegian*, 9 Dec. 1968, p. 1; "What Accreditation Means," *HBC News*, Dec. 1968, 1.

institutional birth and survival, the struggle for agreement in matters of program and policy, the frustration of anonymity in a big city, the constant need for financial resources, and the difficulty of establishing home and family in a new place. Yet, few would have traded these years of founding for any other years anywhere else. For all its stress, the trip had been wonderful. God had blessed this new creation richly.

Upon receiving the call from Atlanta, people seemed to pour from every office on campus to hear the news of our first accreditation by the Southern Association. It was an affirmation of all the years of prayer and dreams, of all the toil and investment of time and resource. Shouts and hugs filled the hallway. Then, suddenly, everyone fell quiet, and the silence of the moment was eloquent. And, as quickly as we had gathered, grateful faculty and staff turned to waiting phones to share the news. I do not know what form joy took in Atlanta, but on the campus on December 4, 1968, there was a moment of heaven on earth. The memory occupies a special place in my heart.[207]

The accreditation honored fifteen years of diligent work in establishing the new college. SACS approval was vital. Regional accreditation would permit the unquestioned admission of HBC graduates into post-baccalaureate study and professional schools. Accreditation for the College was retroactive to the graduation of the first class in 1967. This affirmation would serve to certify the qualitative merit of the College to other sister institutions and pave the way for financial aid that was often reserved for students in regionally-accredited colleges. The HBC *Bulletin of Information* distributed in the spring of 1969 bore the rubber-stamped imprint, "Accredited by Southern Association of Colleges and Schools." The action served as a significant boost to the recruitment of both students and faculty and represented a tangible tribute to the early faculty, staff, and trustees. The popular annual faculty-trustee Christmas dinner two weeks later provided a time for justified celebration.

§

The Student Senate and the Fine Arts Department sponsored a competition for the composition of a new Alma Mater in December.[208] Dr.

---

207 Dr. Don Looser, "Days of Glory," *HBC News*, Feb. 1997, 27.
208 "Christmas Could Mark Semester End," *The Collegian*, 9 Dec. 1968, p. 2.

Hinton had written a text during a "particularly beautiful flight back to Houston" late one afternoon. The setting sun and the billowing clouds had encouraged his hand at a poetic response to the moment. Musical settings were solicited from campus participants. From the anonymous submittals, a jury of music faculty selected the setting done by Assistant to the President Don Looser.

Hail the Orange and Blue was scored for band and quickly became used at campus athletic events and formal convocations.

In the great state of Texas,
Houston, USA,
Stands our noble alma mater,
Christ saying "I Am the Way."

In our search for knowledge,
Tempered with Thy love,
Seeking our place of service
With wisdom from above.

Give us courage, strength, and faith
To face a world filled with fear.
Ever onward to the challenge,
Knowing Thou art near.

God bless our school.
Keep her safe and true!
God bless our alma mater.
Hail the Orange and Blue!

Hinton-Looser

The College finally had a mascot, school colors, and an Alma Mater.

§

In February 1969, the NCAA accepted HBC for membership.[209] This action predictably followed the granting of accreditation by the

---

[209] "HBC accepted to NCAA," *The Collegian*, 19 Feb. 1969, p. 7; "N.C.A.A. Membership Announced," *HBC News*, Feb. 1969, 4; *Ornogah 1970*, 143.

Southern Association of Colleges and Schools. The year 1969-70 marked the first season for basketball as an NCAA team.[210] The baseball team won the district championship in the spring.[211] Golf had its beginning as a walk-on sport coached by Mac Sutton. The *1966 Ornogah* records the team of J. Eige, Kit Haines, Charles Livingston, Mike Norton, and Henry Zepeda.[212] Eige '67 recalled, "We had no HBC hats, windbreakers, shirts, golf bags, or even a towel or travel bag. In fact, I recall that we even had to furnish our own golf balls. Morgan Baker allowed us to play a couple of days a week at Sharpstown and from time to time offered some coaching. Braeburn also allowed us to play there on Mondays."[213] The team, transported by Eige's father, competed in two tournaments that first year, in Fort Worth and Huntsville. One of Eige's cherished memories from his student days was the opportunity to caddy for the President one year in the Houston Open Pro-Am when Dr. Hinton was teamed with Jack Nicklaus.[214] By 1969, an outstanding college golf team—including Steve Buetel, Mike Dorman, John Lewis, Robert Seligman, and Tom Dickey—was coached by Sharpstown Country Club pro Morgan Baker.[215]

A number of other changes occurred during the spring of 1969. A new mascot, Mingo, greeted the season. Mingo would be the mascot for many years and would be the object of affectionate care by the Coreons and ultimately by loving members of the College staff. Pi Kappa Delta, national honorary speech fraternity, was chartered.[216] Frank Fisher resigned as Registrar,[217] and long-time trustee-then-faculty-member Dr. James E. Williamson was appointed to fill the vacancy.[218] Ralph Gibson was named Director of Admissions.[219] Dr. James Massey was announced as Dean of Student Life in March. With the counsel of Dr. W. F. Howard, Director of the Student Department of the BGCT, a new name—Christian Life on Campus—replaced the Baptist Student Union as a title

---

210 "Head Coach Moves to Tech; Richards Replaces Myers," *The Collegian,* 20 Mar. 1970, p. 4.

211 "Baseball Team in Play-offs," *HBC News,* May 1969, 1; "Huskies Nipped in Play-Offs," *HBC News,* June 1969, 1.

212 *Ornogah 1966,* 136-37.

213 (J. Eige to Dr. Don Looser, Aug. 25, 2009).

214 (J. Eige, *From HBC to U,* Houston Baptist University Alumni Association, Founding Classes Reunion, Aug. 8, 2008).

215 "Golfers Gain Few Laurels, Much Experience," *HBC News,* Mar. 1969, 3. Photo.

216 *Ornogah 1969,* 155.

217 Houston Baptist College, Minutes of the Meetings of the Academic Affairs Committee of the Board of Trustees, Meeting on 10 Mar. 1969; Minutes of the Meetings of the Board of Trustees, Meeting on 22 Mar. 1969.

218 Houston Baptist College, Minutes of the Meetings of the Faculty, Meeting on 8 May 1969.

219 "Promotions, Changes and New Division Heads," *HBC News,* Apr. 1969, 3.

for campus religious life at HBC in an effort to embrace the range of denominations represented among students.[220]

In academic life, Dr. Glendola Nash reported that the National League for Nursing had indicated "reasonable likelihood for accreditation" of the new baccalaureate program. Rex Fleming's debaters posted a sweepstakes win at the Southern Methodist University tournament, ranking third in a field of sixty-three colleges. The HBC Student Educators Association placed in the top five in state-wide competition. In medical school admission competition, sixty percent of HBC applicants were admitted to medical school, initiating a long record of acceptances under the leadership of faculty advisor Dr. Joyce Fan. Study-abroad trips were scheduled for the Shakespeare Institute and for the Holy Land. Dr. Calvin Huckabay published the first edition of his internationally-recognized bibliography of John Milton; Texas historian Dr. Marilyn Sibley published two new books.[221] Lew Zailer was elected Dean of the Houston Chapter of the American Guild of Organists.[222] R. Paul Green was selected to lead music conferences in Hong Kong for the Foreign Mission Board,[223] and in a well-documented chapter of Houston cultural history, HBC faculty member Bill Guthrie left his seat in the audience and replaced an ailing featured singer onstage in a Houston Grand Opera performance of *The Barber of Seville*.[224] Doctoral degrees were completed by Molly Wieting, Ed Billings, Elysee Peavy, Troy Womack, Carrie Palmer, and Daton Dodson.[225] Indicative of the close faculty/student relationships, a number of faculty for whom music was a significant personal involvement participated in the College Chorus. In 1967, the spring ensemble included Dean of Students Dr. Williamson, and faculty members Dr. Joyce Fan, Elsa Jean Looser, Opal Goolsby, and Dr. Albert Myers.

Once again, no faculty raises were proposed for the fall; few new faculty positions were approved; several majors were discontinued because of low enrollments; the faculty was told of the possibility of increased teaching loads.[226] The library budget was reduced by $18,000; two faculty and

---

220 "Looser organizes group to study religious life," *The Collegian,* 6 Mar. 1969, pp. 1, 3.
221 Lucille Stewart Krisch, "Twigs and Trees: Early Texas Travelers," *San Antonio Light,* 14 July 1968, sec. G, p. 9.
222 *Flashes & Dashes,* 15 Sept. 1967, p. 2.
223 Houston Baptist College, Minutes of Meetings of the Board of Trustees, Meeting on 21 Mar. 1969.
224 Ibid.
225 Ibid.
226 Houston Baptist College, Minutes of Meetings of the Academic Committee of the Board of Trustees, Meeting on 27 Jan. 1969.

six staff positions were eliminated.[227] As a result of these saving measures, the 1967 operating deficit of $430,000 declined to $130,000 in 1968. A *Report of the President, Houston Baptist College 1968-69* was published in the spring that highlighted the first five years of operation. This report documented the decline of church gifts from $135,765 in 1963-64 to $78,244 in 1968-69. "Non-church" giving increased, however, from $379,334 in 1963 to $747,139 in 1968. The report showed investment in plant in 1969 to be $9,724,308.[228]

Discussion and negotiation continued with the Board to secure a sale to the Gulf Oil Company of a tract on the corner of Beechnut and the Southwest Freeway. At the same time, the lease of a tract at Fondren and Beechnut was consummated with the Humble Oil Company. The leased land was reserved for future campus expansion.[229] The College Property Committee sold twelve acres of college land on the Southwest Freeway just south of Beechnut in the summer of 1969.[230] The *Houston Post* acquired 4.37 of these acres to accommodate new facilities for KPRC-TV, Channel 2.[231] Progress with Imperial Point and Inwood Forest residential developments portended additional revenue for the College. In these projects, the Property Committee continued to work with several friends of the College who had proven their mettle in the fire of the original campus development—Walter Mischer, Bennett Coulson, and Norwood and Monarch Homes.

Ultimately, Imperial Point yielded approximately 800 residential lots and a 6.5 acre future church site that was sold to the UBA. The "Baptist Sections" of Inwood Forest at Antoine Road and Little York Road consisted of 189 acres and ultimately yielded $275,000 for the College. Additionally, commercial reserves from the Inwood projects were valued at $461,448 to provide future income.[232] In 1969, changes in the federal tax law caused the Property Committee to report, "At this time it is not anticipated that any new lands will be acquired by this committee, and

---

227 Houston Baptist College, Minutes of Meetings of the Board of Trustees, Meeting on 21 Mar. 1969.

228 Houston Baptist College, *Report of the President, Houston Baptist College: 1968-69*, 11.

229 Houston Baptist College, Minutes of Meetings of the Board of Trustees, Meeting on 21 Mar. 1969.

230 Ibid.

231 Jack Harris, *The Fault Does Not Lie With Your Set* (Austin: Eakin Press, 1989), 113. "We (KPRC-TV) wanted in the southwest part of the city. . . . We also needed immediate access to a major thoroughfare. . . . Finally, we selected a site now designated as 8181 Southwest Freeway. It had been owned by Houston Baptist College, but the administrators . . . decided they would never expand the campus that far west."

232 Houston Baptist College, Minutes of Meetings of the Executive Committee of the Board of Trustees, Meeting on 18 Mar. 1968.

we anticipate a termination of the functions of this committee within the next year."[233] However, the value of this committee's operation to the financial health of the College and the expertise that was resident in the committee's membership warranted the continuation of real estate activity long into the future under an alternative organizational structure.

§

In 1969, trustee Gilbert Turner introduced a new concept for attracting outstanding students with scholarships funded by gifts to the endowment.[234] The concept provided a means for individuals and churches to contribute affordable gifts to endow a student scholarship. The Endowed Academic Scholarship program ultimately proved to be the most significant resource for this purpose in College history. Based initially on gifts of $30,000 to the endowment, the first four gifts for Endowed Academic Scholarships were received from Gilbert Turner, Stewart Morris, the Strake Foundation, and an anonymous donor.[235]

Trustees organized to support legislative efforts to establish financial aid grants by the State for students attending independent colleges in Texas. Senate Bill 485 by Senator Jack Hightower of Vernon proposed to establish a Tuition Equalization Grant program that would result in a powerful source of aid for students demonstrating financial need. Based on the premise that a scholarship for a student attending an independent college costs the state far less than formula funding for that same student to attend a public institution, the bill drew the early support of Houston Senator Barbara Jordan who was quickly convinced of the economic merits of the proposal.[236]

The spring of 1969 also marked one of the most stellar events in the history of the young College. The President's Council membership at this time represented a powerful cultural cross-section of some ninety businessmen in the city. The Council provided a means of visibility for the College and helped create an advocacy for institutional support in the community. The President's Council annual black-tie dinners enjoyed outstanding celebrity speakers and had outgrown the capacity of several

---

233 Sibley, 76.
234 Houston Baptist College, Minutes of Meetings of the Executive Committee of the Board of Trustees, Meeting on 19 May 1969.
235 "40 Years of Excellence: 1963-2003," *HBU News*, Dec. 2003, 14.
236 "Private School Legislation Pends," *HBC News*, May 1969, 4.

of the city's finest banquet facilities. James E. Lyon, Chairman of the Program Committee, was an active Republican fundraiser. Through his influence, the President's Council Dinner at the Shamrock Hotel in May 1969 featured an address by California Governor Ronald Reagan. Harold Sellers, Chairman of the Council, presided over the gala evening and presented awards to the twenty-two living Founders of the College.[237] The dinner attracted some 500 guests and provided a significant opportunity for Reagan to reaffirm long-term relationships with local Republican Party leadership. For the College, this Reagan event marked a new high for community visibility.

§

The dreams of the founders for a Christian liberal arts college of the first rank had been realized. The first years of operation had created a stalwart group of committed students, faculty, staff, and trustees. In an essay entitled "Halcyon Days," Professor Elysee Peavy recalled,

> That the College had a strong commitment to Christian education was certainly no surprise; what was unexpected was the strong commitment to the liberal arts and to the Christian ideal of learning as an undertaking that includes not merely specialized knowledge, but knowledge that develops the person morally and intellectually. . . . The core curriculum was a model of this ideal. . . . What a wonderful community of scholars such a common curriculum generated. Faculty and students continued class discussions long after classes were over, sometimes standing in halls. . . . Faculty from different disciplines met regularly over coffee in the Student Center . . . to exchange ideas in the spirit of intellectual inquiry. Students complained about the rigor of the curriculum but felt a sense of community derived from common frames of reference. These same students acknowledge to this day that the core curriculum has been invaluable in their personal and professional lives. The camaraderie engendered among these students gave rise to traditions that continue to enrich our campus life. . . . those early years remain a touchstone of what higher education can be.[238]

---

237 "Reagan to be Council Speaker," *HBC News,* Apr. 1969, 1; "Reagan talk Dinner Highlight," *HBC News,* May 1969, 2. Photo.
238 Dr. Elysee H. Peavy, "Halcyon Days," *HBU News,* June 1996, 29.

For the young College, greater obstacles than had been anticipated had resulted in greater accomplishment than might have been expected. Adversity and trial had purged many colleagues who were unable or unwilling to respond to the rigor of those early years. Significantly, there was no attrition among trustees or the executive staff. In 1969, only fourteen of the original faculty of twenty-nine remained.

Virtually all aspects of college life and governance had developed and matured. The College had produced its first graduates who became among its most ardent alumni. Houston Baptist College had gained recognition, respect, and accreditation. The College learned from mistakes and built upon that experience. In the process, these first years reveal themselves to be among the richest in institutional history.

FIVE

1969-1974

Following the graduation of the first classes and the awarding of the first accreditation by the Southern Association of Colleges and Schools, College history became more linear, less generative, and more episodic. College "firsts" still occurred, but long-range solutions and well-considered protocols became more common than short-term fixes. By this time, the academic product was studied and well-defined. Institutional management became more effective, molded by external forces and honed by experience. The College community refined its population to retain those colleagues stimulated by free-ranging opportunity and unafraid of change. Professional roles in the institutional hierarchy became more clearly understood. Colleagues became more confident, trusting, and embracing of each other. A corporate personality began to emerge.

The 1970 federal census showed a population of 1,232,802 residents in the city of Houston—almost double the 1950 population. Houston now ranked fifth among America's largest cities. In this period of extraordinary growth, developer Gerald Hines opened the Galleria shopping complex, established a whole new prototype for retail merchandising, and created a newly-defined area of the city called the "Magic Circle." Texas Eastern Transmission Company bought thirty-three contiguous blocks of downtown real estate on which to build the Houston Center development. Kenneth Schnitzer opened The Summit arena in Greenway Plaza as home of the Houston Rockets.[1]

On the campus, the Morris Columns were dedicated by Mayor Louie Welch and Dr. George M. Low, Deputy Administrator of the National Aeronautics and Space Administration, on October 23, 1969.[2] A gift from historical preservationists Joella and Stewart Morris, ten of sixteen

---

1 Houstonhistory.com, "Booming Economy, Houston History: 1970-1980," http://www.houstonhistory.com/decades/history5q.htm (accessed Sept. 28, 2009).
2 Marilyn McAdams Sibley, *To Benefit a University* (Houston: Houston Baptist University, 1978) 50; *Ornogah 1970*, 229. Photo.

granite columns from the 1899 Galveston County Court House were set upon massive foundations to mark the east end of the Holcombe Mall. These architectural artifacts had personal significance for the Morris family whose grandfather had sought refuge from the 1900 Galveston hurricane inside the 1899 Court House. The pink granite columns, quarried in central Texas in 1898, were thirty feet tall, measured thirty inches in diameter, weighed thirteen tons each, and rested on deep tear-drop shaped foundations.[3] The columns were crowned by capitals carved in both the Corinthian and Ionian style. Because not all sides of all the capitals were fully detailed, they appear to have been carved after having been erected during the original Court House construction. On campus, the capitals were positioned to show only the fully-carved façades from the Holcombe Mall. In the years after their installation, they became the most universally-recognized visual symbol of the College.[4] Their dedication plaque describes their significance to the Morris family:

> Symbolic of justice, law, and order, ten of the sixteen
> columns which guarded the entrance to the Galveston
> County Court House, erected 1899, demolished 1965, where
> William H. Stewart, grandfather, served as district judge. Behind
> these columns, many, including W. C. Morris, father, found refuge
> during the great storm of 1900. May their beauty, magnitude,
> and simplicity remind us of the ageless message of the Word
> of God, the Bible.
>
> Given October 1969, Joella and Stewart Morris,
> Founder, Trustee 1958-1969, Chairman 1966 to 1969.[5]

Stretching westward from the Morris Columns was the Holcombe Mall,[6] dedicated on October 25, 1969. The Mall was funded by a gift that honored former Houston mayor Oscar Fitzallen Holcombe (1888-1968) from his daughter Elizabeth and her husband Markley Crosswell, a

---

3 Frank Carmical, "Columns Have 'Roots,'" *The Collegian*, (undated), Vol. 17 #2, p. 5. Photos.
4 In 1968, the columns stood starkly in isolation on the campus giving rise to the rumor devised by one playful faculty member that they were the first element of construction for an off-ramp from the Southwest Freeway to Beechnut Street. This same faculty member reportedly lectured in *Culture and Human Experience* that the Holcombe Mall bronze lanterns were from the early *Rumpleheimer* period of architectural history. Students taking notes clamored to get the correct spelling of *Rumpleheimer* that, as it turned out, was actually the name of an ice cream parlor in Westbury Square, a popular local Victorian shopping village.
5 The Morris Columns plaque is mounted adjacent to the walk on the north set of columns.
6 "Mall Plans Revealed," *The Collegian*, 13 Nov. 1968, p. 1; *Ornogah 1970*, 228. Photo.

member of the HBC President's Council. The legacy of the ubiquitous mayor Oscar Holcombe can be found throughout the city. Holcombe served as mayor of Houston for twenty-two years in eleven non-consecutive terms. The dedication plaque reads,

> Oscar F. Holcombe (1877-1968). Best known as the long-time Mayor of Houston during the period of its greatest growth, this man was also a devoted Baptist layman. In memory of his selfless, public-spirited and Christian contributions to the community he loved and worked so diligently to develop, the Oscar F. Holcombe Memorial Mall is respectfully dedicated October, 1969.[7]

The Mall marked the new epicenter of the campus connecting the Sharp Gym with the Morris Columns and relating the new Moody Library to the academic quadrangle buildings. The Holcombe Mall became the physical crossroads of the campus, the scene of presidential inauguration and commencement, and the dominant feature of campus land-planning. Sidewalks on the Holcombe Mall were paved a generous ten-feet wide to accommodate the collection of period carriages owned by the Stewart Morris family. During construction, student organizations were invited to "etch" their insignia in sections of the walk leading to the gymnasium.[8]

As work progressed on the Holcombe Mall, Joella Morris became aware of the salvage of several large bronze lanterns that had graced the façade of the old City Auditorium in downtown Houston. This historic structure had been razed in the early 1960s to build Jones Hall on the same site. Mrs. Morris rescued these prized lanterns from the City of Houston storage yard and gave them to the College for restoration and installation on the Holcombe Mall. Bronze parts missing from a third lantern had to be reproduced from the other two—hand cast in sand molds—to provide the components for three complete lanterns. These lanterns, dating from 1910, were installed on the central walk across the Holcombe Mall, and share their *Belle Époque* period with the Morris Columns.[9]

The Moody Library was dedicated on October 31, 1969, by Mrs. Mary Moody Northen in memory of William L. Moody, Jr.[10] The library helped

---

7 The Holcombe Mall plaques are mounted on the east side of the Mall adjacent to the Brown Academic Center.
8 "Mall Walks Inscribed for Posterity," *HBC News,* Feb. 1969, 3; *Ornogah 1969,* 236-7. Photos.
9 (Dr. Don Looser, personal recollections, 1969).
10 "New Mall Area Gives Campus Attractive New Look," *HBC News,* Oct. 1969, 3. Photos.

The campus in 1970 was enhanced by the newly-completed Moody Library, the Holcombe Mall, and the Morris Columns. The campus showed early evidence of landscaping activity.

enclose the Holcombe Mall and provided spacious new housing for study, lectures and receptions, for the library collection, and for the Museum of American Architecture and Decorative Arts. The Museum of American Architecture and Decorative Arts formally opened later on February 23, 1969, in 2,000 square feet of space on the library's second floor.[11] Museum Director Helen Tinch had invested several years seeking acquisitions for the new museum collection and in forming a new Museum Society. Featured in the opening exhibit were the Theo Redwood Blank Doll Collection, paintings by Mrs. Emma Richardson Cherry,[12] silverware and Houston-made furniture from the family of Friedrich Usener,[13] carriages from the Morris collection, and an exhibition of rare books. Miss

11 "Museum Formally Opens with Representative Displays," *HBC News*, Feb. 1969, 1, 3. Photo.

12 Lori Rodriguez, "A brush with history: Emma Richardson Cherry," *Houston Chronicle*, 31 July 2005, p. 4, one-star ed; "Emma Richardson Cherry," *Handbook of Texas Online*, www.tshaonline.org (accessed Dec. 8 2009). Mrs. Cherry saved the home of William Marsh Rice that is now in Sam Houston Park. A student of European artists, Cherry painted the four large murals that reside in the Julia Ideson Building of the Houston Public Library. In 1900, she organized the Houston Public School Art League that later became the Houston Museum of Fine Arts. Cherry's family collection of paintings was donated to HBC in 1969 by her daughter, Dorothy Reid, a friend of founding Museum Director, Helen Tinch.

13 Dorothy E. Justman, *German Colonists and Their Descendants in Houston including Usener and Allied Families* (Wichita Falls: Nortex Offset Publications, Inc., 1974), 76. Photo of "Solid walnut secretary built in Houston by Friedrich Usener in 1842. Donated to Museum of American Architecture and Decorative Arts by Dorothy Eckel Justman in 1969."

Hogg attended the grand opening accompanied by Mr. and Mrs. Stewart Morris and Mr. and Mrs. Cecil Cook and expressed particular appreciation for the Houston-made Usener family furniture.[14] Helen Tinch mounted a series of impressive exhibitions in the new space. These included Frank Horlock's collection of Yena paintings depicting the *Battles of Texas*, *Military Miniatures*,[15] *Portals to the Past along the Gulf Coast*,[16] *The Ming Dynasty*,[17] and *Crèches around the World*.[18] Tinch's series of stimulating exhibits was the subject of a lengthy article in the *Houston Chronicle*.[19]

The Library Lecture Room became the most attractive facility on the campus for events of all kinds. Adjacent to the Lecture Room, looking onto the Holcombe Mall and the Morris Columns, was a handsome new Board of Trustees Room—replete with magnificent hand-carved conference furniture, a gift of the South Coast Life Insurance Company.[20] The realization of the new library facility met the requirement of the Southern Association of Colleges and Schools as a part of its approval for reaffirmation of accreditation.

Another gift to the College provided a benefit of a different kind. On November 18, 1969, Mrs. Frankie Currie, the sister-in-law of Florence Weaver, conveyed her Colorado homestead of 610 acres to the University for the use and enjoyment of the College family.[21] The property rose from the canyon of the South Platte River southwest of Denver on the eastern slope of the front range of the Rocky Mountains and was crowned at an elevation of 7,000 feet by a two-story log house that had been hand-built by Mrs. Currie's husband, Trevor. The Curries had homesteaded the land that was deeded by President Calvin Coolidge in 1928 and had added a ten-acre abandoned gold mine near the river to the original property. In conveying the gift, Mrs. Currie expressed her desire that "the memory of Trevor Currie . . . be perpetuated in the lives of countless generations of students at HBC."[22]

---

14 "Museum Formally Opens," *HBC News,* Feb. 1969, 1, 3.

15 "Museum Shows Miniatures," *HBC News,* Mar. 1970, 1.

16 "New Exhibit at Museum," *HBC News,* Oct. 1970, 1. Architectural motifs including doors, grilles, knobs and hinges.

17 "Museum Exhibit Features Chinese Art," *HBC News,* Sept. 1971, 2. This exhibit featured carved ivory, embroidered tapestries, and porcelain urns.

18 "Crèches of the World," *The Collegian,* 24 Nov. 1970, p. 3.

19 Marie David, "History's More Fun Without the Books," *Houston Chronicle,* 30 Mar. 1969, sec. 7, p. 6; *Houston Chronicle,* 17 Feb. 1971, Southwest sec., p. 8.

20 Houston Baptist College, Minutes of the Meetings of the Board of Trustees, Meeting on 13 Sept. 1962.

21 Don Looser, "Frankie Currie Tribute," *HBU News,* Nov. 1988, 4.

22 "College Deeded Colorado Land," *HBC News,* Dec. 1969, 2. Photo of Currie, Weaver, and Hinton.

Furnishings were left in the house to accommodate College guests along with instructions for managing the property. Set in an isolated location served not even by a county road, access to the house was gained across a highland meadow. At one time, the College considered building a summer camp on the site. However, the terrain was rough and steep and proved virtually impossible to adapt for group use. Nonetheless, HBC families were welcomed to schedule the house for a week in the summer. Over the next fifteen years, the Currie Ranch was the scene of numerous vacations, family reunions, staff retreats, and at least one golden anniversary celebration.[23] The view from the house overlooking Littleton and Denver at night was spectacular. Wildlife abounded; hiking, bird watching, and wildflower photography provided unique experiences for many College families. Scrapbooks of photographs and letters were assembled by the annual occupants of the "cabin" that detailed the many memories that were resident there.[24]

§

In 1969, new action taken by the Baptist General Convention of Texas prohibited persons from serving simultaneously on the board of more than one Texas Baptist institution. In Houston, the policy eliminated a number of potential HBC trustee candidates who were already trustees at other institutions. HBC trustees Kline McGee, Don McGregor, Freland Murphy, and James Riley were forced to resign in order to remain affiliated with longer-standing institutional trusteeships.[25] The BGCT also proposed a new distribution formula for Texas Baptist colleges that would reduce the 1969 HBC grant by $71,596 and redistribute those funds to Baylor University, Baylor Dental Branch, Hardin-Simmons University, and San Marcos Baptist Academy.[26] Chief Financial Officer Troy Womack wrote a strong letter to the Christian Education Commissions opposing the formula:

The proposed new formulas are unacceptable to us. Though they contain some of the trappings and jargon of educational expert-

---

23 Dr. Don Byrnes, "A Wonderful Week in the Rockies," *The Scene*, Vol. 1, #1, pp. 7-8. Photos.
24 These scrapbooks are housed in the Moody Library archives. A book detailing this colorful section of Colorado is *The Upper Side of the Pie Crust* in the Moody Library.
25 "Baptist General Convention of Texas to Meet—Elect Trustees," *HBC News*, Oct. 1965, 1.
26 Houston Baptist College, Minutes of the Meetings of the Board of Trustees, Meeting on 6 Oct. 1969.

ise, they violate the fundamental tenets of the sound and just allocation of funds for higher educational purposes. If it is the purpose of the Christian Education Commission to encourage and support Baptist higher education, then let us add additional money from the convention and get on with the job of giving all our colleges support in the fight for survival.[27]

The new formula had been developed as a result of the report by William Carden, Coordinator of Institutional Affairs for the Christian Education Commission of the Baptist General Convention of Texas, that advocated greater support for Baptist institutions with graduate and professional programs, chiefly Baylor and Hardin-Simmons universities, and less convention support for other Texas Baptist colleges.[28] Significantly, the Carden Report correctly forecast a day of diminishing institutional reliance on BGCT contribution. Funding from the BGCT for higher education increased only four percent over the next two years.[29] In 1968, Baylor College of Medicine separated from Baylor University for related reasons.[30] In 1971, Houston's Memorial Baptist Hospital was released from its ties to the BGCT to attain increased community representation and financial support.[31] The Carden Report also challenged the claim of many Texas Baptist colleges to be "liberal arts institutions" when the majority of their students were majoring in professional areas, i.e. business and education. Additionally, the Carden report questioned institutional claims of academic excellence in a period of declining per-student expenditures for instruction and academic support.[32] McBeth reported, "Despite recommendations of the ill-fated Carden Report in 1968, the universities . . . remained fixed; none closed and no new ones formed.[33]

A number of new faculty members who were recruited in 1969 ultimately contributed many years of College service. These included Dr. Don Byrnes, History (1969-2005); Dr. Robert Linder, Music (1969-1994; 2004-05); Dr. Jerry Modisette, Physics (1969-1980); and Dr. Ed

---

27 Houston Baptist College, Minutes of the Meetings of the Board of Trustees, Meeting on 6 Oct. 1969; (Troy Womack to CECB, BGCT, Aug. 12, 1969).

28 "Carden Report Rejected," *Abilene Reporter-News*, 26 Feb. 1969, p. 1.

29 Houston Baptist College, Minutes of the Meetings of the Board of Trustees Executive Committee, Meeting on 19 July 1971.

30 "Baylor releases medical school," *The Collegian*, 9 Dec. 1968, p. 3.

31 Marianne Miller Anderson, *One Hundred Years of Excellence in Nursing Education* (Houston: Houston Baptist University, 2007), Vol. I, p. 18.

32 "A Report to the Christian Education Commission of the Baptist General Convention of Texas on a Financial Efficiency Analysis", William R. Carden, July 22, 1968.

33 McBeth, 377.

Tapscott, Education and Vice President for Academic Affairs (1969-1983).

Honors and recognition continued to distinguish the College faculty. Dr. Jules Ladner completed a new text in physical chemistry.[34] Dr. Calvin Huckabay became the first HBC faculty member to win the coveted Minnie Stevens Piper Foundation award for superior teaching among faculty in Texas colleges. Huckabay was internationally recognized for his definitive bibliography on John Milton.[35] Moreover, he was the guiding scholar behind the development of the College's Great Books Program for freshman English, the senior seminar model, and the Shakespeare study-abroad program at Stratford-upon-Avon.[36]

A new Preparatory Music Division was begun by Ralph Liese to offer applied lessons for children and non-college adult students.[37] Majors in social work[38] and medical technology were added to the curriculum in 1970;[39] Dorothy Allen succeeded Jefferson Caskey as College Librarian,[40] and the first sabbatical leaves were awarded to faculty members Dr. Robert Parker and R. Paul Green.[41] Under the leadership of Dr. Jerry Modisette, the physics major was reinstated as a result of increased enrollments.[42] Additionally, Modisette secured a NASA weather research grant in stellar ultraviolet spectroscopy for the physics program.[43] At the same time, Dr. Jerry Robinson received continuation of his grant for studies in mental health through the new College Research Council.[44] Academic support for nursing came from the Helene Fuld Health Trust for nursing's highly-mediated instructional program.[45] The Fuld Trust was to become

---

34 Alex Almeyda, "Ladner authors text," *The Collegian*, 2 Apr. 1973, p. 5.

35 Dr. Calvin Huckabay, *John Milton: An Annotated Bibliography, 1929-1968* (Pittsburgh: Duquesne University Press, 1969).

36 "Huckabay Piper Professor," *HBC News*, Mar. 1970, 1. Photo.

37 "Preparatory Music Division Announced," *HBC News*, Oct. 1968, 4.

38 Houston Baptist College, Minutes of the Meetings of the Academic Committee of the Board of Trustees, Meeting on 17 Dec. 1969.

39 "B. S. Degree in Medical Technology now offered," *The Collegian*, 8 Oct. 1970, p. 3; Minutes of the Meetings of the Faculty Academic Affairs Committee, Meeting on 26 Aug. 1970; Minutes of the Meetings of the Board of Trustees, Meeting on 25 Sept. 1970.

40 "Full-Time Faculty Numbers 72 for 1970-71," *HBC News*, Sept. 1970, 2.

41 Houston Baptist College, Minutes of the Meetings of the Academic Committee of the Board of Trustees, Meeting on 15 Oct. 1969; Minutes of the Meetings of the Board of Trustees, Meeting on 2 Mar. 1970.

42 Houston Baptist College, Minutes of the Meetings of the Academic Affairs Committee of the Faculty, Meeting on 14 May 1970.

43 Houston Baptist College, Minutes of the Meetings of the Executive Committee of the Board of Trustees, Meeting on 22 May 1970.

44 Houston Baptist College, Minutes of the Meetings of the Board of Trustees, Meeting on 23 May 1970.

45 "Nursing Program Receives NY Grant," *HBC News*, Sept. 1970, 1.

a major contributor to pedagogical innovation in the HBC nursing program.

The *Senior Seminar* served as the keystone of the HBU curriculum. In 1970, the University conducted opinion surveys of alumni and faculty regarding the senior seminar experience. The results yielded strong levels of support and remarkably parallel assessment. Alumni lauded the senior seminars for development of individual initiative, the development of skills for independent study, for relating the major to a larger macrocosm, and fostering the ability to synthesize. Suggestions for improvement included establishment of a permanent *Senior Seminar* committee and the requirement of both a research paper and a written exit exam in the major. *Senior Seminar* papers from this era were routinely placed in the Moody Library.[46] One of the finest early examples of these projects, an HBC history written by senior Elaine Lowry (McMullen), has served as a significant resource for this book.[47]

One of the most popular holiday traditions, the Renaissance Christmas Dinner for faculty, staff, and trustees, established a long run in 1969 with the initiation by Dr. Jim C. Smith of festive Madrigal Dinners featuring costumed singers, servers, and Elizabethan holiday fare.[48] In 1969-70, the first Student Foundation was established to select outstanding students to represent the College at major public events.[49] Among the College alumni, nine graduates were named to the *1971 Outstanding Young Men in America:* Bob Anderson, Charlie Bonds, Mark Fowler, John Gillespie, Milford Kuhn, Ken McNutt, Ronnie Moore, and Rodney Price.[50]

The first January term in 1970 enrolled 328 students and provided opportunity for enrichment courses and study-abroad programs. These study trips included *Culture and Human Experience* on-site in Europe, Dr. Glen Cain with students in Israel, Dr. Marion Webb with students in

46 Houston Baptist College, Minutes of the Meetings of the Academic Affairs of the Faculty, Meeting on 26 Aug. 1970.

47 Elaine Lowry, "The History of Houston Baptist College," (Senior Seminar Paper, Houston Baptist College, 1967), p. 7. On file in the Moody Library.

48 Beverly Harris, "Arnold Upstages Madrigal Stars," *Houston Chronicle,* 3 Dec. 1970, sec. 5, p. 5; *Ornogah 1975,* 159; "Madrigal Dinner," *HBC News,* Dec. 1969, 2; "Madrigal Dinners Feature Holiday Customs," *HBC News,* Nov. 1970, 1; "Madrigal Dinners Coming Again," *The Collegian,* 24 Nov. 1970, p. 1.

49 Houston Baptist College, Minutes of the Meetings of the Executive Committee of the Board of Trustees, Meeting on 12 Mar. 1970.

50 "Alumni Begin Making Waves," *HBC News,* Sept. 1971, 3.

Guatemala, and Dr. Don Byrnes with students in Philadelphia.[51]   In April, Dr. Calvin Huckabay took his study-abroad students to Stratford-Upon-Avon for Shakespeare's birthday.[52]   Dr. Byrnes's three-week European CORE trip in 1974 included April in Paris, Rome, Venice, Munich, Amsterdam, London, and Stratford and was priced at $876 inclusive.[53]   To expand the January term course options, Don Looser was appointed to work with the Southwestern Consortium for International Study that facilitated the participation of students from member colleges in the study-abroad programs of all other member colleges.[54]

In the fall 1969, Stewart Morris completed a nine-year appointment on the Board of Trustees including three years as Chairman.   In accord with Baptist General Convention of Texas policy, he rotated off the Board membership for a mandatory minimum of one year.   Gilbert Turner, the creator of the Endowed Academic Scholarship program, was elected Chairman.[55]   Turner's Endowed Academic Scholarship program gained quick success; by 1970, ten scholarships had been funded by individual donors.[56]   As a result of this program, the College endowment surpassed $1,000,000 in 1970 for the first time in history.[57]   In the spring, the Board voted to award the first honorary degrees in College history to Dr. Ross Dillon and to Rex G. Baker for their vision and service to the institution.[58]   Additionally, special resolutions of appreciation were approved to recognize Cecil Cook for his time and leadership in consummating a series of complex real estate leases[59] and Mrs. Ethel McDermott for her work in campus beautification.[60]

Mrs. McDermott was a charming, quiet lady and a member of Houston's cultural elite.   She was the near neighbor of Miss Ima Hogg on Lazy Lane.   Her quiet votes at Board of Trustee meetings were typically

---

51 Houston Baptist College, Minutes of the Meetings of the Academic Affairs Committee of the Faculty, Meeting on 12 Oct. 1969.

52 Lou Detwiler, "Students tour London's (sic) cities," *The Collegian*, 17 Apr. 1970, p. 4.

53 "CORE on the way to Europe," *The Collegian,* 25 Jan. 1974, p. 1.

54 Among the regional member institutions were Southern Methodist University, Texas Tech University, Austin College, Southwestern University, and Houston Baptist College.

55 Houston Baptist College, Minutes of the Meetings of the Board of Trustees, Meeting on 25 Nov. 1969.

56 Houston Baptist College, Minutes of the Meetings of the Executive Committee of the Board of Trustees, Meeting on 22 May 1970.

57 Ibid.

58 Houston Baptist College, Minutes of the Meetings of the Board of Trustees, Meeting on 2 Mar. 1970; "College Founders to Receive Honorary Degrees," *HBC News,* Apr. 1970, 1.   Photos.

59 Ibid.

60 Houston Baptist College, Minutes of the Meetings of the Executive Committee of the Board of Trustees, Meeting on 20 Oct. 1969.

accompanied by the statement, "If that is what you think we should do." Yet, her presence in meetings brought a noticeable but subtle order and structure. While discussion had never lacked decorum, interaction became more thoughtful and considerate. Members deferred to each other with greater alacrity. In her own way, Mrs. McDermott was a strong force within the Board and, along with Florence Weaver, pioneered the way for generations of women who followed her in service to the Board of Trustees.

The McDermott home was a regular site on the Spring Azalea Trail of the River Oaks Garden Club and was a frequent backdrop for HBC *Ornogah* Beauty Pageant photographs. As a trustee, Mrs. McDermott turned her attention to campus beautification. Her ongoing interest in campus enhancement encouraged her to provide funds to pave the McDermott Plaza between the Atwood Theology Building and Denham Hall. The large plaza replaced two temporary asphalt walks and mirrored the "cross" motif in the millwork of the Atwood façade.[61]

In 1970, the Morris Columns marked the eastern terminus of the Holcombe Mall. From the Mall, one could look East through the columns across the barren campus to the Beechnut apartments. One morning, without notice or fanfare, a black Cadillac pulled slowly to the curb outside the Atwood Building. Mrs. McDermott and her gardener quietly alighted in their gardening attire and moved to the rear of the Morris Columns where she proceeded to direct the planting of a long row of large ligustrum bushes taken, she explained, from her own gardens on the banks of Buffalo Bayou. This hedge created a backdrop for the stage and a visual terminus for the Holcombe Mall until construction of the Hinton Center nearly thirty years later.[62]

The contributions by Cecil Cook and Mrs. McDermott were indicative of the ongoing involvement of trustees in active personal service for the benefit of the College. In like kind, trustees Howard Lee, Sr. and Rex G. Baker, Sr. provided funds in 1970 to establish annual grants to recognize a male and female faculty member for teaching excellence.[63] In time, these outstanding teaching awards became known as the Opal Goolsby

---

61 "Construction underway on Plaza," *The Collegian*, 7 Apr. 1971, p. 2; Minutes of the Meetings of the Executive Committee of the Board of Trustees, Meeting on 12 Mar. 1970.

62 (Personal recollection, Dr. Don Looser).

63 Houston Baptist College, Minutes of the Meetings of the Academic Affairs Committee of the Faculty, Meeting on 11 Feb. 1971 and 13 Jan. 1972.

Opal Goolsby was the teacher's teacher and a legend, even in her own time.

Awards in recognition of the extraordinary student affection and admiration for this founding faculty member.

§

Over the next several years, the College continued its commitment to the examination of fresh concepts in organization and pedagogy. For the first time, a "New-Faculty Orientation" program was offered that paired new personnel with experienced faculty mentors.[64] The first credit-by-examination was offered to forty-two incoming freshmen in 1971 through the College Level Examination Program (CLEP);[65] the first thirty-nine students received financial aid through the Tuition Equalization Grant (TEG) program;[66] and, the Graduate Record Examination was dropped as a graduation requirement when consideration was given to other assessment exit exam options.[67] The GRE *did* provide empirical assessment data on the graduating seniors from the first five years that enabled comparison with graduates of other colleges.[68]

A 1970 survey by the American Council on Education revealed that the "statistically typical" HBC freshman was eighteen years old, was a "B" student in high school, and ranked in the top quarter of the graduating class. The student's home was within a fifty-mile radius of HBC and was headed by a father who attended college and a mother who did not. Students in the survey described their parents as deeply religious, interested in intellectual and cultural pursuits, politically aware, finan-

---

64 Houston Baptist College, Minutes of the Meetings of the Academic Affairs Committee of the Faculty, Meeting on 15 Oct. 1970.

65 Houston Baptist College, Minutes of the Meetings of the Academic Affairs Committee of the Faculty, Meeting on 1 Sept. 1971.

66 "State Tuition Grants Assist 39 Students," *HBC News,* Sept. 1971, 3.

67 "GRE Replaced By UP Tests," *The Collegian,* 18 Dec. 1972, p. 2.

68 Houston Baptist College, Minutes of the Meetings of the Academic Affairs Committee of the Faculty, Meeting on 8 Aug.1972.

cially comfortable, and deeply concerned for their children. Finally, the typical HBC freshman voted in student elections, was sometimes late to class, played a musical instrument, discussed the future with parents, attended religious services, tutored student friends, read poetry not required in a class, took vitamins, had visited an art gallery or museum in the last twelve months, and occasionally stayed up all night.[69]

In 1970, students voted a self-imposed $10 speaker's fee to improve the quality of Assembly programming.[70] In related action, the Board approved a recommendation to grant academic credit and limit the required attendance at Chapel and Assembly to four semesters.[71] With the additional fee revenue, the satisfaction with Assembly programs improved dramatically. In the fall, assembly programs featured CBS reporter Dan Rather for Dad's Day,[72] NBC News commentator Ellie Abel,[73] attorney F. Lee Bailey,[74] singer-advocate Anita Bryant,[75] White House Press Secretary Dr. George Christian for *Men's Day*,[76] Miss America Marilyn Van Derbur,[77] and music by the New Christy Minstrels.[78] Presenters over the next several months included best-selling author and sociologist Vance Packard,[79] jazz musician Stan Kenton,[80] White House Press Secretary Bill Moyers,[81] heart surgeon Dr. Michael DeBakey, decathlon runner Rafer Johnson,[82] NBC reporter Peter

---

69 "If I were a freshman," *The Collegian*, 28 Jan. 1971, p. 2.

70 Tom Kennedy, "Traditional chapel changes; main difference is speakers," *Houston Post*, 18 Nov. 1970, sec. A, p. 1.

71 "Revamp chapel-assembly," *The Collegian*, 26 Aug. 1970, p. 1.

72 Tom Kennedy, "SE Asian involvement won't end, Rather feels," *Houston Post*, 26 Mar. 1971, sec. A, p. 24; "Rather speaks on administration," *The Collegian*, 25 Mar. 1971, p. 3.

73 Tom Kennedy, "Society's ills reflected in colleges, Abel says," *Houston Post*, 13 Nov. 1970; "Prominent Speakers Featured Next Year," *HBC News*, Dec. 1970, 1; *Ornogah 1971*, 255.

74 Tom Kennedy, "Traditional chapel," *Houston Post*, 18 Nov. 1970, sec. A, p. 1.

75 "Calendar of Events," *HBC News*, Mar. 1970, 4; *Ornogah 1970*, 250, 252-3.

76 "What's Up Next," *The Collegian*, 15 Oct. 1970, p. 1.

77 "Four Baptist College co-eds named as Woman of Year," *Houston Post*, 6 May 1971, Southwest section, p. 2.

78 "New Christy Minstrels Due in Sharp Gym," *HBC News*, Oct. 1970, 4; *Ornogah 1971*, 255; "New Christy Minstrels coming," *The Collegian*, 24 Sept. 1970, p. 1.

79 Tom Kennedy, "Ads blamed for social decay; Packard talks to students," *Houston Post*, 12 Feb. 1971, sec. A, p. 4; "Packard emphasizes change," *The Collegian*, 11 Feb. 1971, p. 1.

80 "Stan Kenton to host clinic and concert," *The Collegian*, 7 Apr. 1971, p. 1; "Big Band Jazz Man Stan Kenton Performs," *HBC News*, Mar. 1971, 3.

81 "Senator Goldwater Will Speak," *HBC News*, June 1971, 3.

82 Ibid.

Hackes,[83] author Reid Buckley,[84] and coach Bud Wilkinson.[85] Over the next years, a number of well-known personalities visited the campus as a part of the Assembly program including entrepreneur Ross Perot for Dad's Day,[86] Senator Lloyd Bentsen,[87] NFL athlete Frank Gifford,[88] Houston mayor Louie Welch,[89] musician John Gary,[90] attorney Melvin Belli,[91] Senator Bob Packwood,[92] author Charlie Shedd,[93] and Houston Symphony Orchestra conductor Lawrence Foster.[94] The weekly schedule of one Assembly and one Chapel service continued. These speakers regularly garnered Section A coverage in the *Houston Post* and molded public awareness of the college's commitment to excellence in the academic environment.

A highlight of the fall term in 1970 was the first *Christianity and the Fine Arts* festival that was sponsored by the Christian Life on Campus (CLC). The festival featured a "student artistic expression competition" in art, music, and creative writing.[95] The speaker for the week was the brilliant scholar Dr. John Newport, author of the new book *Christianity and Contemporary Art Forms*.[96] In October, the combined HBC student organizations sponsored a symposium on student unrest on college campuses. "Man in Revolution" featured Dr. Richard Knudten, Chair of the Department of Sociology at Valparaiso University; "Revolution in Race" featured Dr. Robert Hayes, Texas Conference of the United Methodist Church. Some seventy-one area colleges were invited to participate.[97] A third symposium in December presented Dr. William Glasser in

83 "Correspondent Will Speak October 14," *The Collegian*, 30 Sept. 1971, p. 1. Peter Hackes spoke on the topic, "The Environmental Crisis."
84 "Senator Goldwater," *HBU News,* June 1971, 3; *Ornogah 1971*, 254.
85 Ibid.
86 "Perot says pressure can free POWs," *Houston Post*, 4 Dec. 1970, sec. A, p. 4; "Perot, Newsman, Author on HBC Lecture Series," *Houston Chronicle*, 21 Oct. 1970, Sharpstown sec., p. 5; "Ross Perot and 1500 Men," *The Collegian,* 24 Nov 1970, p. 1; "Perot Will Speak," *HBC News*, Nov. 1970, 3; "Perot urges return of POWs—now," *The Collegian*, 10 Dec. 1970, p. 1; *Ornogah 1971*, 255.
87 Houston Baptist College, 1972 May Commencement program.
88 "Commentator Frank Gifford To Speak at Nov. 2 Assembly," *The Collegian*, 19 Oct. 1972, p. 2; *Ornogah 1974*, 41.
89 "Top Names on Agenda as Speakers," *The Collegian*, 1 Sept. 1972, p. 1.
90 "Gary to headline Homecoming," *The Collegian*, 28 Jan. 1971, p. 1; *Ornogah 1971*, 242-3.
91 "Reflections of Trial Lawyer on Capital Punishment," *The Collegian*, 25 Feb. 1971, p. 1; *Ornogah 1971*, 257.
92 "Sen. Packwood speaks," *The Collegian*, 24 Sept. 1970, p. 4; *Ornogah 1971*, 254; "Graduation—a time for smiles and tears," *HBU News,* June 1975, 1.
93 "Shedd, Writer, Pastor Speaks for Chapel," *The Collegian*, 19 Oct. 1972, p. 2.
94 "Top Names," *The Collegian*, 1 Sept. 1972, p. 1.
95 "CLC sponsors fine arts festival," *The Collegian*, 24 Sept. 1970, p. 1.
96 John Newport, *Christianity and Contemporary Art Forms* (Waco: Word Books, 1971).
97 "HBC to host student unrest meet," *The Collegian,* 22 Oct. 1970, p. 1.

Assembly and in seminars for school personnel on the subject "Schools Without Failure."[98]

The Collegian continued to enjoy a high level of student writing. Jim Cornell won several competitive awards for his "Dateline" humor column. He was the first to announce "that CORE will be on a pass/fail basis in the future; either your pass it or you fail to graduate."[99] From a press conference, Cornell reported that Miss USA was "well rounded."[100] He further predicted that computerized classes would be offered "in the foreseeable future when the professor will come in and lecture to a room full of computers."[101] The University literary anthology *Shank's Mare* was a vehicle for outstanding student writing and art. In 1971, Editor Ken Flournoy announced that cash awards funded by Miss Jessie Millsaps would be initiated for best poetry, prose, and art work.[102] The College also held a first publications award banquet in 1971 with radio talk show host Alvin Van Black as guest speaker.[103] The *Shank's Mare* flourished over the next several years with editors Ada Burk in 1972 and Marijane Rountree in 1973.[104]

Dr. William Guthrie achieved a high level of performance with the College opera workshop program. Beginning in 1970, Guthrie mounted a production of *Gianni Schicchi* that toured area community colleges to provide performance opportunity for the HBC singers, to enhance the visibility of the College in the community, and to recruit students.[105] A 1971 production of *The Marriage of Figaro* garnered praise in reviews carried both by the *Houston Post* and the *Houston Chronicle*.[106] The most notable production of the period was American composer Robert Ward's Pulitzer Prize winning opera *The Crucible* based on Arthur Miller's book that chronicled the Salem Witch Trials. Ward traveled to Houston for the 1973 HBC production that starred Guthrie and Mary Frances Langford and was directed by Lynn Bracewell.[107] The following year, an all-student

---

98 "Dr. William Glasser conducts Seminar," *The Collegian,* 10 Dec. 1970, p. 1.

99 Jim Cornell, "Dateline," *The Collegian,* 7 Apr. 1971, p. 3.

100 "Adams and Cornell Get Well Rounded Education," *The Collegian,* 11 Mar. 1971, p. 4.

101 Jim Cornell, "Dateline," *The Collegian,* 11 Mar 1971, p. 4.

102 "Flournoy to edit Shank's Mare," *The Collegian,* 11 Mar. 1971, p. 1. The poetry award was given to future film and Broadway star Trey Wilson.

103 "Journalists awarded at Publications Banquet," *The Collegian,* 13 May 1971, p. 2.

104 "Shanks Mare Goes On Sale," *The Collegian,* 1 Sept. 1972, p. 5.

105 "Opera Tours," *HBC News,* Feb. 1970, 1. Campuses included Wharton, Blinn, San Jacinto, and Sam Houston.

106 Houston Baptist College, Minutes of the Meetings of the Board of Trustees, Meeting on 11 Feb. 1971.

107 "The Crucible Slated Feb. 18-22," *The Collegian,* 17 Feb. 1972, p. 1; "Composer to attend HBC Opera," *Houston Post,* 18 Feb. 1972; *Ornogah 1972,* 232. Photos.

cast presented Mozart's *Don Giovanni*,[108] and in 1974, the HBC Opera Players presented Benjamin Brittain's classic work, *Albert Herring*.[109]

In drama, the period 1968 to 1974 marked a golden age for theater at HBC. Drama coach Cecil Pickett reached new heights of achievement and recognition. Pickett was recruited from Bellaire High School to the HBU faculty by his good friend and colleague, Rex Fleming. Both Fleming and Pickett were in later years named to the National Forensics League Hall of Fame.[110] At Bellaire High School, Pickett had worked with an outstanding group of students that had included Patrick Swayze and Dennis Quaid. When Pickett came to HBC in 1968, many of his former students transferred from other colleges to complete their degrees and work with their former director.[111]

Among Pickett's productions were Moliere's *The Imaginary Invalid*,[112] Shakespeare's *Midsummer Night's Dream*,[113] *Twelfth Night*,[114] and *Carnival*[115] in the Denham Hall venue, and two elaborate musicals produced at the Houston Music Theater, *Cindy*[116] and Cole Porter's *Anything Goes*.[117] The Pickett style was known for the creative juxtaposition of elements—Keystone cops in Shakespearean plays, for example. For the Shakespeare production, the run had to be extended; more than 1,000 tickets were ultimately sold for the 125-seat Denham Hall venue.[118] Under the musical direction of Robert Linder, the production of *Anything Goes* at the Houston Music Theater featured a number of students who later achieved fame on Broadway, in movies, and on television.[119] The remarkable cast included Randy Quaid (*The Last Picture Show, Saturday Night Live*); Roxie Lucas (*Forbidden Broadway, Damn Yankees!*); Brent Mintz Spiner (Data in *Star Trek: The Next Generation, Sunday in the Park*

108 Mary Sit, "HBC presents opera 'Don Giovanni,'" *The Collegian*, 2 Apr. 1973, p. 1.

109 "Afraid of Opera? Try the HBU Opera Players," *The Collegian*, 26 Apr. 1974, p. 1. Photo.

110 National Forensics League, *Hall of Fame*, www.nflonline.org/AboutNFL/HallofFame (accessed Feb. 24, 2010).

111 "Gallery Theater Announces Season," *HBC News*, Oct. 1968, 1. Photo of Trey Wilson, Brent Mintz (Spiner), Steve Murry, Gene Reppond, and Evin Thayer.

112 "Moliere is last offering of Gallery Players," *The Collegian*, 31 Jan. 1969, p. 1; "Moliere Closes Players Season," *HBC News*, Mar. 1969, 4.

113 "Gallery Theater Announces Season," *HBC News*, Oct. 1968, 1.

114 "Calendar of Events," *HBC News*, Sept. 1969, 4.

115 "Carnival Dec. 2-11," *The Collegian*, 30 Nov. 1971, p. 3. Photo.

116 "'Cindy' Slated for Houston Music Theater," *HBC News*, Dec. 1968, 1. Photo.

117 "'Anything Goes' Feb. Music Theater Feature," *HBC News*, Feb. 1970, 2; *Ornogah 1970*, 238-239. Photo of Trey Wilson, Cindy Pickett, and Brent Mintz (Spiner).

118 "Editorials: Drama Department," *The Collegian*, 13 Nov. 1968, p. 3.

119 "Anything Goes," *HBC News*, Feb. 1970, 2; *Ornogah 1970*, 238-9. Photo.

with George); Trey Wilson (*Raising Arizona, Bull Durham*); and Cindy Pickett (*Ferris Bueuller's Day Off, The Guiding Light*).[120]

The College had no adequate campus theater facility for its outstanding drama program. In 1970, President Hinton engaged in conversation with Frank Sharp about the purchase of the Houston Music Theater by the College.[121] The Theater was a $3,500,000 domed theater in-the-round seating 2865 that had been built in 1966 by Bob Hope and a group of Hollywood luminaries. However, because of the Music Theater's high cost of operations, its configuration in the round, and its distance from the campus, Board Chair Gilbert Turner announced to the local press in August that the acquisition discussions had been curtailed.[122]

Pickett resigned in 1970 to accept appointment at the University of Houston. Most of his students who were nearing graduation remained at HBC and continued to perform in College productions.[123] Lynn Bracewell followed her long-time friend and colleague and joined the drama faculty in the fall of 1970. *The Gallery Theater* mounted a production of Moliere's *Tartuffe* directed by Dr. Jerry Talley[124] and a third musical production, *How to Succeed in Business Without Really Trying* at the Houston Music Theater in the fall 1970 under the direction of Bracewell.[125] Highlights of 1971 were *An Italian Straw Hat,*[126] *Carnival,* and *The Torchbearers* which starred both Pam Whitten and Steve Murry.[127]

§

In September 1970, baseball was discontinued as an intercollegiate sport.[128] A planned retail development was to cover much of the baseball

---

120 Houston Baptist College, Division of Fine Arts, *Anything Goes*, Houston Music Theater, 13 Feb. 1970, performance program.
121 Houston Baptist College, Minutes of the Meetings of the Executive Committee of the Board of Trustees, 9 July 1970.
122 Ann Holmes, "Dark Nights Ahead for Houston Music Theater," *Houston Chronicle,* 11 Aug. 1970.
123 Bruce Westbrook, "Former students salute star-maker—Cecil Pickett," *Houston Chronicle,* 6 June 1989, sec. D, pp. 1, 4.
124 "Gallery Players to raise curtain," *The Collegian,* 8 Oct. 1970, p. 6; "The Collegian focuses on Jerry Talley," *The Collegian,* 9 Dec. 1968, p. 3.
125 "Cast really trying to make music production a success," *The Collegian,* 12 Nov. 1970, p. 1. This production was under the musical direction of Robert Linder and starred Pam Whitten and Steve Murry.
126 Leigh Bishop, "*An Italian Straw Hat* to be staged," *The Collegian,* 30 Sept. 1972, p. 1.
127 Roy George, "Goodwin to direct Torch Bearers," *The* Collegian, 11 Mar. 1971, p. 5.
128 "No more baseball for HBC," *The Collegian,* 8 Oct. 1970, p. 7.

field, and baseball had proved to be an expensive sport to maintain. This action was taken upon the recommendation of the faculty Athletic Committee; however, it was announced after the beginning of the fall semester and met with strong student opposition.[129] The team had a previous year's record of two wins and twenty-two losses. A strongly-worded statement from the Student Senate decried the decision and protested that student athletes had been told as late as September 14 that the sport would be continued—in spite of the need to move the field. A new baseball coach, Bobby McKinley, had been named only in April.[130] Athletic Director Ed Billings announced that scholarships would be honored and that track would replace baseball in order to meet NCAA minimum requirements.[131] The construction of a new track adjacent to the dormitories was planned. In September 1971, the University announced plans to form an NCAA University-division United Athletic Conference with Hardin-Simmons University and Pan-American with basketball as a primary sport. HBU competed in the college division.[132] NCAA regulations required six teams to form a conference.[133] The United Athletic Conference never materialized, however.[134] The University would play as an independent until the formation of the Trans America Conference in 1978.

Basketball coach Gerald Myers resigned in March 1970 to accept a position at his Alma Mater, Texas Tech University. Lonnie Richards was appointed Head Coach of the Huskies[135] and enjoyed a first winning basketball season with a 15-11 record including a Delmar Stadium victory over nationally-ranked LSU New Orleans, 84-75.[136] A new American Basketball Association franchise purchased from San Diego, the Houston Rockets, set up practice and training headquarters in Sharp Gym and created a new lunchtime diversion for campus onlookers.[137] Elvin Hayes and Calvin Murphy were among the popular favorites on the new team.[138]

The 1970-71 golf team, described by *The Collegian* as "the unknown team from the unknown school playing without a coach in its first nation-

129 "Track to Replace Baseball," *HBC News,* Oct. 1970, 2.

130 "New Coach Raises Hopes," *HBC News,* Apr. 1970, 4. Photo.

131 "No more baseball for HBC," *The Collegian,* 8 Oct. 1970, p. 7.

132 "Huskies Join New Basketball Conference," *HBC News,* Sept. 1971, 4.

133 Ibid.

134 "3 Colleges To Compete for Titles," *Mansfield (Ohio) News-Journal,* 8 Nov. 1972, p. 28.

135 "Head Coach moves to Tech; Richards Replaces Meyers," *The Collegian,* 20 Mar. 1960, p. 4; *Ornogah 1971,* 198-99.

136 "Huskies blast nationally ranked LSU-NO," *The Collegian,* 11 Mar. 1971, p. 1.

137 "Rockets Use Gym," *HBC News,* Sept. 1971, 1.

138 "Rockets Sound in Sharp Gymnasium," *The Collegian,* 30 Sept. 1971, p. 4.

al tournament," placed 4th in the NCAA College Division Championships in California[139] and finished the next year ranked 5th in the nation.[140] In the 1971-72 season, the team "climaxed its year with five tournament victories and individual medalist honors."[141] The team was invited to the NCAA championships for the second year.[142] The University golf team participated in its third competition on the Old Course at St. Andrews, Scotland in 1973 and placed second in a field of 17 colleges in the International Collegiate Team Championship;[143] Robert Seligman finished second in the individual competition.[144]

§

Student conduct policy including hair and dress codes continued to be rigidly enforced. An early handbook for women at HBC, *Cues for Coeds*, detailed visiting hours in the dorms, sign-out requirements for women, prohibition of untucked shirts or blouses, and the requirement of shoes and socks daily and "hose-and-heels" or "coat-and-tie" for Sunday meals.[145] "Each student is expected to attend the church of his choice each Sunday."[146] Curfew in the Women's Residence was 9:30 p.m. for freshmen and 11 p.m. for upperclassmen during the week. There were no parallel curfew regulations for men. Until 1970, pantsuits were not allowed for women.[147] Alumnae from this period may remember that a revised policy was visually communicated by Dean of Women, Barbara Brightwell, who emerged from behind the stage at a weekly assembly in a pants suit.

No facial hair was permitted for men (including faculty),[148] and men's hair had to be trimmed above the ears and shirt collar.[149] Jeans were still prohibited, but by 1972, men's sideburns could be as long as the ear lobe, and hair could reach mid-ear on the side but above the shirt collar

---

139 "Golf Team Wins Fourth in NCAA," *The Collegian,* 16 Sept. 1971, p. 3.

140 "The 1972-73 Huskie Golf Team," *The Collegian,* 20 Nov. 1972, p. 4. Photo.

141 Houston Baptist College, *The President's Report 1971-72*, 3.

142 "Hinton, Golfers Earn Laurels During June," *HBC News,* June 1972, 3.

143 "Oral Roberts Wins Golf Championship," *Odessa (Texas) American,* 7 Apr. 1973, sec. B, p. 3.

144 "Golfers finish second in Scotland tournament," *The Collegian,* 16 Apr. 1973, p. 1. Photo.

145 Houston Baptist College, *Cues for Coeds: a handbook for women at HBC,* Association of Women Students, 1967.

146 *Cues,* p. 23.

147"New Pants code suits women," *The Collegian,* 20 Sept. 1970, p. 1.

148 Alex Almeyda, "Face it: to beard or not to beard?" *The Collegian,* 19 Feb. 1973, pp. 2, 4.

149 Houston Baptist College, Minutes of the Meetings of the Faculty, Meeting on 1 Sept. 1970.

in the back.[150] The *Collegian* observed that the College had abandoned its long-standing hair policy, only to replace it with an ear policy.[151] During registration, it was common to see male students in the campus restrooms trimming each other's hair in order to pass Student Affairs' inspection. The *Collegian* reported that Dean of Students Jim Massey "must own stock in the Sharpstown Barber Shop." In May 1972, the Associated Press reported that a member of the graduating class was not permitted to participate in commencement ceremonies because of hair length.[152] Dr. A. O. Collins recalled, "We had strict rules, and students were aware of them when they enrolled. In my CORE discussion group, a male student who was giving a report suddenly fainted. His wig fell off and his shoulder-length hair spread all over the floor. The class gasped in shock as he was revived."[153]

§

For many years, College trustees had worked to develop the land along the Southwest Freeway as income-producing property. In 1970, negotiations with Wayne Duddleston, a Houston-based property developer, yielded a creative, long-term lease of fifteen acres of property at the corner of Fondren Road and the Southwest Freeway.[154] The tract had been the site of the proposed senior citizen's development in 1962. The new fifty-two-year lease served as collateral for an immediate cash advance payment of $1,025,000 from Duddleston to the College. Because of its timeliness and its long-lasting income stream, Dr. Hinton later ranked the lease as second in importance only to the purchase of the original campus among the contributions of the College Property Committee. Duddleston completed a lease with the Woolco Division of the F. W. Woolworth Company to anchor the retail center. The College thus reserved the land for future use and, at the same time, received a cash payment to apply to its outstanding indebtedness.[155] Plans for Fondren I included the 103,000 square-foot Woolco department store

150 "Graduation Not Long-Hair Affair," *Big Spring (Texas) Herald*, 21 May 1972, sec. A, p. 4.

151 Alex Almeyda, "Face it: to beard or not to beard," *The Collegian*, 19 Feb. 1973, p. 2.

152 "Graduation," *Big Spring Herald*, p. 4.

153 A. O. Collins, "Founders' Day Address," *The Collegian*, 15 Feb. 1991, p. 10.

154 Houston Baptist College, Minutes of the Meetings of the Executive Committee of the Board of Trustees, Meeting on 12 Mar. 12 1970; Sibley, 68.

155 Sibley, 69.

and a 22,000 square-foot Weingarten's Food Store.[156] Completion of this lease was critical to the financial health of the College and marked the first large income-producing project to be built on College land. Chrysler Corporation also exercised an option to purchase a seven-acre tract of University property on the Southwest Freeway near Hillcroft Avenue.[157]

In early 1971, the College Property Committee made a monumental effort to attract the Memorial Hospital to the campus, based on a study that showed both phenomenal growth predictions and the potential of the trade-area surrounding the campus.[158] In addition, existing and proposed major thoroughfares and freeways portended excellent access to the hospital site. The city was moving out the Southwest Freeway; Fort Bend County was just beginning its period of extraordinary growth. The hospital seemed very interested; but each party had its own set of concerns. Marilyn Sibley reported,

> Negotiations were lengthy with the two sets of trustees attempting to look after the best interests of the institutions. . . . Although there were personal friendships between the individuals on the two boards and the feelings of denominational kinship still lingered, the negotiations were emphatically at arm's-length. Each set of trustees labeled the other as a "tough bunch."[159]

However, on June 11, 1971, the Memorial Baptist Hospital announced the purchase of a 38.5 acre tract of land on the southwest side of the campus and released plans to move from its downtown facility in 1973.[160] The hospital ultimately bought another 6.5 acres that brought its holdings to forty-five acres.[161] The sale to the hospital system was of particular significance to the College. First, construction of the hospital served to increase the value of College land along the Freeway. Moreover, Memorial Hospital was an appropriate neighbor—also dedicated to the mission of service held by both institutions. Second, the project returned nursing students to the campus for their upper-division work where they could be more successfully integrated into the total student population.

---

156 Houston Baptist College, Minutes of the Meetings of the Board of Trustees, Meeting on 25 Nov. 1969; "Development reduces debt," *HBC News*, Feb. 1970, 4.
157 Houston Baptist College, Minutes of the Meetings of the Board of Trustees Executive Committee, Meeting on 10 Apr. 1970.
158 Sibley, 70.
159 Sibley, 71.
160 "Medical Complex Will Benefit College," *HBC News*, June 1971, 1.
161 Sibley, 71.

Third, the monies received on the sale of land provided critically-needed income for the financial operation of the College.[162]

With some relief to the financial pressure in the offing from real estate sales and leases, Board Chairman Gilbert Turner began to establish models for more effective long-term financial support for the institution. The College finished the 1969-70 academic year with a cash balance of $68,000.[163] In 1971, Turner established a leadership task force composed of Earl C. Hankamer, Rex Baker, Sr., John Lynch, Director of Texas Eastern Transmission, J. Bruce Belin, Jr., and local public relations personality Fred Nahas to lead an Advancement Fund Campaign with a goal of $600,000.[164] The campaign was the first formal annual sustaining drive and utilized the leadership of many community leaders outside the traditional College family.[165] Succeeding sustaining campaigns yielded $615,000 in 1972 and $501,000 in 1973 and were headed by Rex Baker, Sr., Milton Cross, Dan Elkins, Orrien Smith, and R. E. McGee.[166] A full-color *Report of the President: Houston Baptist College 1971* was published that summarized College growth in library volumes and expenditures, number of full-time faculty, student enrollment, endowment growth, instructional expenditures, cumulative church gifts, and institutional student aid for the period 1963-1970.[167] The report detailed an endowment of over $1,000,000 and cumulative church giving near $1,500,000.[168]

In December, Dr. James E. Williamson retired as Registrar. "Dean Will," as he was affectionately known, occupied the unique distinction of service as founding trustee, Chair of the Department of Mathematics, Dean of Student Life, Registrar, and Professor Emeritus.[169] While an original trustee from 1960 to 1963, Williamson had been Dean of Students at the University of Houston. In his work as a founding trustee, he helped secure letters of transferability from neighboring universities before HBC was accredited. Dr. Williamson had provided an invaluable knowledge of Houston to the new administrative staff. He possessed a

---

162 Sibley, 72.

163 Houston Baptist College, Minutes of the Meetings of the Executive Committee, Meeting on 22 May 1970.

164 "Leaders Named to Advancement Program," *HBC News,* Nov. 1971, 1.

165 "Hinton Announces Fund Committee," *The Collegian,* 11 Nov. 1971, p. 3.

166 "Forward Fund Campaign Goal Set at 501K," *The Scene,* Vol. 1, #2, p. 1.

167 Houston Baptist College, Minutes of the Meetings of the Board of Trustees, Meeting on 21 May 1971.

168 Houston Baptist College, *Report of the President 1968-69.*

169 Houston Baptist College, Minutes of the Meetings of the Board of Trustees, Meeting on 19 May 1972.

rich body of university experience and offered a generous gift of self to students.[170]

The College received its formal report of reaffirmation of accreditation from the Southern Association of Colleges and Schools (SACS) in December 1971.[171] As a part of the self-study process, the Statement of Purpose was amended to include the offering of multiple degrees and the substitution of the words "denominationally-related" for "church-related."[172] The Board also approved a *Manual of Board Policy and Organization* that contained detailed information regarding contracts, fringe benefits, professional growth opportunities, and lines of responsibility.[173] This *Manual* was merged with the *Faculty Handbook* to provide a single, comprehensive document.[174] A follow-up response to the SACS reaffirmation report was drafted by the Steering Committee composed of Dr. Calvin Huckabay, Dr. Ed Tapscott, Dr. Joyce Fan, and Dr. James Massey. The HBC response detailed charter and by-Law revisions that provided a written protocol for removing a board member from office for cause.[175] The response also reaffirmed the efficacy of the existing divisional structure of the College and outlined an improved communication process between the administration, faculty, and staff. Additionally, in response to SACS institutional articulation concerns, the general education requirement of sixty-three semester hours was reduced to forty-nine hours to improve the ease of transfer and compare more competitively with the general education core at other colleges.[176] Finally, the response described the plan for the centralization of personnel records and certified the completion of the documentation of all faculty credentials.[177]

---

170 "Dean Will" and his wife Dona were long-time members of the Baptist Temple church in the Heights that was a strong college supporter through student recruiting, financial assistance, and the trusteeship of its pastor, Roy Ladd. Dona later served as President of the Women's Auxiliary

171 Houston Baptist College, Minutes of the Meetings of the Executive Committee of the Board of Trustees, 9 Dec. 1971.

172 Houston Baptist College, *1970 Self Study for the Southern Association of Colleges and Schools,* p. iv; Minutes of the Meetings of the Board of Trustees, Meeting on 21 Mar. 1970.

173 Houston Baptist College, Minutes of the Meetings of the Executive Committee, Meeting on 22 May 1970.

174 Houston Baptist College, Minutes of the Meetings of the Academic Committee of the Board of Trustees, Meeting on 11 Nov. 1970.

175 Houston Baptist College, Minutes of the Meetings of the Executive Committee of the Board of Trustees, Meeting on 11 Nov. 1971.

176 The SACS guidelines stipulated no more than 40% of degree requirements could be mandated in general education requirements.

177 Houston Baptist College, Minutes of the Meetings of the Academic Affairs Committee of the Faculty, Meeting on 13 Apr. 1972.

The SACS visiting committee report expressed concern for the ongoing financial health of the College. Despite heroic efforts by Finance Committee chairs Gilbert Turner and Curtis Hankamer to balance income with expenditures, annual deficits prevailed. Long-term trends included shortfalls in tuition income, sustaining funds, and auxiliary enterprises. Church gifts remained "significantly lower" than budget requirements.[178] Additionally, operational expenses were regularly over budget. In 1971, the University refinanced its short term debt with a $1.8 million loan from First City National Bank.[179] For 1971-72, the operating deficit was $290,000. The trustees ultimately passed an unveiled motion mandating that no administrator could "authorize overspending of line items without the prior approval of the Board."[180]

Analysis of the financial statements from this period reveals the concern not only to have been about overspending but also about continual shortfalls in tuition revenue, gifts, and auxiliary enterprise income. The budget projections for tuition, gifts, and auxiliary enterprises consistently overestimated actual income. Virtually unanimous affirmation of the outstanding performance by HBC students and faculty supported the conviction that funds were being invested wisely. Rather, inadequate income resulted in salary compression, heavy teaching loads, inadequate academic support, and thinly-staffed organizational infrastructure—especially in fund raising. The high achievement of the faculty and students was made even more remarkable in the light of limited financial support.

In 1971, the Sharpstown Bank became the object of action by the United States Securities and Exchange Commission that filed criminal and civil charges against Frank Sharp and a number of Texas state officials.[181] In the course of these events, the neighboring Strake Jesuit College Preparatory School, a Sharp beneficiary, was reported to have lost $6,000,000 in investments.[182] Those organizations associated with Sharp in any way became the objects of some degree of public scrutiny. HBC President Hinton served on the board of the Sharpstown State Bank, but was never the object of any personal legal action.[183] In a statement to the

---

178 Houston Baptist College, Minutes of the Meetings of the Board of Trustees, Meeting on 21 Nov. 1969.
179 Houston Baptist College, Minutes of the Meetings of the Executive Committee of the Board of Trustees, Meeting on 27 July 1971.
180 Ibid.
181 Robert Heard, "Mutscher Stands Alone As Big Target in Trial," *Del Rio (Texas) News-Herald,* 29 Feb. 1972, p. 4.
182 Mickey Herskowitz, *Sharpstown Revisited* (Austin: Eakin Press, 1994), 103.
183 "Dr. Hinton attends Senate proceedings," *The Collegian,* 1 Feb. 1971, p. 1.

faculty, Hinton affirmed that he "had bought and sold stock at a profit, but had done nothing illegal or improper."[184] Nonetheless, the experience caused the Board of Trustees to pass a resolution stating that henceforth "no employee of Houston Baptist College could serve on a Board of Directors in any public corporation or as a general partner of a limited partnership or as a private entrepreneur without prior approval of the Executive Committee" of the Board of Trustees.[185]

§

In the spring of 1971, the HBU nursing program received accreditation by the National League for Nursing —prior even to the graduation of the first class.[186] Subsequently, in July 1972, all thirty-eight of the first nursing graduates passed the licensure examination on the first attempt— an enviable achievement of one hundred percent—equaled only by one other college in the state. The goal of one hundred percent pass rate on the first sitting became the expectation for the new nursing program.

The College administration sought more flexibility in dealing with several majors that were not producing sufficient graduates to be financially viable. In 1972, the University administration recommended to the Board of Trustees that the faculty tenure system be replaced by a term-contract system. Tenure was virtually a universal practice in higher education and provided the protections of academic freedom.[187] There was understandable concern by the faculty about the loss of tenure. Dr. Don Byrnes, President of the Faculty Assembly, speaking for the Assembly, requested that the due process protocol under the tenure system be sustained. "The meeting of the Faculty Assembly was held without rancor, divisiveness, or anger. The consensus seems to be that despite some reservations on some of the changes proposed, they should work to the betterment of the institution that we all serve."[188] In the succeeding months, the trustees 1) approved the recommendation that the tenure system be replaced with a term-contract system; 2) changed to a quarter calendar to

184 Houston Baptist College, Minutes of the Meetings of the Faculty, Meeting on 3 Feb. 1971.

185 Houston Baptist College, Minutes of the Meetings of the Executive Committee of the Board of Trustees, Meeting on 26 Feb. 1971.

186 Houston Baptist College, Minutes of the Meetings of the Executive Committee of the Board of Trustees, Meeting on 23 Mar. 1971.

187 Houston Baptist College, Minutes of the Meetings of the Executive Committee of the Board of Trustees, Meeting on 9 Nov. 1972.

188 Houston Baptist College, Minutes of the Meetings of the Faculty Assembly, Meeting on 9 Nov. 1972.

correspond with the new year-round schedule for public schools in Texas; and 3) changed the institutional name from "College" to "University."[189] Several reasons supported a change in institutional name.[190] The SACS visiting committee had urged an alternate internal organization that could be more clearly perceived than was the divisional structure.[191] The change of name from "College" to "University" had been a matter of discussion among the trustees for several years. Chief among the concerns was the public perception about HBC's mission and confusion that HBC was perhaps a Bible college, a seminary, or a two-year institution.[192] Moreover, the trustees desired a more clearly-perceived name to distinguish the institution from proprietary colleges throughout the city. The College was already participating in the "University" division of intercollegiate athletics; and, finally, the change was sought to enhance fund-raising and student-recruitment potential.[193]

Responding for the Southern Association of Colleges and Schools, Dr. Gordon Sweet offered congratulations on the name change and reorganization and offered his assistance in any way that might be helpful.[194] In the Baptist General Convention of Texas, however, two members of the Program Coordinating Committee of the BGCT opposed the name change, delaying approval, and sending the matter to the Committee on Institutions.[195] Board Chairman Curtis Hankamer, an experienced denominational observer, wrote Dr. Woodson Armes of the Christian Education Commission. "There is a great deal of competition for the educational dollar in Houston. Fortunately, through diligent effort, we have not had to call on the Baptist [sic] Convention of Texas for financial assistance beyond our share of the Cooperative Program."[196] The impact of this latter statement underscored the self-reliance of the University Board of Trustees to provide its own financial support in contrast to repeated requests that had come from other Baptist colleges for additional BGCT funding.

In 1971, the College long-term planning committee—concerned with future institutional funding and church/state restrictions—had

---

189 Houston Baptist College, Minutes of the Meetings of the Board of Trustees, Meeting on 17 Nov. 1972.
190 "HBC Becomes HBU," *The Collegian,* 18 Dec. 1972, p. 4.
191 "Five Colleges to Emerge," *HBC News,* Dec. 1972, 1, 4.
192 "Status Report on Change of School Name," *The Scene,* Fall quarter, 1973, p. 3.
193 Houston Baptist College, Minutes of the Meetings of the Executive Committee of the Board of Trustees, Meeting on 9 Nov. 1972.
194 Houston Baptist College, Minutes of the Meetings of the Board of Trustees, Meeting on 23 Feb. 1973.
195 Houston Baptist College, Minutes of the Meetings of the Board of Trustees, Meeting on 18 May 1973.
196 Houston Baptist College, Minutes of the Meetings of the Board of Trustees, Meeting on 23 Feb. 1973.

recommended that the HBC Board "consider the advisability of all the implications associated with a change of denominational status."[197] At that time, to allay any BGCT anxiety over this recommendation, trustee Curtis Hankamer moved that the "the Board of Trustees reaffirm our position as a Baptist institution affiliated with the Baptist General Convention of Texas and our intention to remain so."[198]

Ultimately, in the fall of 1973, the Baptist General Convention of Texas approved the name change setting in motion a change to the institutional charter on file with the State of Texas.[199] The October 16, 1973, issue of the *Collegian* was the final edition to bear the subtitle, "The Student Voice of HBC." In an editorial on November 9, 1973, that shared its front page placement with the new University seal, the *Collegian* staff wrote,

> It is possible that somewhere another four-year liberal arts college can boast a comparable ten-year record of achievement. However, it is doubtful that one which was founded as a private, non-tax-supported school at a time when many colleges were shuttering their doors because of money problems, that opened with codes of conduct and dress when permissiveness was the order of the day, and that had its beginning at a time when campuses all over the country were being seized by student unrest, could have prospered, grown, and served as HBC has.[200]

§

The Long Range Planning Committee recommended a goal of 1600 full time equivalent students by 1981, a commitment to "quality plus career," a goal of thirty-five percent of undergraduates in residence, and a more balanced gender distribution.[201] The Long Range report affirmed the nature of the HBU curriculum that emphasized 1) academic breadth, 2) sound Biblical knowledge, 3) the American heritage, 4) opportunity to develop depth in selected fields, 5) opportunity to select general electives

---

197 Houston Baptist College, Minutes of the Meetings of the Executive Committee of the Board of Trustees, Meeting on 11 Nov. 1971.
198 Ibid.
199 Houston Baptist College, Minutes of the Meetings of the Academic Committee of the Board of Trustees, Meeting on 2 Aug. 1973.
200 "Houston Baptist University," *The Collegian,* 9 Nov. 1973, p. 1.
201 Houston Baptist College, Minutes of the Meetings of the Academic Committee of the Board of Trustees, Meeting on 15 Nov. 1971.

for intellectual curiosity, 6) the integration of subject matter and team teaching as an effective means of achieving outcomes, and 7) proficiency in written and oral communication.[202]

A major part of the academic reorganization was the replacement of divisions by the creation of colleges. The University established five academic units—in Fine Arts and Humanities, Business and Economics, Education and Behavioral Sciences, Science and Health Professions, and a College of General Studies that came to be named for Dr. H. B. Smith.[203] The commitment of Smith College was to provide a broadly-based liberal arts experience for all students regardless of major, to provide a safe-haven for freshmen and sophomores to explore potential majors without being pressed to make premature choices, to provide a range of support services offered by University personnel, and to ensure the development of effective skills in writing, oral communication, and computer competency. The first Dean of Smith College, Dr. Don Looser, established policy and assumed responsibility for the management and coordination of academic advising, testing and placement programs, academic counseling, student retention, and the commitment of the University to provide a liberal arts platform for all students.[204] Central to this mission was the administrative responsibility for the required interdisciplinary courses.

A Counseling and Guidance Center was established by Drs. Steve Donohue and Stephen Williams staffed by volunteer faculty members A. E. Kannwischer, Kirby Gull, and James Leavell.[205] The Center offered students assistance with vocational guidance, educational support, and personal adjustment.[206] A new Smith College program of peer-to-peer advising pioneered by Dr. Mike Robbins also enhanced the potential for student academic success,[207] and a new tutoring program established by Dr. Stephen Williams yielded student grade improvement of seventeen percent in its first term.[208] The first deans of the other academic units were Dr. Lonnie Nickles, College of Business and Economics; Dr. Ed Tapscott, College of Education and Behavioral Sciences; Dr. Calvin

---

202 Houston Baptist College, Minutes of the Meetings of the Academic Committee of the Board of Trustees, Meeting on 2 May 1972.

203 "Five Colleges to Emerge," *HBC News,* Dec. 1972, 1, 4.

204 Houston Baptist College, Minutes of the Meetings of the Board of Trustees, Meeting on 17 Oct. 1973; "Five deans to head new colleges," *The Collegian,* 12 Mar. 1973, pp. 5-6.

205 "Counseling and Guidance Center in Operation," *The Collegian,* 8 Oct. 1973, p. 1.

206 "Center Set Up to Help Students with Problems," *The Scene,* Vol. 1, #1, Fall 1973, p. 1.

207 "Student Counselors Needed," *The Collegian,* 14 May 1973, p. 1.

208 "Results of Tutoring Experiment Favorable," *The Collegian,* 20 Nov. 1972, p. 1.

Huckabay, College of Fine Arts and Humanities; and Dr. Glendola Nash, College of Science and Health Professions.[209]

Dr. H. B. Smith continued to be a powerful force for academic excellence. He continued to press for academic rigor;[210] he proposed an early admissions program for high school juniors who had completed virtually all high school requirements;[211] he pressed for a "major works" program built upon the framework that supported freshman English and sophomore *World Literature*. He repeatedly sought administrative support for an honors college. He refused to initiate remedial or developmental courses for students with inadequate high school preparation. He worked tirelessly for expansion of the study-abroad programs and for the development of enrichment courses during the January term.[212]

§

Many private higher educational institutions in the United States struggled under increasing financial pressures to survive in the 1970s. In Baptist ranks, both the University of Corpus Christi in 1971 and Atlanta Baptist College in 1972 ceased to exist as originally chartered.[213] A number of Texas Baptist colleges repeatedly requested supplementary funding from the Baptist General Convention of Texas to assist with their financial survival. Baylor Dental College in Dallas moved to independent status in 1971. In Houston, the Catholic Sacred Heart Dominican College closed in 1975. The Dominican nursing program was the only other private college nursing program in the city. The program had accumulated a debt of $235,000 that resulted in its efforts to merge with another local nursing program.[214] The Dominican program eventually moved to the University of St. Thomas where it was later terminated as a part of cost-cutting action. About the same time, the South Texas Junior College, the only private junior college in the state, determined it could no longer

209 "Five deans to head new colleges," *The Collegian,* 12 Mar. 1973, p. 5.

210 Houston Baptist College, Minutes of the Meetings of the Academic Affairs Committee of the Faculty, Meeting on 19 Sept. 1969.

211 Houston Baptist College, Minutes of the Meetings of the Academic Affairs Committee of the Faculty, Meeting on 15 Jan. 1972.

212 Houston Baptist College, Minutes of the Meetings of the Academic Affairs Committee of the Faculty, Meeting on 16 Nov. 1972.

213 Houston Baptist College, Minutes of the Meetings of the Executive Committee of the Board of Trustees, Meeting on 19 July 1971.

214 Houston Baptist College, Minutes of the Meetings of the Executive Committee of the Board of Trustees, Meeting on 13 May 1971.

financially continue and entertained discussion with several local colleges about merger. South Texas College ultimately became the downtown campus for the University of Houston system.[215]

Houston Baptist weathered the financial storm of the 1970s with the same determination as in its founding days of the 1960s. Tenacious resolve by the Board of Trustees to maintain financial responsibility for the institution deterred any appeals to the Baptist General Convention of Texas for additional funding. Bruce Belin, Jr. chaired the trustee Development Committee and elicited a high level of productivity from the administrative staff.[216] The Board adopted five fund-raising goals for itself—$200,000 for endowed scholarships; $60,000 for curtailed library resources; $150,000 for nursing scholarships; $50,000 for intercollegiate athletics; and a special campaign including bank solicitations[217] and foundation proposals.[218] Belin was followed as Chair by Curtis Hankamer who urged strong sales strategies in student recruitment and recommended holding development expenses to twenty-five percent of money raised.[219]

Board minutes confirm the years of dedication and assumption of financial responsibility by trustees both at the personal and corporate levels. The role of the College Property Committee stands as testimony to the personal commitment of its members to use their professional acumen for the accomplishment of a mission they viewed to be spiritually ordained. This trait of institutional self-reliance would reveal itself repeatedly in the history of the University in finance, in curriculum, in hierarchy, and in vision. This resolve would also be manifested in a trait of autonomy, particularly in responding to attempts to control its decision-making by external agencies.

On October 1, 1971, Dr. Ross Dillon completed his ongoing work with the College Property Committee. Dillon had officially retired as Vice President for Development in 1968. The Board of Trustees, acting on the recommendation of the Student Senate, yet again renamed the men's dorm to Ross E. Dillon Hall and the women's dorm to Mrs. Trevor

---

215 Houston Baptist University, Minutes of the Meetings of the Executive Committee of the Board of Trustees, Meeting on 13 Dec. 1973.
216 Houston Baptist College, Minutes of the Meetings of the Executive Committee of the Board of Trustees, Meeting on 10 Sept. 1970.
217 Houston Baptist College, Minutes of the Meetings of the Board of Trustees, Meeting on 2 Mar. 1970.
218 Houston Baptist College, Minutes of the Meetings of the Board of Trustees, Meeting on 25 Sept. 1970.
219 Houston Baptist College, Minutes of the Meetings of the Executive Committee of the Board of Trustees, Meeting on 13 May 1971.

Currie Hall.[220] On campus, Robert Newell was named the director of the Christian Life Council[221] that later changed its name to Christian Life on Campus to be indentified more clearly as an interactive agent rather than an administrative operation.[222]

In 1972, the Student Senate released results of a poll taken to attempt to determine some of the causes for decline in student retention. Reasons ascribed included the high cost of private education, hair and dress codes, too many required interdisciplinary and Christianity courses, Chapel attendance requirements, dorm regulations, and personal matters—marriage, job transfers, and family moves. In the same survey, students strongly praised small classes, close relationships with faculty members, the sense of community, and the Christian environment.[223]

A new Bachelor of Science degree was approved in1972 along with curricular revision that eliminated a foreign language requirement, but retained the requirement of either 1) two courses in *American History*, or 2) a combination of *The American Economic System* and *American and Texas Government*.[224] This curricular requirement had been a matter of great conviction for many trustees, particularly Rex Baker, Sr., since 1963. The integrative outcomes of interdisciplinary learning had proven themselves conclusively to the HBU faculty. As a result, in 1972 an integrated science course completely replaced traditional freshman level courses in biology, chemistry, and physics. The course *Natural Science* met the degree requirement for Smith College and provided the introductory freshman academic experience for the majors in the three sciences.[225]

Dr. Joyce Fan established her reputation early in College history for amassing a record of successful student placements into medical colleges. At that time, the double major in chemistry and biology was the most popular choice of pre-med students—providing them greater academic breadth than students from most other universities. In February 1972, Fan reported a one hundred percent admission acceptance rate for HBC

---

220 Houston Baptist College, Minutes of the Meetings of the Executive Committee of the Board of Trustees, Meeting on 14 Oct. 1971. These had first been named for dorm directors Dr. James Herring and Mrs. Alma Jordan.

221 "CLC has new director," *The Collegian*, 26 Aug. 1970, p. 3.

222 "New Name for CLC," *The Collegian*, 8 Oct. 1973, p. 1.

223 Jim Cornell, "HBC Dropout Students Surveyed by Senate," *The Collegian*, 23 Mar. 1972, p. 2.

224 "New Program Offers Choices," *The Collegian*, 1 Sept. 1972, p. 1.

225 Houston Baptist College, Minutes of the Meetings of the Academic Affairs Committee of the Faculty, Meeting on 30 Aug. 1972.

pre-med students.[226] All HBC student applicants had been admitted to Texas medical colleges, and four of the applicants had been admitted to all five Texas medical colleges.[227] Dr. Fan was a student favorite for her dedication to their success in chemistry. She seemed tireless in her ability to explain, excite, and energize her students. These attributes were recognized in 1972 with her selection by the Minnie Stevens Piper Foundation of San Antonio to receive one of the statewide awards for outstanding teaching.[228] Dr. Fan became the second recipient of this award following the selection of Dr. Calvin Huckabay two years earlier. Her stature among her peers was further affirmed by her selection to receive a sabbatical leave in the following year.[229]

Board Chair Gilbert Turner established a number of models to strengthen the academic quality of the College programs through stronger financial stability and resource. He began the Endowed Academic Scholarship program[230] and, in 1972, secured the first Endowed Chair for the College, the Hermann Brown Chair in Business—named for one of the founders of the Houston-based Brown and Root. The grant of $500,000 from the Brown Foundation established an endowment to underwrite the academic activity of outstanding faculty members.[231] Turner concluded three years as Chairman of the Board of Trustees in 1972.[232] The Board passed a resolution of appreciation for his outstanding service and affirmed his value to the financial health of the University by appointing him as Chair of the Finance Committee.[233]

§

May 19, 1972, marked the tenth anniversary of Dr. Hinton's election as President of the College. These ten years had been difficult and exhausting. However, despite operational tensions over the course of

---

226 Leigh Bishop, "Pre-Meds Build Tradition," *The Collegian,* 17 Feb. 1972, p. 1.

227 Ibid.

228 Houston Baptist College, Minutes of the Meetings of the Executive Committee of the Board of Trustees, Meeting on 9 Mar. 1972.

229 Houston Baptist College, Minutes of the Meetings of the Board of Trustees, Meeting on 25 Feb. 1972.

230 Houston Baptist College, Minutes of the Meetings of the Executive Committee of the Board of Trustees, Meeting on 19 May 1969.

231 Houston Baptist College, Minutes of the Meetings of the Executive Committee of the Board of Trustees, Meeting on 11 May 1972.

232 Houston Baptist College, Minutes of the Meetings of the Executive Committee of the Board of Trustees, Meeting on 10 Feb. 1972.

233 Houston Baptist College, Minutes of the Meetings of the Board of Trustees, Meeting on 19 May 1972.

institutional emergence, the trustees had high personal and professional regard for the President. Turner's concluding remarks as chair complimented the "ability, energy, and enthusiasm" of Dr. Hinton.[234]   A poignant handwritten letter from trustee Stewart Boyle was included with the September 1971 Board minutes:

> Gentlemen, our President has had some hard and trying years at the College, and I feel it is time that this Board says thank you to Dr. Hinton. (I propose) that a special committee . . . be appointed by the chairman this day to arrange a proper and fitting occasion to proclaim to the public our support, thanks, confidence, and love of this devoted man.[235]

Board minutes of the meeting record a spontaneous standing ovation in response to the reading of Boyle's letter. Milton Cross, Howard Lee, Sr. and Bill West joined Boyle in recommending that the fall President's Council Dinner featuring Senator Barry Goldwater be dedicated to Dr. Hinton in celebration of the accomplishments of the first ten years.[236]

§

The first sale of a portion of the Atwood property was consummated in July 1972. The history of development of this property, that included Miss Atwood's homestead, stretched back ten years. The thirteen-acre tract at the corner of Kirby and Richmond contained her home where she had lived since 1906 and some sixty-nine rent houses.[237] The property had been conveyed to the Baptist Foundation of Texas that had valued the property at $900,000. The College had borrowed $250,000 from the Foundation in 1963 to construct the Atwood Building with the understanding that when the property was sold, the capital amount would be repaid plus accrued interest.[238] The dream of Stewart Morris to work with Houston developer Gerald Hines on the creation of a "Houston Rockefeller Center" on the Atwood property had never developed, much

---

234 Ibid.

235 Houston Baptist College, Minutes of the Meetings of the Executive Committee of the Board of Trustees, Meeting on 24 Sept. 1971.

236 Houston Baptist College, Minutes of the Meetings of the Executive Committee of the Board of Trustees, Meeting on 11 Nov. 1971; "Goldwater, Dad of the Year," *The Collegian,* 28 Oct. 1971, p. 1.

237 Sibley, 62.

238 Ibid.

to Morris's great disappointment.[239]   Hines had developed eighty-two projects including fourteen along Richmond Avenue in the general vicinity of the Atwood property. Morris later confided his assessment that protracted legal negotiations had caused Hines to become disinterested.

By 1972, Board Chairman Gilbert Turner became concerned that the Atwood property could become unattractive for development as the city expanded in other directions. Moreover, the property showed a net loss of $61,000 from 1968 to 1970.[240] Stewart Morris offered the services of the College Property Committee to the Baptist Foundation of Texas. Using the Committee's strong networking capability, the members sought to sell the land in smaller parcels. UBA staff member, Ed Best, working with trustee Howard Lee, Sr. helped negotiate the Atwood sale of 116,622 square feet at $4.70 on July 13, 1972. These funds paid off the indebtedness on the Atwood Building nearly ten years after the original gift and also provided a surplus to be used in accordance with Miss Atwood's instructions for a second Atwood Building some years later. At the September meeting of the Board of Trustees, Howard Lee, Sr. reported Atwood sales of $1,300,000 for the College Property Committee.[241] Upon reflection of this significant sale, Stewart Morris estimated the value of property and funds managed by College Property Committee since its founding in 1958 to have been between $15,000,000 and $20,000,000.[242]

§

Since the 1960s, the forty independent colleges of Texas had proposed a statewide program of financial support for Texas students enrolled in independent colleges. The plan was based upon an existing capacity for an additional 15,000 students in the independent colleges. The colleges asserted that the cost to the state of Texas to enable a student to enroll at an independent college was less than that for that same student at a public institution—so long as surplus existed in the private sector. In April 1965, the Independent Colleges and Universities of Texas (ICUT) organization was incorporated. A concerted statewide effort was mounted to

---

239 Sibley, 62-64.
240 Sibley, 64.
241 Houston Baptist College, Minutes of the Meetings of the Board of Trustees, Meeting on 22 Sept. 1972.
242 Houston Baptist College, Minutes of the Meetings of the Board of Trustees, Meeting on 17 Nov. 1972.

inform legislators about proposed issues and to prepare for the introduction of a Senate bill in the 1972 legislative session to provide grants to students.[243] Dr. Hinton asked Dr. Looser to serve as the University's designate to the statewide program. Formal efforts began to document persons of influence in the state to support this project. Chief among these were members of the boards of trustees, development councils, alumni, parents, and students themselves. Among the denominational schools, influential clergy and lay persons were enlisted.[244]

The stakes for the independent colleges were high. An otherwise modest appropriation by public university standards would serve to provide an inordinate base of support for financial aid in the private sector. A kick-off luncheon for state legislators was held at the Houston Club on December 7, 1970, hosted by Earl Hankamer, and featured an address by Rice University Chancellor Carey Croneis.[245] Mayor Louie Welch, a proud 1940 alumnus of Abilene Christian College, added his support to the process.[246] The independent university presidents scheduled visits with Governor Preston Smith,[247] Lt. Governor Ben Barnes, and Speaker of the House Gus Mutscher.[248] Locally, State Senators Barbara Jordan and Hank Grover were provided detailed financial analysis of the proposal and became strong early supporters of the legislation.

Statewide, Dr. Robert Hunter from Abilene Christian College provided tireless leadership for this voluntary lobbying effort.[249] Formal support from the Houston Chamber of Commerce was sought since the city was the residence of five ICUT colleges—HBU, University of St. Thomas, Rice University, Sacred Heart Dominican College, and South Texas Junior College.[250] Busloads of students from the ICUT schools visited with legislators in Austin. Ultimately, Senate Bill 56 was decisively approved after vicious attacks both from anti-Mutscher forces as well as separation of church vs. state proponents.[251] The bill provided for grants

---

243 Houston Baptist College, Minutes of the Meetings of the Board of Trustees, Meeting on 20 Nov. 1970.

244 (Dr. Robert Hunter, Abilene Christian College to Dr. Don Looser, Aug. 3, 1970).

245 Dr. Carey Croneis, "Public Enrichment through Private Endowment," ICUT File, Academic Affairs, Houston Baptist University.

246 (ICUT letter from Houston Mayor Louis Welch (ACC'40) to Abilene Christian College alumni, undated).

247 (Texas Governor Preston Smith to Dr. W. H. Hinton, Aug. 5, 1970).

248 (Texas Speaker of the House Gus Mutscher to Dr. W. H. Hinton, July 21, 1970).

249 "Stevens Announces ICUT Coordinators," *Abilene Reporter News*, 16 Sept. 1970, sec. A, p. 12.

250 (Hugh Patterson, President, Houston Chamber of Commerce to Texas Senator Oscar Mauzy, Chair, and Senator W. E. Snelson, Vice Chair, and members of the Texas Senate Education Committee, Apr. 15, 1971).

251 Houston Baptist University, ICUT Files, Academic Affairs: *Houston Chronicle,* 14 May 1971, sec. 1, p. 14; *Dallas Morning News,* 12 May 1970, sec. A, p. 10.

of up to $600 annually to be awarded needy students at independent colleges in Texas. The Tuition Equalization Grants (TEG), as they were called, quickly became an important enabler for students who desired to attend an independent college and provided significant financial stability to the participating institutions.

Texas Attorney General John Hill questioned the eligibility of students attending HBU on the new TEG grants because of the University's employment restriction to professing Christians as stated in the Preamble to the By-Laws.[252] Though many Christian colleges had such employment restrictions, few had written documents that stipulated such policy. These TEG grants represented potential annual income of $200,000 to HBU at this time. Similar questions of HBU's employment policy and practice had arisen some years earlier with an inquiry from the Anti-Defamation League of B'nai B'rith.[253] Howard Lee, Sr. and the Legal Committee reviewed the Attorney General's opinion and proposed two changes in the Preamble wording that they believed preserved the intent of the founding fathers but clarified the employment issue raised by the Attorney General. Lee proposed to add to the statement, "all those who become associated with the Houston Baptist University as a trustee, officer, member of the faculty or staff" the words "and perform work connected with the educational activities of the University."[254] This addition would ease employment practice in positions not related to students, i.e. maintenance, grounds, or engineering. However, in the U. S. Supreme Court case of *Amos vs. Bishop* the legal right of a private educational institution to restrict employment on the basis of religion had been upheld.[255] In a second suggested rewording, the Preamble statement that "the ultimate teachings in this university shall always be consistent with the above principles" was rephrased to state "the ultimate teachings in this university shall never be inconsistent with the above principles."[256] The opinion and recommendation of the Legal Committee was that the revised statement would be more capable of being legally sustained if challenged. Change to the By-Laws required a unanimous vote of the Board of Trustees. These two recommendations were unanimously approved by

252 "College Hiring Practices Hit—No State Funds," *Galveston Daily News*, 11 Jan. 1974, sec. A, p. 2.
253 Houston Baptist College, Minutes of the Meetings of the Executive Committee of the Board of Trustees, Meeting on 8 Feb. 1973; Meeting of the Board of Trustees 23 Feb. 1973.
254 Houston Baptist College, Minutes of the Meeting of the Board of Trustees, Meeting on 22 Feb. 1974.
255 U.S. Supreme Court: Corp. of Presiding Bishop v. Amos, 483 U.S. 327 (1987).
256 Houston Baptist College, Minutes of the Meetings of the Board of Trustees, Meeting on 22 Feb. 1974.

the Board of Trustees. Coupled with the change in name from "College" to "University" in the Preamble, these changes constitute the only changes made in its history to date. The University's students have participated in the TEG program all the years since its inception.

§

The spring of 1973 marked a number of milestones for student life on campus. Folk-artist John Denver entertained for Homecoming—a winter event now associated with basketball season.[257] Other Assembly speakers during this period included Dr. Joyce Brothers,[258] author Rollo May,[259] Miss America, Vonda Van Dyke who used Dr. Jerry Ford as her ventriloquist "dummy,"[260] nuclear scientist Dr. George Schweitzer,[261] writer Norman Lear, comedian Pat Paulsen,[262] child psychologist Dr. Haim Ginott,[263] author George Plimpton, and NBA stars Bill Russell[264] and Bill Bradley.[265] The President's Council Dinner speakers from this period included Chet Huntley,[266] Bud Wilkinson,[267] Roger Staubach,[268] Phil Crane,[269] and Mark Hatfield.[270]

Greek organizations were active as evidenced by a regular *Collegian* column that detailed the activity of Epsilon Delta Pi, Kappa Alpha,[271] Sigma Phi Chi, Triceans, Alpha Tau Omega, Alpha Pi Kappa,[272] and the Coreons. In the spring of 1973, an announcement was made that an intercollegiate gymnastics program was being added to the University's

---

257 "Denver To Be Featured at Homecoming," *The Collegian*, 18 Dec. 1972, p. 1; *Ornogah 1973*, 33.

258 "Calendar of Events," *The Collegian*, 22 Mar. 1974, p. 2.

259 "Dr. Rollo May visits HBU," *The Collegian*, 13 Dec. 1971, p. 1.

260 "Peavy, Rogers win honor," *The Collegian*, 16 Apr. 1983, p. 5. Photos.

261 Houston Baptist College, Minutes of the Meetings of the Board of Trustees, Meeting on 23 Feb. 1973.

262 *Ornogah 1973*, 41.

263 Ibid.

264 *Ornogah 1973*, 40.

265 "Quarter Calendar," *The Scene*, Fall Quarter 1973, p. 12. Bradley was also a Rhodes Scholar and later U. S. Senator.

266 Houston Baptist College, Minutes of the Meetings of the Board of Trustees, Meeting on 17 Nov. 1972. President's Council Dinner at the Shamrock Hotel Emerald Room.

267 Houston Baptist College, Minutes of the Meetings of the Executive Committee of the Board of Trustees, Meeting on 13 Apr. 1972.

268 Houston Baptist College, Minutes of the Meetings of the Executive Committee of the Board of Trustees, Meeting on 8 Mar. 1973.

269 Houston Baptist College, Minutes of the Meetings of the Board of Trustees, Meeting on 16 Nov. 1973.

270 "Quarter Calendar," *The Scene*, Fall Quarter 1973, p. 12.

271 "Phi Kapps Petition Kappa Alpha," *The Collegian*, 3 Feb. 1972, p. 1.

272 "Alpha Pi Kappa begins fraternity involvement," *The Collegian*, 24 Sept. 1970, p. 2.

sports lineup,[273] and music Professor Robert Linder volunteered to coach a fledgling tennis team.[274] Linder recalled, "In the second year, we got balls, rackets, and uniforms, but no scholarships."[275] In 1974, former collegiate NCAA top-ten ranked Ben Weil began coaching the team.[276] Three University athletes were named as "Outstanding College Athletes of America:" E. C. Coleman, 6'8" NCAA All-District forward; Jim Skaggs, basketball guard; and Robert Seligman, golf.[277] Coleman also received the HBU President's Award in May and was drafted by the NBA Houston Rockets.

An addition to the Sharp Gymnasium, partially financed by a grant from the West Foundation, was constructed to house a new hybrid academic program called paramedical sports therapy.[278] Vernon Eschenfelder developed the program for students that desired to become athletic trainers.[279] In response to the NCAA requirement for additional sports, a new $150,000 Tartan surface track was under construction near Ross E. Dillon Hall.[280] Campus intramurals reached a high level of participation under the leadership of Dr. James Massey. A fine athlete himself, Massey ran the Boston Marathon in the spring of 1973[281] and again in 1976.[282] Intramural competition was a highly inclusive activity on the University campus that involved faculty, staff, organizations, and independent students in the program. Intramural activity has remained important throughout institutional history.[283]

A new gymnastics coach, two-time All American gymnast Dr. Robert "Hutch" Dvorak,[284] joined the University faculty in the fall of 1973.[285] His appointment marked the beginning of one of the most exciting periods of University history. Dvorak began his program with three transfer

---

273 "Gym to Expand," *The Collegian*, 2 Apr. 1973, p. 7.

274 "Netters lose," *The Collegian*, 2 Apr. 1973, p. 7. Bill and Joe Knight, Dick Law, and David Walker were among the first members of the tennis team under Linder.

275 "Linder Readies Rack-Pack," *The Collegian*, 8 Oct 1973, p. 3.

276 "Tennis Team Beginning to Make its Move," *The Scene*, Winter Quarter 1974, p. 5.

277 "HBC's Coleman, Skaggs, Seligman Selected Outstanding College Athletes of America," *HBC News*, Apr. 1973, 4.

278 "Gym to expand," *The Collegian*, 2 Apr. 1973, p. 7.

279 "Program for Trainers Offered for First Time," *The Scene*, Fall Quarter 1973, p. 5.

280 Alex Almeyda, "Track to be completed," *The Collegian*, 2 Apr. 1973, p. 7.

281 "Massey engages in aerobics," *The Collegian*, 2 April 1973, p. 6.

282 "Massey Responsible for Intramurals," *The Collegian*, 18 Jan.1978, p. 6.

283 *Ornogah 1974*, 128-9.

284 "Intercollegiate Gymnastics Next Major Sport," *The Scene*, Fall Quarter 1973, p. 6.

285 Houston Baptist College, Minutes of the Meetings of the Executive Committee of the Board of Trustees, Meeting on 8 Mar. 1973.

students—Bill Austin, Gary Linder, and Steve Turley—who formed the nucleus of the team that competed in tournaments from Tucson to Chicago.[286] The team competed in Division I of the NCAA. *No other collegiate gymnastics program existed in the State of Texas at that time.*

§

In the fall of 1973, the University marked its tenth anniversary of operation and moved smoothly to the new quarter calendar maintaining a semester-hour credit system. Three twelve-week quarters replaced two sixteen-week semesters and the three-week January term. The fall quarter concluded at Thanksgiving, and the winter quarter began immediately thereafter. Students typically enrolled for fewer hours each quarter, but had the potential for taking more hours in three terms over the nine-month academic year.[287] The calendar change was in response to the move of public schools in Texas to year-round operation based on four terms. New faculty appointments from this period included several who would come to contribute some of the University's strongest academic leadership: Dr. Brooke Tucker, History (1972-2004); Dr Joyce DeRidder, Sociology (1973-1984); Dr. Ernie Pyle, Mathematics, (1973-); Dr. James Taylor, Speech (1973-2005); Dr. Avin Brownlee, Biology (1973-); and Dr. Carter Franklin, Business (1974-2001).

The initiation of the quarter calendar was marked by the unveiling of a fresh newspaper publication designed particularly for alumni. *The Scene* presented Volume 1 #1 in September 1973 and committed to provide "more news about people, programs, and activities."[288] In fact, a recently discovered file of issues of this publication offer a more detailed record of "people, programs, and activities" from the several years of its publication than is represented in any other University publication. The surviving issues from 1973 to 1977 contain a wealth of news about alumni, faculty professional activity, campus happenings, and personal insights. The first issue celebrated the accomplishments of University alumni from the first ten years. These recognitions included PhDs James Bannerman, Bill Myers, and Milford Kuhn; MDs Linda Cecil Miller, Mike Armand, John Grauke, and James Barbee; and JDs Tom Cherry, Pat Ellis, Dick Martin,

286 "HBC Welcomes Gymnastics Team," *The Collegian,* 26 Oct. 1973, p. 7. Photo.
287 Mary Sit, "Administrator Answers Questions On New System," *The Collegian,* 18 Dec. 1972, p. 1.
288 "New Publication Launched With High Hopes, *The Scene,* Fall Quarter 1973, p. 1.

Clarence Williams, Rodney Price, Don Hendrix, and Larry Comer.[289] In November 1973, alumnus Don Anderson '68 was selected to receive the first W. H. Hinton Outstanding Alumnus Award that was accompanied by a gold Rolex watch.[290]

Fall 1973 also witnessed enrollment of the first early admission students. Based on a plan proposed by the University and approved by the school boards of participating districts, high school juniors who lacked only government credit could enroll at HBU in lieu of the senior year, take courses for credit, and receive their high school diploma at the end of their freshman year of college. A highly selected ten Houston ISD students pioneered the program that was broadened in 1974 into the Spring Branch, Cy-Fair, Aldine, and Brookshire districts. HISD students that year received an average of nine semester hours of credit on the College Level Examination Program and compiled a quality-point average of 3.21. By 1975, a total of twenty-three freshmen were enrolled at HBU on an early admission basis.[291]

In 1973, the Board approved the purchase of a townhouse on Fondren near the campus to house missionaries-in-residence on the campus. This action was taken in response to a request from benefactor Laura Sampson whose estate had been bequeathed to the University.[292] Since its founding, the University had hosted a missionary-in-residence program that provided housing and adjunct teaching opportunity for furloughing missionaries.[293] These colleagues had included Morris Wright, Britt Towery, Ben Welmaker,[294] Eddie Spann, and Tom Law, Jr. Sampson had been a member of the Ladies Auxiliary, was a frequent hostess for University social gatherings, and lived in a spectacular home that was a re-creation of Washington's Mount Vernon and stood on property adjacent to the Rosewood Hospital on Westheimer near Fondren.[295]

§

---

289 "Ten-Year Record Cause for Real Pride," *The Scene*, Fall Quarter 1973, pp. 1, 3.

290 "Anderson Named Outstanding Alumnus," *The Scene*, Winter Quarter 1973, p. 1.

291 "High school juniors to enter HBC in fall," *The Collegian*, 16 Apr. 1973, p. 4.

292 Houston Baptist College, Minutes of the Meetings of the Executive Committee of the Board of Trustees, Meeting on 12 July 1973.

293 Houston Baptist College, Minutes of the Meetings of the Executive Committee of the Board of Trustees, Meeting on 13 Sept. 1973.

294 "Welmaker Missionary in Residence," *HBU News*, Sept. 1974, 1; *Ornogah 1975*, 99.

295 Madeleine McDermott Hamm, "Mount Vernon on the Brazos," *Houston Chronicle*, 11 April 1993, Texas section, p. 6, two-star ed. Houston socialite Joann King Herring Davis, the great-niece of Mrs. Sampson, eventually acquired the house and moved it to a country site outside the city.

In January 1974, Houston hosted Super Bowl VIII pitting the Minnesota Vikings against the Miami Dolphins. Individual tickets were difficult to acquire. The Pinkerton Detective Agency contacted the University seeking men who could serve as security personnel during the game. Among the younger members of the University staff, there was a spontaneous response to the Pinkerton opportunity. As a result, the Pinkerton staff at Rice Stadium on January 13, 1974, included HBU's Ed Best, Buddy Boyd, Don Byrnes, Daton Dodson, Steve Donohue, Russell Jenkins, Bob Linder, Don Looser, Ken Rogers, Ed Tapscott, and Jim Taylor.[296] The day was cold and wet; the weather was miserable, and not all the HBU personnel were stationed in locations where the game could be seen. Virtually all the HBU personnel, however, reported the similar experience of being unrecognized in their Pinkerton uniforms and caps by personal acquaintances. Larry Csonka led the Dolphins to a 24 to 7 victory over the Vikings.

§

The spring of 1974 marked the retirement of a substantial number of personnel who had profoundly influenced the University's history in these first ten years. One of the most beloved, Christianity professor Dr. Arthur Travis, was feted in the last Assembly of the spring with the gift from students of a three-wheeled velocipede for his daily trips in retirement to the post office and grocery store in Clyde, Texas where he had built a duplicate of his Houston home.[297] To the delight of the students, Travis took a lap around the perimeter of the gym waving his goodbyes and expressing his thanks. Of Travis, Dr. Glen Cain wrote, "Few people have exerted as great an influence on the student body. He has averaged teaching more than 300 students annually for eleven years. He has been friend and counselor to student and faculty alike."[298]

Dr. A. O. Kannwischer, Chairman of the Department of Social Sciences, also announced his retirement.[299] As an ordained pastor, former chaplain, and a brilliant scholar, Kannwischer had built strong majors in sociology and psychology and, along with Travis, had served as an

---

296 Griffin Colvert, "Picture this: three University officials stood guard at Super Bowl VIII held in Houston 30 years ago," *The Collegian,* 29 Jan. 2004, p. 7.
297 "Dr Travis—Professor to deliver farewell address," *The Collegian,* 26 Apr. 1974, p. 1. Photo.
298 "Smith, Travis, and Kannwischer to Retire," *The Scene,* Summer Quarter 1974, p. 2.
299 "Dr. Kannwischer to retire," *The Collegian,* 17 May 1974. p. 1.

approachable mentor. Good friends, Travis and Kannwischer had cut each other's hair weekly since 1965.[300]

The egalitarian nature of these first ten years made title, rank, and status relatively transparent among colleagues. Staff members Sue Hart in Public Relations and Marie Wetzel in Academic Affairs also announced their retirement. Staff members in these days took on significant administrative responsibility and drew the undying affection and appreciation of students for their second-mile devotion to address student needs with skill and enthusiasm. Hart and Wetzel were two of the finest. Hart was named Staff Woman of the Year in 1973 and was an honorary sorority sister.[301]

The greatest moment of change in the history of the young University, however, came with the retirement of Dr. H. B. Smith. Administrative officers Smith, Womack, and Hinton represented the last of a generation characterized by a more authoritarian administrative style. Smith's unrelenting focus on long-term goals and institutional best-interest made him a powerful figure to address the needs of the new college. Smith was invariably consistent in his administrative decisions. Years after his retirement, those whom he mentored could determine with great accuracy how they knew he might analyze a given issue.

In his final meeting with the Board of Trustees, Smith received a standing ovation and was informed that the College of General Studies had been named the Herbert B. Smith College of General Studies. A dedication plaque mounted in the Brown Quadrangle reads:

> The Herbert B. Smith College of General Studies honors the University's first Vice President for Academic Affairs whose vision, education, and tireless service in behalf of the institution in its formative years created a legacy of exemplary achievement which serves to challenge all those who follow in his footsteps. Gratefully dedicated May 24, 1974.[302]

Smith was a man of great contrasts. His friends and colleagues included many of the most innovative pedagogical leaders of his time. He was active in professional matters at the national level. Yet, he could often be found working in his rose garden or picking blackberries on the

---

300 "Smith, Travis, and Kannwischer to Retire," *The Scene*, Summer Quarter 1974, p. 2.
301 "After 9 Years, Hart Hangs 'Em Up," *The Scene*, Summer Quarter, 1974, p. 8.
302 This plaque is mounted in the Bettis Academic Quadrangle of the Brown Academic Center.

Dr. W. H. Hinton and Dr. H. B. Smith, 1974.

eventual site of the Memorial Hospital.[303] His daily schedule was as regular as clockwork. His green Volkswagen Beetle appeared in the same spot each morning at 7:30 and remained until 6:00 each evening. Secretaries arriving at 8 a.m. found their office doors unlocked and their lights on as a daily greeting. Smith had lunch in the cafeteria each day at 12:30 p.m. and then reconnoitered the campus until 2:00 p.m. And each summer, on schedule, he packed his car to drive to the annual meeting of the Association of Southern Baptist Colleges and Universities then on to his home in Kentucky for four calendar weeks of vacation—all the while staying off the Interstate highways in order to enjoy the byways instead.

In 1974, Smith loaded his car in Houston for the last time and drove home to his native Kentucky. His record of contribution to Houston Baptist University over ten momentous years has not been surpassed.

---

303 H. B. Smith was a family man. He lost his wife, Virginia, to cancer during their years in Houston. On weekends, he could often be found watching University of Kentucky basketball games on television with the hope of seeing one of his blonde granddaughter-cheerleaders.

SIX

1974-1984

Academic Affairs

With the retirement of Dr. H. B. Smith, the University concluded a period reflective of one man's profound influence—still palpable more than forty years later. Smith represented the end of an age of classicism in higher education; his was the dream of a liberal arts college on the model of Denison, Davidson, Wheaton, Oberlin, Colorado, Florida Presbyterian, and Austin colleges. He was bolstered in that vision of excellence in Houston by a group of influential founding trustees including Rex Baker, Sr., John Baugh, Dr. William Denham, Stewart Morris, and Robert Ray.

The HBU degree was intentionally distinctive and maintained its fidelity to liberal arts foundations by the requirement of selected courses for all students regardless of major. The model was made distinctive by the interdisciplinary nature of the curriculum, the view of the faculty member as mentor, an emphasis on breadth as reflected in the double major, preparation for graduate study through the senior seminars, and by programs of academic rigor. At the same time, Smith recognized the coming of the global village by his visionary requirement of courses in world literature, communication skills, languages, technology, and creation of the interdisciplinary courses *Culture and Human Experience* and *Great Issues of the Twentieth Century.*

With the dawn of the space age, tension during the undergraduate years became more extreme between the historic role of the liberal arts in the development of the "whole person" and a pragmatic emphasis on career preparation. The University successfully walked a fine line in this struggle with the support of faculty members who reflected both broad cultural literacy and career preparation as a part of their academic allegiance. "Career-oriented liberal arts" became a phrase that had meaning on the campus. The existence of professional colleges in education, business, and nursing reflected the dual character of the HBU academic program. Yet, the

151

requirement of the liberal arts core for all students was uncompromised. As a result, in order to accommodate the general studies core and two majors, the University degree required 130 semester hours in comparison to the traditional undergraduate degree in most other colleges of 120 hours. The requirements of Smith College and its interdisciplinary courses, however, were not so malleable for transfer—a force that began to foster increasingly greater pressure for conformity. In the professional areas, degree completion in four years became virtually impossible.

H. B. Smith's commitment to a core of learning manifested itself in a restricted number of majors and program options. For success, this model relied heavily on a residential student population, a pervasive campus environment for personal growth, and an extended opportunity for faculty and student interaction. Increasingly, the HBU of the 1970s became more incongruent with this model. Residential students began to comprise a smaller portion of the University family. For many families, financial considerations mandated living at home and working extensive hours to pay for private college education. As a result, participation in co-curricular activities assumed a more strategic role in student retention. Student organizations including fraternities and sororities, intercollegiate athletics, and fine arts became inordinately important to the quality of the student experience and a sense of community.

The HBU history of the period 1974–1984 is best viewed thematically. The linear, chronological perspective of the first ten years of University history is more successfully replaced for the 1970's by a view of the functional areas of University activity. Nowhere was change more significant than in academic affairs. The appointment of Dr. Ed Tapscott as Vice President for Academic Affairs in 1974 represented a nod to the professions; Tapscott had served as Dean of the College of Education and Behavioral Sciences.[1] Over the coming years of the University's history, there would be extensive proliferation in fields of study, in alternative course selection, and the addition of career-preparation majors.

The HBU curriculum changed profoundly in both breadth and depth during the 1970s. Previously suspended majors in accounting, art, drama, French, political science, and psychology were reinstated in 1974.[2] Several new professional majors were added to existing degree programs including

---

1 "Hinton names several to higher Posts," *The Collegian,* 8 Apr. 1974, p. 1.

2 Houston Baptist University, Minutes of the Meetings of the Executive Committee of the Board of Trustees, Meeting on 14 Nov. 1974.

bilingual education, special education, and applied science. An interdisciplinary, mass-media major that combined elements of journalism, broadcasting, and reporting was jointly developed by the University's faculty and the city's media professionals who contended that traditional majors in journalism and television frequently lacked current practice.[3] While majors in finance and Spanish were reinstated in 1977,[4] majors in drama, physics, and paramedical sports therapy were suspended.[5] Physics was ultimately reinstated in 1980.[6] The discontinuance of selected majors was largely a financial decision made with little apparent consideration of the liberal arts curriculum as a body of requisite disciplines.

Student support services were thinly staffed. Following the counseling services offered by Drs. Steve Donohue, Stephen Williams, A. E. Kannwischer, Kirby Gull, and James Leavell and in response to a growing student need for testing and counseling, the University's first formal Counseling Center for academic, career, personal, and skill development needs was established in 1975 by Drs. Stephen Williams, Stephen Donohue, Ruth DeHart, Joyce DeRidder and Cheryl Simmons.[7] In 1977, Dr. Muriel Flake assumed responsibility for the leadership of the Center.[8] Born of her recognition that the University needed a visible entity to which students could come for assistance, she added this responsibility to her teaching and chairmanship duties.[9] For the next twenty years, faculty would provide the primary staffing for the counseling needs of students in addition to their teaching responsibilities.

A number of new professional degrees were established in the 1970s. The Bachelor of Music Education degree and the Bachelor of Church Music were approved.[10] A major in social work was established in 1974[11] and became accredited in 1977 by the Council on Social Work Education.[12] The HBU program provided the only accredited, under-

---

3 Houston Baptist University, Minutes of the Meetings of the Board of Trustees, Meeting on 2 May 1976.
4 Houston Baptist University, Minutes of the Meeting of the Board of Trustees, Meeting on 18 Nov. 1976.
5 Houston Baptist University, Minutes of the Meetings of the Executive Committee of the Board of Trustees, Meeting on 13 Dec. 1979.
6 Houston Baptist University, Minutes of the Meetings of the Executive Committee of the Board of Trustees, Meeting on 21 Feb. 1980.
7 "Help Received Through Counseling Center," The Scene, Winter Quarter 1975, p. 3.
8 "Counseling Center," The Collegian, 14 Feb. 1977, p. 6.
9 "University Counseling Center Aids Students," The Collegian, (undated) 1977, Vol. 17, #2, p. 3.
10 Houston Baptist University, Minutes of the Meetings of the Board of Trustees, Meeting on 21 Nov. 1975.
11 "Social Work is now a course offering at HBU," The Collegian, 14 Feb. 1975, p. 6.
12 Houston Baptist University, Minutes of the Meetings of the Academic Committee of the Board of Trustees, Meeting on 7 Feb. 1977.

graduate social work program in a 200-mile radius of Houston.[13] Students graduating from the accredited HBU program could enter directly into the second year of a Master of Social Work program at other universities.

The reputation of the University's pre-medical program resulted in early admission to medical college for a limited number of highly selected students at the end of the junior year of college. HBU developed a protocol whereby such outstanding students could receive their bachelor's degree upon completion of the first year of medical school. Endowed Academic Scholar Tom Wheeler moved in 1975 from this junior year at HBU into his first year at Baylor College of Medicine.[14] In 1997, he was named a Distinguished Alumnus of the University. In 2010, Wheeler was Chair of the Department of Pathology at Baylor College of Medicine.

In 1976, the new Bachelor of Science in Nursing program emerged from its historical relationship with Memorial Baptist Hospital.[15] An education building in the new Memorial complex on campus was planned to house the nursing program and other hospital training programs.[16] However, the Department of Health, Education, and Welfare required that the University, not the Hospital, make the formal grant application. Given the University's historical stance to deny direct federal subsidies, the University declined the Hospital's request.

Memorial Hospital found itself unable to provide funding to construct its education building. The hospital was reported to be considering the sale of 4.2016 acres of freeway frontage for $5 per square foot in order to pay for the educational building.[17] Another 3.38 acres of frontage was also considered "excess property" by Memorial and slated for eventual sale. The University offered to assume responsibility for housing the nursing program in order to avoid the sale by the hospital of any of the contiguous campus land. As a result, the facility needs of the College of Nursing were added to the Cullen Science Center design program.[18]

The decision of the Hospital to move to the HBU campus coupled with

13 "Social Work Receives Accreditation," *HBU News*, Mar. 1977, 2.

14 Baylor College of Medicine, "Dr. Thomas Wheeler receives George T. Caldwell Distinguished Service Award," www.bcm.edu/pathology/tsp.htm (accessed Feb. 25, 2010). In 2007, Dr. Wheeler was awarded the prestigious George T. Caldwell Distinguished Service Award by the Texas Society of Pathologists.

15 Houston Baptist University, Minutes of the Meetings of the Board of Trustees, Meeting on 26 Sept. 1976.

16 Houston Baptist University, Minutes of the Meetings of the Executive Committee of the Board of Trustees, Meeting on 12 Sept. 1974.

17 Houston Baptist University, Minutes of the Meetings of the Executive Committee of the Board of Trustees, Meeting on 12 Sept. 1974.

18 "Nurses To Move From Old to New," *The Collegian,* 15 Dec. 1976, p. 5; "South Wing of Science Center to Open Jan. 24," *HBU News,* Dec. 1976, 1.

its ultimate financial inability to provide instructional facilities for the nursing program created the unusual opportunity for a campus-based nursing program. A nursing program on a college campus, outside a clinical setting, was not an ordinary venue. However, the move was a two-edged sword. The University had a new flagship program of undisputed quality; at the same time, the 10:1 student faculty ratio mandated by the National League for Nursing made the program the University's most expensive major to maintain. Memorial agreed initially to provide scholarships by means of capitation grants to the University based on nursing enrollments. The hospital also continued to lend hospital equipment for nursing instruction and to remain the chief clinical site for HBU nursing students.

So successful did the University's baccalaureate nursing program become that graduates frequently were able to select from multiple employment offers. Moreover, for HBU graduates, these offers were increasingly for nursing supervision, research management, and physician's office assignment rather than for hospital patient care. Therefore, in a further effort to address direct patient care needs, Memorial Hospital proposed the establishment of an Associate Degree program in nursing that would lead to licensure as a Registered Nurse, but would postpone other bachelor degree requirements. Memorial agreed to provide initial financial support for the program that was approved by the University Board of Trustees and accredited by the Texas State Board of Nurse Examiners in November 1982.[19]

The integrative outcomes of interdisciplinary learning had proven themselves conclusively to the HBU faculty. The INDC courses and *Natural Science* were thoroughly ingrained in the University curriculum. In 1981, the University added the requirement of an applied computer course to provide students a functional ability in word processing, database management, and spreadsheet design.[20] Placed in the freshman year, *CISM 1321* provided skill development early in the academic preparation in an era when computer skills were virtually unknown to many incoming students.[21]

§

The most visible change in curriculum, however, was the development of programs of graduate study. In tribute to the quality of the

19 "Nursing Program Approved," *HBU News,* Jan. 1983, 2.
20 Houston Baptist University, Minutes of the Meetings of the Board of Trustees, Meeting on 19 Nov. 1981.
21 Ibid; Shirley Gore, "Development of HBU," *The Collegian,* 2 Sept. 1982, p. 1.

University faculty, pressure for graduate study began to mount. This was fostered by the urban location of the University. For reasons difficult to understand, graduate programs in the city of Houston in the 1970s were relatively non-proliferated. Opportunity was ripe for an expansion into graduate programs, and the University's reputation for strength encouraged the move. Niche areas of study emerged that were otherwise virtually unavailable in the Houston area.

Southwestern Baptist Theological Seminary in Fort Worth established a branch center in Houston in 1975 using the University's campus facilities.[22] Houston was the largest city in the nation at that time without a resident evangelical seminary. Seminary classes met once a week; seminary faculty flew to Houston on Mondays when there were no classes on the Ft. Worth campus.[23] The housing of this program on the HBU campus gave rise to consideration of University programs of graduate study, as well.

The consideration of graduate study, however, marked one of the most significant mileposts in University history. From its beginnings, the University had specifically stated its undergraduate purpose: "Houston Baptist University is a private, four-year institution of higher learning."[24] Since its inception, the University had officially stated that it had no plans for graduate study. However, late in his service as Vice President for Academic Affairs, H. B. Smith privately confided, "Because of the excellence of our faculty, one day the public demand for graduate study will beat a path to our door." HBU's strong faculty credentials supported consideration of graduate study. At issue was the very nature of the institution.

The University Board of Trustees shared the faculty's assessment of a high level of interest within the city—initially for a Master of Business Administration program designed for working professionals. There were related considerations. Library resources would have to be significantly expanded. Approval by the Southern Association of Colleges and Schools would be required to move from undergraduate to master's level degree status. Most significant, however, was the firm resolve of the Board of Trustees that graduate programs be financially self-sufficient. Supporting the move was a window of opportunity within the higher education community in the city at that time. Only the University of Houston and

---

22 Houston Baptist University, Minutes of the Meetings of the Executive Committee of the Board of Trustees, Meeting on 8 May 1975.
23 "SET Prepares to Start Third Year in Fall," *HBU News,* June 1977, 1.
24 Houston Baptist University, *Bulletin of Information 1975-76,* 10.

Texas Southern University offered traditional MBA programs to the Houston business community.

The University's first graduate study was ultimately initiated in September 1977.[25] The University model, created by Dr. Eugene McNeill, Dean of the College of Business, and Dr. Carter Franklin, Director of the MBA program, was designed around cohorts of students that would remain integrated learning units throughout the twenty-four months of the program.[26] Instruction capitalized on peer experience within the cohort; students learned from each other. The innovative design offered a degree in twenty-two weekends and two intensive weeks of work annually.[27] Response to the highly-personalized model was immediate and dynamic. The first MBA class in September 1977 was comprised of thirty-three graduate students.[28] In response to the time and energies of the corporate executives enrolled in the program, an MBA help-desk was created to manage registration, textbooks, and advising for the students. Weekend classes enjoyed food service and offered peer networking opportunity. Breakout sessions enhanced more formal learning processes. The MBA was marketed with a comprehensive fee for the entire degree and profited from employer tuition reimbursement from the outset.

Approval from the Southern Association of Colleges and Schools for Level III status authorizing Master's level programming was granted in December 1979 along with an encouraging letter of support from SACS Executive Director Dr. Gordon Sweet.[29] It was determined that a legal change in the University charter was not required for graduate study— only a redefinition of University purpose. However, the Baptist General Convention of Texas expressed concern over this expansion of role into graduate study and ultimately decided not to provide financial support for graduate study at HBU as it did at Baylor and Hardin-Simmons universities.[30] The BGCT action was based to some degree upon the recommendations of the *Carden Report* that questioned the efficacy of

25 Houston Baptist University, Minutes of the Meetings of the Executive Committee of the Board of Trustees, Meeting on 1 Sept. 1977.

26 "New Weekend MBA Program Initiated," *The Collegian,* 13 May 1977, p. 1.

27 "First Graduate Program to Begin," *HBU News,* May 1977, 1.

28 Houston Baptist University, Minutes of the Meetings of the Executive Committee of the Board of Trustees, Meeting on 15 Sept. 1977.

29 Houston Baptist University, Minutes of the Meetings of the Executive Committee of the Board of Trustees, Meeting on 13 Dec. 1979.

30 Houston Baptist University, Minutes of the Meetings of the Executive Committee of the Board of Trustees, Meeting on 21 Apr. 1977.

proliferated graduate programs among Texas Baptist institutions. Dr. Woodson Armes wrote for the Christian Education Coordinating Board (CECB) and expressed concern "that HBU had not waited for a study committee to be appointed by CECB."[31]

In demonstration of its independent character once again, the University did not hesitate to move forward with other graduate programs. The University trustees approved the Master of Education (MEd) degree beginning in 1979[32] and the Master of Science degree (MSM) in Management and in Accounting beginning in 1980.[33] By 1981, the demand was so great for the MBA that a second program was opened for persons at earlier stages of career development. Headed by Dr. James Callicoat, the Master of Science in Management program was more traditional in curriculum, less dependent on the professional experience of the student, and more inclusive of leadership skill development.[34]

In 1977, the March of Dimes Foundation approached Dr. Glendola Nash, Dean of the College of Nursing, and sought to establish a national research program in perinatal nursing at the graduate level.[35] Since the licensure record of HBU nursing students was so outstanding, the Foundation had selected HBU as the academic unit for the research program. Houston's Jefferson Davis Hospital was selected as the clinical site because of the hospital's history of managing some 10,000 births annually. The Foundation offered to underwrite the program for five years.[36] Therefore, a Master of Science in Nursing degree (MSN) was established in December 1977 with a specialization in perinatal nursing.

The selection of HBU's College of Nursing was a signal honor and bore testimony to the reputation of the program in the medical community. *Perinatal programs existed at only six other colleges of nursing in the United States.*[37] The perinatal program focused on developing medical training for nurses in the care of mothers and infants born anytime after the fourth month following conception.[38] After five years of successful operation

---

31 Houston Baptist University, Minutes of the Meetings of the Board of Trustees, Meeting on 18 Nov. 1976.
32 "HBU to offer Master of Education Degree in June," *HBU News,* May 1979, 1.
33 Houston Baptist University, Minutes of the Meeting of the Board of Trustees, Meeting on 2 May 1976.
34 Houston Baptist University, Minutes of the Meetings of the Board of Trustees, Meeting on 24 Sept. 1981.
35 Houston Baptist University, Minutes of the Meetings of the Board of Trustees, Meeting on 28 Nov. 1977.
36 Houston Baptist University, Minutes of the Meetings of the Executive Committee of the Board of Trustees, Meeting on 19 July 1979.
37 "Founders' Day Presentation Lauds 'Creation' of HBU," *HBU News,* Dec. 1978, 5. Rare photo of Kline McGee, Rex Baker, Sr., and Gus Glasscock.
38 The miniaturization of medical equipment and tools were an outgrowth of this program.

and exceptional achievement, the program was greeted by new policy from the National League for Nursing requiring doctoral faculty for master's level instruction.[39] Doctoral-level nursing faculty was exceptionally difficult to find and attract. Reluctantly, the Foundation and the University sought a partner institution that could continue the work initiated in the pioneering HBU program.

In the summer of 1979, the first fifty-four students enrolled in Master of Education classes;[40] 110 graduate students were enrolled in the MBA program. The first twenty-nine graduates received their MBA degrees in September.[41] Other Texas Baptist colleges quickly saw the opportunity for graduate study in their geographical areas and appealed to HBU for joint-degree assistance while they secured SACS approval for their own graduate programs. By 1980, HBU offered MEd classes for East Texas Baptist College, the University of Mary Hardin Baylor, Howard Payne University, and Wayland Baptist College.[42] By 1981, the University's College of Business also offered the Master of Science in Management program at Bergstrom Air Force Base in Austin and Reese Air Force Base in Lubbock.[43]

Niche marketing emerged as a powerful strategy for the development of graduate programs. By Board policy, these programs were to be sustained only so long as they remained profit centers; graduate study was never to become a financial liability for the undergraduate program. In reality, graduate education quickly became a significant profit center for the University. The University's MBA program fulfilled all expectations for academic and financial success. Ultimately, the program would emerge as an Executive Master of Business Administration program (EMBA) for seasoned professionals offered in addition to the traditional MBA program for less career-experienced applicants.

The University's master plan of growth for undergraduate and graduate enrollments was on target. A 1971 study had projected a 1981 enrollment of 2600 including 600 graduate students. Actual 1981 fall-enrollment was 2643 that included 400 graduate students.[44]

---

39 Houston Baptist University, Minutes of the Meetings of the Academic Committee of the Board of Trustees, Meeting on 6 Feb. 1981, and the Executive Committee of the Board of Trustees, Meeting on 9 Feb. 1981.
40 "First MBA Class Graduates," The Collegian, Sept. 1979 (undated), Vol. 20, #1, p. 1.
41 Ibid.
42 Houston Baptist University, Minutes of the Meetings of the Executive Committee of the Board of Trustees, Meeting on 17 Jan. 1980; "Education Innovation Expanding," HBU News, Sept. 1980, 1.
43 Houston Baptist University, Minutes of the Meetings of the Board of Trustees, Meeting on 26 May 1981.
44 Houston Baptist University, Minutes of the Meetings of the Board of Trustees, Meeting on 24 Sept. 1981.

In 1980, the annual cycle of self-study for reaffirmation of accreditation by the Southern Association of Colleges and Schools was completed. A visiting committee spent time on the campus the following January. Written recommendations from the committee formed the action plan for the next five-year cycle. These included 1) an improved personnel evaluation process; 2) the need for an income stability plan; 3) the continuing need for better campus communication; 4) a word of caution about borrowing above current income; and 5) an encouragement to keep tuition dependence at or below the current level of fifty percent. The committee also called for increased library funding, the realization of a fine arts building, and labeling intercollegiate athletic expenses as such rather than as "instruction."

§

Houston was becoming an international community in the 1970s. It had expanded beyond its Anglo roots with an influx of population from Mexico, South and Central America, the Middle East, India, and Asia. Local schools became more populated by students speaking multiple non-English first languages. In 1968, through the Bilingual Education Act, the federal government began to make available large scholarship programs for students engaged in bilingual education programs that were conceived at the time to be enrichment programs. HBU professor Dr. Sally Wilton recognized the changing demographics of the Houston community and established a new program in bilingual education in 1976. HBU was awarded a first Title VII grant for tuition scholarships in 1981.

Some fifteen graduate students initiated the bilingual education track of the Master of Education degree. At the same time, twenty-five student scholarships were made available for undergraduates in English as a Second Language.[45] The impact of this program and its supporting grant on the growth of graduate study at HBU was profound. HBU quickly became a major source for bilingual teachers in an employment market that was expanding faster than supply could accommodate. The federal scholarship program mitigated against the potential obstacle of private college tuition for many students, much in the way that corporate tuition reimbursement for the MBA eliminated that recruiting disadvantage for higher-cost private universities. In the period 1981 to 2007, over

---

45 "HBU Receives Forty Bilingual Scholarships," *HBU News,* Sept. 1981, 9.

$3,500,000 was awarded to students through the Title VII program.[46]

The expansion of graduate study at HBU during this period culminated with the establishment of the Master of Accountancy degree (MAcct) designed to prepare those already holding an undergraduate accounting major for the Certified Public Accountant examinations.[47] A Master of Arts in Psychology degree (MAP) was approved in 1982 that offered tracks for certification as a clinical psychologist as well as for a school counselor.[48]

The University's master plan of strategic initiatives recommended that graduate education never become more than twenty-five percent of the credit-hour production of the University in order to preserve the undergraduate character of the institution. Graduate program growth was testimony to the urban demand for graduate study and to the attractiveness of HBU's programs among Houston's universities. By 1984, real-time graduate courses for credit in the Master of Education and the Master of Psychology programs were being telecast utilizing the resources of the Texas Region IV Educational Service Center network.

The University also began to provide non-credit programs of professional development for the corporate community. Royce Bach served as the first Director of Continuing Education in 1974 and began to offer evening classes and professional seminars.[49] In 1981, the Office of Continuing Education became the Division of Professional Development under the leadership of Dr. Joan DeRooy. Short-term refresher programs, certification renewal programs, and topical seminars were offered both on and off the campus. Response was particularly strong for certification renewal programs in real estate, insurance, and accounting, some with opportunity for American Management Association certification.[50]

With the proliferation of graduate and undergraduate programs, the academic reputation of the University became more widely recognized in the community. Empirical evidence of student performance and words of affirmation undergirded the image of the University as a place of academic excellence. Elmer Bertelsen, Education Editor of the *Houston Chronicle*, detailed evidence of the University's strength in a 1979 article,

46 (Dr. Lilita Olano to Dr. Don Looser, Jan. 15, 2010).

47 Houston Baptist University, *Bulletin of Information 1984-1985*, 51.

48 Houston Baptist University, Minutes of the Meetings of the Academic Committee of the Board of Trustees, Meeting on 10 Feb. 1982.

49 "Bach to Head Continuing Education," *The Scene*, Fall Quarter 1974, p. 1.

50 "Continuing Education Changes Name," *HBU News*, Sept. 1981, 6.

"Houston Baptist does not share in pessimism of private schools."[51] Bertelsen credited the University's record of excellence to several factors: 1) its location centered in the "robust economic growth" of Houston; 2) assets of $35,000,000 with an endowment of $15,000,000; 3) career-oriented programs; 4) insistence on high academic standards; and 5) the Endowed Academic Scholarship program that enabled competition for the finest of students.[52] The article quoted founding trustee, Rex Baker, Sr., who gave credit to the citizens of Houston who had given of their resources to found the new institution. "I walked up and down Main Street calling on friends for help," Baker recalled. "Others visited every industry on the Ship Channel. Most people contributed; so it is a community success. It is exactly what the founders envisioned—a quality institution with Christian foundations."[53]

In 1975, the State Board of Nurse Examiners reported that HBU was the only baccalaureate degree program in Texas to exceed both the state and national test score averages.[54] In 1978, all of the University's nursing graduates passed the Texas licensure examination on the first attempt,[55] and once again, HBU was the only Texas university whose students exceeded both the state and national averages. By 1982, each of the graduating classes had achieved the hundred-percent pass rate. News circulated in the medical community about the quality of the HBU nursing graduate. HBU's program provided significantly more hours of clinical training than most other nursing programs in the state. For this reason, HBU nurses had the reputation of being mature professionals from their date of initial employment. Dr. Glendola Nash, Dean of Nursing, had guided the transition from diploma to baccalaureate program and from the hospital to the campus location with success and élan.

Another of HBU's highly-visible programs at this time was its premedical program. Chemistry Department Chair, Dr. Joyce Fan, coordinated the work of the faculty in this program and supervised the student recommendation process to the nation's medical colleges.[56] Most premed students selected the biology/chemistry double major combination

51 Elmer Bertelsen, "Houston Baptist does not share in pessimism of private schools," *Houston Chronicle,* 22 June 1979, sec. 2, p. 2.
52 Ibid.
53 Ibid.
54 "Clip-Art for Bulletins Makes Hit," *HBU News,* Sept. 1975, 3.
55 Houston Baptist University, Minutes of the Meetings of the Executive Committee of the Board of Trustees, Meeting on 20 Apr. 1978.
56 "Future doctors accepted to medical schools," *HBU News,* Apr. 1975, 4.

as their fields of study. HBU pre-med alumni felt the double major was particularly strategic in giving them a competitive edge over applicants from other colleges. HBU enjoyed a high level of acceptances into medical schools from the inception of the program. In 1976, twenty-four HBU students were admitted to medical and dental schools.[57] By 1980, the cumulative number of HBU students who had secured medical school admission was 181.[58] Fan summarized her philosophy of individual attention and confidence-building in a *Southern Baptist Educator* article in 1978. She credited the University's acceptance rate of eighty percent as the end-product of instilling hope, faith, and love in her students.[59] Fan was the subject of a *Houston Chronicle* article entitled "Fan's Miracle Factory." *Chronicle* writer Elmer Bertelsen described "crisp lectures designed to create self-confidence and enthusiasm among her students. Admissions officers praise her and give great weight to her evaluations of students seeking to enroll in medical or dental school."[60] Stories of her support—personal and academic—were legion. Fan was named to the rank of Distinguished Professor in 1980 and retired in 1982.[61]

Dr. Joyce Fan and her husband, Paul, surrounded by former students and colleagues.

57 Houston Baptist University, Minutes of the Meetings of the Board of Trustees, Meeting on 2 May 1976.
58 Elmer Bertelsen, "Fan's Miracle Factory," *Houston Chronicle*, 1 May 1980.
59 Dr. Joyce Fan, "Putting Hope Where It Belongs," *HBU News*, June 1980, 1-2.
60 Elmer Bertelsen, "Fan's Miracle Factory," *Houston Chronicle*, 1 May 1980.
61 *WHO Houston '80*, (Houston: WHO Houston, 1980), 137. In 2010, Fan was recognized as the oldest living physics major of Wheaton College where she completed a double major in chemistry and physics in 1942.

§

Rex Fleming, HBU's nationally-honored debate and forensics coach, continued to have winning teams throughout the 1970s. In 1971, HBC debaters were ranked in the top ten teams in the nation by the Speech Association of America.[62] Team photographs from this era show dozens of trophies and awards amassed by the winning debate teams of this era.[63] In 1974, Fleming was named one of the top ten debate coaches in the nation by the National Forensics Association. He was one of only ten coaches ever to hold the Double Diamond Award for both high school and college coaching.[64] In 1978, Fleming's twelfth year as coach, alumnus Tom Pearson returned to help coach a team that was nationally ranked. Fleming modestly observed, "No other college our size is as well known as are we."[65]

Harry Herzog and Mark Haas won tournaments at the University of Southern California and at UCLA. Herzog was regarded as one of the top ten debaters in the nation.[66] The team took first-place honors at LSU and finished the year with a 30-21 record. Further national recognition came to the debate program when HBU was selected for a chapter of Phi Kappa Delta, national honorary debate fraternity.[67] Dale Jefferson and David Slaughter defeated Northwestern University at the Iowa tournament in 1980, and in 1982, the team of Dale Jefferson, David Slaughter, Mark Sandlin, and Don Hernandez received an invitation to participate in the national tournament. The 1983 team won sweepstakes for the third straight year over thirty other colleges at the University of Houston tournament.

By the time he retired in 1985, Fleming had served eighteen years as HBU coach and had been named National Debate Coach of the Year.[68] His forensic teams had won four national championships in extemporaneous speaking, three in original oratory, two in poetry reading, and three

62 "Debaters Ranked in Nation's Top Ten," *The Collegian,* 30 Sept. 1971, p. 1.

63 Fleming recalled using Dr. Troy Womack's HBC car in the early years of competition to drive the team to regional tournaments. In later years, Womack admitted declining Fleming's travel budget request one year because it included travel to the national tournament. Womack responded, "When you get selected for nationals, come see me." As Womack later would proudly tell the tale, one day he looked up and saw Fleming leaning against his doorway. He knew the team was going to nationals.

64 "Fleming Receives Top Honor," *The Scene,* Summer Quarter 1974, p. 6.

65 "Fleming Says Debaters 'Ranked With Top Teams,'" *The Collegian,* 18 Jan. 1978, p. 1.

66 Ibid.

67 "Debaters in Gear from 1979-80 Season," *The Collegian,* Sept. (undated) 1979, Vol. 20, #1, p. 5.

68 "Dr. Fleming Ends Successful Reign as Debate Director," *The Collegian,* 25 Apr. 1985, p. 1. Photo.

in radio speaking. From 1967 to 1985, Fleming's teams amassed over 150 trophies. In 1988, Fleming was named to the National Forensics League Hall of Fame—one of only four college coaches so to be named. Fleming reflected, "I wouldn't change a thing about my career. The best thing I ever did was to come to HBU." In recognition of Fleming's unparalleled contributions, the University readers' theater organization is named "The Rex Fleming Readers."

Music continued to play a major role in campus enrichment and institutional visibility. Under the direction of Dr. Gary Horton, Chairman of the Department of Fine Arts, the music faculty of this era represented one of the strongest in institutional history. Soprano Virginia Babikian joined the College faculty in 1965 as Artist-in-Residence and coordinator of vocal studies. Babikian was an internationally-recognized concert artist. A product of Westminster Choir College with a graduate degree in conducting, Babikian had received the Baumgartner and Williamson awards at Westminster and was the recipient of a Fulbright Scholarship for study at the Teatro dell' Opera di Roma. She had been honored with a Ford Foundation Award for opera study and had recorded a definitive performance of Carl Orff's *Carmina Burana* with Leopold Stokowski.[69] In 1971, she was selected by Robert Shaw to perform the Beethoven Mass in D with the Houston Symphony. In 1971, Babikian formed a men's ensemble at HBU, the Theatre Men, that performed an annual national concert and recruiting tour.[70] The ensemble performed repertoire from opera, the classics, and Broadway. Babikian also established a corresponding women's ensemble, the Bel Canto Singers. Voice students from the studios of Babikian and Dr. William Guthrie were frequent finalists in the National Association of Teachers of Singing (NATS) competitions.[71]

In 1979, Babikian helped recruit Dr. David Wehr as Director of Choral Activities. Wehr followed the era of R. Paul Green's outstanding

---

69 Charles Ward, "Recalling 'Carmina,'" *Houston Chronicle*, 12 Nov. 1995, Zest sec., p. 13, two-star ed. Babikian recalled, "Stokowski asked me how high I could sing. I told him that at Westminster I had to sing a high E in a Gabrielli work with the New York Philharmonic. He hired me to do *Carmina*. Later, he recommended me for a Fulbright fellowship at the Rome Opera." While there, Stokowski called her home to record *Carmina* with him. That recording "made" her career.

70 "HBC's Theatre Men go on tour," *The Collegian*, 11 Mar. 1971, p. 5. Members of the original ensemble were Dr. Bill Guthrie, John Enloe, Ralph Gibson, Michael Wood, David Sullivan, Chris Holcombe, Ed Wittner, and Bob White.

71"Current Events," *HBU News*, Nov. 1976, 3. In 1976, Mark Evans, Dawn Monachino, Jeff Wells, Richard Wolfe, Cathy Torres, Sharon Harris, and Cindy Hamilton were regional NATS winners from a field of six hundred singers. Wells was in his sixth year under contract to New York's Metropolitan Opera Company in 2010.

choral leadership. Also a graduate of Westminster Choir College where he was selected for a Distinguished Alumni award, Wehr was a choral composer and an accomplished organist. An extraordinary 1979 performance of the Vaughan-Williams *Hodie* featured HBU faculty members Virginia Babikian, Norma Newton, William L. Guthrie, Tim Seelig, and Eugene Talley-Schmidt under the baton of Dr. David Wehr.[72] The size and reputation of the vocal faculty during this era represents the finest chapter in University history. By 1982, Babikian had been named Director of the Houston Symphony Chorale with David Wehr as her associate. In addition, Wehr formed the Houston Concert Chorale, a professional ensemble that presented an annual series of concerts. Wehr received multiple annual recognitions by the American Society of Composers, Authors and Publishers (ASCAP) for the "unique prestige value of his published works for chorus and organ" and the number of performances of his works.[73] Under Wehr's direction, the University Singers were engaged by the Houston Grand Opera in 1980 to serve as the opera chorus for the HGO production of Francesco Ciliea's *Adrianna Lecouvreur*.

In 1977, Babikian was instrumental in recruiting another nationally-recognized concert artist to the HBU music faculty. Dr. Clyde Holloway had won the National Young Artists Competition of the American Guild of Organists in 1964 and had become the youngest member of the Indiana University music faculty in 1965. Holloway had also been a Fulbright Scholar at the Amsterdam Conservatory and had studied with Olivier Messiaen in Paris. In 1977, Holloway joined the faculty at HBU and began work to recruit new students, to commission on-campus pipe organs for student practice,[74] and to initiate planning for a new concert instrument for the Weaver chapel. As a result of Holloway's fund-raising skills, two new Schlicker tracker pipe organs for student practice were installed in 1981 in renovated space designed for their acoustical and environmental requirements.

In response to the heightened levels of activities in the fine arts and the breadth of the program in the College of Fine Arts and Humanities, the Board of Trustees approved separating these areas into two colleges in

---

72 "Choral Ensemble Presentation," *The Collegian,* Nov. (undated) 1979, Vol. 20, #5, p. 1.
73 "Wehr Honored by ASCAP," *HBU News,* Oct. 1980, 3.
74 Houston Baptist University, Minutes of the Meetings of the Board of Trustees, Meeting on 26 May 1981.

1977.[75] Dr. Gary Horton was named Dean of the College of Fine Arts; Dr. Calvin Huckabay continued in his role of academic leadership in the humanities. The Board also approved the creation of a College of Graduate Studies in 1977, though the model was never implemented and the graduate academic position was unstaffed until the 1979 employment of Dr. Roger Brooks as Vice-President for Graduate Studies.[76]

In the field of art, faculty member James Busby was the subject of a *Houston Chronicle* article in 1980. Busby had joined the HBC faculty in 1970 and had been honored with a one-man show at the prestigious Dubose Gallery of Houston.[77] The drama program enjoyed renewed success under the talented direction of Dr. Nic Hagler. The Gallery Theatre offered Hagler's one-man show *A Mark Twain Evening,*[78] and the comedy *Harvey.*[79] In 1977, Hagler took his Gallery Theater production of *The Lion in Winter* to the regional American College Theatre Festival.[80] In 1980, the HBU production of *Vanities* was chosen in the American College Theatre competition for performance at the regional festival in Fort Worth.[81]

However, an administrative decision was made to phase out a major in drama in 1981 until such time as an adequate instructional and performance facility could be acquired on the campus. Among some faculty members, it was felt that other concerns may actually have resulted in the decision. In time, Denham Hall was reconfigured as a television studio. The theater major has never returned.

In historical context, the absence of theater from the cultural fabric of the campus has been palpable. The succession of strong drama faculty in the persons of Clift, Pickett, Talley, Bracewell, and Hagler added significantly to the depth of the academic resource. Significant institutional contributions by the theater arts program included the extraordinary talent of the students who were drawn to the campus because of the program and the enrichment of the cultural environment by the presence of

75 Houston Baptist University, Minutes of the Meetings of the Board of Trustees, Meeting on 27 Sept. 1977.

76 "Roger Leon Brooks Named Vice President," *HBU News,* May 1979, 1.

77 Stan Redding, "Jim Busby: On the Road to New Art," *Houston Chronicle.* Reprinted in *HBU News,* Dec. 1980, 3.

78 *Ornogah 1976,* 99.

79 *Ornogah 1977,* 30-31.

80 "Drama Presented at ACTF: Show To Open Here Oct. 24," *The Collegian,* 19 Oct. 1977, p. 1.

81 Sue Dauphin, *Houston by Stages: a history of theatre in Houston* (Burnet: Eakin Press, 1981), 346-348 (history of HBC theater program).

theater as a form of human expression. One has only to reflect on the integrative capacity of drama with the study of literature, history, art, and music to appreciate the depth of its loss from the curriculum. The cohesive effect of theater productions on the campus had functioned to bind the collegiate community more tightly together in shared experience. Additionally, the visceral excitement of basking in the warmth of praise from the city's cultural community provided a qualitative environment that no other art form ever replaced.

Robert Linder was named Dean of the College of Fine Arts in 1980. He had served as director of the University's instrumental program since 1969. Linder was well known in the city, and enjoyed a reputation as an energetic, musical "man for all seasons." He was responsible for HBU's concert band, jazz band, and symphony orchestra and had conducted the Houston Youth Symphony and Ballet, the Houston Civic Symphony and the Municipal Band of Houston. Linder's far-ranging professional work included an NBC television special taped in Nashville. *Performing Arts Magazine* described Linder in an article entitled, "People Who Know the Score."

> Conductor Linder probably has more irons in the fire than any conductor in Houston. He has done televisions specials, Gilbert and Sullivan including the PBS production of *Princess Ida*, and numerous productions by *Theater Under the Stars*.[82]

§

The Endowed Academic Scholarship program had enabled the University to be highly competitive in the recruitment of the finest high school students. The *1982 Ornogah* was dedicated to the donors of these scholarships:

> The heart of any university is its student body. As a direct result of the Endowed Scholarship program, many extremely gifted students have enrolled through the years at Houston Baptist University providing a steady heartbeat for growth. The program was inaugurated in 1969 to meet the following goals: to provide a way for academically able students to attend the university; to enhance the academic standing of the University; to

---

82 "Acting Dean of Fine Arts: Robert Linder," *HBU News,* Sept. 1980, 6.

encourage major gifts to build the university endowment; and to recognize appropriately the gifts of these major donors. It is to the people that have donated these scholarships that we dedicate the 1982 Ornogah Yearbook.[83]

The promise of full-tuition scholarships proved to be a powerful equalizer in the competitive battle for the best and most promising freshman students. By 1981, the EAS program had grown to 130 scholarships. Donors were invited to an annual convocation-lunch where they were hosted by their current scholarship recipient and where graduating EAS students could be honored. In many cases, life-long friendships between donors and students emanated from the four years of college relationship. As the program matured, long-term donors enjoyed an ongoing friendship with a number of former scholarship recipients. Donors often became the best encouragers of friends to establish scholarships of their own. In one known case, a donor "strongly encouraged" her stock broker to establish his own scholarship. He did!

Dr. Hinton speaking to donors at the dedication ceremony
for the first Endowed Academic Scholarships.

---

83 *Ornogah 1982*, 18.

§

The University faculty flourished in the area of professional growth and recognition. Four faculty members completed doctoral degrees— Joyce DeRidder, Florence Gould, Cynthia Rogers, and Doris Warren.[84] Dr. Glendola Nash was elected President of the Texas League for Nursing.[85] Dr. Joe Griska was awarded a Mellon Fellowship for study in English at Duke University.[86] Dr. Marilyn Sibley was honored by the American Association for State and Local History for her book, *George Brackenridge: Maverick Philanthropist*.[87] In April 1976, Dr. Sibley was named one of the state's ten most outstanding college professors by the Minnie Stevens Piper Foundation.[88] She joined HBU faculty members Dr. Calvin Huckabay and Dr. Joyce Fan who in 1970 and 1972 were also recipients of this prestigious recognition for outstanding teaching. Sibley was later elected President of the Texas State Historical Society[89] and authored her fifth book on Texas history in 1983.

Dr. Marion Webb followed her three HBU faculty colleagues in 1982 with her selection by the Minnie Stevens Piper Foundation.[90] This record of four faculty members selected for outstanding teaching distinction within less than the first twenty years of university history was unprecedented. Webb also served as President of the Faculty Assembly in 1983, was named Spanish Teacher of the Year in 1984 by the Texas Foreign Language Association, and was selected for the Opal Goolsby Outstanding Teaching Award at HBU three times in 1974, 1982 and 1987.[91]

Three endowed chairs and two professorships were established during the period of the 1970s. In 1972, through the efforts of trustee Gilbert Turner, the Brown Foundation of Houston announced a gift of $500,000 to fund the Herman Brown Chair of Business and Economics. At the Fall 1983 President's Council Dinner, U. S. Senator Mark Hatfield commended George Brown for the gift "as an example of responsible corporate citizenship." The Brown commemorative plaque reads,

84 "Doctoral Degrees Earned by Four," *The Scene*, Winter Quarter 1975, p. 2.
85 "Nash Elected," *The Scene*, Winter Quarter 1974, p. 4.
86 "Griska Receives Fellowship for Research at Duke," *The Collegian*, 1 Apr. 1977, p. 6; "Griska Named Mellon Fellow," *HBU News*, Mar. 1977, 2.
87 "Faculty Briefs," *The Scene*, Winter Quarter 1974, p. 3.
88 Houston Baptist University, Minutes of the Meetings of the Board of Trustees, Meeting on 15 Apr. 1976.
89 "Faculty Briefs," *HBU News*, Mar. 1981, 5.
90 "Webb Receives Piper Award," *HBU News*, May 1982, 2. Photo.
91 "Awards Day honors students," *The Collegian*, 15 May 1987, p. 1. Photo.

This philanthropic act perpetuates the memory of a pioneer Houston businessman, Herman Brown, whose acumen and perseverance helped create Brown & Root, the world's largest construction company. With this gift, the Brown Foundation has enriched the academic life of this college and enhanced the Business resources of the community.

The funds emanating from the Brown Chair have provided a series of annual lectures delivered by such respected corporate executives as Robert McNair, Jack Blanton, Archie Dunham, Gordon Bethune, Larry Farmer, and Bob Beauchamp '87.

A second endowed chair honoring Robert H. Ray was established in Humanities in 1974 by Ray's daughter Colletta and her husband Don McMillian.[92] The Ray family was profoundly involved in the University's history. Robert H. Ray was a member of the original UBA College Committee, a college Founder, and a former Chair of the Board of Trustees. His son-in-law, Don McMillian, was also one of the College Founders.[93] Ray's daughter, Colletta McMillian, was the first President of the President's Advisors, later served on the University Board of Trustees, chaired its Academic Committee, and headed the Search Committee for the University's second president. The Ray Chair plaque reads,

> Honoring Robert H. Ray whose community interest and Christian concern led Mr. and Mrs. Don F. McMillian to provide the Robert H. Ray Chair in Humanities. Robert H. Ray, 1902-1968. This philanthropic act perpetuates the memory of a pioneer Houston Baptist layman and geophysicist who was interested in Christian education. His acumen and dedication created the Ray Geophysical Company. With this gift, Mr. and Mrs. Don F. McMillian have enriched the academic life of this university and enhanced the cultural life of our community.[94]

This family illustrates several multi-generational families in service to University trusteeship. These families have included Rex Baker, Sr. and his son Rex, Jr.; Howard Lee, Sr. and his son Howard, Jr.; L. D. Morgan and his son John; Dr. Stewart Morris and his daughter Lisa Morris Simon; and Robert Ray and his daughter Colletta Ray McMillian.

---

92 "McMillians Endow Chair in Humanities," *The Scene*, Summer Quarter 1974, p. 1. The McMillians gave a gift of 12.6 acres of land at 7100 Katy Freeway between Wilcrest and Brittmoore valued at $1,000,000 to be divided equally by HBU and Baylor College of Medicine.
93 "Don McMillian: Life Has Been Good to Us," *HBU News,* Mar. 1981, 6. Photo.
94 The Ray Chair plaque is mounted at the entrance to the Brown Administrative Quadrangle.

In 1975, a third endowed chair was established by trustee Jim R. Smith honoring the longtime pastor of Houston's First Baptist Church, Dr. John Bisagno.[95] Smith's father, Founder O. R. Smith, had also served as Chairman of the University's President's Council. The Bisagno plaque reads,

> Honoring John R. Bisagno whose life of dedication to the preaching of the gospel led Jim R. Smith to provide the John R. Bisagno Chair of Evangelism. Provided by Jim R. Smith whose dedicated life as a deacon and Christian layman has been a witness to his community. This chair recognizes the leadership of a pastor whose commitment has been to a New Testament evangelism emanating from the local church, presenting Jesus Christ as Lord and Saviour in the power of the Holy Spirit for the purposes of winning the lost who in turn will go make disciples.

The University also garnered two endowed professorships during this period. In 1977, Hazel and Harry Chavanne established the Prince-Chavanne Professorship of Christian Business Ethics in honor of their parents.[96] Their daughter, Claire Turner, was later to serve as a University trustee. Turner's husband, Oscar, had served as Vice President of Development. The Prince-Chavanne plaque reads,

> Prince-Chavanne Professorship of Christian Business Ethics honoring William Gilbert Prince, Pearl Blackshear Prince, Philip Edward Chavanne, Anna Faucett Chavanne. Provided by Mr. and Mrs. Harry J. Chavanne in appreciation of the Christian example of their parents both in personal life and in business and economics.[97]

Like the Brown Chair, the Prince-Chavanne Professorship sponsored a lectureship series whose presenters included ethicists Dr. Stanley Hauerwas, Dr. William F. May, Dr. Oliver F. Williams, and Dr. Donald P. Robin. The University's commitment to learning in a Christian environment was recognized in 1978 when Dr. Don Anthony, Secretary of the BGCT Christian Education Coordinating Board, observed, "HBU had been more successful in permeating the learning experience with Christian witness than any of our schools."[98]

---

95 "Donated by James R. Smith: New Evangelism Chair Honors Dr. Bisagno," *HBU News,* Feb. 1975, 1.
96 Houston Baptist University, Minutes of the Meetings of the Executive Committee of the Board of Trustees, Meeting on 18 Aug. 1977.
97 The Prince Chavanne plaque is mounted at the entrance to the Brown Academic Quadrangle.
98 Houston Baptist University, Minutes of the Meetings of the Board of Trustees, Meeting on 31 Mar. 1978.

In 1977, University trustee John Baugh established an endowed pro-fessorship honoring Dr. Rex G. Baker, Sr.[99] Both Baker and Baugh were members of the original UBA College Committee and were members of the first Board of Trustees.[100] Baker had also been honored by the University with an honorary Doctor of Laws degree in 1970. Of all the trustees, Baker had been among the most fervent advocates for programs of academic excellence. In expressing his appreciation for the gift, Baker observed, "An exceptional faculty costs money. Endowment makes the difference in quality of education. . . . Endowment is the groundwork for perpetuity."[101] President Hinton lauded Baugh and Baker as "two of the greatest men in the history of the University."[102] The Baker plaque reads,

> The Rex G. Baker Professorship in the College of Business and Economics honors a Christian gentleman, University Founder, and trustee whose generous contribution of self and unswerving allegiance to the highest ideals of Christian living and academic achievement serve to inspire all those generations which benefit from his wisdom and diligent devotion. Provided by John F. Baugh, Dr. Baker's family, and Friends.[103]

Dr. Carter Franklin was named to the Brown Chair in Business and Economics in 1974;[104] Dr. Calvin Huckabay was appointed to the Ray Chair in Humanities in 1974; and Dr. Robert Bush was named to the Prince-Chavanne Professorship in Christian Business Ethics in 1980.[105]

In addition to the gifts to the endowment for chairs and professor-ships, significant library gifts enriched the academic environment of the University during this era. A library of 1,000 volumes on Southern and military history was given to the University by Robert Bradley and Frances Bradley Lummis in 1976.[106] In 1981, Robert Bradley gave a sec-ond gift of books dating from 1794 that included first editions, some autographed, of works by James Joyce, Dylan Thomas, Edith Wharton,

---

99 Houston Baptist University, Minutes of the Meetings of the Executive Committee of the Board of Trustees, Meeting on 18 Aug. 1977.

100 "Rex Baker Endowed Professorship," *HBU News,* Mar. 1978, 1. Photo of Baker and Baugh.

101 Houston Baptist University, Minutes of the Meetings of the Board of Trustees, Meeting on 23 Feb. 1978.

102 Ibid.

103 The Baker Professorship plaque is mounted at the entrance to the Brown Academic Quadrangle.

104 Houston Baptist University, Minutes of the Meetings of the Executive Committee of the Board of Trustees, Meeting on 12 Sept. 1974.

105 "Prince-Chavanne Endowed Professorship," *HBU News,* Feb. 1980, 3. Photo.

106 "Rare Book Collection Donated to Library," *The Collegian,* 17 Nov. 1976, p. 1; Houston Baptist University, Minutes of the Board of Trustees, Meeting on 24 Sept. 1976.

F. Scott Fitzgerald, Wilkie Collins, C. S. Lewis, and Oscar Wilde.[107] The Palmer Bradley Library Special Collection was created and later housed in its own proprietary research center in the Moody Library.

§

In 1975, the Board of Trustees created the rank of Distinguished Professor to honor and recognize significant faculty contribution to the academic life of the University. The first recipients of this honor were Dr. Calvin Huckabay (1975),[108] Dr. Alma Leavell (1978),[109] and Dr. Joyce Fan (1980).[110] The trustees also chose honorary degrees as the means to convey gratitude to those who had played significant leadership roles in the University's history. Among the degree recipients in this era were trustees Rex G. Baker, Sr. (1970), Ross E. Dillon (1970), D. E. Sloan (1972), Opal Goolsby (1974), Stewart Morris (1975),[111] and Gilbert Turner (1977).[112]

Other retiring faculty members including Dr. E. D. Martin and Dr. James E. Williamson received the rank of Faculty Emeritus in 1972 providing lifetime recognition of merit and service. "Dean Will" had the unique distinction of being the only person ever to serve as a founding trustee, a faculty member, and an administrative officer. He had served as a member of the UBA planning committee from 1956 to 1961 and a member of the first Board from 1960 to 1963. His record of dedicated service was acknowledged by the dedication to him of the *1968 Ornogah*.[113]

In September 1978, the University lost one of its icons and greatest treasures with the death of Opal Goolsby.[114] Goolsby had come with Dr. Hinton from Texarkana Junior College in 1963 to teach English and French as a founding faculty member.[115] She had been an early director

107 Shirley Gor, "Library Receives Book Collection," *The Collegian,* 21 Jan. 1981, p. 4.

108 Houston Baptist University, Minutes of the Meetings of the Executive Committee of the Board of Trustees, Meeting on 14 Nov. 1974.

109 "Leavell Named Distinguished Professor," *HBU News,* June 1978, 6.

110 Houston Baptist University, Minutes of the Meetings of the Board of Trustees, Meeting on 15 May 1980.

111 Houston Baptist University, Minutes of the Meetings of the Executive Committee of the Board of Trustees, Meeting on 14 Nov. 1974.

112 "Smith, Ladd, and Turner Honored at Commencement Exercises," *HBU News,* June 1977, 2. Photos.

113 "In Memoriam," *The Collegian,* 25 Sept. 1986, p. 1; *Ornogah 1968,* 4-5.

114 "English Professor Dies of Stroke," *HBU News,* Oct. 1978, 1-2. Photo.

115 At the outset of World War II, Goolsby and her sons fled the Middle East and reached Paris only to become separated from her husband for more than a year. Goolsby enrolled in the Sorbonne to hone her French language skills and taught French the rest of her life.

of the fledgling Baptist Student Union. She had been a sponsor both of the *Collegian* and the *Ornogah.* She was named Faculty Woman of the Year in 1969.[116] The *1969 Ornogah* was dedicated to her contributions to the campus,[117] and she was the recipient of the Outstanding Teaching Award in 1976.[118] In 1982, following her death, the annual awards for teaching excellence at the University were re-named the Opal Goolsby Outstanding Teaching Awards. To her former students, she was in a league of her own—as much for her classroom work as her consummate commitment to a personal relationship with her students. She was honored by the University as the recipient of the degree Doctor of Humane Letters in 1974. A pragmatic, hard-working, tireless teacher, she was for all the years of her service the embodiment of the energy of the new college. Her memory through all the years since has continued to personify the finest traditions of academic advising, instruction, and friendship.

The University lost another exceptional founding faculty member with the death of R. Paul Green in 1981. In the early years, Green, more than any other original faculty member, put Houston Baptist College in the cultural and community limelight with his leadership of the College Singers. From its auspicious debut for Billy Graham Day in 1963, the Singers garnered local and national attention for the new institution. Green responded to the dream for a new college from his position as Director of the Broadman Chorale, a professional recording ensemble based in Nashville.[119] He had served as Director of Choral Activities for Southwestern Baptist Theological Seminary, Director of the Baptist Hour Choir, and was widely known among church musicians for the excellence of his choral work. His recruitment was arguably the greatest coup among the founding faculty.

In the first years of the new College, the Singers became the chief emissary to the Houston community. The College Singers were invited to appear before the Baptist World Alliance in Miami, the Baptist World Youth Conference in Bern, Switzerland,[120] and to premier in Atlanta a new youth musical, *Hello World,* written by Buryl Red and Ragan Courtney.[121] The Singers recorded Mary Caldwell's cantata *Of Time and*

---

116 "Opal Goolsby," *The Collegian,* 21 Sept. 1978, p. 2. Photo.

117 *Ornogah 1969,* 4-5.

118 "Opal Goolsby," *The Collegian,* 21 Sept. 1978, p. 2. Photo.

119 Houston Baptist College, *Destiny,* Jan. Feb. 1964, p. 3. Cover photo.

120 "HBC goes to SBC and BWC," *The Collegian,* 15 Sept. 1965, p. 4.

121 "Singers state 'Hello, World,'" *The Collegian,* 17 Apr. 1970, p. 2.

Eternity for the Broadman Press, and presented annual spring concerts in the Houston Music Hall.[122]

More significantly, Green was a charismatic mentor for his young students.[123] His cutting-edge attire and his jaunty manner reinforced the appeal Green had to students. In 2008 and again in 2010, grateful former members of the College Singers under R. Paul Green held a reunion on the University campus to sing music they had learned, to be led by former members of the College Singers, and to share memorabilia from the Green era. A College Singers website was established to disseminate recordings and photographic records from the R. Paul Green era. Green's pre-mature death from cancer left a void in the heart of the campus and its students that bore testimony to his years of dedicated service.

§

From its earliest history, the University enjoyed a faculty of considerable reputation and experience. Realizing the potential of such a faculty-at-large, the Southern Association encouraged the formation of a faculty organization to represent its professional interests. In this context, a Faculty Assembly was formed in 1968[124] that profited from the leadership of an outstanding group of early presidents including Dr. Newell Boyd, Dr. Don Byrnes,[125] Dr. Stephen Donohue, Dr. Robert Linder, Dr. Robert Parker, Dr. James Riley, and Dr. James Taylor. The purpose of the Assembly was "to serve as the formal vehicle through which the faculty cooperates with the administration in formulating and implementing the policies of the University."[126]

In the period 1975-1978, two legal challenges provided an unusual opportunity for improved institutional protocols. These opportunities also prompted further refinement of the Faculty Assembly's policy dealing with faculty grievance and personal conduct. Ultimately, these events caused the Assembly to develop a protocol to facilitate its role in

---

122 "Singers to present cantata," *The Collegian,* 26 Apr. 1966, p. 4.
123 One alumnus reflected, "Having lost my dad to cancer just 3 days before the start of my freshman year, I thank God for R. Paul Green who pulled me through some difficult times."
124 "Faculty Organizes," *Houston Baptist College News,* Mar. 1968, 2.
125 "Faculty Chooses Byrnes as Leader," *The Collegian,* 20 Apr. 1972, p. 2.
126 Houston Baptist University, Minutes of the Meetings of the Faculty Assembly, Meeting on 19 Feb. 1976.

providing a grievance procedure for faculty. Moreover, the Assembly developed a *Faculty Policy on Professional Conduct*.[127]

Two faculty members were administratively removed from the classroom for cause in 1975. The Faculty Assembly conducted grievance hearings for both faculty members.[128] In both cases, based on the information it had, the Assembly recommended reinstatement to the teaching assignment. However, on legal counsel, the University administration and Board of Trustees affirmed the action taken. Ultimately, both faculty members brought legal action against the University. In the first case, the faculty member agreed to accept a financial settlement, drop legal action, and resign.[129] In the second case that involved a tenured faculty member, lengthy litigation followed the on-campus grievance procedure. A lawsuit was filed against the University in 1978.[130] But, it was not until 1982 that the courts finally ruled—sustaining the University's position on all seven allegations against this faculty member.[131] As a result of these two complex cases, the University Board of Trustees instructed the University administration to "caution any faculty member whose actions tend to portray an image detrimental to the high ideals we should cherish at a Christian institution."[132] The Faculty Assembly also drafted a *Policy on Professional Conduct*. The Assembly *Policy* anticipated the coming era of focus on sexual harassment:

> (Faculty members should avoid) the area of romantic involvement between faculty and enrolled students which tends to portray an image detrimental to the high ideals we cherish at this Christian institution. Such involvement could easily lead to the erosion both of the effectiveness of the faculty member at an institution which functions in a Christian context and the institution itself; therefore, such involvement should be avoided.[133]

---

127 Houston Baptist University, Minutes of the Meetings of the Faculty Assembly, Meeting on 30 Mar. 1976.
128 Houston Baptist University, Minutes of the Meetings of the Faculty Assembly Hearing Committee, Meeting on 1 Dec. 1975.
129 Houston Baptist University, Minutes of the Meetings of the Board of Trustees, Meeting on 16 Jan. 1976.
130 Houston Baptist University, Minutes of the Meetings of the Faculty Assembly, Meeting on 11 Dec. 1978.
131 Houston Baptist University, Minutes of the Meetings of the Faculty Assembly, Meeting on 5 May 1982. Tragically, the faculty member died in the interim, but the case was continued to verdict by the estate. The court decided in favor of the University.
132 Houston Baptist University, Minutes of the Meetings of the Board of Trustees, Meeting on 27 Feb. 1976.
133 Houston Baptist University, Minutes of the Meetings of the Faculty Assembly, Meeting on 30 Mar. 1976.

The broad policy statement also expressed concern for "objective grading, the inappropriate use of student work for faculty research, and the threat to student academic success from excessive scheduling of activities by student organizations."[134]

A third faculty grievance from this era focused on tenure policy. In 1972, the University adopted a term-contract system to replace its previous policy of granting tenure to selected faculty members. All faculty members who had tenure at that time retained the status for the duration of their University service. Under the new system, contracts for faculty were annually renewable and were typically for a period of three years following probationary status. As with tenure, long-term contracts safeguarded academic freedom and the financial security of the faculty member. In May 1975, the Board of Trustees was notified that a grievance had been filed with the American Association of University Professors (AAUP) by a former HBU faculty member. The contract of this faculty member had not been renewed in 1970, but he claimed to have had tenure since his total years of service "at all institutions" exceeded a probationary period of six years.[135]

As stated in the *HBU Manual of Board Policy,* tenure could be granted only by the Board of Trustees upon the recommendation of the President. It was neither automatic after a period of probationary service nor was it universally awarded. The AAUP sided with the complainant and placed the University on its list of censured institutions demanding, in essence, that a de jure tenure system be re-instituted, whatever it be called:[136]

> The Sixty-first Annual Meeting voted to censure the Houston Baptist University administration after it acted without affordance of academic due process to terminate the services of a professor whose years of teaching had exceeded the maximum probationary period permitted under the 1940 Statement of Principles. The published report . . . also dealt with the abrogation of the existing tenure system by the institution's governing board.[137]

---

134 Ibid. The performance calendar of the College Singers frequently took students from classes causing absences to exceed University maximums.
135 Houston Baptist University, Minutes of the Meetings of the Board of Trustees, Meeting on 23 May 1975.
136 "AAUP censures HBU," *Houston Chronicle,* 28 May 1975, sec. 1, p. 14.
137 American Association of University Professors, *Academe,* Spring 1975, (accessed Feb. 27 2010).

Over the next thirty years, the University and the AAUP exchanged policy refinements and participated in conciliatory efforts with little result. Ultimately, as tenure became a more debatable national issue, the AAUP added other concerns to the original charge and focused primarily on a public grievance hearing procedure. Finally, in 2004, as personnel changes occurred in both the AAUP and the University, a process agreeable to both parties was proposed by Dr. Don Byrnes, Legal Counsel to the President, and the University was removed from the AAUP list.[138] A report completed for the 2000 self-study indicated that there had been minimal negative effect on faculty recruiting in the intervening years by the absence of tenure.

The Faculty Assembly continuously addressed areas of faculty well-being and professional environment. In a period of financial uncertainty, the University had begun a practice in 1974 of withholding salary increases from the faculty contracts issued in March with the expectation of giving salary increases in the fall after fall enrollments were known.[139] However, in 1976-77 no fall raises were granted to faculty or staff despite enrollment increases, prompting requests from the Faculty Assembly for an explanation and reconsideration of the current practice. The Assembly passed a resolution that expressed its strong contention that salary adjustments should be part of the good-faith contracts issued in March. The Assembly purported that the "morale of the faculty and staff has been badly shaken by the sudden reversal of an established pattern."[140] A 1976 survey of Baptist colleges by the noted higher education consultant Dr. Earl McGrath confirmed low rankings by the HBU faculty and staff in the areas of democratic governance, academic freedom, and institutional spirit.[141] In 1982, the Faculty Assembly requested further changes in policy regarding summer pay policy, minimum class size requirements, teaching load calculation, and pay for mentoring independent study. These administrative policies were contained in an HBU personnel document referred to as the "White Paper."[142]

138 American Association of University Professors, Press Release, 15 June 2004.
139 Houston Baptist University, Minutes of the Meetings of the Board of Trustees, Meeting on 27 Sept. 1974.
140 Houston Baptist University, Minutes of the Meetings of the Faculty Assembly, Meeting on 12 Oct. 1976.
141 Earl J. McGrath, "Study of Southern Baptist Colleges and Universities, 1976-77," Educational Commission of the Southern Baptist Convention, June 1977; Houston Baptist University, Minutes of the Meetings of the Faculty Assembly, Meeting on 19 Sept. 1977.
142 Houston Baptist University, Minutes of the Meetings of the Faculty Assembly, Meeting on 12 Feb. 1982.

The Assembly also addressed the University's long-term ban on facial hair. The context of the discussion focused on the personal rights of the individual. A formal resolution was sent to the University President and to the Board of Trustees:

> A liberal arts university, by its very nature, recognizes diversity of appearance. Many Christians have begun to recognize that beards are socially acceptable, and one finds bearded leaders in all phases of American life. Therefore, the Faculty Assembly recommends that university policy allow faculty members to grow beards if they wish. Faculty members with beards would naturally recognize the responsibilities to the university and consider their appearance with dignity and discernment.[143]

Ultimately in 1978, the trustees approved a revised policy permitting facial hair for both students and faculty.[144] Shortly thereafter, however, it was wryly noted that bearded faculty member Robert Linder had been appointed conductor of the Boston Pops when he was mistaken for the ghost of Arthur Fiedler.

---

143 Houston Baptist University, Minutes of the Meetings of the Executive Committee of the Board of Trustees, Meeting on 22 Apr. 1977.
144 Houston Baptist University, Minutes of the Meetings of the Executive Committee of the Board of Trustees, Meeting on 21 Feb. 1978.

SEVEN

1974-1984

Campus, Student Life, and Athletics

The period 1974-1984 witnessed significant additions to the campus and its facilities. A challenge grant of $1,000,000 from the Cullen Foundation in 1975 set in motion the realization of a new Cullen Science Center to house the departments of biology, chemistry, mathematics, physics, and nursing.[1] Funding for the Center included a gift of $668,000 from Houston Endowment, $250,000 from the College Property Committee[2] and $150,000 from the M. D. Anderson Foundation.[3]

In further Hospital-University cooperative development, the University and Memorial shared the cost of constructing an underground box culvert to enclose a drainage canal located between the hospital and the college.[4] This feature appeared in early aerial photographs as a "Z" across the campus property. The construction provided uninterrupted land surface between the two campuses and permitted full development of the property. The ground easement over this construction would later accommodate the entry drive for the University Place development.

The prospects of a move to the University campus were traumatic for the nursing faculty. The downtown facility for the Lillie Jolly School of Nursing had provided a multi-story dormitory, an auditorium, a swimming pool, cafeteria, and student-life areas. Additionally, Memorial Baptist Hospital was located just across McKinney Street and provided easy access to clinical facilities, maintenance and supplies, and the professional medical staff of the hospital. The model of a nursing program on a University campus rather than in a medical center was not common.

---

1 "Science Center on Schedule," *The Collegian,* 1 Sept. 1976, p. 1; "Cullen Grant $1,000,000 to HBU," *HBU News,* Feb. 1975, 1.
2 Houston Baptist University, Minutes of the Meetings of the Board of Trustees, Meeting on 28 Feb. 1975.
3 Houston Baptist University, Minutes of the Meetings of the Board of Trustees, Meeting on 2 May 1976.
4 Houston Baptist University, Minutes of the Meetings of the Board of Trustees, Meeting on 26 Sept. 1975.

The Lillie Jolly faculty feared loss of recognition, unfamiliar administrative process, and waning autonomy.

Consequently, the architectural design process for the Cullen Science Center involved faculty and students from both science and nursing. Multiple affinity-relationship designs were "gamed" by students and faculty working with Goleman and Rolfe, Architects.[5] Science students enjoyed the immediate access to the outdoor balconies of the original labs on the academic quadrangle. Science faculty wished to retain personal management of labs and wanted offices nearby, but out of sight along a separate professional corridor. Nursing needed its own proprietary entrance and visibility.

Ultimately, the College of Nursing design reflected the small class, mastery-learning, mediated-instruction model pioneered at HBU in the new degree program. A Learning Resource Center provided technology and instructional media that was funded by a series of grants from the Helene Fuld Health Trust. This trust funded highly-selected programs across the nation and developed a shared-distribution capability whereby instructional media from one college could be made available to all Fuld institutions. The Fuld Trust provided initial grants of $145,000 for staff and technology in the new facility[6] and an additional $75,000 later for conversion to color television capability. Open-landscape faculty offices were designed to facilitate one-on-one learning, to accommodate changing teaching team membership, and to enhance team interaction.

The 40,000 square-foot Cullen Science Center provided chemistry laboratories and science classrooms in a north wing and faculty offices, biology and physics laboratories, and the College of Nursing in a south wing. The north wing was structurally designed so that two additional floors could be added in the future. The College of Nursing completed its move to the Cullen Science Center in advance of the 1977 spring quarter, and the departments of science and mathematics moved into the new building in early summer. Construction of the Memorial Hospital adjacent to the Cullen Science Center eased nursing faculty concerns about professional recognition and physical access. The nursing faculty quickly adapted to the comfort of a campus academic environment with its many support services. The nursing facility became a nationally-noted model of

---

5 "Design Phase Started on Science Center," *The Scene*, Winter Quarter 1975, p. 1. Photo.
6 Houston Baptist University, Minutes of the Meetings of the Board of Trustees, Meeting on 28 Feb. 1975.

effective design that was widely emulated in other collegiate nursing facilities over the next decade.

Wilhelmina Cullen Robertson brought the dedicatory address for the Cullen Science Center in October 1977.[7] Completion of this facility freed space in the north wing of the administrative quadrangle for remodeling and alternative assignment. By 1981, the former Lillie Jolly School of Nursing building and the Memorial Professional Building in downtown Houston had been demolished to make way for the Allied Bank Tower.

In May 1976, a grant of $350,000 from the J. E. and L. E. Mabee Foundation was announced to fund construction of a new 265-seat teaching theater integrally related to the Cullen Science Center.[8] The Mabee Teaching Theater was the largest instructional facility on the campus and featured tiered theater seating in close proximity to a stage with a triple-screen rear-projection capability. In keeping with the University's commitment to build highly-flexible facilities, the theater was also designed to accommodate media presentations, music recitals, concerts, readers' theater, campus lectures, and general assembly.[9] The Mabee Teaching Theater was dedicated in late October 1977 with a series of events designed to highlight the many potential uses of the space.[10] Until construction of the Morris Cultural Arts Center in 2007, Mabee Theater provided the University's best facility for performance and large assembly.

§

One of the more poignant chapters of University history began in December 1976 with the announcement by former HBU trustee Florence Weaver that she was providing funding for a new campus chapel.[11] A chapel was a major element in the University's long-range plan for campus development. The need on campus for a worship center and physical spiritual symbol was felt; however, the chapel was to be designed to accommodate drama and music events as well. At Mrs. Weaver's request,

---

7 "Thanks Given to Foundations for Buildings," *HBU News,* Nov. 1977, 1; "Dedication Fills Week," *The Collegian,* 9 Nov. 1977, p. 1. Photos.
8 "New Teaching Theatre Projected for Fall '77," *The Collegian,* 18 Mar. 1977, p. 3; "Fine Arts Complex Next Major Effort," *HBU News,* June 1976, 1. Photos.
9 "Progress continues on the new Mabee Teaching Theatre," *HBU News,* May 1977, 2; "Excellent working weather," *HBU News,* June 1977, 4. Photos.
10 "Dedication Ceremonies Planned for Oct. 24-28," *The Collegian,* Oct. (undated) 1977, Vol. 17, #1, p. 1.
11 Houston Baptist University, Minutes of the Meetings of the Executive Committee of the Board of Trustees, Meeting on 16 Dec. 1976.

architect Harold Calhoun was engaged to design the new facility.[12] At the same time, noted performing artist Dr. Clyde Holloway was recruited to the HBU music faculty in part by the prospect of a concert organ as a part of the chapel project.[13] The Weaver gift would provide $300,000 initially and another $400,000 ultimately from her estate. The Baptist Foundation of Texas agreed to early release of the additional $400,000 from the Atwood trust to be used for the Chapel construction and repaid in time from the Weaver estate. Trustees were encouraged to write personal notes of appreciation to Mrs. Weaver who had been a member of the UBA Property Committee and a founding trustee.[14]

Funds were provided to visit and critique chapel and church facilities across the nation. *The Scene* reported a design for a massive, architecturally-sculpted chapel that would provide moveable seating for 400, a tracker-action concert pipe organ, and an interior that afforded balconies for performance of antiphonal music.[15] Flexible-seating arrangements with "cathedral chairs" would accommodate configuration for worship, weddings, religious drama, lectures, and concerts. A large model of the chapel was constructed to stimulate thought about creative use of the projected facility.[16]

Mrs. Weaver flew to Denver late in May 1977 to visit her sister-in-law Frankie Currie, the donor of the University's Currie ranch property. On the morning of June 1, she died there in her sleep.[17] HBU was subsequently notified on June 23 that Mrs. Weaver had, in fact, "left no gift in her will for the Weaver Chapel even though her intent to do so was obvious to many people."[18] Her will left approximately thirty-five percent of her estate for ministerial scholarships at HBU, thirty percent for scholarships at Southwestern Baptist Theological Seminary, and thirty-five percent to the Second Baptist School of Houston. In July, the Executive Committee of the trustees initiated discussion with the two other beneficiaries outlining the circumstances of the pledge and requesting that steps be taken to honor the request of Mrs. Weaver to fund the

---

12 Houston Baptist University, Minutes of the Meetings of the Board of Trustees, Meeting on 22 Feb. 1977.

13 "Seven Additional Faculty Employed," *HBU News,* May 1977, 3. Photo of Dr. Holloway.

14 Houston Baptist University, Minutes of the Meetings of the Executive Committee of the Board of Trustees, Meeting on 16 Dec. 1976.

15 "Fine Arts Department Making Big Plans," *The Scene,* Spring Quarter 1977, p. 2.

16 "Plans Crystallized For Chapel; Search For Funds in Progress," *The Collegian,* 18 Jan. 1978, p. 1. Photo.

17 "School Mourns Weaver Passing," *HBU News,* June 1977, 1.

18 Houston Baptist University, Minutes of the Meetings of the Executive Committee of the Board of Trustees, Meeting on 23 June 1977.

Weaver-Currie Chapel at the University.[19] When this proved fruitless, the Board initiated a fund drive in January 1978. Over time, however, this project became displaced by more urgent operational needs of the University and was never fully pursued. Nearly thirty years would pass before the dream for a University chapel would be realized in the Belin Chapel of the Morris Cultural Arts Center.

§

The Board of Trustees in the 1970s became increasingly concerned with preservation of campus property. The "scare" created by Memorial Hospital's consideration to sell part of its property heightened the resolve of the trustees to preserve the integrity of campus land for the University's future. Most commercial development on the campus "reserve" had taken place on leased property that would eventually revert back to the University. In April 1977, the trustees approved a $3,100,000 lease to real estate developer Moody Rambin Interests for the construction of a Howard Johnson motor hotel on four acres of land south of the Memorial Hospital tract. The hotel would feature 162 rooms and a restaurant.[20] Of concern to the trustees was the potential for sale of alcoholic beverages in the hotel restaurant.[21] Of additional concern was the fact that the four acres of land was subordinated to the lease and had the potential liability of being lost in case of foreclosure on the hotel development. However, financial times were hard, and the contract eventually was approved by the Board.[22] All of the University pastor trustees voted against approving the lease on a roll call vote. The hotel was ultimately built, and the University received its first payment of $98,000 in 1982. Neither of the concerns about alcohol sales or the subordinated lease disappeared, however.

A grant from the M. D. Anderson Foundation in 1982 provided additions to the M. D. Anderson Student Center affording increased space for bookstore operation and a campus post office. Increased parking provi-

---

19 Houston Baptist University, Minutes of the Meetings of the Executive Committee of the Board of Trustees, Meeting on 21 July 1977.

20 Houston Baptist University, Minutes of the Meetings of the Executive Committee of the Board of Trustees, Meeting on 22 Apr. 1977.

21 Houston Baptist University, Minutes of the Meetings of the Board of Trustees, Meeting on 17 Mar. 1977. The lease *did* prohibit package liquor sales.

22 Houston Baptist University, Minutes of the Meetings of the Executive Committee of the Board of Trustees, Meeting on 15 Jan. 1981.

sion and improved facilities for music instruction and performance remained as critical needs. As many as 275 cars were parking on grass on days when seminary classes were also being held. In an ongoing effort to increase the number of resident students, the trustees approved $1,000,000 to renovate both University residences adding efficiency kitchen units to each of the suites, replacing plumbing fixtures and existing air conditioning systems, and purchasing all new furniture.

The estate of Enla Atwood had provided for construction of additional instructional facilities. In 1963, Miss Atwood's original dream had been to construct a building for a new seminary in Houston on the College campus. Florence Weaver and Ross Dillon had redirected her thinking toward provision of facilities for Bible study. With this history in mind, in 1982 Dr. Hinton and Dr. Russell Dilday, President of Southwestern Baptist Theological Seminary, began to discuss the possibility of a second Atwood Building to house the seminary offices and provide classrooms on selected days that would be available for University use at other times. The Seminary agreed to provide $300,000 for the project including $50,000 from the Atwood estate that was reserved to provide for seminary instruction. Architect Harold Calhoun designed the Atwood II building to provide 17,000 square feet of space including a suite of offices for the Southwestern Seminary in Southeast Texas (SET) program and ten classrooms for shared use.[23] Groundbreaking for the new facility by representatives from Southwestern Seminary, The Baptist Foundation of Texas, and the University was held February 29, 1983.[24] The Atwood II Building opened on October 1 and was formally dedicated on February 7, 1984, when ribbons were cut jointly by Presidents Hinton and Dilday.[25] The dedication also honored the Rockwell Foundation for a gift that provided a large plaza between the Atwood I and Atwood II buildings. The Atwood II facility represented a rare joint project between a state Baptist university and a Southern Baptist Convention seminary that may have been unique in denominational history.

In the early 1980s, three firms were engaged to do feasibility studies of potential campus building projects. In 1982, Crain/Anderson was employed to develop a prospectus for a combination events center, fine

---

23 Houston Baptist University, Minutes of the Meetings of the Board of Trustees, Meeting on 25 May 1982; "Building On," *The Collegian*, 1 Sept. 1983, p. 1. Photos.
24 "Atwood II Construction Underway," *HBU News*, March/April 1983, cover, 6. Photo.
25 "Atwood II Dedication," *The Collegian*, 16 Feb. 1984, p. 2.

arts performance and instruction space, and television studios. The comprehensive study included a demographic survey of the sports and cultural ticket-buying public in Houston to predict how many days annually the several venues might be rented for community use.[26] Among other considerations, the extensive proposal projected an ideal size for each of the facilities based on need and cost/benefit analysis. Architect Ralph Anderson, whose designs included the *Superdrum* on the University of Texas campus, proposed a complex under one roof that shared lobby and support space and provided a 1200-seat proscenium theater; a 5,000-seat events center for sports and assembly, music, drama, and art instructional space; and a 10,000 square feet television studio. Building Committee chair Otis Brigman estimated the cost of the project to be $16,500,000.

Also in 1982, the firm of Langwith, Wilson, King, and House was retained to develop a proposal for additional student housing. Architect Charles Wilson proposed a six-story facility adjacent to existing housing so configured as to house both men and women residents in separate wings but with shared cafeteria, lobby and infrastructure space.[27] Resident students at that time still had to walk from the residence colleges to the M. D. Anderson Student Center cafeteria for food service. The mid-rise design reflected the growing concern for preservation of campus land. The design featured efficiency kitchens, suites of bedrooms, a "garden" view, and proximity to food service.

The third authorized study was a land-use proposal by the firm 3-D International for thirty-three acres of undeveloped campus land along the Southwest Freeway.[28] Gilbert Turner, in both his roles as Board Chair and as Finance Committee Chair, continually exhorted the Board of Trustees to address the ongoing financial stress of the University by increasing gifts and grants rather than by sale of land. At one point, Dr. Hinton recommended that the Board sell these thirty-three acres in order to pay for construction of an expanded campus.[29]

---

26 Houston Baptist University, Minutes of the Meetings of the Board of Trustees, Meeting on 23 Feb. 1982.
27 Ibid.
28 Houston Baptist University, Minutes of the Meetings of the Executive Committee of the Board of Trustees, Meeting on 13 Apr. 1982.
29 Houston Baptist University, Minutes of the Meetings of the Executive Committee of the Board of Trustees, Meeting on 9 Feb. 1982. Dr. Hinton outlined "present, pressing, and future needs." Immediate needs included $276,000 for athletic maintenance; parking for 275 additional automobiles; a second Atwood Building; renovation of Denham Hall; and a $5,000,000 high-rise apartment building. Future needs included an $11,000,000 activities center, a $5,000,000 theater, library expansion, and a $6,500,000 educational television station. He recommended that all or part of the 33 freeway acres be sold to fund these projects.

In an eloquent response addressed to the Board in 1982, Turner exhorted,

> Over 100 acres have been sold or leased during the past twelve years which, together with subdivision development and other miscellaneous sales, have provided over $10,500,000 for financing deficits and debt retirement. If we still had this property, we could expect over $55,000,000 from its development today. As it is, we have less than 35 acres from which to generate $20,000,000 in an orderly and systematic development program. This is our safety net which should not be used to build more buildings with expanded operations resulting in larger deficits and no means of paying for them. . . . Let us redouble our efforts in gifts, grants, and bequests. . . . We enjoy an enviable reputation in the financial community . . . for prudent and responsible management of our financial affairs. If this is destroyed by hasty actions, the University could be faced with severe financial problems, fiscal and operational constraints, and a damaged image for years to come. *Don't let the present your future hold, nor for the first the last be sold.*[30]

The Board of Trustees did not approve the President's recommendation.

§

Enrollment on campus grew from 1794 students in 1977 to 2738 in 1983. Undergraduate enrollment of 2327 in 1983 marked the historical high point. Under the leadership of Dr. James Massey, the University invested heavily in programs contributing to the quality of student life. Convocation speakers during this era included Tom Brokaw,[31] Pauline Frederick,[32] Jim McKay,[33] Abigail Van Buren,[34] Jack Anderson,[35] Eliot Janeway,[36] Howard K. Smith,[37] Charles Kuralt, Jessica Savitch, Senator William Proxmire, Tommy Lasorda, Shana Alexander, Lou Holtz, Mark

---

30 Houston Baptist University, Minutes of the Meetings of the Board of Trustees, Meeting on 23 Feb. 1982.
31 "Tom Brokaw To Speak In Assembly," *The Collegian*, 17 Nov. 1975, p. 1.
32 *Ornogah 1977,* 20.
33 *Ornogah 1977,* 37.
34 *Ornogah 1977,* 36.
35 Ibid.
36 *Ornogah 1977,* 37.
37 "Journalist Spotlights Convocation Speaker List," *HBU News,* Sept. 1978, 1.

Russell, Wayne Dyer,[38] William F. Buckley, Jeb McGruder, and Paula Zahn.[39]

A number of annual events enjoyed wide-spread student and faculty participation including Freshman Orientation, Tug-of-War, Woman's Day, the *Ornogah* Beauty Pageant, the Christmas Madrigal Dinners, Westward Ho Day, Religious Emphasis Weeks, Songfest, student-mission trips, Homecoming, Gymnastics Slave Sale, International Fair, the Gong Show, Sadie Hawkins Week, Awards Day, and the Endowed Academic Scholarship Day. The first of the HBU sororities became nationally affiliated when Triceans joined Phi Mu in 1978.[40] Epsilon Delta Pi became Kappa Delta.[41] By 1984, the only local fraternity still in existence was Alpha Pi Kappa; the Coreons considered itself a social-service organization. Phi Kappa Epsilon became Kappa Alpha, and Sigma Phi Chi became Alpha Tau Omega.[42]

In religious life, the University began an innovative program for student ministry volunteers in 1976. The pioneering *Support for Every Religious Vocation* (SERV) program comprised a two-phase internship.[43] Early learning opportunity in the program was based on field observation guided by a professional advisor; for upper classmen, the program added formal training, campus debriefing, counseling, and a financial stipend.[44] The SERV program was among the first of its kind in the nation and was widely emulated by other Christian colleges.

A new ministry outreach team called FOCUS was formed in 1977 to relate the University more effectively to the community. This musical performance group represented HBU to high school and church groups and provided spiritual nourishment while extending the visibility of the University.[45] FOCUS was invited to participate in a mission outreach project in Brazil in 1981.[46] FOCUS and its sister ensemble REFUGE provided spiritual development opportunity for its student members and one of the most successful community relation vehicles in University history.

---

38 *Ornogah 1982*, 122.

39 *Ornogah 1983*, 39.

40 "Phi Mu Replaces Triceans," *The Collegian*, 24 Apr. 1978, p. 2. Vol. 17 #2. The issue was actually May 1978.

41 "New Kappa Delta Chapter Initiated Into Conference," *The Collegian*, 2 Feb. 1978, p. 5.

42 "Happy Birthday ATO," *The Collegian*, 1 Nov. 1974, p. 1.

43 "SERV Program Begins," *HBU News*, Oct. 1976, 3.

44 Houston Baptist University, Minutes of the Meetings of the Executive Committee of the Board of Trustees, Meeting on 15 Sept. 1977.

45 "FOCUS At Cloverleaf," *HBU News*, Mar. 1981, 3.

46 "FOCUS Goes to Brazil," *HBU News*, June 1981, 5; "FOCUS News," *HBU News*, Sept. 1981, 7.

Robert Newell, Dean of Religious Affairs, garnered nation-wide recognition for the creative models of student ministry represented by SERV, FOCUS, and CLC. Weekly convocation and chapel services were restructured in 1980 to become a single weekly event that received a grade of "pass" or "fail" and was required of all full-time students. Programs alternated between spiritual and academic emphasis.[47]

Student achievement in competitive arenas reached an all-time high during the 1970s. Of particular merit were programs in publications, music, debate, and athletics. The *Collegian* newspaper received its first recognition by the Texas Intercollegiate Press Association (TIPA) in 1976.[48] Both the *Ornogah* and *The Collegian* won TIPA awards in 1977, and the student literary anthology *Shank's Mare,* funded by Bill Brittain's Fine Furniture,[49] won overall first place and sweepstakes awards that same year[50] under the leadership of Dr. Honora Lynch.[51] Dennis Alexander was recognized by TIPA in 1978 for his outstanding political cartoons, satirical columns, and the general excellence of his writing for *The Collegian.*[52] The student newspaper was plagued by intermittent publication during the late 1970s, but was gifted with some of the most entertaining writing in its history. Barbara Joan Musil can be credited for the finest *Collegian* headline of the era, "For Whom the Bell Curves."[53] The consistently spectacular Doug Spence wrote a series of predictions for the next ten-year period that included "Bertha Opens National Hamburger Chain," "Mabee Adds Balcony for Additional Enrollment," "Massey Wins Olympic Marathon," and "Byrnes Loses to Reagan."[54]

Intercollegiate sports reached new heights of achievement in the 1970s. Eddie Brown emerged in 1972 as a shining light of this era by compiling a record as HBU's all-time high-scorer in men's basketball.

---

47 Houston Baptist University, Minutes of the Meetings of the Academic Committee of the Board of Trustees, Meeting on 7 Feb. 1980; Minutes of the Executive Committee, Meeting on 21 Feb. 1980.

48 "HBU Attends Convention, Wins Awards," *The Collegian,* 15 Apr. 1976. p. 1.

49 "Mr. W. O. Brittain," *HBU News,* June 1977, 4. Photo of Bill Brittain, Dr. Honora Lynch, and Editor Nelda Hughes.

50 Houston Baptist University, Minutes of the Meetings of the Executive Committee of the Board of Trustees, Meeting on 21 Apr. 1977; "Shank's Mare Wins 1st, Sweepstakes," *HBU News,* Apr. 1977, 4.

51 "Shank's Mare Making New Start," *The Collegian,* 19 Jan. 1977, p. 1.

52 "Publications Take Prizes," *The Collegian,* 24 Apr. 1978, p. 1.

53 B. J. Musil, "For Whom the Bell Curves," *The Collegian,* Nov. (undated) 1978, p. 8.

54 Doug Spence, "The Misshape," *The Collegian,* Feb. 1980, p. 2. Spence also predicted the realization of a campus fine arts facility with the vision of all of Shakespeare's plays being performed simultaneously by the Gallery Theatre Players. In 2009, Spence, now a biology professor at the University of Texas Permian Basin, related, "My own college students know of such faculty as Cynthia Young, Joyce Fan, Avin Brownlee, and Jerry Modisette as Olympian gods in my mythological past." (Dr. Doug Spence to Dr. Don Looser, Mar. 6, 2009).

The move to NCAA Division I University Division competition in 1972 was not an easy one for the small athletic program.[55] The institutional costs of maintaining the six-sport program required by the NCAA became a matter of constant concern to the Board of Trustees. Ongoing deficits led the Board to appoint an ad hoc committee in 1978 to review the scope and mission of intercollegiate athletics on the HBU campus.[56] This study followed a year with no raises for University faculty and staff, a projected athletic deficit of $150,000, and trustee concern about limited community awareness of the athletic programs.[57] Nonetheless, in the fall of 1978, the Board of Trustees approved the University's participation in the formation of the Trans America Athletic Conference. The basketball-centered conference was composed also of Centenary College, Hardin-Simmons University, Mercer University, Northeast Louisiana University, Oklahoma City University, Pan American University, and Samford University.[58] HBU's roster of six NCAA sports—all for men—included basketball, golf, gymnastics, soccer, tennis, and track. This marked the end of fourteen years of athletic competition as an independent.

Intercollegiate golf had roots in 1966 when coached by Athletic Director Mac Sutton. By 1969 Morgan Baker, the golf professional at Sharpstown Country Club, assumed the coaching responsibility. For a while in the early 1970s, there was no coach; there was a winning team, however. Dave Mannen became coach of the golf team in 1974, a position he held until the closure of the program in 1989. Mannen was voted Coach of the Year in the Trans America Athletic Conference an unprecedented eight times from 1982 to 1989. Outstanding golfers from this era included four TAAC Players of the Year, Ken Kelley (1982) also named TAAC Athlete of the Year,[59] Darryl Henning (1984), Colin Montgomerie (1985), and Paul Davenport (1988). Seven HBU golfers were named to All-America honors: John Lewis (1972), Robert Seligman (1972), Ken Kelley (1982), Darryl Henning (1985, 1986), Colin Montgomerie (1984, 1986, 1987), Jeff Wagner (1988), and Ulfar Jonsson (1988). Tim Thelen was the first HBU golfer ever to qualify for the U. S. Open in 1983.

55 "Huskies Move Up To University Division," *The Collegian*, 1 Sept. 1972, p. 7.

56 Houston Baptist University, Minutes of the Meetings of the Executive Committee of the Board of Trustees, Meeting on 21 Feb. 1978.

57 Houston Baptist University, Minutes of the Meetings of the Board of Trustees, Meeting on 28 Sept. 1978.

58 Houston Baptist University, Minutes of the Meetings of the Board of Trustees, Meeting on 16 Nov. 1978; "Trans-America Conference Formed," *HBU News*, Oct. 1978, 3; "Trans American Conference Formed, " *The Collegian*, 19 Sept. 1978, p. 1.

59 "HBU Ken Kelley Named Trans-American 'Golfer-of-the-Year,'" *HBU News*, July 1982, 7. Photo.

British Walker Cup team member Colin Montgomerie[60] was a member of the teams that won the TAAC championships in 1984, 1985, and 1986. The HBU Huskies were also conference champions in 1988 and 1989.[61] The Rev. Dr. John Lewis, now an Episcopal priest and faculty member, recalls the "travel opportunities the school provided that were an integral part of my broad liberal arts education, the wonderful Christian nurturing and encouragement of Athletic Director Dr. Ed Billings" and the inspiration of teammate Robert Seligman.[62] Seligman's college and professional careers were tragically altered by a serious automobile accident late in his collegiate experience.

Women's golf was initiated single-handedly in 1973 by a talented student, Mary Beth Morgan. By the following fall, she had recruited two outstanding colleagues, Debbie Skelly and Sherry Donovan.[63] In 1975, Houston's only intercollegiate women's golf team won its first tournament.[64] With the assistance of alumna Dale Green Moore '68, Morgan's team finished the 1976 season ranked seventh in the nation,[65] and in 1977, she was named HBU's Athlete of the Year.[66] The team's first professional coach Sue Little was appointed in 1976 and recruited Stephanie Farwig, Ann Soderman, and Peggy Gustafson to the 1977 team that was ranked 13th in the nation by the Association for Intercollegiate Athletics for Women. Farwig finished tenth in the national AIAW rankings in 1979 and was named to Southwest Regional All-America honors in 1981. Caroline Pierce, the English Girls' International Champion in 1980 and 1981, joined the women's golf team in 1983 and in that year achieved the best individual woman's record in the history of the Dick McGuire Women's Intercollegiate Golf Tournament. Pierce was named to All-America honors in 1986.[67]

Of those golfers, several have gone on to professional careers. Stephanie Farwig began her rookie year on the Ladies Professional Golf Association tour in 1982 and won the LPGA Rookie of the Year Award in 1983. Caroline Pierce was also a member of the LPGA tour for fourteen years. She won her first major title with the Big Apple Classic in 1996 and retired from

---

60 Phil Gordon, "The Interview: Colin Montgomerie," *The Independent* (London), 28 Oct 2001, p. 17.

61 Houston Baptist University, *Golf Sports Information Guide, 2007-08,* p. 15.

62 (J. Eige to Dr. Don Looser, Nov. 15, 2009).

63 "Morgan, Skelley, Donovan: HBU's Female Golf Team," *The Collegian,* 1 Nov. 1974, p. 6. Photo.

64 "Lady Golfers Win First Tournament," *The Scene,* Winter Quarter 1975, p. 1.

65 "Girl Golfers Swinging Good," *The Collegian,* 20 Oct. 1976, p. 2.

66 *Ornogah 1976,* 258, 276-77.

67 "HBU's Caroline Pierce Captures Title in McGuire Women's Golf," *The Collegian,* 27 Oct. 1983, p. 4.

1998 HBU Distinguished Alumnus Colin Montgomerie.

the LPGA in 2001.[68] Tim Thelen was named PGA Professional Player of the Year in 2001, was a member of the PGA U. S. Cup teams from 2000 to 2007, and won the 2000 and 2003 PGA Professional National Championships.

Thelen's teammate, the well-known Scottish professional golfer Colin Montgomerie, was a member of the European Ryder Cup teams from 1991 to 2006. He has been elected captain of the European Ryder Cup team for 2010. "Monty" has been awarded both the Order of the British Empire and Member of the British Empire medals by Queen Elizabeth II. In 1998, Montgomerie was named a Distinguished Alumnus of the University. In his video acceptance speech, Montgomerie admitted, "I must confess I am a different person from the shy young student that arrived in Houston from a strict Scottish boarding school." Coach Dave Mannen recalled, "He had a tremendous amount of talent, but wasn't yet a fierce competitor." In a *London Daily Mail* article in 1999, Husky Montgomerie was remembered as gentlemanly, reserved, and fun—"with a lovely sense of humour."[69]

With the suspension of the baseball program in 1970, basketball became the most visible sport on campus. Except for a self-imposed dormancy in 1990, basketball at HBU is the only sport that has a continuous history dating from 1963. In the spring of 1977, following several years of losing seasons, the University accomplished something of a coup

68 Jack Cavanaugh, "Pierce is Unlikely Winner in Big Apple," *New York Times*, 6 Oct. 1996, Sec. 8, p. 13.
69 Lauren St. John, "Americans who love Monty remember him as teddy bear and model student," *London Daily Mail*, 10 Sept. 1999, p. 89. Interviews include those with Coach Dave Mannen, Athletic Committee Chair Dr. James Taylor, fellow-student now coach Mary Ellen Hall, and Associate Vice President for Public Relations Sharon Saunders.

with the appointment of Gene Iba as head basketball coach.[70] Iba came from a prominent basketball family and had served at the University of Texas El Paso as Assistant Coach. Nonetheless, the next three years were difficult years for the Huskies. Their 1980 season of 14-13 was broadcast on radio station KTRH.[71] This marked the seventh year of NCAA Division I competition but the first winning season in nine years. The following year, Iba was named Coach of the Year in the Trans America Athletic Conference.

Finally, in 1981 HBU won the TAAC conference championship with a record of twenty wins and nine losses for the season.[72] The Huskies also won the 1983 title and, in 1984, became the first Husky team ever to win both the conference title and the tournament championship.[73] In a memorable series of post-season playoff games led by HBU center Anicet Lavodrama, the Huskies defeated Samford for a berth in the NCAA playoffs. President Hinton came home from the TAAC 1984 Tournament with the goal net and an NCAA check for $55,000. Lavodrama shared team leadership in the playoffs with Hamilton Lewis, Scott Bigott, and Boone Almanza who was also named to Academic All-America honors.[74]

In 1985, head basketball coach Gene Iba resigned to accept a position at Baylor University. Iba had compiled a 128-96 record in NCAA competition during his eight years at HBU and was named Coach of the Year in 1981.[75] During his final three seasons against such nationally ranked teams as LSU and Arizona, the Huskies amassed a total of sixty-five wins, won the TAAC Championship in 1984, and played in the national NCAA tournament. Anicet Lavodrama, Matt England, and Terry Hairston garnered All-America honors. Anicet Lavodrama graduated in 1985, was drafted by the Los Angeles Clippers, went on to participate in the 1988 Summer Olympic Games in Seoul playing for the Central African Republic, and has since represented the International Basketball Federation (FIBA). Teammate Matt England was drafted by

70 Louis Ernst, "Iba To Take Over Husky Recruiting and Coaching," *The Collegian,* 1 Apr. 1977, p. 1; "Coach Iba Arrives," *HBU News,* Mar. 1977, 4.

71 Houston Baptist University, Minutes of the Meetings of the Board of Trustees, Meeting on 17 Apr. 1980.

72 Houston Baptist University, Minutes of the Meetings of the Board of Trustees, Meeting on 26 May 1981.

73 Mark Vinson, "HBU No. 1: Wins TAAC Tourney," *The Collegian,* 15 Mar. 1984, pp. 1, 4, 5, 7. Photos.

74 "Basketballer Boone Almanza Named Academic All-American," *HBU News,* Mar. 1983, 10. Photo.

75 "All-Time Results," *HBU Basketball Media Guide 2008,* pp. 53-54.

the Washington Bullets.[76] With the resignation of Gene Iba, Tommy Jones was named head coach for men's basketball.[77]

Several other players from the teams of this era were drafted by National Basketball Association teams. E. C. Coleman '73 was selected to play with the Houston Rockets. Ultimately, Coleman also played for the New Orleans Jazz and the Golden State Warriors.[78] The *New York Times* observed, "During his six National Basketball Association seasons, E. C. Coleman was noted as a defensive specialist and rebounder."[79] Robert Paige graduated in 1976 and played for the next ten years for the Harlem Globetrotters. Randy Martell was drafted by the Washington Bullets following his graduation in 1981. All of these professional players completed their degree requirements and graduated from HBU.

Intercollegiate soccer was begun at HBU in 1979 with Dave Swonke as coach. Soccer had not yet achieved the popularity in Houston that it had in much of the rest of the nation. Swonke's first Division I team was young but showed promise. Two years later, when the team compiled an 18-2 record, tying for the best record in NCAA Division I, Coach Swonke was named TAAC Coach of the Year.[80] By 1982, the HBU team won the Trans America Athletic Conference Championship and finished the season with a record of thirteen wins, two losses, and one tie. Among the players, Carlos Gil was named Player of the Year in 1984 for the third year; Mike Kyei was named to Midwest Region NCAA All-America honors; and, Randy Sorrels was named an Academic All-American.[81] The Huskies took the conference title again in 1984.

The sport that captured the greatest attention of the campus, the Houston public, and news media, however, was intercollegiate gymnastics. Dr. Hinton recruited Dr. Robert "Hutch" Dvorak to the University in 1973 to establish the program.[82] Because gymnastics was new to Houston, gymnasts Bill Austin, Gary Linder, and Steve Turley were asked

76 "NBA Selects Lavodrama, England," *HBU News,* Summer 1985, 14; "NBA Selects Lavodrama, England," *The Collegian,* 5 Sept. 1985, p. 8.

77 "Jones Promoted to HBU's Head Basketball Coach," *The Collegian,* 4 Apr. 1985, p. 1; Vince Santos, "New Head Basketball Coach Tommy Jones: the Future is Now," *The Collegian,* 4 Apr. 1985, p. 4.

78 "E. C. Coleman, the unflashy Jazzman," *The Collegian,* 14 Feb. 1975, p. 4.

79 "A Rookie Sizzles for Rockets," *New York Times,* 21 Nov. 1979, sec. B, p. 8.

80 Houston Baptist University, Minutes of the Meetings of the Board of Trustees, Meeting on 19 Nov. 1981.

81 "Almanza and Sorrels Named To TAAC All-Academic Team," *HBU News,* Summer 1984, 3.

82 "HBC Welcomes Gymnastics Team," *The Collegian,* 26 Oct. 1973, p. 7. Photo.

Coach Dvorak (l) and gymnasts Austin, Linder, and Turley at the Astrodome.

to present a Houston Oilers' halftime demonstration of the sport at the Astrodome that first year.[83]

HBU competed in gymnastics as an independent member of the NCAA Division I Western Region. In November 1974, the first Husky Classic was held in Sharp Gym. HBU hosted teams from the University of Texas, University of Oklahoma, Louisiana State University, and Arizona State University.[84] By 1975, the HBU gymnastics team boasted ten athletes. Gary Linder and newcomer Steve Kinnett advanced that year to the thirty-third annual NCAA National Gymnastics Championships.

In 1976, the Husky Classic moved to the Summit Arena, home of the Houston Rockets. HBU was ranked seventeenth out of seventy-five teams in the nation in 1977, had a season record of eight wins and three losses, and won a berth at the NCAA regional competition. Linder, Kinnett, and Don Smith qualified for the National Tournament, Linder and Kinnett for the second time.[85] The team was ranked eleventh in the

83 "Flying High In the Dome," *The Collegian*, 26 Oct. 1973, p. 4. Photo.
84 "Husky Classic '74," *The Collegian*, 13 Dec. 1974, p. 6.
85 "Linder, Kinnett, Smith Qualify for National Gymnastics Meet," *The Collegian*, 1 Apr. 1977, p. 7.

nation in 1978 with Chris Wiloth, Larry Besong, and Taylor Davis achieving national individual standing.[86] The 1979 *Husky Classic* at the Summit drew Olympic Gold Medalist Kurt Thomas and four other All-America competitors. HBU was ranked fifth in the nation for the 1979 season.[87] Chris Wiloth was named the University's first NCAA All-American in 1979[88] and placed fourth in vaulting in the NCAA Gymnastics Championships. HBU set a national vaulting mark of 47.9 to rank first in the nation in that event. In 1980, both Price and Wiloth were named NCAA All-Americans—both in vault.[89]

By 1980, terms like "iron cross," "pommel horse," "scissoring," and "planche" were becoming more familiar to local gymnastics fans. Tournaments were televised locally. Dvorak was named Coach of the Year for the Midwest Region of the NCAA in 1980, served as Secretary of the National Association of Collegiate Coaches, and was elected President of the National Association of Collegiate Gymnastics Coaches.[90] Touted as the premier vaulting team in the nation, the HBU gymnasts Chris Wiloth, Percy Price, Kyle Brown, and Joel Berry were all individual qualifiers for the national tournament in 1980. Wiloth and Price again were named NCAA All-Americans in vault in 1981. Wiloth attained the position of number one in the national rankings.[91]

Steve Kinnett qualified for the national NCAA tournament four straight years on the still rings. He had lost his right leg to cancer at the age of fourteen; his dismounts were legendary among fans. Dr. Joyce Fan, his pre-med advisor, called him one of the most inspirational people she had ever met. Kinnett elected not to wear a prosthesis that made him feel, he said, "handicapped." After graduation and medical school, Kinnett, a Colorado physician, also mastered snow skiing, backpacking, and ultimately took up sky-diving.[92] His love and talent for technical climbing led to a job at the camp where he learned and eventually taught more than 1,200 mobility-challenged young people.[93] His HBU record

86 "Gymnasts Receive National Rating," *The Collegian*, 18 Jan. 1978, p. 7.
87 "Percy Price—1980 Olympic Hopeful," *HBU News*, Mar. 1979, Cover, 4, 6. Photos.
88 "Chris Wiloth Earns HBU's first All-American Honor," *HBU News*, May 1979, 3; "HBU Gymnasts In Gear For 1979-80," *The Collegian*, Oct. (no date) 1979, Vol. 20 #3, p. 12.
89 "HBU's Chris Wiloth & Percy Price named NCAA All-Americans," *The Collegian*, April (no date) 1980, p. 1; *Ornogah 1980*, 158-59; "Chris Wiloth & Percy Price Named All-Americans," *HBU News*, May 1980, 2.
90 "Dvorak Named Coach of the Year," *HBU News*, May 1980, 2. Photo.
91 "Sports: Gymnastics," *HBU News*, Mar. 1981, 7.
92 Steve Kinnett, "Lucky skydiver tells of desperate jump to safety," *Houston Post*, 19 Apr 1981, sec. A, p. 23.
93 Loretta Sword, "Absence of leg doesn't deter athletic physician," *The Gazette (Colorado Springs)*, 29 Sept. 1999, http://findarticles.com/p/articles/mi_qn4191/is_1999020/ai_n9959203 (accessed May 15, 2010).

of four years at the national championships has never been equaled.

In 1982, the program was rewarded with the first invitation for the team to participate in the national championships.[94] *HBU was the smallest Division I college ever to be invited to the National Tournament; HBU was also the first private college to receive an invitation since 1962.*[95] Four HBU team and individual records were set in the national championships. Dvorak was named Coach of the Year again in 1983. Four gymnasts qualified for the Western Athletic Conference Invitational Tournament in 1984: Declan Fleming, John Romine, John Sweeney, and Zach Thomas. John Sweeney was named a dual All-American in vault and parallel bars in both 1973 and 1974.[96] Declan Fleming also was named to Academic All-America honors.

Other sports during this period were struggling. A new state-of-the-art Tartan-surface track was constructed near the men's residence in 1974.[97] Dr. Ed Billings coached track from 1974 to 1976 when the University employed Johnny Morris, a well-known Southwest Conference track coach from the University of Houston.[98] Jerry Martinez assumed track coaching duties in 1982 and began with an inexperienced group of athletes. Nonetheless, the team won the Trans America Athletic Conference Cross-Country competitions in 1983 and 1984. In 1983, HBU junior Rickie Thompson won the NCAA High Jump Championship by clearing 7 feet 5 ¼ inches. In so doing, Rickie became the first NCAA National Champion in University history.[99]

Throughout the exciting years of the 1970s, the University Husky mascot was a Samoyed named Mingo. Initially cared for by the men's fraternity the Coreons, Mingo had since 1971 been attended by a University staff member, Virginia Crosno. Theirs was a most public love affair. They went everywhere together. Mingo walked the campus several times daily. He ate cooked rice and vegetables, Melba toast, ground meat, and cottage cheese lovingly prepared by Crosno. He enjoyed the finest of medical care from volunteer veterinarians and rarely missed a major campus athletic event. The love and attention of Mrs. Crosno for Mingo became

---

94 "Gymnasts Go To Nationals," *The Collegian,* 24 Apr. 1982, p. 1.
95 Ibid.
96 "Sweeney All-American on Parallel Bars and Vault," *The Collegian,* 23 Apr. 1984, p. 7.
97 "Synthetic Surface Track Complete," *HBU News,* Sept. 1974, 4.
98 "Top Track Coach on Campus," *The Collegian,* 17 Nov. 1976, p. 1; *Ornogah 1982,* 116.
99 "Thompson Wins NCAA High Jump Championship," *HBU News,* Summer 1983, 7; *Ornogah 1983,* 163; "Thompson Wins NCAA High Jump Championship," *The Collegian,* 1 Sept. 1983, p. 10.

one of the great object lessons for students and staff alike to observe.[100]
In 1982, Mingo developed kidney failure and died on June 14. Virginia
Crosno had been his care-giver for eleven years. An emotional remem-
brance service was led by Dr. James Massey. Mingo was buried in the
courtyard of the Sharp Gym where a memorial marks his grave.[101]

Despite the victories in athletics and the publicity the University garnered, the costs related to intercollegiate athletics were of concern to the
faculty and to the Board of Trustees. Trustee Gilbert Turner reported for
the Finance Committee that "the cost of athletics in 1979 was $400,000
with basketball being the most expensive sport to maintain, and golf and
gymnastics only slightly behind."[102] However, the ad hoc committee
appointed by the Board in 1978 to examine the athletic program costs in
view of institutional mission and purpose recommended no curtailment of
athletic programs. However, the Committee recommended responsibility for the athletic deficit be assigned to the development office.

The financial difficulties of the University only worsened in the
1970s. This was not a unique problem. Dallas Baptist College had
reported accumulated debts of $7,500,000, and in July of 1974, asked to
be merged with Baylor University.[103] As late as 1982, DBC "once again
faced bankruptcy and came to the Executive Board asking for a
$3,000,000 loan."[104] Atlanta Baptist College merged with Mercer
University. In Houston, the South Texas College of Law sought to merge
with another local university in response to pressure from the American
Bar Association. Dominican College ceased operation. HBU faculty raises were postponed from the issuing of contracts in the spring of 1974 to
the fall. In 1976, no raises were given other than "humanitarian aid" of
$15,000 divided among a number of the lowest paid staff.[105] Gifts,
grants, and tuition income were consistently under budget. A year-end
shortfall of $350,000 in 1976 was followed by a $400,000 deficit in
1979[106] and a $200,000 deficit in 1980. A line of credit at First City

100 "Mingo + Crosno=Best Friends," *The Collegian,* 19 Jan. 1977, p. 3.

101 "Mingo: HBU Mascot 1966-1982," *HBU News,* July 1982, cover, 2; *Ornogah 1983,* 16. Photo.

102 Houston Baptist University, Minutes of the Meetings of the Executive Committee of the Board of
Trustees, Meeting on 16 Oct. 1980.

103 Houston Baptist University, Minutes of the Meetings of the Executive Committee of the Board of
Trustees, Meeting on 11 July 1974.

104 McBeth, 353.

105 Houston Baptist University, Minutes of the Meetings of the Executive Committee of the Board of
Trustees, Meeting on 21 Oct. 1976.

106 Houston Baptist University, Minutes of the Meetings of the Executive Committee of the Board of
Trustees, Meeting on 19 Apr. 1979.

National Bank increased from $1,800,000 in 1976 to $2,200,000 in 1981. Additional short term borrowing from the quasi-endowment funds (discretionary funds functioning as endowment) totaled $2,220,000 by 1982.

The endurance, patience, and contribution of the University staff and faculty during this era cannot be overlooked. With lagging salaries, no salary and budget increases over several years, heavy teaching loads, and limited assistance, the University's human resource contributed significant financial relief to the University's operation. To the opening faculty meeting in 1980, Dr. Hinton proclaimed, "The philosophy of the 1980s will be to take care of those who come with what we have. Faculty will have to do more than ever. We must be Christian in all that we do, scholarly, outstanding in every area, be what God wants us to be in this place."[107]

The greatest source of financial relief for University operations came from real estate leases and sales. A 1976 real estate report to the board listed the University properties currently managed. Exclusive of the 100 campus acres, those included Fondren I (Woolco), the University Savings site, the Beechnut Exxon station, the thirty-three acre freeway tract, ten other freeway acres, the miniature golf site, commercial acreage in Inwood Forest and Inwood Pines, 437 acres on Old Katy Road, property in Conroe, 610 acres in Colorado, 1000 acres in Blanco County, 7.5 acres in Brazoria County, 159 acres in Fayette County, and notes receivable for a total of $14,865,000.[108] In 1978, the University's smallest lease in history was consummated with John H. Baker, III for a plot totaling forty-eight square feet to erect a billboard bordering the Southwest Freeway.[109] On a per-square foot basis, this became the most productive property in University history.

Some real estate holdings began to yield significant financial benefit. A Toys-"R"-Us lease of 3.67 acres was executed on land south of Memorial Hospital.[110] In 1980, Inwood Pines property yielded $500,000.[111] The 375-acre farm of Jewel Wise near Crockett, first

---

107 Houston Baptist University, Minutes of the Meetings of the Faculty, Meeting on 3 Sept. 1980.
108 Houston Baptist University, Minutes of the Meetings of the Board of Trustees, Meeting on 24 Sept. 1976.
109 Houston Baptist University, Minutes of the Meetings of the Executive Committee of the Board of Trustees, Meeting on 19 Oct. 1978.
110 Houston Baptist University, Minutes of the Meetings of the Executive Committee of the Board of Trustees, Meeting on 16 Oct. 1980.
111 Houston Baptist University, Minutes of the Meetings of the Executive Committee of the Board of Trustees, Meeting on 17 Jan. 1980.

purchased by her family in 1911, was sold to fund endowed scholarships.[112] Another 2.6 acres of land in Inwood Forest yielded $579,000 in 1982. The University still had its valuable thirty-three acres of undeveloped land along the Southwest Freeway for which Gilbert Turner had issued his eloquent plea for preservation.

Remarkably, much critical campus construction was funded during these same years. Qualitative productivity by faculty was at an all-time high; student achievement in multiple competitive areas was unparalleled; institutional maturity and an undying sense of mission continued to fuel the energy of the University leadership, including the Board of Trustees. The commitment of the Board to solve its own financial problems rather than turn to denominational or community resources was unswerving.

From these seeming ashes, a phoenix did rise in the form of a ten-year, $32,000,000 campaign called *On Our Way*.[113] Gilbert Turner accepted the responsibility as campaign chair[114] and enlisted the co-leadership of Rex Baker, Sr., Milton Cross, John Lynch, and Ethel Loos McDermott. The campaign, among other things, was to provide $28,500,000 for construction of a new fine arts complex, a library tower, a chapel, ten endowed chairs, twenty-five endowed professorships, and one hundred endowed scholarships.[115] Turner pledged the first $100,000 that was followed by pledges from trustees Milton Cross, Hank Chamberlain, and Roland Burrows.[116] The goal later was raised to $32,000,000 to include an annual sustaining fund goal of $350,000 for the ten-year period.[117] Turner's goal was to raise the first $11,000,000 in the campaign by 1979.[118]

In addition to gifts to the endowment for chairs and professorships, a number of other significant financial gifts also came to the University during this period. Board members continued their history of personal contribution; major gifts were recorded from trustees John Baugh, Roland Burrows, Milton Cross, Gus Glasscock, Tracy Lawrence, H. A.

---

112 "Wise Donates Acreage for Church Vocation Students," *HBU News*, Sept. 1978, 3; Houston Baptist University, Minutes of the Meetings of the Executive Committee of the Board of Trustees, Meeting on 18 May 1978. Photo of Mrs. Wise and Dr. Hinton.

113 Houston Baptist University, *On Our Way: a decade of proof 1963-1973, a decade of promise 1973-1983*, 1973.

114 "Turner to Lead 10-Year Campaign," *HBU News*, Dec. 1974, 1; Houston Baptist University, Minutes of the Meetings of the Executive Committee of the Board of Trustees, Meeting on 14 Nov. 1974.

115 Houston Baptist University, *On Our Way: a decade of proof 1963-1973, a decade of promise 1973-1983*, 1973.

116 Houston Baptist University, Minutes of the Meetings of the Board of Trustees, Meeting on 28 Feb. 1975 and 21 Nov. 1975.

117 Houston Baptist University, Minutes of the Meetings of the Executive Committee of the Board of Trustees, Meeting on 13 Feb. 1975.

118 Houston Baptist University, Minutes of the Meetings of the Board of Trustees, Meeting on 28 Sept. 1978.

Three giants among the Chairs of the Board of Trustees were
Gilbert Turner (l), Howard. C. Lee, Sr. (c), and Milton C. Cross (r).

Lott, Stewart Morris, Ethel McDermott, and Gilbert Turner. By 1983, the individual members of the E. P. West Class of Second Baptist Church, taught by President Hinton, had funded twenty-eight Endowed Academic Scholarships, raising the total of their individual contributions to approximately $750,000.[119] These scholarships were in addition to those funded by the E. P. West Class itself.

One of the largest estates ever to come to the University was that of Mrs. T. J. Bettis. Early legal documents for this estate stipulated a number of colleges as beneficiaries—the University of Texas, Southern Methodist University, Texas A & M University, Baylor University, and Houston Baptist University. A later document appeared to remove all colleges other than Houston Baptist University. The other college beneficiaries questioned the validity of the final document, and in 1981 the matter ultimately required an opinion by the Attorney General of the State of Texas who specified that grants of $150,000 be given to each of

---

119 "E. P. West Class Completes Another Endowed Academic Scholarship," *HBU News,* Mar./Apr. 1983, 7-8. Scholarships funded by E. P. West Class members as of 1983 included those by Theo Dora Heyne, Jack & Bessie Conner, Mr. and Mrs. Bennett Coulson (3), Dr. and Mrs. Ross Dillon, Dr. and Mrs. W. H. Hinton, Mr and Mrs Howard Luna (2), Rev. and Mrs. M. A. Marshall (2), Mr. and Mrs. Wm. E. Pielop, Jr. (3), David and Essa Hallum (8), Mevis and Nell Smith, Florence Oldham Weaver (2), Judge T. M. Kennerly, and Mrs. Lula B. Kennerly.

the several institutions. Houston Baptist University was awarded twenty-five percent of the residual estate.[120] A 1983 assessment of the gift to the University projected $2,500,000 in cash, $2,400,000 in bonds, and $2,250,000 in mineral rights. Mrs. Bettis had first become a friend of HBC in 1964 when she gave $100,000 to establish a scholarship honoring her first husband.[121] The Bettis estate would emerge as the largest single source for eliminating most of the accumulated University operating deficit.

§

By 1975, two affinity organizations were functioning effectively to create visibility for the University in the community and to raise money in support of University programs. Since 1964, the President's Council membership had grown to 142 men. Vice President for Development Oscar Turner worked with this group of outstanding community leaders that focused on semi-annual black-tie dinners as a vehicle for community awareness and fund-raising. Featured presenters for these dinners during this era included Art Linkletter,[122] Giselle MacKenzie,[123] Jerome Hines,[124] Grady Nutt, and a second visit by Ronald Reagan.[125]

A second organization, the President's Advisors, was formed in 1974 under the leadership of HBU Development Associate Theo Dora Heyne.[126] At their first meeting in December, seventy-eight new members heard President Hinton "whose appeal contained the excitement and challenge of a coach's last minute pep talk. The College Singers, under the magical direction of R. Paul Green, provided extra incentive."[127] By the following year, some ninety members of the Advisors had united to form "an elite group of civic-minded and socially-active Christian women joined together to share mutual interests and concerns for the future

120 Houston Baptist University, Minutes of the Meetings of the Executive Committee of the Board of Trustees, Meeting on 13 Apr. 1982.
121 Houston Baptist College, *Destiny*, Jan. 1964, cover, p. 2.
122 "President's Council Spring Dinner," *HBU News*, Feb. 1976, 1. Photo of Linkletter.
123 Houston Baptist University, Minutes of the Meetings of the Board of Trustees, Meeting on 18 Nov. 1976.
124 "Opera Star to Sing at Annual Dinner," *HBU News*, Mar. 1978, 3; "Tribute Paid at Dinner to Members of President's Council," *HBU News*, Mar. 1978, 1, 3. Photos.
125 "Ronald Reagan Will Address Council Dinner," *HBU News*, Feb. 1977, 1.
126 "Development Adds New Personnel," *HBU News*, Sept. 1974, 1.
127 "New Group, President's Advisors Formed," *The Scene*, Winter Quarter 1974, p. 1.

growth of the University."[128] By 1976, the Advisors had grown to 125 members and had initiated seasonal lunches as a means of gaining visibility for the University and raising funds. Theo Dora Heyne was a Christian business woman who brought her organizational acumen to her University leadership role and enabled the President's Advisors to flourish from the very beginning. This organization would eventually become The Guild and serve as a major provider for student scholarships. Theo Dora Heyne died only four years later in 1978 leaving the legacy of a vibrant organization in University life.[129]

Founder Theo Dora Heyne, seated on the right, and members
of the President's Advisors at an early gala. Mrs. Hinton is seated to the left.

Helen Tinch, founding Director of the Museum of American Architecture and Decorative Arts, retired in 1978. She built the museum collection, opened its first exhibit space in the new Moody Library in 1968, and had worked with the American Museum Society since its founding in September 1965. Tinch had worked with the Harris County Heritage Society and became interested in an HBC museum as a result of

128 "On-campus seminars for President's Advisors," *HBU News,* Mar. 1975, 4.
129 Frank Carmical, "A Tribute to Theo Dora Heyne," *The Collegian,* 24 Apr. 1978, p. 5. (Actually, Vol. 17, #11, May 1978); Houston Baptist University, Minutes of the Meetings of the Executive Committee of the Board of Trustees, Meeting on 20 Apr. 1978.

the architectural symposia of the early 1960s.[130] Rex Baker, Sr. had proposed a separate Board of Directors for the Museum of American
Architecture and Decorative Arts in 1974.[131] Baker's concept was to create a fund-raising and policy entity that would complement the American
Museum Society. In 1977, trustee Otis Brigman suggested a "Museum
Historical Society"[132] along the same lines. Subsequent discussion led the
Board to believe that control should remain with the trustees. The desire
for the museum to be a center for academic history research was also a
dream of founding trustees Rex Baker, Sr. and Stewart Morris. During this
period, the Museum mounted a number of historical exhibits including
The Influence of Primitive Art in Stone and Wood, A Stitch in Time,[133] *Eighteen
Minutes to Glory* that won a Texas Historical Commission award,[134] *City of
Destiny,*[135] *Lone Star and Eagle* that won a "best interpretive exhibit" award
from the Texas Historical Commission,[136] *Texas—Sense of Place, Spirit of
Independence,*[137] and the Smithsonian exhibit *Five Crucial Elections.*[138]

§

University leadership during the period 1974 to 1984 was shared by
a number of dedicated individuals. Dr. Ed Tapscott was appointed Vice
President for Academic Affairs upon the retirement of H. B. Smith.
Herman Barlow '72 succeeded Ralph Gibson and Frank Fisher as
Director of Admissions. Dr. Jerry Ford was named Registrar and
Associate Dean of Smith College in 1975 following Dr. Mike Robbins.[139]
In 1977, four new vice presidents were named: Dr. Don Looser in
Administrative Affairs; Dr. James Massey in Student Affairs; and Dr. Ray
V. Mayfield, Jr. and Barney Walker, Jr. in Development.[140] Additional

---

130 Gay McFarland, "Milady's chamber: a look at 19th century women," *Houston Post,* 23 Jan. 1975, sec. B,
p. 2.
131 Houston Baptist University, Minutes of the Meetings of the Board of Trustees, Meeting on 11 Jan. 1974.
132 Houston Baptist University, Minutes of the Meetings of the Board of Trustees, Meeting on 24 May 1977.
133 Yasmin Islom, "Museum of American Architecture and Decorative Arts," *The Collegian,* 4 Nov. 1982, p.
1.
134 "Local Museum Wins Statewide Award," *The Collegian,* 10 Dec. 1984, p. 9; "HBU Museum Receives
Honors," *HBU News,* Summer 1984, 2.
135 "HBU Museum Displaying 'City of Destiny' Exhibit," *The Collegian,* 4 Oct. 1984, p. 1.
136 "Museum Hosts Christmas Show," *The Collegian,* 10 Dec. 1984, p. 4.
137 "Museum Opens Texas Exhibit," *The Collegian,* 4 Apr. 1985, p. 6.
138 "Museum Features Critical Elections," *HBU News,* May 1980, 4.
139 "Dr. Ford named Registrar," *The Collegian,* 3 Sept. 1975, p. 1.
140 "Four New VPs Named," *The Collegian,* 1 Apr. 1977, p. 5.

leadership in the Development Office was provided by Jack Tweed,[141] Theo Dora Heyne, Oscar Turner, Dr. Ray Mayfield, Jr., Dr. O. D. Martin, Jeff Wells, State Senator Hank Grover, and Dr. B. J. Martin.[142]

Dr. Roger Brooks was appointed the first Vice President for Graduate Studies in 1979 and later served as Vice President for Administration. In 1980, Dr. Carl Wrotenbery succeeded Jefferson Caskey and Dorothy Allen as Director of the Moody Library, moving from a similar position at Corpus Christi State University.[143] The Office of Admissions was re-named Student Development in 1980 and Brenda Cherry Davis '71 was appointed its Director.

In 1982, Dr. Don Byrnes was named Dean of Admissions and Records, and Dr. Jerry Ford was appointed Dean of the Smith College of General Studies.[144] Dr. James Massey served as Vice President for Student Affairs throughout the decade with Frances Curtis as his associate.[145] Joan DeRooy was appointed Director of Continuing Education in 1980 and soon began to pioneer new ventures in instructional television and professional development.

In September 1983, Dr. Ed Tapscott left work on a typical Friday afternoon, going home for the weekend. Several hours later, he collapsed and died at the age of 50.[146] Since the retirement of H. B. Smith in 1974, Tapscott had served nine years as Vice President for Academic Affairs. His tragic death represented a challenge to the stability of the University's administrative structure, particularly coming at the beginning of the new academic year. In due season, Dr. Hinton announced the appointment of Dr. Don Looser as Vice President for Academic Affairs. Looser had been with the University nineteen years. He was currently serving as Vice President for Administrative Affairs, and had previously served as Assistant to the President for Academic Affairs and the founding Dean of Smith College.[147]

§

141 "Jack Tweed New VP for Development," *The Scene*, Fall Quarter 1974, p. 1.
142 *WHO Houston '80* (Houston: WHO Houston, Inc., 1980), 275.
143 "Dr. Wrotenbery Named Library Director," *The Collegian*, Feb. 1980, p. 1.
144 Houston Baptist University, Minutes of the Meetings of the Board of Trustees, Meeting on 25 May 1982.
145 "New Dean Takes Office," *The Collegian*, 16 Sept. 1971, p. 1.
146 "Obituaries: Tapscott," *Houston Post*, 25 Sept 1983, sec. B, p. 6.
147 "Looser Named to Academic Affairs," *The Collegian*, 6 Oct. 1983, p. 1.

Opportunity for more "firsts" abounded in the 1970s. Judy Babb became the first HBU employee in 1970 to have the mayor of the City of Houston name a day honoring her service to University students.[148] Public Relations Director Dan Gorton became the first Convocation speaker ever to receive a standing ovation in advance of his remarks when he asked anyone to leave who didn't want to hear what he had to say.[149] The University's first bomb threat prematurely terminated spring 1978 Commencement Exercises.[150]

The University acquired its first administrative computer, a Microdata mainframe used for registration and institutional accounting.[151] Gilbert Turner gave a Prime I 1000 main-frame computer, soon named "George" by students, to equip the first student computer laboratory in 1981.[152] Atwood II was constructed as the first jointly-funded instructional facility by a state Baptist university and a Southern Baptist Convention seminary.[153] HBU's first graduate degree programs were established. Student publications received their first TIPA awards. HBU's first student athletes were named to All-America and NCAA championship honors.

The 20th anniversary of the University's first classes was marked by multiple ceremonies in 1983.[154] As part of the celebration, the Women's Auxiliary commissioned the weaving of a large wall hanging depicting the University seal that was presented to Dr. Hinton and hung in the lobby of the University administration building.[155] Dr. Troy Womack and Dr. Hinton each began his twenty-first year of service. The University honored its first twenty-year employees that included Judy Babb, Flonnie Brown, Dr. Glen Cain, Dr. A. O. Collins, Dr. William Dacres, Dr. Joyce

---

148 "Birthday Proclamation," *HBC News,* Mar. 1970, 2; "Mrs. Judy Babb Receives Promotion," *HBU News,* Nov. 1976, 2.

149 "Gorton Resigns," *HBU News,* March 1978, 4. Gorton, a cartoonist, served until 1978 and was known for working to keep HBU out of the news during the days of national campus political unrest. The 1969 *Shank's Mare* was dedicated to Gorton, "a true Renaissance man."

150 Houston Baptist University, Minutes of the Meetings of the Board of Trustees, Meeting on 25 May 1978. All student degrees had been conferred. Dr. Hinton directed an orderly evacuation of the building. An honorary rank for Dr. Alma Leavell whose family had come from California had to be conferred at a later time. To the University's surprise, the Houston Police bomb squad directed that a search of the gymnasium be undertaken by University personnel unassisted by the bomb squad. Nothing was ever found.

151 "Microdata Computer Here," *The Collegian,* 1 Apr. 1977, p. 3. Photo.

152 Houston Baptist University, Minutes of the Meetings of the Executive Committee of the Board of Trustees, Meeting on 17 Sept. 1981.

153 Houston Baptist University, Minutes of the Meetings of the Board of Trustees, Meeting on 23 Feb. 1982.

154 "Dr. Hinton Honored for 20 Years of Service," *The Collegian,* 27 Oct. 1983, p. 1.

155 *Ornogah 1981,* 85.

Fan, Dr. Calvin Huckabay, and Dr. Ray V. Mayfield, Jr. The 1983 President's Council Dinner under the chairmanship of Stewart Morris enjoyed a media reflection on the period 1963 to 1983 by *Eyes of Texas* personality Ray Miller. At the 1984 Dinner, John Baugh, U. S. Senator Lloyd Bentsen, and Stewart Morris recalled the formative years of early college planning and expressed gratitude for "the pursuit of excellence that stresses the quality of life as well as the quality of learning."[156]

For the President's Advisors' spring gala on April 19, 1983, Mayor Kathy Whitmire declared Dr. W. H. Hinton Day in the City of Houston in honor of Dr. Hinton's twenty years of service. Later on October 11, 1983, a black-tie dinner at the Westin Galleria for more than 400 guests celebrated the University's twentieth anniversary and honored Dr. and Mrs. Hinton. Five past chairmen of the University Board of Trustees were also honored. The program for the evening featured a multi-media presentation of the story of Dr. Hinton's life from his West Texas beginnings through his tenure as HBU's President. Dr. Edwin Young served as Master of Ceremonies for the program that featured Dr. Charles Allen, former pastor of Houston's First Methodist Church; Dr. Phil Hoffman, former President of the University of Houston and current President of the Texas Medical Center; Dr. Bill Denham, first Chairman of the University Board of Trustees; and friends, students, and representatives of the Board of Trustees. Dr. Hinton received a gold ring fashioned after the University seal and surrounded by twenty diamonds signifying the anniversary years. Additionally, the main campus entrance was named Hinton Drive, and the President's Home was designated as Hinton House. Dr. Hinton's service of more than twenty years was the longest tenure of any serving college or university president in the State of Texas.

§

The decade from 1974 to 1984 clearly stood on the shoulders of the University's first ten years. Despite the University's serious ongoing financial difficulties, the faith of the trustees never wavered. Students, faculty, and administrators achieved new heights of accomplishment that honored the confidence of the trustees. The physical campus expanded. The endowment of the University significantly increased. The University

---

156 "President's Council Dinner Planned for May," *The Collegian,* 23 April 1984, p. 1.

moved from institutional birth to a period of growth and development. A tradition of long-term institutional commitment by trustees, faculty, donors, and administrators was established. The University drew near the passing of the torch from its first and founding President to a new generation of leadership.

EIGHT

1984-1987

By the 1980s, Houston emerged as the fourth largest city in the nation with a population of 1.6 million residents—the largest urban area in Texas. In the midst of economic depression in much of the rest of the nation, Houston became a "promised land" with its wealth of employment opportunity for urban residents in the "rust belt" cities of Cleveland, Pittsburgh, Detroit, and Chicago.[1] *U. S. News and World Report* proclaimed, "This is not a city. It is a phenomenon—an explosive, churning, roaring juggernaut that is shattering tradition as it expands outward and upward with an energy that stuns even its residents."[2] In his book *Houston: A Chronicle of the Bayou City,* author Stanley Siegel observed,

> Only occasionally in the history of a civilization, nation, or city, do all the dynamic forces of existence combine to produce an extraordinary time or historical moment. By the 1980s, Houston stood within the borders of a renaissance with many of the contours of potential greatness apparent. Houston was a city on the verge—an ever-expanding urban metropolis well on its way to becoming one of the most cosmopolitan, ethno-culturally diverse, and economically dynamic cities in the United States.[3]

The sudden influx of American expatriates from the "rust belt" fed suburban home and office building construction and freeway traffic in Houston. Previously undeveloped areas north, west, and south of the downtown area exploded with new subdivisions and office parks. George Mitchell's "The Woodlands" and Gerald Hines' "First Colony" offered some of the finest planned communities in the nation.[4]

Such dramatic urbanization enhanced the potential of Houston Baptist University for growth and stability. A subtle but dramatic change

---

1 Stanley E. Siegel and John A. Moretta, *Houston: A Chronicle of the Bayou City* (Sun Valley: American Historical Press, 2005), 210.
2 Alvin P. Sanoff, "Where supercities are growing fastest," *U. S. News and World Report,* 30 June 1980, 52-55, 56.
3 Ibid.
4 Ibid.

began to be visible in the demographic composition of the student body. The city began to experience considerable immigration from Southeast Asia beginning with refugees from Vietnam, Laos, and Cambodia. Additionally, the 1980s witnessed the increasing migration of a Hispanic population from Mexico and Central America.[5] This pattern of internationalization continued into the 21st century with the influx of Chinese, South Korean, Japanese, Indian, and Pakistani residents.

Between 1980 and 1990, the percentage of Asian students increased from eleven percent to fifteen percent; Hispanic enrollment increased from four percent to ten percent; African-Americans increased slightly from five percent to eight percent. Anglos decreased as a percentage from eighty-one percent to sixty-five percent. Other significant changes occurred in the composition of HBU's undergraduate population. As enrollments grew, the percentage of resident students declined. The *Collegian* began to address issues related to a commuter campus with increasing frequency.[6]

The reputation for excellence in many of the University's professional programs—particularly in pre-medicine, nursing, math, and science—drew students from families for whom a child represented the potential for upward economic mobility. Students from culturally-diverse families were also attracted to small classes, individual attention, a highly personalized environment, a safe campus, and the commitment to excellence. The requirements of courses in Bible and Convocation attendance were not perceived as deterrents for non-Christian students. For the University, the cultural diversity of the campus presented welcome opportunity for inculcation of the Christian faith, a heightened environment for cultural understanding, and a campus population that reflected the demographic diversity of the city.

Toward the end of the Hinton era, subtle evidence verified HBU's blend of pragmatic reality alongside dreams of "what could be." The twenty-year-old University was still buoyed by the same idealism with which it had been born. Long-term members of the faculty and staff who shared the founding dreams remained steadfast in spite of difficult and unpredictable circumstances. However, many colleagues who preferred a more stable environment had moved to other institutions. Founding

---

5 Siegel, p. 219.
6 Alfonso Munoz, "Where is School Unity," *The Collegian,* 8 Nov. 1984, p. 2.

faculty member A. O. Collins recalled, "In spite of the rough times and frustrations, these have been very fulfilling years."[7]

Among the faculty, staff, and trustees, the excitement of achievement continued unabated. Dr. Troy Womack recalled,

> The early days at Houston Baptist College were dominated by young, energetic people who pitched in to work. One of HBC's strongest assets has been its trustees. They have a "go-get-'em" attitude. They put their prestige, time, and energy into making HBC one of our leading Texas Baptist institutions.[8]

A strong commitment to the original tenets of liberal arts education in the Christian context flourished. An innovative spirit found deep roots. Faculty and staff learned the joy of risk and reward. Students shared the sense of adventure and demonstrated high levels of academic and professional achievement.

By 1984, many of the investments of time and resource by the young university were bearing fruit. In 1985, the University's librarian, Dr. Jon Suter, was contacted by Mr. and Mrs. Douglas Ragland seeking to honor the memory of their son. Suter warmly welcomed their son's considerable personal library of books in mathematics and philosophy to the library and established a friendship with the couple. In 1987, Mr. and Mrs. Douglas Ragland pledged a gift of $150,000 to be matched by the Cullen Foundation to establish the Ragland Reading Room in the new Library addition in memory of their son, Douglas Ragland, Jr. This marked the first of many annual gifts from the Raglands who were drawn to the University by its spirit of gratitude and welcome.

A series of major gifts from long-cultivated friends proved to be strategic to the University's growth and maturity. In 1986, the University received its portion of the Delores Welder Mitchell estate that was divided among six institutions. The estate conveyed a gift to HBU of approximately $3,000,000 to be distributed over a twenty-nine-year period for non-operational, enrichment opportunities. Two of the first campus improvements funded by the Mitchell Trust were the construction of a new campus entrance in 1987 and the purchase of a new Hamburg Steinway concert grand piano for the Mabee Theater.

---

7 "Reflections: HBC Beginnings and HBU Today," *HBU News,* Summer 1986, 4.
8 "Reflections: HBC Beginnings and HBU Today," *HBU News,* Summer 1986, 5.

Trustee Whitson Etheridge completed negotiations in 1987 to accept a gift from the Sun Oil Exploration and Production Co. representing property in Texas and Louisiana valued at over $1,000,000.[9] In other action, the Cullen Foundation made an additional grant of $1,000,000 to the University to support construction of the proposed "Library Tower."[10] From the final settlement of the Bettis estate, the University received a refund of an additional $75,000 of windfall profits tax from the IRS.

In gratitude and recognition of these significant gifts, several campus landmarks received new named designations. By means of a formal resolution on June 19, 1984, the University trustees, in recognition of "the magnanimous nature of this gift," renamed the academic quadrangle the Leona Mankin Brown Bettis Quadrangle;[11] the administrative offices became designated as the Stanley P. Brown Administrative Complex—named for Mrs. Bettis' first husband who was an executive of the Hughes Tool Company.[12] These facilities were formally dedicated on May 2, 1986.[13] Additionally, the student housing was renamed, yet again, as the Rebecca Eleanor Bates Philips Residence College for Women and the Reuben Littleton Philips Residence College for Men.[14]

§

The strategic value of the University land bounded by the Southwest Freeway, Fondren Road, and Beechnut Street became increasingly apparent. In 1984, some 600 crepe myrtle trees were planted by 250 volunteers along the 2.2 miles bordering the campus on Fondren Road, Beechnut Boulevard, and the Southwest Freeway.[15] The joint project with Memorial Hospital more formally defined the contiguous campus properties. The collaboration reflected a proposal by Stewart Morris to develop a university/medical/research triangle.[16] The personal generosity of University trustees and friends was again evident with donation of the trees by Sterling Cornelius, site preparation by Andy Sikes and Gilbert

---

9 Houston Baptist University, Minutes of the Meetings of the Board of Trustees, Meeting on 26 May 1987.
10 Houston Baptist University, Minutes of the Meetings of the Board of Trustees, Meeting on 19 Nov. 1985.
11 *Ornogah 1986*, 14. Photo.
12 Houston Baptist University, Minutes of the Meetings of the Executive Committee of the Board of Trustees, Meeting on 19 June 1984.
13 "Building Dedications," *HBU News,* Summer 1986, 2; *Ornogah 1986,* 244. Photo.
14 Commemorative plaques are displayed at the residences.
15 "600 Crepe Myrtles Planted On Campus," *HBU News,* Winter 1984, cover, 1. Photos.
16 Houston Baptist University, Minutes of the Meetings of the Board of Trustees, Meeting on 24 Sept. 1985.

Turner, and provision of irrigation by trustee Otis Brigman.[17] This beautification project visually communicated the expansive University campus for the first time. Coupled with construction in 1986 of an imposing granite campus entrance on Fondren, the trees dramatically defined the campus property. The entrance design by architect Charles Wilson was selected in a formal competition, utilized the same Texas granite as the Morris Columns, and was based on classical Greek elements.[18]

Construction began in 1984 on a second Cullen building of 18,000 square feet to house the College of Nursing Associate Degree and the Department of Mathematics, to afford additional classrooms, and to provide a Cullen Parlor for campus social and professional receptions, lunches, and meetings.[19] Each incremental element of this facility addressed a major campus need. At the same time, a second campus facility was under construction to provide one of the most comprehensive gymnastics training centers in the nation. A gift from Mr. and Mrs. C. Gus Glasscock, the gymnastics facility was given in memory of their son, James Thomas Glasscock.[20] The innovative design for the training center included deep pits filled with foam for protection against dismount injury in the training process. The added importance of this facility to the campus was the easing of the Sharp Gymnasium schedule for physical education classes, basketball practice, and weekly convocations.

One of the most pressing campus needs during the 1980s was for additional library space. A report issued by the Southern Association of Colleges and Schools in 1980 focused on "the insufficiency of funds to support library operations and insufficient space to seat twenty-five percent of the student body."[21] A formal recommendation from SACS in the 1981 reaffirmation process mandated solution of this problem as it had in 1970. The University administration proposed a massive library tower that would connect the Moody Library and the Cullen Science Center. Contained within 75,000 square feet on eight floors of a tower would be space for library shelving, a student center, the museum, classrooms, and

17 Houston Baptist University, Minutes of the Meetings of the Board of Trustees, Meeting on 30 Nov. 1984; *Ornogah 1985,* 28-29. Photos.

18 "Main Entrance near Completion," *HBU News,* Fall 1986, 1; *Ornogah 1987,* 260-61.

19 Farha Ahmed, "Cullen Science Annex," *The Collegian,* 23 Apr. 1984, p. 1.

20 "New Gym Built," *The Collegian,* 30 Aug. 1984, p. 1; "Dedication Glasscock Gymnastic Center," *HBU News,* Summer 1985, 5; *Ornogah 1985,* 64-65. Years later, upon the death of Mr. Glasscock, it was reported that his father and uncles had at one time all been acrobats with a traveling circus. Photos.

21 Houston Baptist University, Minutes of the Meetings of the Board of Trustees, Meeting on 27 Nov. 1984.

executive offices. Fund raising continued for the "Library Tower" project to which the most recent Cullen Foundation gift had been pledged.[22]

In the midst of planning for the library addition, trustees arrived for an Executive Committee meeting on February 18, 1986, and were greeted by a contingent of members of the President's Advisors already seated in the Board Room. Among the delegation were wives of several of the current trustees. Speaking for the group were Lee Lawrence and Dr. Kate Bell who proposed that the library tower be named for Dr. Hinton and that the College of Education and Behavioral Sciences be housed therein. The aggregation was unexpected; their appearance was not on the meeting agenda. Nonetheless, they were invited back to address the full Board of Trustees the next week. At that time, a formal resolution was presented to the trustees who proposed

> that the tower under planning bear the name of Dr. W. H. Hinton as a permanent testimony to his long and distinguished tenure as the only President of HBU. It will be a fitting tribute to the man who has devoted his entire professional life to the growth and development of education in a Christian context. It is also proposed that the College of Education and Behavioral Sciences be incorporated within the Tower to further honor Dr. Hinton for his lifelong participation in education and to magnify the honor he brought to the teaching profession.[23]

The Advisors pledged their assistance in raising the requisite funds for the facility. Following the departure of the delegation and discussion of their resolution, the Board voted to respond positively and name the proposed new facility for Dr. Hinton. Thus ended the only campus sit-in ever recorded in University history.

Still under consideration was the 1982 Crain/Anderson feasibility study for a 100,000 square-foot special events center that would house a field house, fine arts performance facilities, and a television studio. The project was designed to be built in phases as funding became available.[24] Dr. Hinton had at one time recommended sale of the thirty-three acres of

---

22 "The William H. Hinton College of Education and Library Tower," *HBU News,* Fall 1986, cover, 2-3. Photos.

23 Houston Baptist University, Minutes of the Meetings of the Board of Trustees, Meeting on 25 Feb. 1986.

24 Students championed the proposal; the Student Senate sent a resolution to the Board of Trustees offering to "lead a fund raising effort to build the W. H. Hinton Special Events Center for intercollegiate athletics, special convocations, and cultural events."

campus land bordering the Southwest Freeway to fund this proposed facility.[25]

§

The University's first efforts to undertake comprehensive strategic planning began in 1985. A Short-Term Goals Committee was appointed headed by Colletta McMillian, Chair of the Trustee Academic Committee. In the fall, a workshop for faculty and trustees was presented by Dr. Robert Shirley, a consultant in strategic planning. Emanating from this strategic planning process was a 1986 report to the Board from Vice President of Academic Affairs Looser.[26] The report summarized the University's chief assets: an urban location; its small size in proximity to a large population; a strong reputation for excellence; institutional flexibility; the dedication of its faculty and staff; and its potential for growth. The report catalogued a number of critical needs. Critically important was reversal of the declining undergraduate enrollment by providing a testing and guidance center, a career/placement center, and additional administrative support accompanied by more adequate fund-raising. Second was the need to provide more competitive facilities for additional library seating, fine arts instruction, a campus theater, chapel, and recital hall. A third critical need was to strengthen academic programs through more competitive faculty salaries, reduced teaching loads, opportunity for more professional growth, funding of additional endowed professorships and chairs, and discipline-related accreditation. Finally, the report advocated greater visibility in the community, the need for further strategic planning, and greater attention to competitive student life facilities and services.[27]

Despite resource shortages, however, a vibrant academic program continued to characterize the University's achievements. In 1987, the University awarded its 5,000th degree to Phyllis Childress.[28] The number of Endowed Academic Scholarships rose to 162 and represented fifty-four percent of the institutional endowment.[29] The University's Opera Theater productions directed by Dr. Richard Collins caught the

---

25 Houston Baptist University, Minutes of the Meetings of the Board of Trustees, Meeting on 26 Mar. 1985.
26 Houston Baptist University, Minutes of the Meetings of the Board of Trustees, Meeting on 18 Nov. 1986.
27 Houston Baptist University, Minutes of the Meetings of the Board of Trustees, Meeting on 2 Jan. 1985.
28 Houston Baptist University, Minutes of the Meetings of the Board of Trustees, Meeting on 20 May 1987.
29 Houston Baptist University, Minutes of the Meetings of the Faculty Assembly, Meeting on 16 Oct. 1984.

approving eye of *Houston Post* music critic Carl Cunningham.[30] The University's success in medical-school admission reached an all-time high. Dr. Cynthia Young, University pre-med advisor, announced that sixty-six percent of the forty HBU student applicants had received their top choice institution on the first match.[31]

Enrollment data from 1985 showed 468 students enrolled in non-degree professional development courses. Dr. Joan DeRooy, Vice President for Instructional Television and Professional Development, coordinated the work of a large staff and offered programs for upward aspiring working professionals. Continuing education credits were offered for certificate programs in management, human resources, information systems, certified public accounting (CPA), chartered property casualty underwriting (CPCU), real estate, and the Insurance Institute of America. In 1984, a Division of Instructional Television evolved.[32] The University's Master of Science in Management degree began to be offered via live television at workplace sites for employees of HBU's Corporate Alliance including Texas Eastern Transmission, Texas Instruments, Dow Chemical, Phillips Petroleum, Enron, and Aramco.[33] This program graduated its first students—three Texas Eastern employees— in 1986.[34] In further remote-site expansion, the University was asked to offer the Master of Science in Management taught by HBU College of Business faculty on instructional sites at both Bergstrom Air Force Base in Austin and Reese Air Force Base in Lubbock.[35]

One of the University's most innovative graduate programs was established in 1985. The Master of Liberal Arts degree (MLA) was created under the leadership of Dr. Newell Boyd and was based on models of similar programs at liberal arts institutions throughout the nation. The program offered courses restricted to MLA students and was characterized by charismatic teaching and stimulating content. The program was aimed at an adult, non-traditional student who desired a structured but

---

30 Carl Cunningham, "Tartuffe at HBU," *Houston Post* reprinted in *The Collegian,* 16 May 1986, p. 6. "Mechem's clever adaptation of Moliere got a quite sparkling premiere from HBU's Opera Theater."

31 (Dr. Cynthia Young to Dr. W. H. Hinton, Feb. 14, 1986).

32 "HBU/TV—The University's Newest Learning Option," *HBU News,* Fall 1985, 6-7. Photos of Dr. DeRooy, Clay Porter, and Isaac Simpson.

33 Houston Baptist University, Minutes of the Meetings of the Executive Committee of the Board of Trustees, Meeting on 22 Jan. 1985.

34 "Texas Eastern has first grads in HBU's 'workplace' campus TV program," *HBU News,* Winter 1986, 2.

35 Houston Baptist University, Minutes of the Meetings of the Executive Committee of the Board of Trustees, Meeting on 22 Jan. 1985.

flexible course of interdisciplinary study in the liberal arts. Pragmatically, the program drew students who sought intellectual stimulation and learning in a social setting with others of similar intent. A menu of some three or four courses was offered each term with class enrollment limited to twenty students to promote extended discussion. Most students took only one course each term. The program was academically challenging and enrolled sixty students in its first year. By 1986, some 130 students were enrolled in the MLA program.[36] With an average age of forty, the students included attorneys, physicians, teachers, corporate executives, and retirees. The *Houston Post* featured the MLA and the MBA programs in an article on the strengths of the University entitled, "Houston Baptist campus blossoms."[37] The program was the only program in Houston accredited by the Association of Graduate Liberal Studies Programs and produced its first graduates, Les Coy and Mark Sandlin, in November 1986.[38] By 1985, eight years after the inception of graduate study at HBU, graduate students represented twenty-six percent of the University's enrollment. Graduate programs had quickly become a major profit center in support of the undergraduate program.

The College of Nursing received reaffirmation of its accreditation in 1986 in a process distinguished by the absence of any recommendations and by the inclusion of a formal commendation from the Texas Board of Nurse Examiners for a history of stellar student achievement on the state licensure exams.[39] Another professional commendation recognized the work of the Dean of Smith College, Dr. Jerry Ford.[40] The National Academic Advising Association (NACADA) named Dr. James Taylor one of the nation's outstanding faculty advisors in 1984 and named HBU's program as the nation's top academic advising program in 1986. Ford's *Student Advising Handbook* developed for new faculty orientation at HBU was specifically recognized by NACADA for its quality and effectiveness. In 1984, Dr. Don Looser was elected President of the Conference of Academic Deans of the Southern Association of Colleges and Schools.[41] Dr. Ann Gebuhr added to her academic laurels with her selection for a sabbatical in music composition at the famed Edward McDowell Colony

---

36 "Master of Liberal Arts," *HBU News,* Fall 1986, 4-5.
37 Richard Vara, "Houston Baptist campus blossoms," *Houston Post,* 20 Sept. 1986, Religion sec., p. 1.
38 "Hinton Honored at Graduation," *HBU News,* Summer 1987, 7. Photo.
39 Houston Baptist University, Minutes of the Meetings of the Board of Trustees, Meeting on 23 Feb. 1987.
40 "Smith College: HBU wins top advising honors," *HBU News,* Summer 1986, 8.
41 "HBU Official is selected as conference chief," *Houston Chronicle,* 24 Mar. 1985, sec. 3, p. 7, three-star ed.

New Hampshire.[42] Writer-in-Residence Arthur Smith won the national Agnes Lynch Starrett Prize for Poetry and gained publication of his work in *The New Yorker* magazine, the *New England Review,* and *The Nation.*[43] Robert Trevino became the University's first alumnus to receive a Mellon Fellowship for graduate study at Stanford.[44] Three of the University's brightest faculty members, Robert Creech, Keith Putt, and Lois Lawrence, completed PhD work.[45] The University Singers under Dr. David Wehr were invited to participate in the International Beethoven Festival in Nuremberg, Germany in 1984 and 1986.[46]

The University's lecture series, funded by endowments, generated a high level of enrichment for the academic program. Herman Brown Chair lecturers from this period included Dan Arnold, President of First City Bancorporation; Sam Segnar,[47] CEO of Houston Natural Gas/Internorth; and Harold Hook, CEO and Chairman of the American General Corporation.[48] The Prince-Chavanne Ethics lecturers featured Dr. Otto Betz, New Testament scholar from the University of Tubingen, Germany[49] and Dr. Richard Chewning, Professor of Ethics at Baylor University.[50]

In related enrichment, the 1985 President's Council Dinner honored Dr. Denton Cooley who received the Doctor of Humane Letters in an evening focused on HBU's academic achievement.[51]

Dr. Hinton and Dr. Denton Cooley after receiving the Doctor of Humane Letters, 1985.

42 Houston Baptist University, Minutes of the Meetings of the Board of Trustees, Meeting on 24 Feb. 1987.
43 "Arthur Smith Wins Poetry Prize," *HBU News,* Fall 1984, 1; "HBU Poet," *HBU News,* Winter 1984, 5; Sholay Guilak, "Are You Creative?" *The Collegian,* 18 Oct. 1984, p. 3.
44 "Trevino receives Mellon Fellowship," *HBU News,* Summer 1986, 13.
45 "Three new doctorates on campus," *The Collegian,* 26 Sept. 1985, p. 3. Photo.
46 *Ornogah 1987,* 242-3.
47 "The Brown Distinguished Lecture Series," *HBU News,* Winter 1985, 3. Photos.
48 Houston Baptist University, Minutes of the Meetings of the Board of Trustees, Meeting on 9 Apr. 1987.
49 "Chavanne Lectures," *HBU News,* Spring 1986, 5.
50. "1987 Academic Lecture Series: Prince Chavanne Chair," *HBU News,* Spring 1987, 13.
51. "Cooley Honored at President's Council Dinner," *HBU News,* Summer 1985, 6; Allan Rhodes, "Doctor Cooley Receives Honorary Degree at President's Council Dinner," *The Collegian,* 9 May 1985, p. 1; *Ornogah 1985,* 42-43.

The 1986 spring dinner hosted Lord Irwin Bellwin, former member of Margaret Thatcher's cabinet. Chaired by Stewart Morris, Lord Bellwin's appearance featured a campus visit, a lecture on privatization in England under Thatcher, and high tea in the President's home hosted by the Daughters of the British Empire.[52] The 1987 President's Council dinner featured J. Peter Grace, President and CEO of W. R. Grace & Company.[53] In 1987, HBU was selected to participate in the Thomas Staley Foundation's Distinguished Christian Lecture Program. The University's first Staley lectures were given that year by Dr. Kirby Godsey, President of Mercer University in Georgia.[54]

§

Academic losses were also experienced, however. The undergraduate social work major, one of the University's most distinctive programs, became the political victim of a national accreditation battle within the *Council on Social Work Education*. Under the leadership of faculty members Dr. Gerda Smith, Virginia Robbins, and Jeralean Money, HBU enjoyed the only accredited undergraduate social work program in the city. Enrollment was strong, and the program profited from the double-major requirement by being able to pair with sociology as a second major. Graduates of HBU's accredited program could enter directly into the second year of work for the Master of Social Work degree. However, large universities throughout the nation wrested control of the national organization and revised accrediting requirements to mandate a substantial minimum number of faculty positions in social work. The new minimum standard was an unattainable threshold for smaller programs. As a result, several hundred college programs across the nation no longer met the Council's standard. Dr. Gerda Smith represented these smaller programs in a passionate appeal to the Council's national meeting. Political influence prevailed, however, and the standards were changed. HBU was permitted to continue to offer courses needed for degree completion to currently enrolled students. In February 1986, the trustees were formally notified of the Council's termination of social work accreditation.

---

52 "Lord and Lady Bellwin Honored at President's Council Dinner," *HBU News,* Spring 1986, 6-7; *Ornogah 1986,* 90-91. Photos.
53 "President's Council Dinner," *HBU News,* Spring 1987, 4-5; *Ornogah 1987,* 24-25.
54 "1987 Academic Lecture Series: Staley," *HBU News,* Spring 1987, 13.

§

During the 1970s and 1980s, only limited competition in student recruiting was felt from other colleges in the Houston area. Students who matriculated at HBU were typically four-year degree students seeking a private, if not a specifically Christian, institution to attend. The local community college system was not a strong competitor in student recruiting; its campuses were not yet geographically proliferated and focused primarily on trade skill courses. Competitive MBA programs within the city could be found only at the University of Houston. Moreover, many of the professional programs at HBU were viewed as among the best to be found in the region.

In 1985, the University of Houston announced a new campus in Fort Bend County. Concurrently, the Houston Community College began to expand its geographical locations into additional area high schools. For several years, Fort Bend County leaders had been negotiating to acquire a four-year college to enhance the community and compete more favorably with the Clear Lake area for attracting new business and industry. Several years earlier, HBU had begun to work with the Fort Bend Chamber of Commerce to explore program offerings on-site in Fort Bend County. As a result of this collaborative project, a survey of public opinion was taken to determine the University's image with its neighbor to the south. The survey reported surprising results:

> HBU was highly regarded (by the general public), though ill perceived, inaccurately known, and viewed as a cloistered institution of excellent reputation largely for children of the wealthy. There was little knowledge of HBU's graduate program offerings, adult education, professional growth, and televised delivery to corporate sites.[55]

The survey not only confirmed the difficulty of maintaining effective visibility in a major metropolitan area, but also affirmed the University's image with the general public to be one of excellence and high achievement. A *Houston Post* article in September 1986 carried the headline, "Houston Baptist Campus Blossoms."[56] The news article credited the

---

55 Houston Baptist University, Minutes of the Meetings of the Board of Trustees, Meeting on 19 Nov. 1985.
56 Richard Vara, "Houston Baptist campus blossoms: University maintains momentum by keeping focus on academics," *Houston Post,* 20 Sept. 1986, Religion sec., p. 1.

"high level of momentum sustained on the campus to a focus on academics."[57] Specifically mentioned were medical school admission success, the number of students enrolled in the Master of Business Administration program, the burgeoning enrollment in the new Master of Liberal Arts degree program, the Endowed Academic Scholarship program, and the cultural diversity of the student body.[58]

Student life also enjoyed a period of considerable achievement. In 1984 a Center for Exploring Ministry Careers (CEMC) was developed by the leadership team of Dr. Robert Newell, Dr. Joyce DeRidder, Edgar Tanner, and Linda Shook.[59] The center was designed to provide opportunity at the pre-seminary level for students in ministry-career exploration and clarification of call. This innovative mentoring program gained the attention of colleges across the nation and became widely emulated. The program provided financial aid and vocational guidance for students exploring ministry careers. Field-based internships, urban ministry projects, mission trips, and evangelistic teams offered wide-ranging options. The University's partnership with Southwestern Baptist Theological Seminary's Houston campus celebrated its tenth anniversary in 1985 with a banquet at the Sharpstown Country Club. The beloved founding manager of the Houston program was Hilda Moffett.[60]

§

In retrospect, this may well have been the "golden era" for intercollegiate sports at the University. In soccer, the Huskies were Conference West champions in 1984 and 1985 and won the Trans America Athletic Conference (TACC) tournament in 1982, 1983, and 1985.[61] The team was ranked in the top twenty in the nation in 1985. Carlos Gil was named TAAC Player of the Year four times during the years 1982 through 1985, and Coach David Swonke was named TAAC Coach of the Year in 1981 and 1985. Gil and George Cruz also achieved All-America honors in 1985.[62]

---

57 Ibid.
58 Ibid.
59 "HBU Creates New Center for Exploring Ministry Careers," *HBU News,* Fall 1984, 2-3.
60 "Seminary Celebrates 10 Years at HBU," *HBU News,* Summer 1985, 2.
61 Houston Baptist University, *Soccer Media Guide 2008-09,* 29.
62 "Huskies Dominate TAAC," *The Collegian,* 9 May 1985, p. 6; "HBU Soccer Honors," HBU *Soccer Media Guide 2008,* p. 28; *Ornogah 1985,* 204.

In cross county, Charlie Foreman won a second TAAC individual cross country title in 1985 and was named Runner of Year for the second time. In 1986, freshman Magnus Fyhr was named Runner of the Year, and in 1987, Kari Niemela won HBU's fourth straight Runner of the Year title.[63] The Cross Country program under Coach Jerry Martinez, begun only in 1982, attained its fifth TAAC title in 1987.[64] Coach Martinez was named TAAC Coach of the Year for the fourth time in 1986, and a women's track program was initiated.

To meet the NCAA Division I requirement for two women's team sports, in 1986 the women's programs in golf and tennis were discontinued in order to begin programs in soccer and volleyball.[65] HBU had the only women's golf program in the city. Women's gymnastics and track continued as individual sports. Golfer Caroline Pierce was named to All-America honors in the final year of the program.[66] The men's team received NCAA team invitations in 1984, 1987 (finishing #5 nationally), and 1988.[67] The men's golfers were also TAAC conference champion each year from 1984-86, in 1988 and in 1989 when the golf program was discontinued. TAAC Tournament Champions included Darryl Henning (1984), Colin Montgomerie (1985 with a TAAC tournament record score of -11), and Paul Davenport (1988). Men achieving NCAA All-America designation in this era included Darryl Henning (1985, 1986), Colin Montgomerie (1984, 1986, 1987), Jeff Wagner (1988), and Ulfar Jonsson (1988). TAAC Players of the Year included Darryl Henning, Colin Montgomerie, and Paul Davenport. The 1987 team was ranked eleventh in the nation.[68]

The University's gymnastics program moved into its new Glasscock training facility in 1985 and continued to gain national recognition. Mark Ebers and Eric Beardsley competed in the NCAA National Gymnastics Championships.[69] In 1986, Ebers returned to the nationals with teammates Paul O'Neill, Tim Pearson, and Jeff Lamb.[70] By 1987, Coach Hutch Dvorak's Huskies were ranked seventh in the nation. That

---

63 "Indoor Tracksters," *HBU News,* Spring 1987, 18.

64 "HBU Cross-Country captures TAAC championship," *HBU News,* Winter 1986, 14.

65 "Women's soccer and volleyball added," *HBU News,* Summer 1986, 14.

66 "Honor Role," *HBU Golf Media Guide 2008,* p. 15.

67 "HBU Sets 5th Place Record," *HBU News,* Summer 1987, 14; *Ornogah 1987,* 164-169.

68 *Ornogah 1987,* 164-169.

69 "NCAA Gymnastics Championship," *HBU News,* Spring 1985, 14.

70 "Gymnasts in Review," *HBU News,* Spring 1986, 13. Photo.

year, sophomore All-America designee Paul O'Neill scored a perfect "10" on the still rings and won the NCAA national championship in that event.[71] Freshman Alfonso Rodriguez became the first Husky in history to receive All-America recognition in all-around competition. Jose Barrio and Miguel Rubio also received All-America honors. Rubio became the third Husky to record the nation's highest score on an event.

An article in the *Los Angeles Herald Examiner* carried the headline, "Who-Ston Baptist Sleeper in NCAA Men's Gymnastics."[72] The HBU team received coverage from *USA Today* and *CBS Sports,* as well as the *Houston Chronicle,* the *Houston Post, KPRC-TV,* and *KHOU-TV.* By 1987, the gymnastics team boasted seven All-America athletes: Chris Wiloth, Percy Price, John Sweeney, Paul O'Neill, Alfonso Rodriquez, Jose Barrio, and Miguel Rubio.[73] A total of 25 of Dvorak's HBU gymnasts were selected to participate in the national NCAA championship tournaments in 1982, 1986, 1987, and 1988 when the team finished fifth in the nation.[74] The Huskies boasted a total of more than thirty All-Americans and seven individual NCAA champions in the period from 1979 to 1988.

§

The Board of Trustees aggressively continued its real estate development program to provide financial support for the outstanding achievement of students and faculty. Meanwhile, a number of legal issues consumed much of its attention during this period. In 1986, problems related to the Harvest House hotel development grew more threatening. Four acres of land had been subordinated in the hotel lease in 1977 that had the potential threat of the University's loss of the land in the case of the hotel's financial default. In 1986, the hotel was a failing venture with mounting debt.[75] To forestall foreclosure, the Board created a new corporation, Harvest House, Inc., to own the property and appointed the Chairman of the University Board of Trustees to function as a sole director of the corporation.[76] Furthermore, the University embraced Memorial

---

71 *Ornogah 1987,* 164.

72 "All-Americans: Huskies steal the show," *HBU News,* Summer 1987, 14; *Ornogah 1987,* 164-169.

73 "Huskies steal show at NCAA's," *The Collegian,* 15 May 1987, p. 5.

74 Shirley Gor, "Gymnasts travel to Championships," *The Collegian,* 25 Apr. 1986, p. 7; "Gymnasts in Review," *HBU News,* Spring 1986, 13.

75 Houston Baptist University, Minutes of the Meetings of the Board of Trustees, Meeting on 28 Jan. 1986.

76 Houston Baptist University, Minutes of the Meetings of the Executive Committee of the Board of Trustees, Meeting on 22 Aug. 1986.

Hospital as a partner in trying to save the Harvest House land. Foreclosure notice was posted on the hotel in September 1986, and the University entered into direct negotiations with the financing agency CIGNA to attempt to save the property. To forestall the foreclosure process, the University offered to guarantee $200,000 immediately to the lender. The balance of the loan would then be assumed by Harvest House, Inc. to be repaid over a 48-month period.[77]

In addition to financial problems, the issue of sale of alcohol at the hotel resurfaced. A letter from Dr. William Pinson of the Baptist General Convention of Texas called for immediate cessation of the serving of alcohol in the hotel or the relinquishment of hotel operation to a third party.[78] The University, in fact, had never intended to fall heir to the hotel's management and operation though the alcohol issue had been the object of criticism from some members of the Board who voted against the original proposal in 1977. The Board Executive Committee responded to the BGCT concerns in October, pledging resolution of the issue.[79]

Despite the prospects of an interested buyer for Harvest House in September 1987, no sale was consummated. The University was forced to continue to cover operational expenses to protect its property interests. Ultimately, the value of the land to the Memorial Healthcare System for its own expansion led to its acquisition of the Harvest House property and resolution of the attendant issues for the University. Trustee Whitson Etheridge was again recognized by the University Board, this time for his years of professional legal service to the University in resolving the Harvest House matter. A final payment of $59,000 in 1989 settled all third-party claims against the hotel operation. The importance of this experience to the Board of Trustees was to underscore the viability of the contiguous campus property and the need to safeguard the resource at all costs for the University's future. The Harvest House experience became a mantra for all subsequent real estate development.

For most of its history, the University's chief asset had been its land that had, in time, become more attractive to others. Land holdings were its principal leverage in business transactions—whether borrowing, leasing, or developing. The original sale of campus land to Memorial Hospital

---

77 Houston Baptist University, Minutes of the Meetings of the Board of Trustees, Meeting on 16 Sept. 1986.
78 Ibid.
79 Houston Baptist University, Minutes of the Meetings of the Executive Committee of the Board of Trustees, Meeting on 18 Oct. 1986.

was a cash flow salvation for the University; furthermore, the transaction escalated campus land values. However, as the older, wealthier institution, Memorial had negotiated a very favorable agreement for itself in the move from downtown. In the 1980s, however, a change of leadership in the Hospital system occurred (as so with the University) that led to the realization that the original tract of land sold to the Hospital would be inadequate for the projected scope of its operations. New leadership styles in both institutions welcomed dialog, partnerships, and shared benefit. In a critical turn of history, the two institutions began talking about a university/medical complex that might provide land for the Hospital and functional benefits for the University, its programs, and its personnel.

In this emerging climate in 1985, Board Chairman Milton Cross proposed the joint development of the thirty-three acres that Gilbert Turner had so passionately fought to protect for such a moment as this. Cross proposed to name the joint venture the University Medical Triangle. "The concept is to develop a community service center anchored in the fields of education and health in the greater Houston community."[80] In January 1986, the boards of the two institutions met in called session to explore the possibilities. One of the more prominent items on the agenda was the development of a senior retirement center.[81] This project reached formal agreement a year later when Stewart Morris brought a proposal for the Hospital to lease ten acres of land for $3,500,000 for an initial period of fifty years with the University maintaining twenty-three percent equity in the enterprise.[82] The resultant University Place project was the first of several partnership developments between the University and the Memorial System.[83] Significantly, the project was a dream come true for trustee Stewart Morris who, in 1963, had dreamed of a University-owned retirement center at the corner of the freeway and Fondren Road. Funds from the University Place lease were used to apply to re-purchase of the Harvest House property. The partnership was of benefit both to the Hospital and the University. University Place sales and marketing personnel soon discovered that the location of the project adjacent to a college campus was a significant factor in attracting

---

80 Houston Baptist University, Minutes of the Meetings of the Board of Trustees, Meeting on 19 Nov. 1985.
81 Houston Baptist University, Minutes of the Meetings of the Executive Committee of the Board of Trustees, Meeting on 21 Jan. 1986.
82 Houston Baptist University, Minutes of the Meetings of the Faculty Assembly, Meeting on 31 Mar. 1987.
83 Houston Baptist University, Minutes of the Meetings of the Board of Trustees, Meeting on 20 Jan. 1987.

residents. At the same time, the University enjoyed University Place residents at its sports, cultural, and academic events.

Under the leadership of Jim Smith—not yet a University trustee—work was initiated on the development of fifteen acres of land on the freeway feeder road near Fondren for a retail center to be called Fondren II.[84] A new lease agreement with Mervyn's department store in Fondren I was negotiated to generate an additional $900,000 in revenue over the next ten years.[85] Upon the counsel of Stewart Morris, the University also began buying houses facing the campus along Fondren Road to preserve control over the appearance of the main entrance to the campus and to provide convenient, affordable housing for University employees.[86] At the same time, commercial leases at the corner of Beechnut and Fondren became the target of heated criticism from students and from Sharpstown residential neighbors. A miniature golf course, car racing track, and video arcade complex was decried by the neighborhood as an ear and eye sore.[87] The amusement center that once had yielded an income stream for the University was now in continuous default on its lease payments and eventually closed.[88] A large structure in the development, however, was assimilated into a "temporary" new home for the University's Department of Art—one that the department "temporarily" occupied for the next twenty years until the construction of the University Academic Center in 2008.

§

The University's operating budget continued to be underfunded. The expansion of the athletic program was increasingly perceived by the faculty to be diverting funds from academic programs. In 1985, the instructional budget was reduced by $109,473; at the same time, the athletic budget was increased by $93,500 to "fund four women's sports."[89] Library funding as a percentage of the educational budget declined from five percent in 1981 to four percent in 1984 despite the 1981 Southern Association mandate that "the library budget be increased to accommo-

---

84 Houston Baptist University, Minutes of the Meetings of the Board of Trustees, Meeting on 19 Nov. 1985.
85 Houston Baptist University, Minutes of the Meetings of the Board of Trustees, Meeting on 27 May 1986.
86 Houston Baptist University, Minutes of the Meetings of the Board of Trustees, Meeting on 25 Sept. 1984.
87 Houston Baptist University, Minutes of the Meetings of the Executive Committee of the Board of Trustees, Meeting on 22 Jan. 1985.
88 Ibid.
89 Houston Baptist University, Minutes of the Meetings of the Board of Trustees, Meeting on 22 Jan. 1985.

date additional personnel and materials."[90] By 1986, no salary increases had been given faculty and staff in three of the last four years. In a two-year period, the University lost twenty-four faculty members.[91] In many years, faculty members were being asked to sign a contract in March containing no increase with the "carrot" that with good enrollment in the fall, some adjustment might be made. In May 1987, financial consultant S. D. Moore reported a year-end deficit of approximately $600,000 due in equal measure to over-expenditure and a funding shortfall.[92] How best to provide faculty salary equity with other institutions became a divisive issue within the Board of Trustees, particularly in the face of approval for such projects as a new $250,000 campus entrance and athletic program losses.

§

In 1982, trustee Gilbert Turner began to provide leadership for a project that had great promise for the Christian community in Houston. The Federal Communications Commission released notice of intent to grant a permit for operation of Channel 14 in the Houston area as an educational television station. A group of local Christian business leaders committed to secure the station as a Christian educational channel. The leaders applied for incorporation of Educational Television of Houston (ETOH) with the State of Texas, naming Gilbert Turner as President, Dr. Ed Young as Vice President, and William Merrill as Secretary. Houston Baptist University agreed to assist the project by providing initial administrative support and eventual programming.

By mid 1982, the ETOH application had been made to the FCC along with applications from two other local groups of investors for the same license. One competing application was from a group called Amerivision whose investors included comedian Flip Wilson, Houston haberdasher Harold Wiesenthal, home builder Doyle Stuckey, author Mickey Herskowitz, and artist Leroy Nieman.[93] The other application was from a group called K-RAM Corporation of Houston that requested of the FCC that "you help the Houston community better serve this fast-growing black, Hispanic, and female population by redesignating

90 Ibid.
91 Houston Baptist University, Minutes of the Meetings of the Academic Committee of the Board of Trustees, Meeting on 20 Feb. 1987.
92 Houston Baptist University, Minutes of the Meetings of the Board of Trustees, Meeting on 26 May 1987.
93 Ann Hodges, TV Editor, *Houston Chronicle*, undated newspaper clipping, HBU "Channel 14" files.

Channel 14 from educational to commercial so that K-RAM can proceed."[94] Both other non-educational applications were publicly contested prior to FCC consideration because of "alleged interference with other communication operations."[95] ETOH secured expert counsel in Washington for the FCC application process,[96] and in late 1983 the FCC issued a construction permit to ETOH to operate a new Channel 14 station to be called KHBU-TV.[97] Fund raising began immediately. In a letter to University trustees, Dr. Hinton wrote,

> HBU has a once-in-a-lifetime opportunity to embark on a journey into the future of Christian education and, at the same time, use television to reach millions of people for Christ, increase our image and visibility in the community, and serve our denomination.[98]

Programming assistance had been assured from both the Radio-Television Commission of the Southern Baptist Convention in Fort Worth[99] and from the Texas Education Commission's Region IV Service Center in Houston. A bank note for up to $1,500,000 had been personally guaranteed by Gilbert Turner, David M. Smith, Otis Brigman, Robert Brunson, and John H. Baker III.[100] In early 1984, a letter from Dr. Hinton to ETOH directors explained that the project would require approximately $2,000,000 for the television transmitter plant, an additional $1,000,000 for operational equipment, and first-year operating costs of approximately $1,000,000.[101] In addition, television production equipment would be required. The operation was a considerable undertaking for a non-commercial organization.

In order to retain designation as a tax exempt corporation, the station had to provide evidence of its public service character. Therefore, funding was sought from a broad base of support rather than from only a few proprietary sources. The ETOH Board reflected community diversity

---

94 (K-RAM Corporation President Clara McLaughlin to Secretary William J. Tricarico, Federal Communication Commission, undated). HBU "Channel 14" files.

95 (Gilbert Turner to ETOH Directors, July 23, 1982). HBU "Channel 14" files.

96 (Gammon & Grange, Attorneys, Washington, D. C. to Dr. W. H. Hinton, Dec. 28, 1981). HBU "Channel 14" files.

97 "Channel 14 Planning Underway," *HBU News,* Winter 1984, 4.

98 (Dr. W. H. Hinton to current and former HBU trustees, undated). HBU "Channel 14" files.

99 (Dr. Jimmy Allen, President Radio-Television Commission, Southern Baptist Convention, to Dr. W. H. Hinton, Sept. 3, 1982).

100 (Stephen Newman, Capital Bank, Houston, to Gilbert Turner, June 25, 1982).

101 (Dr. W. H. Hinton to Board of Directors, ETOH, Jan. 26, 1982).

and included Turner, Merrill, Young, HISD Superintendent Billy Reagan, and City Council member Martha Wong[102] with advisory trustees Dr. John Coleman, Eleanor McCollum, John Baugh, Dr. Luden Gutierrez, Percy Creuzot, and Father William J. Young. In 1985, Rex Baker, Jr. succeeded Gilbert Turner as President of ETOH, and the advisory board was expanded to include a number of additional community and academic leaders including Mayor Emeritus Louie Welch, George Strake, Eddy Scurlock, Carloss Morris, Leo Linbeck, Jr., and Dr. Charles LeMaistre.[103]

The initial television operation plan was to utilize the HBU studio, but UHF transmission equipment would ultimately be required, as well as access to a broadcast tower. The former Vice President and General Manager of KHOU-TV Channel 11 in Houston, Tom Kenny, was initially employed as technical consultant to get the new station on the air as quickly as possible.[104] In 1985, Fred Frey was named Executive Vice President and General Manager. Programming was intended to provide wholesome educational, religious, cultural, and socially-uplifting content. A 2.5 acre tract of campus land on Beechnut was proposed as a production center for KHBU-TV.

Financing the project proved to be a major obstacle. The University Board voted in 1984 not to assume any direct financial liability for the Channel 14 project.[105] However, the trustees were committed to help raise the needed funds. Milton Cross recommended that HBU contribute $190,000 annually for fifteen years from funds generated by the development of the land along the Southwest Freeway. Proponents suggested that Rice University and Memorial Healthcare Systems become equal financial partners in the venture. Other funding proposals suggested generating initial operating funds by pledges from individuals and churches.[106] Meanwhile, the construction permit deadline was extended from 1985 to 1986 because of incomplete funding.[107] Approximately $3,000,000 was needed for equipment and $1,500,000 for operations.[108]

102 "Channel 14 Planning Underway," HBU News, Winter 1984, 4.

103 Ibid.

104 Houston Baptist University, Minutes of the Meetings of the Executive Committee of the Board of Trustees, Meeting on 24 July 1984.

105 Houston Baptist University, Minutes of the Meetings of the Board of Trustees, Meeting on 25 Sept. 1984.

106 Houston Baptist University, Minutes of the Meetings of the Executive Committee of the Board of Trustees, Meeting on 18 Feb. 1986.

107 Ibid.

108 Houston Baptist University, Minutes of the Meetings of the Executive Committee of the Board of Trustees, Meeting on 22 July 1986.

In the midst of the fund raising efforts, a letter dated August 22, 1985, arrived from the Community Educational Television, Inc. (CET) in California stating, "We understand the Educational Television of Houston may be in the market to sell its construction permit for Channel 14." CET was an arm of Paul Crouch's Trinity Broadcasting Company that owned Channel 44 VHF in Harlingen. Acquiring a UHF station in a major urban television market was part of the Trinity Network's master plan of development. Finally, with the impending expiration of the construction permit in October 1986, the Board of ETOH determined that the best course of action was to maintain Christian programming on the proposed Channel 14 by selling its properties, assets, and rights to Community Educational Television of California. On September 27, 1986, the *Houston Chronicle* reported sale of the construction permit to CET pending Federal Communication Commission approval. CET proposed to lease eighty-two percent of its programming time to the Trinity Broadcasting Network and commit eighteen percent of its time to educational offerings in order to maintain its FCC license as an educational station. The *Chronicle* article addressed some criticism of the decision within the Christian community because of Paul Crouch's charismatic faith. The article explained, "Baptists and charismatics differ widely in their treatment of gifts of the Holy Spirit. These differences are being set aside for the sake of a business deal that would bring another Christian network to Houston."[109]

The University retained access to several hours of educational programming on Channel 14 weekly. Under this arrangement, the University would produce programs that would be funded by residuals paid for each telecast on stations in CET's network.[110] This network ultimately included Houston, Beaumont, Harlingen, San Antonio, and Jacksonville, Florida. Loss of the license was a bitter disappointment for local leaders. Houston was experiencing profound economic stress during the 1980s, and the University had neither the requisite financing nor personnel equal to the demands of the project.[111]

Gilbert Turner retired from the University Board of Trustees in 1986 after nineteen years of membership, having served from 1970 to 1972 as

---

109 Julia Dunn, "Charismatic network could put Baptist TV station on air," *Houston Chronicle,* 27 Sept. 1986, sec. 6, p. 1.

110 Houston Baptist University, Minutes of the Meetings of the Board of Trustees, Meeting on 16 Sept. 1986.

111 Julia Duin, "Charismatic network could put Baptist TV station on air," *Houston Chronicle,* 27 Sept. 1986, sec. 6, p. 1.

Chairman of the Board. No other trustee in University history has so broadly been involved in support of University growth. Turner, along with Stewart Morris, can be credited with the financial survival of the University at several points in its history. Turner was inaugurated as a trustee by Morris in 1967 as one "carefully chosen to work."[112] In his years of service, in addition to his three years as Chairman of the Board, he served as a member of the Academic Committee, as Chair of the Finance Committee, as Chair of the President's Council, Chair of the Development Council, Chair of the $32,000,000 *On Our Way* capital campaign, and President of Channel 14's Educational Television of Houston. He was the founder of the Endowed Academic Scholarship program concept and, along with Stewart Morris, was the first to fund a scholarship. In 1977, he was granted the honorary Doctor of Laws degree in recognition of his extraordinary contribution. A pragmatist and activist, Turner first funded a student recruiting expense fund for the University with fellow trustee Al Parker. He led in the lobbying efforts for the first passage of Tuition Equalization Grant legislation in Texas and was the donor of the University's maintenance facility in 1964 and the University's first mainframe computer laboratory for student use in 1982. Illustrating the breadth of his many areas of operational support, Turner quietly established a marketing expense fund to underwrite the University's advertising in periodic *Education Section* editions of the local newspapers. As Chair of the Finance Committee, he pled for sustained ownership of land along the Southwest Freeway for future development and established protocols and policies for improved institutional financial controls. Turner authored a University gift acceptance policy to prevent "the development of sensitive issues with major donors or with other members of the Board of Trustees."[113] Gilbert and Claydene Turner were honored with the Spirit of Excellence Award in 1992.

§

Bertha Mae Wilson, creator of the famed *Bertha Burger,* announced her retirement in 1985. A favorite of all who knew her, Bertha had been a part of the campus food-service operation since the 1960s. Known in her early career for her soul-food lunches during the summer months,

---

112 Houston Baptist University, Minutes of the Meetings of the Board of Trustees, Meeting on 17 Nov. 1987.
113 (Dr. Gilbert Turner to Dr. W. H. Hinton, Nov. 4, 1994).

Bertha had ultimately been promoted to manager of the snack bar grill.[114] First praised in *The Collegian* by Merrill Blackburn and universally beloved by faculty and student, Bertha "was surrogate mother for many of the students and was always available for advice and scolding when there was need for it."[115] Upon the occasion of her retirement, she was presented a University medallion "with much affection" and honored with a campus reception.[116] Some fifteen years later, HBU flags were lowered to half-mast upon news of the loss of Mrs. Wilson.

In 1986, the University lost one of its strongest visionary leaders. Dr. Rex Baker, Sr. was a member of the first UBA College Committee, a University Founder, a co-author of the University's *Preamble*, and a founding trustee. For many years, he served as chair of the Board's Academic Committee. Baker was a fierce advocate for academic excellence. He was a member of Phi Beta Kappa at the University of Texas and was instrumental in raising that institution to national academic prominence. Baker often reminded colleagues, "I do not have any time to give to this undertaking unless it is to be of a first-class academic and spiritual quality."[117] As General Counsel and Vice President of Humble Oil, Baker had been particularly instrumental in securing powerful early support from the corporate and cultural community in Houston.[118] A resolution passed by the trustees in February 1986

> acknowledged the life and influence of this patriarch on the birth and growth of the University and resolved that the ideals and insistence upon excellence which characterized the life of Rex G. Baker be a constant source of challenge to all future generations of trustees, faculty, and administrators who follow the path he so thoroughly illuminated.[119]

After more than twenty years of extraordinary accomplishment, Dr. Hinton began to experience a series of family and personal health issues that increasingly drew him away from the campus. Mrs. Hinton's health was declining, and both the Hintons experienced hospital stays and med-

---

114 *Ornogah 1983*, 5. Photo of Bertha Wilson and daughter Ronnie Lott at the M. D. Anderson Snack Bar.
115 "Former snack-bar supervisor dished up food for the soul," *The Collegian*, 13 Jan. 2000. Bertha Wilson died on December 30 1999.
116 Sholay Guilak, "Reception Held for Bertha," *The Collegian*, 31 Jan. 1985, p. 1.
117 "In Memoriam: Rex G. Baker, 1892-1986," *HBU News*, Spring 1986, 4.
118 Ibid.
119 Houston Baptist University, Minutes of the Meetings of the Board of Trustees, Meeting on 18 Feb. 1986. Original framed presentation resolution in University archives.

ical concerns. Board minutes of the period reveal increasingly visible leadership from operational Vice Presidents Looser, Womack, and Massey.[120] Private dialog between Chairman Milton Cross and these three vice presidents assured them of Board support for their heightened levels of responsibility during this awkward period of leadership. High levels of mutual trust made such management possible.

The University was managed by a seasoned administrative team who worked together effectively for many years. The strength of their leadership was particularly crucial at this point in University history. The team included Dr. Don Looser, Vice President for Academic Affairs (1964); Dr. Troy Womack, Vice President for Financial Affairs (1962); Dr. James W. Massey, Vice President for Student Affairs (1969); Dr. Herman Barlow, Vice President for University Affairs (1972); Dr. Roger Brooks, Vice President for Administrative Affairs (1979); Dr. Joan DeRooy, Vice President for Instructional Television and Professional Development (1980); Dr. B. J. Martin, Vice President for Church Relations (1980); Dr. Ray V. Mayfield, Jr., Vice President for Development (1963); and Dr. Don Byrnes, Dean of Admissions and Records (1969).[121]

Following the untimely death of Dr. E. V. Tapscott in 1983, a committee was appointed by the trustees to review the matter of administrative succession.[122] In the spirit of that dialog, the Board approved the draft of a letter to Dr. Hinton in March 1985 notifying him of the intent to appoint a committee to search for a new President and to name him as the University's first Chancellor. Contained in the letter were assurances to provide employment until his seventieth birthday, to allow occupancy of the President's home so long as either he or Mrs. Hinton lived, and to extend other expressions of the University's appreciation.[123]

No definite date was set for Hinton's appointment as Chancellor. Cross explained, "The trustees are keenly conscious of the unique and remarkable work of Dr. Hinton as University President. Because of his own expressed desires (and ours), he will continue to be deeply involved in the life of the University in many ways."[124] To the surprise of most trustees, Cross's comments were greeted by an unanticipated peremptory motion in the Board meeting to appoint a Search Committee immedi-

---

120 Houston Baptist University, Minutes of the Meetings of the Board of Trustees, Meeting on 28 May 1985.
121 *Houston Baptist University Bulletin 1986-87,* 159.
122 Houston Baptist University, Minutes of the Meetings of the Faculty Assembly, Meeting on 7 May 1985.
123 Houston Baptist University, Minutes of the Meetings of the Board of Trustees, Meeting on 26 Mar. 1985.
124 Houston Baptist University, Minutes of the Meetings of the Faculty Assembly, Meeting on 7 May 1985.

ately with a prescribed distribution of pastor and lay membership. The motion seemed out of character with the contemplative spirit of Chairman Cross's comments and was overwhelmingly defeated.[125] When a Succession Committee was appointed later in May 1985, Colletta McMillian was named chair. The Committee was comprised of Board Chairman Milton Cross, former Chairs Marvin West, Otis Brigman, Bill Merrill, and Walter Morgan as well as trustees Jim Cabaniss, Doug Tipps, Leah Tucker, and Dr. George Gaston. Dr. Hinton was as an ex-officio member along with advisory members John Baugh, Dr. Howard Lee Sr., and Dr. Stewart Morris.[126] No faculty, staff, students, or alumni were appointed to the Search Committee. Dr. Hinton "reiterated the importance of the Christian emphasis at HBU stating that without an emphasis on Jesus Christ there is no rationale for the existence of the University. He further reminded the trustees that this emphasis must continue if the Lord is to continue to bless the University."[127]

§

The January 1986 meeting of the Board of Trustees bore striking parallel to the poignant meeting of November 1963 in its coincidence with national tragedy. HBU trustees meeting in January 1986 quietly adjourned upon learning of the explosion of the space shuttle *Challenger*[128] as had trustees in 1963 upon learning of the assassination of President John Kennedy.

§

Over the next years, the Board of Trustees showed evidence of less participative decision-making and stronger executive authority. Board committees appeared less active as deliberative and data-gathering entities. The focus of the trustees shifted from policy-making to management of institutional finances and land development. Minutes of trustee meetings reveal extended floor debates, apparent lack of information on many issues, and even occasional reversal of decisions within the same meet-

---

125 Houston Baptist University, Minutes of the Meetings of the Board of Trustees, Meeting on 26 Mar. 1985.
126 Houston Baptist University, Minutes of the Meetings of the Faculty Assembly, Meeting on 7 May 1985.
127 Houston Baptist University, Minutes of the Meetings of the Board of Trustees, Meeting on 28 May 1985.
128 Houston Baptist University, Minutes of the Meetings of the Board of Trustees, Meeting on 28 Jan. 1986.

ing.[129] Some of the few recorded negative votes on motions in University history are documented in this period.[130] A struggle for political power within the Board seemed evident.

Dr. Hinton continued in the role of President for two more years. The Succession Committee, first appointed in 1985, continued to interview candidates, both from within the University family and from the larger community.[131] After a two-year search, in a called meeting in January 1987, the Board of Trustees elected Dr. E. D. Hodo as the University's second President, effective June 1.[132]

The spring of 1987 hosted a flurry of activity honoring Dr. and Mrs. Hinton in gratitude for their twenty-five years of service. As founding President, Dr. Hinton proved to be a man of remarkable leadership qualities. He exhibited strong personal magnetism—on the campus, the speaker's platform, the golf course, in a social setting, or teaching his E. P. West Bible class. People were drawn to him as a person and then to the University. His keen interest in people seemed to pervade all that he set out to do. In 1986, he shared intimate feelings in an article in *The Collegian*:

> Every plaque on this campus represents a person or a family who believed what we said, who shared our enthusiasm, and who was willing to invest their fortune in what we are trying to do here. Every building you see is here because someone believed. People do things because of other people. I would hope that my successor is a dreamer, that he loves people.[133]

Pastor, trustee, friend Dr. LeRay Fowler delivered an eloquent tribute in Dr. Hinton's last Board meeting as President:

> Dr. Hinton is a man of many intangible qualities. He has a burning concern for students—emotionally and financially—especially for students who *want* an education. There is his deep abiding interest in Christian education here and elsewhere. There is that sense of humor and warm personal magnetism for his friends. There is his personal involvement in his church where he has taught the E. P. West Bible Class for over 25 years. There is his

---

129 Houston Baptist University, Minutes of the Meetings of the Board of Trustees, Meeting on 25 Feb. 1986.
130 Houston Baptist University, Minutes of the Meetings of the Executive Committee of the Board of Trustees, Meeting on 18 Feb. 1986.
131 Houston Baptist University, Minutes of the Meetings of the Faculty Assembly, Meeting on 18 Feb. 1986. President James Riley reported the committee had interviewed eight candidates thus far.
132 "Dr. Doug Hodo named HBU President," *HBU News*, Spring 1987, 3.
133 Alan Rhodes, "Celebrating the Past," *The Collegian*, 30 Jan. 1986, p. 7.

deep interest in providing decent retirement programs for Baptist ministers with no personal gain on his part. He will not be forgotten by those he loved.[134]

May 22, 1987, was declared W. H. Hinton Day in the City of Houston by Mayor Kathy Whitmire. Dr. Hinton was recognized by a resolution of appreciation passed by the Texas Senate and signed by Lt. Governor Bill Hobby and was appointed an Admiral in the Texas Navy by Governor Bill Clements.[135] Hinton was awarded the honorary Doctor of Laws degree by the University and also received the Doctor of Letters degree from the University of St. Thomas.[136]

In reflection upon his years of service, Dr. Hinton recalled that the budget of the institution had grown from of $831,000 to over $13,000,000. By 1987, the University held $59,000,000 in current assets, $31,000,000 in endowment funds, $15,000,000 in wills and irrevocable trusts, and $21,000,000 invested in plant. Dr. Hinton expressed his deep appreciation to the Board and offered his prayer that the Board of Trustees would continue to serve with "their life and love for the University every day."[137] Dr. Hinton pointed to the coming of Dr. Hodo as a "fortunate event for the University." In his final Board meeting, Hinton's friend and trustee Leah Tucker moved, "In accordance with the agreement between the Board of Trustees and W. H. Hinton approved in 1985, I move the election of Dr. W. H. Hinton as Chancellor of the University effective June 1, 1987."[138]

§

To his friends, Hinton was as remarkable for who he was as for what he accomplished. He often spoke of his love for people, and he invested the future of the University heavily in them. Founder John Baugh called Hinton "a promoter in the finest sense of the word and a generous encourager to all persons."[139] Dr. Hinton often stated that his "dream job" would be as a student recruiter. More than twenty years after his

---

134 Houston Baptist University, Minutes of the Meetings of the Board of Trustees, Meeting on 26 May 1987; *Ornogah 1987*, 32.

135 Houston Baptist University, Minutes of the Meetings of the Board of Trustees, Meeting on 26 May 1987.

136 "University of St. Thomas Honors Hinton," *HBU News*, Summer 1987, 8.

137 Houston Baptist University, Minutes of the Meetings of the Board of Trustees, Meeting on 26 May 1987.

138 Ibid.

139 John Baugh, "Founders' Day Address," *HBU News*, Winter 1991, 9-11.

retirement, wills and estates, community and foundation networking, memberships in University organizations, and alumni affection still bore the strong imprint of his person. Colleagues who differed with him on issues remained personally drawn to him by his warmth and friendship. Dr. Bill Pinson reflected upon the man:

> The real history of your presidency, Dr. Hinton, may be written in terms of your development of human potential. Because you have always so effectively shown your love for people, because you have given so freely of yourself without limitation, because of your affection for the students of HBU and your constant devotion to their needs and best interest, the Board of Trustees has voted to elevate you to the proud status of honorary alumnus of this University by conferring the Doctor of Laws degree.

Many of Dr. Hinton's achievements were summarized in a "Resolution of Appreciation" adopted by the Board of Trustees in June 1991:

> Whereas Dr. and Mrs. W. H. Hinton were called to serve as the first Presidential family of the newly chartered Houston Baptist College,

> And whereas Dr. Hinton was responsible for the construction of the original campus, the recruiting of the first administrative staff, faculty, and student body, and the perpetuation of the commitment of the institution to "academic excellence in a Christian environment,"

> And whereas Dr. Hinton led the College through its birth and development securing construction of Atwood I and II, the Sharp Gymnasium, the Moody Library, The Cullen Science Center, the Mabee Theater, the Glasscock Gymnastics Center, the Cullen Nursing Center, the Holcomb Mall, and the Morris Columns,

> And whereas Dr. Hinton provided the leadership which led to the endowed academic scholarship program, the accreditation of the College, the move of the Memorial Hospital to College property, the establishment of intercollegiate athletic programs centered in the formation of the Trans America Athletic Conference, the reorganization of the institution from college to university status, the establishment of programs by Southwestern Baptist Theological Seminary on the University campus, the development of programs in education, business, and nursing and the establishment of instructional television capability,

And whereas under the tenure of Dr. Hinton as President, the University grew to be second in size among all Texas Baptist colleges offering both liberal arts and professional programs at both the undergraduate and graduate level,

And whereas Dr. Hinton fostered the University's commitment to academic excellence in a Christian environment through the nurture of publicly-recognized programs in pre-medicine, nursing, the performing and visual arts, debate, and athletics which became tangible symbols of excellence to the City of Houston and its residents,

And whereas Dr. and Mrs. Hinton have cultivated and sustained a genuine affection for the University's students and its alumni in whose eyes they remain symbolic of the significant chapter of the University history in which they played such important roles of leadership,

Therefore be it hereby resolved by the Board of Trustees, acting in behalf of all those who wish for Dr. and Mrs. Hinton the very best of retirement years, which this resolution of appreciation, affection, and sincere gratitude for your work and lifetime of devotion to the University be approved and enacted.

§

Never again would there be a founding president of Houston Baptist University. Never again would there be a first Chancellor of the University. More than anyone, Dr. Hinton was mindful of the great contributions of those who had gone before him in the Union Baptist Association and as visionary pioneering trustees and Founders. Yet, no more gripping visual representation of the extraordinary contributions of this man can be conjured than the image of him standing alone before 200 acres of bare land as he must have seen it on his first day in office on June 1, 1962. There were those who dreamed, and there were those who brought life to those dreams. In 1987, in one way or another, virtually every page of institutional history chronicling the human realization of this dream could be laid at his feet.

NINE

1987-1990

Houston in the mid-1980s was living up to its reputation for change as a constant. The Houston Endowment sold the *Houston Chronicle* to the Hearst Corporation; the *Toronto Sun* sold the *Houston Post;* Dillard's bought Joske's; and the City of Houston bought the Sharpstown Country Club, converting it to a public golf course. Joan Raymond became the first woman superintendent of the Houston Independent School District. Wortham Theater opened in the Arts District. Dominique de Menil mounted her internationally acclaimed art collection in a new museum setting, and Nolan Ryan left the Houston Astros and signed with the Texas Rangers.

The coming of a new president to the campus of Houston Baptist University seemed an appropriate response to the changing urban environment. If a leader's first hundred days are predictive of that which is to follow, then President Hodo's arrival on the campus gave strong indication of the level of reorientation that would characterize his presidency. His first days heralded significant change in management style. Hodo's academic background in the field of economics, his family experience in manufacturing and banking interests, and his previous positions of leadership in colleges of business combined to shape a studied and highly specific level of expectation. Moreover, his personal style emerged as one of high energy, active involvement in all levels of University operation, and focused attention on conservation of resource.

Although the presidential search committee had met and interviewed candidates for many months prior to his selection, Hodo was not surprised by his invitation to serve. In fact, several years before, on a previous visit to the campus as chair of a review committee for the Baptist General Convention of Texas, Dr. Hodo confided to Dr. Hinton that he felt God had called him to be President of Houston Baptist University. At his first official meeting with the trustee Executive Committee, Hodo shared that his goal was "a management style based on scripture—that Jesus be first in his life and in the life of the University—and that evangelism and salvation be paramount in the University's life."[1] After only several weeks, Dr. Hodo wrote the faculty and staff, "I feel the Lord would have us have an early-morning prayer time each week."[2] From that time throughout his presidency, Dr. Hodo hosted a voluntary time for prayer open to all at 7:00 a.m. each Tuesday morning in the Moody Library. The new President scheduled personal conferences with every member of the University faculty and staff.

From the outset of Dr. Hodo's presidency, the financial health and well-being of the University were of paramount concern. His background in business well-equipped him to address the University's long history of deficit financing, first permitted to establish programs of excellence, but later sustained as a result of insufficient fund-raising paired with ambitious goals for high achievement.

In his year-end financial analysis for the Board, consultant S. D. Moore reported a deficit for 1986-87 of $600,000 due both to revenue shortfalls and over-expenditure.[3] The state of the Houston economy in 1987 was depressed. "Oil service companies were folding; drilling rigs were stacked; and, loans were going into default. Local property values declined $16 billion between 1986 and 1990."[4] Savings and loan associations began failing in 1986. In the Houston banking sector, the Bank of the Southwest became M Bank then became Bank One; Texas Commerce Bank became Chemical Bank. John Mecom lost his fabled Warwick Hotel to creditors, and former Governor of Texas and United States Secretary of the Treasury John Connally filed for personal bankruptcy.

The waning years of the Hinton presidency had witnessed greater direct involvement in administrative process by a small group of trustees headed by Board Chair Milton Cross. One form this action took was the employment of several consultants reporting directly to the Board of Trustees. In addition to Vice President Womack, the Board employed S. D. Moore to provide additional financial analysis and advice. Ed Best, the long-time Director of Real Estate, also reported directly to the Board. This latter arrangement was a derivative of the halcyon days of the UBA Property Committee when Best was employed by the Committee. One of Hodo's

---

1 Houston Baptist University, Minutes of the Meetings of the Executive Committee of the Board of Trustees, Meeting on 23 June 1987.

2 (Dr. E. D. Hodo to staff and faculty, Aug. 21, 1987).

3 Houston Baptist University, Minutes of the Executive Committee of the Board of Trustees, Meeting on 23 June 1987.

4 *Houston History: 1836-2010*, http://houstonhistory.com/decades/history5r.htm (accessed Feb. 19, 2010).

first administrative acts was to attach the activity of both men directly to the Office of President.[5]   This act marked a subtle but significant signal to the Board that Hodo planned to manage the whole of the enterprise.

Dr. Hodo announced that he intended to recommend $350,000 for salary increases in September.   His financial goal was to achieve a $650,000 contingency "with personnel and program changes" in the budget that he had inherited.   For an article in the *Houston Chronicle,* he reported, "There is no financial crisis on this campus. I am trying to bring about managerial and financial efficiency."[6]   There were several promising financial developments.   Channel 14 had been purchased by Community Education Television, the educational arm of Trinity Broadcasting Network, the nation's third largest Christian network.[7]   Board Chair Milton Cross reported in June that the University would receive $300,000 from Channel 14 upon the initiation of their program broadcasting.   Additionally, Sun Oil planned to convey approximately $1,000,000 in property designated for the Hinton Tower.   Portions of these funds were to be matched by the Cullen Foundation.   The Falcon Management Group indicated an interest in purchasing the Harvest House Hotel even as negotiations continued on the project buyout with the lender CIGNA.[8]   Moreover, trustee Walter Morgan reported that the Bettis estate had grown to approximately $20,000,000 from its initial estimate of $16,000,000.[9]   The University's approximate share of the estate was twenty-five percent.

In August, Dr. Hodo announced that he had initiated a study of the University's $1,300,000 athletic budget.   The cost of membership in Division I of the NCAA was of major concern.   By the opening of the fall quarter, Hodo had cut $450,000 from the non-academic budget.[10] Nonetheless, students and faculty returning in the fall were greeted with a refurbished Atwood Theology Building, upgraded telephone service, and resurfaced parking lots.[11]   The library budget had been increased by

5 Houston Baptist University, Minutes of the Meetings of the Executive Committee of the Board of Trustees, Meeting on 23 June. 1987.

6 "New President at HBU plans to reduce costs," *Houston Chronicle,* 17 July 1987, p. 19.

7 Julia Duin, "Religious TV network starts broadcasting here," *Houston Chronicle,* 18 July 1987, p. 25.

8 Houston Baptist University, Minutes of the Meetings of the Executive Committee of the Board of Trustees, Meeting on 28 July 1987.

9 Houston Baptist University, Minutes of the Meetings of the Executive Committee of the Board of Trustees, Meeting on 25 Aug. 1987.

10 Houston Baptist University, Minutes of the Meetings of the Faculty, Meeting on 2 Sept. 1987.

11 *SomeTimes,* 31 Aug. 1987.

$25,000.[12] Dr. Hodo announced the University's first *Campus Improvement Day* for faculty and staff to paint, clean, and improve the campus appearance. Approximately 225 volunteers responded to the appeal that was acknowledged by a Certificate of Appreciation from the City of Houston.[13]

Enrollment for the fall 1987 quarter was 2,626 students of whom 650 were graduate students. Analysis of the demographic composition of undergraduate students revealed that fifty-six percent were female; seventy percent were Anglo-American. Baptists comprised thirty-eight percent of the student body. Among the academic disciplines, thirty-six percent of students majored in business, and twenty-seven percent declared majors in science and nursing. Among the faculty, sixty percent held the doctorate; fifty-seven percent ranged in age between thirty-five and fifty; and thirty-eight percent were Baptist.[14]

The University's level of achievement remained high. Dr. Elysee Peavy was awarded a Mellon Fellowship for summer study.[15] HBU gymnast John Sweeney was a double winner at the U. S. Gymnastics Championship with victories in both vault and floor exercise.[16] The HBU debate team was honored as one of the top ten teams in the nation and was selected to compete in the University of Kentucky's Thoroughbred Round Robin Debate Tournament.[17] The University was honored by the National Academic Advising Association as having 1987's "Outstanding Institutional Advising Program."[18]

In his first address to the Faculty Assembly, President Hodo articulated his chief goals—raising admissions standards, lowering faculty teaching loads, providing salary increases for faculty and staff, addressing the "balance" between athletics and academics, and working to complete funding for the Hinton Tower.[19] The President's recommendation for raises was not approved by the trustees in September. A three percent salary supplement pool was later distributed to nineteen key faculty members in January 1988.[20] A September report confirmed that HBU's

---

12 Houston Baptist University, Minutes of the Meetings of the Faculty Assembly, Meeting on 6 Oct. 1987.

13 *SomeTimes*, 28 Sept. 1987.

14 Baptist General Convention of Texas, *Christian Education Coordinating Board Annual Report* (Dallas: Baptist General Convention of Texas, 1987).

15 *SomeTimes*, April 1989.

16 Michael Janofsky, "Gymnastics," *New York Times*, 22 June 1987, sec. C, p. 11.

17 (Martin Sadler to Dr. E. D. Hodo, Sept. 3, 1987).

18 (Dr. Jerry Ford to Dr. Don Looser, Aug. 1, 1987).

19 Houston Baptist University, Minutes of the Meetings of the Faculty Assembly, Meeting on 22 Sept. 1987.

20 Houston Baptist University, Minutes of the Meetings of the Board of Trustees, Meeting on 26 Jan. 1988.

faculty salaries were among the lowest in compensation among master's-degree-granting institutions in Texas.[21] After three years of no raises for most of the faculty, there surfaced discussion of unionization.[22]

In his first report to the Board of Trustees, Dr. Hodo reported a warm reception from the University family. He observed that "academic programs were in very good shape," that the physical plant was in fair condition with renovation needed in the Atwood Theology Building, and that attention was required for maintenance and operation of the plant.[23] The President also reported he was reviewing and renegotiating all third-party contracts and was focusing on the cumulative debt in athletic operations that approached $1,000,000. He announced the appointment of Linda Shook as Assistant to the President for Alumni Relations, and stated that future meetings of the Board of Trustees were to be closed to faculty, students, alumni, and other "non-Board members" except Vice Presidents Looser and Womack.

Planning was initiated in early summer of 1987 for a presidential inauguration to be held in October. Dr. James Taylor, President of the Faculty Assembly, was charged with the responsibility for coordinating the many facets of this assignment. Virtually all University employees became involved in planning and execution of the several days of celebration. Inaugural-week activities began on Monday with a faculty art exhibit and a music recital. Festivities continued on Wednesday with a tea honoring Dr. and Mrs. Hodo hosted by the Auxiliary and the President's Advisors at the home of Lee and Tracy Lawrence. The inauguration itself was held on Thursday, October 29, 1987, on the Holcombe Mall. Delegates from some 125 universities and learned societies participated.[24] The ceremony featured original music composed by Drs. Ann Gebuhr and Dan Kramlich and performances by the University Singers conducted by Dr. David Wehr, and the Symphonic Band and Choralis Brass directed by Dr. Robert Zwick.[25] Dr. Hodo's inaugural address placed emphasis on a redemptive spirit and stressed the University's responsibility for developing both the intellectual and spiri-

---

21 Houston Baptist University, Minutes of the Meetings of the Faculty Assembly Executive Committee, Meeting on 15 Sept. 1987.

22 Houston Baptist University, Minutes of the Meetings of the Board of Trustees, Meeting on 23 Feb. 1988.

23 Houston Baptist University, Minutes of the Meetings of the Board of Trustees, Meeting on 22 Sept. 1987.

24 *SomeTimes*, 23 Oct. 1987.

25 "Ceremony of Inauguration," *HBU News*, Winter 1987, 6; "Special Music Commissioned," *The Collegian*, 17 Dec. 1987, p. 8.

tual life of the student.[26] A Thursday evening banquet honored the new President and his wife and featured an address by Dr. Russell Dilday, President of Southwestern Baptist Theological Seminary.

From the outset, the new President was not without the counsel of others, both solicited and otherwise. He arrived on the campus with a number of goals already shaped by "a high volume of correspondence and discussion" prior even to his assuming office. Vice-President Looser prepared a *State of the University Report* that suggested that the commitment of the faculty and staff in the difficult, recent years was perhaps the University's strongest asset. "Despair has not set in, but there is acknowledged shortfall (of morale) that has frequently belied public utterance."[27] Looser advocated heightened academic support, the development of a Board of Trustees with significant community influence, campus improvements, reduction of administrative hierarchy, reallocation of resources, focus on goals related to mission, and "affirmation of individual contribution to the whole."[28]

The Faculty Assembly also drafted a series of recommendations for the new President—the need for a Dean of Graduate Studies,[29] improved summer-school pay, graduate tuition reimbursement for employees, the selection of "recognized scholars" as speakers for the fall opening convocation, and miscellaneous changes in a number of procedural policies.[30] The Assembly also requested a line of direct access to the Office of the President. Dr. Hodo's response to these several recommendations rejected a faculty senate model of governance and affirmed the role of the office of the Vice President for Academic Affairs in matters relating to academic practice and faculty relations. His response further recognized current budget constraints and the goal of reducing administrative costs by declining the request for a graduate dean. The recommendation for a scholarly speaker for opening convocation was warmly embraced.[31]

In October, Dr. Hodo recommended an alternate facilities plan that would provide a 17,000 square foot addition to the Moody Library and a separate second building composed of three of the proposed eight floors of the Hinton Tower to house the Colleges of Education and Behavioral

---

26 "Inauguration Day Activities," *The Collegian,* 17 Dec. 1987, p. 9. Photos.
27 (Dr. Don Looser to Dr. E. D. Hodo, "State of the University Report", Aug. 6, 1987).
28 Ibid.
29 Houston Baptist University, Minutes of the Meetings of the Faculty Assembly, Meeting on 3 Nov. 1987.
30 Houston Baptist University, Minutes of the Meetings of the Faculty Assembly, Meeting on 5 Jan. 1988.
31 Houston Baptist University, Minutes of the Meetings of the Faculty Assembly, Meeting on 8 Jan. 1987.

Sciences and the College of Business and Economics. The timetable on the library expansion was critical; the project had been mandated by the Southern Association of Colleges and Schools as a requirement for the 1990 re-affirmation cycle.[32] Dr. Hodo delivered a written report to the Board detailing several recommendations: 1) the development of alumni affairs as a major focus; 2) the need for greater visibility of the University in the community; and 3) a request to increase the size of the Board of Trustees beyond twenty-one members.[33]

The November 1987 meeting of the trustees served to mark a symbolic end of the pre-Hodo era. Outgoing Chair of the Board Milton Cross was given a plaque of appreciation for his leadership in "the years of transition, 1983-87."[34] Cross had been a trustee since 1972 and served as Chair of the Board from 1976 to 1978 and from 1985 to 1988. He was a Rice University alumnus, had an insightful concept of University need, and was decisive in his leadership. Cross had a distinguished record of service as a trustee, Chairman, and member of the Presidential Search Committee. His commitment to institutional excellence was rivaled only by that of Stewart Morris. His enlightened service to the University community during the years bridging the University's first and second presidents is of historic significance. The trustees also noted the passing of Dr. Ray V. Mayfield, Sr. who directed the University's real estate ventures from 1968 to 1971[35] and the death of the University's first Vice President for Academic Affairs Dr. H. B. Smith. Dr. Looser's tribute to Dr. Smith and his HBU contributions was read into the November Board minutes:

> Smith conceived and established in a brand new college an academic program highlighted by a double major, interdisciplinary courses, senior seminars, international study, and a commitment to a strong liberal arts foundation supported by outstanding library and faculty resources. At a point in history when few knew anything about HBC, the name and presence of H. B. Smith gave instant credibility to the fledgling college in the academic world. When he retired, the community felt inordinately dysfunctional without his presence because of the difficulties and

---

32 Houston Baptist University, Minutes of the Meetings of the Executive Committee of the Board of Trustees, Meeting on 27 Oct. 1987.

33 Houston Baptist University, Minutes of the Meetings of the Board of Trustees, Meeting on 24 Nov. 1987. To clarify community visibility, Dr. Hodo banned the use of the acronym "HBU" in all written communication on the conviction it was not widely-recognized.

34 Houston Baptist University, Minutes of the Meetings of the Board of Trustees, Meeting on 24 Nov. 1987.

35 "In Memoriam: Ray V. Mayfield, Sr.," *HBU News,* Winter 1987, 4.

victories we had all shared together in those first 10 years. His funeral eulogy in the mountains of his beloved Kentucky concluded with 2 Samuel 3:38: "Know ye not that there is a prince and a great man fallen this day in Israel?"

The pregnant first hundred days of the Hodo administration evidenced the intensity and detailed attention of the new president to all aspects of University life. The year closed with the popular faculty, staff, and trustee Christmas dinner at Braeburn Country Club.[36] Over these years, the Christmas dinners were eagerly anticipated. They provided a forum for University employees and spouses to enjoy social interaction with members of the Board in a setting that helped make the concept of "family" an operational reality.

The opening of the calendar year 1988 marked the University's twenty-fifth year of service. President Hodo recommended the creation of a Student Affairs Committee in the Board structure to complement those existing in academic, financial, and development affairs.[37] The firm of John Farrell and Associates was employed as the architect for the Moody Library addition. *The decision was made to move the site of the Hinton Tower from between the library and the science complex to an alternate campus location.*

At the February 1988 meeting, the Board moved to recommend an amendment of Article 6 of the Articles of Incorporation to eliminate a stated maximum number of trustees. This action was subsequently approved by the Baptist General Convention of Texas and recorded with the Secretary of State's office.[38] The President reported that $750,000 of athletic coaches' salaries that historically had been recorded as "academic expense" had been moved appropriately to "athletic expense." In his ongoing assessment of the role of the athletic program, Dr. Hodo shared his analysis with the trustees:

Gymnastics is the only sport that requires membership in NCAA Division I. We have a lot invested in the Glasscock Center; the crowds are better for gymnastics than for basketball; gymnastics is nationally ranked. Without that sport, we could move to NCAA Division II or NAIA. . . . The question is can we afford to

---

36 Over the years, these dinners proved so popular that they outgrew all campus facilities. The near-by Braeburn Country Club was made available by Dr. and Mrs. James Taylor.

37 Houston Baptist University, Minutes of the Meetings of the Board of Trustees, Meeting on 26 Jan. 1988.

38 Houston Baptist University, Minutes of the Meetings of the Board of Trustees, Meeting on 23 Feb. 1988.

lay down a $1,000,000 deficit annually in the athletic department to the detriment of something as important as academics.

The President further urged the Board to fund salary raises for all faculty in the 1988-89 budget. "I would like to provide a contingency fund; but the risk of not providing for the faculty is a greater risk than not having a contingency." The Board subsequently voted to set up money from the Bettis estate mineral income for one year to fund faculty merit raises.[39] A three-year grant totaling $1,500,000 from the Cullen Foundation for the Hinton Tower was announced. Additionally, the University received $100,000 from Pearl Hillyer for its first Endowed Academic Scholarships specifically for National Merit Scholars.[40]

The decision was made to place the Currie property in Colorado on the market to be sold for the Hinton project. Originally, the Property Committee felt the market should be tested at $1640 per acre; however, Colorado appraisers listed the property at $770 per acre or $470,000 for the entire tract.[41] Mrs. Currie died in September 1988 while the University still owned her homestead.[42] The Faculty Assembly reflected on Mrs. Currie's desire for the use of the ranch by University families and requested that the Currie log house that had been built by Mr. Currie and the surrounding meadow be retained by the University rather than sold.[43]

§

Since their arrival in Houston in May 1987, Dr. Hodo and his family had been living in a leased home in Tanglewood. Because Chancellor and Mrs. Hinton had been granted lifetime use of the President's home on campus, plans were discussed to construct a new president's home that would better provide for campus social functions, for housing University guests, and for the residential needs of the first family. The original Hinton House, as it had become named, might then be used for admissions or alumni activities. Builder-trustee Bruce Belin began working with Dr. Hodo to develop plans for the new project.

---

39 Ibid.

40 *SomeTimes*, 3 Mar. 1988, p. 1.

41 Houston Baptist University, Minutes of the Meetings of the Executive Committee of the Board of Trustees, Meeting on 26 Apr. 1988.

42 "In Tribute," *HBU News*, Fall 1988, 4. Memorials written for Frankie Currie, Rose Dillon, Freland Murphy, and Orrien Smith.

43 Houston Baptist University, Minutes of the Meetings of the Faculty Assembly, Meeting on 4 Oct. 1988.

Dr. W. H. Hinton served as the first President of Houston Baptist College from 1962 to 1987 when he was appointed as the University's first Chancellor.

Dr. E. D. Hodo served as the second President of Houston Baptist University from 1987 to 2006 when he was named President Emeritus.

Dr. Robert B. Sloan, Jr. was elected the University's third President in 2006.

The UBA Property Committee: Cecil Cook, Florence Weaver, Jake Kamin, Dr. Howard C. Lee, Sr., and Dr. Stewart Morris.

The Cullen Science Center Dedication Exhibit commemorates the roles of Jesse Jones, Roy and Lillie Cullen, and M. D. Anderson through their respective foundations in support of the Science Center construction. Shown as partners are Memorial Hospital, the University nursing program, the skyline of the City of Houston, and the images of the major donors.

IV

The ten Morris Columns date from 1898 and were preserved from the Galveston County Court House.

The Holcombe Mall lanterns date from 1910 and were preserved from the Houston City Auditorium.

The Houston Baptist University class ring is distinguished by the triangle representing the Holy Trinity, the open Bible and cross from the college seal, and a shield of faith with the "1960" date of founding.

Dr. W. H. Hinton congratulated Dr. E. D. Hodo on October 29, 1987, upon his investiture as the University's second president.

The dome of the Hinton Center was lifted into place as a part of a topping-out ceremony.

Participating in the ribbon-cutting for the Hinton Center dedication on September 16, 1997, were Elizabeth Hickman, David Nelson, Anna Leal, Robert and Janice McNair, Dr. Tracy and Lee Lawrence, Dr. Hinton and President Hodo.

Lady Margaret Thatcher engaged in fireside chat with Ron Stone for the 1999 Spirit of Excellence Dinner.

The campus in 2000 looking toward the Fondren Road main entrance. New additions include the Moody Library extension, the Hinton Center, the Baugh Center and the Mest Wing under construction.

Jack Carlson, Chair of the Board of Trustees, formally installed Dr. Robert B. Sloan, Jr. as the University's third president.

President Robert B. Sloan, Jr. delivered his inaugural address in a colorful Holcombe Mall setting at the base of the Morris Columns.

Dr. Stewart and Joella Morris were honored as principal donors at the dedication of the Joella and Stewart Morris Cultural Arts Center.

The collections of the University's three museums—the Dunham Bible Museum, the Museum of American Architecture and Decorative Arts, and the Museum of Southern History—reside in the Joella and Stewart Morris Cultural Arts Center.

The Dunham Theater in the Joella and Stewart Morris Cultural Arts Center serves the campus and the city with a facility of exceptional acoustics and performance capability.

The Lake House, dedicated in November 2008, provides residence for 350 students in a spectacular campus setting.

The University Academic Center provides unique learning environments for the School of Art, the Honors College, and the College of Arts and Humanities.

The Belin Chapel and the Sherry and Jim Smith Létourneau Organ in the Joella and Stewart Morris Cultural Arts Center.

The University debaters under Coach Marty Sadler finished in the top five teams in tournaments at Vanderbilt, Wake Forest, University of Kentucky, and Dartmouth College.[44] The University enjoyed the visit of David Vaisey, Bodley's Librarian at Oxford University and longtime friend of Dr. Calvin Huckabay, who delivered the Robert Ray Lectures in Humanities in April.[45] And after twenty-six years of service, Dr. Troy Womack, founding Vice President for Financial Affairs, announced his retirement. Honorary degrees were presented in the spring to Drs. Womack, B. J. Martin, and William Denham, first chairman of the HBC board of trustees.[46]

The University gymnastics team under Coach Hutch Dvorak represented the University at the 1988 NCAA Division I National Tournament, finished with a ranking of sixth in the nation, and boasted the number one and number two all around gymnasts in the nation—Alfonso Rodriguez and Miguel Rubio.[47] This competition was the team's second opportunity to be invited to the national championships.[48] Additionally, the University's men's golf team garnered its second invitation to the NCAA Golf Championships. The team had won the TAAC championship four of the previous five years. Golfer Jeff Wagner was selected for All-American recognition, and coach Dave Mannen was selected TAAC Coach of the Year for the seventh straight year.[49] Exemplifying the University's multi-cultural student body, five HBU students were selected to compete in the 1988 Olympic Games. These included Rubio Gonzales, luge, Argentina; Fred Goporu, basketball, Central African Republic; Bruno Kongawoin, basketball, Central African Republic; and, Rodriguez and Rubio, gymnastics—both from Spain.[50]

In May 1988, Dr. Hodo summarized his first year to the Board of Trustees:

> My first goal continues to be the overall atmosphere, commitment, and thrust of Christianity on this campus. I am convinced that if that is not first, nothing else will be right. . . . Academics are in good shape. Teaching loads are heavy. . . . Dr. Womack is retiring, but we have asked him to serve an unfilled term as

44 Houston Baptist University, Minutes of the Meetings of the Board of Trustees, Meeting on 24 May 1998.
45 "1988 Spring Academic Lecture Series," *HBU News,* Summer 1988, 9.
46 *Ornogah 1988,* 70.
47 Houston Baptist University, Minutes of the Meetings of the Executive Committee of the Board of Trustees, Meeting on 26 Apr. 1988.
48 Alfonzo Rodriguez, "Olympics '88: The Ultimate Dream," *The Collegian,* 12 May 1988, pp. 8-9. Photos.
49 *Ornogah 1988,* 230.
50 Alfonzo Rodriguez, "Olympics '88: The Ultimate Dream," *The Collegian,* 12 May 1988, pp. 8-9. Photos.

trustee. We will finish the year in the red, but I promise it *will* be black. We need to get the enrollment to 3200 students. . . . We should be raising $500,000 in sustaining funds annually. . . . There are those employees who are not needed, who don't reflect the values and image we wish to project. Coaches are being taken from three-year to one-year contracts. Athletics is still a concern. Alumni, placement, and counseling are deficient areas. And, we need to increase our resource base.[51]

Tom Hixson was named Vice President for Financial Affairs to replace Dr. Troy Womack. Hixson held the MBA and had been Vice President at California Baptist College since 1984.[52] Womack's role in the history of the University had been significant. He yielded decision-making influence far beyond that which a chief financial officer might ordinarily provide, i.e. he served as secretary of the faculty Academic Affairs Committee and was member of the faculty Admissions Committee for many years. The confidence Dr. Hinton had in him and Womack's shared vision with the President made their association a powerful influence on University history.

In 1988, Dr. Joan DeRooy was named Vice-President for Advancement, and Dr. Ray Mayfield was made Director of Planned Giving.[53] DeRooy moved to Advancement from Instructional Television following the sale of Channel 14. Mayfield was highly productive in this arena; his community networking capacity stemmed from the service of both himself and his father as pastors and enabled him to have the kind of church influence provided in earlier days by O. D. Martin. Under Mayfield's direction, the Endowed Academic Scholarship program flourished. It is indicative of their institutional commitment that DeRooy, Dean of Nursing Glendola Nash, Mayfield, and Womack all completed doctoral degrees in response to their HBU administrative appointments.

In July, following a visit to review other college athletic programs, Dr. Hodo recommended to the Board that the University athletic program be moved to a lower division with the exception of gymnastics that was required to be in NCAA Division I.[54] The University additionally developed a program of in-kind advertising with KPRC-TV that provided

---

51 Houston Baptist University, Minutes of the Meetings of the Board of Trustees, Meeting on 24 May 1988. The 1987-88 deficit was $445,000, down from $880,000 the previous year.

52 "Hixson Named Vice President," *HBU News*, Fall 1988, 2.

53 "DeRooy Directs University Advancement Team—Mayfield Directs Planned Giving," *HBU News*, Summer 1988, 8.

54 Houston Baptist University, Minutes of the Meetings of the Executive Committee of the Board of Trustees, Meeting on 26 July 1988.

three thirty-second promotional spots weekly over the course of the following twelve months.[55]

During the summer, news of a second presidential home reached the campus community that was laboring under severe budget restrictions.[56] The commitment to permit Dr. and Mrs. Hinton to live in the first President's home for their lifetime necessitated provision of a second edifice. In a *Collegian* interview in the fall, Dr. Hodo answered student questions about the house: yes, he had designed it; the cost was estimated to be $450,000; and tuition would not be increased to pay for it. The house was to include a guest suite and was designed to be used for University functions.[57] Coming as it did in a time of repressed faculty salaries and constricted operational budgets, the scale of the new house represented a matter of questionable judgment to many in the campus community and eroded confidence in the commitment of the trustees to make salaries "a top priority." The size and grandeur of the house became a matter of some animosity on campus as had the new Fondren entrance.[58]

The University's first twenty-five-year employees were honored in 1988—Judy Babb, Flonnie Brown, Dr. A. O. Collins, Dr. Bill Dacres, Dr. Calvin Huckabay, Dr. Ray Mayfield, Jr., and Dr. Troy Womack (retired).[59] For many years, the relative youth of those involved in the early College history held at bay the reality of eventual personal loss—either to retirement or death. Eventually, the demographic composition of the University faculty began to assume a more traditional pattern. The University lost several early supporters during the fall months of 1988. University Founder and former chair of the President's Council, Orrien Smith, died in August. Colorado homestead donor Frankie Currie, founding trustee Freland Murphy, and Rose Dillon all passed away during September. Many donors, trustees, faculty, and staff who had provided a sense of security and fidelity to the early mission were being replaced by younger, newer leaders.

Off the campus, Dr. Hodo effectively bridged the transition from a personal allegiance to a founding President to an institutional allegiance to a strategic mission. The transition among external constituent groups was

55 Houston Baptist University, Minutes of the Meetings of the Board of Trustees, Meeting on 22 May 1990.
56 Houston Baptist University, Minutes of the Meetings of the Faculty, Meeting on 12 May 1988; Minutes of the Faculty Assembly, Meeting on 29 Sept. 1988.
57 "President clears misconceptions about new house," *The Collegian*, 8 Oct. 1988, p. 1.
58 "Letters to the Editor," *The Collegian*, 11 May 1989, p. 2. Once under construction, the three-story profile of the new home dwarfed the adjacent Hinton House fostering the campus nickname, the "Taj Mahodo."
59 "Honors, Honors, Honors," *HBU News*, Winter 1988, 9.

seamless and enthusiastic. The new President's wife Sadie became a distinctive player in her own right. She worked closely with affinity organizations, was accorded the title of "First Lady," and came to have her own personal record of contribution over the years of Dr. Hodo's presidency.

§

Ground was broken in September 1988 for the Moody Library expansion. The addition was to provide additional shelving and study space, house the special book collections, provide for technical support and media services, and offer dedicated space for the Museum of American Architecture and Decorative Arts. Additionally, the existing library was to receive new lighting, additional shelving, and new carpet.[60] Fund surpluses of $1,500,000 for additional construction were carried forward to be used for a separate facility to house the instructional programs in education and business.[61]

The University consummated the purchase of Harvest House from CIGNA for $1,925,000, $75,000 less than originally sought.[62] The property was placed under the management of the University's new wholly-owned subsidiary, Beechnut Street, Inc. Additional discussion ensued regarding the possibility of the University's sale to Memorial Hospital of the site of the *Toys-R-Us* store adjacent to Harvest House.[63] In further financing action, the trustees passed a resolution to refinance some long-term University indebtedness including $3,000,000 for the Hinton Tower project with low-interest bonds available from the Texas Higher Education Authority, Inc.[64] The University consummated the sale with eventual buy-back rights to HBU of 9.7 acres to Memorial Senior Services, a subsidiary of Memorial Care Systems, for a retirement center. Groundbreaking for this facility was held April 7, 1988. University Place, as it came to be called, was to comprise 186 units, of which 92 had been pre-sold prior to groundbreaking.[65]

---

60 Houston Baptist University, Minutes of the Meetings of the Executive Committee of the Board of Trustees, Meeting on 28 Oct. 1988.
61 "Library expansion to begin," *HBU News,* Fall 1988, 6.
62 Houston Baptist University, Minutes of the Meetings of the Executive Committee of the Board of Trustees, Meeting on 19 Oct. 1988.
63 Houston Baptist University, Minutes of the Meetings of the Executive Committee of the Board of Trustees, Meeting on 28 Oct. 1988.
64 Houston Baptist University, Minutes of the Meetings of the Board of Trustees, Meeting on 25 Oct. 1988.
65 "HBU sells 9.7 acres for retirement community," *The Collegian,* 13 Oct. 1988, p. 1.

In the late 1980s, the Faculty Assembly adopted a more assertive role in University governance that proved to be a healthy model for institutional improvement. In contrast to an elected faculty senate model, the Assembly had always been a voluntary membership organization; average attendance comprised about thirty-five percent of the faculty. The role of the Faculty Assembly in relation to responsibilities of Presidentially-appointed committees continued to be a matter of exploration and development. The Assembly's requests for increased summer pay and a tuition-waiver for faculty enrollment in graduate courses were postponed pending an improved financial climate.[66] However, a request for clarification of the salary-decision process elicited the establishment of a new comprehensive policy that featured annual professional goal-setting, faculty performance review, and salary recommendations by the deans. In the new model, it would be the responsibility of the Vice President for Academic Affairs to monitor overall salary equity and the realities of higher market-driven salaries in competitive areas like accounting, nursing, science, and management. Final decisions rested with the President. This new model replaced a long-standing practice of salary decisions being made largely by President Hinton and Vice President Womack with no formal performance assessment.[67] A primary goal of the new model was the elimination of excessive salary variation among faculty at the same rank and approximate years of service.[68] Hixson issued the first staff-benefit document in the University's history. The manual paralleled the comprehensive *Faculty Handbook* developed some years earlier. At this point in history, staff members were still not eligible to participate in the University's retirement program.[69] However, in March 1989, Dr. Hodo implemented a revised retirement policy that provided for inclusion of all employees, but adjustment of the University's long-standing level of generous matching contribution to the faculty plan.[70]

A number of new academic program developments were implemented. A new course, *Human Wellness,* replaced physical education activity courses as the requirement for all baccalaureate degrees, and *World Civilization* replaced *Western Civilization* as the baccalaureate degree

---

66 Houston Baptist University, Minutes of the Meetings of the Faculty Assembly, Meeting on 29 Sept. 1988.

67 Houston Baptist University, Minutes of the Meetings of the Faculty Assembly, Meeting on 4 Oct. 1988.

68 Houston Baptist University, Minutes of the Meetings of the Faculty Assembly, Meeting on 29 Nov. 1988.

69 Houston Baptist University, Minutes of the Meetings of the Faculty Assembly, Meeting on 6 Dec. 1988.

70 Houston Baptist University, Minutes of the Meetings of the Board of Trustees, Meeting on 28 Mar. 1989. All employees would be eligible for 7.5 percent University contribution to the retirement plan.

requirement. A Bachelor of Business Administration degree was established. In a move regarded as a sign of the times, faculty members were required to enroll in a basic computer skills course to establish common foundations of knowledge and to enable standardization of campus software platforms.[71]

Endowed Chair lecturers from this period included John Bradshaw, Chuck Colson, Dr. Gordon Kingsley, Dr. William May, Cal Thomas, Dr. Bill Tillman, Jr., and Sysco CEO John Woodhouse. Academic program grants were received from the National Science Foundation for science equipment, the Exxon Foundation for math education, the Helene Fuld Health Trust for nursing instructional media, and the Rockwell Fund for a writing laboratory.[72] Among the faculty, Dr. James Ulmer's poetry appeared in *The New Yorker*, the *Carnegie-Mellon Journal*, and the *Mississippi Valley Review*.[73] Dr. Ann Gebuhr's scholarly work appeared in the *College Music Symposium* as did that of Dr. Curtis Freeman in *The Reformed Journal*.[74] As signs of the coming era of technology, the Moody Library announced the acquisition of its first telefacsimile machine.[75] The library had also proudly rid itself of "noisy rental typewriters" and installed coin-operated word processors for student use.[76] A note also appeared in the University publication *SomeTimes* requesting the re-inking of dot matrix printer ribbons rather than the purchase of new ones.[77]

§

In November 1988, it was announced that the University had identified several ineligible players on the HBU soccer team. In accord with NCAA response, the University was forced to forfeit all soccer games between 1982 and 1985. At the heart of the issue was assistance from a University alumnus who had recruited internationally for the team, but was later discovered to be a professional sports agent.[78] At issue was the

---

71 Houston Baptist University, Minutes of the Meetings of the Faculty, Meeting on 1 Sept. 1987.
72 Houston Baptist University, Minutes of the Meetings of the Academic Committee of the Board of Trustees, Meeting on 26 Oct. 1988.
73 *SomeTimes*, Feb. 1989.
74 *SomeTimes*, Jan. 1988.
75 *SomeTimes*, Sept. 1987.
76 Dolly Martin, "Old Clunkers Replaced by a Computer," *The Collegian*, 10 Dec. 1984, p. 4. Software pre-loaded on the computer included *Bank Street Writer*, *VisiCalc*, and *Home Accountant*.
77 *SomeTimes*, Dec. /Jan. 1989.
78 Houston Baptist University, Minutes of the Meetings of the Executive Committee of the Board of Trustees, Meeting on 16 Nov. 1988.

allegation of the use of professional players and ineligible students in the athletic program. As a result, the soccer coach resigned, and the Athletic Director was reassigned for the balance of his contract.[79]

In other sports action, the women's gymnastics team under Coach John Pellikan went to the NCAA regional tournament and was ranked #15 in the nation in only its fourth year of competition.[80] The men's gymnastics team beat the University of Nebraska in March 1989 and placed first in every event, including team awards, during competition with Penn State, Southern Illinois University, and the Naval Academy.[81] The Huskies later defeated Iowa to move ahead of UCLA into position as the #1 team in the nation.[82] The team amassed a 21-1 record in competition against large state universities including Arizona State, Iowa State, Brigham Young University, Illinois, Penn State, and the University of Nebraska.[83] *No other athletic team in HBU history had accomplished the remarkable feat of being ranked #1 in the nation in NCAA Division I competition.*

In April, the University announced its decision to move to NCAA Division II status that required participation in only four sports. Men's gymnastics remained in Division I as required by the NCAA. Dr. Hodo spoke to student athletes shortly before an official press release was distributed explaining that the action was a financial decision. Later that same evening, Dr. Hodo spoke with a group of students who had gathered in front of the President's home upon hearing the news. *The Collegian* reported, "Students Stage Protest March."[84] Local press and television covered the event. In the days that followed, Dr. Hodo agreed to meet with members of the Student Senate regarding the athletic decision in response to a Senate charge of "little or no communication between yourself and students."[85]

The President later told the *Houston Chronicle*, "Of all the things I've ever done from a managerial point of view, this was the toughest. It was not a popular decision. But, it was one that had to be made, and I had to make it."[86] The *Houston Post* announced that tennis and track/cross

79 Houston Baptist University, Minutes of the Meetings of the Board of Trustees, Meeting on 22 Nov. 1988.

80 Ernie Petru, "Women's gymnastics: Future beams brightly," *The Collegian*, 8 Dec. 1988, pp. 8-9. Photos.

81 "Coach Dvorak flips over win against Nebraska," *The Collegian*, 16 Mar. 1989, p. 1.

82 "Husky Gymnasts Number 1 in Nation," *HBU News*, Spring 1989, 15.

83 "Men gymnasts rank #1 in nation," *The Collegian*, 14 Apr. 1989, p. 1.

84 "Students stage protest march," *The Collegian*, 11 May 1989, p. 1.

85 Ibid, p. 4.

country for both men and women would be dropped.[87] Basketball was to be suspended for one year to enable players to retain eligibility if they wished to transfer to another Division I institution. Men's baseball and men's and women's riflery were added. Golf, soccer, volleyball, softball, and women's gymnastics were to move to NCAA Division II. The move affected twenty-eight athletes and two coaches. The University assured the student athletes of its commitment to honor scholarship funding.

As a result of the fallout from the soccer infraction, Dr. Ed Billings resigned as Athletic Director. Billings had been Athletic Director since 1966. Basketball coach Tommy Jones was appointed to the Athletic Director position, but vacated it in the fall to take a coaching position at the University of Houston.[88] Dr. Hodo assumed the responsibility of acting Athletic Director in the interim. During Billings' years as Athletic Director, HBU golf teams won the Trans America Conference Championship in 1984-85 and 1988 and participated in NCAA national tournaments in 1974, 1984, 1987-88. HBU basketball teams had won TAAC championships in 1981 and 1984 when they also competed in national tournaments. Gymnastics teams had gone to NCAA national tournaments in 1982, 1984, and 1987-89. Both men's and women's gymnastics had been ranked #1 in the nation.

§

The 1989 Spring Commencement was held on the Holcombe Mall. For many graduating seniors and faculty, Houston's humidity and heat were stifling—particularly in academic robes. Dr. Hodo, under some pressure to return commencement to the campus, deflected charges that the decision to move outdoors was primarily a cost-saving move but asserted his desire to host such significant events on the campus.[89] May and July nursing graduates once again continued the tradition of a hundred percent pass rate on first attempt in the nursing licensure examinations. HBU ranked first among sixty-three colleges of nursing in Texas

---

86 Jayne Custred, "Houston Baptist fans, players, give up game cold turkey," *Houston Chronicle*, 21 Jan. 1990, Sports sec. 2, p. 19, two-star ed.
87 *Houston Post*, 27 Apr. 1989, sec. B, p. 1.
88 *SomeTimes*, April 1989.
89 Paul W. Alli, "Graduation to be held at Holcombe Mall," *The Collegian*, Jan. 1990, p. 1.

based on the licensure results.[90] Over the course of the summer, Ricky Witte and Benny Agosto were appointed new coaches for baseball and soccer.[91] In July, trustee Walter Morgan reported to the Board that all financial claims against Harvest House finally had been put to rest.[92] Harvest House was reopened as the Garden Village Retirement Center.[93]

During the summer months, Dr. Robert Newell resigned his post as Dean of Religious Affairs to accept a local pastorate. Newell's contributions to the religious life area have not been equaled in University history. He joined the University in 1968 and soon formulated a series of creative models for college student ministry that were widely emulated in colleges across the nation. The ministry structures of CLC, CEMC, SERV, and FOCUS were still viable in the University's program in 2010.

Dr. Norman Hackerman, President of the Welch Foundation and former President of Rice University, initiated the new academic year in the fall with an address for the 1989 Opening Convocation.[94] Enrollment was down from 2775 degree-seeking students in 1985 to 2324 in 1989. Correspondingly, the budget was reduced by $559,000 on the basis of these enrollment data.[95] The new library addition and remodeling were completed, and the staff coordinated a ninety-degree rotation of library shelving to take better advantage of stack lighting. Seating capacity with the new addition afforded study space for 400 students. The new Ragland Reading Room provided outstanding lounge and study space for students.[96] *The Library Journal* printed a description and photograph of the new addition in its December issue.[97] The library expansion was dedicated in ceremonies on October 26, 1989.[98] In related activity, architect Arthur Jones of Lloyd, Jones, and Phillpot was selected to begin work on the revised Hinton Tower concept. The University was still $2,000,000 short of needed funds for the project that had been assigned a $5,000,000 budget.[99]

90 *SomeTimes*, 15 Nov. 1989.
91 Paul W. Alli, "Soccer: New coach, new attitudes, new team," *The Collegian,* Sept. 1989, pp. 8-9.
92 Houston Baptist University, Minutes of the Meetings of the Executive Committee, Meeting on 25 July 1989.
93 Houston Baptist University, Minutes of the Meetings of the Executive Committee of the Board of Trustees, Meeting on 24 July 1990.
94 *Ornogah 1990*, 32.
95 Houston Baptist University, Minutes of the Meetings of the Executive Committee, Meeting on 19 Sept. 1989.
96 "New Library Wing Dedication," *HBU News,* Winter 1990, 5.
97 "Ruins Among the Splendor: Library Buildings '89," *Library Journal*, Dec. 1989, 48.
98 Mo Bahamdun, "Dedication marks library completion," *The Collegian,* Jan. 1990, p. 3.
99 Houston Baptist University, Minutes of the Meetings of the Board of Trustees, Meeting on 14 Nov. 1989.

In the fall of 1989, Houston's Steinway dealer, the Forshey Piano Company approached the University with a business proposal that would provide new pianos annually for student and classroom use in exchange for heightened corporate visibility and for hosting an annual sale of these instruments to University constituents. The University received thirty new Young Chang pianos from owner Fred Forshey in the first year of this agreement. The pianos replaced the aging Steinway practice instruments purchased in 1963 and provided grand pianos for teaching studios, the President's home, and performance venues on the campus. The University's students and faculty profited from higher levels of learning and performance made possible by these fine instruments.[100] The University would enjoy the Forshey relationship for the next twenty years.

The Faculty Assembly passed a resolution in 1989 to request the increase of adjunct faculty compensation, frozen since 1981, to be more competitive in employing part-time faculty. In some disciplines, i.e. Christianity, English, and Business, adjunct faculty provided a significant portion of classroom instruction. The resolution further proposed that monthly summer school pay be increased to equal one-twelfth of a basic nine-month contract salary rather than a fixed stipend per course. Finally, in a move further reflective of heightened faculty anxiety, the Assembly requested quarterly meetings by the Assembly President with Dr. Hodo "to minimize the proliferation of rumors, decrease the level of stress, and maintain appropriate communication between important constituencies on the campus."[101]

In September, a report surfaced regarding an NCAA infraction involving an HBU All-America gymnast who had returned to Spain with Coach Dvorak "to testify before the Spanish gymnastics federation to plead his case for Olympic eligibility."[102] Because the University had allegedly paid for the trip, the athlete was declared ineligible by the NCAA.[103] In November, the NCAA stated that the University had also "illegally" recruited and housed several gymnasts and provided "special benefits." The NCAA charged poor athletic management because these actions had by-passed the Athletic Director and the Athletic Business Manager and had been approved directly by the Vice President for

---

100 *SomeTimes*, Oct. 1989.
101 Houston Baptist University, Minutes of the Meetings of the Faculty Assembly, Meeting on 29 Sept. 1989.
102 Mark Evangelista, "HBU Officials give testimony," *Houston Chronicle*, 6 Feb. 1990, Sports sec., p. 9.
103 *Houston Post*, 24 Oct. 1989, sec. B, p. 1.

Financial Affairs. The case involved University monies—later reimbursed—to provide air fare from Spain to the United States and temporary housing for an athlete prior to the opening of the school year.[104] NCAA rules prohibited housing and feeding athletes until they became officially registered students. Dr. Hodo explained that the University had discovered the issue, had self-reported it to the NCAA, and was cooperating at the highest level with the investigation. Women's gymnastics coach John Pellikan was named to replace Dvorak "in a move perceived as a show of compliance to the NCAA."[105]

When the NCAA met in San Diego in January 1990, Dr. Hodo, Legal Counsel to the President Dr. Don Byrnes, Coach Hutch Dvorak, and Athletic Committee Chairman Dr. James Taylor headed a University delegation to testify before the NCAA Rules Infractions Committee. The NCAA Infraction Report called for the suspension of the coach until July 1991. The men's gymnastics program was placed on probation and banned from post-season competition and from awarding new grants through the 1991-92 season.[106] The University was required to vacate all team and individual records in national competition by the two athletes from 1987-89. Significantly, however, the final year of probation "was suspended because of HBU's exemplary cooperation in the investigation, its diligence in uncovering the most serious violation independently, and its candor before the committee."[107] Though the actions may have been made for "humanitarian" reasons to assist student athletes to participate in the Seoul Olympics, these actions violated NCAA policy regarding "special benefits."[108] Meanwhile, the NAIA declared HBU's golf and baseball programs ineligible for district playoffs for failure to meet the deadline for filing requisite conference forms.[109]

In sparkling contrast, in 1990 the women's gymnastics team won their first national championship in history under the coaching of John Pellikan, compiling a 21-2 record for the year. Pellikan presented Dr. Hodo with the team plaque for *Women's Gymnastics Sweepstakes.* Named to All-America honors were Dawn Mulholland, Nicole Williams, Renee

---

104 Houston Baptist University, Minutes of the Meetings of the Executive Committee of the Board of Trustees, Meeting on 6 Dec. 1989.

105 Mark Evangelista, "Pellikan replaces Dvorak," *Houston Chronicle,* 5 Jan. 1990, Sports sec., p. 10, two-star ed.

106 Dr. E. D. Hodo, "From the President," *HBU News,* Spring 1990, inside cover.

107 Associated Press, "Probation for HBU's Gymnasts," *Houston Chronicle,* 27 Mar. 1990, p. 1.

108 Houston Baptist University, Minutes of the Meetings of the Board of Trustees, Meeting on 14 Nov. 1989.

109 *Austin American Statesman,* 3 May 1990, sec. D, p. 10.

Melancon, and Donna Valasquez. Under men's gymnastics Coach Tim Erwin, Carlos Saura, Zavier March, and Miguel Jorge qualified for the NCAA national championships. The women's track team won the district championship and also advanced to national NAIA competition.[110]

§

The University celebrated the thirtieth anniversary of its chartering in 1990. The 1990 federal census established the population of Harris County at nearly three million residents. Bob Lanier moved from his position as Chairman of the Metropolitan Transit Authority—where he had revolutionized Houston's public transportation—to the office of Mayor in 1992. Houston remained the largest un-zoned city in North America. In continuing fallout from the economic straits of the 1980s, the Houston luxury retailer Sakowitz Brothers declared bankruptcy, liquidated its assets, and closed its eighteen stores. Adjacent to the campus, the Southwest Freeway was bearing the full brunt of major construction to widen and reroute feeder roads that resulted in the permanent closing of the southbound Fondren exit to the campus.[111]

On campus, the institutional self-study for the Southern Association of Colleges and Schools was complete—for the fourth time under the leadership of Dr. Calvin Huckabay. Dr. Jerry Ford, Dr. Tom Holland, and Burton Burrus formed a new Student Academic Services Office to offer expanded counseling, testing, and career placement services for students.[112] Dr. James Taylor won a national "Teaching Excellence and Campus Leadership Award."[113] Nursing alumna and faculty member Nancy Yuill '72 received her doctorate and was named Acting Director of the School of Nursing following the unexpected resignation of Dr. Glendola Nash, Dean of the College of Science and Health Professions.

Glendola Nash had joined the HBC faculty in 1968 as a part of the acquisition of the Lillie Jolly School of Nursing diploma program. She served as department chair initially and then was named Dean of Science and Health Professions in 1972. During her years of leadership, more than 500 nursing students graduated, compiling one of the state's highest

---

110 *Ornogah 1990*, 35, 140-145.

111 *SomeTimes,* March 1990.

112 Houston Baptist University, Minutes of the Meetings of the Faculty, Meeting on 10 Jan. 1990.

113 "Taylor Cited for Teaching Excellence and Campus Leadership," *HBU News,* Summer 1990, 8.

records of passing the nursing licensure examination on first attempt. Graduates of the HBU program were widely sought as employees and were known and respected for their thorough preparation and extensive clinical experience. Nash had raised more than $1,500,000 in grants for the nursing program and had successfully managed the move of the program from its inner-city location to new housing in the Cullen Science Center on the University campus. She was named a Distinguished Professor at the 1989 commencement, and an Endowed Academic Scholarship was established in her honor. At her retirement dinner in the spring, Dr. Hodo joined colleagues from the health and medical community across the state to honor her outstanding record of professional leadership.[114]

§

In February 1990, dedication ceremonies were held for the newly-relocated Museum of American Architecture and Decorative Arts. The new wing provided greatly expanded space, windowless protection from harmful ultraviolet rays, custom display cases, exacting humidity and temperature control, a dedicated entrance with affinity to nearby parking, and onsite artifact storage. The American Museum Society continued its long record of financial support with gifts that provided new display cases allowing greatly expanded exhibit space for the Theo Redwood Blank Doll Collection.

The Museum of American Architecture and Decorative Arts had enjoyed an auspicious beginning in the 1960s under the leadership of Mrs. Charles Bybee. Helen Tinch had been appointed as founding Director of the Museum and was largely responsible for acquisition of the collection and establishing its first home in the campus Moody Library. Following Tinch's retirement, Lynn Miller and Sheila Bush, who had served as volunteer docents for Tinch, continued to direct the development of the museum. In 1981, Dr. Doris Anderson assumed the Museum leadership. Dr. Phil Lanasa joined Anderson in 1986 as Co-Director of the Museum. In 1988, Lanasa resigned, and in 1989 Anderson was followed by the return of Lynn Miller as Director.

In 1990, Director Lynn Miller coordinated the complex move of the collection into its new facility. The new wing, for the first time in history,

---

114 "University Honors Dr. Glendola Nash," *HBU News,* Spring 1990, 2. Photo.

afforded dedicated exhibit areas for antique furniture, period room recreations, the Blank Doll Collection, and later the Schissler Miniature Furniture Collection. The new museum wing was the realization of need first articulated some twenty years earlier. In October 1990, the American Museum Society under President Grace Gandy celebrated its twenty-fifth anniversary with a Silver Tea featuring the Blank Doll Collection.

§

The Board of Trustees approved the inclusion of $100,000 in the 1990-91 budget to provide merit raises for selected faculty. The proposed athletic budget was reduced from $1,200,000 in 1988 to $807,000 in 1990. Additional monies were approved for public relations and student recruiting activities. The trustees approved a new faculty application form that presented the Preamble to the By-Laws, a request for a written statement of personal faith, and indication of church membership affiliation. The Board further voted to open its meetings to representatives from the Faculty Assembly, the Student Senate, and the University Alumni Association.[115] The appointment of Dr. Don Byrnes as Legal Counsel and Assistant to the President was announced. Byrnes areas of responsibility included institutional research, assessment, legal counsel, and governmental relations including the Tuition Equalization Grant program of the State of Texas.[116] Carol Elsbury was named Registrar.

In May 1990, Dr. James Massey presented a special report to the Board of Trustees, *Students: Our Most Precious Resource*.[117] Massey spoke from his heart, addressed a rising tide of student dissatisfaction that he felt was developing on the campus, and encouraged the development of facilities and programs to address student morale and retention. During the summer, the University MBA programs mounted their first international study experiences with visits to corporate and business sites in Frankfurt, Stuttgart, Munich, and Paris. A summer trip was also made to corporate sites in Japan.[118] At the same time, thirty-two students in the Master of Liberal Arts program participated in a learning experience based in Scotland and Ireland.

---

115 Houston Baptist University, Minutes of the Meetings of the Board of Trustees, Meeting on 27 Feb. 1990.
116 "Report of the President," *HBU News*, Spring 1990, inside cover.
117 Houston Baptist University, Minutes of the Meetings of the Board of Trustees, Meeting on 22 May 1990.
118 "EMBA's take the classroom abroad," *HBU News*, May 1995, 13.

The University's marketing consultant STAMATS unveiled a new University motto, *Strong in Mind, Strong in Spirit* to spearhead a two-year program of student recruiting and "branding" activity. The new motto was developed after interviews with over 1100 students who reported choosing the University because of its reputation, location, low student/faculty ratio, specific programs, and faculty accessibility. In the STAMATS study, students reported high levels of satisfaction with the University experience. The study documented that the student body was comprised of two specific populations: 1) students with traditional Christian backgrounds for whom the spiritual character of the campus was important; and, 2) students who were attracted to the University primarily for the strength of the academic programs.[119] However, neither attribute was shown to be mutually exclusive. The documentation of this population segmentation was significant for the University's strategic planning and helped chart the path of change from the more homogeneous roots of HBC in its early years. The STAMATS study showed that most students did not select the University primarily because of its Christian commitment.[120]

A number of the University's senior faculty announced plans to leave at the end of the spring quarter.[121] Most of these were moving to positions at other universities. These actions took a particularly heavy toll on academic leadership; especially hard hit were the social and behavioral sciences. However, joining the faculty were several new faculty whose strategic value ultimately served to anchor a new generation of strong academic leadership. These included David Capes, Randy Hatchett, Leslie Kennedy, Alice Rowlands, and Shari Wescott. In other academic developments, the Faculty Assembly President Dr. Lou Shields recommended the creation of a faculty rank of Professor Emeritus.[122] In July, faculty member Dr. John Alexander was named Athletic Director. Alexander had been a longtime member of the University Athletic Committee, had served as a volunteer assistant softball coach, and was active in campus intramural sports.[123]

§

---

119 Susan Stern, "Forum with Hodo addresses issues," *The Collegian*, 6 Nov. 1990, p. 1.
120 "A Look at the University—Stamats," *HBU News*, Fall 1990, 7.
121 These included Dr. Charlene Dykman, Dr. Muriel Flake, Dr. Wallace Hooker, Dr. Keith Putt, Dr. Gerda Smith, and Dr. Stephen Williams.
122 Houston Baptist University, Minutes of the Meetings of the Faculty Assembly, Meeting in May 1990.
123 "Alexander named Athletic Director," *HBU News*, Summer 1990, 13.

In the fall, the MBA 2000 degree was offered via live television to students at the Kingwood campus of North Harris County College. Dr. Robert Bush's *Corporate Finance* was televised to students on the campuses of Wayland Baptist College and Howard Payne University as a part of the BGCT consortium of "Shared Resources."[124] HBU's capacity for leadership in this area of technology among Houston's colleges and those of the BGCT was formidable. Further evidence of an entrepreneurial academic spirit energized the campus. Similar programs bore further testimony to innovative spirit by offering courses in the Master of Education degree by HBU faculty on other Baptist campuses and the Master of Science in Human Resource Management at Reese and Bergstrom Air Force Bases.

In October 1990, the Student Senate passed a resolution decrying an increase in tuition and mailed copies of the resolution directly to members of the Board of Trustees.[125] A Student Forum hosting Dr. Hodo was held in November.[126] Student opinion proposed that the tuition increase was a result of inadequate institutional fund-raising and that the general maintenance of the University dorms, apartments, and classrooms was unsatisfactory.[127] The Faculty Assembly followed with its own request that additional presidential forums be held for faculty and staff, as well. The Assembly called for the creation of a Faculty Welfare Committee to review employment benefits, retirement policies, and salary equity issues.

In the fall, the *Collegian* was provided its own newsroom in which to work. The Faculty Assembly offered kudos to the student newspaper and its new sponsor Alice Rowlands for a greatly improved product.[128] The stated goal of the staff was "to let the newspaper be just that—a newspaper, a sort of a watch dog for campus life and activity, a source of information, and an arena for the exchange of ideas. We try to make the newspaper one that is more attractive, contains more newsworthy information, and is more accessible to students and organizations."[129] Volume 25, No. 1 of *The Collegian* marked the beginning of a long record of service and professional recognition under Rowland's leadership.

124 *SomeTimes*, Sept. 1990.

125 Missie Ludtke, "Tuition increase causes frustration and tension," *The Collegian*, 2 Oct. 1990, p. 4.

126 Sangita Rangala, "Frustration expressed over 'communication breakdown,'" *The Collegian*, 2 Oct. 1990, p. 1.

127 Susan Stern, "Forum with Hodo addresses issues," *The Collegian*, 6 Nov. 1990, p. 1.

128 Houston Baptist University, Minutes of the Meetings of the Faculty Assembly, Meeting on 23 Oct. 1990.

129 Doug Parker, "Collegian staff says 'thank you,'" *The Collegian*, 11 Dec. 1990, p. 2.

In fall events of no apparent direct significance to HBU, the Baylor University Board of Regents surprised the Baptist General Convention of Texas and revised its process for electing members to create greater institutional autonomy and independence. This action pre-dated a later, similar decision by the HBU Board of Trustees, also to the surprise of the BGCT. In the fall of 1990, an Associate Professor of Religion from Baylor, Dr. Robert B. Sloan, Jr., spoke for Convocation. Some seventeen years later, Sloan would be named the third President of Houston Baptist University.

A fire damaged sixteen units of the University Apartments in November. No one was injured, and the thirty-four displaced students were moved to the dorms and other apartments in the area.[130] Also in November, a member of the women's gymnastics team was injured and filed a $125,000 lawsuit against the University. The University had only recently incurred sharply-increased insurance premiums for its comprehensive liability coverage. The combination of both events placed further stress on the financial efficacy of the gymnastics programs at HBU.

The year ended by celebrating twenty-five years of service by Dr. Wallace Hooker and Controller Jackie Williams and twenty years of service by Mildred Boone, James Busby, Nora Hayes, and Dr. Phyllis Nimmons.[131] In December the chair of the visiting committee from the Southern Association, Dr. Robert Burnett, President of Armstrong College in Savannah, made his preliminary visit to the campus in preparation for his committee's onsite visit early in 1991.[132]

§

The first years of the new presidency had proved eventful. Residual problem resolution occupied much of Dr. Hodo's attention. However, he had mounted a sharply-focused set of goals for the University that was expressed in the institutional self-study and in the early work of institutional strategic planning. Dr. Hodo had created an integrated administrative leadership team that resulted in more highly-informed decisions and effective internal communication. He offered himself to students through open forums, the student newspaper, and campus opportunity as had never been done before. Yet, financial problems that were not of his

---

130 *Ornogah 1991*, 29.
131 *SomeTimes*, Dec. 1990.
132 Doug Parker, "Committee Considering Accreditation," *The Collegian*, 15 Jan. 1990, p. 1.

making continued to dominate decision-making. The Board of Trustees bore its own measure of complicity in the accumulated indebtedness of the University, as well as much credit for fund-raising successes. Yet, the Board held the new President responsible for extricating the University from its history of financial imbalance. Remarkably, Houston Baptist University had achieved high levels of achievement in many areas of endeavor—music, debate, nursing, education, pre-medicine, the liberal arts, faculty strength, and athletics—proving its capacity for producing results of excellence. The University had failed historically, however, to provide the financial resources necessary to support such ambitious undertakings. The appointment of President Hodo clearly marked a forced confrontation with the incompatibility of funding shortfalls and over-expenditure, no matter how extraordinary the resulting history of University achievement.

TEN

1991-1994

The United States invaded Iraq and Kuwait in January 1991 in the "shock and awe" of the Desert Storm operation. College students confronted the prospects of required military service for the first time since Viet Nam. The *1991 Ornogah* paid tribute to a number of HBU students among U. S. troops stationed in the Persian Gulf.[1] In Houston, trains loaded with tanks and armored equipment on their way to the Port of Houston were a daily sight at railroad crossings and freeways.

On campus, the visiting committee from the Southern Association of Colleges and Schools arrived in February 1991 to assess the institutional self-study and to work with the University in the reaffirmation-of-accreditation process. Some eighteen colleagues from other campuses representing all phases of college operations comprised the membership of the committee. The University had been working on its self-study for more than two years, addressing issues that appeared to need attention, and documenting areas of concern. At the end of its review, the committee issued its preliminary report to the President summarizing its recommendations.

The SACS committee called for improved process in assessment of institutional effectiveness, in master planning, and in evaluation; mandated were improved learning resources, especially in graduate programs; the development of an adequate financial base to decrease the deficit; improvements to the physical campus including safety and deferred maintenance; greater faculty participation in decision-making with authority for curriculum; a high priority for improved faculty salaries with written criteria for salary decisions; and attention to the distinction between trustee responsibility for policy-making and administrative responsibility for management. The report further called for development of a plan for continuous analysis and improvement of all university operations—not just academics, the coordination of graduate management under one office, greater support for library and instructional media resources, development

---

1 *Ornogah 1991*, 39.

of a "service mentality" in the information technology operation, and the elimination of deficit spending. One particular recommendation reflected faculty anxiety over perceived religious expectation beyond the Preamble. "If there are institutional expectations that faculty and staff must evangelize, attend worship, lead in prayer or perform other religious acts not stated in the Preamble, the Reaffirmation Committee recommends that a written policy be developed for approval by the institution's Board of Trustees after full discussion with the faculty and staff."[2]

To accompany these requirements, an additional number of suggested actions were proposed—improved fine arts facilities, more doctoral faculty in nursing, reduced faculty teaching loads, expansion of student counseling services, establishment of an employee grievance procedure, development of new sources of income, "acceleration" of the *board's leadership in fund-raising*, formulation of an action plan to address campus morale and staff stability, and restriction of the role of instructional television to academic support rather than curriculum development. The report called for a separate SACS visit to the University's graduate degree program in business at Bergstrom Air Force Base.[3] In addition, the SACS committee affirmed several outstanding areas of University academic performance including the programs in communications, pre-medicine, nursing, fine arts, and business.[4]

Among those on the committee was the former President of the University of Richmond, Dr. Bruce Heilman, one of the nation's most respected institutional fund-raisers. Heilman proposed a number of suggestions for improved success with HBU's fund raising: 1) concentrating on the role of fund raising over event-planning, organization liaison, public relations, continuing education, and instructional television; 2) cultivating new donor prospects; 3) the immediate acceleration of fund raising; 4) assigning more of the staff as fund raisers and fewer as "floaters;" and 5) clarifying the responsibility of the President to remove deficits and provide salary raises.[5]

The SACS document was a sweeping report. The depth and strength of the recommendations came as a surprise to many members of the campus community. In February, Dr. Hodo addressed the Board of Trustees

---

2 Southern Association for Colleges and Schools, *Report of the Visiting Committee,* Jan. 1991, Sec. II, #2.
3 A parallel program at Reese Air Force Base in Lubbock had been phased out in 1990.
4 Doug Parker, "SACS calls for campus improvements," *The Collegian,* 14 Feb. 1991, p. 1.
5 Houston Baptist University, Minutes of the Meeting of the Board of Trustees, Meeting on 16 Mar. 1991.

in response to the SACS report. He expressed his conviction of the need to petition the Christian Education Commission of the BGCT for funding of graduate programs at HBU as provided for Baylor and Hardin-Simmons University. In additional response to the SACS report, Milton Cross, Chair of the trustee Finance Committee, wrote a personal letter to members of the Board challenging each to "give or get" $10,000 for immediate faculty salary increases. In his letter, Cross confirmed that the HBU faculty had received only a five to eight percent salary adjustment over the previous five-year period in the face of a twenty percent increase in Houston's consumer price index. Cross wrote, "We have been distracted from our fiduciary responsibility by the press of other matters and the *comfort of forgetfulness*. Our heavy dependence on tuition-driven budgets is a practice we must reduce as have so many other institutions in the independent sector."[6]

An ad hoc committee was appointed to review the specific SACS recommendations that were addressed to the trustees. The Board instructed its own Development Committee to focus greater attention on fundraising. Committee Chair Hank Chamberlain subsequently noted that only two staff members were specifically designated as institutional fundraisers in a development operation that cost $.40 for every dollar raised.[7] In other action, the Board voted to approve a recommendation of the self-study to divide one of the academic units and create two separate colleges—in nursing and in science and mathematics.[8]

The most sweeping action taken by the Board of Trustees, however, related to intercollegiate athletics. "In response to the SACS recommendations, current lawsuits, and twenty-seven years of deficits," the Board voted in 1991 to move intercollegiate athletics from the NCAA to the NAIA Division I in basketball, baseball, softball, and volleyball.[9] The Board further voted to eliminate men's and women's gymnastics and riflery, men's golf, and soccer.[10] For the 1991-92 year, the University would field teams in baseball, softball, volleyball, and basketball. The Glasscock Gymnastics Center would be converted to a wellness facility.[11]

6 (Milton C. Cross to Board of Trustees, March 26, 1991). Minutes of the Meetings of the Board of Trustees, Meeting on 26 Mar. 1991.
7 Houston Baptist University, Minutes of the Meeting of the Board of Trustees, Meeting on 26 Feb. 1991.
8 Houston Baptist University, *Bulletin 1992-94,* 196, 201.
9 Houston Baptist University, Minutes of the Meeting of the Board of Trustees, Meeting on 26 Feb. 1991.
10 *The Chronicle of Higher Education*, 20 Mar. 1991, sec. A, p. 40.
11 Houston Baptist University, Minutes of the Meeting of the Board of Trustees, Meeting on 26 Feb. 1991.

A grant from the Meadows Foundation later provided $80,000 for construction of a second-floor exercise/dance studio in Glasscock.[12] Finally, a new baseball field was to be constructed.[13]

On March 8, some 300 assembled students heard Dr. Hodo announce these changes as well as a tuition increase.[14] The President shared, "After careful consideration, the Trustees and I feel that such realignment in intercollegiate athletics will better reflect the scope and mission of the University. We feel it is time to further streamline the University's budget in athletics based on escalating costs."[15] Student response was predictable. Under the headline, "HBU Cuts Enrage Student-athletes," the *Houston Chronicle* reported,

> Trustees at HBU drop more athletic programs for the second time in two years. President Hodo said the cuts will not immediately lessen the financial burden on the school and its athletic department, but after next year, should realize from $250,000 to $300,000 in savings. . . . Undergraduate enrollment has continued a downward spiral that corresponds to the decreasing emphasis on athletics.[16]

Whether related to athletic cuts or not, undergraduate enrollment had dropped from 2066 in 1984 to 1761 in 1990. On campus, a talented, young sports reporter named Carlton Thompson covered the momentous days of institutional agony for *The Collegian*.[17] Years later, alumnus Thompson would be named the first African-American Sports Editor of the *Houston Chronicle*.

Much of the initial shock of the 1991 decision centered on the particular sports to be eliminated. The *San Antonio Express-News* reported, "Last year, women's gymnastics was ranked #1 in the NCAA Division II and won the national championship. Soccer and golf were nationally ranked."[18] Men's gymnastics had been ranked #1 in the nation, as well. Hodo later elaborated on the decision in his column in the *HBU News*:

---

12 "News Brief," *SomeTimes,* Apr. 1992.
13 Houston Baptist University, Minutes of the Meeting of the Board of Trustees, Meeting on 24 Nov. 1992.
14 *Ornogah 1991,* 39.
15 Doug Parker, "Sports teams cut to balance budget," *The Collegian,* 14 Mar. 1991, p. 1.
16 "HBU Cuts Enrage Student Athletes," *Houston Chronicle,* 9 Mar. 1991, p. 1, two star ed.
17 Doug Parker, "Sports teams cut to balance budget," *The Collegian,* 14 Mar. 1991, p. 7.
18 *San Antonio Express-News,* 10 Mar. 1991, sec. C, p. 9.

We feel changes in our level of intercollegiate competition are warranted so that we may be good stewards and more effectively use our resources. Athletics is an enormous expenditure. This institution cannot allow our athletic program to dictate what dollars will be left to run the academic side of the University. . . . Gymnastics has become a very expensive sport to support. Travel and insurance costs have escalated dramatically.[19]

The final women's gymnastics meet was held in Sharp Gymnasium on March 22, 1991; HBU defeated Centenary College. The HBU women's team wore symbolic black tights for the last event.[20] Rene Melancon set a University record in the all-around with a score of "38.45." The women's team went on to the NCAA nationals in April and placed #4 in the nation. Mulholland, Melancon, Sandi Clayberg, and Nicole Williams were named to All-America honors.[21]

President Hodo agreed to appear at an open student forum attended by several members of the Board of Trustees and other invited university administrators. Students expressed "objections to the lack of communication regarding changes from the administration and the trustees."[22] Alumnus-trustee Robert Creech, Chair of a newly-appointed Student Affairs Committee, reported back to the trustees that students did not feel their questions regarding the rationale for the cuts were being addressed.[23]

In April, the administration announced that the University's debate program also would be discontinued at the end of the academic year in order to further reduce budget costs. From its earliest days, the debate program had established a twenty-seven-year history of regional and national wins. First begun in regional competition in 1964, the program garnered its first national recognition under Coach Rex Fleming in 1966. In the intervening years, debate had been a program with consistent winning seasons. Dr. James Taylor, Chairman of the Department of Communications, lamented the decision. "We have qualified for the National Debate Tournament for four of the last six years, finishing as high as fifth place nationally."[24] Students pointed out that the April announcement was too late for students to apply for scholarships and

19 Dr. E. D. Hodo, "From the President," *HBU News,* Apr. 1991, 2.
20 Carlton Thompson, "Lady Huskies Dazzle," *The Collegian,* 28 Mar. 1991, p. 10. Photo.
21 *Ornogah 1991,* 58-59.
22 Houston Baptist University, Minutes of the Meetings of the Board of Trustees, Meeting on 26 Mar. 1991.
23 Ibid.
24 Vivian Camacho and Doug Parker, "Debate program dropped," *The Collegian,* 18 Apr. 1991, p. 6.

transfer to other institutions.[25]   Ultimately, with the encouragement of Drs. Taylor and Byrnes, a Debate Advisory Council composed predominantly of alumni attorneys offered to underwrite the debate program for a minimum period of three years.   In February 1992, the debate team qualified for the national tournament for the fourth consecutive year and achieved its best team finish since 1987.[26] The team of Brent Benoit and David Yount was coached by Matt Caligur.

In May 1991, the Student Senate passed a resolution calling for the resignation of President Hodo.[27] The *Houston Chronicle* reported, "HBU Student Senate wants the President out."[28]   The Senate resolution expressed student dismay:

> We feel the decisions handed down over the past four years have not been in the best interest of the students and the University. Fundraising efforts have been less than adequate forcing students and faculty to bear much more of the financial burden than necessary. We feel our request is just and should be considered an earnest plea from the student body.[29]

Dr. Hodo responded, "I think the document is a request for dialog. . . . to that end, I stand prepared to visit and dialog with the Senate."[30] In a broader perspective, *The Collegian* offered an editorial reflective of a new day of consumerism, even in higher education:

> Many students have expressed dismay toward the attitude they perceive from both the President and the Board that students, like children, should be seen and not heard. . . . This petition is a rude awakening. As consumers, students have the right to question the decisions made by the administration, and even demand their reversal. The administrative body, however, has thus far turned a deaf ear toward the requests of the student body and refused truly to communicate with them.[31]

The Faculty Assembly applauded Dr. Hodo's offer of dialog with the students. However, the Assembly expressed concern "about our mission

---

25 Ibid.
26 "Debate team vies for national title," *The Collegian*, 19 Mar. 1992, p. 1.
27 *The Chronicle of Higher Education*, 22 May 1991, sec. A, p. 29.
28 "HBU student senate wants president out," *Houston Chronicle*, 10 May 1991, sec. A, p. 28, two-star ed.
29 Mary Hewitt, "Hodo's resignation requested," *The Collegian*, 9 May 1991, p. 1.
30 Ibid.
31 Mary Hewitt, "Sacrifice paternalism for open communication," *The Collegian*, 9 May 1991, p. 3.

as an institution, faculty morale, opening dialog with faculty, opening lines of communication with students, plus addressing the recommendations of the Southern Association."[32]   In an effort to contribute to a greater sense of communication, Vice President Looser began a series of personal newsletters called *Ruminations* in the fall of 1992. These informal notes bore no official imprimatur and were distributed initially to faculty and then ultimately, at their request, to supervisory staff and administrative personnel. The biweekly insider's letter contained news chiefly at the operational level with greater detail than might be found in official announcements and news releases. The communication experiment proved successful, and the newsletters were continued through 1995.[33]

The Board of Trustees stood by the President. In its own resolution, the Board affirmed "its commitment to continue working wholeheartedly with Dr. Hodo and the administration in the development of clear, concrete, specific objectives for achieving the mission of the University while strengthening faculty and student morale, restoring fiscal health, and increasing student enrollment."[34] The trustees again reiterated that it was the Board's decision to make the programmatic cuts, and that this decision was made within the context of approving a budget for the 1991-92 operations.[35]

In the years that followed, President Hodo referred to the years from 1987 to 1991 as "the longest ten years of my life." Despite their difficulty, however, these years were not without notable achievement. Dr. Doris Warren was named as a Piper Professor by the Minnie Stevens Piper Foundation in 1991. She became the University's fifth Piper Professor in its young history to be so recognized as one the state's outstanding faculty members following Calvin Huckabay, Joyce Fan, Marilyn Sibley, and Marion Webb. In the spring, Dr. Ann Gebuhr, the University's most prolific scholar, premiered her new operatic composition *Brian Boru* based on the life of the first king to unite Ireland under one rule.[36] May performances were scheduled for Miller Theater in Hermann Park featuring students, faculty, and alumni in leading roles.

The 1991 Spirit of Excellence Dinner celebrated the thirtieth anniversary of the University's founding and featured Roger Staubach. Master of

---

32 Houston Baptist University, Minutes of the Meetings of the Faculty Assembly, Meeting on 14 May 1991.
33 (Dr. Don Looser, *Ruminations,* Sept. 16, 1992 to Nov. 13, 1995).
34 *SomeTimes,* May 1991.
35 Houston Baptist University, Minutes of the Meetings of the Board of Trustees, Meeting on 14 May 1991.
36 Vivian Camacho, "HBU premieres opera," *The Collegian,* 29 Jan. 1991, p. 1.

Ceremonies Ron Stone helped blow out the candles on a ceremonial cake and voiced recognition of the University's special honorees—Joella and Stewart Morris, Colletta and Don McMillian, and Lee and Tracy Lawrence.[37] Further honored were Memorial Healthcare Systems, Oryx Energy, the Cullen Trust for Higher Education, and The Houston Endowment.[38]

Six outstanding senior faculty and staff members announced their retirement in the spring of 1991.[39] Their collective record constituted a significant body of contribution to the University's record of achievement. In May, the Board passed a resolution of appreciation to Judy Babb, secretary to the President for eleven years and an associate in financial affairs for eighteen years. The resolution expressed gratitude that she had

> endeared herself to generations of University students, manifesting interests in their behalf, offering herself and her personal resources to help meet their individual needs and came to represent . . . the very personification of University commitment to Christian concerns. The name Judy Babb has become synonymous with HBU tradition, with care and concern, with discipline and rigor, and with selfless devotion to the diverse needs of students and the University's best interests.[40]

Other personnel retiring included Dr. Marion Webb who had been a member of the University faculty for twenty-three years. Webb was a Fulbright Scholar, a Piper Professor, three-time winner of the Goolsby Outstanding Teaching Award, Faculty Woman of the Year, and founder of programs in ESL, medical Spanish, and learning for the blind. She was named a Distinguished Professor at commencement in 1991. Dr. Bill Dacres, one of the last of the founding faculty members, also announced his retirement. Dr. Dacres was the first faculty sponsor of the *Ornogah* yearbook in 1963 and had served twenty-eight years as Chair of the Department of Biology. Another retiree, Dr. Stephen Williams, Professor in Psychology, was in his twenty-fourth year of University service.[41] Williams would be remembered particularly for his significant contribution to student counseling needs before the establishment of a campus counseling center.

37 "Lee and Tracy Lawrence," *HBU News,* Apr. 1991, 5.
38 "Spirit of Excellence," *HBU News,* Summer 1991, 10-11.
39 "Retirees share plans for future," *The Collegian,* 9 May 1991, p. 4.
40 Houston Baptist University, Minutes of the Meetings of the Board of Trustees, Meeting on 14 May 1991.
41 "Honorees," *HBU News,* June 1991, 18.

Dr. A. O. Collins, another retiring member of the founding faculty, was Chair of the Department of Christianity and Philosophy. He had organized the University's first Biblical archeology study trips for students, had been an enthusiastic member of the *Culture and Human Experience* teaching team, and had directed a number of INDC study trips to Europe. Collins was particularly admired for maintaining communication with former students. Additionally, Collins had been active in the founding of a chapter of Alpha Pi Kappa fraternity and the establishment of a circle of Omicron Delta Kappa Society. He organized and moderated the annual Awards Day ceremonies in conjunction with Student Affairs. Dr. Collins delivered the Founders' Day address during his final year of service and provided a poignant reflection of his twenty-eight years of service:

> It is my desire that we remain a place where strong liberal arts education is foremost. Students need to learn to think, to deal with life, and to face the ultimate questions. I trust HBU will teach students to think creatively, to cultivate moral values, to care, to be good citizens, to sacrifice, to serve, and to be dedicated to God and to their fellow man. I hope we will continue to recognize we are not a church, nor a mission organization, but a strong academic community. Competence should not be replaced by piety, nor excellence by religious zeal. Christian colleges should expect as much, if not more, in the area of academics than purely secular institutions. Let us learn to be free to laugh, to live, to love, and to be at home in our world.[42]

The sixth retiree was Chancellor Dr. W. H. Hinton. Hinton was honored at the 1991 Spirit of Excellence dinner with wishes for "the very best of retirement years conveyed by this resolution of appreciation, affection, and sincere gratitude for your work and lifetime of devotion to the University."[43] At the May Board meeting, Dr. Hinton summarized those achievements for which he was most grateful. These included the physical campus; the early staff, faculty, and students; perpetuation of "academic excellence in a Christian environment;" the Endowed Scholarship Program; the first SACS accreditation; the creation of the nursing program; the founding of the Trans America Athletic Conference; and, the move from College to University. He expressed gratitude for "the nur-

---

42 "Founders' Day," *HBU News,* Feb. 1991, 7-11.
43 Houston Baptist University, Minutes of the Meetings of the Board of Trustees, Meeting on 26 Mar. 1991.

ture of publicly-recognized programs in pre-med, nursing, performing and visual arts, debate, and athletics that had become tangible symbols of excellence in the city."[44]

The University lost three additional institutional icons during this same period. Dr. Claude Rhea, the University's founding Chairman of the Division of Fine Arts and its first Vice President for Administrative Affairs, collapsed and died at Charles De Gaulle Airport while on business for the Foreign Mission Board in Paris in 1990. Rhea's value in the founding faculty can hardly be overestimated. In 1963, he had recruited the most recognized departmental faculty within the young College ranks and directed creative activity in multiple directions that helped the College establish cultural and social beachheads in Houston. To his credit should be given the early civic impact of the College's fine arts program including the College Singers, the recruitment of Houston Symphony musicians as faculty, the establishment of a museum that elicited the participation of Houston's cultural elite resulting in national summer symposia on historic preservation, the initiation of Fine Arts Festival performances at the Music Hall, and the enticement of musicians like Andre Previn, Doc Severinsen, and Meredith Willson to provide student enrichment workshops. Rhea's boundless vision gave flight to the work of Dr. Hinton to establish influence in the city born on wings of programs of excellence. At the time of his death, Rhea was President of Palm Beach Atlantic College.

In March 1991, Dr. Ross Dillon died at the age of 91. As Executive Secretary of the Union Baptist Association beginning in 1948, Dillon was one of a handful of key players who had fashioned the dream for a college in Houston and worked to make the vision a reality. He had been named HBC Vice President for Development in 1963 and had retired in 1970; Mrs. Dillon died in 1988.[45] The stories of Dillon's indefatigable energy, his deep spiritual faith, his confidence about the endeavor, and his dogged determination were legion. How the new College might have been born without the dynamic leadership of Ross Dillon is difficult to imagine. The profound contribution of Dr. and Mrs. Dillon was honored several years later with the dedication of the Dillon Hall as a part of the Hinton Center project. Portraits of the Dillons, the square grand piano from their home, and a testimonial plaque outlining their role in University history memorialize their legacy in the rooms bearing their name.

---

44 Houston Baptist University, Minutes of the Meetings of the Board of Trustees, Meeting on 19 May 1999.
45 "A final tribute," *HBU News*, Mar. 1991, 9.

Finally, in a tragic construction accident in June 1991, former Chair of the Board of Trustees Milton Cross was killed. Cross had served eighteen years as a trustee and had twice been elected Chair. He was a member of the Board of the Cullen Trust for Higher Education and had been instrumental in a long history of grants from that Trust. He had been a member of the President's Council for twenty-six years, was a member of the Presidential Search Committee, and enjoyed a close personal friendship with President Hodo. Only in May had Cross had been awarded the Doctor of Laws degree by the University in appreciation for his extraordinary record of service. Particularly significant was the award presented him in 1988 by the Board of Trustees in gratitude for his leadership in bridging the years between the first and second presidents. As evidenced by his March letter to trustees challenging them to raise money for faculty salary increases, Cross's dynamic leadership style inspired confidence; his incisive analytical ability provided wisdom; and, his commitment yielded strength. A resolution was prepared noting his years of service and documenting his instrumental role in securing the development of properties for income, particularly along the Southwest Freeway, his staunch advocacy for academic excellence, and his devotion to the concerns of faculty and students.[46]

§

In response to SACS recommendations, the academic support areas of instructional television, media, and continuing education were moved from Advancement to Academic Affairs.[47] Tommy Bambrick was named Vice President for Advancement; Assistant Vice President Lou Shields was assigned to address strategic planning needs; and Dr. Don Byrnes was named Assistant Vice President for Institutional Effectiveness.[48] Drs. Rhonda Furr and Jon Suter directed the summer INDC European study tour, and thirty-four students participated in the Master of Liberal Arts study-abroad program in Greece with Dr. Boyd.[49]

The absence of a theater or field house on campus continued to mandate that such events as commencement ceremonies, drama productions,

---

46 Houston Baptist University, Minutes of the Meetings of the Board of Trustees, Meeting on 24 Sept. 1991.
47 Houston Baptist University, Minutes of the Meetings of the Faculty, Meeting on 8 May 1991.
48 Houston Baptist University, Minutes of the Meetings of the Board of Trustees, Meeting on 24 Sept. 1991.
49 "Travel Abroad Programs," *HBU News,* Fall 1991, 24.

and music concerts be presented off-campus. Despite the model of outdoor ceremonies on other neighboring campuses, the University's well-intentioned efforts to hold its commencement ceremony outdoors on Holcombe Mall proved memorable. Following a first Holcombe Mall commencement in 1989, a second ceremony in May 1991 was greeted with inclement weather. Ignoring the rain that began to fall in mid-ceremony, however, the University's guest speaker proceeded to deliver his full text.[50] Guests scurried to the protection of the administration building; umbrellas dotted the faculty and graduate seating; musicians scrambled to protect their instruments. A letter to the editor of *The Collegian* called the event a "May Debacle . . . in which an otherwise ceremonial occasion was turned into a three-ring circus."[51] Nonetheless, some 433 degrees were conferred bringing the total number of degrees conferred by the University since 1967 to 6,672. In response to outcry over the outdoor ceremony, the Board affirmed to the administration its preference for off-campus May commencement ceremonies to "aid comfort and capacity."[52] The Faculty Assembly recommended terminating the practice of an invited guest speaker in favor of brief presidential remarks. The University's first summer commencement was held in August in the Sharp Gymnasium; sixty-eight students received graduate and undergraduate degrees before a gathering of 500 guests.[53]

The fall quarter of 1991 began with faculty meetings whose agenda chronicled the pertinent professional issues of the day—enrollment management, institutional research, legal counsel, copyright laws, sexual harassment issues, student privacy rights, faculty liability in private practice, the Americans with Disabilities Act, academic dishonesty, strategic planning, and a national conference on Faith and Discipline.[54] Local news commentator Linda Lorelle, Stanford University Phi Beta Kappa member, delivered the address for the Opening Fall Convocation. The former Glasscock Gymnastics Center was slowly but methodically being transformed to a wellness, fitness, and activity center with its own full-time director. *Collegian* reporter Carlton Thompson chronicled the metamorphosis in a poignant article entitled, "Glasscock: an empty building full of memories:"

---

50 Houston Baptist University, Minutes of the Meetings of the Faculty Assembly Executive Committee, Meeting on 15 Oct. 1991.
51 Vivian Camacho, "Graduation site decision applauded," *The Collegian*, 2 Apr. 1992, p. 2.
52 Houston Baptist University, Minutes of the Meetings of the Board of Trustees, Meeting on 24 Sept. 1991.
53 *Ornogah 1992*, 52-53.
54 Houston Baptist University, Minutes of the Meetings of the Faculty, Meeting on 3 Sept. 1991.

The floor has been stripped, the pits have been filled with cement, and the gymnastics equipment has been cleared away. All that remains are memories—memories of what was once considered by informed observers to be one of the finest facilities of its kind. Memories of what? Memories of the nationally ranked gymnastics teams that put HBU on the map.[55]

Dr. Lois Lawrence established an endowment to honor outstanding student achievement in writing. The "Danny Lee Lawrence Writing Awards" were named in memory of her son. The first awards were announced at the initiation of the Delta Lambda Chapter of the Sigma Tau Delta International English Honor Society.[56] In November, English faculty member Lawrence announced the return of the *Shank's Mare* literary anthology. She revealed that the personal financial contributions of Dr. Massey and others were underwriting the publication that received no University funding.[57] In his preface to the 1988-89 edition of the anthology, Faculty Advisor Dr. Wallace Hooker eloquently described the publication as having

walked, tip-toed, stumbled, staggered, and waltzed through the years, and it has usually been afoot; students, friends, professors, and faculty advisors have had to find money wherever their shanks would take them. Publication has not always been sequent, but it has been frequent, and the publication has not yet been delegated to some mysterious *samizdat* read only by a select literati. . . . . One of the most important functions of a university is to foster the creative impulse. . . . It is the fostering of that creative impulse in the literary arts that is most important; this is *Shank's Mare*'s responsibility.[58]

In the fall, Vice President James Massey wrote a spirited letter to the editor of *The Collegian* in praise of achievement on campus. Massey noted that student enrollment had increased; there was a new student activities director, a new Intra-fraternity Council constitution, a vibrant Student Activities Board, and a new Student Affairs Committee within the Board of Trustees. Massey praised the work of Chris White, the first alumni

---

55 Carlton Thompson, "Glasscock Gym, an 'empty building full of memories,'" *The Collegian*, 9 Sept. 1991, p. 7.

56 Vivian Camacho, "Lawrence endowment provides award," *The Collegian*, 9 May 1991, p. 10.

57 Janne Po, "*Shanks' Mare* cost increases," *The Collegian*, 7 Nov 1991, pp. 1, 6.

58 Dr. Wallace K. Hooker, "Preface," *Shank's Mare* 1988-89. Hooker's preface elicited a letter of commendation from Dr. Gordon Kingsley, President of William Jewell College.

director of FOCUS, and Nancy Henderson who directed organized campus programs and concerts including the beauty pageant, International Night, and Husky Revue. Massey concluded by praising the construction of a new baseball field, the provision of a new floor in the gym, and the outstanding leadership of Alice Rowlands with *The Collegian*.[59]

In 1991, intercollegiate basketball returned with a new coach—Ron Cottrell. The program had moved from National Collegiate Athletic Association (NCAA) competition to that of the National Association of Intercollegiate Athletics (NAIA).[60] Dr. James Taylor, chair of the faculty Athletic Committee, proved to be a key player in the transition through the NCAA sanctions to the relocation of the athletic program in the NAIA. The Board approved the fifty-year lease of 7.2 acres along the freeway for construction of a new 30,000 square foot Circuit City store.[61] The trustees further approved a new investment policy that distributed funds between The Baptist Foundation and other investment houses as selected by the Board on a competitive basis.[62] Dr. Hodo began to discuss possible modifications to the proposed Hinton Center design to better fit available funding.

The Southern Association of Colleges and Schools reaffirmed the University's accreditation in December; however, SACS continued to require annual reports to monitor the University's progress in four areas: planning and evaluation; faculty compensation; financial resources; and library resources, especially for graduate programs.[63] These additional annual reports were required for the next three years. As late as 1994, SACS was still monitoring financial resources, the annual audit report, and plans for repaying the endowment funds.[64]

Faculty members were granted a cash bonus in December 1991 in lieu of salary increases. This practice kept salary levels flat. The Faculty Assembly pressed for Board attention to the SACS recommendation to improve faculty salaries. The Assembly compiled a list of HBU faculty salaries by rank and years of experience in an effort to reduce "confusion and uncertainty" about salary equity.[65] Unpopular among some faculty mem-

59 James W. Massey, "Massey offers update, praises achievements," *The Collegian*, 26 Sept. 1991, p. 2.

60 Bobby Sanders, "Basketball team prepares for season," *The Collegian*, 7 Nov. 1991, p. 1.

61 "University leases land to retail outlet," *HBU News,* Fall 1991, 8.

62 Houston Baptist University, Minutes of the Meetings of the Finance Committee of the Board of Trustees, Meeting on 18 Nov. 1991.

63 Doug Parker, "SACS reaffirms campus," *The Collegian*, 19 Dec. 1991, pp. 1, 9.

64 (Dr. James Rogers, SACS Commission on Colleges, to Dr. Hodo, Jan. 18, 1994).

65 Houston Baptist University, Minutes of the Meetings of the Faculty Assembly, Meeting on 21 Jan. 1992.

bers was the practice of differentiated salaries based on market-driven forces in high-demand teaching disciplines, i.e. accounting, physics, and nursing.

In April 1992, the Moody Library purchased its first online information system *FirstSearch* with access to *WorldCat*, the world's largest database of bibliographical information.[66] That month the University also employed a professional fund-raising firm to perform a campaign feasibility study including an analysis of the University's visibility, its perception by the community, as well as public attitudes toward specific potential projects. The report from Tom Herren & Company, Inc. revealed that while the city respected the University's Christian commitment, the general populace did not feel Christian commitment as a civic priority. The limited visibility of the University in the community was a concern. Among those who knew of HBU, the University's programs were regarded highly. Houston's recovering economy was a concern for the success of such a campaign. The study revealed that the current political struggle within the Southern Baptist Convention was a negative influence for the campaign, as was the perception of the University as a commuter campus. The most likely projects for funding seemed to be the Hinton Academic Center, endowed chairs and scholarships, fine arts programs, and a student activities center. Campaign management concerns included the University's current financial condition, the level of alumni involvement and support, concerns about the strength of Board leadership within the community, and a history of limited institutional fund-raising success.[67]

The Spirit of Excellence Dinner in 1992 featured an address by David Aikman, *TIME* magazine's bureau chief in Moscow, Jerusalem, and Beijing.[68] Honorees included Dorothy and Milton Cross (posthumously), Claydene and Gilbert Turner, the Exxon Corporation, and the Good Samaritan Foundation.[69] In May, Board Chair Rex Baker, Jr. led the trustees to adopt a $5,300,000 capital campaign of which $500,000 was to be reserved for faculty salaries. Tom Herren was employed as a fund raising consultant.[70] Bruce Belin, Jr. was selected to take the place of the deceased Milton Cross on the Board of the Cullen Trust for Higher

---

66 Denise Lancaster, "Library boasts new research technology," *The Collegian*, 2 Apr. 1992, p. 1.

67 Tom Herren, "A Report to the Board of Trustees of Houston Baptist University," April 1992. Attached to the Minutes of the Board of Trustees, Meeting on May 12, 1992.

68 "Spirit of Excellence Award Dinner," *HBU News,* Aug. 1992, 9. Photo.

69 "Spirit of Excellence Award Dinner," *HBU News,* Aug. 1992, 10-13. (Exxon Corporation, 10; Good Samaritan, 11; Milton Cross, 12; Gilbert Turner, 13).

70 Houston Baptist University, Minutes of the Meetings of the Board of Trustees, Meeting on 12 May 1992.

Education. Dr. Hodo reported to the trustees in May, "There are many indicators that the University is on the upward trend with emphasis needed on long-term solution to our situation."[71]

In 1992, Dr. Don Byrnes was named Vice President for Enrollment Management and Legal Counsel to the President.[72] At the time, two significant University legal cases were reaching final resolution. A lawsuit against the University and several administrators by a faculty member whose contract had not been renewed was dismissed with no institutional liability.[73] A second suit brought by a female gymnast who had sustained injuries as a member of the intercollegiate team was mediated at a level well within the University's insurance coverage.[74]

§

In shocking action in July, Dr. Hodo announced the resignation of Vice President of Student Affairs Dr. James Massey. Hodo explained that he had conferred with Dr. Massey a number of times over the previous eighteen months and that "he and Massey had philosophical, operational, and management-style differences."[75] Massey responded that he "had a participatory style, was a team builder, and a decision maker."[76] Massey had been a member of the University administrative staff for twenty-three years.

Massey's contributions to the University over those years had been massive. In a *Collegian* article in September, Dr. Massey cataloged some of the highlights of his HBU career including the establishment of national fraternities, creation of the University's extensive intramural program, development of the University's outstanding convocation and speaker's program, the establishment of Spring Fling, renovation of the men's and women's residences, upgrading campus security to a licensed police force, founding the annual Husky Revue event, establishment of the student leadership development programs, his friendship with Virginia Crosno and the University mascot Mingo, and the national win of the women's gymnastics team. Massey further reflected,

---

71 Ibid.
72 "Byrnes named Vice President," *HBU News,* May 1992, 2.
73 Houston Baptist University, Minutes of the Meetings of the Board of Trustees, Meeting on 12 May 1992.
74 Houston Baptist University, Minutes of the Meetings of the Executive Committee of the Board of Trustees, Meeting on 28 July 1992.
75 Carla Craig, "Massey resigns," *The Collegian,* 10 Sept. 1992, pp. 1, 10.
76 Ibid.

It has been a blessing to be a facilitator and advocate for our students for over 23 years. This experience has truly enriched my life. I will miss our close association, the warmth of love and friendship in our Christian campus environment. . . . I will cherish the many fond memories of our times together.[77]

The September *Collegian* included tributes to the Massey years from colleagues Newell Boyd, Don Byrnes, Frances Curtis, Daton Dodson, Nancy Henderson, Saliem Kahleh, Robert Linder, Don Looser, and Melanie Phifer.[78]

Despite general understanding of the Massey personnel decision, the silence on campus resulting from his separation was deafening. For twenty-three years the ubiquitous Massey had been a part of virtually every major campus event, had fashioned much of the character of the campus through his responsibility for planning institutional convocations, had effectively monitored the pulse of the campus community for the University administration, and was generally regarded as friend and advocate to student and colleague alike. Among his lasting contributions was his gift of community-building—molding a core of students dedicated to institutional commitment from the otherwise disparate communities of athletes, student organizations, campus residents, fraternities and sororities, elected student leaders, and those deeply involved in Christian service. This integrated core of students, strongly committed to the University, heavily mitigated against the normal but pervasive erosion of a spirit of community in the largely commuter, urban, student population. Massey later filed a lawsuit claiming he had a lifetime oral and written contract "with which the University and Dr. Hodo tortuously interfered."[79] The University ultimately was awarded a summary judgment in the case.

Dr. Lou Shields was named Acting Vice President for Student Affairs. The selection of Dr. Shields as Acting Vice President was a popular choice. In addition to Shields' history with the University, her academic leadership over many years, and her sense of spiritual calling for commitment to students, she emerged as "a strong student advocate, communicator, and counselor."[80] In 1994, Jack Purcell was named Assistant Dean of

---

77 James W. Massey, "Massey remembers," *The Collegian*, 10 Sept 1992, pp. 8-9.
78 "Colleagues recognize 23 years of service to HBU, '69-'92: Dr. James W. Massey" *The Collegian*, 10 Sept 1992, pp. 2, 8-9.
79 Houston Baptist University, Minutes of the Meetings of the Board of Trustees, Meeting on 22 Feb. 1994.
80 Carla Craig, "Massey resigns," *The Collegian*, 10 Sept. 1992; p. 1.

Student Affairs.[81] The next several years proved to be quiet in the area of student affairs, perhaps in the aftermath of the turmoil of the 1987-92 period.

§

A number of indicators marked these years as a period of strong academic growth. In 1992, a gift from the chair of the trustee Academic Committee Dr. James Hammond provided funds for the computerization of the Moody Library card catalog.[82] This generous grant opened the door to a whole new chapter of digital data-retrieval for the library.[83] Dr. Alvin Reid was named to the Bisagno Chair of Evangelism in October.[84] Reid's involvement in the field of church growth brought a new focus to the work of the Chair.[85] Reid worked tirelessly to network with pastors in the University's behalf and to provide seminars on campus for their professional growth. Dr. Joe Blair was named Chair of the Department of Christianity and Philosophy following the retirement of Dr. A. O. Collins.[86] A new Endowed Academic Scholarship honoring Dr. Joyce Fan was established in 1993 funded by former students and friends. Dr. Fan had retired in 1983 and was celebrating her fiftieth wedding anniversary.[87] During her HBU career, more than 500 students had been admitted to medical and dental colleges.[88] Fan was further honored with selection by the *Houston Chronicle* as one of fifty women who "have made their mark on Houston."[89]

Under Coach Matt Caligur, the debate team compiled an outstanding record and was able to continue successful competition, even with reduced institutional scholarship aid. The commitment of financial support for the program from the Debate Advisory Council was largely unre-

---

81 Annie Phillip, "Purcell named," *The Collegian,* 24 Mar. 1994, p. 9.
82 Houston Baptist University, Minutes of the Meetings of the Board of Trustees, Meeting on 22 Sept. 1992.
83 (Ann Noble to Dr. Don Looser, Dec. 7, 2009). In 1990, the library was using a CD-Rom index system, *General Periodicals Index.* This was replaced in the early 1990s by *ProQuest* that was still CD-Rom based. Several years later, a library use fee was established that permitted access to *ProQuest Direct,* an online product readily available to multiple, simultaneous users.
84 "Reid named to John Bisagno Chair of Evangelism," *HBU News,* Fall 1992, 4.
85 Annie Phillip, "New faculty join the university," *The Collegian,* 22 Oct. 1992, p. 10.
86 Houston Baptist University, Minutes of the Meetings of the Board of Trustees, Meeting on 23 Feb. 1993.
87 "The Joyce Fall Endowed Scholarship," *HBU News,* Feb. 1993, 8-9.
88 Ibid.
89 Cheryl Laird, "Fifty women who have made their mark in and on Houston," *Houston Chronicle,* 4 Apr. 1993, Lifestyle sec., p. 1, two-star ed.

alized. The 1992 team headed by Brent Benoit and Sean Figaro was named one of the top fifty teams in the nation by the National Forensics League.[90] *The Collegian* featured a four-part series of reports on the debate program in 1993 noting that HBU debaters had qualified for the national championship tournament in five of the last six years."[91]

Distinguished speakers filled the campus podium for scholarly and academic lectureships during these years. The noted scholar and author, Dr. Frank Stagg, was the guest of Dr. Curtis Freeman for a lecture to the student organization *Kairos* in January 1992.[92] Prince-Chavanne lecturers in ethics included Dr. David Newell[93] and Dr. Allen Verhey;[94] the A. O. Collins lecturers in Christianity included Dead Sea Scroll scholar Dr. James Charlesworth[95] and Duke Divinity School professor Dr. Samuel Proctor.[96] The Staley Lectures featured Dr. John Newport,[97] writer Calvin Miller,[98] and Dr. Barry Stricker,[99] while the Brown lectures brought Linnet F. Deily, President of First Interstate Bank of Texas[100] and Robert McNair, President of Cogen Technologies.[101]

The Spirit of Excellence dinners continued to honor significant donors, attract the attention of the city to the University, and provide opportunity to promote the development campaigns of the University. The 1993 dinner honored Mr. and Mrs. Bennette Coulson, the Shell Corporation represented by trustee Jack Little, and the John Dunn Research Foundation. The dinner featured a speech by Mrs. James A. Baker III, and guests heard a report on the $5,600,000 capital campaign chaired by trustees Colletta McMillian and Randy Butler.[102] Some $3,500,000 had been raised from the gifts of 120 major donors including one hundred percent of the trustee membership. The campaign includ-

---

90 "Debate team vies for national title," *The Collegian,* 19 Mar. 1992, p. 1.

91 Bindu Adai, "Debate team continues winning tradition," *The Collegian,* 15 April 1993, p. 4.

92 Denise Lancaster, "Noted Southern Baptist scholar delivers speech," *The Collegian,* 30 Jan. 1992, p. 3. *Kairos* was a student organization formed to provide occasions for serious theological reflection on campus.

93 Newell was Chairman of the Department of Philosophy at Washington College, Maryland.

94 Houston Baptist University, Minutes of the Meetings of the Board of Trustees, Meeting on 22 Feb. 1994.

95 Carol Taylor, "Speaker details ancient scrolls," *The Collegian,* 18 Mar. 1993, p. 13. Photo.

96 *SomeTimes,* April 1994; Donia Bhatia, "Graduate student dies of stroke," *The Collegian,* 22 Sept. 1994, p. 4. David Campbell '89, benefactor and founder of the Collins Lectures, died on September 9, 1994.

97 "Lecture series planned," *The Collegian,* 19 Mar. 1992, p. 7.

98 "Briefs," *The Collegian,* 18 Mar. 1993, p. 13.

99 Houston Baptist University, Minutes of the Meetings of the Board of Trustees, Meeting on 22 Feb. 1994.

100 *SomeTimes,* April 1993.

101 "Robert McNair serves as Brown lecturer," *HBU News,* Summer 1994, 8; Houston Baptist University, Minutes of the Meetings of the Academic Committee of the Board of Trustees, Meeting on 11 May 1994.

102 "Spirit Awards," *Houston Chronicle,* 30 Sept. 1993, p. 10.

ed $4,000,000 for the Hinton Center project, $788,000 for campus operations, $485,000 for salaries, and $300,000 for the University nursing
program to match a grant by the Dunn Foundation.[103]   Of the
$5,600,000 campaign goal, $4,900,000 had been raised by 1994; however, only nine percent of the $485,000 goal for faculty salaries had been
secured, and only twelve percent of the $788,000 goal for university
operations had been realized.[104]

Dr. Shields was ultimately named to the position of Vice President for
Student Affairs in March 1993; Dr. Ray Mayfield, Jr. was named Vice
President for Bequests and Trusts;[105] and Estelle Jeu replaced Phil Kimrey
as Director of Admissions.[106] The Board of Trustees approved the establishment of a new Master of Arts in Pastoral Counseling and Psychology
that was marketed to church staff professionals who performed personal
counseling and desired professional credentialing.[107] Dr. Sally Phillips
announced the receipt of a three-year grant totaling $570,000 for schol-
arships in support of the University's strategic graduate program in bilingual education.[108] In January 1994, the University partnered with two
other colleges and three school districts and received a Texas Education
Agency grant for $1,500,000 for a developmental program in instruc-
tional technology.[109]

Dr. Frank Mahoney, Director of the Human Resources Institute,
authored a best-selling book, *The TQM Trilogy*, and served as advisor to
the Malcolm Baldridge National Quality Award for Education program.[110] Dr. Steve Wentland completed a textbook, *Mechanistic Models in
Organic Chemistry*.[111] The University created a new Intensive English
Institute headed by Harold Harris and Avenelle Merritt to provide ESL
instruction for students applying for college admission and for adult professionals needing improved English language facility.[112] The HBU international business programs visited corporate and business sites in

---

103 "Spirit of Excellence Capital Campaign, "HBU *News*, Aug. 1993, 8.
104 Houston Baptist University, Minutes of the Development Committee of the Board of Trustees, 8 Feb.
1994.
105 "Administrative Announcements," *HBU News*, Apr. 1993, 18.
106 *SomeTimes*, Sept. 1993.
107 Denise Lancaster, "Pastoral MA scheduled for Board vote," *The Collegian*, 11 Feb, 1993, p. 1.
108 Houston Baptist University, Minutes of the Meetings of the Board of Trustees, Meeting on 23 Sept. 1993.
109 Leslie E. Tripp, "Grant awarded for pilot program," *The Collegian*, 27 Jan. 1994, pp. 1, 3.
110 *SomeTimes*, Jan. 1994.
111 Mujahed Lateef, "Faculty writes textbooks", *The Collegian*, 11 Dec. 1990, p. 1.
112 Houston Baptist University, Minutes of the Academic Committee of the Board of Trustees, Meeting on 22
Feb. 1994.

Singapore, Hong Kong, London, Paris, Frankfurt, Munich, Berlin, Brussels, and Amsterdam.[113]

By 1994, competition was becoming intense in student recruiting among graduate business programs in Houston. In addition to programs at HBU, Rice University, the University of Houston, and the University of St. Thomas, Houston now was home to programs offered by institutions from outside the city including LeTourneau University, Southern Methodist University, and Our Lady of the Lake University.[114] MBA programs at the University of Texas in Austin and at Texas A&M University were also being heavily marketed in the Houston metropolitan area.

In the spring of 1994, under particular pressure from the College of Business and Economics, sweeping curricular revision was approved by the faculty Academic Affairs Committee. Virtually all undergraduate degree requirements were revised in response to pressure for a more "transfer-friendly" program. Based on the recommendation of an ad hoc committee chaired by Dean Nancy Yuill '72, the new curriculum dropped the requirement for *World Literature* that had accompanied *Culture and Human Experience* in the sophomore year. In its place was a wide selection of upper-division English literature and writing courses. The Interdisciplinary courses *Great Issues of the Twentieth Century* and *Culture and Human Experience* were no longer required for graduation though they were elective options. However, traditional courses in art and music appreciation were added that proved the death knell for the more rigorous, team-taught *Culture and Human Experience*. All students were to be required to complete *College Algebra* and a sequence of laboratory science courses.[115] A new Bachelor of General Studies degree was approved to offer degree completion opportunity through one of several alternative paths.[116] At the graduate level, a new Master of Science in Health Administration was established for health professionals who already held either the MBA or the MSN degree.[117] Students perceived that such dual graduate degree combinations significantly enhanced employment opportunity.

---

113 "EMBA's take the classroom abroad," *HBU News*, Spring 1995, 13.

114 Houston Baptist University, Minutes of the Meetings of the Academic Committee of the Board of Trustees, Meeting on 22 Feb. 1994.

115 Denise Lancaster, "Smith College changes provide more options," *The Collegian*, 28 Apr. 1994, p. 1; Houston Baptist University, Minutes of the Meetings of the Academic Committee of the Board of Trustees, Meeting on 26 Apr. 1994.

116 Houston Baptist University, Minutes of the Meetings of the Board of Trustees, Meeting on 10 May 1994.

117 Houston Baptist University, Minutes of the Meetings of the Academic Committee of the Board of Trustees, Meeting on 26 Apr. 1994.

The Faculty Assembly continued to lobby for annual salary adjustments for faculty and staff. No raises had been given for contracts in the 1992-93 academic year. A resolution from the Faculty Assembly to Dr. Hodo stated,

> Whereas, making raises contingent on extraordinary revenue has resulted in no raises in many years, and whereas the lack of regular raises, even cost of living adjustments, has left deteriorating real income and low morale, and whereas the effort to balance the budget through elimination of programs and personnel have produced neither a balanced budget nor adequate raises, therefore the Faculty Assembly requests budget raises be based on the model developed by the University Planning Committee.[118]

The Planning Committee model was based on budgeted salary increases tied to the projection of fund-raising goals set to meet requisite budgetary demands.

In 1993, the Faculty Assembly requested opportunity to address a meeting of the Board on matters of salaries, reinstating a tenure system, and creating a hearing process for faculty grievances. In response to the grievance hearing request, legal counsel Byrnes clarified that the requirements of due process models "were not required of private institutions." However, a "fair-play" grievance-hearing protocol was cooperatively developed with the Assembly and approved by the trustees in September 1993.[119] Salary increases were approved for 1993-94 within the institutional budget;[120] however, no raises were budgeted in 1994-95.[121] Dr. Hodo explained that no raises were proposed because "our highest priority is a balanced budget."[122]

In March 1993, the Business and Audit Committee of the BGCT Christian Education Coordinating Board expressed concern that the University's "trend for operational deficits is continuing. In fact, there has been an operating deficit of expenses over receipts every year since 1988." The report noted that quasi-endowment funds had been transferred to offset those losses and that endowment funds had recorded an unrealized loss in real estate value of $2,500,000 in 1992. The report

---

118 Houston Baptist University, Minutes of the Meetings of the Faculty Assembly, Meeting on 12 Jan. 1993.
119 Houston Baptist University, Minutes of the Meetings of the Faculty Assembly, Meeting on 21 Sept. 1993.
120 Houston Baptist University, Minutes of the Meetings of the Faculty Assembly, Meeting on 6 May 1993.
121 Houston Baptist University, Minutes of the Meetings of the Board of Trustees, Meeting on 22 Feb. 1994.
122 Houston Baptist University, Minutes of the Meetings of the Faculty Assembly, Meeting on 26 Apr. 1994.

noted operation shortfalls approximating $1,000,000 in each of the years 1990 to 1992. The committee expressed "grave concern about increasing trends and lack of response from trustees in apprising us of corrective measures to deal with the matters."[123]

A report to the March 1993 Board meeting revealed that spring undergraduate enrollment was down to 1811 from an all-time high of 2327 in 1983. The deficit for the year was $550,000 to date with expenses running $141,000 under budget. The goal for the annual sustaining drive was $300,000. The trustees delayed adopting the 1993-94 budget and requested additional administrative reductions of $200,000. Approximately sixty percent of projected 1993-94 income was slated to be received from tuition.[124]

In July, the Christian Education Coordinating Board again wrote trustee Chairman Rex Baker, Jr. requesting a response to its letter of March 9 and requesting a meeting of University representatives, the Coordinating Board, and the Business and Audit Committee. Dr. Hodo responded by letter that the University had reduced its budget by $199,000 and was signing leases with Memorial Hospital System that would generate new monies of $453,000 for operations and repayment of interfund borrowing.[125] The proposed meeting was held in Dallas on July 27. University officials reported on Memorial Hospital System's option on 3.7 acres of land, Memorial's option on eleven additional acres, the University Place project, the Garden Village lease, and other recent gifts and grants.[126] By November Chairman Rex Baker acknowledged the receipt of $1,000,000 from the transactions with Memorial Hospital.[127] A fifty-year lease had also been consummated for a professional building project on Beechnut to house the Texas Eye Institute.[128] Auditors for the University reported that they felt "HBU has turned the corner financially."[129]

§

123 (Business and Audit Committee, Baptist General Convention of Texas Christian Education Coordinating Board, to Dr. E. D. Hodo, Mar. 9, 1993).

124 Houston Baptist University, Minutes of the Meetings of the Board of Trustees, Meeting on 6 Apr. 1993.

125 (Dr. E. D. Hodo to Baptist General Convention of Texas, July 22, 1993).

126 Houston Baptist University, Minutes of the Executive Committee of the Board of Trustees, Meeting on 27 July 1993.

127 Houston Baptist University, Minutes of the Meetings of the Board of Trustees, Meeting on 17 Nov. 1993.

128 Houston Baptist University, Minutes of the Meetings of the Executive Committee of the Board of Trustees, Meeting on 15 Jan. 1993.

129 Houston Baptist University, Minutes of the Meetings of the Faculty Assembly, Meeting on 2 Nov. 1993.

By August of 1992, a total of 7,142 degrees had been conferred by the University.[130] Five HBU alumni served on the Board of Trustees— Dr. Robert Creech '74, C. Pat Ellis '68, Curt Floyd MBA '81, Doug Tipps '67, and Steve Woodall '75.[131] Three alumni served on the University faculty—Dr. Jennifer Ferguson '69, Dr. Linda Roff '69, and Dr. Nancy Yuill '72.[132] In 1990, the Alumni Association had begun to name an annual recipient of the *Distinguished Alumnus Award* honoring contribution to profession as well as a *Meritorious Service Alumnus Award* honoring contribution to advancement of the University. Those so recognized as Distinguished Alumni included Nursing Dean Dr. Nancy Yuill '72 and Steve Woodall '75 in 1990; Marsha Mathis Eckermann '68 and Dick Hudson '75 in 1991; Carol Ann Halliday Bonds '68, Kay Kepler '68, and Dr. John Brady, Jr. '71 in 1992; Dr. Barbara Taylor-Cox '81 and Dr. James Denison '80 in 1993; and Pam Moore '74, MBA '81 and Stephen Pickett '80 in 1994. The *Meritorious Service Alumni Award* was presented to Kay Parker '82 and Randy Garbs '76, MBA '83 in 1990; Jane Jester Marmion '68, Joel Berry III '72, and Dr. Mark Jensen '78 in 1992; Jim Skaggs '73 and Lois Shanks '82 in 1993; and Dawn Nelson '90 and Steve Braun '80 in 1994.

In 1994, the Board of Trustees approved a resolution[133] to sell the Currie Ranch and the Della Lode mining claim in Colorado that had been deeded to the University by Frankie Currie in 1969.[134] Thus was concluded a chapter of history chronicling one of the more treasured fringe-benefits for University employees and trustees. The Currie Ranch had hosted twenty-five years of University families, friends, and colleagues for week-long summer visits. The letters and photographs from these years had been assembled into albums that record many of the joys of the Currie experience including at least one golden wedding anniversary celebration, numerous family reunions, and hundreds of vacations by University families. The friendship of the neighboring John Kuehster family to HBU summer guests was returned in later years by the HBU graduation of

---

130 *Ornogah 1993*, 70-71.
131 Houston Baptist University, Minutes of the Meetings of the Board of Trustees, Meeting on 22 Sept. 1992.
132 Houston Baptist University, *Bulletin 1992-1994*, pp. 216-223.
133 Houston Baptist University, Minutes of the Meetings of the Board of Trustees, Meeting on 4 Jan. 1994.
134 Houston Baptist University, Minutes of the Meetings of the Executive Committee of the Board of Trustees, Meeting on 24 Jan. 1994.
135 A colorful history of this family and rural mountain life in Jefferson County, Colorado is in the collection of the Moody Library: Margaret V. Bentley, *The Upper Side of the Pie Crust* (Conifer, Colorado: Margaret V. Bentley 1978).

Kuehster daughters, Susan in 1993 and Christina in 1995.[135]

In the spring of 1994, the Spirit of Excellence Dinner featured speaker Drayton McLane and honored Hazel and Harry Chavanne, Panhandle Eastern Corporation, and the M. D. Anderson Foundation.[136] The University announced its membership in the Big State Conference of the National Association of Intercollegiate Athletics (NAIA) that included Ambassador College, East Texas Baptist University, Huston-Tillotson University, and LeTourneau University. Membership in the Heart of Texas Conference was deemed too costly.[137] The University would field men's and women's teams in one sport each quarter.[138] A new Samoyed mascot Mingo II was secured for the campus to be cared for by the student organization K-9 Corps.[139]

The University recognized its first thirty-year employees—Flonnie Brown, Dr. Calvin Huckabay, and Dr. Ray V. Mayfield, Jr. Receiving twenty-five-year service recognition were Dorothy Allen, Frances Curtis, and Dr. James Tsao.[140] The University community was saddened by the loss of several former colleagues. In 1992, Dr. Herman Barlow '72, alumnus and former Vice President for University Affairs, died of cancer.[141] In 1993, Bobbie Hinton, wife of the University's first president and first Registrar, passed away after a number of years of declining health.[142] The University's prize-winning debate coach Rex Fleming died of cancer in July 1994.[143]

Tom Hixson resigned as Vice President for Financial Affairs in April 1994 to become the Executive Director of the Northwest Baptist Foundation in Portland, Oregon.[144] Richard Parker was subsequently appointed to the post. Parker was a CPA and moved from a corporate position.[145] In addition, a number of long-time staff members announced plans to retire. These included Bookstore Manager Ellouise Zapalac after

---

136 "Spirit of Excellence," *HBU News,* May 1994, 13-18.

137 Denise Lancaster, "Huskies join new NAIA conference," *The Collegian,* 24 Mar. 1994, p. 1.

138 "University joins Big State Athletic Conference," *HBU News,* May 1994, 6.

139 *Ornogah 1995,* 32; "New Mascot," *The Collegian,* 24 March 1994, p. 3.

140 *SomeTimes,* Nov. 1993.

141 Carla Craig, "Colleague fondly remembered," *The Collegian,* 24 Sept. 1992, p. 2.

142 "Bobbie Ruth Hinton; In Memoriam," *HBU News,* Feb. 1993, inside cover; Denise Lancaster, "Hinton remembered," *The Collegian,* 14 Jan. 1993, p. 2.

143 Stephanie De Los Santos, "Faculty member and friend to many remembered for fervor and success," *The Collegian,* 8 Sept. 1994, pp. 6-7.

144 Denise Lancaster, "Hixson resigns, moves to Oregon," *The Collegian,* 14 Apr. 1994, p. 1.

145 "Parker named Vice President for Financial Affairs," *HBU News,* Spring 1994, 7.

146 Leslie New, "Bookstore director retires," *The Collegian,* 10 Feb. 1994, p. 2.

twenty-seven years of service,[146] Secretary to the President Margil Benedict after twenty years, Secretary to the Vice President Mary Woodward after twenty-three years,[147] Director of Secretarial Services Pauline Wright after seventeen years,[148] and Director of Telecommunication Services Mildred Boone after twenty-six dedicated years.

Mildred Boone was the object of particular affection from students, staff, and faculty. She served as the honorary coach of the faculty/staff intramural teams, was a vocal cheerleader at athletic events, and was caretaker at one time for the University mascot. A colleague wrote of Mrs. Boone,

> She has long been the University's ambassador of good will. Over many years, she has greeted campus visitors, served as honorary coach and unofficial head cheerleader for the University athletic teams. She has functioned as counselor and advocate for generations of University apartment dwellers, and has encouraged countless students, faculty, and staff in her role as good friend. Her winning smile, her indomitable cheer, and her love for this school will long be remembered.[149]

Retirement plans were also announced by Dr. Ray V. Mayfield, Jr., Dr. Calvin Huckabay, and Dr. Robert Linder. Mayfield, Vice President for Planned Giving, had first served as a member of the UBA College Committee in the 1950s and was then a founding member of the Board of Trustees from 1960-63. He joined the University staff as Assistant to the President in 1963 and was completing thirty-one years of administrative service. *Mayfield and his father represent the only father/son administrative appointment in University history.* The growth and development of the University's Endowed Academic Scholarship program was the product of Mayfield's devotion and remains a lasting legacy to his commitment. *The Collegian* reported, "It is impossible to contemplate the University as it presently has matured without the significant labors of Dr. Ray Mayfield, Jr."[150] At the time of his retirement, Mayfield's thirty-one years represented the University's longest record of service.

---

147 "A Special Thanks," *HBU News,* Nov. 1993, 25; Denise Lancaster, "Woodward retires after 22 years," *The Collegian,* 21 Sept. 1993, p. 2. Photo.

148 Denise Lancaster, "Wright announces retirement," *The Collegian,* 16 Dec. 1993, p. 3.

149 *SomeTimes,* May 1993.

150 Denise Lancaster, "Founding trustee retires after 31 years," *The Collegian,* 14 Apr. 1994, p. 8.

Dr. Robert Linder announced his retirement. He had joined the faculty in 1969 to direct the HBC instrumental music program following the retirement of Ralph Liese. Linder's boundless energy, his capacity for flexibility, his commitment to excellence, and his devotion to the University combined to make him virtually unique among colleagues. A *Resolution of Appreciation* passed by the Board of Trustees in 1994 noted, "Linder has provided a model of leadership to his faculty colleagues by his unfailingly positive attitude, by his unflagging energy in the University's behalf, by his creative leadership of the fine arts program, and by his exemplary perspective of the total University."[151]

Linder defied any effort at categorization. His musical involvements included many seasons as conductor of the Houston Civic Symphony, the Houston Youth Symphony, Houston's Theater Under the Stars, Seattle's Fifth Avenue Theater, and as music director of the Gilbert and Sullivan Society of Houston in addition to University ensembles including jazz band, concert band, and pep band. While serving as Dean of the College of Fine Arts, Linder enjoyed faculty intramural athletics in basketball and tennis, fund raising, and the collegiality of friends. He was an avid hunter, an international sports fisherman, and was active in several national wildlife organizations. Dr. Linder was awarded the rank of Distinguished Professor on the occasion of his retirement in 1994 after 25 years of service.[152] Linder was to return ten years later in 2004 at the University's invitation for a one-year interim appointment as Director of the School of Music.

Dean Calvin Huckabay represented the consummate scholar. Head of the humanities for thirty-one years, Huckabay was the first Dean of the College, held the Robert H. Ray Chair in Humanities, was the first University scholar named as a Piper Professor, and was ultimately appointed to the rank of Distinguished Professor.[153] Fellow deans considered him "the Dean of Deans." Huckabay had established the University's first residential study-abroad programs at the Shakespeare Institute at Stratford-upon-Avon. He had pioneered the unique liberal arts core and the interdisciplinary courses of Houston Baptist College. Moreover, he had compiled and published two editions of a definitive international bibliography of works on John Milton. Students and facul-

---

151 Houston Baptist University, Minutes of the Board of Trustees, Meeting on 10 May 1994.
152 Denise Lancaster, "Linder retires, continues conducting career," *The Collegian*, 12 May 1994, p. 13.
153 Denise Lancaster, "Original faculty member retires after 31 years," *The Collegian*, 12 May 1994, p. 12.

ty alike considered him to be the quintessential mentor—wise, kind, patient, and unrelenting. The pervasive influence of his scholarship on the University community was powerful—encouraging and stimulating a high level of academic research and publication by his fellow scholars on the faculty. Four times, Huckabay chaired the institutional self-study for the Southern Association of Colleges and Schools. His summer sabbaticals to the Bodleian Library at Oxford refreshed and returned him to the campus each fall with renewed energy and confidence about the potential of the new college for scholarly achievement. Given Huckabay's moment in time, his role in University history may not soon be equaled.

§

In 1994, Dr. Hodo concluded his eighth year of service as University President. This had been a period of considerable stress, but aggressive resolution of issues. With the difficult decisions involving the appropriate role of intercollegiate athletics in a balanced University program and the requirements of the Southern Association to address issues that would eventually inure to the University's long-term benefit, the period 1987-1994 emerged as an era of wrenching change. A number of managerial initiatives marked strategic mileposts in the process of strengthening the University. Dr. Hodo's direction of the institutional enterprise was steady and resolute.

Academic innovation and entrepreneurship distinguished the era. Student achievement and the quality of the campus environment continued to enrich the collegiate experience. By 1994, the last of the founding faculty were gone, leaving a void, but creating opportunity for a new generation of academic leadership. The University's administrative team had been dramatically reshaped by the coming of new colleagues. Additionally, with the death of Milton Cross, an era of powerful individual influence from within the membership of the Board of Trustees also came to a virtual close.

Many issues remained to be resolved. However, emerging from this period of challenge would be a new era of accomplishment indelibly marked with the brand of President Hodo whose personal clarity of mission and assertive leadership followed a clearly projected path of spiritual conviction.

ELEVEN

1994-1998

With the attainment of greater stability in financial operations, the University was poised for the first time under President Hodo to emerge from an era characterized by the need for reactive decision-making and enter a period of more planned development. The institution was adjusting to the voids of curtailed and eliminated programs and activities. Many of the priorities from the Hinton administration had changed, but the University had not yet fully defined many of the strategic initiatives that would characterize its future. The mandates of the Southern Association of Colleges and Schools required greater emphasis on planning, assessment, and response in all areas of institutional operation. Into this environment, Dr. Hodo introduced stronger emphases on data-gathering and quality control. A Quality Council was established consisting of faculty and staff in designated leadership roles, as well as representative members of the campus community.[1]

Dr. Hodo also restructured the operation of the Board of Trustees to require higher levels of participation and more universal oversight of institutional activity. All trustees were assigned to operational committees that were required to meet regularly with the appropriate administrative officers, prepare written reports, and distribute them in advance of trustee meetings.[2] Oral summaries in the Board meetings were confined to matters requiring either special attention or action and were voiced by the trustee chairs of the committees rather than as previously presented by the University Vice Presidents. Board meetings themselves were moved to a quarterly schedule, were structured by a published agenda, and were contained within a period of several hours. Separate meetings of the Executive Committee were virtually eliminated. In so doing, President Hodo achieved the involvement of the Board as a whole, eliminated dependency on decision-making by a few executive officers, and encouraged an engaged and informed trustee body. Minutes of the Board

---

1 Houston Baptist University, Minutes of the Meetings of the Board of Trustees, Meeting on 28 Nov. 1995.
2 Houston Baptist University, Minutes of the Meetings of the Executive Committee of the Board of Trustees, Meeting on 24 Jan. 1994.

of Trustees from this period reveal much more detail communicated through committee reports, much less extended discussion, and more focused decision-making based on committee recommendations. As a result, the years 1994-98 represent a new plateau of Board of Trustee operation characterized by the purposeful inclusion of all trustees, information-based decision-making, and a new model of shared management by the President and the Board.

In September 1994, the accounting firm of Fitts-Roberts characterized the 1993-94 audit as "the strongest financial picture since the firm began doing the annual audits."[3] The audit showed an unrestricted fund balance of $314,000 for the year just concluded. As a result, the Board voted in September 1994 once again to give all employees a one-time 2.5 percent bonus in lieu of a permanent increase in salary.[4] Interfund debt was reduced from $8,000,000 to $2,000,000.[5] The Board approved a new policy that required, "that the proceeds derived in the future from the sale of significant assets be used solely to retire or decrease existing debt."[6]

A number of grants were received for dedicated use—from the Schissler Foundation for the Museum of Decorative Arts,[7] the Southwestern Bell Foundation for free enterprise education,[8] the Gordon Cain Foundation for biology labs,[9] the Helene Fuld Health Trust for nursing instructional media, Entex for computers for the Language Center, and the Rockwell Foundation and Memorial Healthcare for nursing.[10] The University also began receiving annual grants from the Fred C. and Katherine B. Andersen Foundation with the stipulation that no federal funds be accepted for University operations.[11] An initial grant of $50,000 increased to a maximum annual grant of $250,000 by 2000.[12] Among faculty, the Andersen Foundation restrictions were controversial. Although the grant provided welcomed income, the subsequent restrictions had the immediate effect of forcing the University to withdraw from participation in government contracts for the provision of instructional services and equipment.

---

3 Houston Baptist University, Minutes of the Meetings of the Board of Trustees, Meeting on 27 Sept. 1994.
4 Ibid.
5 Houston Baptist University, Minutes of the Meetings of the Board of Trustees, Meeting on 23 Aug. 1994.
6 Houston Baptist University, Minutes of the Meetings of the Board of Trustees, Meeting on 15 May 1995.
7 "Encore and More," HBU News, June 1996, 17.
8 "Encore and More," HBU News, Feb. 1995, 21.
9 "Encore and More: Gordon Cain Fund," HBU News, May 1995, 15.
10 "Encore and More," HBU News, Aug. 1995, 10.
11 "Encore and More," HBU News, Feb. 1997, 28.
12 Ibid.

Beginning in 1994, the President's Advisors committed to use the funds raised from the annual Silver Tea to fund scholarships for students in the Master of Education program. Moreover, the Advisors established an Endowed Scholarship honoring the University's President to demonstrate "in perpetuity this organization's admiration and regard for Dr. Hodo and his leadership at the University."[13] By May 1997, the Advisors completed funding of the scholarship. In the coming years, the Guild, as the President's Advisors came to be called, would fund a number of endowed scholarships as a part of its role of assistance to the President.

A Covenant Society was formed in 1994 to recognize donors who had made provision for the University through deferred gifts. Those first inducted into membership were Mrs. James (Dona) Williamson, Bill Todd, and Juanita and Phyllis Pool.[14] In subsequent years, additional new members of the Society included Mr. and Mrs. Bennett Coulson, Dr. Kate Bell, Mrs. Robert (Virginia) Bennick,[15] and Meg DeLancey '77.[16]

By February 1995, the University's financial condition had improved; graduate tuition was greater than budgeted; institutional deposits were drawing a high rate of interest; the bookstore and campus housing operations showed profits that helped offset losses in food service.[17] Real estate activity on the University's behalf in 1994-95 yielded $1,765,000 including $500,000 from the sale of the University apartments.[18] Because of increased enrollments, the May 1996 operating surplus was $513,000, $195,000 over budget.[19] However, financial goals were achieved largely by cuts in spending. Endowment income was higher from oil and gas royalty income. Tuition income was higher, but BGCT contributions and sustaining gifts continued lower than budgeted.[20] However by 1998, the Business and Audit Committee reported reductions in expenditures for salary and benefits, television production, and

---

13 Houston Baptist University, *1997 President's Advisors Guild Handbook*, p. 4.

14 "Covenant Council," *HBU News,* May 1994, 10. Photo.

15 Virginia Reeves Bennick worked for the Union Baptist Association as a librarian and set up church libraries throughout the Houston area. She was a member of the Auxiliary; Robert was a member of the President's Council.

16 "Covenant Council Honoree," *HBU News,* Mar. 1996, 12. Meg was the first alumni member of the Covenant Society.

17 Houston Baptist University, Minutes of the Meetings of the Board of Trustees, Meeting on 9 Feb. 1995.

18 Houston Baptist University, Minutes of the Meetings of the Board of Trustees, Meeting on 27 Feb. 1996.

19 Houston Baptist University, Minutes of the Meetings of the Board of Trustees, Meeting on 16 May 1995.

20 Houston Baptist University, Minutes of the Meetings of the Board of Trustees, Meeting on 28 Nov. 1995 and on 19 May 1998.

academic support including computing, student services, and the office of the Registrar.[21]

The Board of Trustees honored the lifetime of contribution from former Chair Howard C. Lee, Sr. by conferring the Doctor of Humane Letters in May 1994.[22] The following year, the trustees also authorized honorary degrees for A. D. Players founder Jeannette Clift George,[23] Christian music artist Cynthia Clawson, and Houston ministers of music Gerald Ray[24] and Gary Moore.[25] The Doctor of Humane Letters was given trustee Marge Caldwell in 1997;[26] the Doctor of Laws was awarded to Board Chair Bruce Belin, Jr.; and, the Doctor of Humane Letters was conferred upon former trustee Dr. Edwin Young in 1998. The friends, Belin and Young, were surprised by the honor, each having been told only that he was reading the citation for the other.[27] The Board further approved a revised institutional Purpose statement drafted to incorporate Southern Association suggestions and requirements.[28]

Under the leadership of Dr. Jerry Ford and Judy Smelser, the 1995 fall enrollments were strong. The number of full-time equivalent students was 2261, up from 2188.[29] The MBA 2000 enrollment increased from 196 to 248 students. Sharon Saunders, Assistant Vice President for Public Relations, unveiled new admissions materials produced by the consulting firm STAMATS. For the first time, separate, focused, marketing publications were designed to provide a campus photography recruiting booklet, a brochure for use in student-search mailings, and a detailed information publication for parents and students attending college-night recruiting events.[30]

The trustees adopted a proposed 1996-97 budget that contained a salary pool of 3.4 percent for merit raises—pending fall 1996 enrollments.[31] Board Chair Pat Ellis announced a "Measure of Excellence" campaign designed to correlate with the fortieth anniversary activities in

21 Houston Baptist University, Minutes of the Meetings of the Board of Trustees, Meeting on 19 May 1998.
22 Houston Baptist University, Minutes of the Meetings of the Board of Trustees, Meeting on 22 Feb. 1994.
23 "Clift George and Moore receive honorary degrees," HBU News, May 1995, 5. Photo.
24 "May Graduates," HBU News, Summer 1995, 4.
25 "Clift George and Moore receive honorary degrees," HBU News, May 1995, 5. Photo.
26 Houston Baptist University, Minutes of the Meetings of the Board of Trustees, Meeting on 25 Feb. 1997.
27 "Belin and Young Honored at Commencement," HBU News, June 1998, 5. Photo.
28 Houston Baptist University, Minutes of the Meetings of the Board of Trustees, Meeting on 26 Sept. 1995.
29 Houston Baptist University, Minutes of the Meetings of the Enrollment Management Committee of the Board of Trustees, Meeting on 26 Sept. 1995.
30 Houston Baptist University, Minutes of the Meetings of the Board of Trustees, Meeting on 28 Nov. 1995.
31 Houston Baptist University, Minutes of the Meetings of the Board of Trustees, Meeting on 27 Feb. 1996.

1997 and provide funds for additional student financial aid to increase the number of dormitory residents.[32] The campaign raised over $90,000.[33] In May, Dr. Hodo observed that the University's endowment had grown to $33,000,000, enrollment had grown from 180 undergraduate students in 1963 to 2200 graduate and undergraduates in 1996, and the institution's operating budget had increased from $679,000 annually to over $17,600,000.[34]

Much of the Board's attention in the years 1994-98 involved the physical development of the campus, construction of new facilities, and management of the University's extensive real estate interests. In the fall of 1994, the Board established the Eastwood Baptist Church Scholarships funded by a gift of property valued at $400,000 from the disbanding church congregation.[35] The following year, Pastor Joe Stutts of the Braes Baptist Church also conveyed property on behalf of his congregation to fund endowed scholarships perpetuating the name of that church.[36]

The Board considered an offer for the purchase of the Garden Village retirement project (Harvest House), but opted for the flexibility of annual rental from the property.[37] Ed Best was elected president and Don Byrnes secretary of Beechnut Street, Inc., a corporation created to "manage property for maximum return to the University" following the disbanding of the UBA Property Committee.[38] In April 1995, the Property Committee reported on lessee refinancing of the Fondren I property, a Memorial Hospital option for eleven acres of additional land, and the status of the partnerships with Toys "R" Us and the Texas Eye Institute. Neither of the latter properties had generated sufficient income for profit sharing in their initial year of operation.[39] Committee Chair Jim Smith further announced that Mervyn's department store and Pier One[40] were moving from the Fondren I development and that Exxon had permanently closed its station at the corner of Fondren Road and Beechnut.[41]

---

32 Ibid.
33 Trina Booher-Haas, "1996 Measure of Excellence Campus Campaign Summary Report," 16 May 1996.
34 "From the President," *HBU News,* June 1996, 2.
35 Houston Baptist University, Minutes of the Meetings of the Board of Trustees, Meeting on 22 Nov. 1994.
36 Houston Baptist University, Minutes of the Meetings of the Board of Trustees, Meeting on 28 Nov. 1995.
37 Houston Baptist University, Minutes of the Meetings of the Board of Trustees, Meeting on 22 Nov. 1994.
38 Houston Baptist University, Minutes of the Meetings of the Board of Trustees, Meeting on 27 Sept. 1994.
39 Houston Baptist University, Minutes of the Meetings of the Board of Trustees, Meeting on 16 May 1995.
40 Houston Baptist University, Minutes of the Meetings of the Board of Trustees, Meeting on 19 May 1998.
41 Houston Baptist University, Minutes of the Meetings of the Board of Trustees, Meeting on 24 Feb. 1998. With the addition of a food store, the station began the sale of lottery tickets that was quickly stopped by University action.

These moves were the first harbingers of changing demographics in the neighborhood and marked the beginning of retail relocation farther south on the Freeway.

In May, the Board Executive Committee established a policy regarding restrictions on the use of leased campus properties. This statement reflected the moral commitment of the trustees but was also a written response to the lesson of Harvest House for the need for such policy:

> All future agreements dealing with real property under ownership or control of the University shall contain protective covenants to prevent the use of the property for any unlawful purpose and to prevent sale or consumption of alcoholic beverages, gambling in any form, provision of abortions or counseling, production, sale or showing of pornographic materials whether written, visual, or audio on property owned by the University.[42]

In 1995, the University engaged the land planning firm of Vernon Henry & Associates to provide a more detailed master plan of campus development including proposed locations for future facilities. The firm proposed a development plan that included a new campus entrance from the Southwest Freeway, additional peripheral parking locations, an internal boulevard connecting Fondren Road and Beechnut, perimeter landscaping and fencing with restricted nighttime entry, locations for student housing clusters and storm water detention, and a strong encouragement to protect the campus reserve from further commercial encroachment. The plan also encouraged the creation of additional student-friendly spaces for study, relaxation, and social gathering throughout the campus.[43]

The University implemented several of the Vernon Henry recommendations with quick responses. The Bettis Quadrangle in the Brown Administrative Complex was effectively enhanced with the addition of a gazebo, tables and chairs, landscaping, and night lighting.[44] New security gates were installed at the Fondren entrance to the campus.[45] A Walk of Honor, unveiled at Homecoming '97, acknowledged the contributions of the University Founders, the original Board of Trustees, former chairs

---

42 Houston Baptist University, Minutes of the Meetings of the Board of Trustees, Meeting on 16 May 1997 and the Executive Committee on 9 May 1995.
43 Vernon Henry, *Campus Master Plan*, Minutes of the Meetings of the Board of Trustees, Meeting on 19 May 1998.
44 "Bettis Quadrangle gets a new look," *HBU News*, Mar. 1996, 8. The enhancements were a part of a student retention plan developed under the leadership of Dr. Don Byrnes.
45 "Newly installed security gates give false sense of security," *The Collegian*, 15 Jan. 1997, p. 5.

of the Board, winners of the Goolsby Teaching Award, the Mayfield Staff Award, the Cross Volunteer Award, the President's Award, the Distinguished and Meritorious Alumni Awards, Spirit of Excellence honorees, and athletic lettermen.[46] The Atwood Theology Building was significantly remodeled to provide improved faculty offices and instructional space. Virtually the entire second floor was reconfigured to provide individual faculty offices to promote improved privacy for student-faculty counseling.[47]

One of the projects Dr. Hodo had inherited upon becoming President was a proposed facility to provide library expansion, facilities for the Museum of American Architecture and Decorative Arts, and housing for the Colleges of Education and Business. The library expansion had been completed in 1990, prior to the reaffirmation visit of the Southern Association. The remaining facility project represented the largest fundraising program ever undertaken by the University. Following a "silent phase" of fund raising, a Spirit of Excellence Campaign for $5,600,000 was announced in 1993. Co-chairs Colletta Ray McMillian and Randy Butler coordinated the work of a team of fifty volunteers who were assigned campaign prospects. Funds totaling $3,500,000 had already been contributed by 120 donors including the Cullen Trust for Higher Education, the M. D. Anderson Foundation, alumni, friends, and one hundred percent of the University trustees.[48] The Cullen grant honored the service of trustee Milton Cross on the Cullen Trust Board. In a surprise development, however, the grant was designated for endowed maintenance of the facility rather than construction.[49] For a number of years, HBU had been striving to budget a maintenance endowment of ten percent of construction cost for new projects. The Cullen restriction set a powerful example for future projects.

In 1994, the Robert and Janice McNair Foundation announced a grant of $1,000,000 to fund a graduate studies center in the new Hinton complex.[50] In August, trustees authorized a working budget of $7,000,000 for the Hinton Center inclusive of a 7.5 percent contingency

---

46 *SomeTimes,* Jan. 1997.
47 Houston Baptist University, Minutes of the Meetings of the Faculty Assembly, Meeting on 21 Apr. 1998.
48 Dr. E. D. Hodo, "From the President," *HBU News,* Aug. 1993, 2.
49 *SomeTimes,* July 1995.
50 *SomeTimes,* Feb. 1994; "McNair Gift to Hinton Center: Graduate Studies Center," *HBU News,* Apr. 1994, 17; Denise Lancaster, "$1 million pledge from McNairs funds Graduate Studies Center," *The Collegian,* 10 Feb. 1994, p. 1.

fund and $150,000 for a requisite retrofit of the University's electric power grid.[51] In 1989, the trustees authorized the employment of architect Arthur Jones with the firm Lloyd, Morgan & Jones to begin preliminary planning for the Hinton building, including a projection of utility infrastructure requirements.[52] As work continued on plan development with Lloyd, Morgan & Jones, however, the University became increasingly concerned with the apparent down-sizing of the architectural firm and the lagging pace of project development. Although the reputation of the firm was stellar, and Herman Lloyd had been the architect for the original campus buildings in 1963, a change of leadership was deemed advisable, and the firm of House, Reh, and Burwell was selected as the new Hinton Center architect.[53]

Vernon Henry detailed specific planning recommendations for the Hinton Center. A site at the east end of the Holcomb Mall behind the Morris Columns was proposed; the site would need to be elevated from twenty-four to forty-eight inches above grade to conform to existing campus buildings. Henry recommended strong vertical design elements to reflect existing campus architecture. He recommended a design that facilitated heavy pedestrian circulation at the first level. The exterior design would need to integrate the Holcomb stage and the Morris columns with the Hinton façade. He recommended large areas of greenspace surrounding the structure and the inclusion of a marked degree of ground-level detail including window penetrations to establish a welcoming pedestrian scale. He observed that the building would be approached and visible from all four sides.[54]

By the time of groundbreaking for the Hinton Academic Center on July 28, 1995, a budget of $6,500,000 had been adopted for a three-story structure of 58,000 square-feet. Trustee Jack Carlson chaired the Building Committee comprised of alumnus/trustee Rick Bailey '69, Board Chair Dr. Bruce Belin, Jr., Vice Presidents Dr. Don Looser and Dick Parker, faculty representative Dr. James S. Taylor, and MBA alumnus Joe Zimmerman '89.[55] Ultimately, the project was financed in part

---

51 Houston Baptist University, Minutes of the Meetings of the Board of Trustees, Meeting on 23 Aug. 1994.
52 Houston Baptist University, Minutes of the Meetings of the Executive Committee of the Board of Trustees, Meeting on 19 Sept. 1989.
53 Houston Baptist University, Minutes of the Meetings of the Board of Trustees, Meeting on 28 Feb. 1995.
54 (Vernon Henry to Dr. Don Looser, Apr. 14, 1995). Minutes of the Meetings of the Board of Trustees, Meeting on 16 May 1995.
55 *Ornogah 1996*, 221. Photo.

by a $4,400,000 bond issue by the Houston Higher Education Finance Corporation.[56] In a little known fact of history, the private issue bonds were all bought by founding trustee John Baugh through the Baptist Foundation of Texas.[57]

A major gift from Lee and Tracy Lawrence in 1995 enabled the establishment of the Sarah Lee Lawrence Academic Center in the Hinton facility in memory of their daughter.[58] Plans for the complex also included a separate conference center funded in-part by the Mary L. Wilson Estate and named for Dr. Ross Dillon that could operate in acoustical and pedestrian isolation from the rest of the facility. Tiered classrooms and corporate-level furnishings would characterize the McNair Graduate Center on the second floor. Faculty offices and academic support for the College of Business and Economics and the College of Education and Behavioral Sciences were to occupy the third level. A central atrium, towering some eighty-five feet, crowned by an illuminated dome would give the campus new visibility from the Southwest Freeway. In addition, the Hinton Center would provide classrooms, computer labs, student and faculty lounges, and a Decision Room for conferences and meetings of the Board of Trustees. The project was to follow a design-build construction process working in close correlation with the contractor Pepper-Lawson Construction Company, Inc. Specialists in acoustics, instructional media, lighting, finishes, graphics, landscaping, and interiors provided a level of expertise that surpassed that of any previous University construction project.[59]

Particular elements of design distinguished the Hinton Center and gave recognition to the contributions of several individuals. A permanent exhibit providing a visual history of the University under Dr. Hinton's leadership was installed in the Hinton Center atrium. A University Seal cast in terrazzo in the floor beneath the dome honored the memory and contribution of former trustee Chair Milton Cross. Large bas-relief University seals cast in architectural stone, a gift of Karen and Jack Carlson, anchored the east and west façades. A prayer garden adjacent to the Dillon Center on the east was given by former trustee Chair Walter Morgan in memory of his wife Ann. The garden was distinguished by James Busby's large sculpture "Descending Dove" inspired by the

---

56 Houston Baptist University, Minutes of the Meetings of the Board of Trustees, Meeting on 13 Sept. 1995.
57 (Hugh McClung to Dr. Don Looser, Aug. 10, 2009).
58 *SomeTimes*, July 1995.
59 "A dream is a reality—Hinton Center," *HBU News*, Aug. 1995, 13-20; *Ornogah 1996*, 20-21. Photos.

Matthew 3:16 description of the Holy Spirit.[60] Within the Dillon Conference Room were placed two large architectural exterior doors from the nineteenth-century headquarters of Lloyd's of London, a gift from trustee John Jemison, to mark the Hinton Center as the home for the University's College of Business.

The impact of the Hinton Academic Center on the visual integration of the campus was profound. By providing a new visual focus, the Hinton Academic Center at once gave the Morris columns a needed backdrop. Furthermore, the Center seemed visually to unite the various buildings around the Holcomb Mall more effectively. The Hinton Center accommodated the various pedestrian axes of the campus connecting college housing, the Atwood buildings, the library, and the Brown Academic Center. Moreover, the Center provided beautiful offices for faculty who had long been operating from virtual closets and professional learning environments for the University's students—particularly those at the graduate level.

The dedication ceremonies for the Hinton Center were held on September 16, 1997. In fitting tribute, the day was proclaimed HBU Day in Houston by Mayor Bob Lanier.[61] Although in failing health, Dr. Hinton attended the ceremonies and was greeted with a standing ovation.[62] His daughter Julie Parton spoke for the family expressing gratitude for the naming of the Center and recalling the many years of devoted service given by both her mother and father.[63] The ceremony solemnized the contributions of many individuals that helped support the University's growth over nearly forty years and marked the attainment of the University's most significant structure to date.

The Hinton Center was a testimony to the commitment of President Hodo as much as a tribute to others. He had inherited the dream for such a facility without the blessing of existing funding and had assumed the responsibility to make the dream a reality as a part of his personal mandate to honor his predecessor. Dr. Hodo was joined in that pursuit by three chairs of the Board of Trustees, Karl Kennard, C. Pat Ellis, and Dr. Bruce Belin, Jr.; by Colletta McMillian and Randy Butler in their leadership of the Spirit of Excellence Campaign; and by the financial support of

---

60 Cindy Wilson, "'Descending Dove' featured at Houston Baptist," *HBU News,* Nov. 1997, 22-23.
61 Allen Jones, "Hodos 'overwhelmed' by Spirit of Excellence award," *The Collegian,* 25 Sept. 1997, p. 1.
62 *SomeTimes,* Sept. 1997.
63 Julie Hinton, "Hinton Center: A foundation built on Jesus Christ," *The Collegian,* 25 Sept. 1997, p. 3. "My father laid a foundation that Doug Hodo has come along and built upon. The true foundation is Jesus Christ."

Dr. Hinton flanked by four of the President's Advisors who staged the Board of Trustees "sit-in," Lee Lawrence, Dr. Kate Bell, Nell Smith, and Marie Kern.

more than one thousand donors—personal, corporate, and foundation.[64] The project had taken more than ten years to bring to fruition. It seemed appropriate, therefore, that at the Spirit of Excellence Dinner on the dedication evening, Dr. and Mrs. Hodo were honored with the 1997 Spirit of Excellence Award.[65]   Additional Excellence awards were given to the Robert A. Welch Foundation, Virginia Marshall, and Mary Claude Thompson. Grace Gandy was the recipient of the 1997 Milton Cross Volunteer Award.[66] The dinner featured Dr. Jeannette Clift George, was hosted by Ron Stone '94, and was attended by more than 600 guests.[67]

The Hinton Academic Center set a new mark for excellence in facilities. Existing campus offices, classrooms, and way-finding signage began to be modeled on the Hinton standard.   The Faculty Assembly expressed its appreciation with a proclamation that delineated specific gratitude for

64 *Ornogah 1996,* 220.

65 "Spirit of Excellence Dinner," *HBU News,* Nov. 1997, 12-13.

66 Ibid.

67 Shelby Hodge, "Houston Baptist hosts spirited awards dinner," *Houston Chronicle,* 19 Sept. 1997, sec. B, p. 3, two-star ed.

beautiful and functional classrooms in a variety of configurations, well designed offices to facilitate accomplishment of tasks away from distraction, an atmosphere that promotes the development of collegiality, a state of the art graduate studies center, a place of spiritual renewal provided by the Prayer Garden and sculpture, and the potential of the Dillon Center for hosting professional conferences and relating more effectively to the public.[68]

All the faculty wish to join the occupants of the Hinton Academic Center in expressing our deep and abiding gratitude to all who dreamt a dream and created a reality whose impact will last far into the future.

Therefore all the faculty wish to express gratitude to our University President Dr. E. D. Hodo; to our Vice President for Academic Affairs Dr. Don Looser; to all members of the Board of Trustees who served from inception to completion; to all donors large and small, and to all the faithful who banded together in an advocacy of a University dedicated to the greater glory of Our Lord and Savior.[69]

The Hinton Center in time became a prototype for academic design, was emulated on other campuses, and enjoyed a high level of national attention in educational and construction journals.[70] Of particular merit was the high quality of the project at nominal incremental cost.

§

Since its founding, the University realized that many of its aspirations could best be achieved with a student population that was primarily residential. Over the first thirty years, the percentage of resident students declined. For many students, apartment living was a family life-style and was preferable to dormitory life. As a part of strategic planning, the University became persuaded that additional campus housing was critical to its institutional mission. Vice President for Student Affairs Jack Purcell recalled, "The sense of community that was present in the early years slowly began to dissipate. There was the need to recapture that feeling

---

68 Houston Baptist University, Minutes of the Meetings of the Faculty Assembly, Meeting on 21 Oct. 1997. Paraphrased.

69 Ibid.

70 Architects for the University of Houston used the Hinton Center as the concept for an administration building for their Fort Bend campus.

of community and collegiality."[71] A goal of 800 students living on campus was articulated.[72]

In May 1995, the University engaged in discussions with Century Development Company about construction of privatized apartment residences on the University campus.[73] Century was responsible for the development of such commercial projects as Houston's Greenway Plaza and had recently entered the college housing market. Century brought design experience that reflected the preferences of college students and brought privatized financing capability in lieu of the requirement for institutional funds. However, HBU represented a smaller institution than any of Century's previous college partners; therefore, the firm's usual bankers ultimately would not provide the needed capital.[74] Efforts were made unsuccessfully to combine HBU financing with other campus projects in which Century was engaged. In order to keep the project moving, Beechnut Street Inc. approved a loan of $300,000 to consummate the ground lease, as well as the management and partnership agreements.[75] The plan was to provide housing for 224 students in garden apartment housing at an estimated cost of $3,600,000.[76] Meanwhile, the University sold the three apartment units at the corner of Beechnut and Fondren.[77]

By the fall 1996, apartment financing had been arranged and construction was underway. The new housing, named Husky Village,[78] was built adjacent to existing campus housing on a portion of the site previously occupied by the University's Tartan-surface track. The new apartment complex provided apartments of varying sizes clustered in five buildings along with a clubhouse and swimming pool.[79] The design of the apartments responded to the particular lifestyle of college students by maximizing space allocation in the common living areas. The ribbon-cutting ceremony for the opening of Husky Village was held in February 1997.[80] The co-ed complex was managed by Century Development in

---

71 "A Community within a community; Husky Village," *HBU News,* Aug. 1997, 8-9.

72 "Campus apartments under construction," *HBU News,* Oct. 1996, 5. Photo.

73 Houston Baptist University, Minutes of the Meetings of the Board of Trustees, Meeting on 16 May 1995.

74 Houston Baptist University, Minutes of the Meetings of the Executive Committee of the Board of Trustees, Meeting on 30 Jan. 1996.

75 Ibid.

76 Stephanie A. De Los Santos, "University proposes new apartments," *The Collegian,* 7 Sept. 1995, p. 1.

77 Stephanie A. De Los Santos, "University Apartments under new ownership," *The Collegian,* 26 Jan. 1996, p. 1.

78 Deana Gentry, "New student apartments dubbed 'Husky Village,'" *The Collegian,* 10 Oct. 1996, p. 2.

79 "Husky Village: Construction Complete," *HBU News,* Feb. 1997, 12.

80 "News in brief," *The Collegian,* 20 Mar. 1997, p. 2. Photo.

conformity with the policies of the HBU Student Code of Conduct. So popular were the new apartments that construction was soon undertaken on an additional three-floor unit that would raise the Husky Village capacity to 272 residents.[81]

Nonetheless, one of the more significant needs of students remained—a larger, more comprehensive student center that would provide both social and recreational opportunity. The M. D. Anderson Student Center served as an effective meeting place and campus crossroads but had no space to provide for additional student activity. Early in 1995, founding trustee John Baugh expressed an interest in making a significant gift to the University to honor his wife Eula Mae. In private consultation with University officials, Baugh became aware of the need for an enhanced student center. In May 1995, he contributed $600,000 as a challenge gift for the construction of a new student services facility.[82] Addressing a student convocation, Mr. Baugh confessed to a lifelong commitment to young people and described students of the 1990s as "inquisitive, intense, and globally-oriented." Baugh recalled his own involvement in the founding of the University and encouraged students to "find favor with God."[83] The Baughs were honored at the 1996 fall Spirit of Excellence Dinner along with ConocoPhillips and the George Foundation.[84] By October 1996, matching contributions for the Eula Mae Baugh Center had been received from the Cullen Trust for Higher Education, the Meadows Foundation, and the J. E. and L. E. Mabee Foundation.[85] Additional gifts were received from Margaret and Emory Carl, Claydene and Gilbert Turner, the Margaret and James Elkins, Jr. Foundation, The Houston Endowment, the Strake Foundation, Compaq Computer Corporation, and Chase Bank of Texas.[86] Trustees authorized a construction budget of $2,800,000.[87] Groundbreaking for the Baugh Center was held in February 1997.[88] The architectural firm of Farrell, Sundlin, and Partners Architects, Inc. and the construction firm of Pepper-Lawson were again selected to build the facility. The 21,000 square feet of the Baugh Center housed a new campus "food court," seating for 300 diners, individual and group study rooms,

---

81 Jessica Rogers, "Husky Village constructing new building," *The Collegian*, 8 Oct. 1998, p. 3. Photo.
82 Houston Baptist University, Minutes of the Meetings of the Board of Trustees, Meeting on 16 May 1995.
83 Deana Gentry, "University honors benefactors at gala event," *The Collegian*, 26 Sept. 1996, p. 1.
84 "Spirit of Excellence Honorees," *HBU News*, Feb. 1997, 9.
85 "Encore and More," *HBU News*, Oct. 1996, 10; "Encore and More," *HBU News*, Aug. 1997, 15.
86 "Baugh Center Dedication," *HBU News*, June 1998, 6-7. Photo.
87 Houston Baptist University, Minutes of the Meetings of the Board of Trustees, Meeting on 20 May 1997.
88 "Baugh Student Center: Breaking New Ground," *HBU News*, May 1997, 6-7.

club meeting and storage space, game rooms, a computer center, television lounge, and Student Affairs offices.[89] The Eula Mae Baugh Center opened in February 1998 and was dedicated on March 24.[90] Eula Mae Baugh, for whom the center was named, reflected, "I consider it an honor to have the Center named after me. It just shows how much my husband loves me."[91]

Eula Mae Baugh and President Hodo at the dedication of the Eula Mae Baugh Center.

The Baugh Center immediately changed the focus of student activity on campus. The move of student life offices and the cafeteria had a profound effect on the M. D. Anderson Student Center. For a while, the student population in Anderson was greatly reduced. For resident students, the Baugh offered supplemental resources in addition to food service that were absent at M. D. Anderson. In addition, the attractive food service of Baugh increased the number of faculty and staff for breakfast and lunch. However, students ultimately also returned to Anderson in great numbers drawn by the bookstore, post office, snack bar, and the large student lounge.

§

89 Davinder Nijar, "$2.8 million student center offers 'needs' of the '90s," *The Collegian,* 11 Dec. 1997, p. 2; Houston Baptist University, Minutes of the Meetings of the Board of Trustees, Meeting on 12 May 1997.
90 "The Eula Mae Baugh Center Dedication: March 24, 1998," Dedication Program, Houston Baptist University archives.
91 Kelly Fitch, "President dedicates Baugh Center," *The Collegian,* 2 Apr. 1998, p. 2. Photo.

In 1997, the University commemorated the tenth anniversary of Dr. Hodo's inauguration by initiating a year-long "Celebration of Decades—Faith, Excellence, and Vision" that also marked the twentieth anniversary of the establishment of the University's first graduate study in 1977, the thirtieth anniversary of the graduation of the first class in 1967, and the fortieth anniversary of the adoption of a resolution to establish a new college by the Union Baptist Association.[92] This year of recognition was initiated by a "Night of the Stars" concert as a part of Homecoming in February.[93] On April 22, 1997, the University presented a Celebration Concert honoring Dr. and Mrs. Hodo at Second Baptist Church featuring faculty and ensembles from the School of Music and tributes from benefactor Archie Dunham, distinguished alumna Marsha Eckermann '68, and past president of the President's Advisors Judy Graham.[94]

As a further part of the Celebration of Decades, Dean Nancy Yuill '72 and the College of Nursing celebrated "30 years of excellence in nursing" on May 8 with an academic symposium. Featured were Allan Graubard and Caroline McGee from the National League for Nursing who spoke on "Sojourns in the Public Trust" and donor/alumna Iris Baker who recalled the history of the nursing program beginning with the Lillie Jolly School of Nursing at Memorial Baptist Hospital.

HBU had long realized the difficulty of maintaining institutional visibility in the Houston urban marketplace. As the competition for students and for financial support became more challenged by additional competition, the importance of clear delineation of institutional character became more vital. "Strong in Mind; Strong in Spirit," developed by STAMATS in the early 1990s, was adopted as the marketing slogan for the University[95] and was the precursor of the 2010 Seventh Pillar of Vision, "Bringing Athens and Jerusalem Together." In the fall of 1998, Fogarty Kline, and Monroe (FKM) urged the use of the acronym "HBU" in University

92 "Celebration: A School of Music Concert in honor of Dr. E. D. Hodo, President, The Tenth Anniversary, April 22, 1997, Second Baptist Church Worship Center," Performance Program, Houston Baptist University archives; Dr. E. D. Hodo, "From the President," *HBU News*, Feb. 1997, 2.

93 "Night of Stars: Celebration of Decades continues," *HBU News*, Feb. 1997, 18-19. "Night of Stars" featured Dr. Rhonda Furr premiering an original composition in tribute to Dr. Hodo, and performances by Lee Melvin '87, Charles Reid '92, Christy Dunham '97, and Veronica Olvera '99 hosted by Ragan Courtney.

94 "Celebration: A School of Music Concert," *HBU News*, Aug. 1997, 6. The elaborate program additionally featured *Interludes* by Ragan Courtney, vocal and instrumental ensembles conducted by Drs. David Wehr and Richard Spitz, Tre Voci, and the University Opera Workshop and Jazz Ensembles.

95 Houston Baptist University, *1997 Publications and Media Guide*, p. 5.

advertising, unveiled a new Husky logo, and created a new slogan, "Houston's Best University, Houston's Blest University."[96] FKM incorporated these elements into their billboard campaign designed to establish a clear identity for the University that also touted institutional strengths.

§

On May 15th, the Thomas Jackson Pipe Organ was dedicated in a concert by organ performance major Carol Nave.[97] The eleven-rank organ, hand-built over many years by Jackson who served as administrator of the Buckner Baptist Haven, had graced the Haven chapel and was given to HBU in memory of Jackson's wife Ruth, a former HBC music faculty member and organist at the Second Baptist Church of Houston.[98] The gift was conveyed for the use of the university's organ students by the Jackson's daughter, Ruth Ann, an HBC music graduate of the class of 1968, and her sister Elaine.

In May, the Board heard a report from Ron Mooney and Jerry Wiles recommending the University's purchase of a significant private library of rare American Bibles and Christian books that had been assembled over a thirty-year period by a devoted collector, Jonathan Byrd.[99] The collection consisted of first editions of significant 18th and 19th-century American printings of the Bible including the only-known existing intact copy of the 1780 Francis Bailey New Testament—the earliest example of Scripture printed in America—and the first English Bible printed in America, the rare 1782 Aitken Bible. Other significant artifacts included the Christoph Saur Bible printed in America in the German language in 1743 and the Columbian Bible of 1792.[100] With Dr. Hodo's strong leadership, the $800,000 purchase was authorized by the Board although no designated funds were in hand; the collection was appraised at a value

---

96 *SomeTimes*, July 1998. *Houston's Best University, Houston's Blessed University*— blessed with the best learning environment with a student-faculty ratio of just 17:1; blessed with the best faculty with 70 percent holding the terminal degree in the field; blessed with classes taught by full-time faculty; blessed with double majors; blessed with the best of both worlds; blessed as a small college in the heart of a big city; and blessed with the best of value and values.

97 Houston Baptist University, *Thomas Jackson Pipe Organ Dedication* program, 15 May 1997; *HBU News,* Feb. 1997, 28. Photo. Houston Baptist University archives.

98 (Neal Knighton, Vice President, Buckner Baptist Benevolences to Dr. Don Looser, August 5, 1996).

99 Houston Baptist University, Minutes of the Meetings of the Board of Trustees, Meeting on 20 May 1997.

100 Juliana Seale, "Campus gets $1.1 million Bible collection," *The Collegian*, 15 Jan. 1998, p. 2. Photo.

of $1,115,000.[101] The Bible in America collection of some 500 items was described as "the most significant American Bible collection assembled in the past half-century, rivaled only by the American Bible Society Library and Archives in New York City."[102] In the transaction, Byrd donated additional artifacts valued at approximately $400,000 to the University. President Hodo commented,

> This collection can heighten awareness of how God has promulgated the Word by different means. While most people have an appreciation for the Word, they don't understand the trials people went through to get it. The Bible in America Museum will stand as a reminder to our students, our city, and our nation that God's eternal Word is the cornerstone of knowledge and education.[103]

A fund-raising campaign was initiated to underwrite the purchase of the collection. Dr. Jerry Wiles, Assistant Vice President for Church Relations, was named Director of a proposed Bible in America Museum.[104]

In contrast to previous years, the working relationship between the Memorial Hospital System and the University became more collaborative under the leadership of Memorial's CEO Dan Wilford. Trustees of both institutions remembered the negotiations regarding sale of the original campus property to Memorial to have been tendentious. Upon Wilford's appointment as President of Memorial, the two institutions began to explore common need and practical relationships. Wilford's long-standing personal friendship with President Hodo facilitated such discussion. In August 1995, to acknowledge Wilford's role in inter-institutional cooperation, the University Board of Trustees passed a resolution of appreciation affirming, "He has led Memorial into an ongoing and close relationship with the University as each institution seeks to carry out its mission."[105]

In 1997, Memorial Hospital revealed plans to construct a wellness center adjacent to its current campus. The Hospital presented a proposal to the University to lease eleven acres of land bordering the Southwest Freeway. Some 51,000 square feet of space were proposed for wellness activity and an additional 20,000 square feet for medical offices. The

---

101 Houston Baptist University, Minutes of the Meetings of the Board of Trustees, Meeting on 25 Mar. 1997.
102 "Word is Getting Around: Museum project gains momentum," *HBU News,* Mar. 1998, 14.
103 Ibid.
104 Juliana Seale, "Campus gets $1.1 million Bible collection," *The Collegian,* 15 Jan. 1998, p. 2.
105 "Wilford Receives Honorary Doctorate," *HBU News,* Nov. 1995, 8; Copy of the Resolution attached to the Minutes of the Meetings of the Board of Trustees, Meeting on 19 Aug. 1995.

project was estimated to cost $12,000,000 and would require the enrollment of approximately 3500 members to prove financially viable.[106] In July, the Chair of the University Board Dr. Bruce Belin, Jr. called a special meeting to approve a Memorandum of Understanding with Memorial for a wellness center "dedicated to the psychological, social, spiritual, and physical aspects of health."[107] The proposal was for only seven acres for the wellness center itself, however, because plans for medical offices had become embroiled in political turmoil within the hospital. In public announcement of the project the next year, the *Houston Chronicle* sardonically reported that the center was designed "for baby boomers past age 50 whose big concerns are privacy and cardiac monitoring."[108] The center proved to be the first major project undertaken by Memorial following its merger with Hermann Hospital. Ground breaking was held in March 1998 for a $13,400,000 facility of 63,000 square feet to be called the Memorial-Hermann/Houston Baptist University Wellness Center.[109]

In May 1998, the Board approved a proposal brought by trustee David Stutts for a 2.5-year lease of two acres of campus land on Beechnut to the KIPP Academy, a then little-known charter school serving 250 students in grades five through eight.[110] Founded by Michael Feinberg, the Knowledge Is Power Program (KIPP) was seeking short-term residency in temporary buildings pending construction of its own new proprietary campus.[111] The program aimed at underserved students in order to build "partnership among parents, students, and teachers that puts learning first."[112] The program provided outstanding teaching, more time in school learning, and a strong culture of achievement. The partnership ultimately brought great satisfaction to the University in its role as a community resource. Eventually, KIPP was to become one of America's great educational success stories with the addition of college-preparatory programs at the high school level. In 2010, KIPP enjoyed national recognition for its network of some eighty-two, free, open-enrollment, college-preparatory public schools in nineteen states serving approximately

---

106 Houston Baptist University, Minutes of the Meetings of the Board of Trustees, Meeting on 25 Mar. 1997.

107 Houston Baptist University, Minutes of the Meetings of the Board of Trustees, Meeting on 29 July 1997.

108 Mary Sit-DuVall, "Total fitness seen as well certain," *Houston Chronicle*, 31 Mar. 1988, Bus. sec., p. 3, three-star ed.

109 "Wellness center project takes off," *HBU News*, June 1998, 4.

110 Houston Baptist University, Minutes of the Meetings of the Board of Trustees, Meeting on 19 May 1998.

111 Merin Brown, "Land leased to middle school," *The Collegian*, 24 Sept. 1998, p. 4. Photo.

112 *Knowledge Is Power Program*, www.kipp.org (accessed Mar. 23, 2010).

20,000 students of whom eighty percent persisted to college enroll-ment.[113]

§

Following the retirement of Dean of Humanities Dr. Calvin Huckabay, the University sought to engage another scholar of stature whose ability to lead and inspire faculty would serve to honor Huckabay's legacy. Such a man was Dr. Harold Raley who was named Dean of Humanities in August 1994. Raley had previously served as Professor of Spanish and Chair of the Department of Modern and Classical Languages at the University of Houston.[114] He was a published author and a devout Christian. Dr. Raley had become greatly interested in the University through his desire to serve in an academic setting where his faith and spiritual values could find free expression. Raley found immediate resonance with his faculty and in the University-at-large. In January 1995, the University announced plans to merge the College of Fine Arts and the College of Humanities into one unit under Raley's leadership.[115] Fine Arts Dean Dr. Robert Linder had retired in June; the moment seemed ripe for such action. Dr. Ann Gebuhr was named acting Associate Dean for the School of Music.[116] At the same time, Dr. James Taylor, Chair of the Department of Communications, was named Associate Dean for Humanities.

Later that spring, Dr. Sebron Williams, the iconic Dean of the College of Education and Behavioral Sciences, announced his retirement after sev-enteen years on the University faculty. Williams had served as Dean since 1982. He had been unusually qualified to manage both education and the behavioral sciences; he had not only school-district superintendence experience, but was a licensed professional counselor as well. Williams had picked up the mantle of student testing and personal counseling upon the retirement of Dr. Steve Williams and had created a student serv-ices operation while serving as Dean. He had initiated the Master of Education, the Master of Arts in Psychology, and the Master of Arts in Pastoral Counseling degree programs. Moreover, Dr. Sebron Williams had played a major role—in concert with his friend and colleague Dr.

---

113 Ibid.
114 *SomeTimes,* Aug. 1994.
115 *SomeTimes,* Jan. 1995.
116 Leslie E. Tripp, "Colleges merge," *The Collegian,* 26 Jan. 1995, p. 1.

Kate Bell—in influencing the decision to house the College of Education and Behavioral Sciences in the Hinton Academic Center. Following his retirement as Dean, Dr. Williams continued to serve on the University faculty and was named Director of Academic Testing in the fall of 1995.[117] Named to succeed Dr. Williams as Dean was Dr. Bill Borgers, Superintendent of the Dickinson Independent School District. Borgers was widely recognized as an expert and a consultant on quality-based, continuous-improvement management.[118]

A third academic dean announced his retirement in 1997. Dr. Jerry Gaultney, a member of the University faculty since 1978, had served as Dean of the College of Science and Mathematics since 1991. A noted microbiologist, Gaultney had first come to the University from medical assignment as a missionary in Nigeria. During Gaultney's years as Dean, the College of Science and Mathematics moved from its early orientation in pre-medicine to a broader definition of the career potential for students. In addition, Gaultney's College preserved the intense commitment to student achievement and high standards of academic rigor established by its noted founding faculty. At the May Commencement, the Board of Trustees conferred on Dr. Gaultney the rank of Professor Emeritus.[119] Dr. Doris Warren was appointed Dean of the College of Science and Mathematics upon Gaultney's retirement.[120]

Dr. Alvin Reid had been named to the Bisagno Chair of Evangelism in 1992. The service of Dr. Reid bore testimony to the fact that one can make extraordinary contributions in a comparatively brief period of time. Reid explored the many opportunities attendant to the Bisagno Chair position and developed effective relationships with pastors, established a newsletter focusing on evangelism and church growth, and maintained a high level of contribution to academic journals. However, in 1995 Reid was named to a position at Southeastern Baptist Theological Seminary. In noting his contributions to HBU, the Academic Committee of the Board reported, "He fostered on the campus a focus of evangelistic fervor through his modeling of effective enthusiastic Christian life. He developed in students from a variety of spiritual backgrounds a renewed zeal for the spreading of the gospel."[121] In the fall of 1996, Dr. Walter

---

117 "Williams named Director," *HBU News,* Nov. 1995, 21. Photo.
118 *SomeTimes,* Aug. 1995.
119 Houston Baptist University, Minutes of the Meetings of the Board of Trustees, Meeting on 20 May 1997.
120 Andrea Smith, "New dean encourages teamwork," *The Collegian,* 15 May 1997, p. 11. Photo.
121 Houston Baptist University, Minutes of the Meetings of the Board of Trustees, Meeting on 16 May 1995.

Lumpkin '81 was named to the Bisagno Chair. Lumpkin was to leave his own extraordinary imprint on University students as well.[122]

Dr. Elysee Peavy, Chairman of the Department of Languages since 1973, announced her May 1997 retirement.[123] Peavy had been a member of the University faculty since 1967 and had been chosen by Dr. Calvin Huckabay to succeed him as Chair of Languages—an honor in itself. Peavy was also the winner of a Woodrow Wilson Fellowship and a Danforth Associate. She was selected to receive the Goolsby Outstanding Teaching Award in 1972, 1975, 1978, and 1984. In 1973, she was elected Faculty Woman of the Year.[124] Peavy had organized a chapter of Sigma Tau Delta, the international honorary English society, on the University campus.[125] In honor of Peavy's career, the Rex Fleming Readers in January 1997 presented Robert Frost's *The Road Not Taken* in recognition of her close personal friendship with Fleming.[126] *The Collegian* devoted a full page in its final issue of the year to express its appreciation for Peavy's contributions to the University. In May, the Board of Trustees conferred on Dr. Peavy the rank of Professor Emeritus.[127]

Dr. Lou Shields, Vice President of Student Affairs, announced her retirement after sixteen years with the University.[128] In 1992, she had been asked by President Hodo to accept the position of Vice President for Student Affairs. Her love for students and her involvement with student activities as a faculty member made her selection particularly appropriate. In 1997, Shields was awarded the Mayfield Outstanding Staff Award for her five years as Vice President.[129] Later in the spring, she was selected as University Woman of Year.[130] *The Collegian* also honored Dr. Shields and her contributions over sixteen years "to make the campus meaningful."[131] At the spring Commencement, Dr. Shields was also awarded the rank of Professor Emeritus.[132]

---

122 "Lumpkin named to Bisagno Chair," *HBU News,* Oct. 1996, 11.

123 Dr. E. D. Hodo, "From the President," *HBU News,* May 1997, 2.

124 *Who Houston '80,* 338.

125 Michelle Francis, "Dr. Elysee Peavy retires after 30 years of service," *The Collegian,* 15 May 1997, p. 8. Photo.

126 Stacy Smith, "Rex Fleming Readers honor Elysee Peavy," *The Collegian,* 30 Jan. 1997, p. 2.

127 Houston Baptist University, Minutes of the Meetings of the Board of Trustees, Meeting on 20 May 1997.

128 Casey Coates, "Student Affairs VP to retire," *The Collegian,* 30 Jan. 1997, p. 1.

129 *SomeTimes,* Feb. 1997.

130 *Ornogah 1997,* 78-79.

131 Andrea L. Smith, "'Goodbye' says Shields," *The Collegian,* 15 May 1997, p. 7. Photo.

132 Houston Baptist University, Minutes of the Meetings of the Board of Trustees, Meeting on 20 May 1997; *SomeTimes,* June 1997.

The length of service by these individuals gave testimony to the commitment and sense of ownership of the University by its faculty and staff. In 1989, the University had begun to make formal acknowledgment of the long-time service of staff and faculty in the annual convocation celebrating Founders' Day. During the period 1994-98 the University's thirty-year service awards were given to Frances Curtis, Dr. Daton Dodson, Dr. Don Looser, Dr. Elysee Peavy, Dr. Cynthia Rogers, Kathleen Strom '87, Dr. James Tsao, Dr. Doris Warren, and Jackie Williams. Recognition for twenty-five years of service was given to Ed Best, Dr. Avin Brownlee, James Busby, Dr. Don Byrnes, Dr. Hutch Dvorak, Nora Hayes, Dr. Robert Linder, Dr. Phyllis Nimmons, Dr. Ernie Pyle, Dr. Verna Peterson, Dr. James Taylor, and Dr. Brooke Tucker. Those recognized for twenty years service included Kay Allen, Virginia An, Marianne Anderson, Carol Elsbury, Judy Ferguson '67, Dr. Ann Gebuhr, Dr. John Green, Dr. Wallace Hooker, Ronnie Lott, Dan Lopez, Dr. John Lutjemeier, Dr. Sally Phillips, Dr. Steve Wentland, and Dr. Gene Wofford.[133] None of these colleagues were a part of the founding faculty and staff. However, their years of service confirmed their arrival at HBC in the early years of college operation. In most cases, this second generation of faculty and staff contributed more years of individual service than many of the founding faculty and, arguably, as a group had provided greater influence on institutional development.

§

Throughout the University, faculty scholarly activity continued to flourish. In June 1994, Dr. Joe Blair completed a new textbook, *Introducing the New Testament*, which was quickly adopted for the University's survey course.[134] Nursing faculty member Barbara Bullock also authored a new text, *Focus on Pathophysiology*.[135] Shortly thereafter, a collection of poems by Dr. James Ulmer, *Notes Toward a City of Rain,* was published by Uroboros Press. Ulmer, HBU's Writer-in-Residence, also had three poems accepted for publication by the literary journal *Touchstone*.[136]

---

133 *SomeTimes,* Nov. 1994; *SomeTimes,* Nov. 1995; *SomeTimes,* Oct. 1996; *SomeTimes,* Oct. 1997; *SomeTimes,* Nov. 1998.
134 Dr. Joe Blair, *Introducing the New Testament* (Nashville: B&H Publishing Group, 1994).
135 Barbara Bullock, *Focus on Pathophysiology* (Philadelphia: Lippincott Williams & Wilkins, 1999).
136 *SomeTimes,* Jan. 1997.

In 1995, Dr. Ann Gebuhr produced her first in a series of scholarly events designed to mark the fiftieth anniversary of the death of theologian Dietrich Bonhoeffer. The seminar "Dietrich Bonhoeffer in a World Come of Age" was held as a cooperative venture of Houston Baptist University, Texas Lutheran University, Grace Presbyterian Church, the Goethe Institute, and St. Martin's Lutheran Church.[137] The keynote speaker, Dr. Larry Rasmussun—the Reinhold Niebuhr Professor of Social Ethics at Union Theological Seminary[138]—was joined by Dr. Eric Gritsch, Barbara G. Green, Bonhoeffer-descendent Ruth-Alice von Bismarck, Dr. Robert Hatten, and Dr. Randy Hatchett.[139] The seminar was prelude to the completion of Gebuhr's opera *Bonhoeffer* premiered in 2000. Gebuhr was recognized as one of "Modern America's Outstanding Women Composers" by *Contemporary Music Review*.[140] In 1996 Dr. Gebuhr was also the recipient of the Creative Artist Award from the Cultural Arts Council of Houston—the first composer ever to be so named.[141] Poet Dr. James Ulmer had been so honored by the Council in 1989 and 1993.[142]

Dr. Rhonda Furr was elected Dean of the Houston Chapter of the American Guild of Organists.[143] Dr. Louis Markos and Leslie Kennedy Adams '86 were selected to participate in summer institutes provided by the National Endowment for the Humanities.[144] Dr. David Capes was elected President of the National Association of Baptist Professors of Religion.[145] Capes and Dr. Louis Markos were editors of a new volume, *The Footsteps of Jesus in the Holy Land*.[146] Dr. Capes manifested his interest in comparative religions by initiating a weekly radio series, "Faith Matters," with Rabbi Stuart Federow, Father Troy Gately, and alternating guest clergy.[147]

At an entirely different level, the noted Old Testament scholar Dr. A. O. Collins in 1995 issued a book of humorous student responses to

---

137 Houston Baptist University, Minutes of the Academic Committee of the Board of Trustees, Meeting on 26 Sept. 1995.

138 Jason Brown, "University honors German theologian," *The Collegian*, 19 Oct. 1995, p. 3.

139 Houston Baptist University, Minutes of the Meetings of the Board of Trustees, Meeting on 28 Nov. 1995.

140 *SomeTimes*, Jan. 1995.

141 *SomeTimes*, Mar. 1996.

142 "Gebuhr wins creative artist award," *HBU News*, June 1996, 5.

143 Houston Baptist University, Minutes of the Meetings of the Board of Trustees, Meeting on 23 Sept. 1997.

144 "Encore and More," *HBU News*, May 1995, 16.

145 *SomeTimes*, Mar. 1997.

146 Dr. David Capes, ed. *The Footsteps of Jesus in the Holy Land* (Houston: N. M. International Enterprises, 1999).

147 "Faith Matters: on the air," *HBU News*, Mar. 1998, 7; (Dr. David Capes to Dr. Don Looser, Aug. 11, 2009).

Christianity test questions entitled, *Don't Tell Me the Bible Says That.*[148] These responses included, "Moses fled to Midland where he took care of his father-in-law's sheep;"[149] "A shofar was a person who drove a chariot in Egypt;"[150] and a personal favorite, "From Dan to Beersheba" refers to Dan's gift to his wife.[151]

§

In September 1996, the University created a new interdisciplinary "Center for Christianity and the Arts" and appointed poet and lyricist Ragan Courtney as its first Director.[152] The Center was designed to be a multi-disciplinary laboratory for relating faith through contemporary art forms. The following year, Dr. Warren Matthews formed a "Center for Economic Education" and was named its first Director. The center was a part of the Texas Council on Economic Education and provided instructional assistance and materials to some 1041 teachers in twenty-six school districts.[153] In 1998, Matthews received the Center of Excellence Award from the Welch Foundation.[154]

Professional growth opportunity was a matter of great interest to faculty. In 1995, HBU administrators participated in a Total Quality Management conference (TQM) at Texas A&M.[155] Dr. Bryan Cole, Chair of the Department of Educational Administration at A&M, was then invited to the HBU campus to conduct a series of seminars on continuous quality improvement for the University's faculty.[156] In April 1996, Dr. Tom Angelo, author of *Classroom Assessment and Classroom Research* and member of the American Association of Higher Education staff, presented a series of seminars on student and program assessment for the HBU faculty, underwritten by a grant from the Strake Foundation.[157]

By 1994, the demand for ever-increasing availability and sophistication of data-based technology was felt as students began to press for

---

148 "Don't Tell Me the Bible Says That," *HBU News,* Mar. 1996, 13.

149 Dr. A. O. Collins, *Don't Tell Me The Bible Says That* (Houston: D. Armstrong Co, Inc, 1995), 31.

150 Collins, 45.

151 Collins, 63.

152 "Courtney to direct arts center," *HBU News,* Oct. 1996, 11.

153 Houston Baptist University, Minutes of the Meetings of the Board of Trustees, Meeting on 23 Nov. 1997.

154 *SomeTimes,* Nov. 1998.

155 Dr. Lou Shields, Dr. Joan DeRooy, and Dr. Don Looser attended the Texas A & M conference in July 1995.

156 Houston Baptist University, Minutes of the Meetings of the Board of Trustees, Meeting on 28 Jan. 1995.

Internet access. The Faculty Assembly formally requested that student and faculty "access to the electronic system known as the Internet"[158] become a major institutional priority. In the spring of 1995, the Moody Library established the first Internet link on the campus.[159] Dr. Hodo's President's Report in the March *HBU News* summarized the University's state of technology as a local area network, the beginnings of an administrative digital database, and an expanded CD-ROM capability in the library by means of CD-ROM "towers" that permitted multiple-user access.[160] Shortly thereafter, upon the recommendation of College of Business Dean Bruce Garrison, the library moved to a ProQuest full text system supported by a self-imposed student fee. Dr. Suter recalls student support for the fee and their delight with the improved product.[161] In 1996, the library moved to an online, Internet-based product called ProQuest Direct.[162] Jim Balkum was appointed Director of Information Services in 1996.[163] Working with the STAMATS group, the University mounted the first two elements of a website late in 1997—the home page and an undergraduate admissions site.[164] Administrative responsibility for the website was assigned to Information Services.

The period 1994-98 witnessed significant curricular revision. The creation of a wider range of options within requisite categories of the Smith College liberal arts core proved popular with students. The revisions maintained the University's commitment to a liberal arts core but provided greater ease of transfer and resulted in higher levels of student enthusiasm.[165] Administratively, the revised Smith College curriculum resulted in significant enrollment shifts away from previously-required courses, a more-even distribution of enrollment between disciplines, larger average class size, and a more efficient operational model.[166] An interdisciplinary Bachelor of General Studies degree was introduced to provide more universal degree-completion opportunities for adults who had

---

158 Houston Baptist University, Minutes of the Faculty Assembly, Meeting on 17 Mar. 1994.

159 Stephanie A. De Los Santos, "Library installs Internet," *The Collegian*, 7 Dec. 1995, p. 1.

160 Donna Rienstra, "Moody Library installs $45,000 computer system," *The Collegian*, 17 Apr. 1997, p. 1.

161 (Dr. Jon Suter to Dr. Don Looser, July 7, 2009). Students responded, "We don't mind paying for something we can use."

162 (Ann Noble to Dr. Don Looser, Dec. 7, 2009).

163 *SomeTimes*, Mar. 1996.

164 *"STAMATS unveils website,"* *HBU News*, Nov. 1997, 6; www.hbu.edu (accessed 12 Sept. 2009).

165 Dr. Don Looser, "President's Report: Academic Affairs," *HBU News*, May 1995, 22.

166 Houston Baptist University, Minutes of the Meetings of the Academic Committee of the Board of Trustees, Meeting on 27 Sept. 1994.

accumulated a significant number of previous hours of academic credit. In 1997, a Bachelor of Liberal Arts (BLA) degree was initiated "to follow in the tradition of a classical Renaissance model featuring honors sections of courses, training in research methods, curricular emphasis in the classics, and a senior thesis."[167] The University anticipated that the undergraduate BLA would provide students for the graduate Master of Liberal Arts degree.

The University's academic program had always had its roots in spiritual conviction. A large part of the guarantee of a spiritual component in the academic process rested upon the employment only of professing believers as faculty. The Preamble at Houston Baptist University made that requirement explicit. In the 1990s, faculty across the nation began to explore the development of more formal structures and a common vocabulary to discuss the relationship of personal faith and teaching discipline in the classroom. The Lilly Foundation and the Pew Trust underwrote conferences across the nation on this topic. In 1992, ten members of the HBU faculty and staff were invited to participate in a conference, "Integrating Personal Faith and Professional Discipline," at Samford University.[168] Upon their return, these colleagues presented a seminar for HBU faculty and distributed copies of a series of books entitled *Through the Eyes of Faith* written for faculty in biology, history, literature, psychology, and business.[169]

The University began to explore cooperative ventures with several other universities in offering a pre-engineering program on the HBU campus. The concept was to offer basic courses from the first two years of a pre-engineering curriculum that would assure admission to the engineering program on another campus. Baylor University and the University of Houston worked with the College of Science and Mathematics to develop program options in chemical, civil, electrical, and mechanical engineering.[170] The pre-engineering program enrolled thirteen students in classes in its inaugural year in 1995.[171]

---

167 Allen Jones, "High standards set for new BLA degree," *The Collegian*, 15 May 1997, p. 1.
168 Representatives from the academic departments and University administration included Marianne Anderson, Dr. Jerry Gaultney, Dr. Doug Hodo, Dr. Don Looser, Dr. Robert Reid, Sharon Saunders, Linda Shook, Dr. James Taylor, Dr. Jerry Wiles, and Dr. Shari Wescott.
169 In 2010, the series contains volumes for music, psychology, biology, history, business, sociology, and literature.
170 Houston Baptist University, *Bulletin 1996-98,* 73-74.
171 Dr. Don Looser, "Presidents Report: Academic Affairs-Science and Mathematics," *HBU News,* May 1995, 23.

At the graduate level, a Master of Science in Health Administration degree was instituted as a joint project of the colleges of Nursing, Business and Economics, and Education and Behavioral Sciences. The innovative program was offered through the newly-created Center for Health Studies headed by Dr. Betty Souther.[172] Within the degree, three majors were available—nursing administration, wellness administration, and personnel management.[173] The program enrolled twenty students in the first year; this number grew to forty students by 1997.[174] Another graduate degree, the Master of Science in Nursing, was reinstituted from its earlier roots in perinatal nursing. The new MSN was designed to prepare graduates for service as a family nurse practitioner, as a congregational care nurse, or as a congregational nurse practitioner.[175] The congregational care concept built on the national model of "parish nursing" whereby the church—rather than a clinical facility—served as the venue for the provision of social services to the community. The HBU program was recognized by the local press and television as *the only program in the nation* offering the nurse practitioner license coupled with training for service in a congregational setting.[176] Surveys by the College of Nursing showed the heaviest concentration of congregational care programs typically existed either in large, urban, mega-church settings or in small, rural communities.[177] Under the direction of Dr. Brenda Binder, the Master's program was approved by the National League for Nursing in 1997.[178] In a history-making event, the program received approval from the Texas Board of Nurse Examiners in November 1997 with special commendations for advanced planning and use of grants, the use of national standards to develop the curriculum, and the innovative adaptation of the traditional field of "parish nursing" to an expanded application.[179] In a written history of the Board's first one hundred years, the *Texas Board of Nursing Bulletin* recorded that HBU's program was "*the first advanced nurse practitioner educational program in Texas approved by the Board.*"[180]

172 *SomeTimes,* Apr. 1995.

173 Houston Baptist University, Minutes of the Meetings of the Board of Trustees, Meeting on 22 Nov. 1994.

174 Houston Baptist University, Minutes of the Meetings of the Board of Trustees, Meeting on 20 May 1997.

175 Houston Baptist University, *Bulletin 1996-98,* 93.

176 "HBU offers new degree," *Houston Chronicle,* 8 Mar. 1997, sec. A, p. 34, three-star ed.

177 Richard Vara, "Nursing the flock," *Houston Chronicle,* 31 May 1997, sec. E, p. 1.

178 Houston Baptist University, Minutes of the Meetings of the Board of Trustees, Meeting on 20 May 1997.

179 Houston Baptist University, Minutes of the Meetings of the Board of Trustees, Meeting on 23 Nov. 1997.

180 "Texas Board of Nursing: 1909-2009," *Texas Board of Nursing Bulletin,* Jan. 2009, p. 7.

In 1995, a Master of Science in Management was established, designed exclusively for individuals who held the MBA and wished to expand their knowledge and skills "in response to the rapid pace of change in the structure of organizations."[181] The popular MBA 2000 program established a Saturday class schedule in response to student demand. This program, historically offered by interactive television in the workplace, had experienced the sociological change of student mindset from the desire for convenience to the desire for personal interaction and the networking opportunities of traditional campus classes.[182] In November 1995, the Executive MBA program celebrated its twentieth anniversary by honoring its founder, Dr. Carter Franklin. The program boasted more than 800 graduates and had a current enrollment of 150 students.[183] The MBA program added a required *Washington Experience* opportunity as an alternative to the international study component for those interested in the not-for-profit sector.[184]

In the humanities, the Master of Liberal Arts program expanded to the Kingwood campus of North Harris Montgomery College with live classes designed to attract graduate students from the north corridor of Harris and Montgomery counties.[185] A Master of Arts in Theology degree (MATS) was approved in 1996. This program was designed to follow a European model of tutorial learning from among Biblical, historical, theological, philosophical, and practical studies.[186] The tutorial method maximized individual attention, minimized program startup costs, and reflected the graduate study model of many of the faculty.

International study flourished in programs at both the undergraduate and graduate levels. In 1994-95, students from *Culture and Human Experience* were on a European "Grand Tour" with Dr. Rhonda Furr and Dr. Jon Suter,[187] forty-four MLA students were studying in Italy, and twenty-three EMBA students were visiting corporate sites in Milan, Zurich, Brussels, and Amsterdam.[188] The EMBA's international study

---

181 Houston Baptist University, *Bulletin 1998-2000*, 99.

182 Stephanie A. De Los Santos, "MBA 2000 Program offers new class day," *The Collegian,* 5 Oct. 1995, p. 1.

183 "EMBA Spotlighted," *HBU News,* Nov. 1995, 10.

184 Houston Baptist University, Minutes of the Meetings of the Academic Committee of the Board of Trustees, Meeting on 26 Sept. 1995.

185 Dr. Don Looser, "President's Report: Graduate Programs," *HBU News,* May 1995, 23.

186 Houston Baptist University, Minutes of the Meetings of the Board of Trustees, Meeting on 14 May 1996.

187 Houston Baptist University, Minutes of the Meetings of the Academic Committee of the Board of Trustees, Meeting on 26 Sept. 1995.

188 "EMBAs take the classroom abroad," *HBU News,* Spring 1995, 12-13.

program alternated between Asia and Europe to enable students to have option of locale during their two years of matriculation.   In 1997, for example, twenty EMBA and MBA2000 students chose to visit the Tokyo Stock Exchange, Fuji Research, Toyota, and Tohmatsu Consulting with faculty mentor Dr. Mohan Kuruvilla.[189]

The period also witnessed additional co-curricular academic activity. In 1994, the University agreed to host an Intensive English Institute (IEI) on campus to offer *English as a Second Language* (ESL) to international adults and college prospects.   The opportunity for ESL study on campus was particularly attractive because the University required a higher score on the Test of English as a Foreign Language (TOEFL) than other local universities.   Harold Harris and Avenelle Merritt formed the IEI from their prior Kaplan Institute experience.   The Institute leased space in the men's residence college and sought to immerse students in spoken English classes, as well as the campus social and academic environment.[190] By May 1995, the Institute for Intensive English had enrolled twenty-eight day students and twenty-seven evening students.[191]

Reflective of the University's commitment to community service, an innovative *Summer Academy* program began in 1996 for promising eighth-grade students in the Sharpstown area.   Tenneco, Inc. provided challenge grants for several years to develop a program to provide academic enrich-ment for selected students.   Teachers at Jane Long Middle School identi-fied thirty students to participate in the first year's program under the leadership of Dr. Ruth Ann Williamson.   The Academy provided four weeks on campus at no cost to the student and utilized both outstanding Jane Long teachers and HBU students and faculty as mentors.   The pro-gram sought to encourage middle school students to persist into the high school years by providing a learning opportunity on a college campus designed to bolster self-image and career visibility.[192]

In 1995, Dr. Jerry Evans was named Director of Extended Education.[193]   Evans had served as a member of the adjunct faculty of the College of Business and Economics for several years.   Extended Education

---

189 "Business Students in Japan," *HBU News,* Mar. 1998, 4.   Photo of students at Toyota Corporate Offices.

190 Houston Baptist University, Minutes of the Meetings of the Academic Committee of the Board of Trustees, Meeting on 22 Feb. 1994.

191 Houston Baptist University, Minutes of the Meetings of the Academic Committee of the Board of Trustees, Meeting on 16 May 1995.

192 Houston Baptist University, Minutes of the Meetings of the Board of Trustees, Meeting on 14 May 1996.

193 *SomeTimes,* Dec. 1995.

at HBU offered non-degree instruction through continuing education, instructional media, and television.[194] Evans also assumed the liaison role with an advisory body called the Corporate Alliance, created by Dr. Joan DeRooy, that provided programming advice for matters related to the televised professional growth offerings.[195] During this period, Instructional Television hosted teleconferencing for such corporate clients as the Southern Gas Association and MedNet in professional development, environmental training, and corporate team building.[196]

The University had been guaranteed several hours of weekly broadcast time as a condition of the sale of Channel 14 to Trinity Broadcasting Network. Dr. Jerry Evans assumed liaison with Trinity's local affiliate, Community Educational Television of Houston (CETH).[197] Negotiations with Paul Crouch, President of Trinity Broadcast Network, indicated that programs on spiritual growth, as well as personal and business skill development, would be topics attractive to both CETH and HBU.[198] CETH agreed to provide funding for production costs. The Channel 14 programming produced by Clay Porter and Isaac Simpson began to air in 1997.[199] The campus-produced programs utilized faculty and staff personnel as presenters for programs that were broadcast by the Trinity Broadcast Network daily in Texas and in Florida. Programming was designed to promote University visibility in the community and address some of the needs for self-improvement among at-home, daytime-viewers of the Trinity Broadcast Network.[200] Such topics were included as *Home Consumer Computer Skills, Personal Financial Management, Marriage and Family Relations, Practical Applications of the Bible, Dealing with Other Cultures, Stress Management,* and *Practical Communication Skills.*[201]

In 1995, the twentieth anniversary of the Southwestern Seminary's SET program was observed. The president of Southwestern Baptist Theological Seminary, Dr. Ken Hemphill, hosted a celebration dinner, addressed alumni and friends of the Southeast Texas program (SET), and honored Hilda Moffett "for her continuous leadership of the Seminary in

---

194 Ibid.

195 "Evans named Director, Extended Education," *HBU News,* Mar. 1996, 17.

196 Houston Baptist University, Minutes of the Meetings of the Board of Trustees, Meeting on 11 Nov. 1994.

197 Houston Baptist University, Minutes of the Meetings of the Board of Trustees, Meeting on 27 Feb. 1996; "Evans named Director, Extended Education," *HBU News,* Mar. 1996, 17.

198 *SomeTimes,* Dec. 1995.

199 Houston Baptist University, Minutes of the Meetings of the Board of Trustees, Meeting on 23 Sept. 1997.

200 Houston Baptist University, Minutes of the Meetings of the Board of Trustees, Meeting on 19 May 1998.

201 Houston Baptist University, Minutes of the Meetings of the Board of Trustees, Meeting on 23 Nov. 1997.

Southeast Texas campus."[202] The SET program continued to grow and, in 1997, added interactive television capability to its instructional resources.[203] Moffett also served as an HBU trustee from 1990-99 and chaired the Academic Committee.

§

A number of the University's programs were honored with significant recognition. The College of Education and Behavioral Sciences was awarded "Exemplary Status" by the Texas Education Agency in 1995, one of only ten colleges in Texas, for achieving a ninety percent pass rate on the state examination for Certification of Educators in Texas (ExCET).[204] The teacher education program won first place honors from the Association of Teacher Education for "emphasizing quality in teacher preparation" and was further honored as a "Distinguished Program in Teacher Education" by the Consortium of Urban Professional Development and Technical Centers. [205]

In 1994, the National League for Nursing issued a glowing report on its review of the University's program and reaffirmed the accreditation of the nursing program under the leadership of its Dean, Dr. Nancy Yuill '72. The League offered specific commendations for faculty excellence, small group instruction, career counseling, a holistic approach to patient care, high program standards and expectations, the reputation of the program, and the ability of the faculty to prepare students to "function confidently in a professional role."[206] The review continued with further commendations for student performance on licensure examinations, innovative approaches to developing critical thinking skills, application of the principles of Continuous Quality Improvement (CQI), and a programmatic commitment to community service. The nursing program was required, however, to revise its commitment to open-office architecture that had fostered team teaching, peer learning, and effective space utilization. In an age of increasing concern for personal rights and privacy,

---

202 *SomeTimes*, March 1995. Board minutes from 16 May 1995 record "repeated expressions of appreciation to Mrs. Moffett for her continuous leadership of the SET program."

203 Houston Baptist University, Minutes of the Meetings of the Board of Trustees, Meeting on 23 Nov. 1997.

204 *SomeTimes,* Oct. 1995; "Education achieves Exemplary Status," *HBU News,* Nov. 1995, 19.

205 *SomeTimes,* Mar. 1996.

206 Houston Baptist University, Minutes of the Meetings of the Board of Trustees, Meeting on 22 Nov. 1994.

the College of Nursing was required to convert its open-concept faculty housing to traditional hard-walled offices.[207]

In the College of Business and Economics, England's noted Henley Business School at the University of Reading chose the HBU MBA program as the American site for its students' 1997 visit.[208] The Henley Business School was one of the oldest in Europe.[209] It was the first business school in the United Kingdom and one of the few business schools globally "to hold triple-accredited status. The Henley students returned in 1998 for a second visit to the HBU campus."[210] At the undergraduate level, the HBU "Students in Free Enterprise" team with faculty sponsor George Flowers advanced to the U. S. National SIFE Congress competition in Kansas City and was ranked in the top ten teams in the nation.[211]

The University's record of success with medical school admissions continued to remain outstanding. A summary report issued in 1998 documented that a total of 459 HBU students had been accepted to medical schools in the period 1974-1997. These included sixty-one students at Baylor College of Medicine, eighty-three at the University of Texas Medical Branch in Galveston, sixty-three at the University of Texas Health Science Center in San Antonio, thirty-four at Texas A&M, twenty-five at the University of Texas Southwestern Medical Center in Dallas, 124 at the University of Texas Medical Branch Houston, and twenty-two at Texas Tech Health Science Center.[212]

Publications at the University also continued to garner recognition and award. In 1995, the student newspaper *The Collegian* under advisor Alice Rowlands was awarded "All American" honors by the Associated Collegiate Press for distinction in news coverage and content, writing and editing, photography-art-graphics, and leadership.[213] The following year the *Collegian* won its second consecutive "All American" award.[214] Additionally, the University's yearbook *Ornogah* received first place honors from the American Scholastic Press Association.[215] Of historic note, the 1994 *Ornogah* was the first HBU yearbook to be produced entirely by

---

207 Ibid.
208 "Henley students visit U.S. and campus," *HBU News,* May 1997, 5.
209 Henley Business School, www.henley.reading.ac.uk (accessed Mar. 23, 2010).
210 Houston Baptist University, Minutes of the Meetings of the Board of Trustees, Meeting on 24 Feb. 1998.
211 Houston Baptist University, Minutes of the Meetings of the Board of Trustees, Meeting on 14 May 1996.
212 Houston Baptist University, Minutes of the Meetings of the Board of Trustees, Meeting on 24 Nov. 1998.
213 "The Collegian receives honors," *HBU News,* Nov. 1995, 8.
214 "Two time winners," *HBU News,* Feb. 1997, 29.
215 "Yearbook captures national award," *HBU News,* Feb. 1997, 29.

computer.[216] The *Collegian* garnered its third "All American" honor from the National Scholastic Press Association in 1997.[217] Dr. James Taylor observed, "The award underscores the consistently high-quality work *The Collegian* staff produces. I am especially impressed by the depth of reporting, something that is missing in most college newspapers."[218] In further Texas Intercollegiate Press Association competition in 1997, the *Collegian* received twelve awards; the *Ornogah* received six including honorable mention for the "best yearbook overall."[219] In 1998, the American School Press Association awarded the *Ornogah* a first place award for yearbooks with a volunteer staff.[220] The *HBU News* also garnered local recognition by winning the 1997 Bronze Quill Award of Excellence given by the Houston Chapter of the International Association of Business Communicators from more than 200 entries.[221] In 1998, the *HBU News* under the direction of Vivian Camacho '91 received the Golden Excalibur Award from the Houston Chapter of the Public Relations Society of American.[222]

§

Academic lectureships brought distinction to the University through the campus residency of outstanding scholars and corporate leaders. Giving the Prince-Chavanne Lectures in Christian Business Ethics were Dr. Allen Verhey, The Institute of Religion; Dr. William F. May and Dr. Richard Mason, SMU; and Dr. Scott Rae, Biola University. The Thomas F. Staley Distinguished Christian Scholar lecturers included Dr. Barry Stricker, Golden Gate Baptist Theological Seminary; Bert Campolo, Executive Director of Kingdomworks; Dr. Leonard Sweet, Drew University; and Dr. Ron Sider, Eastern Baptist Theological Seminary. Honoring one of the founding professors in Christianity, the A. O. Collins Lectures brought the eminent scholars Dr. Samuel D. Proctor, Duke University; Dr. Walter Brueggemann, Columbia Theological Seminary;

216 *Ornogah* 1994, 224.
217 Allen Jones, "Paper wins 3rd award," *The Collegian*, 23 Oct. 1997, p. 1.
218 Ibid.
219 Andrea Smith, "Student publications win 18 awards," *The Collegian*, 17 Apr. 1997, p. 2.
220 Houston Baptist University, Minutes of the Meetings of the Board of Trustees, Meeting on 24 Feb. 1998.
221 *SomeTimes,* June 1997; "News Receives Bronze Quill Award," *HBU News,* Aug. 1997, 5.
222 Rhonda Finley, "*HBU* News brings home the gold," *The Collegian*, 14 May 1998, p. 3.

Dr. John Howard Yoder, University of Notre Dame; and Dr. Luke Timothy Johnson, Emory University. The Herman Brown Chair in Business lectures afforded some of the city's most outstanding corporate leaders for lectures and discussion including Jack Blanton, President, Eddy Refining, Co.; Gene McDavid, President, *Houston Chronicle*; Archie Dunham, President, Conoco, Inc.; and, Gordon Bethune, President, Continental Airlines. Other lecturers during the period included Drayton McLane, Jr., Chairman of the McLane Group; Judge Robert Eckels; A. D. Players founding director Jeannette Clift George; and, U. S. Representative Bill Archer.

§

The period 1994-98 was marked by significant changes in administrative leadership. University Controller Jackie Williams announced her retirement in 1994 after thirty-two years of service. Williams had joined the HBC staff in 1962, officing in the house on Fondren that hosted the first campus offices.[223] In response to the Williams retirement, Hugh McClung was named Director of Investment Accounting, and alumna Loree Watson '80 was named Director of Accounting Operations. Also retiring was Librarian Dorothy Allen, a twenty-seven-year colleague, who had also served in the years immediately preceding the tenure of Dr. Carl Wrotenbery. Allen had supervised the move of the library from its original academic quadrangle location to the new Moody Library in 1967.[224] Other long-term employees retiring included Barbara Owens after twenty-five years as assistant to five Deans of the College of Education and Behavioral Sciences, Mary Ruby after eighteen years with the pre-health professions program,[225] Dr. James Tsao after thirty years as a member of the political science faculty,[226] and Dr. David Wehr after nineteen years as Director of Choral Activities.[227]

In October 1995, the University named Dr. Ronald G. Mooney Vice President for University Advancement. Other new staff members in

---

223 *SomeTimes,* 1 Dec. 1994.
224 Stephanie De Los Santos, "Long-time librarian retires," *The Collegian,* 11 May 1995, p. 1.
225 Lisa Bowlin, "18 years of service comes to a close," *The Collegian,* 12 Jan. 1995, p. 4.
226 "Congratulations to our Colleagues," *SomeTimes,* Nov. 1998.
227 Lucinda Garces, "Owens retires after 25 years," *The Collegian,* 14 May 1998, p. 2.

Advancement included Mary Purcell in Planned Giving[228] and Judy Martin who followed Marsha Mathis Eckermann '68 as Director of Special Activities.[229] Jerry Goree, Director of the Association of Former Students, resigned in 1997 after seven years of service to be replaced by Matthew Diehl '90.[230] In March 1998, Cindy Crane Garbs followed Ron Mooney as Vice President for Advancement; Dr. Joan DeRooy became Vice President for Donor Development and Research.[231]

In 1998, one of the University's most colorful colleagues, Dr. Jerry Ford, was completing a twenty-four-year career with the University. Ford had served as Director of Undergraduate Admissions, Assistant Professor of Education, Dean of Smith College, and University Registrar. Ford was responsible for many years of recognition for HBU's faculty advisors by the National Academic Advising Association (NACADA) for which he had served as Vice President. Under his leadership, NACADA had ranked HBU as the finest academic advising program among private universities in the nation.[232] A member of the noontime faculty-staff joggers "club," Ford was known for his advocacy for students. He also had been recognized by the *Houston Post* as one of the city's ten most notable eccentrics for his passion for LSU, its colors, and its athletic teams.[233] His home and office were decorated in purple that was also often the *couleur du jour* for his attire. Generations of alumni recall Ford's commitment to their best interest and his tireless work in the University's behalf. Over the next several years, Ford continued to assist the University through student recruiting among area community colleges.

§

One of the most significant developments during the presidency of Dr. Hodo was the emergence of the President's wife as an independent figure on her own merit. From the day of the announcement of his election as President, Dr. Hodo clearly indicated that the couple approached their HBU opportunity as a team. With great élan, Sadie Hodo enthusiastically filled the role of a helpmeet to her husband, but also effectively

---

228 *SomeTimes,* Dec. 1996.

229 *SomeTimes*, Mar. 1997.

230 *SomeTimes,* Jan. 1997.

231 Houston Baptist University, Minutes of the Meetings of the Board of Trustees, Meeting on 23 Nov. 1997.

232 Allen Jones, "Director of Admissions resigns after 24 years," *The Collegian,* 20 Mar. 1997, p. 1. Photo.

233 Raequel Roberts, "Just Don't Call them Crazy," *Houston Post*, 6 Nov. 1988, p. 4. Photo.

revealed her own individual persona in activities of support related to the University. Appropriately, in 1995 she was named Woman of the Year by the Association of Women Students.[234] In a series of *Collegian* articles about her, Dr. Hodo commented, "She is a gracious wife, hostess and ambassador for the University who truly has the gift of hospitality and uses it to assist me in my job. . . . We work well together and enjoy our respective roles."[235] A former faculty member herself, Mrs. Hodo was aware of the potential of her role with various constituencies. The birth of the "First Lady" title on the HBU campus emanated from her view of her own sense of mission. Of her a friend observed, "She sees the eternal significance of what she does."[236] She was active as a hostess in the President's Home and was a member of the American Museum Society, the University Auxiliary, and the President's Advisor's Guild. She was also committed to her family, her church, Bible teaching, and to her hobbies. Whether on an early morning campus walk or present at virtually every major campus event, Sadie (as she preferred to be called) was a familiar figure to students, faculty, and staff alike. In 1996, Dr. Hodo established the Sadie Branch Hodo endowed scholarship in her honor.[237]

The years 1994-98 marked one of the most poignant periods of University history in terms of personal loss. Among those who passed away during these years were many of the most outstanding individuals in the University's history including Board Chairs Dr. William Denham, Howard Lee Sr.,[238] and Bill Merrill; trustees Ethel McDermott,[239] Boyd Waltman, and Robbie Robertson; and, benefactors James E. Lyon[240] and Frank Sharp.[241] Of Dr. William Denham, the founding Chair of the Board of Trustees, the *Austin Statesman* observed, "It was through his courage and an uncommon faith in God that he willingly stepped beyond the boundaries of all known security and elected to live what he perceived

---

234 Leslie E. Tripp, "First lady of University honored during convocation," *The Collegian*, 11 May 1995, p. 3.
235 Melodie Francis, "Sadie: Our First Lady," *The Collegian*, 11 Sept. 1997, p. 5. Photos.
236 Melodie Francis, "First Lady, part two," *The Collegian*, 9 Oct. 1997, p. 5. Photo.
237 Melodie Francis, "Sadie: Our First Lady," *The Collegian*, 11 Sept. 1997, p. 5. Photos.
238 "In Memoriam," *HBU News*, Nov. 1997, 34. Lee was a Founder, had served as Chair of the Board of Trustees, Chair of the Academic Committee, a member of the President's Development Council, and was the donor of an Endowed Academic Scholarship and the recipient of an honorary degree from the University in May, 1994.
239 McDermott was a trustee, donor of the McDermott Plaza, and advocate for campus beautification.
240 "Rites set for developer, banker James E. Lyon," *Houston Chronicle*, 2 May 1993, sec. A, p. 27, four-star ed.
241 "Frank Sharp is dead at 87," *New York Times*, 5 Apr. 1993, (accessed Mar. 26, 2010).

to be God's call."[242]   Denham had participated in Founders' Day ceremonies on the campus only twenty days before his death.[243]

Members of the faculty and staff who passed away included Frances Arnold,[244] Molly Middlekauf,[245] Dr. O. D. Martin,[246] Gail Swider,[247] Dr. R. G. Commander,[248] Dr. Frank Mahoney,[249] Cecil Pickett,[250] Dr. Bill Dacres,[251] Dr. Henry Eason,[252] Virginia Babikian,[253] Dr. James Leavell,[254] Dorothy Allen,[255] Dr. Dillard Isabel,[256] Georgia Frazer,[257] Juanita Pool,[258] and Dr. Tom Holland.[259]   In addition to the personal loss, the cumulative effect of the death of so many colleagues who had played significant roles in University history was palpable.

§

---

242 "Tribute to a founding trustee," *HBU News*, Mar. 1998, 10.

243 *SomeTimes*, Oct, 1997.

244 "Founding Staff Member: Frances Arnold," *HBU News*, Feb. 1995, 27. Arnold was the institution's first secretary employed to work with Dr. Dillon before 1962. She also served as an early President of the Auxiliary.

245 "In Memoriam," *HBU News*, June 1996, 21. Middlekauf was a beloved member of the Registrar's staff from 1966-74.

246 "In Memoriam," *HBU News*, Feb. 1997, 38.

247 The 12 Dec. 1996 issue of *The Collegian* was dedicated to custodian Gail Swider. "We will miss your sweet smile, your kind word, and your gentle spirit."

248 "Obituary: R. G. Commander," *Rocky Mountain News*, 22 Feb. 1998, sec. B, p. 10. Commander was an area pastor for 60 years, was active in the formation of the College in the UBA period, and served in the development department of the College from 1963-65. He is the author of a book on UBA history.

249 "Dr. Francis X. Mahoney," *HBU News*, Mar. 1998, 38. Associate Professor Frank Mahoney was a national leader in Human Resources Management. He began teaching as an adjunct in 1979 and was named to a full time position in 1992 upon his retirement from Exxon. He was the founder of the Human Resources Institute and Director of the Masters in Human Resource Management program.

250 Ann Holmes, "Teacher Cecil Pickett touched the lives of many fine acting talents," *Houston Chronicle*, 21 Nov. 1997, Houston sec., p. 3, two-star ed.

251 "In Memoriam," *HBU News*, Nov. 1997, 34. Dacres was a founding faculty member and Chair of the Department of Biology.

252 "In Memoriam," *HBU News*, Aug. 1997, 25. Eason served as Professor in Drama from 1964-67.

253 Charles Ward, "Soprano and Choral Conductor Dies," *Houston Chronicle*, 24 Mar. 1997, Houston sec., p. 3, two-star ed. Babikian was Artist-in-Residence from 1965-82. Charles Ward writing for the *Houston Chronicle* described Babikian as "the revered soprano soloist, choral conductor, and teacher."

254 "In Memoriam," *HBU News*, Feb. 1997, 38.

255 "In Memoriam: Dorothy Allen," *HBU News*, Oct. 1996, 22.

256 Stephanie A. De Los Santos, "Memorial service held to honor sociology professor," *The Collegian*, 7 Sept. 1995, p. 10. Photo. Isabel was Assistant Professor of Sociology from 1990-95.

257 Frazer served on the library staff from 1972-92.

258 "Anna Juanita Pool," *HBU News*, Dec. 1998, 25. Juanita Pool died at 90 having worked for the School of Nursing for only seven years. Photo of Phyllis and Juanita Pool.

259 Allen Jones, "Holland praised as scholar and friend," *The Collegian*, 11 Sept. 1997, p. 3; "In Memoriam: Dr. Thomas Holland, Jr," *HBU News*, Aug. 1997, 25. Photo. Holland was Chair of Behavioral Science and Director of the Counseling and Testing Center until 1993. He was remembered for possessing a good blend of rigor and empathy. His 600-volume library was given to the Moody Library collection.

In 1995, the alumni organization changed its name to the Association of Former Students. At that time, the University had awarded degrees to 8,594 students and had served a total of 29,099 students over the thirty-two years of its history.[260] C. Pat Ellis '68 was elected the first alumnus chair of the Board of Trustees in 1996.[261] In succeeding years, the Board would be headed by other alumni including David Stutts '82 in 2001, Dr. Mark Denison '82 in 2003, Diane Williams '93 in 2005, Ray Cox, Jr. '81 in 2006, Rick Bailey '69 in 2008, Bob Powell '76 in 2009, and Ed Seay '73 in 2010. In 1997, the first graduating class celebrated the thirtieth anniversary of its graduation. The third edition of an HBU alumni directory was published in 1998 under the leadership of Matthew Diehl '90 as Director of the Alumni Association and Dr. Mark Denison '82, Chair of the Alumni Association.[262] Shortly thereafter, the Association of Former Students established endowed scholarships honoring faculty members Dr. James Taylor and Dr. Gene Wofford.[263]

Beginning in 1990, the University annually recognized alumni who had made a distinctive, sustained contribution to their professions. Those alumni so honored were Pamela K. Moore '74 and Stephen Pickett '80 in 1994, Dr. Linda Fix Roff '69 and Rick Bailey '69 in 1995, Elaine Wood '80 and Ron Stone MLA '94 in 1996, and Dr. Elizabeth Harkins '73 and Dr. Thomas Wheeler '75 in 1997. The University also recognized alumni who had made significant, sustained contribution toward the advancement of the University. Dawn Nelson '90 and Steve Braun '80 were the recipients of this award in 1994; Amy Butler Swartz '89 and Ray Cox, Jr. '81 in 1995; Dr. Jennifer Berry Ferguson '69 and Chuck Lang, III '75 in 1996; and Avie Croom Bailey '68 and Saliem Kahleh '84 in 1997.[264] These individuals were permanently recognized by inclusion in the campus Walk of Honor, paved with commemorative tiles detailing the name of the honorees and the date of recognition.[265]

Other alumni achieved notable recognition. Dr. Carol Ann Bonds '68 was the winner of the 1996 Robert Wood Johnson Foundation National

---

260 Houston Baptist University, Minutes of the Meetings of the Business and Audit Committee, Meeting on 15 Nov. 1995.

261 "Alumni lead Board trustees," *HBU News,* Mar. 1996, 11. Chair Ellis '68 and Vice Chair Curt Floyd '81 were both HBU alumni.

262 Houston Baptist University, *1998 Alumni Directory* (White Plains: Harris Publishing Co, Inc., 1998).

263 Alicia Whitehead, "Scholarships named for Taylor, Wofford," *The Collegian,* 19 Mar. 1998, p. 2.

264 Houston Baptist University, *1998 Alumni Directory,* pp. viii and ix.

265 "Walk of Honor: The Tradition Begins," *HBU News,* Feb. 1997, 22.

Community Health Leader award. Superintendent of schools Dr. Bonds was the first person not directly involved in the health care field ever to receive the award.[266] In April 1995, a newspaper headline, "Scores in the Big League," announced the appointment of alumnus Carlton Thompson '92 as Sports Editor of the *Houston Chronicle.* Thompson had moved to the *Chronicle* from *The Houston Post* and was the first African-American to be named sports editor of the *Chronicle.*[267] Angie Sisk '93[268] and Kara Williams[269] were crowned Miss Texas USA in 1993 and 1994. Tenor Chuck Reid '92 won the Jacobson grant from the Richard Tucker Foundation of New York—the first Texan ever to be selected—and began singing roles with the Metropolitan Opera in 1998.[270] Two alumni were elected to become presidents of colleges during this period. Dr. Ron Ellis '77 was named President of California Baptist College in 1994;[271] Dr. Gary Dill '69 was inaugurated as President of McPherson College in Kansas in 1997.[272] A third alumnus, Dr. Herman Barlow '72, served as President of College of the Southwest in Hobbs, New Mexico prior to his death in 1992. HBU alumnus Colin Montgomerie '89 won the World Championship of Golf in 1997 and was the PGA European Tour's leading money winner for six consecutive years, 1993-1999.[273] In *Golf Magazine,* Montgomerie credited his years at HBU as a turning point in his life. Admittedly indecisive about his life before HBU, Montgomerie credits the University and Coach Mannen as significant forces in his career. "My time at HBU had a total bearing on my career. I wouldn't have turned pro if I hadn't gone there."[274] Montgomerie's autobiography, *The Real Monty*, relates his curious coming to HBU in a chapter titled, "Setting Houston Baptist Alight."[275]

§

266 "1996 Robert Wood Johnson Foundation Community Health Leader," www.rwjf.org/pr/product.jps?id=52191 (accessed Mar. 26, 2010).

267 "Carlton Thompson '92 Scores in the Big League," *HBU News,* Aug. 1995, 29.

268 "Hats off to '94 nominees," *HBU News,* May 1994, 4. Photo.

269 "Miss Texas USA," *HBU News,* Aug. 1995, 6.

270 "Charles Reid '92 Winner of Grant," *HBU News,* May 1997, 21.

271 "CBU celebrates ten year anniversary of Dr. Ron Ellis," www.calbaptist.edu/about/media-center/sub-page/default.aspx?id=1661 (accessed Mar.23, 2010). The inauguration was on April 21, 1994.

272 "Dr. Gary Dill '69 Striving for Excellence and building for the future," *HBU News,* May 1997, 11.

273 European Professional Golfers' Association tour website, www.europeantour.com (accessed Sept. 5, 2009).

274 "Colin Montgomerie '87 BIG winner in Arizona," *HBU News,* Mar. 1998, 39.

275 Colin Montgomerie, *The Real Monty* (London: Orion Books, Ltd, 2002), 5-13.

In student life, the freshmen won the tug-of-war following the 1995 opening fall convocation for the first time in twenty-seven years. Charges of tying one end of the rope to a tree were leveled by both the freshmen and the sophomores.[276] Popular student events during the year continued to be the Husky Revue, the Beauty Pageant, Spring Fling, and International Night.[277] For the college residents, a tradition of Midnight Breakfast was begun. Served initially at midnight and in following years at 10:00 p.m., the breakfast by Sodexho's Parker Higdon was a gift to resident students the night before final exams began each quarter. University administrators donned chef hats and manned the serving positions. It was difficult to determine if the crowds of students were due to the novelty of administrators' food service or hunger.

Students of this era were described as "Generation X: the Abandoned Generation"—those born to baby boomers between 1961 and 1982. This "Baby Buster" generation saw the inception of the home computer, the rise of videogames, and the establishment of the Internet as tools for social purposes. Nationally, these students seemed less engaged, distracted to the point of seeming rude, pragmatic, savvy, more focused on money and career, and generally more amoral. So disengaged seemed students in the classroom that a series of professional growth seminars was provided for HBU faculty studying William Willimon's *The Abandoned Generation: Rethinking Higher Education,*[278] Peter Sacks' *Generation X Goes to College,*[279] and *Generations*[280] by William Strauss and Neil Howe. Faculty members quickly learned that multi-tasking was the new norm as student behavior in the classroom. This generation changed pedagogy and redefined learning style. Author Neil Howe would later present seminars on a second book, *Millennials Rising: the Next Generation,* for the HBU faculty and staff under joint sponsorship of the University and STAMATS.[281]

Generation-X students interacted through informal social groups and were generally disinterested in organized activity.[282] On the HBU

276 Lisa E. Bowlin, "Freshmen break 27-year tradition," *The Collegian,* 21 Sept. 1995, p. 3. Photo.
277 *Ornogah 1996,* 40.
278 William H. Willimon and Thomas H. Naylor, *The Abandoned Generation: Rethinking Higher Education* (Grand Rapids: Wm. B. Eerdmans Publishing Co, 1995).
279 Peter Sacks, *Generation X Goes to College* (Chicago: Open Court Press, 1996).
280 Neil Howe and William Strauss, *Generations* (New York: William Morrow and Co., 1991).
281 Neil Howe and William Strauss, *Millennials Rising: The Next Generation* (New York: Vintage Books-Random House, Inc., 2000).
282 "Campus enthusiasm dwindles," *The Collegian,* 15 April 1993, p. 3.

campus, the Greek fraternities and sororities had trouble maintaining pledge class minimum enrollments.[283] The Student Senate virtually disbanded due to student apathy and lack of participation.[284] A Senate policy that required a minimum of twelve members to maintain a student organization charter became a threat to the survival of some clubs.[285] In 1996, the spring student elections had to be postponed until fall for lack of candidates.[286] Student retention became more of an issue as a result of less student commitment to institutional loyalty.[287] Career Services Director Dr. Larry Root reported the wide-spread disinterest of graduating seniors in job-search seminars.[288] The whole fabric of the University required reshaping to remain effective in dealing with this new generation.

In stark contrast to this social phenomenon, the spring medical mission trips from the University enjoyed large student participation. In 1994, the mission trip to Matamoros, Mexico mounted seven medical teams, four children's teams, two construction teams, and translators.[289] Juarez, Mexico was the site of the 1995 trip that drew the participation of students, faculty, construction teams, children's ministry teams, doctors and nurses.[290] President and Mrs. Hodo were a part of the mission team as were nursing faculty members Debra Berry '89 and Dr. Betty Souther, Director of the CLC Chuck Davis, and Coordinator of Student Activities Saliem Kahleh.[291] The 1997 mission trip inspired the participation of fifty-one students, four nurses, and five administrators to work with the Matamoros Baptist Children's Home.[292]

The student Convocation Committee began work on a revised Spiritual Life Program in concert with the Campus Minister.[293] In 1994, the Center for Exploring Ministry Careers (CEMC) and Serving Every Religious Vocation (SERV) programs were moved from Student Affairs to the Department of Christianity and Philosophy to achieve a higher degree of program coordination. Mark Crumpler was named the new Director

---

283 Julissa Guerrero, "Low numbers affect Greeks," *The Collegian*, 5 Oct. 1995, p. 1.

284 Julissa Guerrero, "Committee reorganizes Student Senate," *The Collegian*, 10 Oct. 1996, p. 1.

285 Julissa Guerrero, "Student Senators debate proposal," *The Collegian*, 24 Oct. 1996, p. 1.

286 Julissa Guerrero, "Committee reorganizes Student Senate," *The Collegian*, 10 Oct. 1996, p. 1.

287 Houston Baptist University, Minutes of the Meetings of the Board of Trustees, Meeting on 27 Sept. 1994.

288 Cynthia Wilson, "Career Services blames apathy on students," *The Collegian*, 30 Jan. 1997, p. 1.

289 Houston Baptist University, Minutes of the Meetings of the Board of Trustees, Meeting on 22 Feb. 1994.

290 Stephanie De Los Santos, "Students spend week serving in Mexico," *The Collegian*, 23 Mar. 1995, p. 6.

291 "Students Minister in Mexico," *SomeTimes*, Mar. 1995.

292 Houston Baptist University, Minutes of the Meetings of the Board of Trustees, Meeting on 20 May 1997.

293 Tara McFadden, "Power to the students," *The Collegian*, 26 Sept. 1996, p. 3.

of the CEMC.[294]   Convocation adopted a new format that offered "First Thursday" that was planned to feature more "high profile speakers."[295]   In 1996, a new plan was introduced to meet convocation requirements with alternate Christian activities—mission trips, Bible studies, Spiritual Emphasis Week activities, community service, retreats, seminars, lectures, and concerts.[296]   The articulated purpose of Convocation was "to provide a medium for credible, sensitive, comprehensible witness to life in Christ; the building of community within a diverse student body; and the sharing of ideas, information, and talents for the enhancement of life."[297]

In a Student Forum that spring, President Hodo committed to providing a "greater variety of religious speakers" to appeal more to the diversity on campus;[298] all programs were still to have a Christian focus.[299] The new policy was approved for a one-year trial.[300]   In addition to convocation, the weekly worship service on campus called "Quest" enjoyed strong student participation.[301]   In June 1995, the name of the Christian Life on Campus (CLC) program was changed to Student Ministry led by a Ministry Leadership Council composed of twenty-two student leaders from selected areas of campus activity.   Other spiritual-life activities included Disciple Now teams, FOCUS and REFUGE performance and witness ensembles, and Masterpiece, a Christian fine arts team.[302]   The University's Recreation Team was in its sixth years of service in 1995 and had worked with over 12,000 summer campers.[303]

In 1995, Rob Matchett and Shawn Shannon were respectively appointed Campus Minister[304] and Director of Student Ministries.[305] Jack Purcell was named Vice President for Student Affairs in June of 1997 succeeding Dr. Lou Shields.[306]   Purcell had served as Assistant Dean of Students since 1994.   Other than Frances Curtis and Kay Allen, Student

294 *SomeTimes,* Sept. 1994.

295 Lisa Bowlin, "Greater student appeal sought in new convocation format," *The Collegian,* 26 April 1995, p. 1.

296 Rochelle Ferrada, "40 years of spiritual life," *HBU News,* Dec. 2003, 15.

297 Ibid.

298 Tara Linn, "President Hodo responds to issues," *The Collegian,* 9 Feb. 1995, p. 3.

299 Houston Baptist University, Minutes of the Meetings of the Board of Trustees, Meeting on 8 Sept. 1995.

300 Houston Baptist University, Minutes of the Meetings of the Board of Trustees, Meeting on 14 May 1995.

301 Houston Baptist University, Minutes of the Meetings of the Board of Trustees, Meeting on 8 Jan. 1995.

302 *SomeTimes,* Mar. 1994.

303 Houston Baptist University, Minutes of the Meetings of the Board of Trustees, Meeting on 8 Sept. 1995.

304 *SomeTimes,* June 1995.

305 Houston Baptist University, Minutes of the Meetings of the Board of Trustees, Meeting on 8 Sept. 1995.

306 Melodie Francis, "Purcell named Student Affairs V.P.," *The Collegian,* 11 Sept. 1997, p. 1. Photo.

Affairs experienced an almost complete re-staffing of its personnel during this period. In 1998, eight new staff members joined Student Affairs including Larry Root, Director of Career Services; John Yarabeck, Associate Vice President for Student Affairs; and Andy Morris, Missions Coordinator.

§

In 1994, the NBA Houston Rockets began to use Sharp Gym for their noontime practice. Students enjoyed the sight of expensive cars behind the gym, TV news coverage, and the players themselves whom the *Ornogah 1996* described as "tall, nice, and fun to be around."[307] However, sharing the Sharp Gym facility with the HBU athletic program created scheduling problems for both organizations. In September 1996, the Rockets moved to permanent training facilities in West Houston provided by Jim "Mattress Mack" McIngvale.[308]

Following the downsizing of the University's athletic program in the late 1980s, stability and achievement had become re-established in the new NAIA context. In 1995, basketball enjoyed its first twenty-win season since 1985. The Husky baseball team was ranked twelfth in the nation and boasted a record of 39 wins and 6 losses. Baseball coach Rusty Pendergrass was named Coach of the Year in the Southwest Region of NAIA.[309] In the spring of 1995, all the University's teams—in basketball, baseball, softball, and volleyball—were in playoffs for the first time in history.[310] In August, Kaddie Mahoney '94 was named coach of the volleyball team succeeding Jennifer Ferguson '69.[311] In the fall, the volleyball team again won the district title,[312] and Mahoney was named Big State Conference Coach of the Year.[313] Mingo II, the new campus mascot, proved to be noise-averse and was replaced in 1995 by Butch[314]—

---

307 *Ornogah 1996*, 214-5.
308 Ronnie Gaines, "Rockets leave Sharp Gym for 'Mattress Mac' facility," *The Collegian*, 29 Sept. 1996, p. 2.
309 "Pendergrass receives honor," *HBU News*, Aug. 1995, 22.
310 J. K. Washington, "Baseball, softball slide into playoffs," *The Collegian*, 27 April 1995, p. 1.
311 *SomeTimes*, July 1995.
312 Houston Baptist University, Minutes of the Meetings of the Board of Trustees, Meeting on 28 Nov. 1995.
313 "Mahoney named Big State Conference Coach of the Year," *HBU News*, Nov. 1995, 20.
314 "New mascot, Butch," *The Collegian*, 23 Mar. 1995, p. 4.

a Samoyed who was housed near the campus police during the week and with his trainers on the weekends.[315]

A number of HBU students were recognized for All-America selection in the 1994-98 period. In 1996-97 Kim Lowe became the first Husky ever named to both the All-America volleyball team and to Academic All-American honors.[316] Selected for All-America honors in basketball were David Preston in 1993-94 and 1994-95,[317] Mike Sissel in 1995-96,[318] Kelton Smith in 1996-97,[319] and Gabe Rapier in 1997-98.[320] The All-America team in softball named Cindy Connell, Jennifer Elias, and Diana Lyons in 1995-96; Connell, Elias, and Jennifer Carruth in 1995-96;[321] and Connell, Becky Dudley, and Jennifer Elias in 1996-97.[322] Peer recognition also came to Sport Information Director Jacque Cottrell in October 1997 when the NAIA selected HBU's *Media Guides* among the top ten in the nation.[323]

The *Houston Chronicle* reported in July 1995 that HBU had applied for membership in Division II of the National Collegiate Athletic Association—a three-year process. Athletic Director Ron Cottrell explained the move was one of self-protection. "A lot of good (NAIA) schools and good conferences are jumping to the NCAA for various reasons."[324] The NAIA had 390 college memberships in 1995, down from 466 members five years earlier. The NAIA provided no reimbursement for playoff expenses and required higher membership fees than the NCAA. Cottrell elaborated, "We're putting ourselves in position so if some things come about with other schools, we can act immediately and not have to wait three years."[325] In August, President Hodo announced that the NCAA had approved the University's application.[326] NCAA Division II membership would require two additional sports for both men and women.

---

315 Jason Brown, "Future dog show champion succeeds former mascot," *The Collegian*, 23 Mar. 1995, p. 4. Photo.

316 *Ornogah* 1997, 186.

317 "Husky teams have record-breaking seasons," *HBU News*, Spring 1995, 10-11.

318 "Mike Sissel named NAIA All-America 1995-96," *The Collegian*, 28 Mar. 1996, p. 11.

319 "Smith breaks record named All America," *HBU News*, May 1997, 19.

320 Houston Baptist University, Minutes of the Meetings of the Board of Trustees, Meeting on 19 May 1998; 2008-9 *HBU Basketball Sports Media Guide*, p. 60.

321 *Ornogah* 1997, 200.

322 2008-9 *HBU Softball Media Guide*, p. 44.

323 *SomeTimes*, Oct. 1997.

324 Richard Dean, "Houston Baptist applies for NCAA Membership," *Houston Chronicle*, 22 July 1995, Sports sec., p. 9.

325 Ibid.

326 "Houston Baptist accepted for NCAA membership," *HBU News*, Aug. 1995, 23.

However, the University never elected to make the move to Division II NCAA, remaining instead as an independent institution in NAIA.

In the spring of 1996, the Husky softball team coached by Mary-Ellen Hall '88 was nationally ranked eighth and advanced to the national tournament for the first time in University history.[327]   The Lady Huskies returned to the national tournament in 1997 and were ranked eleventh in the nation.[328] Softball was ranked seventh nationally in 1998, compiled a record of 28-10, and under coach Mary-Ellen Hall, participated in the national tournament for the third consecutive year.[329]   The HBU baseball team was ranked fourteenth in the NAIA. The team won the Big State Conference championship with a record of 15-0 in 1996.[330] Pendergrass was again elected Coach of the Year.[331] However, in the fall, Pendergrass submitted his resignation, became a major-league scout, and was replaced at HBU by Brian Huddleston.[332]

For the first time in University history, in 1997 the basketball team was nationally ranked—ninth in the Division I poll, broke seven existing HBU records, and was playing as an independent.[333] The team was undefeated at home for the first time, achieved a twenty-two game winning streak, and was the winner of the NAIA team-scoring title with an average of 99 points per game.[334] The team received one of ten at-large berths for its first national tournament appearance, but was defeated in regional playoffs.[335]

In the spring of 1998 the University became a charter member of the Red River Conference thus ending HBU's independent status within the NAIA. HBU's athletic teams were now eligible to play for conference championships and all-conference honors.[336] The Red River Conference

---

327 Rusty Thompson, "Softball makes nationals," *The Collegian*, 9 May 1996, p. 1. Photo.

328 Faseeh U. Khaja, "Softball team gears up for playoffs," *The Collegian*, 15 May 1997, p. 12.

329 *Ornogah 1998,* 180.

330 Andrew Foreman, "Husky baseball clinches first in Conference," *The Collegian*, 25 Apr. 1996, p. 9. Photo.

331 *Ornogah 1996*, 134-138.

332 Faseeh Khaja, "Head coach asked to resign," *The Collegian*, 11 Sept. 1997, p. 1. Photo.

333 Kelly Fitch, "Orange and blue support is lacking," *The Collegian*, 14 May 1998, p. 9.

334 "Husky basketball enjoys history-making season," *HBU News,* Mar. 1998, 28.

335 Richard Dean, "HBU receives at-large berth to NAIA tourney," *Houston Chronicle*, 10 Mar. 1998, Sports sec., p. 4, two-star ed.

336 Kelly Fitch, "Huskies join new conference," *The Collegian*, 30 April 1998, p. 1. Member teams included Jarvis Christian College, College of Southwest Oklahoma, Northwest Oklahoma State, University of Texas Permian Basin, Langston University, Huston-Tillotson College, Southwest Assemblies of God University, LSU Shreveport, Northwood University, and Paul Quinn College.

was the largest conference in the NAIA and included fourteen institutions in four states divided initially into North and South divisions.[337]

§

Houston Baptist University was named one of "America's Best College Buys" in 1996. In a survey of 1782 institutions, those colleges selected had above average SAT scores and institutional costs below the national average.[338] In the fall of 1997, Dr. Hodo articulated his own personal institutional priorities for the near future: 1) a balanced budget; 2) faculty and staff rewards; 3) recruitment and retention of students; 4) the attainment of an endowment of $60,000,000 to $100,000,000 by the year 2010 with increased fund-raising to reduce student dependency on loans; and 5) to "impact attitudes on campus by implementing TQI (total quality management)."[339] Interlaced in the process of strategic planning and total quality management was the need for goal clarification and consensus. Dr. Hodo advanced his personal goal that Houston Baptist University become "one of America's premier, Christian, urban, academic institutions."[340]

At the end of the 1997-98 academic year, the University was poised to undertake the attainment of Dr. Hodo's vision. The period 1994-98 had transformed the campus. The physical campus had added the Hinton Academic Center, the Eula Mae Baugh Student Center, the Husky Village Apartments, and the development of income-producing properties along the Southwest Freeway including the new Memorial Hermann/HBU Wellness Center. The University had acquired an extraordinary collection of American Bibles for the edification of its faculty and students and the enrichment of the University's role in the community.

The Board of Trustees had been fashioned into a more efficient, informed partner in University growth. Financial stability had emerged from real estate ventures, operational cost-cutting, and effective management of resources. Reluctant farewells had been expressed to a generation of extraordinary trustees, donors, faculty, and staff. A new generation of friends and donors was nurtured through the Spirit of Excellence

---

337 "University joins Red River Conference," *HBU News,* June 1998, 15.
338 *SomeTimes,* Oct 1996.
339 Dr. E. D. Hodo, "From the President," *HBU News,* Aug. 1997, 2.
340 Melodie Francis, "Hodo's vision: 'excellence,'" *The Collegian,* 12 Feb. 1998, p. 1.

dinners, the President's Advisors Guild, the American Museum Society, and President's Development Council.

Faculty members produced significant scholarly output in addition to their roles as pedagogues and student mentors. University publications achieved new plateaus of recognition and effectiveness in relating the University to its many publics. New programs of study provided increased options for career preparation. Professional agencies and accrediting bodies honored the University's academic programs with commendation. New centers of activity in the health professions, in economics, and in evangelism flourished. Faculty and students developed processes for strengthening personal faith and found effective means for its expression in the face of increasing cultural and religious diversity. Interaction with visiting scholars and business leaders afforded the opportunity for enhanced learning. International study confirmed the reality of the global village.

Dramatic changes in administrative leadership portended new perspectives of institutional potential. The University sought to be a more effective neighbor through a summer academy for community students by hosting the KIPP Academy program and the Intensive English Institute, programming on television Channel 14, and housing Southwestern Seminary activity on the University campus.

The University's alumni brought distinction to their alma mater with selection for admission to graduate and professional schools and the attainment of career recognition. A strategic plan for University development led to increased numbers of resident students and goals for increased student enrollment. The University confronted the new age of technology in administrative and academic process. A new generation of student multi-taskers challenged traditional approaches to relationships. University athletic teams attained national recognition and moved effectively from their NCAA roots during the Hinton years through NAIA independent status to NAIA Red River Conference membership.

The Celebration of Decades marked the fortieth anniversary of the Union Baptist Association resolution to establish a new college, the thirtieth anniversary of the graduation of the first class, the twentieth anniversary of the establishment of graduate study, and the tenth anniversary of President Hodo. In 1998, the University had its vision on the opportunities for the next ten years.

TWELVE

1998-2002

The average cost of gasoline in the United States in 1998 was $1.15. President Bill Clinton was impeached by the House of Representatives for perjury and obstruction of justice. Google was founded. Windows 98 was released by Microsoft. Apple unveiled the iMac. The Winter Olympic Games were held in Nagano, Japan. Bestsellers included *Tuesdays with Morrie, Angela's Ashes, The Greatest Generation, Sugar Busters,* and *9 Steps to Financial Freedom.* Television viewers were watching *JAG, Star Trek: Deep Space Nine, Friends, The Practice,* and *Law and Order.*

The thirty-sixth class of freshmen enrolled at Houston Baptist University. Student demography had changed dramatically since 1963. Some 1730 undergraduates were now joined by 576 graduate students who represented one-third of the student population. By the late 1990s, seventy percent of the University's students were female; sixty percent were Anglo. African-Americans and Asians each comprised fourteen percent of the student population. Nearly eighty percent were Harris County residents. The Intensive English Institute under the direction of Harold Harris and Avanell Merritt saw its enrollment climb to an all-time high of sixty-two students during the period 1998 to 2002.[1]

Student enrollment increased in these years. In the fall quarter of 2000, enrollment was up five percent to 2519—including 343 freshmen and 656 new undergraduates.[2] By 2002, forty-one home-schooled students were among the 2745 students[3] providing the highest enrollment since 1991.[4] Both residence colleges were enjoying ninety-eight percent occupancy.[5] The University conferred a ceremonial 10,000th degree

1 Kristen Craig, "Intensive English Institute spring enrollment peaks," *The Collegian*, 15 Mar. 2001, p. 5.
2 Amy N. Davis, "Fall undergraduate enrollment sets record," *The Collegian,* 5 Oct. 2000, pp. 1, 5.
3 Houston Baptist University, Minutes of the Meetings of the Board of Trustees, Meeting on 26 Feb. 2002.
4 Houston Baptist University, Minutes of the Meetings of the Board of Trustees, Meeting on 26 Sept. 2000.
5 Houston Baptist University, Minutes of the Meetings of the Board of Trustees, Meeting on 26 Feb. 2002.

on the entire class of graduates in August 1998[6] and honored HBU's oldest graduate, 88-year-old Elizabeth Martin, in May 2000.[7]

A number of new institutional initiatives greeted 1998. In July, a new imaging awareness campaign was unveiled that included a revisited husky symbol and logo, a focus on *HBU* as the institutional moniker, a new slogan, and an "aggressive outdoor and print advertising campaign."[8] Spearheaded by the new Vice President for Advancement Cindy Crane Garbs—recruited by President Hodo for her record of success in corporate marketing—the advertising campaign was part of a larger initiative called the HBU Legacy Plan. The plan, developed as a result of institutional strategic planning activity over the preceding several years, consisted of six initiatives: 1) construction of a "Legacy Center for American Culture and the Performing Arts" to house the campus museums and programs in music, art, and drama; 2) additional endowments for named chairs, professorships, and scholarships; 3) a sports and recreation arena; 4) expanded funding for academic enrichment; 5) improvements to student life recreation facilities; and 6) an intensive program of marketing the University.[9]

At the heart of the print media initiative was a new billboard ad campaign designed by Fogarty, Kline and Partners to emphasize selected, marketable University strengths—cultural diversity, a small college feel in the big city, an excellent faculty in a value-oriented environment, an easily accessible campus "oasis" in the heart of the city, and programs of strength committed to excellence.[10] A new slogan—*Houston's Best University; Houston's Blessed University*—emphasized both commitment to excellence and Christian faith. The campaign was mounted at strategic billboard locations on major traffic arteries and ran simultaneously in the programs for the Houston Symphony Orchestra, the Houston Grand Opera, and the Society for the Performing Arts.[11] The campaign proved so successful that it was expanded in 1999 to include the *Houston Chronicle,* the *Wall Street Journal,* the *Houston Business Journal, Houston Lifestyle Magazine,* and the local editions of *Newsweek, TIME* magazine, and *U. S. News and World*

---

6 Joe Balat, "10,000th degree confirmed (sic)," *The Collegian,* 24 Sept. 1998, p. 1. Photo. All the graduates were honored as "10,000th graduate" and received a commemorative medallion.

7 Claudia Feldman, "88 year-old takes on her great-grandson's challenge," *Houston Chronicle,* 19 June 2000, Houston sec., pp. 1-2, two-star ed; *HBU News,* Feb. 1997, cover photograph.

8 *Sometimes,* July 1998.

9 Houston Baptist University, Minutes of the Meetings of the Board of Trustees, Meeting on 11 Aug. 1998.

10 Alicia Whitehead, "Ad campaign launched," *The Collegian,* 24 Sept. 1998, p. 1.

11 "Billboards are up!" *SomeTimes,* Oct.1998.

Report.[12]   The design for phase-one of the campaign featured familiar, triplet acronyms juxtaposed with a concise summary statement, i.e., "NBC, CBS, HBU: three things to do with your evenings."   By the third year of the program in 2002, similar white on black copy proclaimed, "Where your professor knows you from Adam" and "Where business ethics is more than a class."[13]   The campaign was the winner of a Crystal Award from the American Marketing Association.[14]

To the delight of the University family, the new marketing campaign addressed the frustrating charge that HBU was "the best kept secret in Houston."[15]   Market visibility in Houston was a problem for business as well as education.   With extensive competition in the urban environment, the careful market placement of the institution among its competitors was a delicate art.   Tuition of $13,500 at HBU was less than at most area private colleges but among the highest at Baptist institutions.[16]   The *Collegian* labeled tuition increases as "competitive," but chronicled an eighty-six percent increase in HBU tuition over nine years.[17]   Student recruiting had become challenged by a number of distant Texas universities with established Houston campuses; competition was now also coming from a new category of highly-funded, well-managed institutions in the for-profit sector, i.e., the University of Phoenix.[18]   This era gave rise to the ratings of colleges and universities by independent third-party sources—based on a variety of considerations.   In October 1998, the University was named in "America's Best Christian Colleges" and "America's 100 Best College Buys."[19]   Both these recognitions supported the University's marketing strategy for recruiting new students.   The Hall Group, Inc., led by Jackie Hall, was engaged to explore new avenues of "energy and certainty" leading to a marketing study of potential new University initiatives.[20]

---

12 Houston Baptist University, Minutes of the Meetings of the Board of Trustees, Meeting on 23 Nov. 1999.

13 "Ad campaign moves into Phase III," *HBU News*, June 2002, 8.

14 *SomeTimes,* July 2002.

15 Houston Baptist University, Minutes of the Meetings of the Faculty Assembly, Meeting on 20 Oct. 1998.

16 HBU tuition charges were twenty-two percent less than the University of St. Thomas, eighteen percent under Baylor, twenty-five percent under Incarnate Word, twenty-four percent under Texas Lutheran, but two percent over Hardin-Simmons, and ten percent over Dallas Baptist. Of these institutions, only St. Thomas and Baylor represented institutions with which HBU ordinarily competed for students.

17 Alicia Whitehead, "New tuition rates competitive," *The Collegian,* 14 Jan. 1999, p. 1.

18 Nicole Yenkinson, "For-profit universities on the rise," *The Collegian,* 10 Dec. 1998, p. 2.

19 Marlo Holdren, "HBU earns top ranking," *The Collegian,* 8 Oct. 1998, p. 1.

20 Houston Baptist University, Minutes of the Meetings of the Board of Trustees, Meeting on 24 Nov. 1998.

Architect Barry Moore was employed to develop conceptual planning for the new Legacy Center and provide data and renderings for communicating the campaign to prospective donors.[21] The Legacy Center was conceived to accomplish a broad range of objectives uniting the University and the Houston community. The facility was proposed with the strong mandate

> to focus on preserving and heralding the legacy of the Christian perspective of our founding fathers; to be a hub of activity serving the community with family-friendly performances and enriching cultural experience; to be the home of the University's museums and fine arts departments; to feature theaters, galleries, recital halls, classrooms, studios, and a social foyer. It was designed to be viewed as the University's gift to the Houston community.[22]

Initially, the "Legacy Center for American Culture and the Performing Arts" was planned for a portion of the west campus adjacent to the Sharp Gymnasium to provide a "new front door for the campus on the Southwest Freeway."[23] Moore was asked to develop a plan for a "multi-function facility" which would add a field house component to the fine arts plan.[24] This concept reflected the 1982 Crain/Anderson architectural concept for a special events center that provided for assembly, athletics, and performance.[25]

In April 1999, the Board of Trustees under Chair Max Crisp received the Hall Group survey results, Moore's architectural proposals, and the fund-raising proposal from the administration. The Hall Group survey encouraged the plan to "embrace neighbors and develop a center for family entertainment and educational opportunity."[26] However, Hall found the name Legacy Center to have elitist connotations that might be avoided with the title "Center for American Culture."[27] Moore's architectural proposal projected a $42,000,000 complex, parts of which could reasonably be expected to be rented to the community several days weekly.[28]

---

21 Houston Baptist University, Minutes of the Meetings of the Board of Trustees, Meeting on 11 Aug. 1998.

22 Houston Baptist University, Minutes of the Meetings of the Board of Trustees, Meeting on 22 Sept. 1998.

23 Houston Baptist University, Minutes of the Meetings of the Board of Trustees, Meeting on 11 Aug. 1998.

24 Ibid.

25 "Feasibility Study for The University Events Center: Houston Baptist University," Crain/Anderson, Inc., Architects, 1982. Houston Baptist University archives.

26 Houston Baptist University, Minutes of the Meetings of the Board of Trustees, Meeting on 23 Feb. 1999.

27 Houston Baptist University, Minutes of the Meetings of the Faculty Assembly, Meeting on 23 Mar. 1999.

28 Houston Baptist University, Minutes of the Meetings of the Board of Trustees, Meeting on 27 Apr. 1999.

Consideration was given to the conversion of the Sharp Gym for fine arts instruction and simultaneous construction of a "sports and special events center" along with the performing arts complex. The "Center for American Culture" became the working title for the project which received conceptual approval from the Board of Trustees.[29]   Mark Dulworth was employed to assist in developing a fund-raising plan.[30]

Plans for a fine arts complex had been at the forefront of administrative attention from the very beginning of College history. The *1966 Ornogah* contains a portrait of President Hinton standing before an architectural rendering for such a proposed facility.[31] The same rendering was presented in the *On Our Way: a decade of proof 1963-1973—a decade of promise 1973-1983* promotion for Gilbert Turner's ten-year capital needs campaign.[32] The site for the facility, however, had historically been proposed at the east end of the campus with direct access both to Fondren Road and Beechnut Street.

§

The Spirit of Excellence dinners came to be prime fund-raising sources for selected campus projects. The fall 1998 dinner at the Westin Galleria Hotel netted $66,000 for redecorating Hinton House, home of the Office of Admissions.[33] The Milton Cross Award for volunteerism was given to Dona Williamson for her forty years of involvement with the dream for a college along with her husband, founding trustee Dr. James Williamson. She was honored for her own leadership as first president of the Auxiliary and as a member of the President's Advisors, the President's Development Council, the Covenant Society, and the Friends of the Library.[34] Special honorees for the event were former Chair of the Board of Trustees Bruce Belin and his wife Mary Ann, a member of the President's Advisors,[35] who had designed and coordinated the redecoration of Hinton House.[36]

---

29 Alicia Whitehead, "American Cultural Center planned," *The Collegian,* 13 May 1999, p. 1.
30 Houston Baptist University, Minutes of the Meetings of the Board of Trustees, Meeting on 28 Sept. 1999.
31 *Ornogah 1996,* 19.
32 Houston Baptist University, *On Our Way: a decade of proof 1963-1973—a decade of promise 1973-1983,* p. 3.
33 Houston Baptist University, Minutes of the Meetings of the Board of Trustees, Meeting on 22 Sept. 1998.
34 Dona Williamson continued her education by participating in one of Dr. Rhonda Furr's summer European study trips.
35 Alicia Whitehead, "Patrons honored at University annual award gala," *The Collegian,* 15 Sept. 1998, p. 1. Photo of Belins.
36 "PDC celebrates Hinton House Renovation," *HBU News,* Aug. 1990, 4. Photo.

The spring 1999 dinner was the most ambitious of any such University undertaking since the 1969 President's Council Dinner featuring Ronald Reagan. The featured speaker in 1999 was the former British Prime Minister, Margaret Thatcher. Donors Robert and Janice McNair served as honorary chairs for the evening.[37] Proceeds from this dinner were designated to provide marketing funds for the "Center for American Culture" project. Ron Stone, popular television newscaster and MLA '94 graduate, moderated the evening and interviewed Lady Thatcher in a "fireside chat" setting. More than 530 guests contributed $548,000 for University advancement.[38] Lady Thatcher endeared herself by making time for students, by greeting personal friends, and by her candor and directness in response to selected questions posed from the guests.

President Hodo expressed his excitement about the University's future in his April 1999 *HBU News* greeting:

> The Thatcher event helped launch the University into greater circles in the Houston community. . . . From a fund raising standpoint, this was a milestone in University history. . . . We were able to showcase the University to new friends. . . . With our *Houston's Best University; Houston's Blessed University* campaign . . . we take our message to new audiences. . . . The University's financial undergirding is sound. . . . We are in a place to address the daily needs of the institution, build our endowment, and embark on new and exciting opportunities as we face the next decade.[39]

§

President Hodo initiated a concentrated period of infrastructure improvement for the campus. In 1998, the College of Arts and Humanities offices were reconfigured and upgraded along with an academic suite for the Department of Communications that provided a darkroom facility and a newsroom for *The Collegian*.[40] Additional remodeling provided improved housing for Information Technology, the Intensive English Institute, the Office of Advancement, and the Department of Music.[41] In April 1999, the Board approved $395,000 for remodeling of

---

37 "A Legacy Evening with Lady Margaret Thatcher," *HBU News,* Apr. 1999, 4-5. Photos.
38 Alicia Whitehead, "Thatcher dinner grosses $548,000," *The Collegian,* 18 Mar. 1999, p. 1.
39 Dr. E. D. Hodo, "From the President," *HBU News,* Apr. 1999, 2.
40 Houston Baptist University, Minutes of the Meetings of the Board of Trustees, Meeting on 24 Feb. 1998.
41 Houston Baptist University, Minutes of the Meetings of the Board of Trustees, Meeting on 22 Sept. 1998.

the twenty-two-year-old Cullen Science Center laboratories, classrooms, and offices.[42] In addition, funds were provided for construction of a new jogging trail adjacent to the residence colleges and for perimeter fencing along Beechnut Street.[43]

Upon completion of the remodeling of Hinton House, the President's Development Council provided an additional $80,000 for the remodeling of the M. D. Anderson Student Center.[44] After the opening of the Baugh Center, many students had experienced a "loss of community" and a sense "that the well-established pattern of socialization in the M. D. Anderson Center failed to transfer to the Baugh Center."[45] Non-residential students seemed particularly affected. The Anderson location of the Campus Store, the post office, Student Life offices, and the snack bar were prime attractions. Vice President Jack Purcell developed a plan to provide "balanced" and complementary facilities between the two venues. A new Enrichment Center, housed in the former Anderson cafeteria space, was created to combine the University's career guidance and personal counseling services in a single location that would elicit heightened student participation.[46] In the fall of 2000, the Fire House Grill in Anderson was upgraded to "benefit commuters and encourage community activity."[47] The resultant Bone Appétit Café opened in December to enthusiastic student and staff reception.[48] In addition, the remodeled M. D. Anderson Student Center featured new furniture, carpeting, and vending in addition to the new food court concept.[49]

Not all such improvements to the campus infrastructure were so apparent. With significant but less visible action, the campus chillers and boilers were replaced; the campus electrical system capacity was doubled; and extensive additions were made to the campus storm drainage capacity. In a *2001 President's Report* in the *HBU News*, campus improvements were delineated that included completion of the Hinton Center, the Baugh Center, the 256-bed addition to Husky Village, the 104-bed Mest wing on the women's residence, new courts— for tennis, sand volleyball,

---

42 Ayesha Shaikh, "Science building renovated," *The Collegian,* 23 Sept. 1999, p. 12.

43 Houston Baptist University, Minutes of the Meetings of the Board of Trustees, Meeting on 27 Apr. 1999.

44 "PDC Honored," *HBU News,* May/June 2000, 18.

45 Joe Balat, "Forum focuses on loss of community," *The Collegian,* 11 Feb. 1999, p. 1.

46 "Campus Updates," *SomeTimes,* Sept. 1999, p. 2; Houston Baptist University, Minutes of the Meetings of the Board of Trustees, Meeting on 28 Sept. 1999.

47 Melissa Torres, "Fire House Grill renovated, timing 'inconvenient,'" *The Collegian,* 21 Sept. 2000, p. 4.

48 Tricia Musser, "Bone Appétit Café open to students," *The Collegian,* 7 Dec. 2000, p. 3.

49 Houston Baptist University, Minutes of the Meetings of the Board of Trustees, Meeting on 21 Nov. 2000.

and outdoor basketball, a jogging track, and campus perimeter fencing. Atwood I, the Cullen Science Center, and the Brown Quadrangle had been dramatically upgraded.[50]

§

Many elements of Dr. Hodo's personality had dramatic influence on the nature of campus operation. He delighted in an early start to the day, ordinarily following his morning devotion with a physical workout, arriving at his office before 8 a.m. Time management shaped his practice. It was not unusual for him to attend a daytime meeting in a distant city and return to his office before 5 p.m. His attention characteristically fell on specific opportunities for improved service and support; it was his penchant to reconnoiter the campus on a regular basis, key in hand, to discover underutilized space. Not since H. B. Smith had the campus been the attention of such scrutiny. Dr. Hodo was known on campus for his campaigns to turn off room lights and computer terminals, conserve water, reduce the use of paper and envelopes for campus announcements, and darken campus parking lots after midnight. Presidential responses were usually hand-written on the original memo and returned to the sender; submitted reports were often returned rather than kept after reading. The President traveled "quick and light;" a ride in his Chevrolet Suburban was often a memorable experience. Nonetheless, Hodo's perspicacity for conservation was often realized in annual spending well-under budgeted allocation.

From the first announcement of his election as President, Dr. Hodo clearly communicated that the decision to accept was a joint one with his wife Sadie. She shared the spotlight at his first introduction to the campus and was a familiar participant in all aspects of University life and activity. In acknowledgement and appreciation of her role of involvement, the Board of Trustees presented a Resolution of Appreciation to her in 1999:

> Whereas for over twelve years, Sadie Hodo has continuously given of her time, her talent, and herself to further the interests of Houston Baptist University, and whereas the Board of Trustees wishes to recognize her for her efforts and achievements at the University, be it resolved by the Board of Trustees of Houston Baptist University that Tuesday, November 23, 1999 is hereby

---

50 Dr. E. D. Hodo, "President's Report: Facilities," *HBU News*, Spring 2001, 43.

recognized as *Sadie Hodo Day* at HBU in appreciation of her service rendered to the University.[51]

§

New campus leadership characterized this period. In January 1999, Dr. Clint Grider was appointed Assistant Vice President for Development and moved from a similar position at Baylor College of Medicine.[52] David Melton was appointed Director of Undergraduate Admissions replacing Judy Smelser who had been advanced to Director of Development for Information Management.[53] HBU alumnus Don Anderson '68 was appointed Director of Alumni Development. Anderson's appointment marked a point of institutional maturity at which HBU alumni were becoming more represented in University leadership roles. He joined the other HBU alumni on the faculty, staff, and Board of Trustees that included Leslie Kennedy Adams '86, Deb Berry '89, Vivian Camacho '91, Lucindra Campbell '94, Ray L. Cox, Jr.'81, Dr. Mark Denison '82, C. Pat Ellis '68, Jennifer Berry Ferguson '68, Rebecca Helmreich '82, David House '96, Eloise Hughes '93, Saliem Kahleh '84, Walter Lumpkin '81, Lisa Penafiel '87, Kaddie Platt '94, Bob Powell '76, Linda Fix Roff '69, David Stutts '82, Rita Tauer '85, Loree Watson '80, Brenda Whaley '79, Diane Williams '93, and Nancy Yuill '72 among others. With Anderson's appointment in 1999, the recent name of Association of Former Students reverted to Alumni Association.[54]

Distinguished Alumni Awards were given in 1998 to Dr. Judith Wallis '81 and Colin Montgomerie '87, Lisa Morris Simon '76 and Dr. Mark Denison '82 in 1999, Dr. Ron Ellis '77 in 2000, Bob Beauchamp '87 in 2001, and Dr. Cliff McGee, Jr. '89 in 2002. Meritorious Service Alumnus Awards were given Rita LaRue '94 and Dick Hudson '75 in 1998, Rosemary Laird '87 and Rick Bailey '69 in 1999, Bob Powell '76 in 2000, Judi Vogel Pyburn '94 in 2001, and Vivian Camacho '91 in 2002.[55]

One of Dr. Hodo's goals was to affiliate with the Council of Christian Colleges and Universities (CCCU). In the fall of 2000, HBU joined ninety-five other institutions in the Council whose mission was "to advance the

---

51 Houston Baptist University, Minutes of the Meetings of the Board of Trustees, Meeting on 23 Nov. 1999.

52 "Grider joins Advancement Team," *SomeTimes*, Dec. /Jan. 1999, 1.

53 Donald Kinyanjui, "Smelser named director of development," *The Collegian*, 29 Apr. 1999, p. 2.

54 (Vivian Camacho to Dr. Don Looser, Aug. 24, 2009).

55 Houston Baptist University, *2008 Alumni Today Directory*, pp. viii, ix.

cause of Christ-centered higher education and effectively integrate biblical faith, scholarship, and service."[56]   CCCU membership offered expanded entré to prospective students through the organization's marketing activities.   The Council offered a community of Christian colleges—in addition to the Baptist college family—and afforded national recognition through CCCU's recruiting, marketing, and lobbying programs.

Among the faculty, the appointment of two new deans proved to alter the course of institutional achievement dramatically.   Dr. James S. Taylor was named Dean of the College of Arts and Humanities in 1998 succeeding Dr. Harold Raley who elected to move to the position of Scholar-in-Residence.[57]   A member of the University faculty since 1973, Taylor had served as Chair of the Department of Communications and, in 1996, had been named Associate Dean of the College.   Taylor received the Opal Goolsby Teacher of the Year Award in 1977 and 1989.   He was recognized by the University's Association of Former Students with the establishment of an Endowed Scholarship in his name for "his excellence in teaching and outstanding contributions to higher education."[58]   A self-professed "teacher at heart," Taylor had nonetheless anchored a number of administrative responsibilities including Chair of the Athletic Committee.   He was universally respected as an influential colleague in promoting faculty/administration communication and understanding.[59] With Taylor's appointment as Dean, Dr. Phyllis Thompson was named Associate Dean of the College of Arts and Humanities.[60]

In the College of Business and Economics, Dr. Lynn Gillette was appointed Dean in June 1998.   Gillette came from Hardin-Simmons University where he had served as Dean for four years.[61]   A *Collegian* article introduced Gillette as a man of intense energy and keen intelligence who firmly believed student learning to be his top priority.   "I want the focus to be on what the student learns, not on what the teacher teaches." Gillette proposed a pedagogical model based on "active learning," hands-on experience, and the development of a wider variety of skills—how to listen, communicate, solve problems, work as a team, and gain interna-

---

56 "CCCU extends membership to HBU," *SomeTimes,* Sept. 2000, p. 2.
57 "Raley appointed Scholar-in-Residence," *HBU News,* Oct. 1998, 21.
58 "College welcomes new deans," *SomeTimes,* July 1998.
59 "Taylor, Gillette lead colleges," *HBU News,* Oct. 1998, 5.
60 Merin Brown, "Thompson 'honored, challenged' by promotion to Associate Dean," *The Collegian,* 13 Apr. 2000, p. 3.
61 "College welcomes new deans," *SomeTimes,* July 1998.

tional perspective.[62] Gillette predicted, "We expect industry to court our graduates with a different level of enthusiasm as soon as word of our resources and their use reaches the business community."[63]

With these two appointments, Toto was no longer in Kansas.[64] Neither College had ever before been so transformed by such leadership. Both new deans brought immediate energy and creativity to their programs. Taylor sprang from the advantage of long-term observation and analysis of the existing academic program. Gillette's new perspective and enthusiasm combined with his commitment to pedagogical revolution. *The Collegian* found many shared values in the two colleges. Taylor emphasized active learning and problem-based learning in the classroom. He stressed the commitment of the College to the inculcation of "Judeo-Christian values and beliefs, critical thinking, effective communication skill, aesthetic appreciation, information literacy, life and career management skills, and a global perspective in a multicultural world."[65] Within several months, Taylor established a departmental honors program[66] and created an Academic Resource Center staffed by faculty volunteers to provide assistance for student papers, speeches, applications, and résumés. No institutional program of tutoring was provided at this time.[67]

Entrepreneurial development of new programs flourished in all the academic colleges. A series of *Collegian* articles addressed the wave of curricular expansion. Under Dean Doris Warren's leadership, the College of Science and Mathematics exploited the potential of the double major and created a complementary second major in Biochemistry/Molecular Biology (BCMB).[68] The biology major had long ranked among the two most popular majors in the University. The new program was paired with the traditional major. The new major acknowledged rapid interdisciplinary changes in scientific thought and marked a path toward visibility of wider career choices in addition to medicine.[69] The BCMB major quickly became one of the most popular options for students in science.[70] The College initiated a study of freshman performance in science courses

62 Reese Nash, "Students' learning is top priority for new dean," *The Collegian,* 24 Sept. 1998, p. 2.

63 Houston Baptist University, Minutes of the Meetings of the Board of Trustees, Meeting on 18 May 1999.

64 The paraphrase is a reference to Dorothy's famous line to her dog in the 1939 movie *The Wizard of Oz.*

65 Jess Rogers, "Colleges share many common goals," *The Collegian,* 7 Oct. 1999, p. 1.

66 Alicia Whitehead, "Honors program proposed for fall," *The Collegian,* 13 May 1999, p. 1.

67 Michelle Cavazos, "Resource center focuses on writing, speech," *The Collegian,* 19 Oct. 1999, p. 4.

68 "College of Science and Mathematics," *HBU News,* May/June 2000, 33.

69 "New Academic Programs developed for 2000," *HBU News,* Mar. 2000, 24.

70 Houston Baptist University, Minutes of the Meetings of the Board of Trustees, Meeting on 26 Sept. 2000.

called "Fish at Risk" to enhance the level of academic success. Eventual analysis of this study established departmental tutorial programs and the revision of the sequence of freshman biology courses. The College further developed a composite science major for teacher education and pioneered *Math for Critical Thinking* as an option for non-science majors.[71] Finally, finding competition for recruiting the finest students increasingly competitive, the College secured a $500,000 multi-year grant for science scholarships from the Gordon and Mary Cain Foundation.[72]

Dr. Doris Warren was one of the University's strongest proponents of the value of a broad liberal arts education. Throughout University history, Warren's record of advocacy for a pervasive liberal arts foundation for students in all majors has been a significant force of support for the University's vision. It is significant that the Deans of Science and Mathematics and Nursing, Warren and Yuill '72, stood historically as strong proponents of curricular fidelity to the University's liberal arts roots. Over the years, Yuill '72 chaired committees for review of Smith College requirements, revision of the University's mission and purpose statements, and advocacy for cultural literacy throughout the curriculum.

In 1998, the University was approached by the Fort Bend Independent School District, working in concert with the for-profit National School Conference Institute, to explore the possibility of mounting an online Master of Education degree to be delivered to some 200 school districts nationwide.[73] Under the plan, Fort Bend personnel would assist in developing a curriculum in instructional technology; the Institute would market the degree with its other professional growth products; and, the University would provide faculty and administrative support to include SACS accreditation, admissions, registration and grading, and the conferring of the degrees.[74] Given the limited capacity of the College of Education faculty for additional assignment, the expansion was a considerable step. However, the opportunity was a bold and exciting move into an academic area that was also needed within the campus major. Dean Bill Borgers and Dr. John Lutjemeier assumed planning and management for the many aspects of the University's responsibility.[75] The first term enrolled 175 teachers in school districts from Trenton, New

---

71 "College of Science and Mathematics," *HBU News,* May/June 2000, 33.
72 "Encore and More," *HBU News,* Sept. 2000, 20.
73 Houston Baptist University, Minutes of the Meetings of the Board of Trustees, Meeting on 19 May 1998.
74 Houston Baptist University, Minutes of the Meetings of the Board of Trustees, Meeting on 22 Sept. 1998.
75 Merin Brown, "University offers long-distance degree," *The Collegian,* 11 Feb. 1999, p. 5.

Jersey to San Antonio, Texas. Students in district cohorts were taught via interactive classes directed to on-site Internet labs that were mentored by local instructional "facilitators."[76] By fall 2001, some 350 graduate students all across the nation were enrolled in the Masters Online program.[77]

College of Business Dean Gillette began the 1999 academic year with dramatic change. Faculty members were instructed in "active teaching" techniques. Gillette asked, "If your class is not the best, why not?" He characterized the teacher as the manager of learning rather than the purveyor of content; every course syllabus was revised to state goals for skill development as well as content. At registration, students were fêted in a social environment with food and refreshments to communicate the message, "You are valued and are the object of our focus."[78] The *Collegian* reported, "The College of Business and Economics is creating a 'buzz' on campus."[79] Gillette initiated a peer advising system by training a group of highly-selected undergraduates,[80] offered a new *Senior-Seminar* in E-commerce, and developed a new Master of Science in Accounting and Information Technology (AIS). Business enrollment for the 1999-2000 year was up forty-five percent over 1998.[81] The stated goal of the College was "to build a strong learning community around great teaching, active learning, and engaging and inspiring students."[82]

Dr. Mike Bourke solicited the cooperation of computer giants Compaq, Oracle, and SAP to establish a Computer Literacy Center in the Hinton Center—one of only six in the nation funded by Compaq.[83] Designed initially to provide specialized training for students in the Master of Science in Management, Computing and Systems, the facility served to bring access to the specialized software to the campus-at-large.[84] At the same time, the College responded to the needs of accountants to prepare for the CPA examination by creating a five-year Master of Accountancy degree—"an innovative program that the accounting profession has been asking education to produce."[85]

---

76 Tomie Lunsford, "Graduate degree available via Internet," *The Collegian,* 7 Dec. 2000, p. 5.
77 "Extending the classroom—on-line," *HBU News,* Dec. 2001, 21.
78 Jess Rogers, "Creating a buzz on campus," *The Collegian,* 23 Sept. 1999, p. 1.
79 Ibid.
80 Jess Rogers, "Peer advising gives students an advantage," *The Collegian,* 21 Oct. 1999, p. 3.
81 "College of Business and Economics," *HBU News,* May/June 2000, 27.
82 Houston Baptist University, Minutes of the Meetings of the Board of Trustees, Meeting on 20 Nov. 2001.
83 Houston Baptist University, Minutes of the Meetings of the Board of Trustees, Meeting on 18 May 1999.
84 Rease Nash, "College of Business gets high-tech computer lab," *The Collegian,* 28 Jan. 1999, p. 1.
85 Jess Rogers, "Masters to be offered in Accounting," *The Collegian,* 18 Mar. 1999, p. 2.

Dean Nancy Yuill '72 fostered the development of a new Associate and Bachelor's nursing curriculum that featured "cutting edge emphasis on the practical applications of content, health management concepts, integration of the Christian faith, career preparation, community involvement, and greater emphasis on wellness and preventions."[86] The new curriculum received written commendation from the Texas Board of Nurse Examiners based on outstanding student performance on the licensure examination.[87] Dr. Yuill described the new curriculum for the National League for Nursing: "The University produces strong graduates who tend to pass the licensure examination on their first attempt and are sought by employers due to their critical thinking, leadership, and therapeutic intervention skills."[88] In 2000, the new Center for Health Studies under the leadership of Dr. Harold Griffin graduated thirteen Master of Science in Health Administration students including the University's first graduate in congregational-care nursing.[89] In testimony to its reputation for excellence, the College received a grant from the Robert Wood Johnson Foundation research in the field of health care strategies.[90]

More than any other college, Arts and Humanities had responsibility both for majors in its disciplines as well as for providing seventy-five percent of the instruction in the Smith College of General Studies. The commitment to learning in the College of Art and Humanities was supported by its record of having sixty-one percent of the Goolsby Teacher recipients selected from among its faculty.[91] Dean Taylor encouraged the development of a Bachelor of Liberal Arts degree designed to "follow in the tradition of a classical Renaissance model—with honors sections, research, emphasis in the classics, and a senior thesis."[92] This program, established in 1999, was also designed to lead directly to admission in the University's Master of Liberal Arts degree. Taylor's dream was that the Bachelor of Liberal Arts would serve to foster the establishment of a University Honors College program as well.

---

86 Sinty Chady, "Nursing Curriculum Improved," *The Collegian,* 21 Oct. 1999, p. 13.
87 Houston Baptist University, Minutes of the Meetings of the Board of Trustees, Meeting on 27 Feb. 2001.
88 Houston Baptist University, Minutes of the Meetings of the Board of Trustees, Meeting on 20 Nov. 2001.
89 Richard Vara, "Nursing the flock: HBU trains students for care giving in churches," *Houston Chronicle,* 31 May 1997, Religion sec., p. 1, two-star ed; "College of Nursing," *HBU News,* May/June 2000, 31; *SomeTimes,* Aug. 2001, p. 4; "Parish nursing program takes holistic approach to health," *Houston Chronicle,* 3 June 2001, Health Care Careers sec., p. 1.
90 *SomeTimes,* "College of Nursing tapped for grant project," May 2001, p. 1.
91 Jess Rogers, "Colleges share many common goals," *The Collegian,* 7 Oct. 1999, p. 1.
92 Houston Baptist University, *Bulletin of Information 1998-2000,* 68.

The Department of Christianity and Philosophy established a Master of Arts in Theological Studies (MATS) degree in 1998 designed to support students in vocational church ministry.[93] Conceived as an alternative to the traditional Master of Divinity program offered by seminaries, preparation for ministry was a commitment of the University through its CEMC program for undergraduates. In 2000, the program was supplemented by an option for a five-year degree that would permit enrollment in nine hours of graduate work in the senior year.[94] The program was based in tutorial study with faculty in one of four areas of theological studies. This instructional model intensified the potential for learning and responded to the uncertainty of initial program enrollments. In 2001, Dr. Walter Lumpkin '81, holder of the Bisagno Chair in Evangelism, established the Antioch Center "for regional, interdenominational ministry emphasis, prayer mobilization, and evangelism."[95]

Through the continuing work of Dr. Sally Phillips, in 1999 the University received a $1,250,000 Title VII grant for scholarships in bilingual education to serve teachers in elementary and secondary programs.[96] This renewable grant provided considerable financial security for the University in support of graduate education over a three-year period and enabled HBU to continue to offer this urgently-needed program to the community. The University's history of contribution in graduate bilingual education began in 1976. The first Title VII grant for scholarships was awarded in 1981, and in the period from 1981 to 2007, over $3,500,000 was awarded to fund tuition for training bilingual and ESL teachers at the undergraduate level and for Master's degree completion at the graduate level.[97]

In 1999, the University's oldest graduate program, the Master of Business Administration, redirected its resources exclusively to the MBA 2000 option and curtailed admission into the Executive program. Dr. Carter Franklin was the founder and pioneer of both programs that were directed toward professionals at different stages of career advancement. For several years, the Executive program had struggled under the heightened competition for executive students with the proliferation of new programs in Houston, particularly the establishment of similar programs at

---

93 Houston Baptist University, Minutes of the Meetings of the Board of Trustees, Meeting on 22 Sept. 1998.
94 Paige Canon, "Christianity majors rewarded with new master's program," *The Collegian*, 10 Feb. 2000, p. 1.
95 "Academic Affairs," *HBU News*, Spring 2001, 41.
96 "Bilingual Scholarships Available," *HBU News*, Nov. 1999, 17.
97 (Report from Dr. Lilita Olano to Dr. Don Looser, Houston Baptist University, Jan. 15, 2010).

Rice University and by Texas A&M at its Woodlands campus.[98] A trend-setter for innovation on the campus, the EMBA was the University's first graduate program and the first University program to issue computers to students. This program was the first to initiate international study as a requisite element of the curriculum. The EMBA focused on experienced executives, offered an innovative evening/weekend schedule of classes, created infrastructure for addressing the particular needs of the executive student, and established an outstanding reputation for excellence in instruction. Consequently, the degree was the pride of the University. For the whole of its history, the EMBA had been a profit center. The program had graduated more than 1,000 professionals who established a powerful alumni community in Houston.[99] In 2001, following Y2K, the name of the MBA 2000 degree was changed to the Professional MBA.[100]

Jennifer Mosley was named Director of Extended Education in November 1999 succeeding Dr. Gerald Evans.[101] One of her first respon-sibilities was to host a week-long conference for the Land Title Institute of the American Land Title Association that attracted one hundred exec-utives from across the nation for a period of intense study and re-certifi-cation.[102] The new Hinton Center facility proved ideal for the conference which returned to the campus again in 2000[103] and in 2001.[104]

In 2000, Southwestern Seminary celebrated the twenty-fifth anniver-sary of its program on the University campus. At the same time, Seminary President Ken Hemphill announced plans to establish an inde-pendent campus.[105] The University and the Seminary had cooperatively funded construction of the Atwood II Building in 1983 and had includ-ed an option for the University to acquire full use of the facility at some future time. As University programs had expanded, critical shortage of both classroom and office space impacted the University programs. Hilda Moffett guided the seminary program that enrolled approximately 200 students in the Doctor of Ministry degree program.[106] Moffett was hon-ored by the Seminary for her service at an April 2000 celebration on

98 Houston Baptist University, Minutes of the Meetings of the Board of Trustees, Meeting on 28 Sept. 1999.
99 "Farewells and transitions," *HBU News,* 15 Sept. 2001, 27.
100 "Academic Affairs," *HBU News,* Spring 2001, 41.
101 "Mosley named director of extended education," *SomeTimes,* Nov. 1999.
102 Houston Baptist University, Minutes of the Meetings of the Board of Trustees, Meeting on 22 Feb. 2000.
103 Ibid.
104 Houston Baptist University, Minutes of the Meetings of the Board of Trustees, Meeting on 27 Feb. 2001.
105 "Seminary celebrates 25th anniversary," *SomeTimes,* April 2000.
106 Houston Baptist University, Minutes of the Meetings of the Faculty Assembly, Meeting on 20 Apr. 1999.

campus.[107] In 2001, Moffett—who also served as a University trustee—announced her retirement from her position of leadership.[108] HBU and the Seminary agreed on an effective date of fall 2002 for the program to move to a new campus in southeast Houston.[109]

§

The period from 1998 to 2002 were years of fecundity for faculty scholarly activity. Among the most prolific individuals was Dr. David Capes, Associate Professor in Christianity. In 1999, Capes was named a Visiting Fellow by the faculty of the School of Divinity at Edinburgh University to permit an eight-month sabbatical study. Additionally, in competition with faculty from a number of research universities, Capes received the Junior Scholar award from the Society of Biblical Literature and the American Academy of Religion for work on his concept "of the imitation of Christ in the early Church."[110] Capes' work later appeared in the *Bulletin for Biblical Research,* and he was appointed a fellow of the Institute for the Study of Christian Origins.[111] In 2002, Capes established a World Religions Forum on campus to promote religious understanding of Christianity, Judaism, Hinduism, Buddhism, and Islam.[112]

The scholarly work of Dr. Ann Gebuhr represented an impressive body of musical composition. Her first opera, *Brian Boru,* had premiered in 1991. In May 2000, after more than twenty years of dreaming and six years of active research, travel, correspondence, composition, fund-raising, and seminars, Dr. Gebuhr's opera, *Bonhoeffer,* received its world premiere at the Moores Opera House in Houston. The three premiere performances were underwritten by a grant by the Cultural Arts Council of Houston, were conducted by former Dean of Fine Arts Dr. Robert Linder, and featured an international cast and production team that included students, alumni, faculty, and staff.[113] Charles Ward, Music Critic for the *Houston Chronicle*, provided an extensive full page Sunday preview article

---

107 "Moffett recognized for 25 years of service," *HBU News,* May/June 2000, 10.

108 Houston Baptist University, Minutes of the Meetings of the Board of Trustees, Meeting on 15 May 2001.

109 Jami Clayman, "Seminary home to be relocated," *The Collegian,* 11 Apr. 2002, p. 12.

110 Paige Canon, "Capes named junior scholar," *The Collegian,* 15 Apr. 1999, p. 1.

111 "Updates," *HBU News,* Mar. 2000, 24.

112 "World Religions Conference," *HBU News,* Mar. 2002, 10-11.

113 Tom Behrens, "Former HBU professor's theme to life as vast as great outdoors," *Houston Chronicle,* 14 Feb. 2002, p. 2, two-star ed.

on the work itself and followed the performances with a review affirming the composition and its performance.[114]

Following the *Bonhoeffer* premier, Gebuhr continued her work in a series of conferences on the topics of faith, creativity, and the arts. In 2001, Gebuhr and Michael Collins hosted a three-day conference, "Synthesis: Creative Spirit in the Arts," which experienced realization on both the campuses of HBU and SMU.[115] Gebuhr was selected by the Rockefeller Foundation Study Center in Bellagio, Italy to be one of fifteen scholars in a period of residence for creative work.[116] Her symphony, *Voyage d'Anima,* was premiered by the Bucharest Philharmonic Orchestra[117] and, in 2003, won the prized annual Louisville Symphony Orchestra competition.[118]

The work of Melanie Leslie was selected for a juried exhibit on equine art in Lexington, Kentucky. Dr. Lou Markos completed recording a twelve-lecture video series on the *Life and Writings of C. S. Lewis* and a twenty-four-lecture series on literary theory for the "Master Teacher Series" of The Teaching Company.[119] Music faculty members John Hendrickson, Rodica Weber and Min Cao toured China on a concert tour of the University's faculty trio Tre Voce[120] and later, in 2002, performed at Carnegie Hall to a "sell-out audience" including Dr. and Mrs. Hodo and a large contingent of Houston friends.[121] Writer-in-Residence Dr. James Ulmer was published in a collection called *The New Generation of American Poets.*[122] Artist Michael Collins was awarded the Grand Prize from the Art League of Houston for his one-man exhibition.[123] Lynda Keith McKnight performed the Bernstein *Kaddish Symphony* with the Nuremberg Symphony Orchestra,[124] and Dr. Michael Bordelon published his history of the Republic of Venice, *La Serenissima,* in 2002.[125]

---

114 Charles Ward, "HBU's 'Bonhoeffer' needs less reflection, more dramatic conflict," *Houston Chronicle,* 23 May 2000, p. 4, two-star ed.

115 La'Qunta Dixon, "University hosts three-day conference on spiritual arts," *The Collegian,* 1 Nov. 2002, p. 1.

116 "Updates," *HBU News,* Mar. 2002, 26.

117 Edrina Newman, "Gebuhr to create symphony in Italy," *The Collegian,* 21 Mar. 2002, p. 4.

118 Houston Baptist University, Minutes of the Meetings of the Board of Trustees, Meeting on 13 May 2003.

119 "Updates," *HBU News,* May/June 2000, 12.

120 "Seminary celebrates 25th anniversary," *SomeTimes,* Apr. 2000; Houston Baptist University, Minutes of the Meetings of the Board of Trustees, Meeting on 23 Nov. 1999.

121 "Carnegie Hall hosts faculty duo," *HBU News,* June 2002, 4; Kristen Brock, "Weber, Hendrickson duo sell out Carnegie Hall," *The Collegian,* 25 Apr. 2002, p. 3.

122 *SomeTimes,* 29 Oct. 1999.

123"Updates," *HBU News,* Mar. 2000, 25.

124 "People on the go," *SomeTimes,* May 2001.

125 "Bordelon introduces book," *HBU News,* Mar. 2002, 26; Amanda Dean, "Bordelon's La Serenissima first book on fall of Venice," *The Collegian,* 14 Feb. 2002, p. 4.

Those faculty selected to receive the Opal Goolsby Teacher of the Year Award in 1998 were Dr. Ann Owen and Dr. Avin Brownlee winning his fourth award,[126] Dr. Jackie Horn and Dr. James Taylor winning his third award in 1999,[127] Dr. Susan Cook and Dr. Randy Hatchett in 2000,[128] Dr. Constantina Michalos and Dr. Joe Blair in 2001,[129] and Dr. Brenda Whaley '79 and Dr. Randy Wilson in 2002.[130] Those granted sabbatical leaves for scholarly study were Dr. David Capes in 1999,[131] Dr. Shari Wescott and Dr. Lou Markos in 2000,[132] Dr. Linda Brupbacher '69 and Dr. James Ulmer in 2001,[133] and Dr. Joe Blair, Dr. Constantina Michalos, and Dr. Stephen Wentland in 2002.[134]

The 1999-2000 year marked the tenth anniversary of the appointment of Alice Rowlands to the faculty and to the position of Advisor to *The Collegian*. Prior to 1990, *The Collegian* had been under the purview of the Public Relations Office.[135] Rowland's appointment in 1990 marked an important institutional move to view the paper as an integral part of the instructional program. Her arrival at HBU brought heightened professionalism to *The Collegian* that was a matter of immediate notice and formal recognition by the Faculty Assembly.[136] In the spring of 2000, Rowlands was selected as a Fellow by the Institute for Journalism Excellence of the American Society of Newspaper Editors, received a cash award, and was afforded a six-week professional internship with the *San Mateo County Times*.[137] In the years after 1990, *The Collegian* realized its goal to become "the window on the campus world" and produced generations of graduates who became outstanding media professionals. A special edition of *The Collegian* in May 2000 was dedicated to Rowlands' ten years of personal and professional contribution.

In the period 1990-2000, *The Collegian* compiled a record of continuous professional recognition by the Associated Collegiate Press, the National Scholastic Press Association, and the Texas Intercollegiate Press

---

126 "Opal Goolsby Award," *HBU News*, Oct. 1998, 13. Photo.

127 "Opal Goolsby Award for Outstanding Teaching," *HBU News*, Aug. 1999, 12.

128 "Opal Goolsby Outstanding Teaching Awards," *HBU News*, Sept. 2000, 16-17.

129 "Opal Goolsby Award for Outstanding Teaching, *HBU News*, Sept. 2001, 8.

130 "Opal Goolsby Award," *HBU News*, Sept. 2002, 8.

131 Houston Baptist University, Minutes of the Meetings of the Board of Trustees, Meeting on 23 Feb. 1999.

132 Houston Baptist University, Minutes of the Meetings of the Board of Trustee, Meeting on 22 Feb. 2000.

133 Houston Baptist University, Minutes of the Meetings of the Board of Trustees, Meeting on 27 Feb. 2001.

134 Houston Baptist University, Minutes of the Meetings of the Board of Trustees, Meeting on 26 Feb. 2002.

135"Publications," *HBU News*, Dec. 2003, 20.

136 Houston Baptist University, Minutes of the Meetings of the Faculty Assembly, Meeting on 23 Oct. 1991.

137 Houston Baptist University, Minutes of the Meetings of the Board of Trustees, Meeting on 15 May 2000.

Association. In 1999, the Texas Intercollegiate Press Association (TIPA) conferred forty-one awards of excellence on the *Ornogah* yearbook and *The Collegian*. In 2000, *The Collegian* received twenty-two TIPA awards in seventeen categories, including seven first-place recognitions.[138] In 2001, the newspaper won TIPA's Sweepstakes Award for the first time in history[139] and repeated the achievement in 2002.[140]

Individual recognition followed group award. The quality and creativity of student journalism during the period was particularly strong as represented by the work of Josh Pease, Rease Nash, Merin Brown, Josh Rowlands, Tomie Lunsford, Dale Peacock, and Amy Davis. In 2001, *Collegian* writer Dale Peacock received the President's Award from Morris Chapman, President of the Southern Baptist Convention, at the "Excellence in Student Journalism Conference" for work that showed "great depth and scope and a strong sense of Christian commitment as a journalist."[141] In the summer of 2000, Amy Davis was awarded an internship with the *New York Times*[142] and followed this recognition the following summer with her selection as an intern with *CBS Network News* in New York. In the summer of 2002, Davis served on the staff of Mayor Michael Bloomberg of New York. In testimony to the University's academic strength, Bloomberg observed, "Her unique double-major combination of mass-media and political science plus her internships at the *New York Times* and *CBS* made her perfect for the mayor's office."[143] Other HBU students were selected for internships with *CNN Atlanta* and the Washington-based *Institute for Journalism*. Seniors Brett Mosher and Joshua Pease were two of only fourteen students selected nation-wide for a semester as Witherspoon Fellows in Washington, D.C.[144]

The *2000 Ornogah* tied for a first-place award from the American Scholastic Press Association,[145] received a bronze medal from the Columbia Scholastic Press Association,[146] and was selected to be included

---

138 "College of Arts and Humanities," *HBU News*, May/June 2000, 25; "HBU newspaper wins honors," *SomeTimes*, Sept. 2000, 4.

139 "Student publications sweep awards: Collegian nets top honors in Texas contest," *The Collegian*, 10 May 2002, p. 35.

140 "Collegian awarded 1st place by TIPA," *HBU News*, June 2002, 5.

141 Amy N. Davis, "Peacock named top journalist," *The Collegian*, 4 Oct. 2001, p. 4.

142 Amy N. Davis, "Cup o'Joe," *The Collegian*, 21 Sept. 2000, p. 7.

143 "Alumna garners top internship with NYC mayor," *HBU News*, Sept 2002, 26.

144 Vivian Camacho, "Ideas take form in Washington, D.C.," *HBU News*, Mar 2003, 13. Photos.

145 Michelle Cavazos, "2000 Ornogah ties for first in scholastic competition," *The Collegian*, 11 Jan. 2001, p. 3.

146 "Ornogah garners awards," *HBU News*, Spring 2001, 5.

in the Taylor Publishing Company's *2001 Yearbook-Yearbook*.[147] *Breaking New Ground, Ornogah 2001* received the University's first Silver Medal Award from the Columbia Scholastic Press Association (CSPA) and a first-place award from the American Scholastic Press Association.[148] In 2002, the *Ornogah* received ten awards from the Texas Intercollegiate Press Association.[149]

The student literary anthology known variously over the years as *The Binding Cord, The Raft,* and *Shank's Mare* was renamed *Crossroads* in 1998. The anthology's remarkable trove of student writing had been gathered since 1967 by faculty sponsors Drs. Wallace Hooker, Daton Dodson, Honora Lynch, June Farrell, and Lois Lawrence. With the establishment of the Danny Lee Lawrence Creative Writing Awards and the founding of the HBU chapter of Sigma Tau Delta honorary English Society, the winning entries of the Lawrence Awards became a significant part of the literary anthology each year.[150] *Crossroads 2001* returned after a year's hiatus, "reborn and remodeled," under the guidance of Dr. James Ulmer[151] and was honored by the Texas Intercollegiate Press Association in 2002.[152]

In the fine arts, HBU's Department of Art was enjoying burgeoning student enrollment. By 2002, enrollment in art had tripled since 1995.[153] The art department had been given "temporary" occupancy rights in 1990 to the University-owned building on Beechnut at Fondren previously occupied by "Games People Play."[154] In an effort to provide better academic housing for art instruction, the move had provided greatly increased space with better lighting and ventilation and had freed several academic quadrangle classrooms for administrative expansion.[155] However, over the years, roof leaks, security concerns, and maintenance difficulties made the "temporary" facility increasingly unusable. Despite its housing in the ignominious "art barn," the department boasted an outstanding faculty of studio artists including its Chair, the thirty-two-year

147 Houston Baptist University, Minutes of the Meetings of the Board of Trustees, Meeting on 25 Sept. 2001.

148 Tomie Lunsford, "Ornogah wins 1st CSPA silver in school history," *The Collegian,* 17 Jan. 2002, p. 1; "Ornogah wins first place," *Houston Chronicle,* 14 Feb. 2001, p. 2, three-star ed.

149 "Yearbook breaks new ground," *HBU News,* June 2002, 4.

150 "Initiation and Awards," *The Collegian,* 29 Apr. 1999, p. 5.

151 Tomie Lunsford, "Literary journal reborn, remodeled," *The Collegian,* 11 Nov. 2001, p. 5.

152 Megan Baumgardner, "Student publications educate, inform, entertain," *HBU News,* Dec. 2003, 20.

153 "HBU Art Department: Painting a Powerful Picture," *HBU News,* Mar. 2002, 14-15.

154 "Movie Stars take 5 on HBU turf," *The Collegian,* 12 Feb. 1998, The Scoop sec., p. 2. Photo. The HBU Art Barn was used as the backdrop for filming scenes in the movie *Arlington Road* starring Jeff Bridges and Tim Robbins in 1998.

155 *SomeTimes,* Aug. 1990.

HBU veteran James Busby,[156] Melanie Leslie,[157] Michael Collins,[158] and Margaret Losinski.[159]

In music, Dr. John Yarrington was appointed Director of Choral Activities in 1999 succeeding Dr. David Wehr.[160] Yarrington was active in the American Choral Directors Association and, in his first year, conducted Houston's Masterworks Chorus and All-State and Honors choirs in Seattle and Birmingham.[161] In 2001, Yarrington's University Singers and Schola Cantorum participated in a concert at Carnegie Hall with the noted British composer John Rutter conducting.[162] Yarrington established a pattern of inviting an American composer to be in residence on campus with students for a week each spring. In 2001, composer-arranger-conductor Alice Parker, the renowned colleague of conductor Robert Shaw, was in residence working with students. In 2002, the noted composer Martin Lauridsen, a member of the faculty at the University of Southern California, was on campus in February for final rehearsals and the performance of a number of his choral works.[163]

The University intellectual environment was greatly stimulated by the appearance of a number of prominent guest lecturers and speakers in the 1998-2002 period. Guests for the Opening Fall Academic Convocations were the President of the University of St. Thomas Dr. Michael Miller, the President of Wheaton College Dr. Duane Litfin, and the former President of Oklahoma Baptist University Dr. Bob Agee. The Thomas F. Staley Distinguished Christian Scholar lectures were given by Dr. Elizabeth Achtemeier,[164] Dr. Calvin Miller,[165] Dr. Os Guiness,[166] and Duke University Chapel Dean Dr. Bill Willimon.[167] Lecturers for the A. O. Collins series included Professor Alan Segal, Professor of Judaica at Columbia University;[168] Dr. Ellen Cherry, Princeton Theological

156 "James Busby," *HBU News,* Fall 2007, 31.
157 "Melanie Wade Leslie," *HBU News,* Fall 2007, 33.
158 Marlo Holdren, "Lasting Impressions," *The Collegian,* 29 Apr. 1999, p. 9. Photos.
159 Annette Baird, "Sculptor immerses herself in healing power of art," *Houston Chronicle,* 7 Mar. 2002, p. 4, two-star ed.
160 "Dr. John Yarrington joins HBU faculty," *HBU Upbeat,* Fall 1999, p. 3.
161 *SomeTimes,* May 2000.
162 Matasha Rauf, "HBU storms Carnegie Hall," *The Collegian,* 25 Nov. 2001, p. 1.
163 "Martin Lauridsen visits campus," *HBU News,* June 2002, 4.
164 Lyn Armstrong, "Christian Marriage in Peril," *The Collegian,* 28 Jan. 1999, p. 1.
165 Teresa Kipp, "Miller Tells Witty Tales," *The Collegian,* 27 Jan. 2000, p. 9.
166 Billy Thomas, "Noted author to speak," *The Collegian,* 11 Jan. 2001, p. 12.
167 "Willimon Lectures," *HBU News,* Mar. 1992, 4.
168 Houston Baptist University, Minutes of the Meetings of the Board of Trustees, Meeting on 18 May 1999.

Seminary;[169] and Dr. John Wilson, Pepperdine Institute on Archeology and Religion.[170]

Delivering the Prince-Chavanne Lectures in Christian Business Ethics were Dr. Oliver Williams, Director of the Center for Ethics and Religious Values at Notre Dame;[171] Dr. Archie B. Carroll, the University of Georgia's Robert Sherer Chair;[172] Baylor University's Dr. Stan Madden;[173] and Dr. Donald Robin, Tylee Wilson Professor of Business Ethics at Wake Forest University.[174] Several of Houston's most prominent business leaders appeared under the aegis of the Herman Brown Chair in Business. Walter Johnson, CEO of Southwest Bank of Texas, provided the Brown Lecture[175] and was followed in 2001 by Larry Farmer, CEO of Halliburton, UK.[176] Other campus guests included Guggenheim Fellow, poet Stephen Dunn;[177] the Federal Reserve Bank's Edward Kelley, Jr.;[178] and Viet Nam war poet William Erhardt presented by the Robert Ray Chair in Humanities.[179]

§

In 1998, as time grew near for the ten-year cycle of reaffirmation of accreditation, the Southern Association's Dr. John Dwyer visited the campus for a preliminary survey. Dwyer described the self-study process as one that critiqued "everything from the President to the parking lot."[180] Dr. Cynthia Young was appointed to coordinate the University's reaffirmation process.

A strategic plan for the period 1999-2002 was unveiled in February 1999. Eight comprehensive goals described the University's mission for the immediate future: 1) foster a supportive Christian environment; 2) provide "highest-quality" academic programs, faculty, services, and facil-

169 "Cherry speaks at lecture series," *HBU News,* June 2000, 4.

170 "Archeology Discussed at Collins Lecture," *HBU News,* Dec. 2001, 6.

171 "Prince Chavanne Lecture," *HBU News,* June 1998, 5. Photo.

172 "Prince Chavanne Lecture features Carroll," *HBU News,* Apr. 1999, 21.

173 Houston Baptist University, Minutes of the Meetings of the Board of Trustees, Meeting on 15 May 2001.

174 "Around the Campus," *HBU News,* June 2002, 6.

175 Jennifer Diehl, "Management, customer service keys to successful businesses," *The Collegian,* 15 Apr. 1999, p. 4.

176 Joshua Pease, "Businessman shares success," *The Collegian,* 10 May 2001, p. 7.

177 Tomie Lunsford, "Award winning poet visits HBU," *The Collegian,* 2 Nov. 2000, p. 7.

178 "Anticipating Y2K," *HBU News,* Dec. 1998, 14.

179 Houston Baptist University, Minutes of the Meetings of the Board of Trustees, Meeting on 15 May 2001.

180 Alicia Whitehead, "Taking a look in the mirror," *The Collegian,* 8 Oct. 2000, p. 1.

ities; 3) provide the necessary human and financial resources; 4) provide relevant professional programs that prepare students for "meaningful and prominent" roles in their community; 5) provide for the development of the whole person; 6) increase the size of the student body to 2,000 full-time equivalent undergraduate and 650 graduate students; 7) respond to the needs of faculty and staff; and 8) market the University to its constituencies for financial support.[181]

The self-study process involved every facet of institutional operation. The HBU committees appointed to appraise the University's performance against the 437 standards of the SACS Criteria were composed of trustees, faculty, students, and administrators.[182] By September 2000, the Self-Study Steering Committee had articulated nineteen internal recommendations to address the SACS requirements. These goals involved institutional research, assessment, faculty salaries, fidelity of programs to institutional purpose, the appropriate role of Information Systems in academic decision-making, and the appropriate role of the trustee Academic Committee in budget approval. As an outcome of the self-study recommendations, the Board approved a change to the By-Laws that specified how a trustee might be removed from office for cause.[183]

The SACS committee visited the campus in October 2000. After nearly a week of residency, the committee issued a preliminary report that delineated forty-eight specific issues requiring University action.[184] Of these, twenty-three of the recommendations were in the area of institutional effectiveness, eleven concerned written policies and procedures, and fourteen related to institutional research. All of HBU's nineteen self-identified recommendations were echoed in the SACS report. Steering Committee Chair, Dr. James Taylor, summarized these requirements for *The Collegian,* "SACS has identified things we have not been doing, and now we have to develop a plan to fulfill those requirements."[185]

Following the SACS review of HBU's written response to the recommendations, the Southern Association voted to place the University on "warning" for a period of extended review to be reconsidered in June 2002.[186] Found lacking by the review committee was a basic "Condition of

---

181 Houston Baptist University, Minutes of the Meetings of the Board of Trustees, Meeting on 23 Feb. 1999.
182 Houston Baptist University, Minutes of the Meetings of Faculty Assembly, Meeting on 11 Apr. 2000.
183 Houston Baptist University, Minutes of the Meetings of the Board of Trustees, Meeting on 26 Sept. 2000.
184 Amy N. Davis, "Team pinpoints 48 deficiencies," *The Collegian,* 2 Nov. 2000, pp. 1, 6.
185 Joshua Pease, "Report of 48 solutions due to SACS in 4 days," *The Collegian,* 15 Mar. 2001, p. 1.
186 "Q & A SACS," *HBU News,* Sept. 2001, 28.

Eligibility" requirement for planning and evaluation process in *all* areas of University operations. The report noted lack of such assessment in a number of non-academic areas, i.e. plant operations, admissions, auxiliary enterprises, alumni, human resources, and business operations. In the academic area, the articulated concerns included excessive dependency on part-time faculty, employee credential documentation, and the requirement of doctoral faculty for graduate nursing instruction.[187] The "warning" status had no effect on current accreditation. It is significant that virtually all the recommendations had to do with the requirement of protocols and procedures for assurance of quality control and effective decision-making. The quality of the University's academic program was never challenged.

The University administration reported to the Board in September, "Some operational areas lag behind others in their degree of understanding about assessment. A good beginning has been made in defining a more comprehensive strategic plan. Aggressive attention to existing evaluative processes and formation of assessment models where absent is a critical priority."[188] In the fall, Dr. Cynthia Young was named Assistant Vice President for Institutional Effectiveness and Research to coordinate the University's response to the SACS requirements.[189]

The Southern Association appointed a second visiting committee to visit the campus in the spring 2000 to assess institutional compliance with fourteen remaining criteria.[190] The result of this second visit was a recommendation to remove HBU from "warning" status and to reaffirm institutional accreditation for the next ten years. The two years of self-study and response had exhausted the emotion and the energy of the campus, but had developed a model for better institutional health and prosperity. With a large measure of relief, the Faculty Assembly drafted a resolution of appreciation for the self-study leadership:

> The Assembly recognizes the overwhelming importance of accreditation to the well-being of the University and all its enterprises. The Assembly particularly recognizes the contribution of many individuals without whose efforts the work might not have been complete; these include (the University executive officers) and the person who became the icon of the project, Dr. Cynthia Young.[191]

---

187 *SomeTimes*, Aug. 2001.
188 Houston Baptist University, Minutes of the Meetings of the Board of Trustees, Meeting on 25 Sept. 2001.
189 Kristen Brock, "Young accepts inaugural Assistant Vice President," *The Collegian,* 20 Sept. 2001, p. 3.
190 Houston Baptist University, Minutes of the Meetings of the Board of Trustees, Meeting on 26 Feb. 2002.
191 Houston Baptist University, Minutes of the Meetings of the Faculty Assembly, Meeting on 7 May 2002.

The University administration later reported to the Board, "Perhaps no SACS reaffirmation in University history since the first visit in 1968 has required more diligent work, but yielded results that are more positive."[192]

§

The Faculty Assembly played a significant role in professional growth and the development of academic support. From the outset of his administration, Dr. Hodo had pledged to reduce faculty teaching loads to more nominal levels. This goal was made more complex by the quarter calendar; any reduction needed to be equally divided across the three terms. In December 1998, the teaching loads were reduced from four courses each term to three.[193] President Hodo stressed, however, that the financial health of the University required greater productivity resulting from fully enrolled classes and, in some cases, fewer sections. Greater financial stability permitted the budgeting of a 4.25 percent salary pool for 2001. Greater reliance on adjunct faculty at lower cost and unfilled faculty positions also contributed to reduce annual spending below budgeted amounts. In spite of the concerns expressed by SACS about use of adjunct faculty, twelve full-time faculty and nine staff positions were unfilled in the fall of 2001.[194]

The Strategic Plan became more articulate in the process of self-study. A revised "Mission Statement" was drawn from the original purpose statement for HBC. "HBU is a Christian, liberal arts institution that prepares students for meaningful lives of work and service to God and to the peoples of the world."[195] The institution's core values were defined as strong academic programs; a liberal arts foundation; the fulfillment of career expectations; a faculty dedicated to teaching excellence; an innovative, entrepreneurial curriculum; and focus on scholarship, professionalism, creativity, and life-long learning. The core values further responded to the recommendations of the many committees involved in the planning process. A proposed comprehensive Vision Statement voiced the University's desire—as first articulated by President Hodo—"to be

---

192 Houston Baptist University, Minutes of the Meetings of the Board of Trustees, Meeting on 24 Sept. 2002.
193 Houston Baptist University, Minutes of the Meetings of the Faculty Assembly, Meeting on 15 Dec. 1998.
194 Houston Baptist University, Minutes of the Meetings of the Board of Trustees, Meeting on 20 Nov. 2001.
195 "HBU Vision, Mission, and Goals . . . ," HBU News, June 2002, 31.

recognized as one of metropolitan America's premier Christian academic institutions."[196]

The Strategic Plan process began with an analysis of institutional strengths and weaknesses, as well as a critique of opportunities and threats (SWOT analysis). Recognized strengths included emphasis on learning, a nurturing Christian environment, the liberal arts core, faculty strength, reputation, academic innovation, and cultural diversity. Identified weaknesses included community visibility, limited finances, a non-residential campus, tuition dependency, facility needs, and compensation. Perceived environmental threats included competition for students and funding, the cost of technology, and a suburban location. Among the perceived opportunities were expansion of undergraduate programs, development of alumni relations, marketing of "flagship" programs, and enhancement of the campus social climate.[197]

From this analysis and the assessment by the visiting committee, a Strategic Plan 2001-2006 was developed. The institutional commitments under this plan were 1) to meet SACS Criteria for assessment and institutional effectiveness, 2) improve academic advising, 3) increase the residential population, 4) broaden the doctrine of faith, 5) employ experienced leadership in corporate and sustaining fund raising, 6) initiate a targeted marketing program incorporating institutional branding, 7) strengthen flagship programs with student and resource improvement, 8) increase undergraduate retention, 9) develop an executive succession plan, 10) explore alternate instructional learning models and delivery systems, and 11) increase salaries in strategic positions.[198] During the winter of 2001, Dr. Jairy Hunter, President of Charleston Southern University, provided a series of seminars for the Institutional Strategic Planning Committee (ISPC) on strategic planning and SACS expectations.[199]

§

In February 2000, the trustees appointed a Charter and By-Law Review Committee.[200] Among the needed revisions were matters of

---

196 Houston Baptist University, *Bulletin of Information 2002-04*, 12.
197 "HBU Vision, Mission, Goals," *HBU News,* June 2002, 31.
198 Houston Baptist University, Minutes of the Meetings of the Board of Trustees, Meeting on 26 Feb. 2002.
199 Houston Baptist University, Minutes of the Meetings of the Board of Trustees, Meeting on 20 Nov. 2001. President Hunter was a friend of the University and was a recognized SACS authority on strategic planning.
200 Houston Baptist University, Minutes of the Meetings of the Board of Trustees, Meeting on 22 Feb. 2000.

conformity with the Texas Non-Profit Corporation Act. Additionally, the University wished to provide more specificity about administrative management policy to guard against potential future litigation. The University's legal counsel, Bracewell & Patterson, was engaged to guide the process. The proposed By-Laws additions affirmed the authority of the University President to appoint, "one or more Vice Presidents as he shall deem advisable, such officers to have the authority and perform the duties assigned by the President. . . . Any Vice President appointed by the President may be removed by the President whenever in his judgment the best interest of the corporation would be served."[201] This addition addressed the University's legal experience in a previous termination case. The changes also specified the role of the President as the "Chief Executive Officer" and limited the number of trustees from any one church to five members, while allowing all those who currently served on the Board to complete full nine-year terms if re-elected.[202]

On May 16, 2000, in an act of major historic importance, the HBU Board approved the restated Articles of Incorporation that revised the process for electing trustees. The Board moved to grant itself authority to appoint seventy-five percent of the members of the Board of Trustees "who will continue to be Texas Baptists."[203] In the future, only one-fourth of the trustees would be elected by the Baptist General Convention of Texas. In the preceding weeks, the BGCT had announced its intention not to appoint trustees from "non-cooperating" Baptist churches in the state "that did not comply with financial contribution requirements to the state body."[204] Moreover, according to BGCT guidelines, two of the ten current HBU trustees to be re-elected were declared ineligible because their election would exceed the allowable number from any one church.

On May 18, 2000, the *Houston Chronicle* reported, "HBU trustees have stunned Texas Baptist officials by declaring autonomy from the state convention."[205] The article stated that the action was taken "to assure broad representation among current and future trustees."[206] President

---

201 Houston Baptist University, Minutes of the Meetings of the Board of Trustees, Meeting on 16 May 2000.
202 Houston Baptist University, Minutes of the Meetings of the Board of Trustees, Meeting on 20 Nov. 2001.
203 Dr. E. D. Hodo, "From the President," *HBU News,* May/June 2000, 2.
204 Richard Vara, "HBU Surprises state Baptists, OKs autonomy," *Houston Chronicle,* 18 May 2000, sec. A, p. 2, three-star ed.
205 Richard Vara, "HBU trustees have stunned Texas Baptist officials by declaring autonomy from the state convention," *Houston Chronicle,* 18 May 2000, p. 21, three-star ed.
206 Ibid.

Hodo explained, "This is an issue of Board autonomy."[207] At stake was approximately $1,500,000 in BGCT annual funding toward HBU's $28,000,000 budget. In the May 24 edition, the *Chronicle* reported that the Executive Committee of the Baptist General Convention of Texas had voted to escrow HBU's annual appropriation while the Convention continued to provide direct student scholarship funds and faculty loans.[208] The Convention appointed a committee to "carefully study the unilateral action taken by the trustees of Houston Baptist University."[209]

Board Chair David Stutts '82, former chair Karl Kennard, and President Hodo met with the BGCT response committee and Keith Bruce, Director of the Christian Education Coordinating Board, in January 2001. The BGCT committee asked the HBU Board to rescind its action.[210] Dr. Hodo explained that the action was taken "to protect at-risk trustees."[211] HBU liaison committee chair Karl Kennard conveyed the news to the HBU trustees that the action would likely result in the loss of the escrowed BGCT funds. In such event, half of the annual BGCT allocation for HBU was to be distributed to the other Texas Baptist colleges and schools.[212] Among the BGCT concerns was HBU's proposed "informal relationships" with other Texas Baptist denominational organizations for the stated purpose of student recruiting, fund raising, and effective church relations. In May 2002, the HBU Board voted "to continue relationships as in the past with the BGCT, Southern Baptists of Texas, and the Cooperative Baptist Fellowship, as well as other Baptist and non-Baptist organizations."[213]

The Board of Trustees enjoyed strong leadership in this period of unusual demands. In 1999, Dr. Charles Wisdom became only the second pastor to serve as Chair of the Board following in the steps of Dr. William Denham, the founding Chair of the Board. In this period of BGCT realignment, a pastor as chair was particularly propitious. Of historic and personal significance was the re-election of Dr. Stewart Morris in 2001 to

---

207 Dr. E. D. Hodo, "From the President," *HBU News,* May/June 2000, 2.

208 Richard Vara, "Texas Baptists to review HBU decision," *Houston Chronicle,* 24 May 2000, sec. A, p. 27, three-star ed.

209 Mark Wingfield, "BGCT will escrow funds for HBU while trustees' action reviewed," *Baptist Standard,* 29 May 2000.

210 Houston Baptist University, Minutes of the Meetings of the Board of Trustees, Meeting on 27 Feb. 2001.

211 Ron Nissimov, "HBU, Baptist convention reach accord over school's control," *Houston Chronicle,* 27 Sept. 2001, sec. A, p. 25, three-star ed.

212 Houston Baptist University, Minutes of the Meetings of the Board of Trustees, Meeting on 25 Sept. 2001.

213 Houston Baptist University, Minutes of the Meetings of the Board of Trustees, Meeting on 14 May 2002.

serve as Chair of the Board for an unprecedented fifth term. Morris was well-versed in HBU/BGCT history. At the end of his term as Chair, Dr. Morris announced his intention to resign his active status as a trustee. Upon his return to Advisory Trustee status, he continued to maintain regular attendance and participation in all meetings of the Board.

The size of the Board was a matter of additional discussion. Upon Dr. Hodo's arrival, he encouraged an expansion of the Board's membership beyond twenty-one trustees.[214] In February 1988, the trustees voted to amend the Articles of Incorporation to eliminate a stated maximum number of members.[215] However, in February 1999, the Board approved a change that would have permitted expanding the Board to thirty-nine trustees by 2001.[216] In November 1999, thirty-three trustees approved an amendment stating that the By-Laws would specify the total number of trustees with a minimum of seven pastors and at least seven lay trustees.[217] In May 2000, the Board amended Article III, Section 2 of the By-Laws to change the size of the Board to thirty-six members—twenty-seven elected by the University and nine by the BGCT.[218] As a part of the Board's decision to elect seventy-five percent of its own membership, the University sustained the requirement of membership in a Baptist church but deleted the phrase "affiliated with the Baptist General Convention of Texas." The term "denominationally related" also became defined as "pastors, spouses, or church and seminary staff members."[219] In 2001, in addition to limiting the trustees from any one church to five members,[220] the Board authorized changes which precluded any University administrator, faculty member, or employee from serving on the Board of Trustees.[221]

§

In March 1998, ground was broken for the Memorial Hermann-HBU Wellness Center cooperatively developed by Memorial Healthcare

---

214 Houston Baptist University, Minutes of the Meetings of the Board of Trustees, Meeting on 24 Nov. 1987.
215 Houston Baptist University, Minutes of the Meetings of the Board of Trustees, Meeting on 23 Feb. 1988.
216 Houston Baptist University, Minutes of the Meetings of the Board of Trustees, Meeting on 23 Feb. 1999.
217 Houston Baptist University, Minutes of the Meetings of the Board of Trustees, Meeting on 23 Nov. 1990.
218 Houston Baptist University, Minutes of the Meetings of the Board of Trustees, Meeting on 16 May 2000.
219 Ibid.
220 Houston Baptist University, Minutes of the Meetings of the Board of Trustees, Meeting on 25 Sept. 2001.
221 Houston Baptist University, Minutes of the Meetings of the Board of Trustees, Meeting on 20 Nov. 2001.

Systems and the University.[222]   The 65,000 square-foot facility was designed to offer a fitness center, an aquatics center, basketball and hand-ball courts, classrooms, a counseling center, and Memorial's Mind Body Institute.[223] Dedication ceremonies were held in November 1999 for the facility, a welcomed new resource for students and employees of the University. In an era characterized by elaborate "climbing wall" university recreation facilities across the nation, the Wellness Center addressed one of the great needs of the campus and echoed the strategic plan goal for an "enhanced social climate." On the Center's first anniversary in 2000, 1691 HBU students and ninety-one faculty and staff were enrolled for membership.[224] The Wellness Center occupied seven acres of land which would ultimately revert to the University. Memorial had an option on an additional four acres for related development.[225]

The confidence, trust, and warm friendship of Memorial's CEO Dan Wilford and the University's President Hodo nurtured the consideration of many proposals of benefit to both institutions. The Wellness Center was one example of this cooperative relationship, even though it was a difficult project to conceive, fund, and manage. Nonetheless, the original concept of benefit both to the institutions and their constituencies fueled the eventual emergence of programs that represented the latest thought in the field of human wellness.

§

The financial health of the University was improved. The year-end report to the trustees in 1998 noted higher-than-expected endowment income of $3,900,000 due largely to oil and gas recovery income.[226] The report further chronicled savings in instructional expenses due to "lower salary and benefit costs, lower academic support, and student services."[227] The year-end surplus approximated $800,000 in 1999.[228] A scheduled surplus of $650,000 was an integral part of the 2000-01 budget.[229]

---

222 Alicia Whitehead, "Complex to house state-of-the-art equipment: Memorial Hermann-HBU Wellness Center," *HBU Collegian,* 13 May 1999, p. 4.
223 "Wellness Center opens for business," *HBU News,* Nov. 1999, 6.
224 Houston Baptist University, Minutes of the Meetings of the Board of Trustees, Meeting on 21 Nov. 2000.
225 Houston Baptist University, Minutes of the Meetings of the Board of Trustees, Meeting on 24 Sept. 2002.
226 "Financial Affairs," *HBU News,* Spring 2001, 42.
227 Houston Baptist University, Minutes of the Meetings of the Board of Trustees, Meeting on 18 May 1998.
228 Houston Baptist University, Minutes of the Meetings of the Board of Trustees, Meeting on 28 Sept. 1999.
229 Houston Baptist University, Minutes of the Meetings of the Board of Trustees, Meeting on 27 Feb. 2001.

One element of savings was achieved by holding selected budgeted positions vacant and employing part-time faculty. The extent of this practice was challenged by the Southern Association. In the fall 2001, a report to the trustees showed twenty percent of all courses were taught by adjunct teachers. Some six full-time faculty positions were vacant.[230] Though the supply of qualified doctoral personnel in Houston was corpulent, the SACS concern was for balance in staffing to provide stability and staff the ancillary services of student advising, committee participation, curriculum building, professional growth, and campus involvement which only full-time faculty served.

Several businesses in the Fondren I retail development were experiencing financial stress. In 2001, Weiner's Stores declared bankruptcy,[231] and the Mervyns Department Store closed and vacated the property.[232] In June 2002, Toys-R-Us announced its intention to close its store adjacent to the Memorial Hospital.[233] The Garden Village Retirement Center continued to struggle. The HBU trustees approved funds for refurbishing the facility in April 2001 and voted to defer some of its overdue payments.[234] The project reopened in October with eighty-five percent occupancy.[235]

A major acquisition for Fondren II, however, was the LifeWay Christian Store—the former Baptist Bookstore. In this financial environment, Stewart Morris advised against extending any of the Fondren I leases beyond the end of their fifty-two-year terms in 2022.[236] Despite the turnover, the income stream from leases in the retail projects continued to remain a significant source of income for the University. At the east end of the campus, the University entered negotiations with CVS Pharmacy for a fifty-year ground lease at the corner of Fondren and Beechnut, site of the former Exxon station.[237]

Significant gifts were received for capital projects and endowed professorships and scholarships. The Houston Endowment conveyed a grant of $250,000 in 1998 for a major improvement project in student

---

230 Houston Baptist University, Minutes of the Meetings of the Board of Trustees, Meeting on 25 Sept. 2001.
231 Ibid.
232 Houston Baptist University, Minutes of the Meetings of the Board of Trustees, Meeting on 15 May 2001.
233 Houston Baptist University, Minutes of the Meetings of the Board of Trustees, Meeting on 14 May 2002.
234 Houston Baptist University, Minutes of the Meetings of the Executive Committee of the Board of Trustees, Meeting on 11 Apr. 2001.
235 Houston Baptist University, Minutes of the Meetings of the Board of Trustees, Meeting on 20 Nov. 2001.
236 Houston Baptist University, Minutes of the Meetings of the Board of Trustees, Meeting on 25 Sept. 2001.
237 Houston Baptist University, Minutes of the Meetings of the Board of Trustees, Meeting on 27 Feb. 2001.

housing.[238] Also in 1998, Roland Burrows, a University trustee from 1973-79, and his wife Sharon, President of the President's Advisors in 1977, established the Sharon Burrows Endowed Professorship in the College of Education to assist in the education of public school counselors.[239] Moreover, in 1998, the Texas Attorney General's office reported recovery of "several hundred thousand dollars" for the University from the Dumraese estate.[240]

In 1999, the trustees received an offer of $450,000 to settle the Mest estate—after fifteen years of legal effort following the death of Mrs. M. Catharine Mest.[241] Funds from this estate were applied to construction costs for the new Mest Wing of the Rebecca Philips Women's Residence.[242] In May 2000, the Board approved the sale of bonds not to exceed $7,300,000 for construction of the Mest wing, repayment of $3,700,000 on 1995 bonds, remodeling the women's residence college, four new boilers, remodeling the College of Nursing offices as required by the Board of Nurse Examiners, and construction of a new Beechnut entry drive. In July, the Houston City Council approved the sale of these bonds through the Houston Higher Education Finance Corporation, a city-owned authority.[243] The Henry H. and M. Catharine Mest Wing of the Philips Residence College was formally dedicated in September 2000 that added 104 beds to the University's residential capacity.[244]

The Cullen Trust for Higher Education committed $1,200,000 in December 1999 for "student life"—related to the Legacy of Excellence campaign.[245] By May, this gift had been increased to $2,000,000, Cullen's largest gift in history to HBU.[246] HBU trustee Dr. Bruce Belin served on the Board of the Cullen Trust for Higher Education. Other year-end gifts were received from the John S. Dunn Foundation and the Cain Foundation.

---

238 Houston Baptist University, Minutes of the Meetings of the Board of Trustees, Meeting on 23 Feb. 1999.

239 "Sharon Burrows Endowed Professorship," *HBU News,* Dec. 1998, 9. Sharon Burrows was instrumental in the formation of the President's Advisors which she served as President in 1977-78. Roland and Sharon Burrows endowed an academic scholarship in 1976.

240 Houston Baptist University, Minutes of the Meetings of the Board of Trustees, Meeting on 24 Nov. 1998.

241 Houston Baptist University, Minutes of the Meetings of the Board of Trustees, Meeting on 11 Oct. 1999.

242 Rease Nash, "104 beds set for new Women's Residence College," *The Collegian,* 4 Nov. 1999, p. 1.

243 *Bond Buyer,* 20 July 2000, p. 3.

244 "Mest Wing added to women's residential college," *HBU News,* Winter 2000, 6; *Ornogah 2001,* 5; "New Wing for Houston Baptist," *Houston Chronicle,* This Week, p. 6, two-star ed.

245 *SomeTimes,* Aug. 2001; Houston Baptist University, Minutes of the Meetings of the Board of Trustees, Meeting on 28 Sept. 1999.

246 Houston Baptist University, Minutes of the Meetings of the Board of Trustees, Meeting on 15 May 2001.

In February, one of the largest gifts in University history was announced from the Michel J. and Gwen A. Mellinger estate. The gift, estimated to be $4,500,000, was designated for scholarships in nursing and in music.[247] The gift was realized through the generosity of Yolande Frazier, a friend of the University's School of Music and former voice student of Virginia Babikian[248] and her daughter, Halisia Frazier Cannon, who received her nursing degree from HBU in 1985.

Financial assistance also came from the several affinity organizations who worked to support University growth. In 2001, President Hodo expressed specific acknowledgement of the Alumni Association, the American Museum Society, the Covenant Society, The Guild, the President's Development Council, and the University Retirees Association in his *HBU News* column.[249] In addition to the funds provided by the President's Development Council for the Hinton House, M. D. Anderson, and Mabee remodeling projects, the President's Advisors generated considerable financial and marketing assistance. Among its annual fund-raising events was a spring Silver Tea. From these events in the period 1995-2002, over $430,000 was donated for scholarships.[250] An annual Christmas Brunch marked the occasion of the December founding of the organization and afforded visibility for the University and its students. In the fall of 1999, the President's Advisors organization began to refer to itself formally as The Guild.[251] Ruth Graham McIntyre was invited to be the guest speaker for the twenty-fifth anniversary of the Guild's founding.[252]

Another affinity organization, the American Museum Society was one of the University's oldest organizations and traced its beginnings from 1965. The Museum Society created an avenue of involvement for Houston's cultural community. International attention gained through three years of extraordinary historical symposia in the mid-1960s firmly established awareness and the reputation of the Museum Society in the early days of College history. The Society prospered with the involvement

---

247 Houston Baptist University, Minutes of the Meetings of the Board of Trustees, Meeting on 22 Feb. 2000; "HBU gets $4.5 million for scholarship fund," *Houston Chronicle,* 21 June 2001, ThisWeek sec., p. 3, two-star ed.

248 "HBU receives $4.5 million gift, Mellinger Estate," *HBU News,* Sept. 2001, 17.

249 Dr. E. D. Hodo, "From the President," *HBU News,* Spring 2001, 2.

250 "HBU Guild Silver Tea," *Houston Chronicle,* 1 May 2002, p. 3, two-star ed. Photo of Kandy Brittain, Linda Higginbotham, Allene Lucas, Dr. Hodo.

251 Houston Baptist University, Minutes of the Meetings of the Board of Trustees, Meeting on 23 Nov. 1999.

252 "McIntyre discusses 'Real Life' at Christmas," *HBU News,* Mar. 2000, 12-13. Photos.

of women who might otherwise not have affiliated with the University or its programs. Most of its members were vitally interested in the Museum of American Architecture and Decorative Arts and were often avid personal collectors or devotees of historical preservation. Each year, the Society hosted a Christmas brunch and a springtime Museum Day Seminar that featured a noted expert. Moreover, the organization served as a touchstone for other affinity organizations that had strong interests in certain aspects of the Museum collections, i.e., doll clubs, needlework societies, and firearms and antique collectors.

In 1999, the University's oldest affinity organization,[253] the Auxiliary, determined to begin a tradition of annual reunions rather than more frequent meetings.[254] Jeannette Clift George was the speaker for the first of these reunions.[255] A campus favorite, George had received the Woman of the Year Award and had been granted a Doctor of Humane Letters degree in 1995.[256] In succeeding years, Mrs. George was followed as speaker by Marge Caldwell in 2000[257] and Margaret Bolding in 2001.[258] The Auxiliary dated from 1963 and had provided a record of unparalleled response to University needs over the decades. In 1973, the membership of the Auxiliary approximated 280 women.[259] The early fund-raising "tasting bees" in Denham Hall eventually were replaced by a Silver Tea and book reviews.[260] Significant gifts from the Auxiliary included the marquee at the Fondren entrance to the campus,[261] night lighting for the campus, dormitory furnishings, campus landscaping, funds for library acquisitions,[262] and on the University's twentieth anniversary in 1980, a custom wall hanging of the University Seal.[263]

The Covenant Society represented one of the newer University responses to institutional donors. Comprised of those who had included HBU in their estate planning, the Covenant Society was chartered in

---

253 "News of Note: Ladies Auxiliary," *Houston Baptist College News,* Nov. 1964, 3.

254 Houston Baptist University, Minutes of the Meetings of the Board of Trustees, Meeting on 18 May 1999.

255 "Auxiliary holds reunion luncheon," *HBU News,* Nov. 1999, 5.

256 "George Named HBU Woman of the Year," *HBU News,* Aug. 1999, 5. Photo.

257 Houston Baptist University, Minutes of the Meetings of the Board of Trustees, Meeting on 26 Sept. 2000.

258 "Auxiliary Reunion," *HBU News,* Dec. 2001, 23.

259 "Auxiliary helps HBC (sic)," *HBU News,* June 1973, 1.

260 Participants who had purchased tickets for one early "tasting bee," arrived in Denham Hall at noon to find most of the food had been eaten by the members of the Auxiliary.

261 "HBC Auxiliary Bulletin Board," *Houston Baptist College News,* Apr. 1968, 3.

262 "Ladies Auxiliary formed February, 1963," *HBU News,* June 1973, 1.

263 *Ornogah 1981,* 85. Following the destruction from Hurricane Ike in 2008, the seal was relocated to the Moody Library.

2000 with sixty-two members representing forty-nine estates. By 2002, the membership had grown to one hundred members who represented the very heart of the institution. Members included the elected leaders of other University support organizations, donors to the Endowed Scholarship program, and University friends who had given of their time and expertise in the University's behalf over many years.[264]

§

Following the Spirit of Excellence Dinner hosting Margaret Thatcher, the winter 2000 dinner recognized donors Mr. and Mrs. Gus Glasscock, Jr. and Dr. Bill Pinson, Executive Director Emeritus of the Baptist General Convention of Texas. Mrs. Mevis "Nell" Smith, President of the President's Advisors in 1988 and a member of the Auxiliary, was awarded the 2000 Milton Cross Volunteer Award.[265] These dinners also became the occasion for public recognition of winners of the Opal Goolsby Teaching Award, the Mayfied Staff Award, the Distinguished Alumnus Award, and the Meritorious Alumnus Award.[266]

In October 2001, General Norman Schwarzkopf was the featured speaker at the Spirit of Excellence Dinner that honored Robert and Janice McNair, Eleanor McCollum, and the Houston Livestock Show and Rodeo.[267] Mr. and Mrs. Archie Dunham served as honorary chairs for the evening that attracted 730 guests. Sherry and Jim Smith joined friends Kim and Michael Stevens as chairs of the gala.[268] While in Houston, Schwarzkopf visited the Bible in America Museum on campus and received a pair of custom boots to remember the occasion. Proceeds from the dinner were designated for the renovation of the Mabee Teaching Theater.[269]

The Schwarzkopf evening marked the final event to be planned by Vice President Cindy Garbs who tendered her resignation shortly thereafter.[270] Garbs joined the University administrative staff in 1998 and brought a new marketing and branding campaign to the University. She helped propagate the concept of the Legacy Center to relate the

---

264 "Covenant Society," *HBU News,* Mar. 2002, 23. Photo.

265 Merin Brown, "Thirteen honored at awards gala," *The Collegian,* 27 Jan. 2000, p. 1.

266 A list of the recipients of these awards may be found in the Appendix of this volume.

267 "Schwarzkopf speaks at HBU," *Houston Chronicle,* 15 Oct. 2001, Houston sec., p. 4, two-star ed.

268 "Spirit of Excellence Gala," *HBU News,* Dec. 2001, 7.

269 Kristen Brock, "Schwarzkopf emphasizes character at fundraiser," *The Collegian,* 18 Oct. 2001, p. 1.

270 "Garbs announces departure," *HBU News,* Dec. 2001, 25. Photo.

University to the community, elicited the marketing assistance of the Hall Group, and executed two of the largest fund-raising events in University history with the Thatcher and Schwarzkopf dinners. The ultimate completion of the Morris Cultural Arts Center in 2006 bore testimony to the brief but significant record of leadership Garbs provided.

In September 2001, climate-controlled exhibit cases were added in the Bible in America Museum to display items from the collection including the rarest item in the collection—the only remaining copy of the Francis Bailey New Testament of 1780, and one of eleven known Aitken Bibles dating from 1782.[271] The Bible in America Museum had opened in the spring of 1998 in space formerly occupied by the Moody Library Lecture Room. President Hodo observed, "Most people don't understand the trials people went through to sustain the Word. The museum will stand as a reminder to our students, our city, and our nation that God's eternal Word is the cornerstone of knowledge and education."[272]

The Moody Library converted the catalog of the collection to a searchable database in late 2000.[273] Using the expanded capability of the Internet, the catalog became available from off-campus as well.[274] In November 2000, Norma Lowder gave her collection of Gilbert and Sullivan memorabilia to the Library in honor of Dr. Robert Linder, conductor of the Houston Gilbert and Sullivan Society.[275] The University Place resident and former principal of the High School for the Performing and Visual Arts had amassed the collection of books, compact disks, posters, libretti, figurines, music boxes, costume designs, and other memorabilia over some thirty years.[276] A formal dinner presentation ceremony honoring Lowder's gift was attended by the British Consul Peter Bacon and by former D'Oyle Carte actor Alistair Donkin.[277] Lowder was a faithful member of the audience for Convocations, Music Forums, recitals, and concerts over all the years of her University Place residence; she was the favorite of students and faculty alike. In 2001, the *Houston*

---

271 Richard Vara, "Rare Good Books: Houston Baptist University opens Museum of American Bibles," *Houston Chronicle,* 8 Sept. 2001, Rel. sec., p. 1, two-star ed.

272 "Museum project gains momentum," *HBU News,* Mar. 1998, 14.

273 Melissa Torres, "New library card catalog adds information, speed," *The Collegian,* 2 Nov. 2000, p. 3.

274 Michelle Cavazos, "Library accessible from home," *The Collegian,* 25 Jan. 2001, p. 2.

275 "A celebration of friends," *HBU News,* Winter 2000, 7.

276 Joshua Pease, "Rare library donation to benefit museum students," *The Collegian,* 2 Nov. 2000, p. 7.

277 "Gilbert and Sullivan," *HBU News,* Winter 2000, 7.

Chronicle noted, "The University has named her Distinguished Mentor Emeritus in the School of Music."[278]

§

In the late 1990s, the University's intercollegiate athletic programs matured, enjoying an unbroken record of achievement and recognition. The University joined the Red River Athletic Conference in 1998. With fourteen member institutions in four states, the Red River was the largest conference in the NAIA and was split into a north and south division.[279] In the fall of 1999, the campus was gifted with a new mascot—its first actual Husky—from Sherry '04 and Billy '03 Thomas.[280] Wakiza, "determined warrior" in the American Indian language, adapted quickly to the campus environment and enjoyed a celebrity status among students and staff.[281] Kiza was handled by Kerry Nolen '99, Director of Student Programming.[282] With Coach Kaddie Platt '94, the women's volleyball team in 1999 was ranked among the top twenty-five teams in the nation for the first time in history.[283] In the University's first season as a member of the Red River Conference, the team won both the conference and tournament championship, and two players, Kara Williams and Crystal Kubena, were named to the All America team.[284] In 2000, the Huskies achieved a 13-0 season and advanced to the national tournament for the first time.[285] By 2002, Coach of the Year Kaddie Platt's team won its fourth conference championship and was ranked twelfth in the nation.[286] Students named to All-America honors in volleyball during this era included Rachael Dinkins, Elele Ekadeli, Sarah Emmer, Crystal Kubena, and Kara Williams. Ekadeli was named to the NAIA All America first team in volleyball in 2001 and 2002[287] and was named national MVP and Player of the Year in 2002.[288]

---

278 Daniel Vargas, "A key player: Retired teacher devotes time, talent and financial aid at HBU," *Houston Chronicle,* 8 Apr. 2001, Lifestyle sec., p. 3, three-star ed.
279 "University joins Red River Conference," *HBU News,* June 1998, 15.
280 Amy N. Davis, "Mascot draws 'good response' from students," *The Collegian,* 7 Oct. 1999, pp. 1, 6.
281 Tammy Sacky, "New Husky mascot to bring spirit, tradition to HBU," *The Collegian,* 7 Sept. 2000, p. 4.
282 "Wakiza graduates," *HBU News,* Winter 2000, 20.
283 Kelly Fitch, "Volleyball team ranks in top 25," *The Collegian,* 5 Nov. 1998, p. 1.
284 Kelly Fitch, "Volleyball players earn top honors," *The Collegian,* 14 Jan. 1999, p. 11.
285 "Volleyball wins conference and region titles," *HBU News,* Winter 2000, 22.
286 "Each sport won its conference championship," *HBU News,* June 2002, 23.
287 "Elele Ekadeli named NAIA All American first team," *HBU News,* Dec. 2001, 27.
288 Houston Baptist University, *2008 Volleyball Media Guide,* 42.

In its initial year, the women's basketball team under Coach Chris Harris won the conference championship and advanced to the NAIA national tournament. Shane Brown was appointed coach in 2000 and led the team to the conference championship and tournament; the Huskies finished the year ranked twenty-first in the nation. In 2001, the team advanced to the third round of the national tournament in their second visit in as many years.[289] In 2002, the team ranked sixth in the NAIA having advanced three rounds to the "Elite Eight" in the national tournament.[290]

The men's basketball team won the RRAC trophy in 1999 and participated in the first round of the national tournament.[291] The following year, men's basketball won the conference title, advanced to the second round of the national tournament, and was ranked tenth in NAIA.[292] It was the Husky's third trip to the NAIA tournament.[293] The Huskies finished a 31-5 season in 2001 tournament and were ranked fourth by the NAIA.[294] The team advanced to the first round of the national tournament in 2002 and finished the year ranked fourteenth in the NAIA— amassing a record of forty consecutive home game wins.[295] All America team members during this time included Michael LeBlanc, Charles Fordjour, Chad Hartley, and Chris Johnson.[296]

The Huskies baseball team wrapped up a 40-19 season, won the NAIA south division championship in 1999 under new coach Brian Huddleston, and participated in the Southwest Regional Tournament.[297] Russell Chandler, Chris Fadal, and Chris Hill were named to All America honors.[298] In the fall of 2000, a Husky alumnus, pitcher Trevor Enders '98, was called up to play for the Tampa Bay Devil Rays. Enders was the first HBU baseball player ever to be tapped for baseball's major leagues. The Huskies won the conference championship for the fourth consecutive year in 2001 but were eliminated in the regional tournament.[299] In 2002, baseball enjoyed a 40-17 season, won the conference championship once

289 Shauna Couri, "Cinderella goes to the ball," *The Collegian,* 29 Mar. 2001, p. 1.
290 Shauntelle Jones, "Women end season with record 33 wins," *The Collegian,* 11 Apr. 2002, p. 15.
291 *Ornogah 1999,* 173.
292 Josh Rowlands, "Men's team paints road orange and blue," *The Collegian,* 16 Mar. 2000, p. 1.
293 Gabriel Rapier, "Red River Conference Champions," *The Collegian,* 13 Apr. 2000, p. 16.
294 "Huskies finish season 31-5," *HBU News,* Spring 2001, 18.
295 Shauntelle Jones, "Women end season with record 33 wins," *The Collegian,* 11 Apr. 2002, p. 15.
296 *Ornogah 1999,* 173.
297 Gabe Rapier, "Huskies clinch championships, *The Collegian,* 13 May 1999, p. 15.
298 "Three named to All America baseball team," *HBU News,* Aug. 1999, 17.
299 Josh Rowlands, "Huskies go to the show," *The Collegian,* 5 Oct. 2000, p. 16.

again, and finished the year ranking thirteenth in the NAIA. Coach Huddleston was recognized as Coach of the Year.[300]

Huskies softball boasted more All-America honors from 1998 to 2002 than any other HBU sport. These included Erin Bolton, Loralyn Hinze, Christine Phillips, Charity Rychlik, and Kathy Spies. In 1999, the team won its conference championship and advanced to the Southwest Region Tournament where they finished ranked thirteenth in the nation.[301] By the spring of 2000, the team was ranked seventh nationally. Its repeat performance in the spring of 2001 marked the third consecutive championship. In 2002, the Huskies finished their season ranked fourth in the NAIA.[302]

In 1999, HBU received the first All Sports Trophy ever awarded by the Red River Athletic Conference for championships in volleyball, men's basketball, softball, and baseball. Coaches Cottrell, Platt, Hall, and Huddleston were all named to Coach of the Year honors.[303] In 2000, HBU won the All-Sports Trophy a second time; Cottrell, Huddleston, and Hall were named to second Coach of the Year awards.[304] In 2001, the Huskies won their third All Sports Trophy. Mary Ellen Hall, Kaddie Platt, and Brian Huddleston were named Coach of the Year for the third consecutive year.[305] Wearing another hat, Ron Cottrell was also named Athletic Director of the Year by Region IV of the NAIA in 2001.[306] To the credit of the student athletes, the NAIA recognized nineteen HBU Scholar Athletes between1998 and 2002.[307] Of sixty-nine athletes in University intercollegiate competition in 2000, thirty-six had grade-point averages of 3.0 or higher. The University's distinguished graduation rate for student athletes was over ninety percent.[308]

Students and alumni also excelled in other areas. In 1999, education majors achieved a ninety-two percent pass rate on state licensure exams; nursing graduates once again achieved a hundred percent pass rate on their professional license examinations.[309] Under the direction of Keri

---

300 "Huskies sweep RRAC championship again," *HBU News,* June 2002, 23.

301 *Ornogah 1999,* 183.

302 Erica Smith, "Softball swept RACC, advance to tournament," *The Collegian,* 9 May 2002, p. 18.

303 "Hall and Huddleston receive '*Coach of the Year*' honors," *HBU News,* Aug. 1999, 16. Photo.

304 "HBU claims second straight All Sports trophy," *HBU News,* Sept. 2000, 22.

305 "Huskies enjoy another banner year," *HBU News,* Sept. 2001, 29.

306 Houston Baptist University, Minutes of the Meetings of the Board of Trustees, Meeting on 20 Nov. 2001.

307 "NAIA All-time honors," National Association of Intercollegiate Athletics, www.naiasports.org/honors (accessed Mar. 31, 2010).

308 "Student Life," *HBU News,* May/June 2000, 35.

309 Houston Baptist University, Minutes of the Meetings of the Faculty Assembly, Meeting on 5 Oct. 1999.

Lilley, FOCUS announced the release of its second CD album. The organization was in its twenty-third year of ministry to the church and civic communities.[310] A new ministry team, Masterpiece, mounted "drama for the Master" as an outreach for the University.[311]

Dr. Carol Ann Bonds '68 was awarded the *Reader's Digest* Health Hero Award in 2001 and was featured in the February issue of the magazine.[312] Bonds was named Texas Principal of the Year, was a finalist for Texas Superintendent of the Year in 2001, and was the first person outside the health care field to receive the national Robert Wood Johnson Community Health Leadership Award for her work with school children in low-income schools.[313] Bonds was later named Superintendent of Schools in San Angelo and was elected to the HBU Board of Trustees.[314]

§

As in succeeding periods of history, the aging of the University was inevitably accompanied by the loss of colleagues who played pivotal roles. Though most had been retired for several years, their influence on campus had remained strong. Bertha Wilson died in January 2000. Her love for the campus and its students eclipsed her defined responsibility. In tribute, *The Collegian* observed that more than anything else, "Bertha dished up food for the soul."[315] The loss of another great friend was Mildred Boone. The telephone voice of HBU for twenty-six years, Boone was the unofficial coach and cheerleader for campus athletic events. Her joy, energy, and selfless enthusiasm were a model for students and staff alike.[316] Appropriately, her memorial service was held on the campus which she loved so greatly.

The University lost several distinguished faculty members. Dr. Alma Malone Leavell died in January 2000. The former Dean of the College of Education and Behavioral Sciences, Malone had been awarded the HBU President's Award and had been named to the rank of Distinguished

310 Mignon Francois, "Focusing on CD release," *The Collegian,* 5 Nov. 1998, p. 8.

311 "Masterpiece: drama for the Master," *HBU Collegian,* 22 Oct. 1998, p. 12.

312 "The Healing Touch," *Reader's Digest,* Feb. 2001.

313 "Robert Wood Johnson Foundation Community Health Leader," www.rwjf.org/pr/product.jsp?id=52191 (accessed Apr. 19, 2010).

314 "SAISD Hires Carol Ann Bonds as New Superintendent," www.saisd.org (accessed Apr. 19, 2010).

315 Paige Cannon, "Former snack bar supervisor dished up food for the soul," *The Collegian,* 13 Jan. 2000, p. 1.

316 "Mildred Boone," *HBU News,* Winter 2000, 31.

Professor.[317] Dr. A. O. Collins passed away in June. His contributions as Chair of Christianity and Philosophy were equaled only by his dedication to student life, his commitment to alumni, and the scholarly nurturing of his department. Among the tributes to Collins were those of Dr. Robert Newell, Dr. Robert Creech, and Dr. Jim Denison '80 who called him "my spiritual father." Inside Collins' Bible was found the prayer, "From the laziness that is content with half-truth, from the fear that shrinks from new truth, from the arrogance that thinks it knows the truth, Oh God of Truth, deliver us."[318]

The founding Dean of the College of Nursing, Dr. Glendola Nash, died in October. Nash had guided the transfer of the Lillie Jolly nursing diploma program to college baccalaureate success, gaining accreditation even before the graduation of the first class. Her student and successor, Dr. Nancy Yuill, paid tribute:

> HBC's early accreditation in 1972 (before the graduation of its first class of nursing students) had never before been achieved. Dr. Nash mentored fine nurses without educational experience to develop faculty. She established a competency-based curriculum that allowed students to develop a strong knowledge base with skills while instilling values of caring, integrity, and compassion. She raised over $1,000,000 for scholarships, programs, and academic support including a state-of-the-art learning resource center, a prototype skills lab, and early computer and media delivery.[319] She set a standard of excellence that established the University's College of Nursing as first in its class in the nation. We continue to strive to maintain that excellence.[320]

A third dean, Dr. Calvin Huckabay, passed away in April, 2001. Huckabay had been a member of the founding faculty and was the University's chief scholar.[321] He had served as President of the South Central College English Association, as President of the Texas Association of Departments of English, had received the Piper Award for outstanding teaching, and was the author of three internationally-recognized bibliographies on John Milton.[322]

---

317 "Obituary," *The Collegian,* 21 Jan. 2000, p. 3.
318 "Dr. A. O. Collins: remembering a friend, mentor, teacher," *HBU News,* Sept. 2000, 14-15.
319 Dr. Nancy Yuill, "Dr. Glendola Nash: a tribute to school of nursing founder," *HBU News,* Winter 2000, 16.
320 "Obituary," *The Collegian,* 19 Oct. 2000, p. 2.
321 Denise Lancaster, "Original faculty member retires," *The Collegian,* 12 May 1994, p. 12.
322. Candace Bush, "Former dean dies at 71," *HBU News,* Sept. 2001, 23.

Dr. Ray V. Mayfield, Jr. was the last of the founding College administrators. Like faculty member Dr. James E. Williamson, Mayfield had been a member of the UBA College Committee, a founding trustee in 1960, and had joined the first College administration in 1963. Mayfield died in February 2002 after having retired in 1994 as Vice President for Bequests and Trusts.[323] Reflective of his college football career, Mayfield "took the ball" of the Endowed Academic Scholarship concept and "ran" with it to establish the most successful ongoing fund-raising program in University history.[324] He was the first member of the University family to receive thirty-year service recognition in 1993. In honor of his institutional contribution, the annual staff recognition award was named the Ray V. Mayfield, Jr. Outstanding Staff Award.[325] At the annual Endowed Scholarship brunch in 2002, Mayfield's thirty-one-year legacy was honored. From the inception of the program to 2002, more than 250 scholarships had been established.[326]

The Mayfield Awards annually honor an outstanding group of University staff. This award was given to Sharon Saunders and Jack Purcell in 1998,[327] Judy Ferguson '67 and Dick Parker in 1999,[328] Loree Watson '80 and Anthony Martin in 2000,[329] Maydeen Wells and David Melton in 2001,[330] and Dr. Cynthia Young and Hugh McClung in 2002.[331] Recognition for years of service was also formalized with acknowledgements and the presentation of gifts in the annual Founders' Day Convocation. The increasing number of long-term employees was an indication of their commitment and their value to the University. Those receiving the University's first thirty-five year recognitions were Kathleen Strom '87[332] and Dr. Don Looser in 1999.[333] Articles on the

---

323 "A Founding Trustee Remembered," *HBU News*, News, Mar. 2002, 8.
324 "The Rev. Ray Mayfield, HBU co-founder," *Houston Chronicle*, 10 Feb. 2002, sec. A, p. 46, two-star-edition.
325 Joshua Pease, "Founding father dies at age 75," *HBU Collegian*, 14 Feb. 2002, p. 4.
326 "Endowed Scholarship Brunch: honoring traditions," *HBU News*, Jun. 2002, 10-11.
327 "HBU honors outstanding staff," Houston Baptist University, Minutes of the Meetings of the Board of Trustees, Meeting on Sept. 1998, p. 3.
328 "Faculty, staff receive recognition," *SomeTimes*, June 1999.
329 "Mayfield Outstanding Staff Awards," *HBU News*, Winter 2000, 18.
330 "Mayfield Outstanding Staff Awards," *HBU News*, Sept. 2001, 24-25.
331 "Mayfield Staff Awards," *SomeTimes*, July 2002.
332 Alicia Whitehead, "Still Active," *The Collegian*, 23 Sept. 1999, p. 8. Kathleen Strom matriculated while she was employed at HBU to complete her degree in 1987 after 20 years of enrollment.
333 Theresa Kipp, "Founders Day Convocation honors employee anniversaries," *The Collegian*, 9 Dec. 2000, p. 3.

careers of both these two long-term personnel appeared in *The Collegian*.[334] Recognitions for thirty years of service were awarded Frances Curtis and Dr. James Tsao in 1998,[335] Dr. Don Byrnes in 1999,[336] and James Busby, Nora Hayes, and Dr. Phyllis Thompson in 2000.[337]

Recognition for twenty-five years was given Dr. Avin Brownlee, Dr. Hutch Dvorak, Dr. Ernie Pyle, and Dr. James Taylor in 1998;[338] Dr. Rick Denham, Dr. Carter Franklin, and Dr. Newell Boyd in 1999;[339] Marianne Anderson, Dr. John Hooker, Dr. John Lutjemeier, and Dr. Gene Wofford in 2000;[340] and Ed Best and Dr. Verna Peterson in 2001.[341] Service awards for twenty years were given to Virginia An, Carol Elsbury, Judy Ferguson '67, Dr. Ann Gebuhr, Dr. John Green, and Ronnie Lott in 1998;[342] Nancy McCreary and Dr. David Wehr in 1999;[343] Dr. Joan DeRooy, Loree Watson '80, and Maydene Wells in 2000;[344] and in 2001, Dr. John Alexander, Linda Clark '87, Margie Coventon, Dr. Dan Kramlich, Sharon Saunders, Dr. Sebron Williams, and Dr. Nancy Yuill '72.[345]

A number of senior faculty and staff joined their retired colleagues during this era. The University's Director of Choral Activities, Dr. David Wehr, retired in 1998. Wehr had followed in the proud choral tradition at HBU and added his own record of outstanding accomplishment to the University's history. A member of the faculty for twenty-one years, Dr. Wehr had anchored a position for the University that involved both academic and public relations responsibility. University choral ensembles toured internationally and performed in Germany with the Nuremberg Symphony and in New York at Lincoln Center. In addition to his role of leadership in the School of Music, Wehr had served as Associate Conductor of the Houston Symphony Chorale, the co-founder of a professional ensemble—the Concert Chorale of Houston, as Music Director for Houston's First Methodist Church, and as composer, organist, and carillonneur.[346]

---

334 Alicia Whitehead, "She Remembers," *The Collegian*, 9 Sept. 1999, p. 7; Merin Brown, "Both ends of the road," *The Collegian*, 13 Jan. 2000, p. 9; Merin Brown, "Living a Legacy," *The Collegian*, 27 Jan. 2000, p. 1.
335 "Congratulations to our Colleagues," *SomeTimes*, Nov. 1998.
336 "Founders Day," *HBU News*, Mar. 2000, 4.
337 "Founders Day," *HBU News*, Spring 2001, 6.
338 "Founders Day," *HBU News*, Apr. 1999, 14-15.
339 "Founders Day," *HBU News*, Mar. 2000, 6-7.
340 "Employee service to be recognized," *SomeTimes*, Nov. 2000.
341 "Founders Day November 29," *SomeTimes*, Nov. 2001.
342 *SomeTimes*, Nov. 1998.
343 "Founders Day," *HBU News*, Mar. 2000, 6-7.
344 "Employee service to be recognized," *SomeTimes*, Nov. 2000.
345 "Founders Day," *HBU News*, Mar. 2002, 6-7.
346 "Dr. David Wehr retires from HBU: 1979-1998," *HBU Upbeat*, Fall 1998, pp. 3-5.

In 2001, Carol Elsbury, a devoted and strategic administrative officer, announced her plans to retire as Registrar after twenty-three years of distinguished University service.[347] Elsbury had guided the University through several generations of increasing sophistication in data gathering and student services. Dr. Bill Borgers, Dean of the College of Education and Behavioral Sciences, decided to move to his beloved Creede, Colorado for "uninterrupted fishing."[348] Borgers' contributions to the University-at-large were significant. He brought expertise in the area of quality-based continuous improvement management at a time when the University greatly profited from his leadership.[349] He developed the University's first distance education program, the Masters Online, in an innovative partnership with the Fort Bend ISD and the for-profit National School Conference Institute.[350] Moreover, Borgers networked effectively for the University with the local and state teacher education community as a result of his experience as school superintendant. Dr. John Alexander was named interim Dean of the College.

Two of the additional retirees were directors of the University's most successful graduate programs. Dr. Carter Franklin, Director of the Master of Business Administration program, served as Associate Dean of the College of Business and Economics and held the Rex G. Baker Professorship. Franklin was honored for twenty-five years of distinguished service in 1999. Dr. Franklin established the University's first graduate program and guided its development as one of the most pre-eminent, entrepreneurial programs in the city. Franklin had created a second MBA program along more traditional models for professionals earlier in their career. He also pioneered protocols for addressing student need by innovative class scheduling and administrative absorption of repetitive matriculation processes. From the outset, the MBA program was a profit center. Moreover, the University found its reputation and standing in the city greatly enhanced by the creation of the program. Franklin maintained high academic standards both for program admission and instruction and proved to be one of the most effective program directors in University history.

Similarly, Dr. Newell Boyd, the founder of the Master of Liberal Arts program, announced his plans to leave the University in 2001. The MLA

---

347 "Farewells and transitions," *HBU News,* Sept. 2001, 27.
348 Josh Rowlands, "Borgers retires as dean of College," *The Collegian,* 20 Sept. 2001, p. 1.
349 "Borgers Named Dean," *SomeTimes,* Aug. 1995.
350 "University offers long-distance degree," *The Collegian,* 11 Feb. 1999, p. 5.

program dated from 1985. Enthusiastic response in the Houston community served to solidify the University's commitment to develop niche programs at the graduate level.[351] In 1995, the program had expanded to the Kingwood campus of the North Harris Montgomery Community College (NHMCC).[352] The HBU program was a member of the Association of Graduate Liberal Studies and one of only three accredited programs in the region—with Southern Methodist University and Tulane University.[353] A member of the faculty for twenty-seven years, Boyd guided the MLA program in its growth and development for the sixteen years of program history. Like Franklin's MBA model, Boyd's MLA was at once innovative and responsive to student need. The program offered a selection of high profile courses that appealed to those whose formal education was complete but who desired study "for the joy of learning."[354] In 2001, the program boasted 350 alumni and had forty-nine currently-enrolled students. Dr. Jon Suter observed, "In many ways, the MLA embodies what the University is all about as a liberal arts institution."[355] Upon Boyd's resignation, Dr. Harold Raley was appointed Interim Director of the program.

Dr. Joan DeRooy, a member of the University staff since 1980, also announced her retirement. Her years of service involved some of the most creative and developmental co-curricular activity in University history. She developed the continuing education and instructional television programs of the University. Through her direction, the Corporate Alliance was created whose member employees took classes in the MBA degree program from their work site via real-time interactive television.[356] DeRooy was also the principal University staff liaison with the Channel 14 television project. In 1998, DeRooy gave direction to the Living the Vision task forces to identify potential donors, heighten visibility in the community, and strengthen donor recognition.[357] This work became the backbone of the first institutional strategic plan. Dr. DeRooy was later named Vice President for Advancement, then Vice President for Donor Development and Research, and finally Vice President for Special Projects.[358]

351 Amy N. Davis, "MLA director professor leaves after 27 years," HBU Collegian, 25 Jan 2001, p. 5.
352 Dr. E. D. Hodo, "President's Report," HBU News, May 1995, inside cover.
353 Houston Baptist University, Minutes of the Meetings of the Board of Trustees, Meeting on 23 Nov. 1999.
354 "Boyd leaves MLA legacy," HBU News, Spring 2001, 21.
355 Amy N. Davis, "MLA director leaves after 27 years," The Collegian, 25 Jan. 2001, pp. 1, 5.
356 "The Division of Continuing Education and Instructional Television," HBU Bulletin 1990-92, 170.
357 Houston Baptist University, Minutes of the Meetings of the Board of Trustees, Meeting on 24 Feb. 1998.
358 Houston Baptist University, Minutes of the Meetings of the Board of Trustees, Meeting on 23 Nov. 1997.

In a meeting of the Faculty Assembly in 1999, President Rhonda Furr proposed the formation of an organization for retired staff and faculty.[359] With the affirmation of the Assembly, an implementation committee was formed to build a database and to develop a Constitution and By-Laws.[360] In the absence of institutional records, much of the staff employment database from 1963 had to be rebuilt utilizing campus telephone direc-tories, *Ornogah*s, the *HBU News,* and archival records. The first meeting of the Association was held on February 16, 2001. The first officers of the new HBU Retirees Association were Dr. Robert Linder, Chair, Dr. Sebron Williams, Barbara Owens, Dr. Robert Creech, and Pauline Wright. Linder observed, "This is an organization whose time has come. The asso-ciation brings together long-time friends whose common bond is their years at HBU. As we evolve, members can remain actively involved in the events and the progress of the institution they served."[361] Assembly President Rhonda Furr was the object of a resolution of appreciation from the Assembly in 2002 and served as Faculty Liaison Officer from 2001 through May 2010.

§

The period 1998 to 2002 reflected an era of challenge and opportunity. The process for reaffirmation of accreditation by the Southern Association of Colleges and Schools resulted in significant process and policy changes in the University's operation. By 2002, the University responded to a clearer view of itself to determine new courses of action. The bold move of asserting institutional autonomy with the Baptist General Convention of Texas was an act foretold by multiple examples of institutional independence from earliest history. The effect of such challenge on the Board of Trustees was to galva-nize resolve and re-engage the commitment of all of its members. Rather consistently, HBU had historically determined to chart its own course, pay its own way, and enjoy the fruits of its freedom to pioneer and innovate. This independent spirit attracted faculty, staff, and students who supported its entrepreneurial spirit. Both Dr. Hinton and Dr. Hodo, each from his own perspective, fostered that institutional characteristic.

---

359 "The Genesis of the HBU Retirees' Association," *2009-2010 Retirees' Association Directory,* 4.
360 Dr. Jerry Gaultney chaired the Implementation Committee whose other members were Dr. Sebron Williams, Teresa Boyd, Dr. Rhonda Furr, Dr. Robert Linder, Dr. Don Looser, Dr. Harold Raley, and Dr. Elysee Peavy. All of the faculty on the Implementation Committee later served a term as Association President.
361 "HBU retirees form association," *HBU News,* Spring 2001, 22.

This era was a time of significant change. A number of new programs and centers of activity were added. Effective control of spending made financial decision-making important but difficult. Academic and non-academic programs vied for available resources. Recurrent faculty issues such as competitive salaries, promotion policy, and the role of the faculty in governance remained significant issues. Recurrent student demand for a more vibrant campus social life remained a concern even after construction of the Baugh and Wellness Centers.

The period 1998-2002 saw the departure of forty-five faculty members. Some departures represented professional advancement. Dr. Curtis Freeman, a member of the Christianity faculty for fourteen years, was appointed Director of the Baptist House of Studies at Duke University Divinity School.[362] Other resignations such as that of graduate program directors Boyd and Franklin hinted of hierarchical fatigue. Senior faculty and staff were often replaced by younger, less experienced though gifted colleagues. As a reflection of generational change, younger faculty members typically professed greater allegiance to their discipline than to the institution-at-large. They seemed less willing than their predecessors to assume quasi-administrative assignment, preferring to concentrate on scholarly and instructional activity. This placed greater stress on already-stretched institutional infrastructure.

Because of this discipline orientation, the critical functions of committee responsibility, strategic planning, retention activity, and academic advising became more difficult to sustain while becoming more important to institutional mission. The University's focus on high profile events and the concentration of the *HBU News* on affinity organizations caused some faculty to feel the academic campus existed as a secondary parallel universe. The Faculty Assembly noted, "The academic 'side of the campus' does not seem to receive as much emphasis and university publicity as do social activities."[363] Faculty also expressed concern that the emphasis on fund raising for the Legacy Center curtailed sustaining fund efforts.[364]

§

---

362 Candace Bush, "Freeman leaves HBU, takes job offer at Duke," *The Collegian,* 10 May 2001, p. 7.

363 Houston Baptist University, Minutes of the Meetings of the Faculty Assembly, Meeting on 19 Jan. 1999.

364 Houston Baptist University, Minutes of the Meetings of the Faculty Assembly, Meeting on 29 Sept. 1998.

The University in 2002 was significantly stronger, more capable, more poised for the future than in 1998. Campus facilities were dramatically expanded and improved. The security of sound financial management contributed to confidence. New academic leadership brought excitement and energy. The campus community began to look beyond the current administrative leadership to the potential for long-range vision and fresh opportunity.

Retirement plans were not unique to faculty and staff. Among the President and Vice Presidents in 2002—Hodo, Looser, Parker, Purcell, Byrnes, and Anderson—all but Parker were at retirement age. These senior executives recognized the vulnerabilities resulting from a virtually complete exchange of administrative leadership over a brief period of time. Consideration of timing and sequence became a matter of internal discussion. Dr. Hodo never articulated plans for "retirement" for himself, but described "moving from the University to new pursuits" at some point. However, he confided his desire first to complete the fund-raising required for the Legacy Center. Fortunately, personal or health circumstances were not mitigating factors for any of these officers; therefore, optimal planning for succession seemed possible. Dr. Hodo led the trustees to adopt a presidential succession plan. He also revised operational policy to address University governance in his extended absence or inability to perform the duties of President. The future portended dramatic change of leadership within the foreseeable future.

THIRTEEN

2002-2006

Enron. Sarbanes-Oxley. World Trade Center. Euro. iPod.

In 2002, the lyrics to a popular song observed, "the future is not what it used to be."[1] Y2K anxiety had provided but a subdued entry to the decade that ultimately was called "the aughts." Houston was still reeling from Tropical Storm Allison and 9/11 when the nation's seventh largest corporation, Enron—Houston's proudest model of excellence and entrepreneurship—collapsed in full view of the world, leaving thousands unemployed, countless others with shattered retirement funds, and the city's newest skyscraper empty. Enron Field, the city's new major league baseball stadium, stood as a stark reminder of unthinkable reversals of fortune. Psychologists and sociologists noted a cultural loss of innocence, the end of an era of euphoria, heightened anxiety stemming from loss of control, and a reversal of meaning for the belief, "All things are possible." Yet, typical of Houston's history, there was also much to celebrate. The neighboring University of Houston marked its seventy-fifth anniversary. HBU—Houston's Blessed University—planned a fortieth anniversary celebration and experienced one of the most significant periods of qualitative growth in its history. The University was named one of 200 *Colleges of Distinction* in 2005.[2] These colleges shared the characteristics of being 1) recognized for excellence, 2) strongly focused on undergraduate education, 3) home to a wide variety of innovative learning experiences, 4) an active campus with opportunities for personal development, and 5) highly valued by graduate schools and employers for outstanding preparation.[3] The Fogarty Kline Monroe imaging campaign moved into its third phase.[4] The new Bible in America Museum was dedicated with a fundraising brunch that featured Pastor Kirbyjon Caldwell, Jeannette Clift George, and a video presentation on the Bible collection narrated by Ron

---

1 Ronnie Milsap, "The Future is Not What It Used To Be," *Ronnie Milsap Live*, RCA Victor, 1976, track 14.
2 "Colleges of Distinction," *HBU News*, Winter 2005, 18.
3 Houston Baptist University, Minutes of the Meetings of the Board of Trustees, Meeting on 17 May 2005; www.collegesofdistinction.com (accessed Jan. 7, 2010).
4 "Go far without going far away." "Where your professor knows you from Adam."

Stone '94.[5] Dr. Hodo marked his fifteenth anniversary as the University's President.[6]

It was a time of change in leadership. New colleagues joined the University. Dr. Joe David Brown was named Dean of the College of Education and Behavioral Sciences in 2002 following Dr. Bill Borgers.[7] In 2003, Dr. Ray Newman, newly appointed Brown Endowed Chair of Business and Dean of the College of Business and Economics, followed the interim service of Ritamarie Tauer MAcct '85.[8] A third new dean, Dr. Brian Runnels '81, was named Dean of the College of Arts and Humanities in 2005 following the retirement of Dr. James Taylor.[9]

Dr. Renee Borns joined the University as Director of Academic Advising.[10] Norm Slosted succeeded Jack Purcell as Vice President for Student Affairs.[11] Dr. Diana Severance was named Curator of the Bible in America Museum.[12] Rick Ogden '98 was appointed Assistant Vice President for Church Relations;[13] Martha Morrow was named to the University's marketing staff;[14] and Colette Cross was appointed Director of Spiritual Life.[15] Additionally, internal reassignments included Dr. Don Byrnes who was named Legal Counsel and special project officer for the Office of the President,[16] Don Anderson '68 who was promoted to Vice President for Development, and Sharon Saunders who was named Vice President for Marketing.[17] Dr. Harold Raley retained his appointment as Scholar-in-Residence, but relinquished the directorship of the Master of Liberal Arts program to Dr. Chris Hammons.[18]

Both the Southern Association and the National League for Nursing reaffirmed the University's accreditation. The purchase of the remaining interest in the Atwood II building from Southwestern Seminary yielded

---

5 "Museum Dedication," *HBU News,* Dec. 2002, 8.

6 "Founders' Day," *HBU News,* Dec. 2002, 10.

7 "Brown named Dean of COEBS," *HBU News,* Sept. 2002, 4.

8 "Newman Named COBE Dean," *HBU News,* Sept. 2003, 4.

9 "Runnels comes home to serve as dean of COAH," *HBU News,* Mar. 2005, 11. Photo.

10 Tomie Lunsford, "Borns named director of academic advising," *The Collegian,* 18 Oct. 2003, p. 2; "Borns named director, academic advising," *HBU News,* Dec. 2003, 25.

11 "Norm Slosted named Vice President for Student Affairs," *HBU News,* Sept. 2003, 5.

12 "Updates," *HBU News,* Sept 2003, 21.

13 "Ogden joins Development," *HBU News,* Dec. 2003, 25.

14 "Morrow joins HBU marketing team," *HBU News,* Spring 2004, 16.

15 Joshua Goldman, "Cross named director of spiritual life," *The Collegian,* 15 Jan. 2004, p. 1; "Cross to lead Spiritual Life program," *HBU News,* Mar. 2004, 16.

16 Ibid.

17 Dr. E. D. Hodo, "From the President," *HBU News,* June 2002, 2.

18 "Hammons leads MLA," *HBU News,* Sept. 2003, 6.

new offices for Financial Affairs, new classrooms, and expanded computer laboratories. New majors were initiated in international business,[19]
entrepreneurship,[20] public policy,[21] and Biblical languages.[22] An honors
track was developed in music.[23] A revised graduate program was initiated in accounting, and an enhanced degree program in Christian
Counseling provided a Licensed Professional Counselor (LPC) option.[24] In
2005, Dr. Carol McGaughey developed an alternative teacher certification plan (ACP) that yielded credit hours toward a Master of Education
degree. The ACP quickly became one of the University's largest graduate programs; most ACP students persisted through the completion of
the graduate degree.[25] The Master of Science in Health Administration
degree was moved to the College of Business and Economics to respond
to student interest in an expanded business core and to profit from Dean
Newman's extensive experience in health administration.[26]

Dr. Newman buttressed the strategic initiative begun by Rita Tauer
to achieve accreditation for the College of Business and Economics. This
symbol of professional affirmation had emerged as a critical element in
the recruiting of graduate students in business. The accrediting process
consumed several years of intensive work and entailed revision of certain
elements of the business curriculum, redefinition of teaching load calculation, an increased requirement for assessment data, and an expanded
definition of professional activity for faculty. In 2005, the College of
Business accreditation was approved by the Association of Collegiate
Business Schools and Programs (ACBSP).[27]

Competition for graduate students in business was keen in the
Houston marketplace, and graduate enrollments at HBU decreased. In
2005, MBA programs were active on five Houston university campuses;
twenty-one programs were offered in Houston by non-resident universi-

---

19 Brie Moore, "COBE offers major in international business," *The Collegian*, 3 Nov. 2005, p. 1.

20 "Entrepreneurship Major Revised," *HBU News,* Mar. 2002, 4.

21 Jeremy James, "COAH to offer public policy major," *The Collegian,* 27 Jan. 2005, p. 4.

22 Cher Cambridge, "Greek, Hebrew studies added as Biblical languages major," *The Collegian*, 18 Sept. 2003,
p. 19. The goal of the major was to be able to read and interpret ancient texts including Apocrypha and the
Dead Sea Scrolls.

23 Tremaine Asberry, "New honors program option for music majors," *The Collegian,* 19 Sept. 2002, p. 3.

24 Scottie Fresch, "New degree prepares students for state exam: MA in Christian Counseling," *The Collegian,*
19 Sept. 2002, p. 5.

25 Houston Baptist University, Minutes of the Meetings of the Board of Trustees, Meeting on 17 May 2005.

26 Newman had been an executive officer at Parkland Hospital, Dallas and St. Luke's/Roosevelt General
Hospital, New York.

27 Brie Moore, "COBE awarded accreditation," *The Collegian,* 15 Dec. 2005, p. 1.

ties; sixty-two institutions reported online programs.[28]   A marketing research study done by the Gelb Group confirmed that HBU's program enrollment was negatively impacted by the limited funds for program advertising.[29]   In response, the Board approved a budget addition of $100,000 for targeted graduate business advertising through the Fogarty Kline marketing campaign.[30]   No institutional funds were provided for graduate financial aid.

The University's faculty was universally recognized to be the chief asset of its program of academic excellence. Longevity in appointment had historically resulted in faculty members with strong institutional allegiance. A 2005 survey revealed the average length of HBU service for faculty at the rank of Professor was twenty years; Associate Professors had served an average of eleven years; Assistant Professors had taught a notable average of nine years.[31] These periods of service are made more significant by the absence of tenure. Concomitantly, some forty percent of the faculty was over fifty-five years of age; each of the five-year increments between thirty-five years and fifty-five years of age represented approximately fifteen percent of the faculty population. An increased rate of retirement by senior faculty due to age was predicted for the period 2010 to 2015.

Each winter, Founders' Day provided opportunity for campus recognition of those long-term employees. The period 2002-2006 witnessed the University's first forty-year service award—presented to Dr. Don Looser who was also honored as a part of 2004 Commencement.[32] Those receiving gifts and awards for thirty-five years of service included James Busby, Dr. Don Byrnes, Frances Curtis, Dr. Daton Dodson, Nora Hayes, Ken Rogers, Dr. Phyllis Thompson, Dr. Doris Warren, and Dr. Cynthia Young. Awards for thirty years of service were presented to Dr. Avin Brownlee, Dr. Hutch Dvorak, Dr. John Lutjemeier, Dr. Verna Peterson, Dr. Ernie Pyle, Dr. James Taylor, Dr. Brooke Tucker, and Dr. Gene Wofford.   Those honored for twenty-five years included Dr. John Alexander, Linda Clark '87, Margie Conventon, Judy Ferguson '67, Dr.

---

28 Houston Baptist University, Minutes of the Meetings of the Board of Trustees, Meeting on 16 May 2005.
29 Houston Baptist University, Minutes of the Meetings of the Board of Trustees, Meeting on 27 Sept. 2005.
30 Houston Baptist University, Minutes of the Meetings of the Board of Trustees, Meeting on 22 Nov. 2005.
31 Houston Baptist University, Minutes of the Meetings of the Board of Trustees, Meeting on 17 May 2005.
32 Rocky Red, "The Man Who Has Done So Much," *Ornogah 2004*, 56-57; "May 2004 Graduation," *HBU News*, June 2004, 5. Looser wrote, "The joy of being here in the early days and still being here today is an experience I never anticipated."

Ann Gebuhr, Dr. Sally Phillips, Sharon Saunders, Loree Watson '80, Maydene Wells, Dr. Stephen Wentland, and Dr. Nancy Yuill '72. Those recognized for twenty years of service included Dr. Linda Brupbacher '69, Nan Donahoe, Linda Hammack, Saliem Kahleh '84, Ann Noble, Clay Porter, Isaac Simpson, Dr. Jon Suter, Don Teltschik, Dr. James Ulmer, and Dr. Treacy Woods.[33] The Mayfield Outstanding Staff Member Awards went to Dr. Cynthia Young and Hugh McClung in 2002,[34] Mary Purcell[35] and Charles Miller in 2003,[36] Mary Ellen Spore[37] and Dr. Don Looser in 2004,[38] Linda Clark '87 and Dr. Don Byrnes in 2005,[39] and Elaine Higginbotham and Roger Wilhite in 2006.[40]

The faculty continued to bring distinction and recognition to the University. Virgil Grotfeldt was named "Texas Artist of the Year" by the Art League of Houston in his first year of eligibility—a once-in-a-lifetime honor.[41] Grotfeldt also enjoyed a solo exhibition of his work at the Jason-McCoy Gallery in New York and was the subject of a new book by Patrick Healy.[42] Dr. Lou Markos completed his new book, *Lewis Agonistes: How C. S. Lewis Can Train Us to Wrestle with the Modern and Postmodern World.*[43] The "Christa McAuliffe In Search of Excellence Award" for demonstrating spirit, energy, enthusiasm, and love of learning was awarded to Dr. Brenda Whaley '79 in 2003[44] and Dr. Melissa Wiseman in 2004.[45] Dr. Rosemary McCarthy was elected President of the Texas Association of Nurse Attorneys.[46] The National Academic Advising Association selected 2000 alumna Alexis Knapp in 2004[47] and Dr. Melissa Wiseman in

---

33 "Founders' Day," *HBU News,* Dec. 2002, 10; "Founders' Day," *HBU News,* Dec 2003, 8-9; "Founders' Day," *HBU News,* Dec. 2004, 14-15; "HBU notes 42 years," *Houston Chronicle,* 22 Dec. 2005, ThisWeek sec., p. 2, two-star ed; "Founders' Day, *HBU News,* Winter 2006, 26.

34 "Mayfield Award," *HBU News,* Sept. 2002, 9. Photos.

35 "Awards, Awards, Awards," *HBU News,* Sept. 2003, 9.

36 Ibid.

37 "Mayfield Outstanding Staff Award," *HBU News,* Sept. 2004, 9. Photo.

38 "Models of Excellence," *Ornogah 2004,* 154.

39 "Mayfield Outstanding Staff Award," *HBU News,* Fall 2005, 12.

40 "Mayfield Outstanding Staff Award," *HBU News,* Fall 2006, 16.

41 David Resch, "Faculty member receives honor for artistry," *The Collegian,* 10 Apr. 2003, p. 7; "Grotfeldt Named Texas Artist of the Year," *HBU News,* Mar. 2003, 6.

42 *HBU News,* Mar. 2005, back cover. Photo.

43 "Markos releases book," *HBU News,* Dec. 2003, 25. Photo.

44 Scott Sweeney, "Educator earns top honor," *Houston Chronicle,* 10 July 2003, This Week sec., p. 7, two-star ed. Whaley's cash award was conveyed to the HBU Christian Medical Fellowship composed of students "who have a commitment to God and an interest in health-related fields."

45 Houston Baptist University, Minutes of the Meetings of the Board of Trustees, Meeting on 28 Sept. 2004.

46 "Updates," *HBU News,* Dec. 2003, 24.

47 "Knapp Wins Advising Award," *HBU News,* June 2004, 17.

2005[48] as one of ten faculty members to receive its Outstanding Faculty Advising Award.

Goolsby Outstanding Teaching Awards during the era were presented to Dr. Brenda Whaley '79[49] and Dr. Randy Wilson in 2002,[50] Dr. Melissa Wiseman and Dr. Chris Hammons in 2003,[51] Dr. Ruth Ann Williamson and Dr. Robert Towery in 2004,[52] Dr. David Capes and Debra Berry '89 in 2005,[53] and Dr. Martha Maddox and Dr. Chris Salinas in 2006.[54] Dr. Ann Gebuhr's compositions continued to enjoy global recognition with the premier of *Pax Vobiscum* for the New York Society for Ethical Culture,[55] a performance of *Voyage d'Anima* by the Bucharest Philharmonic Orchestra,[56] and a new cantata, *Friedenskantate*, commissioned by the St. Thomas Church in Leipzig for the dedication of its "Peace Window."[57]

A gift of $500,000 from Nell Smith and her son Larry established the Dr. Larry D. Smith Endowed Award for Teaching Excellence. The gift provided an annual cash award of $3,000 to $5,000 to a faculty member for outstanding teaching as well as supplementary funds for institutional programs of learning enhancement.[58] Dr. Brenda Whaley '79 was the first recipient of the Smith Award that was subsequently given annually to the University's nominee for the Piper Outstanding Professor competition.[59] An additional gift from the estate of longtime-supporter Jean Scullin yielded an endowment of $1,200,000 for music scholarships.[60] A pianist, herself, Miss Scullin had provided the University's first Steinway pianos for class instruction in 1964.[61]

Ron Stone '94, called by the *Houston Chronicle* "the most revered television anchor Houston has ever seen," had long been the host of the Spirit of Excellence dinners and was the frequent narrator for University promotional presentations. In 2002, Stone shared his love for Texas history by

---

48 "Wiseman Receives National Faculty Advising Honor," *HBU News,* Summer 2005, 28. Photo.

49 Martha Morrow, "Defining Relationships," *HBU News,* Mar. 2005, 4-5. Photo.

50 Candace Desrosiers, "Opal Goolsby Award," *HBU News,* Sept. 2002, 7- 8. Photos.

51 "Awards, Awards, Awards," *HBU News,* Sept. 2003, 7-8.

52 "Opal Goolsby Award for Outstanding Teaching," *HBU News,* Sept. 2004, 10. Photos.

54 "Goolsby Awards," *HBU News,* Fall 2006, 16.

55 Angela Anderson, "Gebuhr gives performance in New York," *The Collegian,* 2 Nov. 2005, p. 1.

56 "People on the Move," *SomeTimes,* July 2002, p. 1.

57 Dr. Ann Gebuhr, www.anngebuhr.com/personal (accessed 7 Jan. 2010).

58 "Smith Donation to Benefit Faculty," *HBU News,* Dec. 2003, 23. Photo.

59 Houston Baptist University, Minutes of the Meetings of the Board of Trustees, Meeting on 27 Sept. 2005.

60 "Brunch honors scholarship donors," *HBU News,* June 2004, 12.

61 "Encore and More," *HBU News,* Dec. 2003, 23.

offering a popular course in the Master of Liberal Arts program.[62] Stone was joined in the MLA program by Peter Roussel, former Staff Assistant to President Gerald Ford and Deputy Press Secretary to President Reagan, who also offered a new MLA course "The Presidency and the Media."[63] The contribution of these two professionals served to illustrate the wealth of expertise available to a university in an urban setting. The goal of the MLA to offer high visibility courses provided the ideal opportunity for incorporating the unique abilities of such distinguished colleagues. HBU's MLA program was the first of its kind in Houston, was the only accredited program in the city, and boasted more than 300 graduates. In 2005, the MLA program celebrated its twentieth birthday.[64]

Those faculty members holding appointment to an endowed position included Dr. John R. Brooks, Prince-Chavanne Professor in Christian Business Ethics; Dr. James Furr, Bisagno Chair of Evangelism; Dr. Ray Newman, Herman Brown Chair of Business and Economics; Dr. Phaedon Papadopoulos, Rex G. Baker Professor of Management; Dr. James S. Taylor, Robert H. Ray Chair of Humanities; and Dr. Nancy Yuill, John S. Dunn Professor in Nursing. The academic lectureships provided by many of these endowments continued to enrich the intellectual experience for the University community. Sherron Watkins, one of *TIME* magazine's "Persons of the Year," delivered the Prince-Chavanne Professorship lectures in 2003. Other Chavanne lecturers included Dr. Donald P. Robin,[65] Dr. O. C. Ferrell,[66] Dr. L. Murphy Smith,[67] and Dr. Rick Lytle.[68] The Brown Chair lectures were given by BMC Software President and CEO Bob Beauchamp '87[69] and by Anadarko Petroleum Corporation President and CEO James Hackett.[70] A. O. Collins Lectures were delivered by Baylor University's Dr. Charles Talbert[71] and Indiana University scholar Dr. Paul Gutjahr.[72]

§

62 Vivian Camacho, "Stone shared love of Texas in MLA class," *HBU News,* Sept. 2002, 6.

63 "Reagan Advisor joins MLA for Spring," *HBU News*, Dec. 2003, 5.

64 "Happy Birthday MLA," *HBU* News, Winter 2005, 4-5. Photos.

65 "Prince Chavanne Lectures," *HBU News,* June 2002, 6.

66 "Prince Chavanne," *HBU News,* June 2004, 4. Photo.

67 "Prince Chavanne," *HBU News,* Mar. 2005, 12. Photo.

68 "Prince Chavanne," *HBU News,* Spring 2006, 14. Photo.

69 "Doing Business in a Global Economy," *HBU News,* Summer 2005, 18. Photo.

70 "The Brown Lecture Series," *HBU News,* Spring 2006, 14. Photo.

71 "A. O. Collins Theology Lectures," *HBU News,* June 2003, 5.

72 "Gutjahr speaks at Collins Lecture," *HBU News,* June 2004, 4.

The quality and excellence of undergraduate scholarly activity was increasingly recognized as an indicator of institutional academic strength, i.e., HBU's inclusion in *Colleges of Distinction*. In 2002, Dr. Treacy Woods represented the University at the National Conference on Undergraduate Research.[73] The HBU research emphasis was further strengthened by the participation of Drs. Gardo Blado, Lucindra Campbell, and Doris Warren in a "Celebration of Scholarship" symposium given by the Council on Undergraduate Research at Claremont, California.[74] In 2003, a "Celebration of Undergraduate Scholarship" symposium was established at HBU as a University-wide project pioneered by Dr. Blado and members of the University's Research and Development Council. By 2004, in recognition of outstanding undergraduate scholarship, the second annual undergraduate research symposium[75] joined with the University's third annual "Arts and Humanities Spring Symposium" that presented student writing, research, and creative output from the College of Humanities.[76] These specific symposia were supplemented in their support of undergraduate research by such additional academic programs as the senior seminars and the Welch Foundation grant in chemistry. Additional scholarly recognition was provided by the establishment of a new chapter of Phi Alpha Theta honor society in history.[77]

Student academic recognition remained strong. In 2004, one hundred percent of the students taking the nursing licensure exams again passed on the first sitting. With the State Board of Nurse Examiner's report came a commendation for outstanding student performance. In like kind, one hundred percent of the University's education students passed the Texas Examination of Education Standards Test.[78] Sidra Qasim was one of seven students in Texas to gain a scholarship and guaranteed admission to one of Texas's medical colleges through the Joint Admission Medical Program (JAMP). Senior Medeeha Saeed was named as a

---

73 Houston Baptist University, Minutes of the Meeting of the Board of Trustees, Meeting on 24 Sept. 2002.
74 Houston Baptist University, Minutes of the Meetings of the Board of Trustees, Meeting on 28 May 2006.
75 "Learning from research," *HBU News,* June 2004, 6. Photos.
76 DJ Warren, "Third annual Spring Symposium displays student, faculty research," *The Collegian,* 1 Apr. 2004, p. 3.
77 Kristen Drymalla, "New history honor society inducts charter members," *The Collegian,* 6 May 2004, p. 9; "Phi Alpha Theta Inducts Charter Members," *HBU News,* June 2004, 5. Photo.
78 Houston Baptist University, Minutes of the Meetings of the Board of Trustees, Meeting on 18 May 2004.

summer research fellow at the University of Texas Health Science Center.[79] Stephanie Torreno was awarded the "Promethean Award" from the Texas Rehabilitation Association for "a person with a disability who has demonstrated motivation and personal courage in overcoming her disability."[80]

Student achievement in the performance areas of mock trial, music, publications, and athletics was impressive. Schola Cantorum was invited to perform for the American Choral Director's Association Southwest Division Convention in St. Louis in March of 2003.[81] Selected by competitive audition, the ensemble was asked to premiere a new work by composer Dan Forest.[82] In 2004 and again in 2005, the American composer Daniel Gawthrop was in residence on campus with students in the School of Music.[83] Dan Forest also served as composer in residence in 2008.

The University's Mock Trial team coached by Dr. Chris Salinas established itself as a national contender. At the Quaker State Classic in 2003, the team placed third—ahead of Columbia, George Washington University, Villanova, and MIT.[84] The team was invited to the 2004 national tournament for the first time in University history,[85] and Justin Kelly and Derrick Owens were named to All America honors.[86] In 2006, the team was invited to the Yale University Invitational Tournament and finished tenth in the nation, competing in a field of seventy colleges and universities.[87]

Student publications had long been an area of achievement for the University. So consistent were competitive awards at the national level for both *The Collegian* and the *Ornogah* yearbook that they became the expectation. The *2002 Ornogah* was the most recognized edition in HBU history winning first place with distinction from the Associated Collegiate Press (ACP), first place overall from the Texas Intercollegiate Press Association (TIPA) and the Baptist Press Association, and a Silver Medal from the Columbia Scholastic Press Association.[88] In 2003, the *Ornogah* won a first-place gold medal from the Columbia Scholastic Press Association and Sweepstakes recognition from TIPA.[89]

79 Ibid.

80 Martha Morrow, "Overcoming the Odds," *HBU News,* Sept. 2004, 14. Photo.

81 Laura Cockburn, "Schola sings in St. Louis," *The Collegian,* 16 Mar. 2006, p. 1.

82 "HBU performs in St. Louis for ACDA," *HBU News,* Winter 2006, 21.

83 DJ Warren, "Gawthrop ends residency in live radio broadcast, concert," *The Collegian,* 6 May 2004, p. 1.

84 Kellye Dorey, "Mock trial team earns third at Quaker Classic," *The Collegian,* 18 Dec. 2004, p. 1.

85 Tomie Lunsford, "Mock trial team advances to nationals," *The Collegian,* 12 Dec. 2004, p. 1.

86 "Mock Trial competes at Nationals," *HBU News,* Mar. 2004, 5.

87 "Mock trial team at nationals," *HBU News,* Winter 2006, 20.

88 "2002 Ornogah takes first place," *HBU News,* Dec. 2002, 5.

89 Kimberly Crowder, "Ornogah earns Gold," *The Collegian,* 29 Jan. 2004, p. 1.

The Collegian won a fourth Sweepstakes recognition from TIPA in 2006.[90] The paper had won TIPA awards every year since 1992 and received the All American Award from the Associated Collegiate Press in each year from 2002-2006.[91] *The Collegian* won the Gold Medal Award from the Columbia Scholastic Press Association in 2003 and also repeated first place awards in the "Excellence in Journalism" competition from the Baptist Press Association.[92] In the Gold Circle competition, Amanda Dean won the Certificate of Merit from the Columbia Scholastic Press Association.[93] Megan Baumgardner and Dale Peacock won the "President's Award for Excellence in Student Journalism" from the Baptist Press Association.[94] However, the crowning honor for *The Collegian* was the ACP Pacemaker award—"the Pulitzer Prize of the collegiate press"— in 2005.[95] *Collegian* staffer Jayna Desai secured a coveted position with the *Associated Press* following summer internships with the *New York Times* and *Good Morning America*.[96]

Faculty advisor to The Collegian, Dr. Alice Rowlands, was the subject of a *Houston Chronicle* article on student achievement in 2006.[97]

The Huskies enjoyed the most comprehensive record of athletic victories in University history. The University's intercollegiate teams dominated the Red River Athletic Conference. In 2001-2002, all five HBU teams were ranked in the top fifteen NAIA teams in the nation.[98] Men and women's basketball finished in the Elite Eight, and softball advanced to the national tourna-

2002 volleyball team celebrates its semifinal victory in the NAIA National Tournament.

90 Audrey La, "Newspaper wins top award," *The Collegian*, 20 Apr. 2006, p. 5.

91 Kimberly Crowder, "ACP honors Collegian," *The Collegian*, 20 Jan. 2006, p. 1.

92 Jeri Tabor, "Baptist Press honors Collegian," *The Collegian*, 15 Dec. 2005, p. 4.

93 Houston Baptist University, Minutes of the Meetings of the Board of Trustees, Meeting on 17 May 2005.

94 "Baumgardner Receives President's Award," *HBU News*, Dec. 2003, 4. Photo.

95 William Taylor, "Collegian nominated for Pacemaker—prestigious journalism award," *The Collegian*, 20 Oct. 2005, p. 5.

96 Rebecca Voholetz, "News wire draws alumna to New York," *The Collegian*, 24 Mar. 2005, p. 5.

97 Flori Meeks, "Houston Baptist professor guides student-run newspaper to honors: adviser instills high standards, strong work ethic," *Houston Chronicle*, 26 Jan. 2006, ThisWeek sec., two-star ed. p. 1.

98 "Huskies sweep RRAC championships—again," *HBU News*, June 2002, 12.

ment.[99] Rachel Werner, Laura Hess, Katelyn Griffin, and Sarah Franz were named to the 2002-03 All America softball team.[100] HBU's volleyball team was runner-up for the national championship;[101] Sarah Emmer and Elele Ekadeli were named to the All America first team. Ekadeli was also named the national tournament's Most Valuable Player and HBU's first national Player of the Year.[102] Mary Ellen Hall, Kaddie Platt, and Brian Huddleston were each named 2002 Coach of the Year.[103] In 2003, the men's basketball team won its fifth conference championship, was ranked first in the nation, and advanced to its sixth national tournament. Rod Nealy was named *Basketball Times* Player of the Year.[104]

National NAIA Player of the Year Elele Ekadeli at the 2002 National Tournament.

All America Rod Nealy, NAIA Player of the Year

The NAIA also named Nealy and Michael Holmquist to its All America teams.[105] The women's basketball team was ranked second in the NAIA. Tiffany Andrews was named to the All America first team

99 *2008 Softball Sports Information Guide*, p. 40.
100 Heather Mooney, "Standing Ovation," *Ornogah 2003*, 202.
101 Heather Mooney, "We are the Champs," *Ornogah 2003*, 185.
102 "Ekadeli Named National Player of the Year," *HBU News*, Dec. 2002, 20-21.
103 Houston Baptist University, Minutes of the Meetings of the Board of Trustees, Meeting on 19 Nov. 2002.
104 Heather Mooney, "Standing Ovation," *Ornogah 2003*, 194.
105 "Nealy and Holmquist named All America," *HBU News*, June 2003, 25.

and Player of the Year, and coaches Ron Cottrell, Shane Brown, and Mary Ellen Hall were each named Coach of the Year.[106] In 2003, Sports Information Director Jacque Cottrell won six publication awards from the College Sports Information Directors of America for *HBU Media Guides*.[107] John Lopez, writing in the *Houston Chronicle,* recorded a fuller story:

> HBU's athletic rise has been an inspirational journey. Ron Cottrell has built the quietest monster in the college game. (The campus) is a place known for an understated way of life. This program has risen from literally nothing (in 1990) to, as the billboards say, the blessed alternative. Coats and ties are required on road trips. Every player lives on campus. Cottrell asks his players to enter intramurals and the Husky Revue. Religious values play a huge role, because that is what the University is. The team is known for its group visits to University Place Retirement Center, University choral concerts, hospital visits, and church attendance on the road.[108]

In 2003-2004, the University claimed its fifth Red River Athletic Conference All Sports Award. In the six-year history of the conference, HBU had won twenty-eight of twenty-nine conference championships. Women's basketball advanced to the Final Four of the national tournament.[109] Volleyball won its sixth consecutive conference championship, returned to the national tournament, and placed three students on All America teams—Sarah Emmer, Elinor Smith, and Nicole Westerterp. Coach Kaddie Platt was named conference and regional Coach of the Year.[110] The women's softball team won its sixth Red River championship and finished the year ranked #3 nationally. Four of its players were named to All America honors—NAIA Pitcher of the Year Laura Hess, Rachel Werner, Cheri Wood, and Katelyn Griffin.[111] The HBU baseball team advanced to regional competition and finished the season ranked ninth by the NAIA.[112] All American Michael Holmquist was honored with the

105 "Nealy and Holmquist named All America," *HBU News,* June 2003, 25.
106 Ibid.
107 "Sport Information wins publication awards," *HBU News,* Dec. 2003, 6.
108 John Lopez, "HBU's rise has been inspirational journey," *Houston Chronicle,* 6 Mar. 2003, Sports sec., p. 1, three-star ed.
109 Tracy Upton, "Huskies fall two games shy of national championship," *The Collegian,* 1 Apr. 2004, p. 1.
110 "Volleyball finishes season with return trip to National Tournament," *HBU News,* Dec. 2003, 26.
111 "Huskies finish best season in school history," *HBU News,* June 2004, 18.
112 Houston Baptist University, *2008 Baseball Sports Media Guide,* p. 45.

Champion of Character Award by the NAIA for exhibiting the core values of leadership, community involvement, and academic achievement.[113]

The year 2004-2005 witnessed the selection of volleyball All Americans Nicole Westerterp and Elinor Smith for the second year, Coach Kaddie Platt's 300th volleyball victory, and Platt's selection as Coach of the Year.[114] The team made a third national tournament appearance. Women's basketball advanced to the second consecutive Final Four and placed three athletes on the All America teams——RRAC Player of the Year Stephanie Stoglin, Dominique Thomas, and Arie Wilson.[115] Softball won a seventh conference title, finished the year ranked second in the nation,[116] and had three athletes named to All America recognition— Rachel Werner, Morgan Anderson, Katelyn Griffin.[117] Men's basketball won its seventh straight conference title and advanced to the national tournament for the eighth consecutive year.[118] Ricky Bennett and Chris Miller were named to the All America team.[119] In 2005, HBU baseball copped its sixth RRAC title, finished the year ranked eleventh in the NAIA, and was honored by six of its players being named to All America teams—Archie Panfilli, Jason Pickett, Lance Casey, Wes Smiley, Aaron Garrison, and Danny Henry.[120] HBU was awarded its sixth Red River Athletic Conference All-Sports Award.[121] Coaches Ron Cottrell[122] and Brian Huddleston each achieved his 300th win.[123] Bryn Caulkins became the second Husky to be awarded the Champions of Character Award.[124]

In the 2005-2006 season, HBU again dominated the conference. In September 2005, Jared Moon '96 was appointed as the Huskies' new baseball coach.[125] Todd Buchanan assumed the responsibilities as women's basketball coach.[126] The women's volleyball team under coach Kaddie Platt won the conference title and reached the quarterfinals of the national tournament; Nicole Westerterp and Andrea Bishop were named to the All

---

113 Ibid, p. 19.

114 Natasha Avey, "Team gives Platt 300th career win after 10-year reign," *The Collegian*, 7 Oct. 2004, p. 16.

115 Houston Baptist University, Minutes of the Meetings of the Board of Trustees, Meeting on 17 May 2005.

116 Houston Baptist University, *2008 Softball Sports Media Guide*, p. 40.

117 "History in the Making," *Ornogah 2005*, 180.

118 "Basketball wins 7th straight RRAC crown," *HBU News*, Mar. 2005, 22.

119 "Men's Basketball," *Ornogah 2005*, 170.

120 "Baseball," *Ornogah 2005*, 186.

121 "Huskies Win Sixth All-Sports Award," *HBU News*, Summer 2005, 25.

122 Steven Key, "Cottrell honored for 300th career victory," *HBU News*, Mar. 2005, 23. Photo.

123 Natasha Avey, "Baseball goes 42-5, *The Collegian*, 5 May 2004, p. 4.

124 "Caulkins receives Champions of Character Award," *HBU News*, Summer 2005, 25. Photo.

125 "Moon Elevated to Head Baseball Coach," *HBU News*, Fall 2005, 24. Photo.

126 DJ Warren, "New head coaches named," *The Collegian*, 22 Sept. 2005, p. 5.

America team.[127] The men's basketball team finished the season ranked eighth in the NAIA and advanced to the Sweet Sixteen. Dwight Jones and Ben McCain were selected for All America honors; Pablo Avila was honored with the NAIA Champions of Character Award.[128] Women's basketball finished the season ranked sixth in the national poll under new coach Todd Buchanan; the team won the conference title with a perfect record of 20 wins, no losses in conference play. Named to the NAIA women's All America team were Jeré Adams, Sherrill Hadrick, Velencia Kuykendall, and Dominique Thomas.[129] In December 2005, the University announced the return of men's and women's soccer to intercollegiate activity after an absence of fifteen years;[130] the University had participated in NCAA competition from 1979 to 1990. HBU's soccer team was to be the only men's intercollegiate team in Houston.[131]

In 2006, the HBU softball team won the conference title while gifting Coach Mary Ellen Hall with her 500th coaching win; the team finished eleventh in the national rankings.[132] Senior Laura Hess was elected to the NAIA All America team.[133] Jared Moon was elected Region VI baseball Coach of the Year in his first season as head coach, and Michael Crabtree and A. J. Fenanes were named to the All America team.[134] The baseball team won a seventh RRAC title, was ranked thirteenth in the NAIA, and had a 35-14-1 record for the season.[135] Men's basketball coach Ron Cottrell had compiled a record of 336 victories in fifteen seasons at HBU. His teams had eight RRAC titles and nine consecutive NAIA national tournament appearances. Cottrell had been elected Coach of the Year five times.[136] In addition to his other responsibilities, he had also served as University Athletic Director since 1994.

§

In 2005, a strategic plan for a campus "culture of engagement" was initiated to encourage campus residency and enhance student activi-

---

127 "Volleyball," *Ornogah 2006,* 166.
128 "Avila receives Champions of Character Award Scholarship," *HBU News,* Summer 2006, 33. Photo.
129 "Volleyball," *Ornogah 2006,* 174.
130 "Men's Soccer is Coming This Fall," *HBU News,* Fall 2005, 16.
131 Kris Bagley, "Soccer returns," *The Collegian,* 15 Dec. 2005, p. 1.
132 "Hall Honored for 500 Career Wins," *HBU News,* Summer 2006, 32. Photo.
133 "Softball," *Ornogah 2006,* 182.
134 "Baseball," *Ornogah 2006,* 186.
135 Houston Baptist University, Minutes of the Meetings of the Board of Trustees, Meeting on 23 May 2006.
136 "Cottrell Selected to USA Basketball," *HBU News,* Summer 2006, 32. Photo.

ties.[137]   Author Neil Howe, in a seminar for HBU staff and faculty, described the new "Millennial Generation" student as reluctant to leave home and heavily dependent on continuing parental involvement. This was the generation of sheltered, "trophy" children (Baby on Board)— "special" to their parents, pressured, achievement-oriented, highly conventional, and data consumed.[138]   The cell phone and other technology encouraged a digitally-linked family unit resulting in the emergence of hovering, "helicopter" parents. The personal privacy rights of college students often seemed contrary to an era when parents were occasionally seen even in the classroom.   A 2004 national Cooperative Institutional Research Program (CIRP) survey revealed that eighty-eight percent of HBU's new freshmen were drawn from a four-county area within fifty miles of the campus; fifty-four percent of the freshmen planned to live at home.[139]   As a result, many students continued to be focused in home churches, neighborhood entertainment, and high school friendships— remaining detached from a new collegiate orientation with the University at the center.   Additionally, *U. S. News and World Report* documented that HBU was noted for its "ethnic diversity index" of .68/1.0—"one of the highest reported throughout the nation."[140]   In the face of such demography, the vitality of campus life and institutional commitment was a challenge.[141]   In 2006, a new marketing slogan, "Write your own story," was designed to respond both to the millennial generation and the diversity of the campus.[142]

To address the concerns of non-residency and diversity, facility and program improvements were critical. The Board addressed these concerns with a $750,000 supplement to the 2005-06 budget.[143]   The Bone Appétit Café was added to the newly remodeled M. D. Anderson Student Center; Starbucks came to *The Pawz* coffee bar and met with immediate success.[144]   Club sports were initiated to augment the historically-strong degree of participation in intramural athletics.   Intercollegiate soccer was

---

137 Houston Baptist University, Minutes of the Meetings of the Board of Trustees, Meeting on 17 May 2005.
138 "The Millennial Comes To Campus," *HBU News,* Fall 2005, 4.
139 Houston Baptist University, Minutes of the Meetings of the Board of Trustees, Meeting on 17 May 2005.
140 "Magazine ranks HBU in top tier of schools," *Houston Chronicle,* 16 Sept. 2004, ThisWeek sec., p. 2, two-star ed.
141 In reporting on student government elections, *The Collegian* headlined, "SGA is MIA."
142 Brie Moore, "Marketing campaign initiated," *The Collegian,* 20 Apr. 2006, p. 4.
143 Houston Baptist University, Minutes of the Meetings of the Board of Trustees, Meeting on 22 Feb. 2005.
144 Kristen Peters, "Starbucks comes to campus," *The Collegian,* 2 Oct. 2003, p. 1; Jayna Desai, "Pawz and smell the coffee," *The Collegian,* 28 Apr. 2004, p. 1.

"reinstated because the move would have the greatest impact on campus life" by providing a fall sport.[145] Phi Kappa Psi was formed as a new fraternity.[146] The Wellness Center was built and the Glasscock Center was remodeled to afford additional opportunity for recreational activity. The University's live mascot, Kiza, returned to campus residence after a two-year absence.[147] The Baugh food court and dining areas were redesigned to encourage lounge function. More spaces were added for informal gathering around the campus; the creation of a pervasive wireless network encouraged extended campus stays. The Bookstore expanded its retailing to address the personal needs of students and become a campus source for clothing, snack foods, greeting cards, and gift ware as well as textbooks.

A block tuition plan was initiated to encourage full-time enrollment with financial incentives; such students would presumably spend more time on campus with a higher degree of involvement.[148] Enhanced scholarship aid supported community-building through music ensembles, forensics, team cheer, club sports, and campus leadership to "help students tie in to areas they feel passionate about."[149] A new *Husky Central* student services venue was established near *The Pawz* to provide "one-stop shopping" for students interfacing with the registrar, financial services, academic advising, student affairs, and admissions.[150] One of the most dramatic actions, however, was Board approval for on-campus dances sponsored by chartered student organizations.[151]

Student life activities on campus were planned for the diversity of the campus population and for the integration of the University's spiritual concerns for students and their growth. A 2005 report to the Board of Trustees provided a comprehensive perspective of the breadth of these activities that included student government, fraternities and sororities, intramurals, career planning, personal counseling, residence life, recreation, event planning and coordination, convocation and spiritual life point programs, community service, and student ministries—Quest, Disciple Now, student missions, spring mission trips, and prayer teams.[152]

---

145 Kris Bagley, "Soccer returns," *The Collegian*, 15 Dec. 2005, p. 1.
146 Lindsey Schenck, "Men organize new fraternity," *The Collegian*, 20 Oct. 2005, p. 1.
147 Sam Byrd, "Kiza's home," *The Collegian*, 27 Jan. 2005, p. 1.
148 Houston Baptist University, Minutes of the Meetings of the Board of Trustees, Meeting on 27 Sept. 2005.
149 Christen Coyle, "Budget increases; rising endowments, tuition result in 2.5 percent growth," *The Collegian*, 7 Apr. 2005, p. 1.
150 Houston Baptist University, Minutes of the Meetings of the Board of Trustees, Meeting on 22 Nov. 2005.
151 Houston Baptist University, Minutes of the Meetings of the Board of Trustees, Meeting on 23 May 2006.
152 Houston Baptist University, Minutes of the Meetings of the Board of Trustees, Meeting on 22 Feb. 2005.

The University's alumni continued to bring distinction to their Alma Mater. In 2002, twenty of the University's graduates gained admission to medical, dental, or pharmacy schools.[153] Colin Lathrop '03 received one of eight post-baccalaureate research internships at the National Institutes of Health in Bethesda.[154] Dr. James Sterling '78 was named chief physician for the USA Winter Olympic team in Turin, Italy.[155] Senior George Atallah was admitted to the Vanderbilt School of Medicine's joint MD/PhD program.[156] Joel Finney became the first HBU student to be accepted into the Edward Herbert School of Medicine— established by the Department of Defense to provide physicians for specialized programs in public health and defense.[157] In 2005, thirty HBU alumni working in the Texas Medical Center were honored by Baylor College of Medicine's President Peter Trauber in gratitude for their outstanding volunteerism in staffing the Houston Astrodome medical center for victims of Hurricane Katrina.[158] Randy Sorrels '84 was elected President of the Houston Bar Association.[159] Dr. Larry Rager '79 was named a Fulbright Scholar for study in Albania.[160] Colin Montgomerie '87 received the Order of the British Empire from Prince Charles at Buckingham Palace.[161]

An *HBU News* article entitled "Making Music" chronicled the professional careers of six music alumni: Dalma Boronkai '00, winner of the Verismo Opera Competition at Carnegie Hall;[162] Kaytha Coker '95 performer with Theater Under the Stars and Masquerade Theater;[163] Kevin McBeth '85, Assistant Conductor of the St. Louis Symphony Chorus and Minister of Music to Missouri's largest Methodist congregation;[164] Chanda Dancy '02, USC graduate student and winner of the Carpenter Fellowship in Film Scoring;[165] Kevin Klotz '99, conductor and Music

---

153 Megan Baumgardner, "Science and math grads taking it to the next level," *HBU News*, Sept. 2003, 16.
154 Baumgardner, "Science," 14-15.
155 Sarah Conn, "A Gold Medal Experience," *HBU News*, Summer 2006, 9-11. Photos.
156 Houston Baptist University, Minutes of the Meetings of the Board of Trustees, Meeting on 13 May 2003.
157 Houston Baptist University, Minutes of the Meetings of the Board of Trustees, Meeting on 17 May 2005.
158 Houston Baptist University, Minutes of the Meetings of the Board of Trustees, Meeting on 22 Nov. 2005.
159 "Named President of Houston Bar Association," *HBU News,* Summer 2005, 33. Photo.
160 "Rager Named Fulbright Scholar," *HBU News,* Summer 2006, 34.
161 "Montgomerie Receives Order of the British Empire," *HBU News,* Spring 2006, 27.
162 "On the Road to Divahood," *HBU News*, June 2003, 11. Photo.
163 "Singer, actress, artist, and teacher," *HBU News*, June 2003, 12. Photo.
164 "Houston to St. Louis," *HBU News*, June 2003, 12. Photo.
165 "Composing music for the movies," *HBU News*, June 2003, 13. Photo.

Director of Houston's St. Laurence Catholic Parish;[166] and Charles Reid '93, in his sixth season with the Metropolitan Opera at Lincoln Center.[167]

Distinguished Alumni Awards were given Dr. Cliff McGee, Jr. '89 in 2002, Manfred F. Jachmich '69 in 2003, Raymond Denson '74 in 2004,[168] Charles Reid '93 in 2005, and Edwin B. Young '84 in 2006.[169] Meritorious Alumni Awards for outstanding service to the University were presented to Vivian Camacho '91 in 2002, Candace Adams Desrosiers '94 in 2003, Monica Hodges '94 in 2004,[170] Catherine Neben '89[171] in 2005, and Tadd Tellepsen '99 in 2006.[172] A new Hallmark Award was established to honor members of the faculty and staff who had shown significant support of the Alumni Association; recipients of the award were designated "Honorary Alumni." The first recipient of the Hallmark Award was Dr. Don Byrnes in 2000. In 2001, the award was given to Dr. E. D. Hodo and Sharon Saunders. Successive honorees included Anthony Martin in 2002, Ken Rogers in 2003, Frances Curtis in 2004, Dr. Larry Ruddell in 2005, and Job Garcia in 2006.[173]

Ongoing networking and professional growth opportunity were developed by the Alumni Affairs Office through a series of noon, professional luncheons on-campus that featured outstanding civic and community leaders. Speakers for these Business Connections events included Conoco President and CEO Archie Dunham,[174] Memorial Hermann CEO Dan Wilford, Warren Electric President Cheryl Thompson, Gallery Furniture's Jim McIngvale, investigative reporter Wayne Dolcefino,[175] Goodwill Industries CEO Steven Lufburrow, Everyone's Internet founder Roy Marsh,[176] City of Houston First Lady Andrea White,[177] contractor Howard Tellepsen, Jr., Houston Bar Association President Randy Sorrels '84,[178] and restaurateur Nina Hendee.

---

166 "Musical multi-tasking," *HBU News*, June 2003, 13-14. Photo.

167 "Charles Reid: Distinguished Alumnus Award," *HBU News*, Fall 2005, 8-9. Photo.

168 Martha Morrow, "The Distinguished Alumnus Award," *HBU News*, Dec. 2004, 10-11. Photo.

169 Houston Baptist University, *2008 Alumni Today*, p. viii.

170 "The Meritorious Service Alumnus Award," *HBU News*, Dec. 2004, 12-13. Photo.

171 "Leading the Pack," *HBU News*, June 2004, 21.

172 Houston Baptist University, *2008 Alumni Today*, p. ix.

173 Houston Baptist University, *2008 Alumni Directory*, p. xi.

174 "Business Connections schedules events," *HBU News*, June 2002, 29. Photo.

175 *SomeTimes*, July 2002, p. 2.

176 "Catching up at Alumni Connections," *HBU News*, June 2004, 27. Photo.

177 "Houston's First Lady Andrea White," *HBU News*, Summer 2005, 33. Photo.

178 "Alumni Networking Luncheon," *HBU News*, Spring 2006, 27. Photo.

The University sought opportunities for faculty leaders to participate in conferences dealing with faith and learning. Over the years, more than thirty faculty and staff members had engaged in such conferences.[179] In 2002, Dr. Jackie Horn participated in a conference sponsored by the Council of Christian Colleges and Universities (CCCU) at Gordon College. Dr. Gardo Blado was selected for a seminar offered by the Center for Theology and Natural Science[180] and subsequently developed a new elective course on the subject at HBU.[181] Dr. Rhonda Furr participated in a "Music, Faith, and Culture" conference offered by the Center for Christian Study in Charlottesville, Virginia, and Dr. Eloise Hughes attended a Pepperdine University "Faith in Learning" conference. Dr. Nancy Yuill and Dr. David Capes were participants in a special Lilly Foundation conference at Samford University on the topic, "Faith, Vocation, and the Core Curriculum."[182] On campus, the Department of Christianity and the Office of Spiritual Life offered a "Christian Streams Forum" moderated by Dr. David Capes that afforded local clergy from evangelical, charismatic, protestant, and Catholic churches the opportunity to discuss the tenets of their faith.[183] Dr. Ann Gebuhr offered a campus/community conference entitled "Synthesis: Creative Vessels of the Soul."[184] Dr. Renata Nero hosted a conference on "Ethics in Christian Counseling" in conjunction with the University's new Master of Christian Counseling degree.[185] Dr. David Capes began an annual "Race and Religion Forum" that presented the Director of Notre Dame's Center for Race and Religion, Dr. Michael Emerson, and Dr. George Yancey from the University of North Texas.[186] In 2006, Dr. Nancy Yuill '72 announced an HBU conference on "Spirituality and Healthcare" featuring Dr. John Swinton.[187]

The HBU faculty exhibited a high level of professionalism by engaging in a process of continual assessment of their classroom effectiveness.

179 These included Gardo Blado, Linda Brupbacher, David Capes, Curtis Freeman, Rhonda Furr, Randy Hatchett, Doug Hodo, Jackie Horn, Eloise Hughes, Don Looser, Marie Mater, Martha Maddox, Connie Michalos, Mary Austin Newman, Jeffrey Quiett, Harold Raley, Robert Reid, Ron Rexilius, Chris Salinas, James Taylor, Bobby Towery, Doris Warren, Shari Wescott, Jerry Wiles, Randy Wilson, and Nancy Yuill.

180 Houston Baptist University, Minutes of the Meetings of the Board of Trustees, Meeting on 24 Sept. 2002.

181 Houston Baptist University, Minutes of the Meetings of the Board of Trustees, Meeting on 13 May 2003.

182 Houston Baptist University, Minutes of the Meetings of the Board of Trustees, Meeting on 22 Nov. 2005.

183 "Christian Streams Forum," *The Collegian*, 31 Oct. 2002, p. 7.

184 "COAH Hosts Synthesis," *HBU News*, Mar. 2003, 7. Photo.

185 Houston Baptist University, Minutes of the Meetings of the Board of Trustees, Meeting on 13 May 2003.

186 "Race and Religion Forum," *HBU News*, Dec. 2004, 19. Photo.

187 Houston Baptist University, Minutes of the Meetings of the Board of Trustees, Meeting on 23 May 2006.

The University's course syllabus format required delineation of stated learning outcomes and evidence of their achievement. Formal student assessments using the *Individual Development and Educational Assessment* (IDEA) instrument were required in all courses. In addition, all members of the faculty prepared portfolios of professional activity as a part of their annual review. In 2002, Dr. Bill Pallett from the University of Kansas presented a series of faculty professional growth seminars designed to help faculty use the IDEA results more effectively for teaching improvement.[188]

Dr. Chip Anderson, a leading authority in student advising and retention, conducted a series of faculty seminars on personal strengths development in 2003. Anderson's visit followed a faculty symposium led by his colleague Dr. Laurie Schreiner dealing with spiritual gifts, innate individual strengths, group and individual performance enhancement, and mentoring models utilizing the understanding of strengths and abilities.[189] Anderson, the co-author with Don Clifton of *StrengthsQuest: Discover and Develop Your Strengths in Academics, Career, and Beyond*, was instrumental in changing the national paradigm in higher education from deficit-remediation to strengths development. His training of the University staff enabled the adoption of a strengths-based program for the University's Enrichment Center and for the Human Resources' activities.[190]

§

In 2003-04, the University celebrated the fortieth anniversary of its opening to students. All current and former trustees and University Founders were invited to return for the Founders' Day Convocation in December 2003. Four of the twenty-five original founding fathers were still living—Senator Lloyd Bentsen, Jr., Jake Kamin, Don McMillian, and Dr. Stewart Morris, Sr. Each was presented the Spirit of Excellence Award at the fall dinner featuring Bush presidential advisor Karen Hughes. A special edition of the *HBU News* presented a centerfold timeline, photographs, history, and reflections on "40 Years of Excellence: HBU 1963-2003."[191] President Hodo wrote,

---

188 Houston Baptist University, Minutes of the Meetings of the Board of Trustees, Meeting on 24 Sept. 2002.
189 Houston Baptist University, Minutes of the Meetings of the Board of Trustees, Meeting on 20 Nov. 2001.
190 Houston Baptist University, Minutes of the Meetings of the Board of Trustees, Meeting on 23 Sept. 2003.
191 "40 Years of Excellence," *HBU News*, Dec. 2003, 14-20.

One can see a history rich with the many people who have built the institution from the ground up—founders who shared a vision for a Baptist college in southeast Texas, administrators who have executed the University's mission, trustees who have guided and counseled the University leadership, faculty who have planted and nurtured seeds of knowledge, staff who have provided the support for consistent operations, students who have made up the life-blood of the institution, alumni who have gone on to become leaders, and of course, the many friends who have supported the University with their time and resources. All have woven unique and integral threads into the University fabric.[192]

Judy Bennatte Ferguson '67, a member of the first freshmen class, reflected,

Today, 40 years later, two lines in the *Alma Mater* hold special meaning for me as an alumnus and employee. As I reflect on the lines, "Seeking our place of service with wisdom from above," I think of one tradition that has become a hallmark of the HBU experience. Students' lives have been blessed by the many faculty, administrators, and staff members who have found a place of service on this campus. . . . We all share a common purpose that transcends our diverse functions. More than any other tradition, this dedication to Christian service helps make HBU Houston's Blessed University.[193]

Homecoming and other traditional University events carried the "Forty Years of Excellence" theme. At the conclusion of the year, the *Houston Chronicle* gave special recognition to the anniversary and the 2004 Founders' Day Convocation.[194]

One of the realities of forty years of history was dealing with the loss of colleagues. With each succeeding year, the ranks of those who forged the earliest chapters of institutional history grew thinner. One of the University's last remaining Founders, Senator Lloyd Bentsen, Jr., died in 2006.[195] Former trustees Judge Clyde Kennelly,[196] Dr. James

---

192 Dr. E. D. Hodo, "From the President," *HBU News,* Dec. 2003, 2. Photos.

193 Judy Ferguson, "From HBC to HBU," *HBU News,* Dec. 2003, 14.

194 Maurice Bobb, "HBU marks 40 years with Founders' Day ceremony," *Houston Chronicle,* 9 Dec. 2004, p. 1, two-star ed; "Founders' Day Convocation," *HBU News,* Dec. 2004, 14-15. Photos.

195 Alexis Grant, "The nation is saying goodbye to a treasure," *Houston Chronicle,* 30 May 2006, sec. A, p. 1, two-star ed; "In Memoriam," *HBU News,* Summer 2006, 38. Photo.

196 "Services pending for former Fort Bend County Judge Clyde Kennelly, *Fort Bend Herald,* 21 Feb. 2005. "Kennelly was a founding trustee of Houston Baptist University and was a Kentucky colonel and admiral in the Texas Navy."

Hammond,[197] Gus Glasscock, Jr.,[198] Roland L. Burrows,[199] and past-Chair Rex 'Pete' G. Baker, Jr.[200] also passed away—each leaving a personal record of strong contribution to the University's history.

Two donors, Juanita and Phyllis Pool, represented a particularly poignant story in University history. Juanita Pool devoted thirty years of her career to the U. S. District Court before she began working for Dr. Glendola Nash and the Lillie Jolly School of Nursing in the 1970s. Phyllis worked for Humble Oil and the U. S. Securities and Exchange Commission. Both Juanita and Phyllis became greatly involved with the HBU College of Nursing upon its move to the campus. Juanita died in 1998, and Phyllis was in nursing care until her death in 2005. Prior to Juanita's death, the Pool sisters had announced their intention to convey their assets to the University to establish the A. Juanita Pool and Phyllis F. Pool Endowed Chair of Nursing.[201] The 2006 Endowed Academic Scholarship luncheon celebrated the Pool estate gift of more than $1,500,000 for the endowed chair.[202]

Loss was sometimes also compounded with tragedy, particularly when colleagues died while in active service. In the space of only a few months, the University lost three of its finest. Dr. Walter Lumpkin '81, holder of the Bisagno Chair in Evangelism and Executive Director of the Antioch Center, succumbed to cancer in 2002.[203] A second colleague Rick Crittenden '82—Director of Academic Advising—died suddenly in 2003.[204] The shock of the death of these two greatly-loved young men bore testimony to the impact of their service on the University. A third colleague, Dr. Rod Cotton, donned his Scottish tam for his last campus visit in April 2004. A favorite of students, Cotton had been named the Robert Griswold Outstanding Teacher of the Year in the College of Business and Economics.[205]

---

197 "In Memoriam," *HBU News*, Dec. 2003, 30.

198 Jamie Powell, "Glasscock was innovator of oil drilling practices," *Corpus Christi Caller-Times,* 25 Oct. 2005, sec. B, p. 5. Glasscock had given the HBU Glasscock Gymnastics Center in memory of his late son, James Thomas Glasscock. Of related interest was the fact that his father and his three brothers had, at one time all been acrobats with the Ringling Brothers Circus.

199 "Roland Lee Burrows," *Roanoke Times and World News,* 29 May 2006, sec. B, p. 5.

200 Lynwood Abram, "Pete Baker, 83, entrepreneur and community leader," *Houston Chronicle,* 27 Mar. 2004, sec. A, p. 36, three-star ed.

201 "In Memoriam," *HBU News,* Summer 2005, 34.

202 Houston Baptist University, Minutes of the Meetings of the Board of Trustees, Meeting on 23 May 2006.

203 "Beloved professor leaves legacy of faith," *HBU News,* Dec. 2002, 29.

204 Tomie Lunsford, "Crittenden dies suddenly," *The Collegian,* 10 Apr. 2003, p. 1; "In Memory: Rick Crittenden," *HBU Upbeat,* Fall 2006, 14.

205 "Saying goodbye to a beloved colleague," *HBU News*, June 2004, 15. Photo.

The University family also lost other retired faculty members including the husband-wife couple Gene[206] and Jeanette (Lombard)[207] Talley-Schmidt,[208] Dr. Arthur Travis,[209] Bill Bolton,[210] Dr. Richard Collins,[211] Dr. Paul Brooks Leath,[212] Ray Fliegel,[213] and Dr. Marilyn Sibley, former history department chair and author of the UBA Property Committee's history *To Benefit a University*.[214]

In the span of one month in 2004, the final chapter to the Hinton era was closed with the deaths—only three weeks apart—of former President W. H. Hinton and his good friend and long-time colleague Dr. Troy Womack. Dr. Hinton was living in Colorado near his oldest daughter Julie and had required increasingly more care in recent years. He was 82. Hinton was the University's founding president and its first chancellor; he had retired from the latter position in 1991. Dr. Hodo reflected, "Dr. Hinton's vision is evidenced on the campus. His Christian commitment, his enthusiasm, and his tenacity during the formative years laid the foundation for creating an institution of academic excellence in Christian education."[215] At his memorial service, his former pastor Dr. H. Edwin Young described the man he knew. "He was tenacious; he was alive. When he saw something he wanted, he went after it with unerring tenacity. He was a leader, and there was no goal that was too high."[216]

Dr. Troy Womack, 85, had served with Hinton for twenty-four years as Vice President for Financial Affairs. He was a member of the founding administrative cabinet and had moved to Houston along with the Hinton family in 1962. Colleague Loree Watson '80 reflected, "He was a man of strong opinions and considerable confidence who cared intensely for students, faculty, and staff."[217] Ken Rogers recalled, "He taught me to be

---

206 "In Memoriam," *HBU News,* Dec. 2004, 29.

207 Lynwood Abram, "Jeanette Lombard, opera singer, teacher," *Houston Chronicle,* 27 Aug. 2003, p. 29, three-star ed.

208 "In Memoriam," *HBU News,* Dec. 2004, 29. Photo.

209 "Obituaries," *Abilene Reporter-News,* 11 July 2002, www.newspaperarchive.com (accessed Feb. 1, 2010).

210 "Bill Bolton," *New Orleans Time Picayune,* 24 Dec. 2003, p. 4. Bolton was the first HBC Director of Public Relations and Vice President for Advancement.

211 "In Memoriam," *HBU News,* Dec. 2003, 30.

212 Ibid.

213 Lynwood Abram, "Ray Fliegel, HSO violinist for 55 years," *Houston Chronicle,* 28 July 2005, sec. B, p. 9, three-star ed.

214 "A Scholar and Mentor with a Gentle Spirit," *HBU News,* Spring 2006, 28.

215 Lynwood Abram, "Hinton, founding president of HBU," *Houston Chronicle,* 16 Apr. 2004, sec. A, p. 27, three-star ed.

216 Tomie Lunsford, "A legend: past and present," *The Collegian,* 22 Apr. 2004, pp. 8-9.

217 Christen Coyle, "Former administrator remembered," *The Collegian,* 6 May 2004, p. 2.

compassionate and to listen to student needs. I appreciate that part of the man who was my mentor."[218] Hinton, Womack and H. B. Smith formed the founding administrative triumvirate. That the College survived—even flourished—during its first ten years was a tribute to the gifts of these three men. As founders, they are remembered in reverential terms.

§

Jack and Mary Purcell retired to the Hill Country town of Boerne in 2003. As Vice President for Student Affairs, Jack Purcell had brought a highly personal dimension to the management of student life—one focused on the individual rather than the event or organization. His management style was based on discussion with colleagues and informality with students, and his impact on the lives of students was as a presence rather than a personality. Purcell was an encourager and advocate. During his vice presidency, an increase in campus residents was achieved; the Enrichment Center was developed to address student personal needs;[219] spiritual life development expanded beyond the convocation requirement; Welcome Days became a pervasive force in student retention; and convocations adopted a more direct approach to addressing the spiritual needs of students.

Mary Purcell had served as Director of Planned Giving and was a winner of the Mayfield Outstanding Staff Award.[220] She created the Covenant Society and the Hinton Center Tree of Life to recognize and honor those who had included the University in their estate planning.[221] Additionally, she worked with the University Auxiliary organization, published the donor newsletter *Harvest*, and established a professional Advisory Committee for planned giving.[222] She became the face of the University to many individual donors and guided the implementation of their wishes to the benefit of the University's growth.

Pat Lassonde retired from her position as Administrative Assistant to President Hodo in 2003 having served sixteen years in that capacity.[223] Lassonde was effective both with campus-based constituencies as well as

---

218 Ibid.
219 Paige Hewett, "College freshmen learn about coping, studying, and ethics," *Houston Chronicle,* 20 Aug. 2003, sec. A, p. 26, three-star ed.
220 "The Mayfield Outstanding Staff Award," *HBU News,* Sept. 2003, 8-9.
221 "The Covenant Society," *HBU News,* Mar. 2003, 21.
222 Bethany Lopez, "Purcells head to the Hill Country," *HBU News,* Sept. 2003, 20.
223 "Lassonde retires," *HBU News,* June 2003, 27. Photo.

external publics. She was described as the model of "efficiency, gracious-
ness, skill, and commitment.[224] Lassonde was joined by two other colleagues of long service to the University—Maydene Wells, Director of
Financial Services for twenty-five years[225] and Mary Ellen Spore, Secretary
to the School of Music for eighteen years. Wells effectively bridged from
the Womack to the Parker years of administrative structure and guided
Financial Services through a significant period of legal and technological
change. Her quiet and steady demeanor coupled with her dedicated spirit resulted in an effective advocate for the financial needs of students.
Music students referred to Mary Ellen Spore as the "glue" of the department. "When she is not here, students act like the world is ending."[226]
Mayfield Outstanding Staff Award winner Spore reflected, "So many
wonderful, talented, creative people have enriched my life beyond all
expectation. This *is* a 'blessed' University."[227] Following retirement,
Spore remained active in the leadership of the Retirees Association and
was Chair-elect in 2010.

From 2004 to 2006, the first wave of the predicted retirement of senior faculty and staff began to be felt. Dr. Brooke Tucker announced her
retirement after thirty-four years of University service. Her role as Chair
of the Department of History and Political Science for the previous twenty years passed to Dr. Chris Hammons.[228] Tucker had been awarded the
Goolsby Outstanding Teaching Award on three occasions and was named
Faculty Woman of the Year.[229] Others who moved from University leadership included Dr. Beth Boyce, Professor of Spanish since 1991 and
recipient of the Goolsby Award;[230] Nancy McCreary, Assistant Professor
in Music since 1983;[231] Goolsby Award winner Dr. Ruth Ann
Williamson, Professor of Education since 1990 and founder of the
Summer Academy program;[232] and Dr. Sebron Williams, Professor of
Education and Psychology and former Dean of the College of Education
and Behavioral Sciences from 1978 to 1995.[233]

---

224 Ibid.

225 "Maydene Wells," *HBU News,* Summer 2005, 11. Photo.

226 Amy Bazemore, "Spore retires from music department," *The Collegian,* 5 May 2005, p. 3.

227 "Mary Ellen Spore," *HBU News,* Summer 2005, 11. Photo.

228 Brie Moore, "Dr. Brooke Tucker retires after 34 years," *The Collegian,* 4 May 2006, p. 8.

229 "New Chapters Begin as Faculty Members Retire," *HBU News,* Summer 2006, 12.

230 "Dr. Beth Boyce," *HBU News,* Summer 2005, 11. Photo.

231 Joshua Goldman, "Changing of the Guard," *The Collegian,* 6 May 2004, p. 11.

232 DJ Warren, "Changing of the Guard," *The Collegian.* 6 May 2004, p. 10.

233 Nina Greenhouse, "Williams retires after 26 years of service," *The Collegian,* 23 Sept. 2004, pp. 3-4. The
article captured Williams' favorite greeting, "Is there anything constructive going on around here?"

Dr. Daton Dodson, Professor of Languages, twice the recipient of the Opal Goolsby Outstanding Teaching Award and Coordinator of International Studies, announced his plans to retire in 2004 after thirty-seven years of dedicated service. Many colleagues considered Dr. Dodson to be the academic's academic. His intellectual honesty, his wit, his energy for learning, and his creativity made him a valued and popular professor among students. He taught both German and English, directed a *Culture and Human Experience* teaching team, pioneered courses based in film, and dominated intramural sports for the years of his service. Dodson was a ubiquitous presence at student concerts, recitals, lectures, theater performances, and athletic events and was described by his dean as "the personification of a Renaissance man."[234]

In 2005, Dr. Harold Raley—Scholar-in-Residence, former Dean of the College of Arts and Humanities, and Director of the MLA program—determined to redirect his full-time attention to an emerging book-publishing enterprise.[235] Since his appointment to the University in 1994, Raley followed in the scholarly tradition of Dr. Calvin Huckabay and led his college to new plateaus of academic achievement.[236] Leading by example, Raley fostered the development of a college of active scholars devoted to research in their disciplines as well as their commitment to student learning. Following his official retirement, Dr. Raley maintained close ties to the University by his service as Chairman of the University Retirees Association from 2008-2010. In his corporate role as a publisher, Raley produced several books by HBU faculty including *From Ruins to Resurrection: Sacred Landscapes of Michael Roque Collins*[237] and this volume, *An Act of Providence, a history of Houston Baptist University, 1960-2010.*

Dr. Stephen Wentland also announced his retirement after twenty-six years on the University faculty.[238] He had served as Chair of the Department of Chemistry and Physics since 1983. Wentland was the first HBU faculty member to use computers in chemistry. He was instrumental in the development of the popular biochemistry/molecular biology major and achieved curricular integration of *Organic Chemistry* and *Physical Chemistry* with the assistance of funding from the Welch

---

234 Kris Bagley, "Changing of the Guard," *The Collegian,* 6 May 2004, p. 11.
235 Michael Rubash, "Changing of the Guard," *The Collegian,* 6 May 2004, p. 11.
236 "Dr. Harold Raley," *HBU News,* Summer 2005, 11. Photo.
237 Michael Roque Collins, *From Ruins to Resurrection: Sacred Landscapes of Michael Roque Collins* (Houston: Halcyon Press, Ltd., 2009).
238 "Wentland Says Goodbye," *HBU News,* Winter 2005, 26. Photo.

Foundation. To his students and colleagues, he represented one who both worked and played hard. At the end of each quarter, he held a pizza party for chemistry majors and showed James Bond films; he was the sponsor of the Vietnamese Student Association.[239]

Two of those retiring first came to the University as faculty members in 1967 and ultimately moved to administrative positions. Both were multi-dimensional professionals. Mayfield Outstanding Staff Award winner Dr. Cynthia Young served as Assistant Vice President for Institutional Effectiveness and Research. Her academic roots were in biology as a faculty member and health professions advisor to students. She became the institutional coordinator of the Southern Association re-affirmation process and later moved into an emerging interest in institutional research.[240] Dr. Young proved particularly effective in working with faculty colleagues for the improvement of learning and institutional assessment.[241] Dr. Doris Warren observed, "She worked to help everyone get to a point where assessment is a part of our culture, and the practice of using research and data is part of our everyday decision-making process. And, she did it all with humor and her own personal cachet."[242] Young enjoyed the lifelong gratitude of the many generations of University students who were admitted to medical college while under her care.

Dr. Don Byrnes was a "man for all seasons." In 2005, Byrnes was serving as University Legal Counsel after thirty-six years of highly particularistic institutional contribution—much unobserved by the public, yet critical to the University's effective operation.[243] As an ordained Methodist minister and the holder of doctoral degrees in history and law, Byrnes was a man of diverse personal interests. Known for his quick wit and his ability to facilitate change, Dr. Byrnes utilized his effective working relationship with the many elements of the campus community to affect growth and professionalism. He was valued for his courage in confronting issues in order to maintain good institutional health. Board Chair Ray Cox '81 observed, "His impeccable character defines him personally and professionally."[244] His responsibilities over the years included the teaching of undergraduate history and graduate MLA courses, pro-

---

239 Renee McGruder, "Esteemed chemistry professor retires," *The Collegian,* 15 Dec. 2005, p. 5.

240 Martha Morrow, "Dr. Cynthia Young," *HBU News,* Summer 2005, 10-11. Photo.

241 Natasha Avey, "Young retires after 38 years," *The Collegian,* 5 May 2005, p. 4.

242 Martha Morrow, "Dr. Cynthia Young," *HBU News,* Summer 2005, 11.

243 Sarah Conn, "Embarking on a New Journey in Life," *HBU News,* Summer 2005, 9. Photo.

244 Meredith Warren, "36 years of service: Dr. Don R. Byrnes retires," *The Collegian,* 12 Apr. 2005, pp. 8-9.

viding leadership for enrollment management, institutional coordination with the Independent Colleges and Universities of Texas, service as University Registrar, Legal Counsel to the President and the Board of Trustees, and member of the Academic Affairs Committee for more than twenty years. Dr. Byrnes was a former President of the Faculty Assembly and in 2005 received the Mayfield Outstanding Staff Award.[245] In formal resolution, the Faculty Assembly expressed its "deep gratitude for (his) long and tireless service to the University as a teacher, administrator, and a counselor."[246] At a retirement dinner given to honor Dr. Byrnes, nearly $10,000 was raised for student scholarships.[247]

In thirty-two years of service, it was conceivable that Dr. James Taylor actually accomplished forty years of contribution. His early arrival on campus each morning was confirmed by time stamps on emails sent while most colleagues still slept. Taylor's self-professed dedication was to teaching. He won the Opal Goolsby Outstanding Teaching Award on three occasions. He was named to the rank of Distinguished Professor. Through his roles as department chair, Associate Dean, and Dean of the College of Arts and Humanities, Taylor's impact on several generations of students and colleagues was profound.[248] In addition, Dr. Taylor also earned the trust and respect of all branches of the University including trustees, alumni, and administration. He served as President of the Faculty Assembly an unprecedented three times. Upon his retirement, the Faculty Assembly wrote in resolution, "We honor your abilities as a communicator, an organizer, and a synthesizer. We also value your integrity and commitment to excellence."[249] Echoing the gratitude of his colleagues, this author wrote, "One is fortunate to have at least one Jim Taylor in your life, someone who causes you to stretch to meet his example, someone who challenges your instincts, someone who supports you as friend even when he may not support your position. He is a man of great consistency, dedication, loyalty, reflection, and action."[250] In addi-

245 Sarah Conn, "Embarking on a New Journey in Life: Dr. Don Byrnes, Legal Counsel," *HBU News,* Summer 2005, 9. Photo.

246 Houston Baptist University, Minutes of the Meetings of the Faculty Assembly, Meeting 19 Apr. 2005.

247 "Celebrating a New Endeavor While Honoring Past Accomplishments," *HBU News,* Summer 2005, 30. Photo.

248 Sarah Conn, "Embarking on a New Journey in Life: Dr. James Taylor, Dean, College of Arts and Humanities," *HBU News,* Summer 2005, 9-10. Photo.

249 Houston Baptist University, Minutes of the Meetings of the Faculty Assembly, Meeting on 19 Apr. 2005.

250 (Don Looser remarks, Retirement Dinner for Dr. James Taylor, Dean of the College of Arts and Humanities, May 2005).

tion to his many designated roles, Taylor was viewed as one of the most effective mediators and catalysts in University history.

Dr. Robert Linder returned to University service in 2004 after a ten-year absence to fill a one-year vacancy as Interim Director of the School of Music.[251] The year was an idyllic experience reuniting the Taylor-Linder team of leadership for a "last hurrah." The Faculty Assembly expressed appreciation to Linder for "heeding the Macedonian call." In further expression of gratitude, the Assembly formally elected Byrnes, Linder, Taylor, and Young to the honorary position of "Hero of the University."[252] In 2005, the University trustees conferred the rank of Distinguished Professor upon retiring faculty members Dr. Beth Boyce, Dr. Harold Raley, Dr. James Taylor, and Dr. Stephen Wentland.[253]

§

One of the great institutional challenges in the decade of "the aughts" was maintaining pace with technological advancement. The sophistication of the personal technology of the "millennial" student frequently eclipsed the ability of the University to keep pace.[254] The gap at HBU was more pronounced in administrative support than in academic instruction. Significant change was accomplished on campus during this period, however. New computer labs added in Atwood II were made possible by the departure of Southwestern Seminary.[255] By the spring 2003 quarter, students were able to use online "E-registration" to enroll in courses for the following term.[256] The acquisition virtually eliminated long waiting lines and the limitations of the Registrar's 8-5 day.[257] The system offered higher levels of student satisfaction while maintaining the faculty advising process.[258] Students wanted "hands-on" access to enrollment and class change without the perceived oversight by a data entry clerk. At the same time, the Moody Library purchased extensive collections of retrospective periodicals in online databases from *Journal Storage* (JSTOR) that

---

251 Candace Bush, "The Music Man Returns," *HBU News,* Sept. 2004, 20. Photo.
252 Houston Baptist University, Minutes of the Meetings of the Faculty Assembly, Meeting on 19 Apr. 2005.
253 "May Commencement," *HBU News,* Summer 2005, 20. Photo.
254 "The Millennials Come to Campus . . . and with them their technology," *HBU News,* Fall 2005, 4-5.
255 Griffin Colvert, "Computer labs relocated," *The Collegian,* 31 Oct. 2002, p. 6.
256 "E-Registrations Comes to HBU," *HBU News,* Mar. 2003, 5. Photo.
257 "From long lines to online," *SomeTimes,* 15 Feb. 2003.
258 Tomie Lunsford, "E-Registration debuts spring quarter 2003," *The Collegian,* 16 Jan. 2003, p. 1.

introduced a new acronym into the everyday academic vocabulary.[259] A third software addition addressed the subject of academic integrity. Through the program *Turnitin*, faculty members could submit student work online to be checked against an international database for plagiarism.[260]

In October 2003, the trustees responded to an administrative plea for the acquisition of integrated software for the campus. A report prepared by all the operational vice presidents and proposed by President Hodo presented the imperative for better accuracy, articulation, data consistency, and speed. The proposed HuskyNet was planned to integrate all digital information on campus and to feature single-portal user access for all requisite functions.[261] The Board approved an internal loan of $1,000,000 to be repaid over a five-year period[262] to purchase SCT *Banner* software.[263] The lengthy process of installation, adaptation, training, and implementation continued over the decade and was brought online by operational units—business operations, student records, and finally academic advising.[264] *Banner* provided "administrative synthesis" and replaced *FirstClass* as the vehicle for communication and instruction. The campus availability of wireless Internet connection soon followed.[265]

New *Recruitment PLUS* software was acquired for the Office of Enrollment Management to provide effective tracking and communication with prospective students.[266] Moreover, the University website emerged as a prime vehicle for recruiting communication and information.[267] STA-MATS was engaged to develop website design, content, and programming. In 2004, a new theme, "Defining Relationships, Defining Lives," became the focus for student recruitment materials.[268] The new theme was developed by working with student focus groups and joined the University slogan, "HBU: Houston's Blessed University," to enhance institutional visibility and image.[269] The final increment in the campus digital

---

259 Brittany Adams, "Moody Library purchases collections for online Journal Storage databases," *The Collegian,* 16 Jan. 2003, p. 7.

260 David Fresch, "Software checks for plagiarism," *The Collegian,* 16 Jan. 2002, p. 7.

261 DJ Warren, "HuskyNet implementation begins fall quarter," *The Collegian,* 23 Sept. 2004, p. 1.

262 Houston Baptist University, Minutes of the Meetings of the Executive Committee of the Board of Trustees, Meeting on 21 Oct. 2003.

263 DJ Warren, "HuskyNet software chosen," *The Collegian,* 7 Oct. 2004, p. 2.

264 Renee McGruder, "Banner system installed," *The Collegian,* 6 Apr. 2005, p. 1.

265 Christen Coyle, "Wireless Internet now available," *The Collegian,* 22 Apr. 2004, p. 1.

266 Houston Baptist University, Minutes of the Meetings of the Board of Trustees, Meeting on 23 Nov. 2004.

267 "A new look with more changes to come!" *HBU News,* Mar. 2005, 11.

268 "Defining Relationships; Defining Lives," *HBU News,* Dec. 2004, 4.

269 Houston Baptist University, Minutes of the Meetings of the Board of Trustees, Meeting on 28 Sept. 2004.

revolution was the acquisition of content-management software to simplify content change and insure consistency throughout the network.[270]

§

Several critical facility improvements enhanced the functional capabilities for the campus. In 2003, a gift of $1,000,000 over three years from the President's Development Council enabled the upgrading of the Glasscock Center, the Mabee Teaching Theater, and the Sharp Gymnasium.[271] Mabee Theater was completely refurbished with a new sound system, enhanced lighting, stage reconfiguration, new seating, and carpeting.[272] An addition to the Holcombe Mall entrance of the Glasscock Center afforded a large reception area, dressing rooms for visiting athletic teams and officials, offices, and support space. The facility could be entered directly from the Mabee Theater lobby and provided a venue for recital and concert receptions as well as a theater setting for events to follow dining events in Glasscock.[273] The second floor was removed from Glasscock—opening the length of the facility for a second basketball court and full access to the total space. The crowded conditions existing in the Cullen Science Center were alleviated in 2004 when two large classrooms in the Cullen Nursing Center were converted to biology laboratories.[274]

The Board continued with significant involvement in the management of University real estate. The Fondren II retail development contributed approximately $500,000 annually to the University and enjoyed a fully-leased position.[275] However, other properties were more problematic. Toys-R-Us closed in 2001,[276] and the Garden Village Retirement Center filed for bankruptcy in 2003. The retirement center's accumulated debt over the previous eleven years of its lease approximated $600,000.[277] In other real estate activity, Circuit City terminated its lease in February 2005 and prepaid its remaining rent.[278]

---

270 Houston Baptist University, Minutes of the Meetings of the Board of Trustees, Meeting on 22 Feb. 2005.

271 "PDC holds spring dinner," *HBU News,* June 2003, 9.

272 Houston Baptist University, Minutes of the Meetings of the Board of Trustees, Meeting on 24 Sept. 2002.

273 "Renovation adds needed space," *HBU News,* June 2003, 5.

274 Katelyn Griffin, "Science lab renovation now finished," *The Collegian,* 21 Oct. 2004, p. 5.

275 Houston Baptist University, Minutes of the Meetings of the Board of Trustees, Meeting on 28 Sept. 2004.

276 Houston Baptist University, Minutes of the Meetings of the Board of Trustees, Meeting on 19 Nov. 2002.

277 Christen Coyle, "Garden Village files bankruptcy," *The Collegian,* 18 Sept. 2003, p. 6.

278 Houston Baptist University, Minutes of the Meetings of the Board of Trustees, Meeting on 22 Feb. 2005.

In 2003, the University's real estate enterprise, Beechnut Street, Inc. (BSI), purchased Husky Village student housing from Century Campus Housing. The University maintained ground rights and twenty-five percent of the profit, but BSI became the owner and manager of the facility. The move enabled rent for students to be lowered and provided a solid investment for the University.[279] Memorial Healthcare System purchased the sites of Toys-R-Us, Garden Village, the Texas Eye Institute, and the Wellness Center (with a reversion clause) for $10,500,000.[280] In 2004, the trustees also approved a fifteen-year ground lease to Memorial Hermann Healthcare Systems for 3.5 additional acres of campus land immediately adjacent to the Wellness Center for parking to be installed and maintained by the Hospital.[281]

§

Faculty salaries continued to be an object of increasing concern to the Board of Trustees. In 2003, the trustee Finance Committee adopted a more active role in budget preparation by addressing the manifested goal of the University to "be one of America's premier, Christian, urban, academic institutions." The committee observed "that the most important aspect of building an organization is to attract and retain outstanding faculty and personnel."[282] The trustee committee initiated a recommendation that money be transferred from proposed contingency funds to underwrite salary increases for the coming year. The committee further requested a formal report on average salaries at other institutions and the development of a multi-year plan to result in more competitive salary levels.

The University reported a year-end surplus of $108,000 in 2003 marking the tenth consecutive year to report a net operating surplus. However, a two-year economic slump and lower-than-anticipated enrollments in the fall of 2003 required budget adjustment in September[283] and additional cuts totaling five percent of budget in January.[284] In 2004, the Finance Committee again revised the proposed 04-05 budget to include

---

279 Amanda Dean, "Husky Village changes owners: lower rent now available for students," *The Collegian*, 18 Feb. 2003, p. 1.
280 Houston Baptist University, Minutes of the Meetings of the Board of Trustees, Meeting on 25 Feb. 2003.
281 Houston Baptist University, Minutes of the Meetings of the Board of Trustees, Meeting on 23 Nov. 2004.
282 Houston Baptist University, Minutes of the Meetings of the Board of Trustees, Meeting on 25 Feb. 2003.
283 Ibid.
284 Christen Coyle, "Lower enrollment forces budget cuts," *The Collegian*, 15 Jan. 2004, p. 1.

monies for salary increases while calling for budget reduction overall.[285] The University finished the 2003-04 year $860,000 under budget.[286]

The budget proposed for 2005-06 included a planned surplus of $611,000. Under the leadership of its Chair Dr. Jack Little, the Finance Committee again responded to the proposed budget with a formal request for salary increases more reflective of "an organization seeking to achieve 'premier' status."[287] In response, the University developed a plan designed to address declining enrollments that included: 1) more competitive salaries; 2) enhanced scholarships in music, forensics, team cheer, club sports, and expanded intramurals; 3) expansion of student recruiting beyond a seventy-five-mile radius; 4) a redesigned website for recruiting emphasis; and 5) physical enhancements to the M. D. Anderson Student Center.[288] The February 2005 report of the trustee Academic Committee also contained results of the requested survey of Texas college faculty salaries in Master's degree granting institutions. In further compensation-related matters, Vice President Parker reported that the University would no longer be able to support one hundred percent of the cost for employee healthcare insurance.[289]

In 2005, the Finance Committee requested a five-year strategic plan that included a three-year budget emphasis on qualitative growth.[290] This multi-year budgeting model marked a significant change in process as a part of strategic planning. Throughout its history, the University had budgeted only one year at a time. The 2005-06 budget recommendation included a 2.75 percent pool of funds to provide merit raises for faculty and staff. An additional allowance—part of a three-year commitment— was provided to raise the salaries of senior faculty to Category IIA averages—the target goal from the SACS institutional self-study. The Faculty Assembly drafted a formal resolution of gratitude for the attention given the matter of salary equitability.[291]

The Board of Trustees elected to recognize several University friends with honorary degrees during the period 2002-2006. In 2003, Archie Dunham, Chairman of ConocoPhillips, delivered the spring commence-

---

285 Houston Baptist University, Minutes of the Meetings of the Board of Trustees, Meeting on 24 Feb. 2004.
286 Houston Baptist University, Minutes of the Meetings of the Board of Trustees, Meeting on 18 May 2004.
287 Houston Baptist University, Minutes of the Meetings of the Board of Trustees, Meeting on 22 Feb. 2005.
288 Ibid.
289 Christen Coyle, "Budget increases," *The Collegian,* 7 Apr. 2005, p. 1.
290 Houston Baptist University, Minutes of the Meetings of the Board of Trustees, Meeting on 17 May 2005.
291 Ibid.

ment address and was awarded the Doctor of Humane Letters degree. The University conferred its 12,932nd degree to graduates that included those from San Antonio, Austin, and Trenton, New Jersey enrolled in the Master of Education Online degree.[292]   In February 2004, Dr. Carol McDonald, President of the Independent Colleges and Universities of Texas, assisted former trustee Representative Charlie Howard in reading Doctor of Laws citations honoring the legislative support of Representatives Scott Hochberg and Talmadge Heflin for the Tuition Equalization Grant program.[293]   Finally, in 2006, Harvey Zinn and trustees Allene Lucas and Tracy Lawrence were awarded the Doctor of Humane Letters degree.[294]

§

In 2003, the Woodland Baptist Church "felt led to close their doors" after 87 years of service to the community.[295]   Led by its pastor Greg Gower '84, the congregation conveyed its assets to the University's Endowed Scholarship fund resulting in a gift of $936,000—one of the largest in history—to benefit future generations of HBU students.[296]   As with other earlier church gifts, the Woodland Baptist Church name lives in perpetuity as a testimony to years of service in the community.[297]

In its ongoing effort to relate to the several Baptist constituencies in the state, in May 2002 the University Board of Trustees committed "to the continued relationships as in the past with the Baptist General Convention of Texas, the Southern Baptists of Texas Convention, and the Cooperative Baptist Fellowship, as well as other Baptist and non-Baptist organizations."[298]   The University explained that the relationship with agencies other than the BGCT would be "fraternal."   Dr. Robert Campbell, pastor of the Westbury Baptist Church of Houston and current President of the BGCT, responded, "We have received reassurances from HBU trustees that they do not want to interrupt the relationship with

---

292 "May commencement honors graduates, Dunham," *HBU News,* June 2003, 8. Photo.
293 "February commencement honors state representatives," *HBU News,* March 2004, 9.
294 "A Milestone Graduation," *HBU News,* Summer 2006, 15. Photos.
295 Dr. E. D. Hodo, "From the President," *HBU News,* Sept. 2003, 2.
296 "The Spirit of Woodland Baptist Church," *HBU News,* Sept. 2003, 12-13.
297 "Brunch honors scholarship donors," *HBU News,* June 2004, 12. Photos.
298 Houston Baptist University, Minutes of the Meetings of the Board of Trustees, Meeting on 14 May 2002.

Texas Baptists."[299] HBU Board Chair and pastor, Dr. Mark Denison, reiterated, "We must respond to *all* the Baptists in Texas."[300] At the annual meeting of the BGCT in November 2003, former trustee Dr. Robert Creech '74 moved that the convention "evaluate fully the implications of HBU entering into a fraternal relationship with another state convention and clarify the status of the relationship between HBU and the BGCT including future levels of funding."[301] Creech asked for a report to the BGCT Executive Committee no later than May 2004. The *Baptist Standard* reported in January 2004 that committees had been appointed to study the HBU relationship.[302]

In February 2004, the HBU Board of Trustees under Chair and pastor Dr. John Morgan, adopted the following statement:

> The Board of Trustees of Houston Baptist University, recognizing our formal relationship with the BGCT and our fraternal relationship with the SBCT, affirm our openness for appropriate cooperation with all Baptists and other evangelicals who share the convictions represented in our Preamble. This cooperation will be determined by verbal agreement between the University President along with the pertinent officials of other entities on a case-by-case basis. This statement is intended to give expression to our common bonds with other groups within the Kingdom of God in Jesus Christ.[303]

In May, the Associated Baptist Press News reported that the BGCT had asked the University to rescind its previous action.[304] At the same time, the Christian Education Coordinating Board (CECB) voted on May 17 to recommend escrowing $581,000 of the funds intended for HBU, not including $169,000 for student ministerial scholarships.[305] An HBU Denominational Relations Committee was appointed with Dr. Robert

---

299 Richard Vara, "Campbell looks back at 2 years of progress and strife," *Houston Chronicle,* 8 Nov. 2003, pp. 1-2, two-star ed.

300 Mark Wingfield, "Houston Baptist University forges new link to SBTC, keeps ties with BGCT," *Baptist Standard,* 1 Oct. 2003, www.baptiststandard.com (accessed Nov. 29, 2009).

301 Mark Wingfield, "Motions call for study of HBU's ties and fund for restorative justice," *Baptist Standard,* 14 Nov. 2003, www.baptiststandard.com (accessed Nov. 29, 2009).

302 Ferrell Foster, "Committees to study HBU relationship," *Baptist Standard,* 23 Jan. 2004, www.baptiststandard.com (accessed Jan. 13, 2010).

303 Houston Baptist University, Minutes of the Minutes of the Board of Trustees, Meeting in Executive Session on 24 Feb. 2004.

304 Ferrell Foster, "BGCT to ask HBU to rescind pacts with conservative group," *Associated Baptist Press News,* 19 May 2004.

305 Ibid.

Overton serving as Chair along with James Clark, Dr. Mark Denison '82, Dearing Garner, Karl Kennard, and David Stutts '82 to address, in part, a request from the Cooperative Baptist Fellowship for a formal relationship.[306] Meetings with the HBU representatives and the Administrative/ Finance Committee of the Christian Education Coordinating Board were held through the summer and fall. Ultimately, in October 2004, a Memorandum of Understanding was developed to be approved by the University trustees and the BGCT:

> These meetings have all been held in a mutual spirit of good will and a desire for a positive relationship. . . . (they) have resulted in much greater understanding on the part of both entities. The CECB . . . committee has discerned that the HBU trustees were genuine in their desire to remain a part of the BGCT while relating informally with another state convention. . . . they acted in accordance with a legitimate understanding of the agreement and in what they believed to be in the best interest of the University. . . . They (HBU) have affirmed again that their relationship with the BGCT is to be their priority focus and have agreed upon the importance of this commitment being observable in programs, ministries, and governance. . . . it is now agreed that the term "unique affiliation" means "exclusive affiliation" and that the phrase 'establishing a formal relationship' refers to a situation wherein HBU and another denomination, convention or religious entity both agree to enter into a formally written "contractual" relationship that involves conditional expectations or administrative requirements.[307]

The Memorandum of Understanding set forth the terms that HBU "will elect only trustees who have affirmed a commitment to carrying out the purposes and mission of HBU . . . and who are positively supportive of the Baptist principles upon which HBU and the BGCT were founded."[308] The funds held in escrow would be released with the exception that the Block Grant Funds withheld when "HBU unilaterally changed its trustee selection process" would continue to be withheld indefinitely.[309] The Block Grant funds represented some $600,000 in 2004 in comparison with a $35,000,000 HBU budget. The agreement was approved by

---

306 Houston Baptist University, Minutes of the Meetings of the Board of Trustees, Meeting on 23 Sept. 2003.
307 Houston Baptist University, Minutes of the Meetings of the Board of Trustees, Meeting on 23 Nov. 2004.
308 Ibid. Memorandum of Understanding between the Christian Education Coordinating Board and the HBU Board of Trustees.
309 Ibid.

the HBU Board of Trustees on November 23, 2004, and by the CECB on November 24.[310]

§

Since 1964, the President's Council had sponsored a series of formal dinners designed to inform the Houston community about the University and offer an opportunity for constituencies to gather and refresh their energies in the University's behalf. In 1991, the President's Council formed in 1964 for men became the President's Development Council for all and continued its tradition of providing financial support for selected University projects.

The 2003 Spirit of Excellence Dinner was distinguished by its honorary chairs, President and Mrs. George H. W. Bush. Presidential advisor Karen Hughes spoke on "Excellence in Leadership" for the event that also recognized Distinguished Alumni Dr. Cliff McGee '90[311] and Manfred Jachmich '69,[312] as well as Meritorious Alumnae Vivian Camacho '91[313] and Candace Desrosiers '94.[314] Former trustee Allene Lucas and former Guild and Museum Society President Linda Higginbotham received the Milton Cross Service Awards.[315] Also recognized were Goolsby Outstanding Teaching Award winners Dr. Brenda Whaley '79, Dr. Melissa Wiseman, Dr. Randy Wilson, and Dr. Chris Hammons,[316] as well as Mayfield Outstanding Staff Award winners Dr. Cynthia Young, Mary Purcell, Hugh McClung, and Charles Miller.

The 2005 Spirit of Excellence Dinner was a victim of Hurricane Rita. In a later dinner at the Houstonian, the University honored Gala Chairs Laura and Bob Beauchamp '87 and Spirit of Excellence awardees Nell Smith, JPMorgan Chase Bank, and the Rudy Tomjanovich Foundation.[317] Dr. Bruce and Mary Ann Belin received the Milton Cross Service Award;[318] Dr. Brenda Whaley '79 received her cash prize as winner of the

---

310 Greg Warner, "BGCT, University reach compromise over ties to conservative group," *Associated Baptist Press News*, 24 Nov. 2004.
311 "Distinguished and Meritorious Alumni Awards," *HBU News*, Sept. 2002, 10. Photos.
312 "Recognizing service and achievement," *HBU News*, Sept. 2003, 9-10.
313 "Distinguished and Meritorious Alumni Awards, *HBU News*, Sept. 2002, 10. Photos.
314 "Recognizing service and achievement," *HBU News*, Sept. 2003, 10.
315 "Spirit of Excellence," *HBU News*, Dec. 2003, 10-11. Photos.
316 "Recognizing service and achievement," *HBU News*, Sept. 2003, 8.
317 "Spirit of Excellence Award," *HBU News*, Winter 2005, 11. Photos.
318 "Milton Cross Outstanding Volunteer Award," *HBU News*, Winter 2005, 12. Photo.

Dr. Larry D. Smith Award for Teaching Excellence.[319] Guests for the original Hurricane Rita evening were offered refunded contributions. Virtually all refused a refund resulting in a $300,000 gift to the University for the dinner "that never was."

A series of Presidential lunches at the St. Regis Hotel was initiated by the President's Development Council. Council Chair Bob Rule explained, "This is an initiative designed to attract business leaders with topics of interest to make them aware of the University's mission and to recruit them as friends."[320] Over the period 2003 to 2007, these speakers included Harris County Tax Collector Paul Bettencourt, Halliburton Energy Services CEO John Gibson, David Weekly Homes President David Weekly,[321] Brunswick Corporation former President Jim Dawson,[322] Genesis Park Chairman Paul W. Hobby,[323] Houston Astros owner Drayton McLane, Jr.,[324] Federal Reserve Director Bill Gilmer,[325] Parkway Investments CEO and University trustee Ned Holmes,[326] Amegy Bank Chairman Walter Johnson,[327] BMC Software President Bob Beauchamp '87, and Pride International President and CEO Louis A. Raspino.

The Guild, the descendant of the President's Advisors established by Theo Dora Heyne, enjoyed a membership of 290 in 2002. In 2004, the Guild celebrated its thirtieth anniversary. The Guild built a network of support for the University among Houston's cultural community through an annual Christmas brunch and springtime Silver Tea. Among the other University affinity organizations, the University Auxiliary held its final formal meeting in September 2002. Past presidents of the organization, formed by Mrs. Hinton in 1963, were honored.[328] The members committed to maintain an annual reunion meeting.[329] All remaining assets and funds of the Auxiliary were transferred to the Moody Library.[330]

---

319 "Spirit of Excellence Gala," *HBU News,* Winter 2005, 12. Photo.

320 "President's Development Council," *HBU News,* Mar. 2004, 15.

321 "President's Development Council," *HBU News,* June 2004, 23. Photo.

322 "President's Development Council," *HBU News,* Dec. 2004, 18. Photo.

322 "President's Development Council," *HBU News,* Dec. 2004, 18. Photo.

323 "President's Development Council," *HBU News,* Mar. 2005, 18. Photo.

324 "President's Development Council," *HBU News,* Summer 2005, 22. Photo.

325 "President's Development Council," *HBU News,* Winter 2005, 19. Photo.

326 "President's Development Council," *HBU News,* Spring 2006, 23. Photos.

327 "President's Development Council," *HBU News.* Summer 2006, 28. Photos.

328 "Encore and More," *HBU News,* Dec. 2002, 24. Photo.

329 Houston Baptist University, Minutes of the Meetings of the Board of Trustees, Meeting on 24 Sept. 2002.

330 Houston Baptist University, Minutes of the Meetings of the Board of Trustees, Meeting on 19 Nov. 2002.

In 2002, under the leadership of Board Chair Dr. Stewart Morris, one hundred percent of the trustees participated in a capital campaign, raising $1,500,000 for the Cultural Arts Center.[331] The *HBU News* honored Dr. Morris's years of service in an article entitled, "One Man, One Vision, One Commitment." Morris was recognized as the "one man whose thread has continually woven and rewoven itself into the fabric of University history."[332] His record of contribution of personal time, expertise, financial support, and advocacy was gratefully acknowledged. In September, Dr. and Mrs. Morris announced a gift of $250,000 to the College of Nursing. Morris had championed this program from its inception when he first envisioned Memorial Baptist Hospital's Lillie Jolly School of Nursing joining the University's academic program. In 2004, trustee Lisa Morris Simon presented the first of an annual grant from the Stewart and Joella Morris Foundation to the University.[333]

In November 2002, trustee Dr. Bruce Belin was named Chairman of the Cultural Arts Center Steering Committee, as well as the Building Committee for the project. The Board approved a plan to employ an architect and contractor and to approach the project as a design/build process.[334] In April, the Cullen Trust for Higher Education on which Dr. Belin served announced a $3,000,000 challenge grant for the Cultural Arts Center over a three-year period to be used for an operational endowment for the facility.[335] By early 2004, approximately $12,500,000 had been raised including $3,300,000 reserved for facility endowment. The trustees formulated a plan to raise eighty-five percent of the $28,500,000 needed before breaking ground for the facility.

In February 2004, the Robert and Janice McNair Foundation announced a gift of $5,000,000 in support of the Center.[336] With both Cullen and McNair, the commitment of the University to provide a facility of excellence for community use was a persuasive force. The Building Committee engaged Morris Architects, designers of the Wortham Center, and W. S. Bellows Construction Corporation, builders of the Wortham

331 Houston Baptist University, Minutes of the Meetings of the Board of Trustees, Meeting on 24 Sept. 2002.
332 Vivian Camacho, "One man, One vision, One Commitment," *HBU News*, Sept. 2002, 14-15.
333 Houston Baptist University, Minutes of the Meetings of the Board of Trustees, Meeting on 24 Feb. 2004.
334 Houston Baptist University, Minutes of the Meetings of the Board of Trustees, Meeting on 19 Nov. 2002.
335 Houston Baptist University, Minutes of the Meetings of the Board of Trustees, Meeting on 13 May 2003.
336 Houston Baptist University, Minutes of the Meetings of the Board of Trustees, Meeting on 24 Feb. 2004.

Center, the Kinkaid Theater, and the Alley Theatre expansion.[337] Charles Ward reported for the *Houston Chronicle* in August that the city was "abuzz" with plans for the new Cultural Arts Center that was to include a 1200-seat music theater and a 350-seat chapel/recital hall. "For musicians the big news is the hiring of Jaffe Holden Acoustics, Inc. The firm has produced increasingly impressive work in Houston beginning with the Wortham Theater. Acoustically, the Moores Opera House and Zilkha Hall are two of the city's best."[338]

Christen Coyle, writing for *The Collegian,* stressed the importance of the facility for student recruiting and enhanced learning opportunity. Moreover, Coyle observed that the Center would help identify the University as a major force in the Houston cultural community.[339] A planned second phase of the project would provide for teaching and rehearsal facilities at a later time. In January 2005, the University announced a gift of $1,000,000 from Dr. Archie and Linda Dunham for the Bible in America Museum in the new Center.[340] Dr. Dunham was the Chairman of ConocoPhillips at the time of the gift, and the Dunham's son Cary was a 1993 graduate of HBU's College of Business and Economics. The Bible Museum was to be named the Dunham Family Bible Museum.[341]

In 2005, Diane Williams '93 was serving as the first woman to chair the University Board of Trustees. As an alumna, member of The Guild, seven-year member of the Board, and former Chair of the Academic Committee, Williams proved providentially placed in her position of leadership at this time. Within a year, she would be chairing the strategic Presidential Search Committee. Her friendship with Dr. Hodo as co-Bible Study leaders together at their church, her marriage to Stanley Williams who was to emerge as a dynamic catalyst in the construction of the Cultural Arts Center, and her love of the University's students combined to make her one of the most effective Board chairs at any moment in University history.[342]

---

337 The principal architect for Morris, Pete Ed Garrett, formed his own firm in the early days of construction. Studio Red, Architects therefore supervised construction and provided additional architectural design for the Center.

338 Charles Ward, "HBU building toward an artistic tomorrow," *Houston Chronicle,* 29 July 2004, Zest sec., p. 15, two-star ed.

339 Christen Coyle, "New center to house arts," *The Collegian,* 21 Oct. 2004, p. 1.

340 DJ Warren, "Donation promised," *The Collegian,* 10 Jan. 2005, p. 1.

341 "The Dunham Family Bible in America Museum," *HBU News,* Mar. 2005, 30. Photo.

342 Martha Morrow, "An Evolving Relationship Brings New Opportunities," *HBU News,* Dec. 2004, 6-7. Photo.

In February 2005, Dr. Stewart Morris accepted the position of Honorary Chairman for the Cultural Arts Center Capital Campaign.[343] This act would prove to be a milestone in the ultimate realization of the project. In order to maintain momentum in the fund-raising process, the trustees approved construction of a new boulevard from Fondren Road to Beechnut Street that would provide access to the new Cultural Arts Center. This project included lighting, drainage, and infrastructure as well. A building-site dedication was held in May with a ceremonial groundbreaking.[344] By November, Dr. Belin and Dr. Hodo reported to the Board that funds were available to begin first phase construction of the project to include the chapel,[345] the Bible and Decorative Arts museums, a grand central hall, and all the supportive infrastructure for the center—virtually everything except the 1200-seat theater and its attendant facilities. Construction time of eighteen months was anticipated; the first phase was not to exceed $15,000,000.[346] The following February, however, the Board also approved the purchase of steel for the entire project.[347]

§

With the anticipation of funding completion for the Cultural Arts Center project, Dr. Hodo announced his intention to resign his position as President effective June 30, 2006. "In the providence of God, we have notified the Board of Trustees of our intention to devote our energies to other ministry opportunities."[348] The move was not unanticipated. The President had often shared his plan to resign upon raising the funds for the Cultural Arts Center.[349] A succession plan had been developed by the Board in 2003 in the event of the death, disability, termination, or resig-

---

343 Houston Baptist University, Minutes of the Meetings of the Board of Trustees, Meeting on 22 Feb. 2005.
344 "Cultural Arts Center Site Dedication," *HBU News,* Summer 2005, 15. Participants included President Hodo, Board Chair Diane Williams, Building Committee Co-chairs Bruce Belin and Stanley Williams, Campaign Chair Dr. Stewart Morris, Student Government President Christi Swift, and School of Music Director Dr. John Yarrington.
345 "A Dream Long Held: The Cultural Arts Center Chapel," *HBU News,* Winter 2005, 20. A successful fund-raising Chapel Committee was chaired by Donna Dee Floyd and Diane Williams '93.
346 Houston Baptist University, Minutes of the Meetings of the Board of Trustees, Meeting in Executive Session on 22 Nov. 2005.
347 Houston Baptist University, Minutes of Meetings of the Board of Trustees, Meeting in Executive Session on 28 Feb. 2006.
348 Dr. E. D. Hodo, "From the President," *HBU News,* Spring 2006, 2.
349 Tracy Upton, "Answering another call," *The Collegian,* 12 Jan. 2006, p. 1.

nation of the University President. In such case, a team of the vice presidents appointed by the Chair of the Board of Trustees would manage University operations until the appointment of an Interim President—who would not be a candidate for the position.[350] For several years, open discussion between Dr. Hodo and his Vice Presidents had facilitated plans for a phased change in the senior administrative leadership. By the time of Dr. Hodo's announcement, Vice President Purcell and Legal Counsel Byrnes had already retired. Dr. Hodo announced his decision to the campus family in University Forum on January 6, 2006:

> My hope is that the Cultural Arts Center project will be underway by spring. . . . With the success of this major project, it is the right time for me to go. The University is poised to take its next steps forward. . . . Sadie and I look forward with expectancy to great days ahead for HBU. It has been a privilege to serve as President. . . . We have wonderful memories of our time here.[351]

A presidential search committee was appointed by Board Chair Ray Cox[352] consisting of Dr. Diane Williams '93 as Chair, Karl Kennard, Jack Carlson, Dr. Mark Denison '82, David Stutts '82, Dr. Bruce Belin, and Dr. Stewart Morris—all former Chairs of the Board of Trustees. The Board also approved the appointment of an advisory committee to consist of two members of the faculty, two students, and one staff member.[353]

Dr. Hodo recalled the early days of his presidency in a lengthy January interview for the *Houston Chronicle*:

> I never dreamed I would be president of an institution for nearly 19 years and impact lives for eternity. It has been a blessing. . . . The first five years were really difficult. Enrollment began declining because jobs were plentiful and private colleges cost more than the publics. . . . Faculty and staff morale was down because salaries were not being raised. . . . But the biggest problem was NCAA Division I athletics. . . . We were going $500,000 to $1,300,000 in the hole every year. . . . We announced the school

---

350 Houston Baptist University, Minutes of the Meetings of the Board of Trustees, Meeting 13 May 2003. Dr. Hodo referred to himself as "President and CEO" and deferred from naming an Executive Vice President during his tenure.
351 "A Legacy of Faith and Learning," *HBU News*, Spring 2006, 6-9. Photo.
352 "Defining Relationships: Ray Cox," *HBU News*, Winter 2005, 6-7. Photo.
353 Houston Baptist University, Minutes of the Meetings of the Board of Trustees, Meeting on 22 Nov. 2005. Named to these positions were Dr. Brian Runnels, Dr. Brenda Whaley, Colette Cross, Edward Batinga, and Mon'Sher Spencer.

would downgrade its athletic program. That brought the wrath of students and alumni but the decision was supported by faculty and staff. . . . We had to get the budget down to what we could afford. . . . Two years later, we resumed intercollegiate sports in the NAIA. We reduced faculty teaching loads. . . . When I came here, the academic and athletic environments were excellent. The spiritual environment was here but not an emphasis, not paramount, not a priority. . . . We strengthened that. . . . We also redefined our relationship with the BGCT. Some trustees were members of conservative churches that supported the newer Southern Baptists of Texas Convention. BGCT funding went from $1,400,000 to $700,000.[354]

The Faculty Assembly named Dr. and Mrs. Hodo as "Heroes of the University" and prepared a resolution of appreciation to them both:

> The Faculty Assembly commends President Hodo for numerous accomplishments and recognizes that Mrs. Hodo has been a constant source of strength and inspiration. Among those accomplishments we include gracious hospitality, the courage to make and implement difficult decisions which in turn have led to a vastly improved financial foundation, an academically and spiritually stronger faculty and staff, a larger and better physical plant, a more attractive campus, a strong emphasis on stewardship, increased transparency in decision-making, and a strong Christian witness on campus and in the larger community.[355]

In further action, Dr. and Mrs. Hodo were named *President Emeritus* and *First Lady Emeritus* by the University Board of Trustees:

> Whereas for more than nineteen years, Dr. E. D. Hodo and his wife, Sadie B. Hodo, gave tirelessly of their time and talents in service to Houston Baptist University as President and First Lady; and

> Whereas, during these years the University achieved a position of financial solidarity and was richly blessed due to the efforts and their unwavering devotion to the cause of Christian education; and

> Whereas, the University is grateful for and wishes to express its enduring appreciation for this long relationship; now

---

354 Richard Vara, "Terms of Endearment: A final semester after 19 years at the helm," *Houston Chronicle*, 14 Jan. 2006, Religion sec., p. 1, two-star edition.
355 Houston Baptist University, Minutes of the Meetings of the Faculty Assembly, Meeting on 4 Apr. 2006.

Therefore be it resolved that the Board of Trustees of Houston Baptist University in recognition of their dedication and commitment to this University, its students, and the cause of Christian education does hereby confer upon Dr. E. D. Hodo and Sadie Branch Hodo the honorary and lifelong titles of President Emeritus and First Lady Emeritus with all the rights and privileges thereunto pertaining.[356]

At the May 20 Commencement, Dr. Hodo spoke on one of his favorite scriptures—Proverbs 9:10, "The fear of the Lord is the beginning of wisdom, and the knowledge of the Holy One is understanding." At the request of the Faculty Assembly, the President had for several years brought the commencement remarks rather than a guest speaker. His frequent introduction to these remarks was that, "Shortnin' was good for two things, biscuits and commencement addresses." At his final commencement, President Hodo was thanked for being "long on commitment and short on commencement."[357]

The President's Development Council honored the Hodos at its spring dinner.[358] In additional recognition, the Board of Trustees of the University hosted a gala celebration at the Post Oak Doubletree Hotel on May 22. Emceed by trustee Jack Carlson, the evening featured presentations of a proclamation declaring May 22, 2006, as E. D. Hodo Day in Houston and a bound book of letters from community leaders, university presidents, church and denominational leadership, alumni, faculty, staff, and trustees.[359]

At the Board meeting the next day, Dr. Hodo continued his role of leadership looking forward to his June 30th departure. The May 23 Board meeting emerged as one of the most significant in history. The University ended the year with a surplus of approximately $200,000 and a net worth of $47,000,000. Total assets were estimated to be approximately $150,000,000. The Sun Oil property donated in 1989 had generated over $2,000,000 in income in the intervening years. In a surprise action, Dr. Stewart Morris announced a gift of $4,000,000 to be matched for the Cultural Arts Center campaign to help meet the $23,000,000 goal.[360] In the same meeting, Dr. Bruce Belin announced that the Cullen

356 Houston Baptist University, Minutes of the Meetings of the Board of Trustees, Meeting on 26 Sept. 2006.
357 "A Milestone Graduation," *HBU News,* Summer 2006, 15. Photos.
358 "PDC honors Hodos at Spring Dinner," *HBU News,* Summer 2006, 29.
359 "A Fond Farewell," *HBU News,* Summer 2006, 25. Photos.
360 Houston Baptist University, Minutes of the Meetings of the Board of Trustees, Meeting on 23 May 2006.

Foundation had paid off its previous grant of $3,000,000 and had approved an additional gift of $3,000,000 that could be applied to the matching requirement of the Morris gift.[361] Completion of the remaining funding would enable immediate construction of the theater in addition to the first phase of construction that had already been authorized. An additional gift of $500,000 was announced from the John S. Dunn Research Foundation for nursing faculty recruitment and retention.[362]

These latest gifts marked a high point in the Presidency of Dr. Hodo. During his tenure as President, the number of alumni increased from 4917 to over 14,000 graduates; the value of the physical plant increased from $19.7 million in 1987 to $37.7 million in 2006.[363] Endowment funds increased from $30 million to $75 million. Revenue rose from $13 million to $33 million in 2006.[364] New facilities constructed in his term of office included the Moody Library expansion, the Hinton Center, Husky Village, the Bible in America Museum, the Baugh Center, the Wellness Center, the Mest Wing of the Women's Residence College, the Glasscock lobby expansion, remodeling of Hinton House and the M. D. Anderson Student Center, and the Cultural Arts Center.[365] Of him was said, "He has given the University the most valuable 20 years of his life. He has brought maturity, focus, commitment, and clarity. His support of strong academic programs, concern for personal spiritual dedication, and his expertise as a financial leader have established a platform for the next twenty years."[366]

In June 2006, as the announced date of President Hodo's departure approached, the presidential search committee reported on interviews with candidates but had yet no recommendation to bring. Dr. Hodo agreed to remain in office through July 31 but emphasized that a new chief executive was needed to assume responsibility August 1 as planning for the new academic year reached fruition. The Board of Trustees turned to its own experienced membership and asked Jack D. Carlson to accept appointment as Interim President effective Aug 1. Carlson was a retired Vice President of Sysco Corporation and had been a member of the Board

---

361 Ibid.
362 Ibid.
363 "Hodo to Retire as Houston Baptist University President," *Southern Baptist Educator,* First Quarter 2006, 14.
364 "A Legacy of Faith and Learning," *HBU News,* Spring 2006, 6.
365 Gigi Arendt, "A Time for new beginnings," *Ornogah 2006,* 56.
366 Brie Moore, "Dr. Doug Hodo's legacy in quotes," *The Collegian,* 4 May 2006, p. 4.

of Trustees for eleven years.[367] A three-member Executive Management Committee was appointed to assist the Interim President composed of Vice Presidents Dr. Don Looser, Richard Parker, and Sharon Saunders.[368]

On August 1, 2006, the University bade formal farewell to its second President. His nineteen years of service chronicled a history of leadership in difficult but productive times. Hard decisions, stressful results, powerful faith, uncompromising commitment, and extraordinary reward characterized his years of service. A beautiful home near Boerne awaited his engagement in new ministry.

---

[367] "Jack D. Carlson to serve as interim president at Houston Baptist University," *Southern Baptist Educator,* 3rd Quarter 2006, 12.

[368] "Around the Area," *Houston Chronicle,* 30 June 2006, sec. B, p. 4, three-star edition.

FOURTEEN

2006-2008

Marking another "first" in University history, the Board of Trustees elected Jack D. Carlson as Interim President of Houston Baptist University to become effective August 1. The Baptist General Convention of Texas was notified of the action, and announcement was made to the campus community in the University Forum meeting in June.[1] Carlson had recently retired as Vice President of Real Estate and Construction with SYSCO Corporation and had served as a University trustee for twelve years.[2] An Executive Committee composed of Dr. Don Looser, Vice President for Academic Affairs; Richard Parker, Vice President for Financial Affairs; and Sharon Saunders, Vice President for Marketing was named to work with the Interim President to coordinate the daily operations of the University.[3]

In late July, the Presidential Search Committee scheduled an executive session of the Board of Trustees to give its report. Board Chair Ray Cox, recovering from surgery, presided over the historic meeting. Trustees heard a report from Chair Diane Williams '93 and the members of the Committee who described an extensive search process and interviews with three final candidates. The unanimous recommendation of the committee was that Dr. Robert B. Sloan, Jr. be elected to the position of University President.[4] At the time, Dr. Sloan was serving as Chancellor of Baylor University.

Sloan was well-known as a scholar. In Baptist circles, he was also known from his years as President of Baylor. Moreover, he had in past years served as the interim pastor of several large Houston churches. In the called meeting, Dr. Mark Denison '82 introduced Dr. Sloan to the Board and described him as an "academic giant, a proven fundraiser, and a product of a Baptist heritage recognized for his years of visionary leader-

---

1 Houston Baptist University, Minutes of the Board of Trustees, Meeting on 14 June 2006.
2 Houston Baptist University, Minutes of the Board of Trustees, Meeting on 14 June 2006.
3 Tim Fields, "Jack D. Carlson to serve as interim President of HBU," *The Southern Baptist Educator,* Vol. LXX, #4, third quarter 2006; "Around the Area," *Houston Chronicle,* 30 June 2006, sec. B, p. 4, three-star ed.
4 Houston Baptist University, Minutes of the Board of Trustees, Meeting on 1 Aug. 2006.

ship at Baylor University."[5] A day of exchange and dialogue between the members of the Board and Dr. Sloan was followed by Sloan's election as the University's third President.[6] Dr. and Mrs. Sloan were introduced to members of the faculty and staff the following day and immediately scheduled briefing sessions for themselves with representatives of the many campus constituencies. Sloan later recalled, "I sensed a real willingness to grow and change from Day One. People love the school. They have aspirations for it and they've lived under the burden of enormous potential."[7]

The University family regarded the election of Dr. Sloan as a major coup. Search Committee Chair, Diane Williams '93, was elated. "This is a phenomenal opportunity in the life of HBU."[8] Dr. Sloan expressed his own thoughts:

> The men and women who worked to build HBU were energized by the idea of building a Christian University right in the middle of the metropolis. The result is a young university with the wonderful combination of a diverse student body and a strong sense of mission for the community, the world, and the Lord. It is good to have important work, indeed, the work of God's kingdom, to which we can put our hands.

In August, Interim President Carlson delivered the Summer Commencement address and assisted with the presentation of diplomas. Of the interim experience, Carlson later reported, "I could only have imagined how wonderful and enlightening this experience has been. The University family has seamlessly performed over these weeks in the professional, exceptional, and excellent manner in which they are accustomed."[9] Significantly, Carlson was on the cusp of inheriting the responsibility of Chairman of the Board of Trustees for the 2006-2007 year. His administrative tenure had provided invaluable insight for his understanding of University operational dynamics, personnel, and needs.[10]

Dr. Robert B. Sloan, Jr. assumed the office of President of the University on September 1, 2006. In his first public appearance, Sloan welcomed fellow-president Dr. Craig Turner as guest speaker for the

---

5 Houston Baptist University, Minutes of the Board of Trustees, Meeting on 1 Aug. 2006 in Executive Session.
6 Ibid.
7 Matthew Tresaugue, "Campus Moving Forward," *Houston Chronicle,* 2 Sept. 2007, sec. B, p. 1, four-star ed.
8 Matthew, Tresaugue, "Search panel taps Robert Sloan as its choice for Baptist school's next President," *Houston Chronicle,* 3 Aug. 2006, sec. A, p. 1, three-star ed.
9 "Jack D. Carlson, Interim President, August 2006," *HBU News,* Fall 2006, 10.
10 "Defining Relationships: Jack D. Carlson," *HBU News,* Winter 2006, 12.

Opening Fall Convocation.[11] The University was beginning the forty-fourth year of academic operation and celebrating the forty-sixth anniversary of its chartering. The new president inherited a campus full of activity at the beginning of a year of considerable momentum. The Cultural Arts Center was nearing completion, and plans had been announced to bring the Museum of Southern History into the University museum complex.[12] U. S. News and World Report again ranked the University in the top tier and named HBU an institution of "best value."[13] Nursing students again achieved a pass rate of one hundred percent on the RN licensure examinations. The University had just completed its thirteenth year of operation with a year-end surplus. Endowment fund earnings were up 9.4 percent over 2005.[14]

Sloan's first avowed commitment was to undergird and develop the infrastructure for critical administrative functions. "I am moved by the commitment of the faculty and staff to the University and to its students. We need to relieve responsibility overload. I want to get them some help."[15] At the September meeting of the trustees, Sloan requested approval to add three positions immediately to the Information Technology team to hasten implementation of the Banner Enterprise Resource Planning software. As a result of his small group meetings with all members of the University family, Sloan's immediate concerns were for revenue and enrollment management.

Fall 2006 enrollments confirmed Sloan's concerns. Reports to the Board documented student retention lower than budget assumptions resulting in lower-than-projected income. Graduate program enrollments in 2006 were half those of 2002; undergraduate enrollment was down fifteen percent from 2001.[16] By spring 2007, credit-hour production had fallen twenty-five percent over the previous five years, and overall enrollment was the lowest in eleven years.[17] However, the average

---

11 "Fall Convocation: A New Beginning," HBU News, Fall 2006, 7. Turner was President of Hardin-Simmons University. Photo.

12 "The Changing Face of Campus: Cultural Arts Center," HBU News, Fall 2006, 8-9.

13 Brie Moore, "Sloan's on the job," The Collegian, 21 Sept. 2006, p. 1. The University was ranked in the category of Master's level institutions in the Western region. HBU was ranked #11 in the category of "Great Schools, Great Prices."

14 Houston Baptist University, Minutes of the Board of Trustees, Meeting on 26 Sept. 2006.

15 Brie Moore, "Sloan's on the job," The Collegian, 21 Sept. 2006, p. 1.

16 Houston Baptist University, Minutes of the Board of Trustees, Meeting on 26 Sept. 2006.

17 Houston Baptist University, Minutes of the Board of Trustees, Meeting on 22 May 2007.

freshman SAT score was up, and forty-four percent of the freshmen had finished high school in the top quarter of the graduating class.[18]

In strategic response, President Sloan announced the employment of James Steen as Vice President for Enrollment Management in October 2007.[19] Steen had earned national recognition in thirteen years of service at Baylor University for a "superb" record of increasing inquiries, focusing on retention, and providing multiple levels of student academic support. Steen served as a consultant to the enrollment management firm Noel-Levitz.[20] Dr. Sloan further announced that Vice President for Advancement Don Anderson and Director of Institutional Research and Effectiveness Dr. Cynthia Young had agreed to postpone retirement and serve in an interim capacity until new personnel could be added. The President voiced the need for a Director of Strategic Planning, for a master plan to address campus capacity and facility expansion, for a fresh look at the congruency of the athletic program with the goals of the University, and for reviewing, refining, and realigning academic programs including an Honors College.[21] Sloan's most public and constant advocacy, however, was for the University's faculty and staff.

In November, Dr. Phil Rhodes was appointed Director of Institutional Research and Assessment. Rhodes, a former senior research analyst, held the PhD in statistics with an emphasis in applied mathematics and was also a former Sloan colleague.[22] Steen and Rhodes represented a powerful addition to the University's executive capability. President Sloan later named Brian H. Hurd as Vice President for Development; Hurd moved from fund-raising responsibility in the not-for-profit sector.[23] The University engaged the land planning and design firm of JJR in Ann Arbor, Michigan to provide an overview of future facilities, residential housing, parking, and the feasibility for growth to 7,000 undergraduate and 2,000 graduate students.[24] In further action, food service areas in the Baugh Center and the M. D. Anderson Student Center were renovated in response to student critique.

---

18 Ibid.
19 "HBU names James Steen as enrollment VP," *Houston Chronicle,* 5 Oct. 2006, sec. ThisWeek, p. 7, two-star ed.
20 Audrey La, "Sloan recruits former Baylor Vice President," *The Collegian,* 2 Nov. 2006, p. 5.
21 Houston Baptist University, Minutes of the Board of Trustees, Meeting on 26 Sept. 2006.
22 Houston Baptist University, Minutes of the Board of Trustees, Meeting on 28 Nov. 2006.
23 "Hurd Appointed VP for Development," *HBU News,* Winter 2006, 17.
24 Ibid.

Into the maelstrom of campus activity came a literal storm in the form of Hurricane Rita that threatened the whole Gulf Coast on September 20th.[25] The "Category 5" hurricane caused thirty-one deaths in Harris County and dozens more on the gridlocked highways north and west of the city as Houston residents fled inland.[26] The threat stimulated a re-examination of the University's disaster response protocols and resulted ultimately in the creation of a highly-effective emergency warning system.[27] Though the University had never in history suffered damage from such storms, Hurricane Rita presaged the catastrophic damage to the campus from Hurricane Ike two years later.

Vice President Steen presented a new *Smart Approach* to student recruiting based on profiling the characteristics of current students to which potential prospects could be compared for a likely match. The object was to recruit students who wanted to enroll at HBU who also matched the University's long term goals. The result was a process that actively sought students for whom there was a high probability of enrollment success and long-term retention. The shotgun approach to recruiting was replaced by a highly personalized, data-driven model. Steen summarized, "It is all about making sure students have every opportunity to succeed."[28]

At the November Board meeting, Dr. Sloan described his approach to budget preparation. He described the past approach as "making revenue estimates and forcing expenses to levels that resulted in a balanced budget plus a surplus but with a backlog of unmet necessities."[29] He described a new model based on estimating budget needs to achieve stated goals and assigning resource acquisition to accomplish the plan. Of immediate jeopardy was a three-year program of salary upgrades supported by Sloan that had been initiated by President Hodo. Increased resources were also needed for the new program of student recruitment that was projected to result in significant increases in enrollment and tuition income. Dr. Sloan requested an immediate infusion of $2,000,000 to be borrowed from quasi-endowment funds and the implementation of technology and general student fees to provide additional income for services rendered.[30]

---

25 Paddy Meda, "Weathering the Storm," *Ornogah 2006*, 18-19.
26 Eric Berger, "Houston's top five weather events since 1992: No. 2," *Houston Chronicle*, 30 May, 2008, http://blogs.chron.com/sciguy/archives/2008/05/houstons_top_fi_4.html (accessed 23 May 2010).
27 Caleb Feese, "University hurricane evacuation plan updated," *The Collegian*, 19 Oct. 2006, p. 2.
28 Houston Baptist University, Minutes of the Board of Trustees, Meeting on 28 Nov. 2006.
29 Ibid; Matthew Tresaugue, "HBU President aims to transform the University; trustees and professors are ready," *Houston Chronicle*, 2 Sept. 2007, sec. B, p. 1, four-star ed.
30 Ibid.

Trustees responded to the vision and budget modification request with approval for adjustment to the current year's budget.

§

The inauguration of the University's third President was held on November 28, 2006. Guided by Sharon Saunders and Dr. Don Looser, whirlwind planning for the event had been completed in a record time of only six weeks. Over one hundred delegates from other universities, academic organizations, and civic and denominational bodies added color and festivity to the ceremonies. Held on the Holcombe Mall with the backdrop of the Morris Columns and the Hinton Center, the afternoon ceremony was blessed with clearing skies and the gift of a sunny afternoon. Those bringing formal greetings to the new president included Rice University President Dr. David Leebron, Founder Dr. Stewart Morris, Board Chair Ray Cox, Jr. '81, Faculty Assembly President Dr. Constantina Michalos, Executive Director of the Baptist General Convention of Texas Dr. Charles Wade, President of the Student Government Association Edgar Gonzalez, Chair of the Alumni Association Board Monica Hodges '96, and Dean of Students Frances Curtis.

Dr. Sloan's pastor, Dr. H. Edwin Young, delivered the keynote address. Others participating on the program included President Emeritus Dr. E. D. Hodo, Interim President Jack D. Carlson, Dr. Duane Brooks, Dr. David Capes, Dr. Mark Denison '82, Dr. James Denison '80, Robert McElroy, Jim Richards, Jack Ridlehoover, and Dr. John Yarrington.[31] Following the formal investiture of the new President by Dr. Hodo and Mr. Carlson, Dr. Sloan's response reflected his sense of call to a Christian institution of higher learning in the heart of a flourishing city:

> We celebrate Houston Baptist University and . . . also the *kind* of university that we are. . . . Christian institutions derive their identity from Jesus Christ, the foundation stone. . . . That has come to be a daunting task here at the beginning of the twenty-first century. . . . But in the face of confessional and practical attrition over the last half century or more, Houston Baptist University, founded in the latter part of the twentieth century, has attempted something very unusual. . . . HBU has sought to embrace the Christian faith as an institution of higher learning in an *urban* setting. . . .

31 Houston Baptist University, *The Inauguration of Robert B. Sloan, Jr.*, Inaugural Program, 28 Nov. 2006.

For Christians who have become perhaps timid about the role of the Christian faith in higher education, I would say that we cannot be faithful to . . . Jesus Christ, who is Lord over all things visible and invisible, over every sphere of reality, unless we also say that the *content* of the intellectual traditions of the Christian faith has an impact upon the kind of university we are, not merely with respect to our environment, our attitude, and our chapel services, but also . . . the intellectual and academic engagement that goes on in the classroom.

We ask questions. We are not afraid of questions. We seek to engage because this is God's world. He made it, and it is good. There is no sphere of reality – not a single corner of this universe – that falls outside the sphere of the Lordship of Jesus Christ, and we therefore need not fear asking any question. . . .

There is a great opportunity for a place like Houston Baptist University. While Christian institutions are called to serve all over the Earth, there is also a calling in the urban setting. The two witnesses of Revelation 11 bear their witness in "the great city." . . . The prophet's deliberate trope [on "the great city" in verse 8] suggests that the One to whom we bear witness is Lord of all, and the witness we bear to Him is a witness that likewise must be borne in "the great city" – where the peoples of the earth come together, where there is language and literature, where there are the atrocities of crime and violence, where there is also learning, culture, business, and commerce. In this environment, our Lord was crucified; in this environment . . . the forces of the spiritual empire of evil . . . must be engaged. As witnesses to the truthfulness of God in Jesus Christ, we bear our witness here . . . where ethnicities and races, peoples and nations are drawn together, as they were in Jerusalem on the day of Pentecost. . . . The world has come to us. Let us take up the cross and follow Him. Thank you.[32]

Following the ceremony, a reception was held in the Great Hall of the Cultural Arts Center, still under construction. The day was shared with Dr. Sloan's wife, Sue, and their extended family and friends. The President later characterized the inaugural as "very personal," recalling the "attentiveness of the audience, the beauty of the procession, the music, and the care and efficiency of the ceremony planning." Alumnus Dr. James Denison reflected, "He taught us that it is possible to be a person of remarkable intellect who is passionately committed to the foundational truths of the Christian world view."[33]

---

32 "Inauguration Day," *HBU News,* Winter 2006, 4.
33 Brie Moore, "Man of Vision," *The Collegian,* 7 Dec. 2006, p. 1.

Presiding over the Sloan inauguration as he had the Hodo ceremonies in 1987 was Dr. Don Looser, Vice President for Academic Affairs. In December, Dr. Sloan made formal announcement of Looser's plan to retire from the position of Vice President of Academic Affairs in May 2007. "His dedication and commitment to the University are unparalleled, and I know the HBU family will join me in thanking Don for his historic and substantial contributions."[34] In February, Dr. Sloan announced that Looser would continue full-time with the University, completing his liaison role with the Cultural Arts Center construction, developing plans for the exhibits in the three museums, and formulating plans with the architects for the University Academic Center. As time permitted, he was to begin research in preparation for writing a history of the University's first fifty years.[35]

Dr. and Mrs. Sloan enjoyed a relaxed, casual lifestyle that was quickly apparent in events held in the President's home. As the parents of seven young adult children, the Sloans were on the wavelength of college students and quite accustomed to the informality of having a house full of company with little or no notice. Sue Sloan endeared herself to HBU students by hosting a series of do-it-yourself food fests featuring her favorite "omelet-in-a-bag" recipe. In the first few months, the student leadership of every major organization on campus enjoyed social time with President and Mrs. Sloan in their home.[36] The Sloans were even known to transport food remaining after an entertainment event to the dorms for student consumption. The student leadership quickly felt at one with the new President and his wife.

In January 2007, the University School of Music joined with the Houston Symphony Orchestra in a performance of Polish composer Krzysztof Penderecki's monumental choral work, *Credo*. The performance was the climax of a three-day conference on campus that addressed the arts and "the many ways in which they are engaged as expressions of faith."[37] A parallel event was an art exhibit, *The Talmud in the Works of Ben*

---

34 "Dr. Don Looser to step down as Vice President of Academic Affairs," www.houstonbusiness.com/mediaroom/pres_release_hbu32.html (accessed Mar. 16, 2009). Several years earlier, Dr. Hodo and Dr. Looser had prepared a document of proposal for a next president's consideration. They expressed a mutual desire that Looser be given opportunity to write a history of the University's first 50 years. In addition, Dr. Looser pledged his willingness to be of service to a new president in his first year of service, should such an offer be accepted by a new chief executive officer.

35 Houston Baptist University, Minutes of the Meetings of the Board of Trustees, Meeting on 27 Feb. 2007.

36 Ashley Marchand, "Sloan nears 500 days," *The Collegian*, 10 Jan. 2008, p. 1.

37 "Credo: Expressing Belief through the Arts," *HBU News*, Spring 2007, 14-15. Photo.

Zion and Marc Chagall that was mounted at the Museum of Printing History. The concert featured the HBU Choral Union, the Treble Chorus from the High School for the Performing and Visual Arts, five soloists, and was conducted by Jahja Ling, musical director of the San Diego Symphony Orchestra. The *Credo* performance was the dream of Dr. Ann Gebuhr who had negotiated the performance with the composer over several years and had raised the funds required to underwrite the concert. Charles Ward, writing for the *Houston Chronicle,* called the Houston premier "memorable" and praised the work of Dr. John Yarrington and the students.[38] Some 2600 persons filled Jones Hall for the concert. The evening was a milestone event for the University with Houston's cultural community. The concert was perhaps the most significant musical event in University history.

The HBU School of Music in performance of Credo with
the Houston Symphony Orchestra at Jones Hall, 2007.

In February 2007, the institutional planning firm of JJR presented its recommendations to the Board of Trustees.[39] The consultants confirmed the capacity of the 125-acre academic campus to support an enrollment of 7,000 undergraduate and 2,000 graduate students, with seventy per-

---

38 Charles Ward, "'Credo' premier dour but memorable," *Houston Chronicle,* 27 Jan. 2007, Star sec., p. 6, two-star ed.

39 JJR, *Houston Baptist University Campus Vision Plan,* Ann Arbor: JJR, 2007.

cent of the undergraduates living on-campus, while maintaining the green "oasis in the heart of the city" campus environment. The firm further recommended upgrading plans for a temporary art instruction facility to a permanent Class A building that could be strategically located to mark the termination of a new campus mall in the master plan of development. The master plan also called for the eventual recapture of land bordering the Southwest Freeway from the intersection of Fondren road south as a location for athletic fields and a special events center.[40]

The official name for the new arts complex was the Joella and Stewart Morris Cultural Arts Center at Houston Baptist University.[41] The Cullen Trust for Higher Education requested that the new chapel be named for Dr. J. Bruce Belin, Jr. who served both on the Cullen and the University boards. The Morris designation honored the unprecedented financial contributions of the Morris family to the University and the nearly fifty years of leadership contributed by Dr. and Mrs. Morris.[42] The naming of these facilities was formally announced in ceremonies in April and was consecrated by prayers of dedication led by Dr. H. Edwin Young, pastor of the Morris and Belin families.[43] Dr. Sloan noted, "The Morrises have spent their lifetime helping to establish HBU as one of America's premier, Christian education institutions. The Morris Center firmly positions us to attract students, faculty, and staff who strive for academic excellence and possess our shared sense of duty for the community."[44]

President Sloan addressed several additional areas of critical need. He confirmed that repairs to the central plant that had been identified prior to his coming were imperative. He expressed his view that the University's strong faculty and academic programs were "undervalued and underappreciated." He pledged his commitment to add value enhancements to existing elements of University life. Dr. Sloan spoke to the need for new residential housing reflective of the quality of the academic programs. He called for campus environment enhancements to include more spaces for informal student gathering, additional recreational and fitness opportunity, and improved food service facilities. In the spirit of these concerns, Dr. Sloan announced a major gift from Dr. Tracy and Lee Lawrence to enable construction of Lawrence Park, an area

---

40 Houston Baptist University, Minutes of the Meeting of the Board of Trustees, Meeting on 27 Feb. 2007.

41 Josh King, "Cultural Arts Center, Chapel named for long-time donors," *The Collegian,* 3 May 2007, p. 1.

42 Ibid.

43 "A Dream Realized: Morris Cultural Arts Center," *HBU News,* Summer 2007, 16.

44 "HBU unveils arts center," *Houston Chronicle,* 3 May 2007, ThisWeek sec., p. 6, two-star ed.

of campus beautification bordering the new cultural arts center boulevard, the Belin chapel, the Ann Morgan Prayer garden, and the Atwood II Theology Building.[45]

For the Board's February meeting, James Steen presented an ebullient report on student recruiting for the coming year. He reported more than 12,000 inquiries, 3200 current applications, and 1289 student admissions vs. 232 at the same time the previous year. Steen projected 500 freshmen for the fall of 2007. Dr. Sloan noted that these extraordinary results reflected only the first three months of Steen's service on the University team.[46] Steen called attention to the series of promotional radio spots recorded by Dr. Sloan that were currently blanketing the Houston-area marketplace. A *Houston Chronicle* article featured Steen's revolutionary work and similar activity at Rice University.[47]

By April, Dr. Sloan announced that a new food service vendor, Aramark, was contracted for the coming year.[48] He also announced enhancements to the Baugh Center that included provision for a fitness center and an adjacent "energy station" coffee/smoothie bar that would remain open late into the evening. Dr. Kathy Anzivino and Randy Worden joined the staff of Norm Slosted as Assistant Vice Presidents for Student Life.[49] In May, Board Chairman Carlson reported on a financial plan to provide funds through a bond issue for the new University Academic Center, a new student residence facility, and repairs and enlargement of the central plant.[50]

One of President Sloan's first commitments to the University faculty was improved housing for the outstanding Department of Art. Dr. Sloan turned to the design team of architect John Rhebergen and Dr. Don Looser working with members of the faculty to realize the creative potential for the facility. On the advice of construction consultants, a concept that began as a steel building with large open spaces and plenty of exterior light, by February had become a plan for a permanent structure of some 25,000 square feet to house art, intercollegiate athletics offices, and information technology.[51] Upon study, information technology was removed as a potential tenant because of its unique infrastructure require-

---

45 Houston Baptist University, Minutes of the Meetings of the Board of Trustees, Meeting on 27 Feb. 2007.

46 Ibid.

47 Matthew Tresaugue, "Colleges Mining Data for Students: HBU and Rice use math models to draw more applicants," *Houston Chronicle,* 18 Mar. 2007, p. 1, four-star ed.

48 Audrey La, "New food service: quality will cost students," *The Collegian,* 5 Mar. 2007, p. 1.

49 Julie Pankey, "From zero to two," *The Collegian,* 22 Mar. 2007, p. 1.

50 Houston Baptist University, Minutes of the Meetings of the Board of Trustees, Meeting on 22 May 2007.

51 Brie Moore, "Art, offices to inhabit $1.8 million building," *The Collegian,* 8 Feb. 2007, p. 1.

ments. Ultimately, administrative offices for the College of Arts and Humanities and faculty offices for the Department of Languages seemed to be more integrated with the Honors College program than the proposed housing for the athletic coaching staff. The design that emerged was tailored to these specific occupants and became one of the most creative design projects in University history.

Another matter of conviction for the new President was the return to an NCAA athletic program. The University had enjoyed many years of domination of all sports in the NAIA Trans America Athletic Conference. However, the new President believed that association with the elite membership of the NCAA Division I schools was more reflective of the University's high academic aspirations and would afford greater public visibility. Apparently, he was not alone in this conviction, for the aspiration was reported to have been a matter of some discussion with the Board of Trustees in his interview process. In April 2007, Dr. Sloan announced application to the NCAA for membership in Division I. Since HBU was a former NCAA member, this reapplication was to be an expedited process.[52] At the same time, Sloan recruited an experienced colleague familiar with NCAA affairs, Steve Moniaci, as Associate Athletic Director to Cottrell. Moniaci had been a member of the Rice University staff for over twenty years.[53]

§

A team of nationally-recognized college residence planners was assembled to design what came to be called the Lake House. The new facility was to be six floors in height, conserving campus land by maximizing use of the facility's footprint. The hall was designed for freshmen on the lower floors and upper classmen on the top levels that featured a rooftop patio. Men and women were to occupy separate wings of the residence that featured a living/learning center, student activity spaces, a fitness center, a chapel, study rooms, laundry facilities, and public spaces for informal gathering. The crescent shape of the facility would cradle a large lake with a fountain feature to provide a beautiful focal point on campus.

In May, the President reflected on the accomplishments of his first nine months of service. He expressed his appreciation of the Board's sup-

---

52 Jessica Brantley, "Changing Brands: University seeks visibility, prestige," *The Collegian*, 1 Apr. 2007, p. 1.
53 Jennie Kleinworth, "Moniaci brings Division I insight," *The Collegian*, 1 Apr. 2007, p. 3.

port for more competitive faculty salaries. Sloan noted his gratitude for the service of James Steen and Dr. Phil Rhodes. President Sloan reported that the Baugh Center remodeling was underway and that the University's NCAA application would be reviewed in June. He stressed the potential for student and faculty recruiting contained in the three new campus facilities—the Morris Cultural Arts Center including the Belin Chapel and the three museums, the new Lake House, and the University Academic Center. In summary, Dr. Sloan reminded the trustees, "We are spending for growth. We must reach the point where prospective students view us as their first choice for college enrollment."[54]

The *Houston Chronicle* described the momentum of Dr. Sloan's first year in an article titled, "Campus Moving Forward: President aims to transform the university—and the trustees and professors are ready."[55] "Sloan has lost no time in barreling forward. He has talked about increasing enrollment fivefold to 10,000 students, adding an honors college and PhD programs, and raising the caliber of the student body and faculty."[56] James Busby, Chair of the Art Department, shared, "There is more excitement than at any time in my previous 37 years on campus. I had planned to retire this year, but I've decided to stay on to see what happens."[57]

With the end of May 2007, Dr. Don Looser retired as Vice President for Academic Affairs, a position he had held since 1983.[58] Looser was in his forty-third year with the University and enjoyed the longest record of service to date of any colleague. Looser had served both Presidents Hinton and Hodo and was invited by President Sloan to continue in Academic Affairs in 2006-07 to bridge the new President's first year of service. In addition, he began work on a long-held dream shared by President Emeritus Hodo and President Sloan to compile a history of the University's first fifty years since the granting of the HBC charter in 1960.

Looser's record of contribution and personal history was chronicled through the spring with a series of articles in *The Collegian*.[59] The University hosted a gala retirement reception for Dr. and Mrs. Looser in the spring at which time it was announced that an endowed scholarship

---

54 Houston Baptist University, Minutes of the Meetings of the Board of Trustees, Meeting on 22 May 2007.
55 Matthew Tresague, "Campus Moving Forward," *Houston Chronicle,* 2 Sept. 2007, sec. B, p. 1, four-star ed.
56 Ibid.
57 Ibid.
58 Brie Moore, "Looser steps down," *The Collegian,* 25 Jan. 2007, p. 1.
59 Merin Brown, "In the beginning, there was . . . Don Looser," *The Collegian,* 8 Feb. 2007, p. 10; "The Looser Legacy," *The Collegian,* 22 Mar. 2007, 8.

had been created to honor the couple for "lifelong commitment to excellence in Christian higher education."[60] Over the course of his career at HBU, Dr. Looser had served as a member of the music faculty, Assistant to the President for Academic Affairs, founding Dean of Smith College of General Studies, Vice President for Administrative Affairs and, since 1983, Vice President for Academic Affairs. As a part of the spring commencement ceremonies, Looser was presented with a formal resolution from the Board of Trustees naming him Vice President Emeritus of the University. Dr. Sloan expressed, "If one person represents the excellence of the HBU family over a long period of time, it is Don Looser. It is very unlikely that the University will ever have someone serve more faithfully over a long period of time than he. He is a marvelous representative of the outstanding faculty and staff who are here."[61]

In May, upon the eve of his retirement, Dr. Jon Suter was named Distinguished Professor by the University Board of Trustees.[62] Director of the University Library since 1984, Suter made plans to retire from that position in the summer of 2007. So great was Suter's influence as a scholar, pedagogue, team member, Renaissance man, fund-raiser, sage, and wit that his exceptional gifts in directing the growth of the library were taken almost for granted. As an MLA faculty legend, a Faculty Assembly president, a former member of the University's INDC teams, and a dedicated member of the Academic Affairs Committee, Suter was recognized by faculty and student alike as a teaching colleague. As a master of the English language, his counsel was often sought by his fellow faculty members. Suter's "third life" was his personal love of books—from the classics to the esoteric to the comics. A lifelong friend observed, "His love for books is almost pathological."[63] Dr. Suter had an extraordinary record of personal contribution to the library collection, often acquiring materials needed for academic support at his own expense. To the delight of his colleagues, Suter maintained an office on campus following his retirement where his affable contribution to progress and environment continued to be a blessing through his role as a member of the MLA faculty.

60 "Dr. Don Looser retires after 43 years," *HBU News,* Summer 2007, 10; "HBU announces new scholarship," *Houston Chronicle,* ThisWeek sec., p. 25, two-star ed. Elsa Jean Looser had been a member of the HBC English faculty from 1965-1969.

61 Dr. Robert B. Sloan, Jr, "Message from the President," *HBU News,* Summer 2007, 2.

62 "Resolution of appointment: Dr. Jon Suter: Distinguished Professor," Houston Baptist University, Minutes of the Meetings of the Board of Trustees, Meeting on 22 May 2007.

63 Jack A Samosky, "Old friend remembers Jon Suter," *The Collegian,* 8 May 2003, p. 12.

During the summer months, the first weddings were held in Belin Chapel,[64] and the University's first commencement ceremonies took place in the University Theater in August. Dean of the College of Nursing Dr. Nancy Yuill was appointed interim Vice President for Academic Affairs. Vivian Camacho was named Director of Alumni Relations,[65] and Gregg Stapleton was appointed as the new Vice President for Financial Affairs and Chief Financial Officer.[66]

President Sloan's second year was introduced with the announcement of a five-year, $1,500,000 grant to train bilingual and English-as-a-Second-Language teachers guided by Dr. Sally Phillips and Dr. Lilita Olano.[67] Freshman enrollment was up seventy percent over 2006; residential housing was full. The Honors College was approved to begin in the 2008-09 academic year. The University contracted with the firm Churchworx working with Gensler Architects and Carter & Burgess Consultants to prepare an infrastructure study for campus expansion including utilities, traffic, parking, and space utilization. An envisioning process was initiated to project fundamental goals for the University's immediate future. James Steen began work with Noel Levitz to use its Enrollment Revenue Management System to accomplish a comprehensive retention study for the University using analysis of the *Student Satisfaction Inventory* and the *College Selection Inventory*.[68]

In October, Mr. and Mrs. Jim Smith announced a major gift to the University to provide a new pipe organ for the Belin Chapel. The 58-rank organ was to be built by Orgues Létourneau Limitée of Quebec and was designed to embrace the circular acoustical configuration of the chapel to maximize the tonal beauty of the instrument. Working with Dr. Rhonda Furr, the organ builders designed the instrument for both worship service and concert performance. In further development, the family of Stanley and Dr. Diane Williams '93 announced the gift of a large fountain and plaza to be located between Belin Chapel and the

---

64 "First wedding ceremony celebrated in Belin Chapel," *HBU News,* Fall 2007, 17. Ryan Yarrington '05 and Alyssa Johns '07 were united in marriage on July 28. The daughter of Dr. and Mrs. Sloan, Sophie, was married in the Belin Chapel on August 25 with Dr. Sloan officiating.
65 "Camacho named Director of Alumni Relations," *HBU News,* Summer 2007, 39.
66 Houston Baptist University, Minutes of the Meetings of the Board of Trustees, Meeting on 25 Sept. 2007.
67 "Around the Area," *Houston Chronicle,* 23 Aug. 2007, sec. B. p. 1; "University receives Title III grant," *HBU News,* Fall 2007, 35; "Houston Baptist to Receive $1.499 Million in 5-Year Grant," *The Baptist Educator,* Fourth Quarter, 2007, p. 15.
68 Ibid.

Hinton Center.[69]   Adjacent to the Williams Fountain was to be the Lawrence Park to provide landscaped walks, benches, and lighting that would complete the landscape of the new east campus bordering the Morris Center Boulevard.

The Honors College was also formally announced in October. This curriculum was designed to provide quality undergraduate students with a unique general education core curriculum in the liberal arts, social sciences, and natural sciences. The Honors College student would begin as a freshman and follow a special four-year curriculum featuring interdisciplinary courses, study abroad, undergraduate research, cultural opportunities, and the integration of faith and learning.[70]   Dr. David Capes was appointed Interim Director of the Honors College to begin developing curriculum, recruiting students, and securing an initial faculty.[71]

§

The week-long celebration of the opening of the Morris Cultural Arts Center was held in October.   The October 8, black-tie gala welcomed guests to the new Grand Hall and University Theater.[72]   The evening opened with antiphonal brass fanfares and presented the University Choral Union under the direction of Dr. John Yarrington and the Houston Civic Symphony under the direction of Dr. Brian Runnels, '81. Master of Ceremonies, Dr. Robert Sloan, Jr. was joined by Dr. Doug Hodo, President Emeritus of the University, for presentation of gifts to donors whose generosity made the Morris Center a reality.   These donors included Dr. and Mrs. Bruce Belin, the Cullen Trust for Higher Education, Dr. and Mrs. Archie Dunham, the Robert and Janice McNair Foundation, the RSMIS Foundation, and Dr. and Mrs. Stewart Morris. Dr. Sloan expressed his particular gratitude to Dr. Hodo for his role in securing the funding for the Center and for its realization.   Dr. Hodo recognized Stanley Williams, Dr. Bruce Belin, Jr., Dr. and Mrs. Stewart Morris, and Dr. Don Looser for their individual contributions to the Morris Center project.   The Hodos were presented a commemorative gift of Boehm porcelain.   The evening concluded with a buffet dinner and

---

69 "We're growing," *HBU News,* 1 Oct. 2007, 4.
70 "HBU Announces New Honors College," *HBU News,* Fall 2007, 5.
71 Houston Baptist University, Minutes of the Meetings of the Board of Trustees, Meeting on 25 Sept. 2007.
72 "HBU Celebrates Morris Cultural Arts Center Gala," *HBU News,* Fall 2007, 7-15.

time of celebration in the Grand Hall. Dr. Stewart Morris, whose generosity ultimately had completed funding for the Center, reflected, "Today is like awakening from a dream. . . . The Lord moves in strange ways his wonders to perform. No longer is HBU a dream. It is real."[73]

The Belin Chapel and Recital Hall dedication on Tuesday evening honored the Cullen Trust for Higher Education, Dr. and Mrs. Bruce Belin, Jr., and Jim and Sherry Smith. The noted actress Jeannette Clift George and members of the Grace Theater company presented an evening called "Connecting the Bridges."[74] In 1985, the Doctor of Humane Letters had been conferred upon Mrs. George whose A. D. Players company was established forty years earlier on the HBC campus. Dr. George shared, "I believe God has cleared a time for the believer artist to speak as the believer artist has never spoken before. You have established a place where the artist of the future can learn and grow."[75] A prayer of dedication was given by the Belin's son, Greg.

Wednesday's dedication was a time of celebratory worship led by Colette Cross, Dr. Randy Hatchett, Dr. Sloan, the University Schola Cantorum and Brass Quintet under the direction of Dr. John Yarrington. Thursday's program presented the first full-scale, large-ensemble concert in the new theater. The concert featured the University Singers and Orchestra, the Choral Union, Schola Cantorum, and faculty members Melissa Givens, Lynda McKnight, and Richard Piersall in a performance of an original composition by Dr. Ann Gebuhr.[76] Not only was the evening viewed as an artistic and aural success, the event marked the end of forty-four years of dependency on off-campus performance facilities. The week was further enhanced by Ron Stone, Jr.'s presentation on the history of Houston,[77] the Prince-Chavanne Lecture by Dan Cathy, and a pastor appreciation luncheon featuring Jack Graham.[78]

The success of the Morris Cultural Arts Center's two performance venues was trumpeted in the *Houston Chronicle* by fine arts editor Charles Ward:

> HBU celebrates the opening of new performance facilities—two new halls with top-notch acoustics. . . . People not associated with the university should rejoice as well. The Center's two acoustical-

73 "University Celebrates Morris Cultural Arts Center Gala," *HBU News,* Fall 2007, 7.
74 "Jeannette Clift George 'Connecting the Bridges,'" *HBU News,* Fall 2007, 10.
75 Ibid.
76 "School of Music in the University Theater wow audience," *HBU News,* Fall 2007, 14.
77 "Ron Stone, Jr. Revisits Houston landmarks," *HBU News,* Fall 2007, 12. Photo.
78 "HBU hosts pastor appreciation luncheon," *HBU News,* Fall 2007, 15.

ly first-rate halls will be available for public use. Laudably, HBU is planning to offer the halls to outside groups as much as possible. . . . Things will get even better when a large pipe organ commissioned from Canada's Orgues LéTourneau Limitée is installed. At the opening ceremonies, the sound was clear and impressive from seats on the main level, the parterre, and the balcony."[79]

Dr. Sloan reiterated, "The concept has always been to provide a state-of-the-art facility for our community's use by churches, performing arts organizations, schools, and cultural groups. The Morris Cultural Arts Center is a gift to the City of Houston."[80]

Groundbreaking ceremonies were held for the University Academic Center in December.[81] The site for the new center was west of the Fondren campus entrance at a location that would eventually mark the terminus of an extension of the Holcombe Mall. University representatives teamed with architect John Rhebergen and contractor Don Woo to turn the first shovels of earth. This new addition to the campus was designed to meet the special requirements of its resident programs—art, mass communications, languages, the Honors College, and *The Collegian*. Contained within the Department of Art facilities were studios for painting, drawing, sculpture, print-making, welding, and ceramics—all of which were to enjoy natural light from a clerestory feature. Also within the art space were a large display atrium, a gallery, classrooms, offices, individual faculty studios, individual senior student studios, a computer lab, a resource materials library, and student lounge. The Honors College would enjoy a suite of offices on the main atrium for the administration of its new program. The goal of construction was to have the facility ready for occupancy by the fall semester 2008.

Financial concerns continued to dominate the attention of the Board of Trustees. Finance Committee Chair David Brooks explained that the University was still trying to recover from declining enrollments over the previous five years. He challenged the trustees

to lead the way in generating funds for operations. We must be committed to raising funds, increasing headcounts, and develop-

---

79 Charles Ward, "HBU celebrates opening of new performance facilities," *Houston Chronicle*, 10 Oct. 2007, p. 1, Star sec., two-star ed.

80 "Morris Cultural Arts Center Grand Opening," *HBU Advancing the Vision*, 26 Oct. 2007, p. 1.

81 "Groundbreaking ceremony kicks off center's construction," *Houston Chronicle*, 6 Dec. 2007, ThisWeek sec., p. 1, two-star ed.

ing the endowment to $100,000,000. Meeting the current challenge is not the measure of success. Success will come through the strength of people with enough faith to press on until goals are realized. We must realize that our tuition is substantially below peer institutions with similar academic programs.[82]

President Sloan pledged his continuing allegiance to improving salaries and stressed that additional revenue was the principal need of the University.[83] On the table was an offer from Dr. Stewart Morris for a gift of $1,000,000 for operations to be matched by the members of the Board of Trustees by May 31.

During January 2008, in response to the threat of Hurricane Rita in the fall, a new two-pronged crisis alert plan was unveiled by Assistant Vice President Martha Morrow. When emergency communication might be warranted, the new system would use a combination of email, text messages, phone calls, and the University website to reach students and employees with critical messages, instructions, and information.[84] In parallel action, CFO Gregg Stapleton reported he was reviewing "disaster recovery and business continuity procedures."[85]

The working draft of a proposed institutional vision statement was released in February responding to the exhortation of Habakkuk 2:2-3, "Write the vision and make it plain on tablets, so he may run who reads it. For still the vision awaits its time."[86] Drafted by President Sloan and Dr. Hunter Baker following envisioning sessions and interviews with faculty, staff, students, trustees, alumni and members of the community, the statement used the ten Morris columns as inspiration for expressing the vision for the University's future. "Ten Pillars: Faith and Reason in a Great City" was a document for renewal of Christian higher education through a twelve-year vision plan for the University that included: build on the classics; recruit for national influence; embrace the challenge of Christian graduate education; establish a residential society of learning; increase the cultural impact of the faculty; renew our campus and community; bring Athens and Jerusalem together; expand our commitment to the creative arts—visual, musical, and literary; cultivate a strong global focus; move to

---

82 Houston Baptist University, Minutes of the Meetings of the Board of Trustees, Meeting on 27 Nov. 2007.
83 Ibid.
84 Ashley Marchand, "Two-pronged crisis alert plan installed," *The Collegian,* 24 Jan. 2008, p. 1.
85 Houston Baptist University, Minutes of the Meetings of the Board of Trustees, Meeting on 19 Feb. 2008.
86 Ashley Marchand, "Sloan discloses draft of vision," *The Collegian,* 7 Feb. 2008, p. 1. Revised Standard Version.

the next level as an institution.[87]   The vision statement was formally adopted by the Board of Trustees in February and soon began appearing on University documents as a rationale for proposed actions.[88]

The University's application for reinstatement to NCAA Division I membership met with revised NCAA policy that eliminated the three-year probationary period for previous member institutions and required a seven-year approval process for all applicants.   Reluctantly but upon the advice of legal counsel, the University filed a lawsuit against the NCAA seeking a reduction in the probationary period from seven years to three. The NCAA informed the University that its policy had been "editorially revised" by its staff to change the terms of the probationary period retroactively.   The suit sought "temporary and permanent injunction to bar the NCAA from enforcing the seven-year probationary period as a violation of HBU's due process rights."[89]   The University had first made application to rejoin the NCAA in order to take advantage of the three-year probation policy while it still was in effect.

Athletic Director Ron Cottrell marked his sixteenth season in 2006-07.   Arriving in 1990 with Ty Bailey as the sole player from the previous basketball era, Cottrell had forged a proud history of athletic achievement.   HBU's student athletes boasted a ninety-two percent graduation rate.   Over one hundred Huskies had been named to All-America honors with fifty-one student athletes named to Academic All America awards. Under Cottrell's coaching, Rod Nealy had been named NAIA Player of the Year in 2002-03.[90]

The 2006-07 athletic season was one of the most successful in history. The baseball Huskies achieved their first win of the regional tournament and competed in the World Series for the first time.   Greg Gosset was named to All America honors for the second year.[91]   Men's basketball won a ninth straight conference championship and played in its tenth consecutive National Tournament.   Dwight Jones was named to the NAIA All America first team.[92]   HBU's softball team won its ninth straight Red

87   Houston   Baptist   University,   "Ten   Pillars: Faith   and   Reason   in   a   Great   City," www.hbu.edu/hbu/Ten_Pillars_A_Vision_for_HBU.asp (accessed Feb. 19, 2010).
88 Houston Baptist University, Minutes of the Meetings of the Board of Trustees, Meeting on 19 Feb. 2008; Ashley Marchand, "Board of Trustees approves University's draft of 'Vision,'" *The Collegian,* 13 Mar. 2008, p. 2.
89 Brandon C. Williams, "HBU wants 3-year path to Division I; lawsuit against NCAA seeks cut in proba-tion period," *Houston Chronicle,* 8 Mar. 2008, Sports sec., p. 9, three-star ed.
90 Houston Baptist University, www.hbuhuskies.com (accessed Mar. 22, 2010).
91 "Baseball competes in first-ever World Series," *HBU News,* Summer 2007, 31.
92 Ibid.

River Athletic Conference title finishing sixth in the national rankings. Cherie Wood was named to All America honors for the second time.[93]

HBU ended its affiliation with the NAIA on June 1, 2007. The University was returning to the NCAA Division I for the first time since 1990. President Sloan elaborated on the decision. "This is something our alumni are very interested in and our student body is very excited about. I think it is something that helps on college campuses, having a good commitment to athletics. The NCAA Division I is the best."[94] Cottrell anticipated the move to the NCAA because of the increased visibility and prestige. "In the past, we've lost recruits we would have otherwise signed. The NCAA provides much better visibility for the University."[95] Cottrell explained, "We will use the probationary time to get our overall program in a solid position to compete in areas like fund-raising, administrative and coaching staff, conference affiliation, and facilities. We will have a mix of opponents for the next several years and will aim for a NCAA schedule for 2009-10."[96]

The University family engaged in further celebration of the Morris Cultural Arts Center with the dedication of the three museums on March 25, 2008. The third of the principle elements of the Center, the museums were so designed to share a central entry and public exhibit space—always open to visitors—and to provide preview viewing of museum exhibits through a continuous window wall in the Great Hall.[97] The Museum of American Architecture and Decorative Arts, the Dunham Bible Museum, and the Museum of Southern History offered the visitor a breadth of experience and extended an additional option to guests who were attending an event in the Belin Chapel or the University Theater.[98] President Sloan, Dr. Don Looser, and exhibit designer Charles Paramore detailed the concept of adjoining the three museums and assigning them a catalytic role in the heart of the Morris Center.[99] The official ribbon-cutters for the Grand Opening included benefactors Archie and Linda Dunham, Dr. Stewart and Joella Morris, and Dr. J. Bruce Belin. Assisting

93 Ibid.
94 Ronnie Turner, "HBU ready for NCAA plunge," *Houston Chronicle,* 12 July 2007, Sports sec., p. 5, three-star ed.
95 Jessica Brantley, "Changing Brands: University seeks visibility, prestige," *The Collegian,* 1 Apr. 2007, p. 1.
96 Scott Hainline, "HBU's Cottrell happy to bide his time," *Houston Chronicle,* 2 Aug. 2007, ThisWeek sec., p. 6, two-star ed.
97 "Home at Last," *HBU News,* Fall 2008, 15.
98 "Home at Last: Museums celebrate a new home," *Ornogah 2009,* 53. Photos.
99 "The Dedication," *Dunham Bible Museum News,* April/May 2008, p. 1.

were Interim Vice President Dr. Nancy Yuill '72 and museum directors Dr. Danny Sessums, Dr. Diana Severance, and Lynn Miller. Prayers of dedication and benediction were offered by trustee Chair Rick Bailey '69 and President Emeritus Dr. E. D. Hodo.[100]

In April, Dr. Sloan announced the appointment of Dr. Paul Bonicelli to the position of University Provost. Bonicelli was serving as Assistant Administrator for Latin America and the Caribbean for the U. S. Agency for International Development. From 2002 to 2005, he had served as Vice President for Academic Affairs at Patrick Henry College.[101] In other action, Dr. Kathy Anzivino was named Associate Vice President for Student Life, the Board of Trustees established a Presidential Advisory Board open to persons of all faiths, and the President assigned administrative responsibility for The Guild to the Office of Advancement.[102] Marketing was renamed the Office of University Communications.[103]

The operational areas of enrollment management and student affairs were combined under the direction of James Steen to better coordinate admission, housing, registration, student life, and advising programs;[104] and, the Spiritual Life office refocused its program to more broadly recognize student community service under the new name Community Life and Worship.[105] A new Center for Christianity in Business was established "to edify and equip current and future business leaders so that they may apply God's transforming principles in the world community of business. The Center (will pursue becoming) a global resource for integrating the Christian worldview with the practice of business leadership."[106]

The *Collegian* announced in May that the University was seeking to employ as many as twenty-six new faculty members to reduce the dependence on adjunct appointees, to maintain a low student/faculty ratio, to gain fresh perspective, to strengthen the University's commitment to undergraduate education, and to staff new areas of study.[107] In

100 Houston Baptist University, *Dedication of the University Museums*, Dedication Program, 25 Mar. 2008.

101 Mauricio Guerrero, "Sloan named Bonicelli provost," *The Collegian*, 1 May 2008, p. 1; Jeannie Kever, "USAID exec named HBU provost," *Houston Chronicle*, 23 Apr. 2008, sec. B, p. 2, three-star ed.

102 Houston Baptist University, Minutes of the Meetings of the Board of Trustees, Meeting on 19 Feb. 2008.

103 Ibid.

104 Mauricio Guerrero, "Enrollment, student life under same department," *The Collegian*, 13 Mar. 2008, p. 1.

105 Kelly Keneshceck, "Spiritual Life office refocuses program to community life," *The Collegian*, 3 Apr. 2008, p. 7.

106 Houston Baptist University, "Center for Christianity in Business," www.hbu.edu/hbu/HBU_Center_for_Christianity_in_Business.asp (accessed 21 Mar. 2010).

107 Editorial, "Incoming faculty assets for students," *The Collegian*, 1 May 2008, p. 13.

the midst of all the whirlwind of change, a *Collegian* headline asked, "Is the University making changes too quickly?"[108]

The Williams Family Fountain was dedicated on May 8. A gift from the family of Dr. Diane and Stanley Williams, the beautiful addition provided a water feature first advocated for campus enhancement in the Vernon Henry campus planning recommendations of 1996.[109] The fountain plaza provided bench seating around a cross motif in the flagstone paving, and integrated the Belin Chapel, the Ann Morgan Prayer Garden, and the Lawrence Park in completion of the University's east campus. For the University family, the Williams Fountain served as reminder of the powerful leadership of Stanley Williams in managing the construction of the Morris Center complex and of Diane Williams' Board leadership and her role in fund raising for the facility.

Two highly respected members of the University family announced plans to retire in 2008. Ken Rogers was completing forty-one years of service in financial aid and admissions. He had been the first recipient of the Mayfield Outstanding Staff Award, was the recipient of the Hallmark Award as an honorary alumnus, and was the proud father of two HBU alumnae.[110] His love for students, his care about his responsibilities, and his dedication to the University placed him deeply in the hearts of the University alumni. Rogers' tireless commitment to students and his love of the University shaped him to be one of the most strategic contributors to the University's success over the life of his career. In like kind, Associate Dean of Students Frances Curtis announced her retirement after forty years at HBU. Curtis had been named Woman of the Year in 1982 and 1998, Employee of the Quarter in 1999, and recipient of the Hallmark Award as an honorary alumna in 2004. Curtis's responsibilities over the years had covered the spectrum from student organizations to housing, cheerleaders, and the Pan-Hellenic Council. She had served with every Vice President for Student Affairs in University history.[111] Her knowledge of institutional history and its players was encyclopedic. Rogers and Curtis were valued friends to all who knew them—student and colleague alike. Their roles of contribution and continuity would likely never be exceeded.

---

108 Editorial, "Antithesis: Is the University making changes too quickly?" *The Collegian,* 1 Apr. 2007, p. 13.

109 Mary Lou Henry, *A Campus Plan for Houston Baptist University,* Vernon Henry and Associates, 8 Apr. 1996.

110 Ashley Marchand, "Legacy Trails: Ken Rogers," *The Collegian,* 1 May 2008, p. 8.

111 Curtis began her career working with Dr. James W. Massey who was the first Vice President for Student Affairs. Previous administrators had carried the title of Dean of Students.

The May 2008 meeting of the Board of Trustees offered a time for evaluation, reflection, and prayers of gratitude for God's leadership during Dr. Sloan's first two years. At the spring commencement, the number of degrees conferred by the University since 1967 passed the 15,000 mark. President Sloan presented a video highlighting the year's accomplishments that included the opening of the Morris Cultural Arts Center, the Belin Chapel, and the three museums; the dedication of the Williams Family Fountain; the master plan of campus development begun by JJR; the renovation of the Baugh and Glasscock Centers; the construction of the new Lake House Residence; the move to rejoin the NCAA; the creation of the Honors College and the College of Continuing Studies; and, the formulation of the "Ten Pillars" vision statement.[112]   Dr. Sloan stressed three imperatives for University action: 1) the recruitment and retention of outstanding faculty; 2) the construction and adherence to a powerful financial model; 3) the creation of a campus with the amenities that students need and want.[113]

Board Chair Rick Bailey expressed appreciation to Karl Kennard for the completion of eighteen years of service as a trustee. Kennard had served as Board Chair, as Chair of the negotiation committees with the Baptist General Convention of Texas on two occasions, Chair of the Finance and Building Committees, and member of the Presidential Search Committee. Kennard confirmed that The Houston Endowment had provided a grant of $850,000 to fund a study of the campus infrastructure to include analysis of deferred maintenance, HVAC needs, utilities, site drainage, planning for technology, traffic, security, and parking—including plans to replace lots with garage facilities. The Athletic Committee reported on the season just concluded and charted the growth of intercollegiate sports at HBU from five sports in 2005-06 to fourteen sports in 2007-08 involving thirty-two coaches and 200 student athletes.

The University had recovered most of the unanticipated shortfalls for the year by sharp reductions in spending. The Board approved a Finance Committee recommendation to sell the campus-related ground leases to the endowment funds and to form a 501(c)(3) corporation to acquire the land and lease holding of the Husky Village campus residence. The budget for the 2008-09 year provided a substantial sum for continuing the multi-year program of salary increases, for a year-end operating sur-

---

112 Houston Baptist University, Minutes of the Meetings of the Board of Trustees, Meeting on 27 May 2008.
113 Ibid.

plus, for the increased athletic program costs, for additional faculty and staff, and for new facility operations.

Dr. Nancy Yuill '72 was completing her service as Interim Vice President for Academic Affairs and was accorded the praise and appreciation of President Sloan and the Board of Trustees. She was returning to her position of leadership as Dean of the College of Nursing. Dr. Sally Phillips was awarded the rank of Professor Emeritus.[114] Phillips was the founder and director of the University's proud program in bilingual education that had enjoyed grants of $5,000,000 in student scholarship funding for the period 1981 to 2011.[115] In the weeks that followed, Charles Bacarisse was named Vice President for Advancement. Bacarisse had served in the White House Office as Associate Director of Media Relations under President Ronald Reagan, as Assistant Director of the office of Public Liaison under President George H. W. Bush, and more recently held the position of District Clerk in Harris County.[116] A new scholarly journal, *The City,* began publication and was initially mailed to 10,000 homes in a move to expand the University's donor base and affirm the University's scholarly mission.

A resolution of appreciation was approved by the Board honoring the Distinguished Alumnus of 1996, institutional spokesperson, MLA faculty member, and remarkable friend Ron Stone '94. Over many years, Stone had opened doors of opportunity for the University, recruited students, facilitated media productions, hosted the Spirit of Excellence Dinners including the visit of Lady Margaret Thatcher, and enriched the campus environment with his inclusion of HBU as one of his "neighbors." Stone was further honored with the announcement that the annual MLA Lectures would henceforth be called the Ron Stone Lectures in Liberal Arts. Three weeks later in May 2008, Ron Stone died. Of him, Dr. Chris Hammons said, "Ron really embodied the MLA spirit. He had a passionate desire to learn and a fantastic command of history and literature. He embraced the intellectual life in an unpretentious manner."[117] Stone's Distinguished Alumnus tile in the campus Heritage Walk reads, "How wonderful it is to learn."[118]

114 Houston Baptist University, Minutes of the Meetings of the Board of Trustees, Meeting on 27 May 2008.
115 Kristen Crawley, "Leaving a Legacy of Language," *The Collegian,* 1 May, 2008, p. 5.
116 "Charles Bacarisse named vice president of advancement," *Advancing the Vision,* July 2008, p. 1.
117 "Remembrances," *HBU News,* Fall 2008, 51.
118 "Ron Stone," *HBU News,* Fall 2008, 51.

In the summer of 2008, the Huskies were admitted to membership in the Great West Athletic Conference with Pan American University, the Universities of North and South Dakota, Utah State University, California Polytechnic University, the New Jersey Institute of Technology, and the University of Southern Utah.[119] Soccer continued to compete in the Atlantic Soccer Conference until the sport was added by the Great West Athletic Conference.

§

As in previous years, the loss of leaders from the University's history seemed to mount with each passing year. During the period 2006-2008, the University gave thanks for Founding Father U.S. Senator Lloyd Bentsen, Jr;[120] trustee and donor Roland Burrows;[121] founding faculty member Dr. Albert L. Myers;[122] trustee and contractor for the first campus buildings H. Alvin Lott;[123] UBA Committee Member, Founding Father, trustee, and donor John Baugh[124] and his wife Eula Mae;[125] donor and lifetime member of The Guild, Claydene Turner;[126] gifted soprano, donor, and Guild member Yolande Frazier;[127] former Chair of the Board and longtime Building Committee Chair Otis Brigman;[128] and Distinguished Professor and Piper awardee Dr. Marion Webb.[129]

Dr. Sloan's stature as a scholar placed its imprint on the examination of every facet of University life. The first two years of the Sloan administration had affirmed the strength and dedication of the faculty and staff and the potential of the academic programs. The President established new levels of infrastructure support and provided professional expertise to address critical needs. The University achieved new plateaus of campus development. Enrollment leapt exponentially. Four new Vice Presidents

---

119 Brandon Williams, "Houston Baptist makes move to Great West Conference, *McClatchy-Tribune Business News,* 10 July 2008.
120 "Founding Father: Senator Lloyd Bentsen, Jr.," *HBU News,* Summer 2006, 38.
121 "Roland Lee Burrows," *Roanoke Times and World News,* 29 May 2006, sec. B, p. 5.
122 "In Memoriam: Dr. Albert Myers," *HBU News,* Fall 2006, 26. Myers' son, Bill '67, was among the first HBC students to receive the Ph.D. Myers serves as Professor of Chemistry at the University of Richmond.
123 "In Memoriam," *HBU News,* Fall 2006, 26.
124 "John F. Baugh, 91, Founder of Sysco, Dies," *New York Times,* 9 Mar. 2007.
125 John Hall, "Eula Mae Baugh dies," 30 Aug. 2007, www.bgct.org/texasbaptists/Page.aspx?pid=4558 (accessed 27 Mar. 2010).
126 "In Memoriam," *HBU News,* Fall 2007, 41.
127 "In Memoriam," *HBU News,* Fall 2008, 51.
128 "In Memoriam: Otis Hobbs Brigman," *HBU News,* Fall 2008, 50.
129 "In Memoriam: Dr. Marion Railsback Webb," *HBU News,* Fall 2008, 50.

joined the administrative team. Dr. Sloan enjoyed the enthusiastic response of the faculty to his leadership and envisioning of the University's future. The Honors College and NCAA membership evidenced renewed commitment to academic and athletic excellence. The University was responding to the vision of its new President.

FIFTEEN

2008-2010

"It seemed . . . thereafter that all their days would be warm and fair."[1]
Ragtime
—E. L. Doctrow

(AP) *Friday, September 12, 2008.* The National Weather Service Hurricane Center bulletin #48 reports that at 10:00 p.m. on September 12, 2008, Hurricane Ike is 55 miles southeast of Galveston Island. The center of Ike will be very near Galveston by early Saturday morning. Ike could reach the Texas coast as a category three major hurricane; hurricane force winds extend outward up to 120 miles from the center. Coastal storm surge flooding with dangerous and battering waves of up to 20 feet above normal tides can be expected.[2]

Classes had been cancelled on Thursday, September 11, and the campus had been battened down. Martha Morrow, Assistant Vice President for University Communications, later reported that the new campus emergency alert system had performed flawlessly to notify students and employees of the impending threat and inform them of news throughout the post-hurricane period.[3]

The storm hit in the early morning hours of September 13. Remaining students equipped with sleeping bags, cell phones, and Bibles, plus twelve police, student life staff, and emergency personnel were sheltered in the University Theater of the Morris Cultural Arts Center that was windowless and equipped with emergency generators.[4] Dr. and Mrs.

---

1 E. L. Doctrow, *Ragtime* (New York: Random House, Inc. 1975), 3.

2 www.nhc.noaa.gov/archive/2008/a109/a1092008.public.048.shtml?

3 Mauricio Guerrero, "Alert system highly successful," *The Collegian,* 25 Sept. 2008, p. 1.

4 Noelle Marchand, "Students, staff, shelter in University Theater," *The Collegian,* 25 Sept. 2008, p. 9. The campus of Mary Hardin Baylor University in Belton was an evacuation site had that plan been deemed necessary.

Sloan remained on campus in the President's House throughout the storm. All were unharmed.[5]

Reporting some of the first news from the campus after the landfall of Hurricane Ike, the *Houston Chronicle* stated, "Most area schools just need electricity. Others require crucial repairs. HBU has suffered devastating damage to its student center and administrative office buildings."[6] Hardest hit were the M. D. Anderson Student Center and the Brown Administrative Complex housing Student Life offices, Admissions, the Registrar's and Business Office, the School of Music, administrative offices, classrooms, and the University Bookstore and Post Office.[7] The television studio in Denham Hall suffered significant wind and water damage. Virtually all its fixed equipment was ruined. Additional damage was reported to Mabee Theater, the Cullen Science Center, and Hinton Academic Center.[8] Later inspection, however, showed no apparent structural damage to the Brown Quadrangle buildings. Dr. Sloan praised the work of the campus police, as well as Student Life and Aramark Food Service personnel who ensured student needs were met during the height of the storm.

Power had been lost on Friday night, September 12, and remained off until September 22. Because of the ten days without electricity, mold and air quality issues developed in the damaged buildings making their immediate rehabitation impossible.[9] Vice President for Operations Eileen Crowell was appointed to head an Office of Disaster Recovery to coordinate insurance matters, environmental issues, relocation, restoration, and repairs.[10] In mid-October, the *Collegian* reported that the future of the Brown complex was "undecided." The cost of repair and the response of the property insurance carrier were unknowns.[11] Tellepsen Builders, the contractor for the Lake House project, was engaged to manage and perform requisite repairs to campus facilities. The Academic Quadrangle was secured with chain link fencing with locked gates to prevent access to the quadrangle and prohibit entrance into the damaged buildings. In November, the *HBU News* reported, "The University considers the refur-

5 Noelle Marchand, "Students, staff shelter in University Theater," *The Collegian,* 25 Sept. 2008, p. 9.
6 Ericka Mellos, "Most area schools just need electricity," *Houston Chronicle,* 12 Sept. 2008, sec. B, p. 1, four-star ed.
7 Martha Morrow, "Hurricane Ike has significant impact on HBU," *Baptist Standard,* 16 Sept. 2008, p. 1.
8 Houston Baptist University, Minutes of the Meetings of the Board of Trustees, Meeting on 23 Sept. 2008.
9 Ashley Marchand, "Ike Strikes: Brown Suffers Catastrophic Blow," *The Collegian,* 25 Sept. 2008, p. 1.
10 Kristen Crawley, "President initiates office of recovery," *The Collegian,* 25 Sept. 2008, p. 1.
11 Ashley Marchand, "Brown Complex future undecided," *The Collegian,* 22 Oct. 2008, p. 2.

bishment or replacement of the central location for student interaction of critical importance to the renewal of the campus."[12]

During and immediately after the storm, of critical importance was also the re-establishment of the reliability of the University's computer network. With only emergency generators providing power on campus, Information Technology staff members addressed the need to move the campus data servers to a safe, remote location. Alumnus Bob Beauchamp '87 and his staff at BMC Software along with Troubadour, Ltd. arranged for space to be made available at CyrusOne's Houston Data Center, a secure facility that hosted data storage operations for many local corporations.[13] Once the move was made, Information Technology Services Director Charles Fix recommended the new location be made permanent to maintain uninterrupted operation of the Oracle Communication System and HuskyNet service.[14] Contributing to this recommendation were space shortage issues on the campus and the need for proprietary utility and HVAC provision for computer server operations.

University staff and faculty personnel returned to campus in the days immediately following the catastrophe to salvage materials from their offices and assist with moving. Students helped move furniture from the M. D. Anderson Student Center and clean up debris. Expressions of prayer and support were received from students on other college campuses and from the agencies of the Baptist General Convention of Texas.[15] The University's administrators began the considerable task of reassigning all the displaced offices and operations to alternate campus locations. Providentially, the availability of some flexible space in the new University Academic Center and the Morris Cultural Arts Center enabled the relocation of many offices. The Admissions, Registrar's, and Financial Services offices were moved to the University Academic Center; the displaced *Collegian* operation was moved to the Executive Conference and Board Room of the Hinton Center.[16] The bookstore moved initially to the new Lake House residential facility, then briefly to the Glasscock Center. Ultimately, the Campus Store took residence in remodeled space formerly occupied by the Museum of Decorative Arts in the Moody Library.[17]

---

12 "M. D. Anderson Foundation awards HBU $500,000 grant," *HBU News,* Fall 2008, 33.

13 Houston Baptist University, Minutes of the Meetings of the Board of Trustees, Meeting on 23 Sept, 2008.

14 Nathan Cadis, "Servers moved off-site," *The Collegian,* 25 Sept. 2008, p. 9.

15 "Hurricane Ike," *The Baptist Educator International,* Fall 2008, p. 3.

16 "Trading Spaces," *The Collegian,* 25 Sept. 2008, p. 11.

17 Noelle Marchand," "Store relocates to Moody Library," *The Collegian,* 4 Dec. 2008, p. 5.

The Post Office moved to the ticket booth of the Cultural Arts Center. Dr. Sloan and his office staff moved to the President's House, and Provost Bonicelli moved his operation to the Atwood Theology Building. The School of Music moved to the dressing rooms, Green Room, kitchen, and backstage support space of the Morris Center and to offices in the Atwood Theology Building. Pipe organs and other equipment were dismantled and relocated or placed in off-campus storage.[18] Student and Spiritual Life offices moved to the Baugh Center; Human Resources management moved to the Hinton House; and Information Technology moved to the former Board Room of the Moody Library and to the Hinton Center. University Communications was moved into modular buildings set up adjacent to Sharp Gymnasium.[19] Many files and documents were hurriedly boxed and moved to storage in off-campus PODS. The *Collegian* published a "Hurricane Ike Special Issue" utilizing the home of its faculty advisor, Dr. Alice Rowlands, as a temporary news room.[20] The staff would later be recognized by the Texas Intercollegiate Press Association for "exemplary performance" on the Hurricane Ike Special Issue.[21]

The fall quarter resumed on September 22 in the confusion of damage and relocation. New to the campus environment were some 565 freshmen, the Lake House residence, the University Academic Center, and the Honors College.[22] To address the loss of the M. D. Anderson facilities, a new "Grab 'n go" food service was added to the Moody Library in the former Bible in America Museum location.[23] The Student Counseling Services office reported a significant increase in the number of clients, including several cases of severe depression, as a result of the panoply of confusion and stressors resulting from the storm.[24]

Of significance was the leadership of Dr. Kathy Anzivino in the area of Student Life during the pivotal period surrounding Hurricane Ike. She had guided the opening of the Lake House campus residence, coordinated the accommodation of a record number of students living on campus, and led in the enhancement of programming opportunities for the entire campus community.

---

18 "Organs go into storage," *The Collegian,* 9 Oct. 2008, p. 3. Photo.
19 "Where on campus is everything?" *The Collegian,* 9 Oct. 2008, p. 7.
20 "Special Hurricane Ike Issue," *The Collegian,* 22 Sept. 2008.
21 "Collegian Wins Awards," *HBU News,* Summer 2009, 23.
22 "Hurricane Ike fails to shatter dedication of HBU family," *Advancing the Vision,* Oct. 2008.
23 Houston Baptist University, Minutes of the Meetings of the Board of Trustees, Meeting on 25 Nov. 2008.
24 Ibid.

At the same time as Hurricane Ike, global financial markets faltered significantly. In September 2008, "the world financial crisis hit its most critical stage."[25] In spite of strong enrollments by new students, the fall tuition revenue was less than budgeted. A rise in the number of students registering for part-time enrollment added to the uncertainty of financial predictions.[26] *The Collegian* reported in October that the current institutional budget had been cut by six percent to $48,500,000 as a "precautionary measure" in view of the bond repayment schedule for the Lake House and the University Academic Center.[27] The reduced 2008-09 budget still represented a 13.6 percent increase over 2007-08.[28] In March 2009, the *Houston Chronicle* reported that the University anticipated a ten percent reduction in faculty for the coming year. Tuition at HBU and at neighboring University of St. Thomas accounted for approximately eighty percent of income.[29]

In May 2008, the President outlined an agenda for change. Framed within a "Ten Pillars" outline, Dr. Sloan proposed revision of the Smith College curriculum to a liberal arts core; addressed barriers to "recruiting for national influence;" emphasized a residential society of learning for students and faculty; underlined the need for new facilities in music, nursing, science, and education; advocated stronger study abroad programs; urged the addition of selected doctoral programs by 2012; and, projected growth of the current graduate enrollments by twenty percent over the coming five years.[30] The following year, Dr. Sloan reported to the Board on academic reorganization and announced a number of faculty non-renewals.[31]

Over the course of the summer, 120 parking spaces were added adjacent to the Morris Center and the athletic fields; 82 additional spaces were constructed near the University Academic Center and Sharp Gymnasium.[32] Provost Bonicelli reported the employment of thirty new

25 "The Financial Crisis: This Day—September, 2008," *CNBC.com*
www.cnbc.com/id/32558173/The_Financial_Crisis_This_Day_September_2008 (accessed Apr. 15, 2010).
26 Houston Baptist University, Minutes of the Meetings of the Board of Trustees, Meeting on 23 Sept. 2008.
27 Beth Zapach, "Budget remains high despite cuts," *The Collegian*, 30 Oct. 2008, p. 3.
28 Ibid.
29 Jeannie Kever, "Private colleges take steps to ward off recession," *Houston Chronicle*, 1 Mar. 2009.
30 Houston Baptist University, Minutes of the Meetings of the Board of Trustees, Meeting on 27 May 2008.
31 Houston Baptist University, Minutes of the Meetings of the Board of Trustees, Meeting on 24 Feb. 2009.
32 Houston Baptist University, Minutes of the Meetings of the Board of Trustees, Meeting on 23 Sept. 2008.

faculty members for fall 2008[33] and announced plans for sweeping changes in the University's academic program, many of them reflective of the HBC original curriculum in the 1960s.

In November, as an integral part of Family Weekend, a "Day of Dedication" was held for the University Academic Center, the Lawrence Park, and the Lake House Residence.[34] The various elements of the Lake House and the University Academic Center had been consecrated during a "prayer walk" by students, staff, and faculty prior to their official opening.[35] Along with the completion of the Morris Cultural Arts Center, the realization of these three projects created a new east campus that became a symbol for the University's commitment to excellence.[36]

The Lake House became the tallest structure on the campus and afforded sweeping panoramas from its rooftop patio. The residence was designed to encourage living/learning cohorts and to support continuing residency throughout the four years of college by providing additional amenities for upper-division students. The quality of the Lake House project was the object of a *Houston Chronicle* article focusing on the return of students to campus living as a national trend.[37] The Hatton Chapel and stained glass window in the Lake House were the gifts of Patti '08 and David Hatton who helped manage the Lake House project, as well as the Morris Center and the University Academic Center projects.[38] The new $35,000,000 Lake House residence provided housing for an additional 350 students bringing the campus resident capacity to 815 students.[39]

Lawrence Park, the gift of Dr. Tracy and Lee Lawrence, completed the east campus landscape with walks, benches, and lighting uniting the Belin Chapel, the Ann Morgan Prayer Garden of the Hinton Center, and the Atwood II Theology Building around a central park. Trustee Lawrence and his wife Lee, a former Guild President, were also the donors for the Sarah Lee Lawrence Academic Center in the Hinton facility and the Endowed Academic Scholarship program.[40] The Lawrences were early friends of Houston Baptist College and instrumental in campus

33 Houston Baptist University, Minutes of the Meetings of the Board of Trustees, Meeting on 20 Aug. 2008.
34 "A Day of Dedication," *HBU News*, Fall 2008, 16-17.
35 "New facilities to be consecrated during prayer walk," *Advancing the Vision*, 7 Aug. 2008.
36 "HBU dedicates three new campus amenities during Family Weekend," *Advancing the Vision*, Nov. 2008.
37 Jeannie Kever, "Area universities welcome campus life: more dorms are added to bring students home," *Houston Chronicle*, 22 Aug. 2008, sec. B, p. 2, three-star ed.
38 "David and Patti Hatton Chapel: a gift from the heart of parents," *HBU News*, Fall 2008, 36.
39 Ibid.
40 Mauricio Guerrero, "Lawrence Park completion due in late spring," *The Collegian*, 7 Feb. 2008, p. 3.

beautification over many years. Many of the first trees planted on campus were from the Lawrence family properties.

The innovative University Academic Center was designed to meet the special requirements of its resident programs—art, mass communications, languages, the Honors College, and the *Collegian*.[41] Contained within the Department of Art facilities were studios for painting, drawing, sculpture, print-making, welding, and ceramics—all of which enjoyed natural light from a clerestory design feature. Also within the art space were a large display atrium, a gallery, classrooms, offices, individual faculty studios, individual senior student studios, a computer lab, a resource materials library, and student lounge.[42] Additionally, the Honors College established its home in a suite of offices adjoining the atrium. On September 4, the Grand Opening of the Art Gallery was held that featured an exhibit of ceramics, paintings, drawings, photography, sculpture, and mixed media.[43] The University's new Gallery Director and Curator, Associate Professor Jim Edwards, organized this first "Showcase of Art" in a series of outstanding gallery exhibits during the inaugural year.[44]

§

The University's students and faculty maintained their achievement of significant academic recognition. Dr. Will Rutherford had his contribution on "Monotheism" published in the *Oxford Encyclopedia of Ancient Greece and Rome*.[45] Dr. Rosemary McCarthy was elected President of the American Association of Nurse Attorneys in February 2008.[46] Dr. Chris Hammons produced *The Constitutionalism of American States* for the University of Missouri Press.[47] This publication was nominated for the J. David Greenstone Award by the American Political Science Association as the best book of the year in politics and history. Dr. Constantina Michalos edited a new anthology on writers of the "Old and New South," *Haunted Voices, Haunted Places*.[48] Dr. James R. Claycomb's new text

---

41 Beth Zapach, "Construction nears August completion," *The Collegian*, 1 May 2008, p. 2.
42 Lindsay Brehm, "Art department finds home," *The Collegian*, 11 Sept. 2008, p. 4.
43 "University Academic Center Gallery Grand Opening," *Advancing the Vision*, Aug. 2008.
44 "The Gallery at HBU: Celebrating a season of exhibition," *HBU News*, Fall 2008, 14; "Home at Last," *HBU News*, Fall 2008, 15.
45 "Faculty/Staff Updates," *Campus Connections*, 16 Apr. 2010.
46 Houston Baptist University, Minutes of the Meetings of the Board of Trustees, Meeting on 19 Feb. 2008.
47 "Hammons co-edits Volume," *HBU News*, Winter 2008, 15.
48 Dale Meadows, "Anthology surveys haunted past," *The Collegian*, 13 Nov. 2008, p. 10.

Introductory Biophysics was published in March.[49] Dr. David Capes collaborated on the book *Israel's God and Rebecca's Children* and, in addition to Dr. Jim Ulmer, was given sabbatical leave to complete work on yet other volumes.[50] Dr. Richard Fiese was elected Chair of the College Division of the Texas Music Educators Association.[51] The 2005 Opal Goolsby Teaching Award winner, Dr. Miguel Estrada, was honored by The College Entrance Examination Board for offering one of the ten best language courses in the nation;[52] as a result, he was also named to the Advisory Board for the Advanced Placement Examinations in Spanish.[53]

In 2008, Dr. Linda Brupbacher was named the University's sixth faculty member to receive the prestigious Piper Foundation Outstanding Teaching Award recognizing faculty members in Texas. She joined the distinguished ranks of Drs. Calvin Huckabay, Joyce Fan, Marilyn Sibley, Marion Webb, and Doris Warren.[54] Dr. Yuri Yatsenko was awarded sabbatical leave to serve as Visiting Professor at the Catholic University of Belgium.[55] Dr. Robert Towery's Welch Foundation research with students was selected for presentation at the World Congress on Biosensors Conference in Shanghai.[56] Dr. Hunter Baker's new book *The End of Secularism* was released,[57] and the University's new scholarly journal *The City* garnered national attention in the *Wall Street Journal*.[58]

With the creation of the Honors College, the establishment of lectureships by the Dunham Bible Museum, and heightened emphasis on scholarly activity by students and faculty, the number of academic presentations on campus burgeoned. Lecturers included Dr. Charles Ryrie on "Production, Teaching, and Marketing of English Bibles,"[59] Dr. Naseeb Shaheen on "Shakespeare and the Bible,"[60] Mercer University

49 "Faculty/Staff Updates," *Campus Connections,* 16 April 2010.

50 Noelle Marchand, "Professors translate Bible drama," *The Collegian,* 13 Nov. 2008, p. 1.

51 "Faculty/Staff Updates," *Campus Connections,* 19 Feb. 2010.

52 Sonia Reyes, "Spanish lit course top 10 in nation," *The Collegian,* 25 Oct. 2007, p. 3.

53 "Estrada lauded for outstanding course," *HBU News,* Fall 2007, 34.

54 Justin Lacey, "Brupbacher '69 is honored as 2008 Piper Professor," *HBU News,* Fall 2008, 22.

55 Minutes of the Meetings of the Board of Trustees, Meeting on 19 Feb. 2008.

56 "Faith and Learning at the Molecular Level," *HBU News,* Fall 2008, 18.

57 "Associate Provost's new book offers strong critique of secularism," *Advancing the Vision,* Aug. 2009; Erica Drexler, "Secularism as Baker knows it," *The Collegian,* 10 Sept. 2009, p. 7.

58 Jonathan Fitzgerald, "Winning Not Just Hearts but Minds," *Wall Street Journal,* 18 Dec. 2009, http://online.wsj.com/article/SB10001424052748704597704574487532250568304.html (accessed Apr. 7, 2010).

59 "Dunham Bible Museum Lecture Series," *Dunham Bible Museum News,* Oct. /Dec. 2008, p. 2.

60 Ibid.

Distinguished Professor of Christian Ethics Dr. David P. Gushee,[61] former U. S. Secretary of State Madeleine Albright,[62] author Ronald C. White on "The Bible and Lincoln,"[63] and Dr. Thomas Rossin on "Johann Sebastian Bach: his Bible and his Music."[64] Additional presentations were made by Honors College Assistant Professor Dr. Evan J. Getz on "Beauty and God's Visible Providence,"[65] American University Professor of Law Dr. Daniel Dreisbach,[66] Wheaton Professor Dr. Leland Ryken on "The Bible as a Literary Classic,"[67] and Houston Mayor Bill White for a conference on student leadership.[68] Further lectures were given by Dr. Donald Brake on "Greek texts used in English Translations of the Bible,"[69] Dr. David Lyle Jeffrey,[70] former Reagan Secretary of Education Bill Bennett,[71] Tyndale House Warden Dr. Peter Williams,[72] and Archbishop Charles Chaput on "Christianity and the State."[73] In March, Cardinal Daniel DiNardo, archbishop of the Galveston-Houston diocese, addressed the convocation audience as the first Cardinal invited to speak at the University. DiNardo offered congratulations to the University on its fiftieth anniversary and spoke to the University's scripture, John 14:6, on Christ's revelation in the book of John.[74]

The lectures afforded by the University endowments continued to enrich the academic program. The Brown Chair of Business sponsored a campus lecture by National Oilwell Varco Chairman Merrill A. "Pete" Miller."[75] The Prince-Chavanne Lectures in Christian Business Ethics were given by Northwestern Mutual Life Insurance Financial Group

61 "Professor of ethics challenges HBU students, faculty," *Advancing the Vision,* Nov. 2008.

62 "Your Neighborhood Events," *Houston Chronicle,* 15 Jan. 2009, ThisWeek sec., p. 11, three-star ed. Albright's appearance was sponsored by the Houston Holocaust Museum.

63 "Coming Events," *Dunham Bible Museum News,* April/June 2008, p. 4

64 "Fall Events at the Dunham Bible Museum," *Dunham Bible Museum News,* Sept./Dec. 2009, p. 2.

65 "Inaugural Honors College Lecture," *Advancing the Vision,* Apr. 2009.

66 "Coming Events," *Dunham Bible Museum News,* Fall 2009, p. 2.

67 "Fall Events at the Dunham Bible Museum," *Dunham Bible Museum News,* Sept./Dec. 2009, p. 2.

68 Daniel Cadis, "Mayor White lectures on leadership," *The Collegian,* 8 Oct. 2009, p. 1.

69 "Coming Events," *Dunham Bible Museum News,* April/June 2008, p. 4.

70 "Coming Events," *Dunham Bible Museum News,* Sept./Oct. 2009, p. 2.

71 Daniel Cadis, "Bennett praises liberal arts," *The Collegian,* 3 Dec. 2009, p. 2.

72 "Fall Events at the Dunham Bible Museum," *Dunham Bible Museum News,* Sept./Dec. 2009, p. 2.

73 "Campus Announcements," *Campus Connections,* 19 Feb. 2010.

74 Mauricio Guerrero, "DiNardo speaks at Convocation," *The Collegian,* 12 Mar. 2010, www.hbucollegian/religion/dinardo-speaks-at-convocation-1.2190474 (accessed May 2 2010).

75 "Brown Lecture," *HBU News,* Spring 2010, 29. Photo.

Managing Partner Jeff Reeter[76] and Texon Corporation President Terry Looper.[77] The Rex G. Baker Professorship in Business hosted Marathon Oil's Daniel J. Sullenbarger.[78] The A. O. Collins Lectures were given by Dr. Merold Westphal of Fordham University on the topics "The Many Faces of Faith and Reason" and "Philosophy and Prayer."[79] In new activity, the Honors College hosted its first Roundtable Dinners for its students. Speakers for these times of enrichment and exchange were HBU President Dr. Robert B. Sloan, Jr., Houston Mayor Bill White, KPRC Vice President Larry Blackerby, and the Ambassador of Greece to the United States, The Honorable Alexandra Theodoropoulou.[80]

The School of Music provided opportunity for its students to enjoy extended master classes with several nationally-known musicians in December. Dr. James Jordon, professor of conducting at the Westminster Choir College, and award-winning composer Dan Forrest worked with HBU students during their winter visits on campus.[81] The prominent American classical and multi-genre violinist and composer Mark O'Connor appeared in concert with Dr. Melissa Marse in April. Marse and Dr. Ann Gebuhr formed the Houston Chamber Music Society that offered two initial performance projects in Dunham Theater, "Soulscapes" and "World Passport."[82]

Faculty and staff were honored for distinguished service to the University by the Goolsby Outstanding Teaching and the Mayfield Outstanding Staff awards. Faculty honored with the Goolsby Award in 2008 were Associate Professor Dr. Valerie Bussell and Assistant Professor Dr. Miguel Estrada.[83] In 2009, Goolsby awards went to Assistant Professor Dr. Ron Homann and Associate Professor Dr. Melissa Wiseman, and in 2010, to Dr. Saul Trevino.

The Dr. Larry D. Smith Award for Teaching Excellence was established in 2003 by University donor Nell Smith and her son. The award

76 "Jeff Reeter to deliver Prince-Chavanne Lecture," *Advancing the Vision,* Oct. 2008.

77 "Prince-Chavanne speaker to share 'secret weapons' with faculty, students," *Advancing the Vision,* Spring 2010.

78 "College of Business hosts first annual Rex Baker Lecture," *HBU News,* Winter 2008, 26.

79 Houston Baptist University, "The 2009 A. O. Collins Theology Lectures," 24 Mar. 2008.

80 (Dr. Robert Stacey to Dr Don Looser, Mar. 9, 2010).

81 "School of Music hosts famous conductor and award winning composer," *HBU News,* Winter 2008, 21.

82 "HBU partners with Houston Chamber Music Society," *HBU News,* Winter 2008, 21.

83 "Opal Goolsby Award for Outstanding Teaching," *HBU News,* Fall 2008, 28.

provided for an annual cash stipend of $3500 for a faculty recipient and additional funds for the institutional improvement of teaching. These awards were made to the University's annual nominee for the Piper Foundation Outstanding Teaching Awards in the state of Texas. Recipients of the Dr. Larry D. Smith Award were Dr. Brenda Whaley in 2005, Dr. Randy Wilson in 2006, Dr. Susan Cook in 2007, Dr. Linda Brupbacher (who also was named a Piper Professor) in 2008, Michael Collins in 2009, and Dr. Rhonda Furr in 2010. Mayfield Outstanding Staff Awards were given in 2008 to Associate Dean of Student Life Frances Curtis[84] and Director of Information Technology Operations Bill Sisk.[85] In 2009, the awards recognized Assistant Director of Financial Services Debora Burnett and the Director of Instructional Media Isaac Simpson; in 2010 the Mayfield awards went to Patricia Evans, Assistant Director of Human Resources, and Clay Porter, Director of Instructional Television.[86]

Service awards were made to long-term University colleagues. In the years 2006-2010, staff and faculty marked new plateaus of service. Dr. Don Looser was recognized for forty-five years with the University—the first person to achieve this record of longevity. Marking forty years of employment were Ken Rogers and Dr. Doris Warren. Honored for thirty-five years of service were Dr. Avin Brownlee, Dr. Hutch Dvorak, and Dr. Ernie Pyle. Judy Ferguson '67, Dr. Ann Gebuhr, and Dr. Sally Phillips were recognized for thirty years with the University. Marking twenty-five years were Dr. Linda Brupbacher '69, Saliem Kahleh '84, Ann Noble, Clay Porter, Isaac Simpson, Dr. Jon Suter, and Dr. Treacy Woods. Awards for twenty years of service were presented to Dr. Rusty Brooks, Debora Burnett, Pam Clopton, Rosemary Fojtik, Dr. Rhonda Furr, Josefina Gonzalez, Dr. Jackie Horn, Venda Johnson, Laurel Motal, Dr. Darlene Serrato, and Ritamarie Tauer.[87]

The academic year 2008-09 witnessed many curricular changes. A new Mission Statement was adopted: "The mission of HBU is to provide a learning experience that instills in students a passion for academic, spiritual, and professional excellence as a result of our central confession,

---

84 Ashley Marchand, "Legacy Trails," *The Collegian,* 1 May 2008, p. 8.

85 "Mayfield Outstanding Staff Award," *HBU News,* Fall 2008, 28.

86 "HBU recognizes dedication to excellence among faculty, staff," *News at HBU,* 11 May 2009, www.hbu.edu/hbu/NewsBot.asp?MODE=VIEW&ID=877&SnID=2 (accessed 22 May 2010).

87 "Founders' Day," *HBU News,* Winter 2008, 16-17; Printed program, "Rolling through the Decades," 24 Apr. 2009; (Candace Desrosiers to Dr. Don Looser, April 15, 2010).

'Jesus is Lord.'"[88] This document paired with the "Ten Pillars" became the structure from which all revision was constructed. In September, the College of Arts and Humanities initiated a new major in philosophy.[89] At the same time, the major in public policy was suspended.[90] Revised processes began to speed and ease the evaluation of transfer credits and to return the Smith College of General Studies to a core of required disciplines—reflective of the First Pillar of Faith and Reason, "Build on the Classics."[91] The College of Continuing Studies re-established activity first begun in 1974 by Dr. Royce Bach and Dr. Joan DeRooy.[92] In February, the double major requirement for degrees was eliminated in favor of a major/minor system.[93] At the same time, it was announced that the capstone Senior Seminars would no longer be an institutional requirement for the degree.[94]

Dr. Archie and Linda Dunham continued to contribute significantly in support of the Dunham Bible Museum to help acquire the extensive Brake-Hellstern collection of papyri, manuscript Bibles, incunabula, early European Bibles, and artifacts.[95] In gratitude, the University Theater in the Morris Center was named the Dunham Theater in 2008.[96] A festive onstage dinner party was held honoring the Dunham family and friends featuring a concert by HBU faculty musicians.[97]

A highlight of 2009 was the first series of concerts by the Houston Symphony Orchestra under conductor Hans Graf in the Dunham Theater of the Morris Cultural Arts Center. A "Bach vs. Vivaldi Festival" was staged in March that utilized all of the facilities of the Center.[98] Over a weekend, orchestra and children's concerts were held in Dunham Theater; solo and chamber concerts were held in the Belin Chapel; McNair Hall was the scene of shops, strolling costumed actors representing the Bach

---

88 "New Mission Statement," *Advancing the Vision,* Apr. 2009.

89 Daniel Cadis, "College of Arts and Humanities launches philosophy major," *The Collegian,* 11 Sept. 2008, p. 3.

90 Mauricio Guerrero, "Students urged to go 'single,'" *The Collegian,* 2 Apr. 2009, p. 1.

91 Houston Baptist University, Minutes of the Meetings of the Board of Trustees, Meeting on 23 Sept. 2008.

92 Robin Foster, "Learning never ends at HBU's newest college," *Houston Chronicle,* 24 Sept. 2009, ThisWeek sec., p. 6, three-star ed.

93 Mauricio Guerrero, "Students urged to go 'single,'" *The Collegian,* 2 Apr. 2009, p. 1.

94 Houston Baptist University, Minutes of the Meetings of the Board of Trustees, Meeting on 24 Feb. 2009.

95 "Brake-Hellstern Collection," *Dunham Bible Museum News,* Spring 2010, p. 10. Photos. Dr. Donald Brake and Dr. John Hellstern had assiduously assembled this collection over their lifetimes. They generously loaned the collection to the Dunham Museum for its opening exhibits in faith that a donor would provide the funds needed to transfer the vast collection to the University.

96 "HBU names Morris Center Theater in honor of Archie and Linda Dunham," *Advancing the Vision,* Jan. 2009.

97 "Dunham Theater Dinner onstage," *Advancing the Vision,* Feb. 2009.

98 Hans Graf, "The Bach vs Vivaldi Experience," *Houston Symphony Performance Program,* Mar. 2009, pp. 12-13.

and Vivaldi, and both Italian and German food in the *Café Baroque*. Highlights of the concerts included performances of both the Bach *Magnificat* and the Vivaldi *Gloria* with the Orchestra and Symphony Chorus in addition to the *Goldberg Variations* and the *Brandenburg Concerti*.[99] The Morris Center proved popular with symphony goers, and the two performance halls were praised by the performers. Graf expressed his personal delight with the excellence of the theaters.

§

Student achievement through publications continued to maintain an outstanding record. *The Collegian* was awarded its ninth All American rating by the Associated Collegiate Press for 2008-09.[100] President Sloan wrote, "The Collegian staff has a strong work ethic and high standards that serve as an outstanding example for their classmates. I have been consistently pleased with their reporting of events on campus."[101] In the spring of 2009, the *Collegian* received twenty-seven awards for excellence from TIPA including a first place for the Hurricane Ike special issue and for online edition excellence.[102] *The Collegian* also won the Lone Star Award from the Houston Press Club as "Best Student Newspaper" in a competition not restricted to size categories. *The Collegian* was "smartly edited, well-assembled, and never let its small size limit it."[103] In further competition, *The Collegian* received a first-place award for "overall newspaper" in Division I from the Baptist Press Collegiate Journalism Conference.[104] Additionally, *The Collegian* won twelve certificates from the Columbia Scholastic Press Association including first place awards for both editorial page and overall design.[105]

The 2008 yearbook *Ornogah* won eighteen TIPA awards including one for overall excellence. However, in the aftermath of Hurricane Ike and the resultant financial pressures, it was announced in September 2009 that production of the *Ornogah* would not be continued after forty-

---

99 Tara Dooley, "Bach vs. Vivaldi: Houston Symphony series," *Houston Chronicle*, 23 Mar. 2009, Star sec., p. 1, three-star ed.
100 "Collegian receives All American rating," *Advancing the Vision,* Dec. 2009.
101 Dr. Robert B. Sloan, Jr., "A Message from Dr. Sloan," *HBU News,* Fall 2008, 2.
102 "Collegian wins Lone Star Award and 27 TIPA awards," *HBU News,* Summer 2009, 23; Beth Zapach, "Collegian takes 27 TIPA awards," *The Collegian,* 16 Apr. 2009, p. 3.
103 "Collegian wins first place," *Advancing the Vision,* July 2009.
104 Kristen Crawley, "Collegian sweeps national awards, receives top honors," *The Collegian,* 2 Dec. 2009, p. 1.
105 "Collegian Receives All American Rating," *HBU News,* Spring 2010, 32.

nine years of publication. A number of additional factors influenced the decision. Assistant Vice President Martha Morrow credited waning student interest, the high cost of production, difficulty in securing staff, and consistent surplus inventory from previous years as contributing factors. The coming of age of digital communication also played a role. *Facebook, MySpace, Twitter,* and *LinkedIn* were voiced as preferable options by students for creating and maintaining records of friends and events. Nonetheless, the value of the *Ornogah* as a comprehensive institutional history remains a prized resource.

Additional student achievement was spotlighted in the April edition of the *Advancing the Vision* online newsletter.[106] The University's Mock Trial team under Dr. Chris Salinas was selected a second time for a berth at the 2008 national tournament—one of only five teams from the Southern region.[107] The *Houston Chronicle* headlined, "HBU's mock trial team earns national recognition" and reported victories over Duke, Emory and the University of Georgia at the National Mock Trial Tournament.[108] Sophomore Jonathan Rodgers was named "All National Attorney."[109]

This also marked the final year of outstanding leadership by Coach Dr. Chris Salinas who resigned to accept a position at SMU. In 2009, under interim coaches Vivian Camacho '91 and Derrick Owens '07, HBU ranked twelfth in a field of sixty-eight teams at the National Invitational Open.[110] In 2010, the teams placed second overall at Baylor's Green and Gold Invitational[111] and hosted their own tournament for the first time. Only HBU and UT placed two teams in the top eight of the twenty-four-college roster. Senior Laurie Balkum was honored as "Best Lawyer" and was awarded a full scholarship to Baylor Law School.[112] Tim Rothberg '02 served as coach for the HBU team.

Blessy Varughese became the University's fifth health-career sophomore to be admitted to the coveted Joint Medical Admission Program (JAMP) for entrance to the nation's medical colleges.[113] The HBU

106 "HBU students excel in business, mock trial, nursing competitions," *Advancing the Vision,* Apr. 2009.

107 Nathan Cadis, "Mock trial earns place at nationals," *The Collegian,* 13 Mar. 2008, p. 4.

108 "HBU's mock trial team earns national recognition," *Houston Chronicle,* 10 Apr. 2008, ThisWeek sec., p. 6, three-star ed.

109 Ibid.

110 Aaron Pizaña, "Mockers rank 12 of 68 teams," *The Collegian,* 12 Feb. 2009, p. 2.

111 "Mock trial season opens," *Advancing the Vision,* Jan. 2010.

112 Emily Klotz, "HBU hosts 'mockers,'" *The Collegian,* 11 Feb. 2010, p. 1.

113 "Lindsey Brehm, "Students guaranteed medical school spot," *The Collegian,* 13 Mar. 2008, p. 4; Clay Carnes, "Sophomore receives Texas medical award," *The Collegian,* 12 Mar. 2009, p. 7; "Varughese receives University's 5th JAMP Award," *HBU News,* Summer 2009, 23.

"Students in Free Enterprise" won state honors and advanced to the USA National Exposition in Philadelphia.[114]   The University's Nursing Students' Association was named the most outstanding chapter in Texas and received the "Breakthrough to Nursing" and the "Outstanding Community Service" awards.[115] HBU's Suhare Adam was selected for the summer undergraduate physics research program at Harvard University following her work at Cornell the previous summer.[116] In 2010, Adam was awarded a full-tuition scholarship for the PhD program at Harvard.[117] The work of *Collegian* editor Mauricio Guerrero, while serving an internship with the *New York Times,* was recognized when his report on the Stanford Financial Group Ponzi scheme was printed by the *Times* with his byline—a significant professional nod of approval.[118]

In 2008, HBU placed fourteen students in medical schools; another nine students were admitted to other medical and health professions programs.[119] In 2010, the *Collegian* reported a historical medical school acceptance rate near ninety percent. HBU science faculty members provided these students intensive mentoring, skill development programs for personal statement preparation, and techniques for a successful interview. Dr. Susan Cook, Director of Health Professions Programs, reported the *early acceptance* of eight outstanding HBU students in 2010.[120]

The University's alumni continued to honor their alma mater by their achievements. From 2006 to 2010, the University's Board of Trustees was led by alumni Ray Cox '81, Rick Bailey '69, Robert Powell '76, and Dr. Ed Seay '73. Meritorious Alumni Awards were given to Tadd Tellepsen '99,[121] Francis Bui '00,[122] Carol Lavender '92, Dee Pate '92,[123] and Terry Lewis '88.[124] Distinguished Alumnus Awards were given Pastor Edwin B. Young '84 of the Fellowship of Las Colinas,[125] former all-pro NFL safety

---

114 Clayton Carnes, "SIFE warrants spot at nationals," *The Collegian,* 16 Apr. 2009, p. 2.
115 Cristina Del Canto, "NSA brings home statewide honors," *The Collegian,* 13 Mar. 2008, p. 3.
116 "Suhare Adam selected for physics research at Harvard," *HBU News,* Summer 2009, 23.
117 "HBU alumna admitted to Harvard Graduate School," *Advancing the Vision,* Mar. 2010.
118 "HBU students excel in journalism and scientific research," *Advancing the Vision,* July 2009.
119 Houston Baptist University, Minutes of the Meetings of the Board of Trustees, Meeting on 23 Sept. 2008.
120 Justin Schneewind, "Building on a reputation of acceptance," *The Collegian,* 28 Jan. 2010, p. 10.
121 "Meritorious Alumnus," *HBU News,* Spring 2007, 10-11.
122 "Around the State," *Baptist Standard,* 27 Nov. 2008, (accessed 20 Apr. 2008).
123 "Meritorious Alumni Awards," *HBU News,* Winter 2008, 6.
124 Heidi Sigmarsdottir, "University honors top alumni," *The Collegian,* 12 Nov. 2009, p. 2. Lewis was the "Voice of the Huskies" for 22 years, announcing home basketball games from Sharp Gym.
125 "Distinguished Alumnus," *HBU News,* Spring 2007, 8-9.

Mike Reinfeldt '84,[126] *Houston Chronicle* Sports Editor Carlton Thompson '92,[127] and Houston Bar Association President Randy Sorrels '84.[128] The Hallmark Award for outstanding service to the Alumni Association was given Dr. Don Looser,[129] First Lady Sue Sloan,[130] Clay Porter,[131] and Dr. Shari Wescott.[132] In the Spring 2010 Commencement ceremony, Dr. Wescott was appointed to the rank of Professor Emeritus by action of the Board of Trustees for her twenty years of service. Wescott had served as Assistant Dean of the College, as Prince-Chavanne Chair in Christian Business Ethics, and had been awarded the Robert Griswold Outstanding Faculty award in business.

The Dean of the College of Nursing Dr. Nancy Yuill '72 was named one of Houston's "Outstanding Nurses of 2008" by the Texas Nurses Association.[133] The University named the family of Rick '69 and Avie '68 Bailey as "Family of the Year" in 2009. Believed to be the University's first three generation family, the Baileys were honored for their significant contributions to the University.[134] Distinguished Alumnus Carlton Thompson '92 was named Executive Editor of Major League Baseball's New York-based *MLB.com* website. Carlton's latest promotion, which provided him a staff of more than one hundred professionals including thirty team reporters, placed him in a position of national prominence in sports reporting.[135]

In 2008, the "founding classes" of 1967-1970 held another in their series of summer reunions and were the guests of Dr. and Mrs. Sloan in the President's Home. Of additional interest was the gathering of sixty former members of the College Singers under Dr. R. Paul Green who enjoyed reunion, a day of rehearsal under alumni conductors, and an evening concert of works first performed with Dr. Green.[136] In November, alumnae of Phi Mu celebrated the organization's thirtieth anniversary with a reunion of fifty members. Houston Mayor Bill White spoke for alumni of the University's MBA program on the occasion of its thirtieth anniversary in

---

126 "Around the State," *Baptist Standard*, 27 Nov. 2008, www.baptiststandard.com (accessed 20 Apr. 2008).

127 Geoffrey Lawrence, "Alumnus garners award," *The Collegian*, 10 Jan. 2008, p. 1.

128 Heidi Sigmarsdottir, "University honors top alumni," *The Collegian*, 12 Nov. 2009, p. 1.

129 *Houston Baptist University Alumni: Today 2008*, xi.

130 "Sue Sloan gets Hallmark Award at Homecoming," *HBU News*, Mar. 2009, 33.

131 "Around the State," *Baptist Standard*, 27 Nov. 2008, www.baptiststandard.com (accessed 20 Apr. 2008).

132 Heidi Sigmarsdottir, "University honors top alumni," *The Collegian*, 12 Nov. 2009, p. 1.

133 "CON Dean, alumna named," *Advancing the Vision*, Nov. 2008.

134 Phanuel Roxas, "Bailey family receives University honor," *The Collegian*, 22 Oct. 2009, p. 1.

135 Richard Prince, "Houston's Carlton Thompson leaving for *MLB.com*," *The Maynard Institute*, www.mije.org (accessed Apr. 9, 2010).

136 "Founding Classes Reunion," *HBU News*, 44-45. Photos.

2008.[137] Members of Alpha Pi Kappa, including five returning fraternity founders, celebrated the organization's fortieth anniversary in 2009.[138]

In 2008, softball coach Mary Ellen Hall '88 earned her 600th career victory in her seventeenth season at HBU. Hall '88 served with fellow coaches Kaddie Platt '94 and Jared Moon '96 as proud alumni of the University. Alumni Randy Sorrels '84 and Cheryl Sorrels '85 contributed $250,000 to create the "Randy and Cheryl Sorrels Field" for the University's soccer program.[139] A four-year letterman, Randy had been a member of the HBU teams that won the Trans-American Athletic Conference championships in 1982, 1984, and 1985. The Sorrels Soccer Field anchored the east campus with an improved playing field, lighting for nighttime play, a grandstand, and physical amenities for vehicular and pedestrian traffic. The Field was dedicated in October with ceremonies honoring the Sorrels family and a dinner in Lawrence Park. HBU competed in the Atlantic Soccer Conference and, with SMU, represented the only Division I soccer programs in Texas.[140] In April, the Huskies scrimmaged the Houston Dynamo and hosted a pre-season exhibition match between the Chicago Fire and the Houston Dynamo at Sorrels Field.[141]

The biggest athletic news of the season was the settlement of HBU's suit against the NCAA to prevent a seven-year delay in tournament eligibility for previous member institutions.[142] The *Houston Chronicle* reported, "Time and a pair of solid attorneys are on the side of the HBU athletic department."[143] The NCAA had rewritten its policy in what the organization termed "an editorial revision that did not require a membership vote."[144] The University claimed that the NCAA had violated U. S. anti-trust laws by preventing new Division I entrants from the post-season tournament. Still required of the University were the NCAA's mandated compliance review, an athletic self-study, a strategic plan, and

---

137 "30th anniversary of MBA in Cultural Arts Center," *HBU News,* Mar. 2009, 26; "MBA 30th," *The Collegian,* 8 Nov. 2007, p. 1. Photo.

138 "Brotherhood lives on," *HBU News,* Summer 2009, 29. Photo. The five founders included Aaron Jefferson '71, Michael Wood '70, Terry Johnson '71, Doug Henry '71, and Ed Seay '73.

139 Kristen Crawley, "Soccer field takes Sorrels' name," *The Collegian,* 11 Sept. 2008, p. 3; "Soccer Field Honors Alumni," *HBU News,* Fall 2008, 40.

140 Jusué Elizondo, "Family ties," *The Collegian,* 22 Oct. 2009, p. 1.

141 Brandon Porter, "Soccer becoming big-name program," *The Collegian,* 14 Apr. 2010, www.hbucollegian.com/sports/soccer-becming-big-name-program-1.2223680 (accessed May 2, 2010).

142 Brandon C. Williams, "HBU settles suits to upgrade sports/full Division I status attainable after 4-year span," *Houston Chronicle,* 4 Feb. 2009, Sports sec., p. 3, three-star ed.

143 Ibid.

144 Ibid.

annual reports; but the time period required for re-admission was reduced to four years. Therefore, a full Division I schedule started in 2009-2010, and only two more years of provisional status would lead to full membership in the NCAA in the spring of 2011.

The University named Steve Moniaci to the position of Athletic Director. Moniaci was experienced with NCAA relations from his twenty-six years at Rice University and his five years as HBU's Associate Athletic Director. The move was not unforeseen.[145] Ron Cottrell directed his energy to the heightened rigor of NCAA play as head basketball coach and Associate Athletic Director. Cottrell had held both the AD and coaching titles for the previous fifteen years. He was the winningest coach in HBU history with a record of 379 wins in eighteen seasons. Cottrell's teams had qualified for the NAIA national tournament for ten consecutive seasons.[146]

The 2008-09 season proved to be a "difficult year of transition" for the Huskies in the Great Western Athletic Conference (GWC). The HBU volleyball team won the National Transition Championship; Daniel Martinez won HBU's first GWC championship in cross country.[147] Men's golf, however, won the GWC championship in the University's first year of competition. The women's team captured second place.[148] The 2010 season proved more favorable for the Huskies. Men's basketball finished second in the GWC with a conference play record of 9-3,[149] but women's coach Todd Buchanan announced his resignation to accept the position as head coach of the women's team at the University of Houston.[150] In 2010, HBU's women's golf team won its first Great West Conference championships. Freshman Gaia Olcese was named Player of the Year, and Coach David Shuster was named Coach of the Year.[151]

The passing of an era in athletics was marked in 2010 by the death of the University's mascot, Wakiza. Kiza had been away from the campus from 2003 to 2005, but then returned as the Husky's live mascot to

---

145 "New roles announced for Cottrell, Moniaci," *HBU News,* Summer 2009, 32.

146 Joseph Duarte, "Cottrell steps down as the AD at HBU," *Houston Chronicle,* Sports sec., p. 6, three-star ed.

147 Caleb Beames, "Program has success and difficulties in first year of conference play," *The Collegian,* 30 Apr. 2009, p. 16.

148 Caleb Beames, "Men prove best in the Great West," *The Collegian,* 20 Apr. 2009, p. 16.

149 Justin Schneewind, "Rising above expectations," *The Collegian,* 1 Apr. 2010, p. 16.

150 Justin Schneewind, "Coaching search begins after Buchanan takes UH job," *The Collegian,* 22 Apr. 2010.

151 "HBU women claim first Great West golf title, sweep individual awards," *Advancing the Vision,* May 2010.

the delight of the campus family.[152] Wakiza was ten years old when she became suddenly and seriously ill. The "determined warrior" was buried in the courtyard of the Sharp Gym near another icon mascot of a bygone era, Mingo.[153]

§

In an effort to sharpen the distinction between professional schools and the liberal arts, a sweeping reorganization of the academic structure was announced. The College of Business and Economics became the School of Business. The College of Education and Behavioral Sciences became the School of Education; the behavioral sciences were transferred to the College of Arts and Humanities; kinesiology was moved to the new School of Nursing and Allied Health. The Department of Christianity and Philosophy became the School of Theology. The Department of Political Science became the Department of Government; Speech Communications became Communications and Rhetorical Studies. Unchanged were the Colleges of Arts and Humanities, Science and Mathematics, Honors, and Continuing Studies.[154]

A number of personnel changes were announced during the course of the 2008-09 year. Dr. Diane Martin was named interim Dean of the College of Arts and Humanities effective January 1, 2009;[155] Dr. Randy Wilson assumed the position of Associate Dean of the College. At the same time, Ann Noble was appointed Director of the Moody Library following a period of interim service.[156] In January, Dr. Mohan Kuruvilla, a member of the University faculty since 1997, was named Dean of the College of Business and Economics.[157] Dr. Marie Mater was named chair of the Department of Communications,[158] and Dr. Ron Rexilius was similarly appointed in the Department of Government.[159] Dr. Melissa Wiseman was named chair of the Department of Accounting, Economics,

152 Sam Byrd, "Kiza's home after two-year absence," *The Collegian,* 27 Jan. 2005, p. 1.

153 Nathan Cadis, "Passing of an icon," *The Collegian,* 25 Feb. 2010, p. 1.

154 "HBU realigns academic divisions, announces new nomenclature," *Advancing the Vision,* June 2009; "Academic Realignment," *HBU News,* Summer 2009, 8.

155 Justin Schneewind, "Martin heads College of Arts and Humanities, raises profile of faculty," *The Collegian,* 29 Jan. 2009, p. 4; Houston Baptist University, Minutes of the Meetings of the Board of Trustees, Meeting on 25 Nov. 2008.

156 Ibid.

157 "HBU College of Business and Economics names Kuruvilla new dean," *Advancing the Vision,* Jan. 2009.

158 Scott Florence, "Mater propels Department of Communications," *The Collegian,* 29 Jan. 2009, p. 4.

159 Samantha Williams, "Rexilius named chair," *The Collegian,* 29 Jan. 2009, p. 4.

and Finance, and Dr. Jackie Horn was appointed Chair of the Department of Biology.[160] Dr. Rusty Brooks and Dr. Mike Bourke were appointed Associate Deans of the School of Business for Undergraduate and Graduate programs respectively. Dr. Lou Markos was named to the Ray Endowed Chair in Humanities and to the position of Scholar-in-Residence.[161] Dr. Hunter Baker was named Associate Provost, and Sandra Mooney was appointed Vice President for Financial Operations.[162] In March, Dr. Robert Stacey, Associate Professor of Government at Regent University, was named Dean of the Honors College at HBU.[163]

In May 2009, the Dean of the College of Nursing, Dr. Nancy Yuill '72, submitted her resignation. Yuill had been a member of the faculty since 1982, was appointed as the second Dean of the College of Nursing in 1990, and had served as Interim Vice President for Academic Affairs in 2007-08. She was the recipient of the "Hero of the University" award and was the author of a new curriculum in nursing that had been successfully implemented in 2000. During her tenure as Dean, the graduate programs in nursing and in health administration had produced seventy-two graduates from the University. Under her leadership, the tradition of one hundred percent of the nurses passing the state licensure examination on first sitting had been maintained.[164] Moreover, Yuill had taken powerful leadership positions on committees relating to reaffirmation of institutional SACS accreditation and revisions of the Smith College of General Studies requirements. At the May 2009 commencement, Yuill was honored and named to the rank of Professor Emeritus.[165]

The Doctor of Humane Letters was conferred upon Distinguished Alumnus '01 Bob Beauchamp (MSM '87) in recognition of professional achievement and in gratitude for his distinguished service to the University in the aftermath of Hurricane Ike.[166] Beauchamp had been a Brown Chair lecturer and had served as Honorary Chair for the 2005 Spirit

---

160 Houston Baptist University, Minutes of the Meetings of the Board of Trustees, Meeting on 27 May 2008.

161 "Academic Leadership," *HBU News,* Summer 2009, 9.

162 "New Financial Operations Vice President," *Advancing the Vision,* Apr. 2009; "VP for Financial Operations: Sandy Mooney," *HBU News,* Summer 2009, 6; Mauricio Guerrero, "Mooney fills CFO position," *The Collegian,* 12 Mar. 2009, p. 1.

163 Beth Zapach, "Quest for Honors College dean concludes," *The Collegian,* 2 Apr. 2009, p. 4. Dr. David Capes had been serving as Interim Dean at the request of President Sloan.

164 "Yuill moves on," *HBU News,* Summer 2009, 12-13.

165 "Retiring Dean Dr. Nancy Yuill named Professor Emeritus," *Advancing the Vision,* June 2009; "December nursing graduates achieve 100 percent pass rate," *Advancing the Vision,* Mar. 2010.

166 "HBU recognizes Bob Beauchamp," *HBU News,* Summer 2009, 6; "HBU awards honorary doctorate to HBC software CEO Bob Beauchamp," *Advancing the Vision,* June 2009.

of Excellence Dinner. In further but little-known service, Beauchamp had extended access to BMC's digital video production facility to HBU students until such time as the campus studio was restored.

Other staff changes marked the 2009-2010 period. In September, the *Collegian* announced, "Dr. Alice Ledford becomes newest interim dean."[167] Since 2008, every dean except Dr. Doris Warren had been replaced. Ledford had been a member of the University education faculty since 2007. Dr. Margaret Ugalde was appointed Associate Dean of the School of Nursing; Dr. Lucindra Campbell-Law '94 was named Interim Director of Nursing. Dr. Doris Warren's duties were expanded to included academic management of the School of Nursing and Allied Health and the College of Science and Mathematics.[168] Dr. Randy Hatchett was appointed Chair of the newly-created Department of Philosophy, and Dr. Matthew Boyleston was named Interim Chair of the Department of Languages.[169]

Dr. Robert Stacey was in his first year of service as Dean of the Honors College. President Sloan was effusive in his praise and gratitude for the work of Dr. David Capes in initiating the Honors College by teaching, curriculum building, and recruiting both students and faculty. Sloan called the program a "jewel."[170] In further action, Dr. Capes was selected to lead the new Graduate School and serve as Director of the School of Theology. The coordination and administration of all the University's graduate programs were part of Capes' new assignment.

In the spring, the University hosted *Rolling through the Decades* to honor colleagues celebrating significant anniversaries of University service and those who were retiring. Among the retirees in 2009 were former Interim Dean of Nursing Debra Berry '89, psychologist Dr. Doug Fitzgerald after twenty-one years of service, Director of the Museum of American Architecture and Decorative Arts since 1984 Lynn Miller '77, Director of the Museum of Southern History Dr. Danny Sessums, and Dean of the College of Nursing Dr. Nancy Yuill '72, a member of the faculty since 1982.

§

167 Daniel Cadis, "Ledford becomes newest interim dean," *The Collegian*, 10 Sept. 2009, p. 4.

168 Christina Burden, "New leadership in school of nursing," *The Collegian*, 20 Sept. 2009, p. 2; "School of Nursing," *Advancing the Vision*, Sept. 2009.

169 "New Arts and Humanities Chairs," *HBU News*, Spring 2010, 6.

170 Dr. Robert B. Sloan, Jr., "A Message from Dr. Sloan," *HBU News*, Summer 2009, 2.

In May 2009, Joella Morris was named "Woman of the Year" for giving "tirelessly of her time and talents throughout HBU's first fifty years."[171] In special convocation ceremonies on campus, the Morrises were specifically recognized as donors of the ten columns from the Galveston County Court House that "served as inspiration for the 'Ten Pillars of Faith and Reason in a Great City.'"[172] Dr. and Mrs. Morris were further recognized as principal donors of the Morris Cultural Arts Center. Mrs. Morris was also recognized as a longtime advocate of historical preservation and as founder of the Museum of Southern History. It was she who guided the Museum from its Jeffersonian venue in Fort Bend County to a new home within the Morris Cultural Arts Center. Mrs. Morris was a founding member of the American Museum Society. As a part of the ceremony, Stewart Morris recognized his three children, Stewart Jr., and alumnae Carlotta Barker '68 and Lisa Morris Simon '76.

The history of financial contribution by the Morris family over 50 years has been an extraordinary record. In one manifestation of support, Dr. Morris challenged members of the Board of Trustees to match his gift of $1,000,000 for University operations. The trustees met the challenge, and it was the "opportunity" of Mrs. Morris to present the check to the University on behalf of the family. In a moment of humor typical of her personality, Mrs. Morris reminded the trustees that the occasion was her first Board meeting ever to attend in University history, and she said, "This invitation cost me $1,000,000."[173]

For several years, Dr. and Mrs. Morris had been working with representatives of the Virginia Historical Society to arrange for the Houston residency of an extraordinary exhibition on the lives and influence of Civil War generals Lee and Grant. In fact, the configuration of the permanent Museum of Southern History exhibit was designed to accommodate the 2009 Houston visit of the Lee and Grant exhibit. Supported by the National Endowment for the Humanities, the exhibit presented a comprehensive reassessment of the lives, careers, and historical impact of Robert E. Lee and Ulysses S. Grant. The Houston exhibition was one of only five venues in the nation.[174]

---

171 "Long-time friend, supporter, Joella Morris named Woman of the Year," *Advancing the Vision,* May 2009.
172 Ibid.
173 Houston Baptist University, Minutes of the Meetings of the Board of Trustees, Meeting on 20 Aug. 2008.
174 "Lee and Grant," *HBU News,* Summer 2009, 11; "Museum of Southern History hosts 'Lee and Grant' traveling exhibit," *Advancing the Vision,* May 2009.

The Lee and Grant Exhibit opened in the Morris Cultural Arts Center in 2009 and featured documents, portraits, family artifacts, Grant's original terms of surrender, Lee's farewell orders, period military equipment, and the uniforms each wore at the surrender at Appomattox. The exhibit marked the first time the two uniforms had been "together" since the historical event at Appomattox.[175] A commemorative pictorial volume was published by the Morris family who also underwrote the Houston appearance of the exhibition. The exhibit drew some 4200 visitors and was instrumental in drawing many guests to the campus for the first time.[176]

§

In August, 2009, representatives of Memorial Hermann Southwest Hospital issued a surprise announcement that a non-binding letter of intent had been signed with the Harris County Hospital District to sell the Beechnut medical complex to the District for up to $165 million.[177] By so doing, the Harris County Hospital District had "hopes of expanding access to medical care for the uninsured and underprivileged."[178] The story was front page news. The hospital complex had just been expanded by the construction of two new treatment and professional towers. The announced plan gripped the University family because of the implications it had for campus property values. In addition, concerns were voiced about security, vehicular traffic, noise, cooperative involvement with the School of Nursing, and the effects on University Place and the Wellness Center.

Almost immediately, the Hospital professional staff registered its strong opposition; many threatened to leave.[179] A petition signed by some 200 doctors and the hospital's medical staff leadership recommended that county commissioners reject the proposal.[180] The *Houston Chronicle* reported, "Opposition has come from multiple directions, and virtually no

---

175 Caroline Gallay, "Reassessing the lives of Lee and Grant," *Houston Chronicle,* 5 June 2009, Star sec., p. 2, three-star ed. The exhibit itinerary was ultimately extended by the Virginia Historical Society through 2011.
176 (Suzie Snoddy to Dr. Don Looser, Apr. 13, 2010).
177 "Intriguing deal, bold plan to buy hospital for county system," *Houston Chronicle,* 9 Aug. 2009, sec. B, p. 13, three-star ed.
178 Peggy O'Hare, "County adding beds to hospital district," *Houston Chronicle,* 7 Aug. 2009, sec. A, p.1, three-star ed.
179 Todd Ackerman, "Proposed sale to hospital district met by firestorm," *Houston Chronicle,* 15 Aug. 2009, sec. B, p. 1, three-star ed.
180 Todd Ackerman, "Hospital staff vows to resign; President of Memorial downplays the petition," *Houston Chronicle,* 20 Aug. 2009, sec. B, p. 1, three-star ed.

important player has rushed forward to endorse the plan."[181]   In September, Memorial's President Dan Wolterman delivered to the county an eight-point ultimatum for answers to relevant questions; he demanded a response within forty-eight hours.[182] Three days later, the *Chronicle* summarized that the matter "ran into a firing squad of critics, culminating in an unpleasant . . . demand letter . . . to the district and a unanimous vote by the district board . . . to back out of the deal."[183]   Ultimately, a group of doctors called for the resignation of Memorial Hermann Healthcare System's President Dan Wolterman. The outcome of this series of events was a shaken relationship for the hospital with some whose future would have been most dramatically impacted by the consummation of the sale— the medical staff and the residents of University Place. In the midst of the melee, University Place residents cautiously celebrated the twentieth anniversary of its opening.

§

In the spring 2009, a sign was attached to the chain-link fence around the Brown Administrative Complex main entrance that read, "Please pardon our disarray (thanks to Hurricane Ike!) Plans for restoration underway and construction to begin SOON." In late summer 2009, on the advice of counsel, the Board of Trustees reluctantly authorized a lawsuit to be filed against the University's property insurance carrier related to Hurricane Ike damage on the campus. Engineering estimates of replacement value were $20,795,829.[184] Because of the extent of the damages, repairs to the existing structures would be required to include upgrades to current building codes, including electrical specifications, disability provisions, replacement of environmentally compromised HVAC systems, and asbestos abatement. The lawsuit also included an amount

---

181 Todd Ackerman, "Hospital district faces tough sell," *Houston Chronicle,* 23 Aug. 2009, sec. B, p. 1, three-star ed.

182 Todd Ackerman, "Memorial Hermann threatens to ax deal," *Houston Chronicle,* 16 Sept. 2009, sec. B, p. 1, three-star ed.

183 "Undone deal: poor politicking and an outdated image sink a hospital purchase," *Houston Chronicle,* 19 Sept. 2009, sec. B, p. 8, three-star ed.

184 Mauricio Guerrero, "Lawsuit seeks justice," *The Collegian,* 10 Sept. 2009, p. 1.

for covered loss of revenue due to business interruption resulting from the effects of the hurricane. In all, the loss of the Brown Administrative Complex was a serious financial blow to the University, not to mention the resulting lack of social gathering places for students and the loss of the M. D. Anderson Student Center.

University enrollment in the fall 2009 was strong. The *Houston Chronicle* reported HBU's undergraduate enrollment up six percent over the previous year.[185] Fall 2009 marked the third year of record growth.[186] The College of Continuing Studies offered courses that targeted professional and workforce development, wealth management, and music industry careers. Dean Ritamarie Tauer reported the successful use of Twitter to promote course offerings.[187] *U. S. News and World Report* again named HBU among the nation's "most diverse universities."[188] The *Collegian* reported heightened interest in sorority membership among HBU's women students;[189] campus residential living continued to increase.

The University initiated a new Master of Arts in Biblical Languages degree in response to student interest and demand. The degree was unique in Houston and emphasized study in Greek, Hebrew, linguistics, hermeneutics, and Aramaic.[190] In September, ITS Director Charles Fix recommended an additional move of the University's computer servers from CyrusOne to Southern Union's Data Center. The move was to permit growth, to provide better service, and to lower institutional cost.[191] The Banner data management support system continued to expand its range of services. In the fall, the "Curriculum Advising Program Planning" (CAPP) module was implemented that culminated preliminary staff work and data input that began in 2006. The CAPP made evaluation of transfer credit and the construction of degree plans virtually instantaneous and greatly enhanced the success of admissions recruiters in attracting transfer students.[192]

---

185 Jeannie Kever, "Sour economy can't keep higher learning down," *Houston Chronicle,* 18 Sept. 2009, sec. A, p. 1, three-star ed.

186 "Enrollment reaches new heights," *HBU News,* Spring 2010, 7.

187 Robin Foster, "Learning never ends at HBU's newest college," *Houston Chronicle,* 24 Sept. 2009, ThisWeek sec., p. 6, three-star ed.

188 "U. S. News and World Report," *Advancing the Vision,* Sept. 2009.

189 Mauricio Guerrero, "Sorority life flourishes," *The Collegian,* 8 Oct. 2009, p. 3.

190 "Master of Arts in Biblical Languages to enrich opportunity for Christian service," *Advancing the Vision,* July 2009.

191 Justin Schneewind, "ITS relocates campus servers," *The Collegian,* 24 Sept. 2009, p. 10.

192 Nathan Cadis, "Advising empowers students," *The Collegian,* 12 Nov. 2009, p. 1.

The Honors College hosted a regional Southwest Conference on Christianity and Literature in October. The three-day conference featured some forty-eight panelists from Japan, Latvia, Canada, and the United States presenting on twenty-one topics. Eight HBU faculty members served as chairs or presenters, and Dr. Louis Markos delivered one of the plenary session presentations. The Conference reflected the fourth of the University's "Ten Pillars: Establish a residential society of scholars."[193]

§

The realization of the dream for a performing arts center continued to create waves of new opportunity for excellence. An early decision in the planning for the Morris Cultural Arts Center was to meet the needs for both a recital hall and a place for worship in one setting. The resultant Belin Chapel was a triumph of beauty and acoustical acclaim. Architects and engineers designed the room to be conceived around a pipe organ as a visual and acoustical focus.

Trustee Jim Smith and his wife Sherry were long term University donors and powerful instruments of institutional development. Smith's father, Orrien, was an early president of the President's Council organization. The Bisagno Chair in Evangelism was underwritten by the Smiths. Over many years, Jim Smith served to develop properties for the University as income-producing investments—prior even to his becoming a member of the Board of Trustees. Active in Houston cultural and social life, the Smiths' commitment to the University served as a catalyst for encouraging the involvement of their friends and associates.

Early in Dr. Sloan's administration, Jim Smith introduced discussion about an organ for the Belin Chapel.[194] Sherry Smith was an accomplished keyboard musician, and music had long been a part of the family experience. The Smiths were active in their church and committed to the importance of worship in personal spiritual development. Ultimately, the naming of the Chapel for the Smith's close friends, Dr. Bruce and Mary Ann Belin, proved to be an anointing of their provision of the chapel organ. In 2007, the Smiths pledged $1,500,000 to provide the Smith Organ for the Belin Chapel.[195]

---

193 "Honors College Events," *HBU News,* Spring 2010, 16.
194 Houston Baptist University, Minutes of the Meetings of the Board of Trustees, Meeting on 28 Feb. 2006.
195 Houston Baptist University, Minutes of the Meetings of the Board of Trustees, Meeting on 25 Sept. 2007.

Acting with the leadership of Dr. Rhonda Furr from the School of Music and third-party design consultants, the firm of Orgues Létourneau Limitée was selected as the builder.[196] The Smith Organ consists of fifty-eight ranks totaling 3200 pipes and was designed to serve both the needs of worship and performance.[197] After two years of off-site construction and months of campus installation, the Sherry and Jim Smith Létourneau Organ was dedicated in September 2009.

Dr. Joby Bell was the featured performer for the Inaugural Concert in September.[198] Typical of their generous spirit, the Smiths also commissioned the creation of new hand-carved entry doors for the Belin Chapel embellished with scriptural reference and symbols of the Christian faith. The dedication evening was described as "a visual and aural feast."[199] The Smiths were honored for their significant gift. Dr. Furr was recognized for her tireless work with the project. Dr. and Mrs. Hodo were thanked for their leadership in the Cultural Arts Center project, their devotion to the completion of the Belin Chapel, and their long-standing friendship with the Smiths. A second concert on Sunday was paired with the lecture by Dr. Thomas Rossin on the personal Bible of J. S. Bach, one volume of which was concurrently on display in the Dunham Bible Museum.[200] Dr. Rhoda Furr gave the inaugural faculty recital on the Smith Organ on November 17, 2009. The Sherry and Jim Smith Organ was the cover feature of the May, 2010 issue of the *American Organist* magazine published by the American Guild of Organists.[201]

Along with the organ, Dr. Sloan set about to commission the design of stained glass windows for the Belin Chapel as a future, ongoing project. In another "act of providence," Sloan and Looser individually recalled art glass installations that each had found particularly outstanding—the Robbins Chapel at Baylor University and the Alice Millar Chapel at Northwestern University. The same firm, Willet Hauser Architectural Glass, was found to have been the artist for both designs—some fifty

196 Charles Ward, "HBU celebrates opening of new performance facilities," *Houston Chronicle,* 10 Oct. 2007, Star sec., p. 1, two-star ed.

197 "Gifts of Music and Light," *HBU News,* Summer 2009, 7. The chancel window "reflected the phenomenon of light as presented in Genesis."

198 Houston Baptist University, "Smith Organ Dedication and Inaugural Concert," Dedication Program, 26 Sept. 2009.

199 "Smith Organ Dedication," *HBU News,* Spring 2010, 22-23. Photos.

200 "J. S. Bach's Bible on Exhibit," *Dunham Bible Museum News,* Fall 2009, p. 1.

201 "Belin Chapel, Houston Baptist University, Houston, Texas, Létourneau Pipe Organs," *The American Organist,* May, 2010, 40-42. Photos.

years apart. The work of Crosby Willet was honored across the nation from Houston's St. Martin's Episcopal Church to the National Cathedral in Washington, D. C. Willet was intrigued by the design potential of the clerestory and the chancel cross in Belin Chapel and made several trips to Houston to refine his work. Sloan, Looser, and Willet developed designs for a large chancel window to focus on the cross and for side windows representing Old and New Testament events. The Hamill Foundation provided a gift to move the project forward.[202] Ultimately, Dr. Bruce and Mary Ann Belin assisted in underwriting the installation of the chancel window that was coordinated with the installation of the Smith organ. For the future, the opportunity remained to complete the stained glass installation in the clerestory and transept windows.

§

Faculty devotion to mentoring students had long been a quality of the HBU campus. One of the more dramatic stories of devotion to students could be found in the life of Texas Artist of the Year, Virgil Grotfeldt. Grotfeldt was an internationally known and exhibited artist who joined the HBU faculty in 2001.[203] Grotfeldt's life and commitment to students was made more intense by his personal battle with brain cancer since 1993.[204] In February 2009, Virgil Grotfeldt lost his battle with the disease.[205] His last exhibit, entitled 274296, was a series of sixteen "exquisite oil paintings executed on scans of Grotfeldt's brain."[206] The exhibit title was Grotfeldt's patient number at M. D. Anderson Hospital. Writer Douglas Brit reflected, "It will be a long time before you have as profound an encounter with art as the one you have here. The paintings don't need sympathy. They stand their ground as top-tier, powerfully intimate works."[207] Grotfeldt's memorial service overflowed the Belin Chapel with friends from across the nation. His art was featured on the cover of the *Houston Chronicle's Zest Magazine* to introduce art highlights of 2009.[208]

---

202 "Hamill Foundation helps HBU move forward with Belin Chapel master plan," *Advancing the Vision,* Dec. 2008.

203 "Faculty, students shine on local and international art scene," *HBU News,* Fall 2007, 30.

204 Kristen Crawley, "Portrait of a Painter," *The Collegian,* 9 Oct. 2008, pp. 10-11.

205 Douglas Britt, "Acclaimed Houston artist dies of cancer," *Houston Chronicle,* 25 Feb. 2009.

206 Douglas Britt, "Artist leaves intimate legacy," *Houston Chronicle,* 28 Feb. 2009, Star sec., p. 3, three-star ed.

207 Ibid.

208 Douglas Britt, "Art highlights in 2009," *Houston Chronicle,* 24 Dec. 2009, Zest Magazine, cover.

The University also lost retired College of Education Professor Dr. Ruth DeHart,[209] former music faculty member and New York City Opera soprano Norma Newton Simmons,[210] and retired Professor of Finance Dr. Robert C. Bush.[211] Don McMillian—University Founder, President's Council member, and donor—died in October. McMillian and his wife, trustee and Guild President Colletta Ray McMillian, were the donors of the Ray Endowed Chair in Humanities.[212] The University also lost Prince-Chavanne Professorship donor Harry Chavanne. In the months following his death, it was announced that a Prince-Chavanne Chair in Christian Business Ethics had been created by his estate.[213] The Chavanne's daughter, Claire Turner, was a past member of the Board of Trustees.

The 99-year old Nell Smith molded and shaped the University over the years of her life with an energy and determination matched by few others in institutional history. Hers was a focused, selective engagement in areas of development that struck her interest. Her style was intensely personal, direct, unyielding, persuasive, yet affable and celebratory. A twinkle in her eye characterized her every pursuit. Her earliest roots in institutional history sprang from her membership in the E. P. West Bible Study Class taught by Dr. Hinton. Smith's enthusiasm and example sparked the contributions by other members of the class to endowed scholarships, membership in development organizations, and active participation in direct contribution to the University. The remarkable attribute of her leadership was that she accomplished her agenda in most cases without benefit of elective office. "Nell" influenced outcomes.

Nell Smith was a charter member of Mrs. Hinton's Ladies Auxiliary, a founding member of Dr. Hinton's President's Advisors, a President of The Guild, and a member of the American Museum Society. She was honored with the Milton Cross Outstanding Volunteer Award and the Spirit of Excellence Award.[214] She was the donor of an Endowed Academic Scholarship honoring her parents, furnished a classroom in the Hinton Center, and established the annual Dr. Larry D. Smith Award for Teaching Excellence in honor of her son.[215] In later years, her effective-

209 "In Memoriam: Dr. Ruth DeHart," *HBU News,* Fall 2008, 50.
210 "Norma Newton," *Evening Times,* 7 Nov. 2008, (accessed Apr. 10, 2010).
211 "Dr. Robert C. Bush," *HBU News,* Spring 2010, 43.
212 "In Memoriam: Don F. McMillian," *HBU News,* Fall 2008, 50.
213 (Veronica Cantu to Dr. Don Looser, Apr. 12, 2010).
214 "Nell Anderson Smith," *Alvin Sun-Advertiser,* 2 Dec. 2009 (accessed Apr. 13, 2010).
215 "Smith Donation to Benefit Faculty," *HBU News,* Dec. 2003, 23.

ness from her wheelchair seemed undiminished; she rarely missed a University event. Her death in November 2009 marked the passage of a kind of unrelenting zeal that so characterized the early College pioneers.

One of the last of the University Founders passed away in August 2010. Jake Kamin was one of the first laymen involved in the quest to establish Houston Baptist College in 1957. Kamin had partnered with Stewart Morris and Don McGregor to establish the Union Baptist Association Property Committee with its proud record of financial contribution to the new institution. Kamin was a member of the first Board of Trustees appointed in 1960 and was instrumental in the financial management of the young College in the 1960s. With Kamin's death, Dr. Stewart Morris became the sole Founder still living.

§

President Sloan returned to the classroom for the spring semester 2010; *The Collegian* headlined, "One class students won't skip."[216] Dr. Sloan elected a course on the book of Revelation for his first return to the classroom since 2002. Like President Hodo before him, Sloan regarded teaching as one of his gifts and most enjoyable responsibilities.

In January 2010, Dr. Sloan announced the appointment of Kimberly Gaynor as the Vice President for University Communications. Sloan described institutional branding as one of Gaynor's areas of expertise. As the University marked the celebration of the fiftieth anniversary of its founding, the adoption of the "Ten Pillars of Faith and Reason," and the reorganization of its faculty and curriculum, Gaynor expressed his commitment to "synthesize the President's vision."[217] Gaynor had guided Baylor University's "Above and Beyond" capital campaign.[218] Gaynor soon announced the launch of a Brand Awareness and Reputation Study for HBU.[219] The research project was designed to measure and explore the perceptions, awareness, and reputation of the University among key external and internal audiences.

In recognition of the fiftieth anniversary of the University's founding, The Guild announced a gift of $50,000 in January to establish an

216 Justin Schneewind, "One class students won't skip," *The Collegian,* 28 Jan. 2010, p. 1.

217 Nathan Cadis, "Ten Pillars shepherds marketing campaign," *The Collegian,* 28 Jan. 2010, p. 1.

218 "Dr. Sloan appoints Kimberly Gaynor as VP for University Communications," *Advancing the Vision,* Jan. 2010.

219 "HBU to conduct Brand Awareness and Reputation Study," *Advancing the Vision,* May 2010.

Institute in Christian Family Studies. President Kandy Brittain explained the purpose of the Institute was "to provide scholars, ministers, students, parents, and other policy-making and community leaders a place to come together to support Christian understanding regarding the traditional family."[220] The inaugural speaker for the Institute was Dr. Jennifer Roback Morse, founder of the Ruth Institute, a project of the National Organization for Marriage.[221] This gift along with current annual scholarship contribution from The Guild brought the organization's lifetime giving through 2009-2010 to $1,214,161.[222]

The Hamill Foundation also announced an additional gift to the University to "support key nursing and student life initiatives."[223] The grant was made to support updating the skills development lab in the School of Nursing and Allied Health and to create new intramural fields.[224] The Hamill grant was to be supplemented in nursing with a $94,000 grant from the Health Resources and Services Administration.[225]

"In continuation of its tradition of supporting HBU at pivotal moments in its history,"[226] the Cullen Trust for Higher Education also announced a $1,500,000 gift to help the University upgrade its information technology and communication infrastructure." The grant was provided to help insure that HBU students continue to have access to cutting–edge, web-based educational resources. The grant continued a long history of support from the several Cullen foundations and addressed a critical area of need to enhance the University's growth and capacity for excellence.

The Morris Cultural Arts Center functioned as a community resource at a level far beyond even the dreams of its planners. During 2009-2010, the Morris Center hosted events representing Chinese, Persian, Hungarian, Russian, Peruvian, and Columbian cultures.[227] The spring hosted a series of campus events, but boasted a crowded calendar of community lectures, dance recitals, high school concerts and graduations, and concluded the season with the Houston Masterworks Chorus and Orchestra presenting

---

220 Erica Drexler, "Donation launches institute," *The Collegian,* 28 Jan. 2010, p. 6.

221 "Guild Institutes inaugural lecture to feature Ruth Institute founder, president," *Advancing the Vision,* Mar. 2010.

222 (Loree Watson to Dr. Don Looser, June 2, 2010).

223 "Hamill Foundation grant," *Advancing the Vision,* Feb. 2010.

224 Daniel Cadis, "Grants aim to upgrade lab," *The Collegian,* 11 Feb. 2010, p. 10.

225 Ibid.

226 "Cullen Trust grant to help fund upgrades to IT, communications infrastructure," *Advancing the Vision,* May 2010.

227 (Candace Desrosiers to Dr. Don Looser, May 25, 2010).

the Brahms' *Requiem*. Promotion for the next season's events included a reference to "the acoustically stunning Belin Chapel."[228]

In the spring, William and Sharon Morris conveyed to the University the 17th century masterpiece, *Saint John the Baptist in the Wilderness,* by the Flemish Baroque artist Anthony Van Dyck (1599-1641). The Morrises expressed that the painting, installed in the Belin Chapel, was given with the wish that the masterpiece would "touch the lives of people who see it and promote more meditation on God's Word." At a dedication ceremony in June, Dr. Sloan responded, "We are honored that William and Sharon have entrusted the University with this very special gift. . . . In this magnificent work, we witness a painting whose sublime rendering of the human capacity for sacrifice and resolution is a testament to the Morrises and their faith, as well as the faith that underpins our mission and work at HBU."[229]

On May 25, present and past members of the Board of Trustees and their spouses responded to the invitation of President and Mrs. Sloan to gather for a dinner in their honor. The evening marked a special opportunity for past and current leaders to celebrate both HBU's 50th year and its vision for the future. Dr. Sloan presented a historical overview, "From Our Founding to the Future" and introduced the debut of a video presentation by Clay Porter showcasing *The Ten Pillars: Faith and Reason in a Great City.*[230]

§

With the achievement of the fiftieth anniversary of its chartering, Houston Baptist University looked forward to the realization of ever-expanding strategic goals and the fulfillment of the dreams of its founders. Each of the University's three Presidents marked the institution by his own brand of leadership. The chapters of the Hinton and Hodo years can be seen and evaluated with the benefits of time and perspective. With the University's fiftieth anniversary, the Sloan administration was still in its relative youth.

The first four years in office for each of the University's three Presidents marked periods of difficulty. For Dr. Hinton, the challenge was the extraordinary stress of gaining momentum and surmounting waves of unforeseen

---

228 Houston Masterworks Chorus performance program, 15 May, 2010.
229 "HBU unveils Van Dyck masterpiece, pays tribute to Morrises," *Advancing the Vision,* June 2010.
230 Ibid.

threats to institutional survival. For Dr. Hodo, the assignment of restoring financial health to the institution made his early administration the most difficult years of his career. For Dr. Sloan, the reorganization of the University and the refocusing of priorities combined with the catastrophic damage from Hurricane Ike and a world economic crisis resulted in the need for unprecedented innovation and malleability. Yet in each era, peaks of achievement emerged that belied the valleys of difficulty.

The *Houston Chronicle* headline from September 2007 had prophesied, "President Sloan aims to transform the University."[231] The Sloan years witnessed the opening of the Morris Cultural Arts Center, the Belin Chapel, and University Museums. To the campus were also added the spiritual and aesthetic contributions of the Williams Fountain and Lawrence Park. A master plan of campus development and a study of infrastructure needs were completed. Student enrollments significantly increased, and numerous student amenities were added across the campus that included enhancements to the Baugh and Glasscock Centers. The University returned to the NCAA. The Lake House Residence and the University Academic Center marked new peaks of excellence for campus facilities. The establishment of an Honors College and the drafting of the "Ten Pillars of Faith" charted the University's path for the future. The College of Continuing Studies re-established this role of service to the community, and Smith College of General Studies returned to its roots as a core of requisite disciplines.

Significant organizational, curricular, and personnel changes were affected. With change inevitably came anxiety. Financial pressures continued to shadow the University's operation. Despite the realization that "the replacement of the central location for student interaction (was) of critical importance to the renewal of the campus,"[232] the loss of the use of the M. D. Anderson Student Center was a blow to the energy and function of the campus community. As the 2009-10 academic year drew to a close, the future of the Brown Academic Center was unknown.[233]

§

---

231 Matthew Tresaugue, "Campus Moving Forward," *Houston Chronicle,* 2 Sept. 2007, p. 1.

232 "Houston Endowment awards HBU "$850,000 grant," *HBU News,* Fall 2008, 33.

233 Ashley Marchand, "Brown Complex future undecided," *The Collegian,* 23 Oct. 2008, p. 2.

President Sloan established a task force to plan and guide the University's 2010 celebration of the fifty years since its chartering.[234] A large committee composed of representatives from alumni, students, faculty, staff, affinity organizations, friends, and community leaders was formed to guide preparations for the fiftieth anniversary celebrations.[235] The University commissioned a history by Dr. Don Looser of the University's first fifty years that was scheduled to be released in the fall 2010. Homecoming and the return of the Spirit of Excellence Dinner in November 2010 would mark the first of the fiftieth anniversary celebrations.[236] Former President George W. Bush accepted the University's invitation to be keynote speaker for this gala evening.[237]

Houston Baptist University in 2010 was on a new course. There was no question that Dr. Sloan had been given a mandate for change upon his coming. There was no question that the same Preamble that was a light unto the path in 1960 still remained illuminating in 2010. From its inception, the chronicle of Houston Baptist University has been one of providential blessing and extraordinary human contribution. This, then, is the history that time has recorded.

This is a story written as much by the lives of people
as by the events they shared. It is a story of faith;
it is a story of confidence; it is a story of inspiration;
it is a story of courage. More than anything else,
it is a story of Providence.

234 "HBU celebrates 50th anniversary," *Advancing the Vision,* Apr. 2010.
235 "HBU celebrates 50th anniversary," *News at HBU,* 16 Mar. 2010, (accessed Apr. 13, 2010).
236 Dr. Robert B. Sloan, Jr., "Message from the President," *HBU News,* Spring 2010, 2.
237 "University plans 50th anniversary," *HBU News,* Spring 2010, 5.

EPILOGUE

"The past is never dead. It's not even past."

Requiem for a Nun, Act I, Scene III
—William Faulkner

Through the years, as HBU and I have grown older together, colleagues have urged the writing of a history of the University. Because I came to HBC in 1964 as one of its youngest faculty members, there always seemed to be many older, wiser, more knowledgeable colleagues for such an assignment. However, as the years passed without others taking up the gauntlet, the responsibility of penning this remarkable chapter in history seemed naturally to be swinging my way. In the 1990s, Dr. Hodo and I began to talk seriously about the institutional imperative that such history be preserved while still at the finger tips. As we moved nearer the time when our own days at HBU would be behind us, Dr. Hodo and I prepared a letter of proposal for the consideration of the unknown president who would follow. The letter indicated my interest in the project and Dr. Hodo's support of its importance. Upon his coming as the University's third president, Dr. Sloan was generous in his adoption of the book project and his encouragement of it. He is the one who has made it possible for me to take on the reality of the task. I am grateful to him for the intensity of his interest and the physical support he has provided.

§

The book has taken longer to compile than I anticipated. The research has taken nearly thirty-six months of concentrated effort. Like many compelling projects, the book has consumed full weeks of work on the campus and evenings and weekends at home. Once begun, it became difficult to put out of mind. In the process, exhaustive review of related serial records has been made. The research included every edition of the *Houston Baptist College News*, the *HBU News, The Collegian,* and many various shorter term publications from a variety of offices within the

499

University. Additionally, this study has examined significant primary source materials including all the minutes of the meetings of the Board of Trustees, the faculty, the Faculty Assembly, and various governing committees, many of which have never been previously available. Online digital resources have enabled newspaper and periodical research including a surprising number of reports from geographically distant locales. All the notes taken on these fifty years have been recorded in digital spreadsheet format that will be available for the daily use of the University staff and future researchers.

The research has included correspondence and personal records dating from the 1950s which have been made available. Dialogue was initiated with a number of alumni, former trustees, and colleagues to ask help, seek clarification, and solicit material from their personal files. Telephone conversations have proven a particular delight; this interaction with former associates has been a most pleasant, personal experience. Many friends of the University have given cherished personal memorabilia. All material used in the preparation of this book that does not reside under the care of a designated University official will be placed in a newly-created University Archive in the Moody Library. Providentially, the threat from Hurricane Ike for the potential loss of historical files, publications, and materials was largely unrealized. There are some related historical records—particularly photographs—that were ferreted away to off-campus storage following the storm where they remain and have not been available for this project.

§

There are choices to be made by the author in such a massive project as this. I have chosen to write the history as full of citation references as possible in order to aid the future researcher and to present virtually all the sources of information I have been able to discover. I encourage your reading the footnotes. After reading the book, I urge you to re-read the footnotes from beginning to end for content synthesis and as a reminder of the wealth of historical resource.

Another author's choice was how to deal with oneself as a historical figure. My choice has been to attribute my personal role only when leaving it out would result in an incomplete or inaccurate record. It is a dilemma. I feel content with my decision.

The book is not a novel; the story is not of my creation. Along the path, there have been the sweet and sour, the "near misses," and an abundance of brilliant successes. In the midst of providential blessing, there have also been difficult days for the University. Mistakes and unwise choices were sometimes made along the way. I have tried to be scrupulously fair, balanced, and ultimately positive in the telling. To our delight, there have been colorful people, eccentric habits, and humorous events. More than all else, there have been generational waves of extraordinary people in all roles drawn to the dream for a university.

An early realization in my research was that people who shared the campus at the same time—but in different roles—experienced dramatically different perspectives of the same events and issues. All participants—students and parents, faculty and staff, administrators, trustees, donors, and the public—had varying knowledge about the actual experience of others. It soon became apparent that an assignment for this volume was the presentation of the varying perspectives by the many constituencies. In so doing, my hope is that readers who helped chart this history will discover the alternate paths taken by others who shared the campus at the same time.

The task of selecting which events and persons to include in these pages has caused more personal angst than any other issue. Clearly, because of space limitations, the names and events contained herein are representative and illustrative, not exhaustive. For purposes of comprehensive inclusion, the University's serial publications are the best sources of detail. These include *Advancing the Vision,* the several editions of the *Alumni Directory, The Binding Cord, Bulletins of Information, The Collegian, Crossroads, Flashes and Dashes, HBColleague, HBUpbeat, Houston Baptist (College) University News, Orange and Blue, Ornogah,* annual editions of the *University Personnel Directory, Points of Interest, The Raft, Ruminations, The Scene, Shank's Mare,* and *Sometimes.* I am particularly indebted and grateful to the staffs of these publications for their generous support of this project.

§

Many friends and colleagues have been generous in their assistance with this work. Among those who shared from their personal memorabilia are Tim Austin '68, Judy Babb, Frances Curtis, Dr. Honora Lynch Finkelstein, Dr. Wallace Hooker, Dr. Lois Lawrence, Howard Lee, Jr., Dr.

Lou Markos, Jane Jester Marmion '68, Richard Meek '71, Dr. Bill Myers '67, Joella Morris, Bill Roberts '70, and Kathleen Strom '87. Many others have shared of their own recollections and memories. These friends of the University were invaluable to enrich the narrative and understand the historical context. These have directly included Dr. Leigh Bishop '75, Merrill Blackburn '68, Tucker Bonner '69, Bill Chambles '68, Jim Cornell, Esq. '75, Dr. Gary Dill '69, Dennis Douglas '70, J. Eige '67, Dr. Sheila Ford, Bonnie Bates Fowler '67, Dr. John Grauke '68, Dr. John Hoskins, Dr. Frank Josserand, John Lewis '74, Elaine Lowry McMullen '67, Mary Beth Morgan '77, Dr. Tim Oesch '76, Dr. Robert Parker, Lillian Turner Porter , Dr. Doug Spence '80, Suzanne Clark Webb '67, Jeffrey Wells, and Michael Wood '70.

Additionally, there are colleagues who maintain historical records related to the University who have responded to inquiries with timeliness, enthusiasm, and professionalism. Such colleagues are Vivian Camacho '91, Veronica Cantu, Linda Wigger Clark '87, Jacque Cottrell, Candace Adams Desrosiers '94, Nan Donahoe, Patricia Evans, Judy Bennatte Ferguson '67, International Association of Baptist Colleges and Universities Director Tim Fields, Dr. Rhonda Furr, Dr. Jackie Horn, Justin Lacey, Hugh McClung, UBA historian Royce Measures, Martha Morrow, Laurel Motal, Ann Noble, Rick Ogden '98, Clay Porter, Alan Presley, Dr. Phil Rhodes, Dean Riley, Dr. Alice Rowlands, Sharon Saunders, Dr. Diana Severance, Michael Tims, Stephanie Walker, Loree Watson '80, and Sharon Wiser. Other associates who have kept the physical and technological process of researching and writing on a steady pace have included Melanie Barber, Linda Clark, Joanna Donovan and Classic FM London, Edith Gabbard, Karen Hanschke, Miguel Morales, Bill Sisk, and Stephanie Walker.

Linda Clark in particular has assisted wisely and well in much of the University's administration since 1990. It was my daily good fortune to enjoy her intellect, her wit, and her friendship over the last twenty years. Without her skills and devotion in remarkable complement to mine, this history might have been dramatically different. We shared our love for the University and dedicated our efforts to its behalf. Linda has guided the University's academic management from days of paper trails into the digital age with tireless commitment to successful outcomes. She remains the fount of knowledge and information for the campus. For the opportunity to work together, I shall always be grateful.

Finally, there are friends who have given personal time to proof text and offer correction, editorial comment, and suggested content. Their work has refined, corrected, redirected, clarified, and tightened the text. I am grateful for the friendship and expertise of Dr. Carol Ann Bonds, Dr. Don Byrnes, Ron Cottrell, Dr. Rhonda Furr, Dr. Robert Linder, Dr. Diane Lovell, Jane Marmion, Dr. Jon Suter, and Dr. James Taylor. Above all, however, have been the professional editorial assistance and the daily personal support and encouragement of my wife Elsa Jean who has shared all these years with me at HBU. As a former faculty member, it is she who has strengthened this work so greatly by her gifts which have been so freely given.

There is the realization that despite best efforts, inevitably there are omissions and errors. For these, I apologize. Countless hours have been spent to assure the reduction of such incidence. In this regard, the encouragement of Dr. Stewart Morris has been immeasurable. As a wise friend, he advised, "Write the history the way you see it. Anyone who doesn't agree can write his own."

§

What began as a professional writing assignment soon became personal reward—greater even than anticipated. The flood of memories triggered by the research has been a gratifying means of reconstructing my personal history as well as bringing my formal association with the University to a point of healthy closure. The experience of learning the HBU story serves as a constant reminder of God's overwhelming grace and power in the face of human adversity.

William Faulkner's reminder to us helps us view our history as a part of our present. What have I learned? God needs no man to accomplish His will, but uses all who are willing to be instruments of His purpose.

Don Looser
Vice President Emeritus
June, 2010

APPENDIX A

ALUMNI AWARD HONOREES

Anderson '68	Don	Outstanding	1973
Bailey '68	Avic Croom	Meritorious	1997
Bailey '69	Rick	Distinguished	1995
Bailey '69	Rick	Meritorious	1999
Barlow, Jr. '72	Dr. Herman	Outstanding	1975
Beauchamp, MS '87	Bob	Distinguished	2001
Berry III '72	Joel H.	Meritorious	1992
Bonds '68	Carol Ann Halliday	Distinguished	1992
Bonner '68	Kay Kepler	Distinguished	1992
Bonner, Jr. '69	Thomas Tucker	Outstanding	1979
Brady, Jr. '71	Dr. John I.	Distinguished	1992
Braun '80	Steve L.	Meritorious	1994
Bui '00	Francis	Meritorious	2008
Byrnes	Dr. Don R.	Hallmark	2000
Camacho '91	Vivian	Meritorious	2002
Cox '81	Dr. Barbara Taylor	Distinguished	1993
Cox, Jr. '81	Ray LaDon	Meritorious	1995
Curtis	Frances	Hallmark	2004
Daniel '73	Art	Outstanding	1976
Denison '82	Dr. Mark	Distinguished	1999
Denison '80	Dr. James C.	Distinguished	1993
Denson '74	Raymond	Distinguished	2004
Desrosiers '94	Candace Adams	Meritorious	2003
Eckermann '68	Marsha Mathis	Distinguished	1991
Elkins '70	Dr. David	Outstanding	1981
Ellis '68	C. Pat	Outstanding	1977
Ellis '77	Dr. Ronald L.	Distinguished	2000
Fabianki '71	Rosalyn Beavers	Outstanding	1978
Ferguson '68	Dr. Jennifer Berry	Meritorious	1996
Garbs '76, MBA '83	Randy	Meritorious	1990
Garcia	Job	Hallmark	2006
Gillespie '67	Dr. John	Outstanding	1982
Harkins '73	Dr. Elizabeth Ann	Distinguished	1997
Hodges '94, MEd '00	Monica McGaughey	Meritorious	2004
Hodo	Dr. E. D.	Hallmark	2001
Hudson '75	Richard L.	Distinguished	1991
Hudson '75	Richard L.	Meritorious	1998
Jachmich '69	Manfred	Distinguished	2003
Jensen '78	Dr. Mark E.	Meritorious	1992
Kahleh '84	Saliem Robeen	Meritorious	1997

Laird '87	Rosemary	Meritorious	1999
Lang III '75	Arthur "Chuck"	Meritorious	1996
LaRue '94	Rita	Meritorious	1998
Lavender EMBA '92	Carol	Meritorious	2007
Lewis '88	Terry	Meritorious	2009
Looser	Dr. Don	Hallmark	2007
Marmion '68	Jane Jester	Meritorious	1992
Martin	Anthony G.	Hallmark	2002
Mayfield '69	Kathryn	Outstanding	1980
McGee, Jr. '89	Dr. Cliff	Distinguished	2002
Montgomerie '87	Colin S.	Distinguished	1998
Moore '74, MBA '81	Pamela K.	Distinguished	1994
Neben '89	Catherine	Meritorious	2005
Nelson '90	Dawn	Meritorious	1994
Parker '82	R. Kay	Meritorious	1990
Pete-Jones EMBA '92	Derenda	Meritorious	2007
Pickett '80	Stephen	Distinguished	1994
Platt '83	Karen Thomas	Meritorious	1991
Porter	Clay	Hallmark	2008
Powell '76	Robert M.	Meritorious	2000
Pyburn '94	Judy Vogel	Meritorious	2001
Raley '71	Dr. Marvin R.	Outstanding	1982
Reid '93	Charles	Distinguished	2005
Reinfeldt '84	Mike	Distinguished	2008
Roff '69	Dr. Linda Fix	Distinguished	1995
Rogers	Kenneth W.	Hallmark	2003
Ruddell	Dr. Larry	Hallmark	2005
Saunders	Sharon	Hallmark	2001
Shanks '82	Lois	Meritorious	1993
Simon '76	Lisa Morris	Distinguished	1999
Skaggs '73	James M.	Meritorious	1993
Sloan	Sue	Hallmark	2008
Sorrels '84	Randy	Distinguished	2009
Stone MLA '94	Ron	Distinguished	1996
Stutts '82	David	Meritorious	1991
Swartz '89	Amy Butler	Meritorious	1995
Tellepsen MBA '99	Tadd	Meritorious	2006
Thompson '94	Carlton	Distinguished	2007
Wallis '81, MEd '85	Dr. Judith	Distinguished	1998
Wescott	Dr. Shari	Hallmark	2009
Wheeler '75	Dr. Thomas	Distinguished	1997
Wood '80	Elaine	Distinguished	1996
Woodall '84	Ronald "Steve"	Distinguished	1990
Young '84	Edwin B.	Distinguished	2006
Yuill '71	Dr. Nancy	Distinguished	1990

APPENDIX B

BOARD OF TRUSTEES CHAIRS

APPENDIX C

FACULTY ASSEMBLY CHAIRS

1968-69	Parker	Robert	First Chair of Faculty Assembly; Music
1969-70	Reynolds	Jerry	Speech
1970-71	Hooker	Wallace	English
1971-72	Reynolds	Jerry	Speech
1972-73	Byrnes	Don	History
1973-74	Cain	Glen T.	Christianity
1974-75	Donohue	Steve	Psychology
1975-76	West	Bill	Christianity; partial year
1975-76	Peavy	Elysee	English; serving as Acting President
1976-77	Linder	Robert	Music
1977-78	Taylor	James	Speech
1978-79	Boyd	Newell	History
1979-80	Taylor	James	Speech
1980-81	Smith	Gerda	Social Work
1981-82	Riley	James	Christianity
1982-83	Hooker	John	Biology
1983-84	Webb	Marion	Spanish
1984-85	Sartain	Robert	Mathematics
1985-86	Riley	James	Christianity
1986-87	Riley	James	Christianity
1987-88	Taylor	James	Speech
1988-89	Smith	Gerda	Social Work
1989-90	Boyd	Newell	History
1990-91	Shields	Lou	Education
1991-92	Fleming	Rex	Speech
1992-93	Hansen	John	Computer Information Systems
1993-94	Zwick	Robert	Music
1994-95	Bohac	Darlene	Accounting
1995-96	Horn	Jackie	Biology
1996-97	Caligur	Matt	Communications
1997-98	Woods	Treacy	Chemistry
1998-99	Furr	Rhonda	Music
1999-00	Lumpkin	Walter	Christianity
2000-01	Suter	Jon	Library
2001-02	Quiett	Jeffrey	Psychology
2002-03	Hammons	Chris	Political Science
2003-04	Wilson	Randy	Sociology
2004-05	Whaley	Brenda	Biology
2005-06	Whaley	Brenda	Biology
2006-07	Michalos	Constantina	English

Faculty Assembly Chairs (cont.)

2007-08	Wiseman	Melissa	Economics
2008-09	Horn	Jackie	Biology
2009-10	Wilson	Dawn	Education
2010-11	Fabre	Taiye	Chemistry

APPENDIX D

FOUNDERS OF THE UNIVERSITY

Dr. Rex G. Baker, Sr.

Keith Beeman

Sen. Lloyd Bentsen, Jr.

W. D. Black, Jr.

Stewart Boyle

Frank Breaker

Lester Cain

Cecil Cook

Dr. Ed Crocker

Tom S. Gandy

R. Graham Jackson

Jake Kamin

Dr. Howard C. Lee, Sr.

Ralph Lee

Milton McGinty

Don McGregor

Don McMillian

Dr. Stewart Morris

Freland Murphy

Robert Ray

Newton Rayzor

Joseph Russell

O. R. Smith

John Wooters

W. M. Wright

APPENDIX E

GOOLSBY OUTSTANDING TEACHING AWARDS

Outstanding Teaching Award until 1982; thereafter called the Goolsby Award.

Adcock	David	Opal Goolsby Outstanding Teaching Award	2007
Alexander	Dr. John	Opal Goolsby Outstanding Teaching Award	1990
Berry '89	Debra	Opal Goolsby Outstanding Teaching Award	2005
Blair	Dr. Joe	Opal Goolsby Outstanding Teaching Award	2001
Boyd	Dr. Newell	Outstanding Teaching Award	1976
Boyce	Dr. Beth	Opal Goolsby Outstanding Teaching Award	1994
Brownlee	Dr. Avin	Outstanding Teaching Award	1978
Brownlee	Dr. Avin	Opal Goolsby Outstanding Teaching Award	1982
Brownlee	Dr. Avin	Opal Goolsby Outstanding Teaching Award	1988
Brownlee	Dr. Avin	Opal Goolsby Outstanding Teaching Award	1998
Bussell	Dr. Valerie	Opal Goolsby Outstanding Teaching Award	2008
Byrnes	Dr. Don	Outstanding Teaching Award	1972
Capes	Dr. David	Opal Goolsby Outstanding Teaching Award	1996
Capes	Dr. David	Opal Goolsby Outstanding Teaching Award	2005
Collins	Dr. A. O.	Outstanding Teaching Award	1972
Collins	Dr. A. O.	Outstanding Teaching Award	1981
Colvin	Dr. Marilyn	Opal Goolsby Outstanding Teaching Award	1983
Cook	Dr. Susan	Opal Goolsby Outstanding Teaching Award	2000
Creech '74	Dr. Robert	Opal Goolsby Outstanding Teaching Award	1985
Denham	Dr. Rick	Outstanding Teaching Award	1975
Denham	Dr. Rick	Outstanding Teaching Award	1980
Dodson	Dr. Daton	Outstanding Teaching Award	1973
Dodson	Dr. Daton	Opal Goolsby Outstanding Teaching Award	1991
Dominguez	Patricia	Opal Goolsby Outstanding Teaching Award	1992
Donohue	Dr. Stephen	Outstanding Teaching Award	1972
Donohue	Dr. Stephen	Outstanding Teaching Award	1974
Estrada	Dr. Miguel	Opal Goolsby Outstanding Teaching Award	2008
Fan	Dr. Joyce	Outstanding Teaching Award	1980
Fleming	Dr. Rex	Opal Goolsby Outstanding Teaching Award	1993
Freeman	Dr. Curtis	Opal Goolsby Outstanding Teaching Award	1994
Furr	Dr. Rhonda	Opal Goolsby Outstanding Teaching Award	1995
Goolsby	Opal	Outstanding Teaching Award	1976
Hammons	Dr. Chris	Opal Goolsby Outstanding Teaching Award	2003
Hatchett	Dr. Randy	Opal Goolsby Outstanding Teaching Award	2000
Homann	Dr. Ron	Opal Goolsby Outstanding Teaching Award	2009
Horn	Dr. Jackie	Opal Goolsby Outstanding Teaching Award	1999
Johnson	Grace	Outstanding Teaching Award	1975
Knapp, MS '00	Alexis	Opal Goolsby Outstanding Teaching Award	2007
Leath	Dr. Paul Brooks	Outstanding Teaching Award	1981
Leath	Dr. Paul Brooks	Opal Goolsby Outstanding Teaching Award	1986

Goolsby Outstanding Teaching Awards (cont.)

Maczali	Monteen	Outstanding Teaching Award	1977
Maddox	Dr. Martha	Opal Goolsby Outstanding Teaching Award	2006
Markos	Dr. Louis	Opal Goolsby Outstanding Teaching Award	1992
Marley	Bob	Opal Goolsby Outstanding Teaching Award	1987
Michalos	Dr. Constantina	Opal Goolsby Outstanding Teaching Award	2001
Miller	Marianne	Outstanding Teaching Award	1971
Nimmons	Dr. Phyllis	Outstanding Teaching Award	1973
Nimmons	Dr. Phyllis	Opal Goolsby Outstanding Teaching Award	1988
Owen	Dr. Ann	Opal Goolsby Outstanding Teaching Award	1998
Pando	Dr. Patricia	Opal Goolsby Outstanding Teaching Award	1985
Parker	Dr. Robert	Outstanding Teaching Award	1968
Peavy	Dr. Elysee	Outstanding Teaching Award	1971
Peavy	Dr. Elysee	Outstanding Teaching Award	1975
Peavy	Dr. Elysee	Outstanding Teaching Award	1978
Peavy	Dr. Elysee	Opal Goolsby Outstanding Teaching Award	1984
Phillips	Dr. Sally	Opal Goolsby Outstanding Teaching Award	1991
Pyle	Dr. Ernie	Opal Goolsby Outstanding Teaching Award	1997
Reynolds	Dr. Jerry	Outstanding Teaching Award	1969
Roff '69	Dr. Linda	Opal Goolsby Outstanding Teaching Award	1997
Rowlands	Dr. Alice	Opal Goolsby Outstanding Teaching Award	1993
Salinas	Dr. Chris	Opal Goolsby Outstanding Teaching Award	2006
Sibley	Dr. Marilyn	Outstanding Teaching Award	1971
Sibley	Dr. Marilyn	Outstanding Teaching Award	1974
Simmons	Cheryl	Outstanding Teaching Award	1976
Smith	Dr. Gerda	Outstanding Teaching Award	1978
Strittmatter	Ruth	Outstanding Teaching Award	1981
Strittmatter	Ruth	Opal Goolsby Outstanding Teaching Award	1990
Taylor	Dr. James	Outstanding Teaching Award	1977
Taylor	Dr. James	Opal Goolsby Outstanding Teaching Award	1989
Taylor	Dr. James	Opal Goolsby Outstanding Teaching Award	1999
Towery	Dr. Bobby	Opal Goolsby Outstanding Teaching Award	2004
Trevino	Dr. Saul	Opal Goolsby Outstanding Teaching Award	2010
Tsao	Dr. James	Outstanding Teaching Award	1979
Tsao	Dr. James	Opal Goolsby Outstanding Teaching Award	1983
Tucker	Dr. Brooke	Outstanding Teaching Award	1980
Tucker	Dr. Brooke	Opal Goolsby Outstanding Teaching Award	1986
Tucker	Dr. Brooke	Opal Goolsby Outstanding Teaching Award	1989
Ulmer	Dr. James	Opal Goolsby Outstanding Teaching Award	1995
Webb	Dr. Marion	Outstanding Teaching Award	1974
Webb	Dr. Marion	Opal Goolsby Outstanding Teaching Award	1982
Webb	Dr. Marion	Opal Goolsby Outstanding Teaching Award	1987
Wentland	Dr. Stephen	Outstanding Teaching Award	1979
Wentland	Dr. Stephen	Opal Goolsby Outstanding Teaching Award	1984

Goolsby Outstanding Teaching Awards (cont.)

Whaley '79	Dr. Brenda	Opal Goolsby Outstanding Teaching Award	2002
Williamson	Dr. Ruth Ann	Opal Goolsby Outstanding Teaching Award	2004
Wilson	Susan	Outstanding Teaching Award	1979
Wilson	Dr. Randy	Opal Goolsby Outstanding Teaching Award	2002
Wiseman	Dr. Melissa	Opal Goolsby Outstanding Teaching Award	2003
Wiseman	Dr. Melissa	Opal Goolsby Outstanding Teaching Award	2009
Woods	Dr. Treacy	Opal Goolsby Outstanding Teaching Award	1996
Young	Dr. Cynthia	Outstanding Teaching Award	1973
Young	Dr. Cynthia	Outstanding Teaching Award	1977

APPENDIX F

GUILD PRESIDENTS

1975-76	Mrs. Don McMillian
1976-77	Mrs. Norris Tucker
1977-78	Mrs. Roland Burrows
1978-79	Mrs. Orval A. Brown
1979-80	Mrs. Edward Thiele
1980-81	Mrs. Bennett Coulson
1981-82	Ms. Kathryn Mayfield
1982-83	Mrs. Charles F. Cockrell
1983-84	Mrs. James A. Davis
1984-85	Mrs. Roy Olsen
1985-86	Mrs. Otis Brigman
1986-87	Dr. Kate A. Bell
1987-88	Mrs. C. V. Kern
1988-89	Mrs. Mevis Smith
1989-90	Mrs. Tracy Lawrence
1990-91	Mrs. Buddy Boek
1991-92	Mrs. Ken Wall
1992-94	Mrs. Wenzel Gandy
1994-96	Mrs. Geren Graham
1996-97	Mrs. Bob Gregg
1997-98	Mrs. Ray Dunwoody
1998-99	Mrs. Joe Reid
1999-2000	Mrs. J. Bruce Belin, Jr.
2000-2001	Mrs. David Harman
2001-2002	Mrs. Earle Higginbotham
2002-2003	Mrs. L. D. Eckermann
2003-2004	Mrs. Mack Boykin
2004-2005	Mrs. Jack Little
2005-2006	Mrs. John Lucas
2006-2007	Mrs. Emmitt Nelson
2007-2008	Mrs. Charles H. Asel, Jr.
2008-2009	Mrs. Saib Saour
2009-2010	Mrs. Bill Brittain
2010-2011	Mrs. H. Todd Corry

APPENDIX G
HONORARY DEGREE RECIPIENTS

Atkinson	James H .	Doctor of Letters	1970
Baker, Sr.	Rex G.	Doctor of Laws	1970
Beauchamp	Robert Elliot	Doctor of Humane Letters	2009
Belin, Jr.	J. Bruce	Doctor of Laws	1998
Bisagno	John	Doctor of Divinity	1974
Bradley	Robert	Doctor of Humane Letters	2008
Brigman	Otis	Doctor of Laws	1991
Caldwell	Marge	Doctor of Humane Letters	1997
Clawson	Cynthia	Doctor of Humane Letters	1995
Cooley	Dr. Denton	Doctor of Humane Letters	1986
Cross	Milton	Doctor of Laws	1991
DeLoach	Jim	Doctor of Divinity	1984
Denham	William	Doctor of Humane Letters	1988
Dillon	Ross E.	Doctor of Divinity	1970
Dunham	Archie	Doctor of Humane Letters	2003
George	Jeannette Clift	Doctor of Humane Letters	1995
Glass	Grayson	Doctor of Divinity	1979
Goolsby	Opal	Doctor of Letters	1974
Heflin	Talmadge	Doctor of Laws	2004
Herrington	Cliff	Doctor of Divinity	1979
Hinton	W. H.	Doctor of Laws	1987
Hochberg	Scott	Doctor of Laws	2004
Jordan	Arthur L.	Doctor of Divinity	1982
Ladd	Roy E.	Doctor of Divinity	1977
Lawrence	Tracy	Doctor of Humane Letters	2006
Lee, Sr.	Howard C.	Doctor of Humane Letters	1994
Linder	Robert	Doctor of Humanities	1986
Lowder	Norma	Doctor of Humane Letters	2007
Lucas	Allene	Doctor of Humane Letters	2006
Martin	O. D.	Doctor of Divinity	1988
Mathis	T. Lamar	Doctor of Divinity	1980
Moore	Gary Winston	Doctor of Humane Letters	1995
Morris, Sr.	Stewart	Doctor of Humane Letters	1975
Parker	Bobby	Doctor of Laws	1990
Patterson	LeRoy	Doctor of Divinity	1984
Ray	Gerald	Doctor of Humane Letters	1995
Robinson	Darrell	Doctor of Divinity	1982
Sewell, Jr.	Cecil O.	Doctor of Divinity	1982
Sloan	D. E.	Doctor of Divinity	1972
Sternberg	Daniel	Doctor of Humanities	1975
Stewart	Charles Allen	Doctor of Fine Arts	1972

Honorary Degree Recipients (cont.)

Strake, Jr.	George W.	Doctor of Laws	1982
Turner	Gilbert	Doctor of Laws	1977
Walker	Arthur	Doctor of Humanities	1985
Walker	Barney	Doctor of Divinity	1975
Weatherford	Carolyn	Doctor of Literature	1984
Wilford	Dan S.	Doctor of Laws	1995
Williams	A. Diane	Doctor of Humane Letters	2007
Williams	Sen. Lindon	Doctor of Laws	1980
Womack	Troy	Doctor of Letters	1988
Young	H. Edwin	Doctor of Humane Letters	1998
Zinn	Harvey	Doctor of Humane Letters	2006

APPENDIX H

HONORARY RANK RECIPIENTS

Boyce	Dr. Beth	Distinguished Professor	2005
Brupbacher	Dr. Linda	Piper Professor	2008
Collins	Dr. A. O.	Distinguished Professor	1994
Fan	Dr. Joyce	Distinguished Professor	1980
Fan	Dr. Joyce	Piper Professor	1972
Gaultney	Dr. Jerry	Professor Emeritus	1997
Hodo	Dr. E. D.	President Emeritus	2006
Huckabay	Dr. Calvin	Distinguished Professor	1975
Huckabay	Dr. Calvin	Piper Professor	1970
Leavell	Dr. Alma Malone	Distinguished Professor	1978
Linder	Dr. Robert	Distinguished Professor	1994
Looser	Dr. Don	Vice President Emeritus	2007
Martin	Dr. E. D.	Professor Emeritus	1972
Nash	Dr. Glendola	Distinguished Professor	1989
Peavy	Dr. Elysee	Professor Emeritus	1997
Phillips	Dr. Sally	Professor Emeritus	2008
Raley	Dr. Harold	Distinguished Professor	2005
Shields	Dr. Lou	Professor Emeritus	1997
Sibley	Dr. Marilyn	Piper Professor	1976
Suter	Dr. Jon	Distinguished Professor	2007
Taylor	Dr. James	Distinguished Professor	2005
Warren	Dr. Doris	Piper Professor	1991
Webb	Dr. Marion	Distinguished Professor	1991
Webb	Dr. Marion	Piper Professor	1982
Wentland	Dr. Stephen	Distinguished Professor	2006
Wescott	Dr. Shari	Professor Emeritus	2010
Williamson	Dr. James E.	Professor Emeritus	1972
Yuill	Dr. Nancy	Professor Emeritus	2009

APPENDIX I

MAYFIELD OUTSTANDING STAFF AWARDS

Borges	Eduardo	2007
Burnett	Debora	2009
Byrnes	Dr. Don	2005
Clark	Linda	2005
Curtis	Frances	2008
Evans	Patricia	2010
Ferguson	Judy	1999
Higginbotham	Elaine	2006
Kahleh	Saliem	1997
Looser	Dr. Don	2004
Martin	Anthony	2000
McClung	Hugh	2002
Melton	David	2001
Miller	Charles	2003
Noble	Ann	2007
Parker	Richard	1999
Porter	Clay	2010
Purcell	Jack	1998
Purcell	Mary	2003
Rogers	Ken	1996
Saunders	Sharon	1998
Shields	Dr. Lou	1996
Simpson	Isaac	2009
Sisk	Bill	2008
Spore	Mary Ellen	2004
Watson	Loree	2000
Wells	Maydene	2001
Wilhite	Roger	2006
Young	Dr. Cynthia	2002

APPENDIX J

AMERICAN MUSEUM SOCIETY PRESIDENTS

1965-67	Mrs. Christine Imber
1967-69	Mrs. Pat Daniel
1969-71	Mrs. Cecelia Talley
1971-73	Mrs. Ann Wilson
1973-74	Mrs. Jody King
1974-75	Mrs. Pat Gambrell
1975-76	Mrs. Jerry Eversole
1976-77	Mrs. Donna Hott
1977-78	Mrs. Charlyne Davis
1978-79	Mrs. Joan Barker
1979-80	Mrs. Jody King
1980-82	Mrs. Claudia Moursund
1982-84	Mrs. Irene Turner
1984-85	Mrs. Darlene Pease
1985-87	Mrs. Johnnie Knight
1987-88	Mrs. Darlene Pease
1988-89	Mrs. Margaret Riley
1989-91	Mrs. Grace Gandy
1991-92	Mrs. Rusty Garrison
1992-94	Mrs. Blanche Largent
1994-96	Mrs. Annette Duggan
1997-99	Mrs. Margaret Hutton
1999-2001	Mrs. Linda Higginbotham
2001-03	Mrs. Mattie Stevenson
2003-04	Mrs. Joan Cullinane
2004-05	Mrs. Lois Shanks
2005-07	Mrs. Sharon Corry
2007-09	Mrs. Judy Elleson
2009-10	Mrs. Pat Ingram
2010-11	Mrs. Marsha Eckermann

DIRECTORS, MUSEUM OF AMERICAN ARCHITECTURE AND DECORATIVE ARTS

1964-1978	Mrs. Helen Tinch, Founding Director
1978-1980	Mrs. Lynn Miller, Sheila Brush
1980-1989	Dr. Doris Anderson
1980-1982	Mrs. Dale Thees, Co-Director
1981-1984	Mrs. Robert W. Bailey, Co-Director
1986-1989	Phil Lanasa, Co-Director
1989-2009	Mrs. Lynn Miller
2009-	Mrs. Susie Snoddy, Interim Director

APPENDIX K

PRESIDENT'S (DEVELOPMENT) COUNCIL DINNERS

Date		Speaker	Venue
October 26, 1964	Howard Lee, Sr.	Dr. Kenneth McFarland	Warwick Hotel
April 23, 1965	Howard Lee, Sr.	Meredith Willson	Houston Club
April 5, 1966	Gilbert Turner	Dr. Walter Kerr	Sheraton Lincoln Hotel
November 15, 1966	Gilbert Turner	Max Rafferty	Warwick Hotel
April 3, 1967	Gilbert Turner	Pat Boone; H. L. Hunt	Warwick Hotel
November 21, 1967	Curtis Hankamer	Paul Harvey	Warwick Hotel
May 13, 1968	Curtis Hankamer	Bob Murphey	Warwick Hotel
May 14, 1969	Harold Sellers	Gov. Ronald Reagan	Shamrock Hotel
November 25, 1969	Harold Sellers	W. A. Criswell	Shamrock Hotel
March 24, 1970	Harold Sellers	Mrs. Gertrude Behanna	Shamrock Hotel
November 11, 1971	Milton Cross	Illinois Rep. Phillip Crane	
April 13, 1972	Milton Cross	Bud Wilkinson	River Oaks Country Club
November 22, 1972		Chet Huntley	Shamrock Hotel
March 15, 1973		Roger Staubach	River Oaks Country Club
November 13, 1973		Rep. Phillip Crane	River Oaks Country Club
April 11, 1974		Jerry Clower	
November 14, 1974	Orrien Smith	Dr. W. H. Hinton	River Oaks Country Club
April 27, 1975	Orrien Smith	Gov. Meldrim Thompson	Sheraton Lincoln Hotel
April 15, 1976	Orrien Smith	Art Linkletter	Hyatt Hotel
November 4, 1976	Bob McQuistion	Gisele MacKenzie	Hyatt Hotel
April 28, 1977	Bob McQuistion	Gov Ronald Reagan	Shamrock Hotel
November 4, 1977	Gilbert Turner	Norma Zimmer	Hyatt Hotel
March 31, 1978	Gilbert Turner	Jerome Hines	Galleria Plaza Hotel
October 26, 1978		Dr. William Guthrie	Galleria Plaza Hotel
April 5, 1979		George Friedensohn	Galleria Plaza Hotel
April 4, 1980		Harold Chamberlain	Galleria Plaza Hotel
May 1, 1981	James Cabaniss	Grady Nutt	Adams Mark
April 1, 1982			Galleria Plaza Hotel
September 15, 1983	Stewart Morris	Ray Miller	HBU Sharp Gymnasium
May 1, 1984	Stewart Morris	Sen. Lloyd Bentsen, Jr.	Westin Galleria Hotel
October 23, 1984	Stewart Morris	Dan Arnold	J. W. Marriott
April 23, 1985	Stewart Morris	Dr. Denton Cooley	Westin Galleria Hotel
March 18, 1986	Stewart Morris	Lord Irwin Bellwin	HBU Sharp Gymnasium
March 10, 1987	Stewart Morris	J. Peter Grace	HBU Sharp Gymnasium
March 29, 1988	Stewart Morris	Dr. Clement Conger	HBU Holcombe Mall
April 18, 1989	Stewart Morris	Chuck Colson	Westin Oaks Hotel
April 30, 1991	Bob Sale	Roger Staubach	HBU Sharp Gymnasium
March 15, 1992	Bob Sale	David Aikman	HBU Sharp Gymnasium
September 28, 1993	Bob Sale	Susan (Mrs. James) Baker	Doubletree Post Oak
September 20, 1994	Max Grigsby	Drayton McLane, Jr.	Doubletree Post Oak
September 19, 1995	Kay Parker	Grant Teaff	Westin Oaks Hotel
September 24, 1996	Dick Hudson	Rep. Jack Fields	Doubletree Post Oak
September 16, 1997	Rick Bailey	Jeannette Clift George	Doubletree Post Oak
September 15, 1998	Richard Meek	Dan Wilford	Westin Galleria Hotel

President's (Development) Council Dinners (cont.)

February 26, 1999	Richard Meek	Margaret Thatcher	Doubletree Post Oak
January 18, 2000	Richard Meek	Voddie Baucham '92	Doubletree Post Oak
October 9, 2001	Donna Dee Floyd	General Norman Schwarzkopf	Doubletree Post Oak
September 23, 2003	Bob Rule	Karen Hughes	Doubletree Post Oak
September 22, 2005	Kay Parker	J. C. Watts	(Cancelled due to Hurricane Rita)
November 16, 2010	President George H. W. Bush		Hilton Americas

APPENDIX L

RETIREES ASSOCIATION CHAIRS

2001-02	Linder	Robert
2002-04	Williams	Sebron
2004-06	Gaultney	Jerry
2006-08	Peavy	Elysee
2008-10	Raley	Harold
2010-12	Looser	Don
2012-14	Spore	Mary Ellen

APPENDIX M

SPIRIT OF EXCELLENCE AWARD WINNERS

1991	Dr. Tracy and Lee Lawrence
1991	Don and Colletta McMillian
1991	Dr. Stewart and Joella Morris
1991	Kerr-McGee Oil and Gas
1991	Cullen Trust for Higher Education
1991	Houston Endowment
1991	Memorial Hermann Healthcare System
1992	ExxonMobil Corporation
1992	Good Samaritan Foundation
1992	Dr. Gilbert and Claydene Turner
1992	Mrs. Dorothy L. Cross
1993	Bennett and Ruth Coulson
1993	Shell Oil Company
1993	John S. Dunn Research Foundation
1994	M. D. Anderson Foundation
1994	Duke Energy Corporation
1994	Harry and Hazel Chavanne
1995	Jim and Sherry Smith
1995	Baptist General Convention of Texas
1995	El Paso Corporation Foundation
1996	George Foundation
1996	ConocoPhillips
1996	John and Eula Mae Baugh
1997	Robert A. Welch Foundation
1997	Mrs. Virginia Marshall
1997	Dr. Doug and Sadie Hodo
1997	Mrs. Mary Claude Thompson
1998	Dr. Bruce and Mary Ann Belin, Jr.
1998	Sterling-Turner Foundation
1998	Southwestern Bell Communications
1999	Gus and Lucille Glasscock
1999	Dr. William M. and Bobbie Pinson

Spirit of Excellence Award Winners (cont.)

2001	Mrs. Eleanor McCollum
2001	Houston Livestock Show and Rodeo
2001	Robert and Janice McNair Foundation
2005	Mrs. Nell Smith
2005	JPMorgan Chase
2005	Rudy Tomjanovich Scholarship Tournament
2010	Dr. Archie and Linda Dunham
2010	Tellepsen Builders
2010	The Hamill Foundation

APPENDIX N

THE NATURE OF THE INSTITUTION

The Houston Baptist University is a Christian liberal arts university dedicated to the development of moral character, the enrichment of spiritual lives, and the perpetuation of growth in Christian ideals. Founded under the providence of God and with the conviction that there is a need for a university in this community that will train the minds, develop the moral character and enrich the spiritual lives of all people who may come within the ambit of its influence, HOUSTON BAPTIST UNIVERSITY shall stand as a witness for Jesus Christ expressed directly through its administration, faculty and students. To assure the perpetuation of these basic concepts of its founders, it is resolved that all those who become associated with Houston Baptist University as a trustee, officer, member of the faculty or of the staff, and who perform work connected with the educational activities of the University, must believe in the divine inspiration of the Bible, both the Old Testament and New Testament, that man was directly created by God, the virgin birth of Jesus Christ, our Lord and Savior, as the Son of God, that He died for the sins of all men and thereafter arose from the grave, that by repentance and the acceptance of and belief in Him, by the grace of God, the individual is saved from eternal damnation and receives eternal life in the presence of God; and it is further resolved that the ultimate teachings in this University shall never be inconsistent with the above principles.

Preamble to the Bylaws of HBU

SELECTED BIBLIOGRAPHY

Abram, Lynwood. "Hinton, founding president of HBU." *Houston Chronicle,* 16 April 2004.

_____. "Jeanette Lombard, opera singer, teacher." *Houston Chronicle,* 27 August 2003.

_____. "Pete Baker, 83, entrepreneur and community leader." *Houston Chronicle,* 27 March 2004.

_____. "Ray Fliegel, HSO violinist for 55 years." *Houston Chronicle,* 28 July 2005.

Ackerman, Todd. "Hospital staff vows to resign." *Houston Chronicle,* 20 August 2009.

_____. "Proposed sale to hospital district met by firestorm." *Houston Chronicle,* 15 Aug. 2009.

_____. "Undone deal: poor politicking and an outdated image sink a hospital purchase." *Houston Chronicle,* 19 September 2009.

Adair, Wendy and Oscar Gutiérrez. *Our Time: Celebrating 75 Years of Learning and Leading.* Virginia Beach: Donning Company Publishers, 2001. University of Houston.

"A. D. Players." *Houston Town and Country Magazine,* December 1975.

Advancing the Vision. Houston: Houston Baptist University, 2007-2010.

Alumni Directory. Houston: Houston Baptist University, 1972-2008.

American Museum Society Yearbook. Houston: 1965-2009.

Anderson, Marianne Miller. *One Hundred Years of Excellence in Nursing Education.* Houston: Houston Baptist University, 2007. A history of the nursing program from its roots to Houston Baptist University. Faculty publication.

A New Dimension in Christian Culture. Houston Baptist College promotional film, 1963.

"Arabic Studies Unit Planned by College." *New York Times,* 10 March 1968.

"A Rookie Sizzles for Rockets." *New York Times,* 21 November 1979.

Baker, Hunter. *The End of Secularism.* Wheaton (IL): Crossway Books, 2009.

Baptist General Convention of Texas. *Christian Education Coordinating Board Annual Report.* Dallas: BGCT, 23 November 1987.

"Baptists Start Drive for Houston College." *Paris (TX) News,* 24 March 1960.

Baptist Standard. 1959-2010.

Bentley, Margaret. *The Upper Side of the Pie Crust.* Conifer (CO): Margaret Bentley, 1985.

"Bill Bolton." *New Orleans Times Picayune,* 24 December 2003.

"Billy Graham." *San Antonio Express/News,* 27 October 1963.

The Binding Cord 1965-66. Houston: Houston Baptist College, 1966. Student literary anthology.

Birth of a College. Houston: Union Baptist Association of Texas, 1960.

Blair, Joe. *Introducing the New Testament.* Nashville: B&H Publishing Group, 1994. Faculty publication.

Bobb, Maurice. "HBU marks 40 years with Founders' Day ceremony." *Houston Chronicle,* 9 December 2004.

Bond Buyer, 20 July 2000.

Bordelon, Michael. *La Serenissima: The Republic of Venice From Its Founding To Its Fall.* Ojai (CA): Laureate Publishing, 2000. Faculty publication.

Brantley, Rabun L. "Hinton Begins Presidency of Houston College." *Southern Baptist Educator,* June 1962.

Britt, Douglas. "Acclaimed Houston artist dies of cancer." *Houston Chronicle,* 25 February 2009. Virgil Grotfeldt.

Bulletin of Information. Houston: Houston Baptist University (College), 1963-2009.

Bullock, Barbara. *Focus on Pathophysiology.* Philadelphia: Lippincott Williams & Wilkins, 1999. Faculty publication.

Byrnes, Don. "A Wonderful Week in the Rockies." *The Scene,* Fall quarter, 1973. This publication was produced from 1973 to 1977 for alumni to provide more detailed news than that printed in the *HBU News.*

Camacho, Vivian and Doug Parker. "Debate program dropped." *The Collegian,* 18 April 1991.

Capes, David. *The Footsteps of Jesus in the Holy Land.* Houston: N. M. International Enterprises, 1999. Faculty publication.

Carden, William R. *A Report to the Christian Education Commission of the Baptist General Convention of Texas.* Dallas: Baptist General Convention of Texas, 22 July 1968. A financial efficiency analysis.

"Carden Report Rejected." *Abilene Reporter-News,* 26 February 1969.

Casler, Diane. "Historical Symposium Planned." *Galveston News,* 19 March 1967.

Cavanaugh, Jack. "Pierce is Unlikely Winner in Big Apple." *New York Times,* 6 October 1996.

Celebrating 100 Years, 1908-2008. Fort Worth: Southwestern Baptist Theological Seminary, 2008.

"Channel 14 Planning Underway." *HBU News,* Winter 1984.

"Charter Application Made for New College." *Waco Tribune,* 17 November 1960.

City by Design: an architectural perspective of Texas. Plana: Panache Partners, 2008.

"College Hiring Practices Hit—No State Funds." *Galveston Daily News,* 11 Jan. 1974.

The Collegian. 1967-2010.

Collins, A. O. *Don't Tell Me the Bible Says That.* Houston: D. Armstrong Co, Inc., 1995. Faculty publication.

Commander, R. G. *The Story of Union Baptist Association.* Houston: D. Armstrong Publishers, 1977.

"Crowds Attend Services in Palacios Auditorium." *Galveston Daily News,* 11 July 1908.

Cues for Coeds. Houston Baptist College. Houston: Association of Women Students, 1967.

Cummins, Light Townsend. *Austin College: A Sesquicentennial History, 1849-1999.* Austin: Eakin Press, 1999.

Custred, Jayne. "Houston Baptist fans, players, give up game cold turkey." *Houston Chronicle,* 21 January 1990.

Dauphin, Sue. *Houston by Stages: A History of Theatre in Houston.* Burnet (TX): Eakin Press, 1981.

Dean, Richard. "HBU receives at-large berth to NAIA tourney." *Houston Chronicle,* 10 March 1998.

"Debate team vies for national title." *The Collegian,* 19 March 1992.

"Decade of Decision: 1961-1970." Foreword to *Decade of Decision*, edited by Dr. E. N. Jones. Dallas: Baptist General Convention of Texas, 1960.

Detwiler, Louis. "Spartans, Alligators, Huskies, Mystery Colors Disclosed." *Houston Baptist Collegian,* 10 September 1970.

Dooley, Tara. "Bach vs. Vivaldi: Houston Symphony series." *Houston Chronicle,* 23 March 2009.

Elliott, Frederick C. *The Birth of the Texas Medical Center.* College Station: Texas A&M Press, 2004.

"Emma Richardson Cherry." *Handbook of Texas.* www.tshaonline.org (accessed 8 December 2009).

"Expanding the mind, Exploring the arts, Nourishing the soul...," *Baptist Standard,* 30 April 2007.

Feldman, Claudia. "88 year-old takes on her great-grandson's challenge." *Houston Chronicle,* 19 June 2000.

Fitzgerald, Jonathan. "Winning Not Just Hearts but Minds." *Wall Street Journal,* 18 December 2009. Dr. Hunter Baker's *End of Secularism.*

Flashes and Dashes. Houston Baptist College. 1966-1968.

Foster, Ferrell. "BGCT to ask HBU to rescind pacts with conservative group." *Associated Baptist Press News,* 19 May 2004.

_____. "Committees to study HBU relationship." *Baptist Standard,* 23 January 2004.

Francis, Ted, and Carole McFarland. *The Memorial Hospital System: the first Seventy-Five Years.* Houston: Larkadale Publishing, 1982.

Gallay, Caroline. "Reassessing the lives of Lee and Grant." *Houston Chronicle,* 5 June 2009.

Gordon, Phil. "The Interview: Colin Montgomerie." *The Independent (London),* 28 October 2001.

"Graduation Not Long-Hair Affair." *Big Spring (TX) Herald,* 21 May 1972.

Graf, Hans. "The Bach vs. Vivaldi Experience," *Houston Symphony Performance Program,* March 2009.

Grant, Alexis. "The nation is saying goodbye to a treasure." *Houston Chronicle,* 30 May 2006. Founder, Senator Lloyd Bentsen, Jr.

The Guild Yearbook. Houston: 1975-2009. Formerly the President's Advisors.

Harris, Jack. *The Fault Does Not Lie With Your Set.* Austin: Eakin Press, 1989. The history of KPRC-TV whose 2010 studio occupies land purchased from the University.

HBColleague. 1968-1972.

"HBU Cuts Enrage Student Athletes." *Houston Chronicle,* 9 March 1991.

"HBU gets $4.5 million for scholarship fund." *Houston Chronicle,* 21 June 2001.

HBUpbeat. Houston: School of Music. 1998-2010.

"HBU's mock trial team earns national recognition." *Houston Chronicle,* 10 April 2008.

Heard, Robert. "Mutscher Stands Along As Big Target in Trial." *Del Rio News-Herald,* 29 February 1972.

Henry, Vernon. *Campus Master Plan.* Houston: Vernon Henry and Associates, 1998.

Herskowitz, Mickey. *Sharpstown Revisited.* Austin: Eakin Press, 1994.

Hewett, Paige. "College freshmen learn about coping, studying, and ethics." *Houston Chronicle,* 20 August 2003.

"Hinton Houston School President." *Abilene Reporter-News,* 1 June 1962.

"Hodo to Retire as Houston Baptist University President." *Southern Baptist Educator,* First quarter, 2006.

Houston Baptist College (University) Personnel Directory. Houston: 1966-2005.

Houston Baptist University Retiree Association Directory. Houston: 2001-2009.

Holmes, Ann. "Teacher Cecil Pickett touched the lives of many fine acting talents." *Houston Chronicle,* 21 November 1997.

Hooker, Wallace. "Preface." *Shank's Mare 1988-89,* 1989. Successor to *The Binding Cord* and *The Raft.*

Horn, Brian. "Opening Doors." *Smart Business,* December 2009. Malcolm Morris remembers the 1963 Billy Graham visit.

Howe, Neil, and William Strauss. *Generations.* New York: William Morrow and Co., 1991.

Howe, Neil, and William Strauss. *Millennials Rising: the Next Generation.* New York: Vintage Books-Random House, Inc., 2000.

Houston Baptist Alumni Today: 2008. Chesapeake (VA): Harris Connect, Inc., 2008.

Houston Baptist College News. 1963-1972.

"Houston Baptist College Proposed." *Odessa American,* 23 March 1960.

Houston Baptist (College) University Bulletin of Information. 1963-2010.

Houston Baptist Collegian. 1963-1972.

Houston Baptist University (HBU) News. 1971-2010.

Houston Chronicle. 1956-2010.

"Houston Fascination in Houston Heritage." *Houston Tribune,* 25 August 1966.

Houston History: 1836-2010.
http://houstonhistory.com/decades/history5r.htm (accessed 19 February 2008).

Houston Post. 1949-1995.

"Houston Society." *Houston Town and Country Magazine,* May 1966.

Huckabay, Calvin. *John Milton: An Annotated Bibliography, 1929-1968.* Pittsburgh: Duquesne University Press, 1969. Faculty publication.

"Hurricane Ike." *Baptist Educator International,* Fall 2008.

Hurley, Marvin. *Decisive Years for Houston.* Houston: Houston Chamber of Commerce, 1966.

"Intercollegiate Gymnastics Next Major Sport." *The Scene.* Fall quarter, 1973.

"Intriguing deal, bold plan to buy hospital for county system." *Houston Chronicle,* 9 August 2009.

"Jack D. Carlson to serve as interim president at Houston Baptist University." *Southern Baptist Educator,* Third quarter, 2006.

JaffeHolden Acoustics. *Acoustic Manual for the HBU Cultural Arts Center.* Norwalk (CT): JaffeHolden, 2007.

Janofsky, Michael. "Gymnastics." *New York Times,* 22 June 1987.

"John F. Baugh, 91, Founder of Sysco, Dies." *New York Times,* 9 March 2007.

Johnston, Marguerite. *Houston: the Unknown City.* College Station: Texas A&M University Press, 1991.

Jones, E. N. (ed.) *The Future Development of the Christian Education Program of the Baptist General Convention of Texas.* Dallas: Baptist General Convention of Texas, 1963.

Justman, Dorothy E. *German Colonists and Their Descendants in Houston including Usener and Allied Families.* Wichita Falls: Nortex Offset Publications, Inc., 1974.

Kever, Jeannie. "Area universities welcome campus life: more dorms are added to bring students home." *Houston Chronicle,* 22 August 2008.

Koch, Rudolf. *The Book of Signs.* New York: Dover Publications, Inc., 1965.

Krisch, Lucille Stewart. "Twigs, Trees: Symposium Success." *San Antonio Light,* 18 June 1967.

Laird, Cheryl. "Fifty women who have made their mark in and on Houston." *Houston Chronicle,* 4 April 1993. Dr. Joyce Fan.

Lopez, John. "HBU's rise has been inspirational journey." *Houston Chronicle,* 6 March 2003.

Lowry, Elaine. "The History of Houston Baptist College." Senior Seminar Paper, Houston Baptist College, 1967.

"Lucky skydiver tells of desperate jump to safety." *Houston Post,* 19 April 1981. Personal history of former gymnast, Dr. Steve Kinnett.

"Magazine ranks HBU in top tier of schools." *Houston Chronicle,* 16 September 2004.

Martin, William. *A Prophet With Honor: The Billy Graham Story.* New York: William Morrow and Co., Inc., 1991.

McBeth, Harry Leon. *Texas Baptists: A Sesquicentennial History.* Dallas: Baptistway Press, 1998.

McComb, David G. *Houston: the Bayou City.* Austin: University of Texas Press, 1969.

"McMillians Endow Chair in Humanities." *The Scene.* Summer quarter, 1974.

Meiners, Fredericka. *A History of Rice University, the Institute Years, 1907-1963.* Houston: Rice University Historical Commission, 1982.

"Men gymnasts rank #1 in nation." *The Collegian,* 14 April 1989.

Miller, James D. *A Centennial History of the Southern Association of Colleges and Schools, 1895-1995.* Decatur (GA): Southern Association of Colleges and Schools, 1998.

Miller, Ray. *Ray Miller's Houston.* Austin: Capital Printing, 1982.

"Minutes of the Meetings of the Board of Trustees of Houston Baptist (College) University." 1960-2010.

"Minutes of the Meetings of the Faculty of Houston Baptist (College) University." 1963-2010.

"Minutes of the Meetings of the Union Baptist Association." 1921-2010.

"Modern Man's Uncertainty Oratorio Theme," *Miami Herald,* 25 June 1965.

Moffett, Hilda. "The History of the Southeastern Texas program." *20th Anniversary Celebration,* 1995. Celebration program.

Montgomerie, Colin. *The Real Monty.* London: Orion Books, Ltd., 1998.

"Museum plans Flea Market." *The Mirror,* 29 September 1965.

Musil, B. J. "For Whom the Bell Curves." *The Collegian,* November 1978.

National Forensics League. *Hall of Fame.* www.nflonline.org/AboutNFL/HallofFame (accessed 24 February 2010).

"Nell Anderson Smith." *Alvin Sun-Advertiser,* 2 December 2009.

"New Group, President's Advisors Formed." *The Scene,* Winter quarter, 1974.

"New Houston Baptist College To Be Dedicated in Sunday Rite." *Galveston News,* 7 September 1963.

"New Museum Society." *Houston Tribune,* 23 September 1965.

"New President Hodo at HBU plans to reduce costs." *Houston Chronicle,* 17 July 1987.

Nicholson, Patrick J. *In Time: An Anecdotal History of the First Fifty Years of the University of Houston.* Houston: Pacesetter Press, Gulf Publishing Co., 1977.

"Nine Faculty Members Are Employed By HBC." *Fourth Estate,* 11 September 1967. This was the only issue of the student newspaper ever to carry this title.

"Obituaries: Arthur Travis." *Abilene Reporter-News,* 11 July 2002.

"Obituaries: R. G. Commander." *Rocky Mountain News,* 22 February 1998.

"On the Cover." *River Oaks Times,* Vol. 21, no. 42. American Museum Society.

On Our Way: a decade of proof 1963-1973; a decade of promise, 1973-1983. Houston Baptist University, 1973. Dr. Gilbert Turner's capital campaign for scholarships and facilities.

Orange and Blue. Houston Baptist University. 1975-1981.

Ornogah. Houston: Houston Baptist University, 1963-2009. Yearbook.

Pais, Wilson. *River Oaks Baptist Church: A Brief History.* Houston: River Oaks Baptist Church, 1995.

"Parish nursing program takes holistic approach to health." *Houston Chronicle,* 3 June 2001.

Petit, Burle. "Gerald Myers Named Cage Coach at Houston Baptist." *Lubbock Avalanche Journal,* 18 March 1967.

Points of Interest. 1996-2010.

Powell, Jamie. "Glasscock was innovator of oil drilling practices." *Corpus Christi Caller-Times,* 25 October 2005.

Presidents Report, 1971-72. Houston Baptist College, 1971.

Prince, Richard. "Houston's Carlton Thompson leaving for MLB.com." *The Maynard Institute* www.mije.org (accessed 9 April 2010).

"Probation for HBU's Gymnasts." *Houston Chronicle,* 27 March 1990.

"Quicksand Halts Search for Phantom Cannon." *Houston Baptist Collegian,* 2 November 1965.

Ratheal, Dale (ed). *The Raft.* Houston: Houston Baptist College, 1967. Student literary anthology, descendent of *The Binding Cord.*

Report of the President 1968-69. Houston Baptist College, 1969.

Rhea, Claude. *With My Song I Will Praise Him.* Nashville: Broadman Press, 1977.

Roberts, Raequel. "Just Don't Call them Crazy." *Houston Post,* 6 November 1988.

"Roland Lee Burrows." *Roanoke Times and World News,* 29 May 2006.

Rosenfeld, Ruth. "Hinton House...Gracious New Home for A College President." *Bellaire Texan,* 28 August 1963.

Rosenfeld, Ruth. "Dr. Tidwell Dept. of Christianity Head at New Houston Baptist College." *Bellaire Texan,* 31 July 1963.

Rosenfeld, Ruth. "Houston Baptist College Prof. Has Served Local Pastorates." *Bellaire Texan,* 17 July 1963. Dr. Arthur Travis.

Rosenfeld, Ruth. "Meet the Musical Rheas." *Bellaire Texan,* 9 October 1963.

Rosenfeld, Ruth, "Language Instructor's Home Filled With Travel Memories." *Bellaire Texan,* 14 August 1963. Opal Goolsby.

Rosenfeld, Ruth. "Over 3000 Hear Billy Graham at Houston Baptist College." *Bellaire Texas,* 6 November 1963.

Routh, E. C. "Romance of a College." *Baptist Standard,* October 1956.

Ruminations. Houston Baptist University. 1992-1995.

Sacks, Peter. *Generation X Goes to College.* Chicago: Open Court Press, 1996.

St. John, Lauren. "Americans who love Monty remember him as teddy bear and model student." *London Daily Mail,* 10 September 1999.

Sanoff, Alvin P. "Where supercities are growing fastest." *U. S. News and World Report,* 30 June 1980.

The Scene. Houston Baptist College. 1973-1977.

Schwartz, Marc. "Change in Course: the Committee of 75." *McCombs School of Business Magazine,* December 2002. http://www/texasexes.org/involved/daa.aspx (accessed January 16, 2009).

"Schwarzkopf speaks at HBU." *Houston Chronicle,* 15 October 2001.

"Severinsen, Smith Hold Spring Band Festival at HBC." *Houston Baptist Collegian,* 22 February 1967.

Sibley, Marilyn McAdams. *To Benefit a University.* Houston: Houston Baptist University, 1978.

Siegel, Stanley E., and John A. Moretta. *Houston: Chronicle of the Bayou City.* Sun Valley: American Historical Press, 2005.

"Simpson College." *Des Moines Sunday Register,* 24 Dec. 1967. Theo Redwood Blank doll collection.

SomeTimes, Houston Baptist University. 1987-2003.

Southern Association of Colleges and Schools. "Report of the Visiting Committee to Houston Baptist University." November 1967.

Spence, Doug. "The Misshape." *The Collegian,* February 1980.

"Status Report on Change of School Name." *The Scene,* Fall quarter, 1973.

Sweeney, Scott. "Educator earns top honor." *Houston Chronicle,* 10 July 2003. Dr. Brenda Whaley.

"Texas Eastern has first grads in HBU's 'workplace' campus TV program." *HBU News,* Winter 1986.

"Three Colleges To Compete for Titles." *Mansfield (OH) News-Journal,* 8 November 1972.

Thompson, Carlton. "Lady Huskies Dazzle." *The Collegian,* 28 March 1991.

"Tom Brokaw To Speak In Assembly." *The Collegian,* 17 November 1975.

Tinch, Helen. *Days in Colonial Texas.* Houston: American Museum Society, 1963. Faculty publication.

Travis, Arthur. *Where on Earth is Heaven?* Nashville: Broadman Press, 1974. Faculty publication.

Tresaugue, Matthew. "Campus Moving Forward." *Houston Chronicle,* 2 September 2007.

_____. "Colleges Mining Data for Student: HBU and Rice use math models to draw more applicants." *Houston Chronicle,* 18 March 2007.

_____. "HBU President aims to transform the University; trustees and professors are ready. *Houston Chronicle,* 2 September 2007.

_____. "Search panel taps Robert Sloan as its choice for Baptist school's next President." *Houston Chronicle,* 3 August 2006.

"Trevino receives Mellon Fellowship." *HBU News,* Summer 1986.

Vara, Richard. "Campbell looks back at 2 years of progress and strife." *Houston Chronicle,* 8 November 2003.

_____. "HBU trustees have stunned Texas Baptist officials by declaring autonomy from the state convention." *Houston Chronicle,* 18 May 2000.

_____. "Houston Baptist campus blossoms." *Houston Post,* 20 September 1986.

_____. "Nursing the flock." *Houston Chronicle,* 31 May 1997.

_____. "Rare Good Books: Houston Baptist University opens Museum of American Bibles." *Houston Chronicle,* 8 September 2001.

_____. "Terms of Endearment: A final semester after 19 years at the helm." *Houston Chronicle,* 14 January 2006.

Vargas, Daniel. "A key player: Retired teacher devotes time, talent, and financial aid at HBU." *Houston Chronicle,* 8 April 2001. Dr. Norma Lauder.

Virgil Grotfeldt: 274296. Houston Baptist University, 2009.

Ward, Charles. "'Credo' premier dour but memorable." *Houston Chronicle,* 27 January 2007.

_____. "HBU building toward an artistic tomorrow." *Houston Chronicle,* 29 July 2004.

_____. "HBU celebrates opening of new performance facilities." *Houston Chronicle,* 10 October 2007.

_____. "Soprano and Choral Conductor Dies." *Houston Chronicle,* 24 March 1997.

Warner, Greg. "BGCT, University reach compromise over ties to conservative group." *Associated Baptist Press News,* 24 November 2004.

Who's Houston '80. Houston: Who Houston, Inc., 1980.

The World Here. Center for Exploring Ministry Careers. 1983-1985.

Williams, Brandon C. "HBU settles suits to upgrade sports/full Division I status attainable after 4-year span." *Houston Chronicle,* 4 February 2009.

_____. "HBU wants 3-year path to Division I; lawsuit against NCAA seeks cut in probation period." *Houston Chronicle,* 8 March 2008.

_____. "Houston Baptist makes move to Great West Conference." *McClatchy-Tribune Business News,* 10 July 2008.

Willimon, William H., and Thomas H. Naylor, *The Abandoned Generation: Rethinking Higher Education.* Grand Rapids: Wm. B. Eerdmans Publishing Co., 1991.

Wilson, Ann Quin. *Native Houstonian: A Collective Portrait.* Norfolk: Donning Company/Publishers, 1982. Premier publication of the HBU Press.

Wingfield, Mark. "BGCT will escrow funds for HBU while trustees' action reviewed." *Baptist Standard,* 29 May 2000.

_____. "Houston Baptist University forges new link with SBTC, keeps ties with BGCT." *Baptist Standard,* 1 October 2003.

_____. "Motions call for study of HBU's ties and fund for restorative justice." *Baptist Standard,* 14 November 2003.

G

Q

R

Tribune, Houston 67, 68, 75, 97, 530, 533
Tribune, Waco 24, 528
Triceans 70, 77, 144, 189
Trinity Broadcasting 231, 242, 325
Tsao, Dr. James 99, 291, 317, 329, 386, 511
Tucker, Dr. Brooke 146, 317, 395, 416, 511
Tucker, Leah 513
Tug-of-War 70, 189, 335
Tuition Equalization Grant 105, 119, 232, 262, 425
Tulane University 4, 95, 97, 388
Turley, Steve 146, 195, 196
Turman, Peggy 82
Turner, Arthur 79
Turner, Claire 172, 493
Turner, Claydene 232, 308, 463, 523
Turner, Gilbert vii, 32, 54, 77, 83, 91, 105, 117, 124, 129, 131, 139, 140, 141, 170, 174, 187, 188, 189, 199, 201, 202, 207, 213, 214, 226, 228, 229, 230, 231, 232, 281, 308, 347, 506, 515, 520, 523, 533
Turner, Irene 518
Turner, Martha 16
Turner, Oscar C. 172, 203, 206
Turner, Ronnie 458
Turner, Roy 58
Tweed, Jack 206
Tyson, Mrs. Knox 67

U

UBA (See also Union Baptist Association) 7, 8, 10, 11, 12, 13, 14, 17, 19, 20, 22, 23, 24, 31, 59, 60, 68, 98, 104, 141, 171, 173, 174, 184, 233, 241, 292, 299, 332, 385, 414, 463, 502
UH (See also University of Houston) 49, 95, 482
Ulmer, Dr. James 254, 317, 318, 360, 361, 396, 472, 511

Union Baptist Association (see also UBA) 6, 7, 8, 9, 10, 12, 13, 14, 15, 17, 18, 19, 20, 21, 22, 23, 24, 54, 68, 239, 276, 297, 310, 342, 494, 527, 528, 532
United Athletic Conference 125
University of California 97
University of Dallas 11
University of Houston 2, 4, 42, 49, 95, 124, 129, 137, 156, 164, 198, 208, 221, 256, 287, 306, 314, 321, 392, 482, 526, 533
University of Oklahoma 4, 196
University of Texas at Austin 4, 7, 19, 20, 97, 187, 190, 194, 196, 202, 233, 287, 327, 340, 400, 532
University Place 181, 226, 227, 252, 289, 379, 403, 487, 488
University Singers (See also College Singers) 166, 219, 244, 364, 454
Uphouse, Lynda 42
Usener family 112
Usener, Friedrich 111, 112, 531

V

Valasquez, Donna 260
Vale, Wiley 58
Van Black, Alvin 122
Van Buren, Abigail 188
Van Derbur, Marilyn 120
Van Dyck, Anthony 496
Van Dyke, Vonda Kay 62, 144
Vara, Richard 536
Vargas, Daniel 380
Vargas, Frances 83
Vass, Peck 58, 79
Verhey, Dr. Allen 285, 328
Verheyden, Clyde 32, 33
Vice President Emeritus iii, 451, 503, 516
Vice President for Academic Affairs vii, 7, 115, 149, 152, 156, 205, 206, 234, 245, 246, 253, 306, 438, 445, 450, 451, 452, 459, 462, 484